MICHELIN

Motoring Atlas Europe

Contents

Inside front cover
Climates in Europe

II **Route Planning**
VI **Driving in Europe**

1 **Key to symbols**
2 **Western Europe** at a scale of 1: 1 000 000
54 **Greece** at a scale of 1: 700 000
66 **Scandinavia** at a scale of 1: 1 500 000
78 **Eastern Europe** at a scale of 1: 3 000 000

82 **Index of place names**

Inside back cover
Distances in Europe
Outside back cover
Key to map pages

Plans of cities and principal towns

83 • Amsterdam
84 • Antwerpen
62 • Athina
85 • Barcelona
86 • Basel
86 • Belfast
88 • Berlin
87 • Bern
87 • Birmingham
88 • Bologna
89 • Bonn
16 • Bordeaux
36 • Bremen
34 • Brugge
90 • Bruxelles-Brussel
89 • Budapest
93 • Dijon
92 • Dublin
93 • Düsseldorf
94 • Edinburgh
94 • Essen
95 • Firenze
95 • Frankfurt a. M.
95 • Genève
96 • Genova
96 • Gent
97 • Glasgow
77 • Göteborg
97 • Den Haag
98 • Hamburg
98 • Hannover
99 • Helsinki
99 • Istanbul
100 • København
101 • Köln
102 • Lausanne
102 • Liège
103 • Lille
103 • Lisboa
106 • Liverpool
104 • London
107 • Luxembourg
106 • Lyon
107 • Madrid
108 • Manchester
109 • Marseille
110 • Milano
109 • Monaco
111 • München
110 • Nantes
111 • Napoli
112 • Nice
112 • Nürnberg
113 • Oslo
48 • Palermo
114 • Paris
116 • Porto
45 • Roma
118 • Rotterdam
120 • Salzburg
120 • Sevilla
121 • Stockholm
122 • Strasbourg
123 • Stuttgart
124 • Torino
125 • Toulouse
33 • Valencia
126 • Venezia
127 • Wien
128 • Zürich

First published 1989 by
The Hamlyn Publishing Group Limited
a division of the Octopus Publishing Group
Michelin House, 81 Fulham Road, London SW3 6RB

Second edition 1991
First impression 1991

All maps © Michelin et Cie Propriétaires-Éditeurs 1991

Creation, graphic arrangement, text pages VI-VIII and Index
© The Hamlyn Publishing Group Limited 1991

Mapping of Great Britain on pages 2-7
based upon Ordnance Survey mapping with the permission of the Controller of Her Majesty's Stationery Office, Crown copyright reserved.

Mapping of Northern Ireland on page 4
based upon Ordnance Survey mapping with the permission of the Controller of Her Majesty's Stationery Office, Crown copyright reserved. Permit No 223.

Mapping of the Republic of Ireland on pages 8-9
based on Ordnance Survey by permission of the Government of the Republic of Ireland. Permit No 4990.

All rights reserved. No part of this publication may be reproduced, stored in a retrieval system or transmitted, in any form or by any means, electronic, mechanical, photocopying, recording or otherwise without the permission of the Publishers and the copyright owners.

In spite of the care taken in the production of this book, it is possible that a defective copy may have escaped our attention. If this is so, please return it to your bookseller, who will exchange it for you, or contact The Hamlyn Publishing Group Limited.

The representation in this atlas of a road is no evidence of the existence of a right of way.

Spiral bound edition ISBN 0 600 57209 9

Printed in Great Britain

MICHELIN
Touring Services

PAUL HAMLYN

Route planning

Jan Mayen
Ísafjörður
Akureyri
IS
REYKJAVÍK
Seyðisfjörður
Vatnajökull
2119
CERCLE POLAIRE ARCTIQUE
SEA
NORVÈGE
NORWEGIAN
DE
MER
0
300 km
Føroyar
Hitra
Kristiansund
Ålesund
2470
Jotunheimen
OCEAN ATLANTIQUE
Shetland
N
Bergen
Orkney
Thurso
Hebrides
Stavanger
Skie
Kristiansand
ATLANTIC OCEAN
Skye
Inverness
Loch Ness
1344
Ben Nevis
Aberdeen
Skagerrak
Dundee
NORTH SEA
Glasgow
Edinburgh
DK
Londonderry
Stranraer
Belfast
Carlisle
Newcastle
MER DU NORD
Esbjerg
IRL
Galway
Man
DUBLIN
Shannon
IRISH SEA
York
Liverpool
Leeds
Limerick
Manchester
Sheffield
GB
Nottingham
Groningen
Cork
St. George's Channel
Ijsselmeer
NL
Bremen
Birmingham
Coventry
Norwich
AMSTERDAM
Hann
Cardiff
Oxford
Cambridge
Den Haag
LONDON
Rotterdam
Thames
Waal
Essen
Dortmund
Southampton
Dover
Brugge
Ka
Plymouth
Portsmouth
Antwerpen
Düsseldorf
Calais
Gent
B
Aachen
Köln
Land's End
Lille
BRUSSEL
BONN
ENGLISH CHANNEL
BRUXELLES
Liège
LA MANCHE
Cherbourg
Channel Is.
Le Havre
Amiens
LUXEMBOURG
Frankfurt a.M
Rouen
Brest
Caen
Reims
L
Heidelberg

MER DE BARENTS
BARENTS SEA
Nordkapp
Hammerfest
Kirkenes
Murmansk
Kanin Poluostrov
Tromsø
Vesterålen
Lofoten
Ivalo
Inarijärvi
LAPLAND
Kol'skij Poluostrov
ARCTIC CIRCLE
Mezen
Narvik
Kiruna
2 111 Kebnekaise
Kousomen
MER BLANCHE
WHITE SEA
Bodø
Malmberget
Rovaniemi
Kuusamo
Kem
Archangel'sk
Tornionjoki
Torneälven
Kemi
Severnaja Dvina
Dønna
Mo i Rana
Luleå
Oulu
Oulujärvi
BOTHNIA
BOTNIE
S
Umeå
SF
Pielinen
Kuopio
Joensuu
Petrozavodsk
Onežkoje Oz.
Trondheim
Östersund
Vaasa
Jyväskylä
Sundsvall
GULF OF BOTHNIA
GOLFE DE BOTNIE
Päijänne
Saimaa
Ładozskoje oz.
Tampere
Vologda
Pori
Lahti
Čerepovec
Lillehammer
Glomma
Mora
Turku
HELSINKI
GULF OF FINLAND
GOLFE DE FINLANDE
Leningrad
Rybinsk
Rybinskoje Vdchr.
Gävle
Dalälven
OSLO
Uppsala
Åland
Tallinn
Novgorod
Västerås
Moss
STOCKHOLM
Čudskoje Oz.
Volga
Örebro
Vänern
Saaremaa
Kalinin
Norrköping
Pskov
Zagorsk
Linköping
Vättern
Gotland
BALTIC SEA
Rižskij Zaliv
MOSKVA
SU
Göteborg
Jönköping
Frederikshavn
Ålborg
Kattegat
Riga
Daugava
Kalmar
Öland
Århus
Vitebsk
Smolensk
KØBENHAVN
Klaipéda
Malmö
MER BALTIQUE
Odense
Sjælland
Fyn
Kaunas
Vilnius
Mogil'ov
Br'ansk
Or'ol
Bornholm
Kaliningrad
Minsk
Kiel
Lolland
Rügen
Gdańsk
Nemunas
Desna
Dnepr
Lübeck
Rostock
Gomel'
Hamburg
Szczecin
Toruń
Prip'at
Černigov
Elbe
Oder
Wisła
BERLIN
Poznań
WARSZAWA
Brest
PL
Łódź
Odra
Magdeburg
Lublin
Kijev
Poltava
DDR
Dresden
Erfurt
Leipzig
Wrocław
Częstochowa
Žitomir
Kremenčugskoje Vdchr.
Erzgebirge
Labe
Kraków
L'vov
Vinnica
PRAHA
CS
KARPATY
Južnyj Bug
Krivoj Rog
Plzeň
Nürnberg
Tatry
2 655
Brno
Dnestr
Černovcy

(A) Austria. 1: 1 000 000	(CS) Czechoslovakia. 1: 3 000 000	(FL) Liechtenstein. 1: 1 000 000
(AL) Albania. 1: 700 000	(D) West Germany. 1: 1 000 000	(GB) Great Britain. 1: 1 000 000
(AND) Andorra. 1: 1 000 000	(DDR) East Germany. 1: 1 000 000	(GR) Greece. 1: 700 000
(B) Belgium. 1: 1 000 000	(DK) Denmark. 1: 1 500 000	(H) Hungary. 1: 3 000 000
(BG) Bulgaria. 1: 3 000 000	(E) Spain. 1: 1 000 000	(I) Italy. 1: 1 000 000
(CH) Switzerland. 1: 1 000 000	(F) France. 1: 1 000 000	(IRL) Ireland. 1: 1 000 000

Lübeck
Hamburg
Szczecin
Toruń
Gomel'
Prip'at
Černigov
Elbe
Oder
Wista
BERLIN
Poznań
WARSZAWA
Brest
PL
Magdeburg
Odra
Łódź
Lublin
Kijev
Poltava
DDR
Žitomir
Kremenčugskoje Vdchr.
Erfurt
Leipzig
Dresden
Wrocław
Częstochowa
Erzgebirge
Labe
Kraków
L'vov
Vinnica
Main
PRAHA
CS
K A R P A T Y
Južnyj Bug
Krivoj Rog
Nürnberg
Plzeň
Tatry 2 655
Dnestr
Brno
Černovcy
Regensburg
Košice
Prut
Dnepr
Donau
Tisza
Augsburg
Inn
Linz
Bratislava
Kišin'ov
Cherson
Iaşi
München
WIEN
Odessa
C A R P A T I I
Salzburg
BUDAPEST
Cluj-Napoca
Innsbruck
A
H
A L P E N
Graz
Großglockner 3 797
Duna
Balaton
Braşov
Moldoveanu 2 543
Bolzano
2 863 Triglav
Sibiu
Timişoara
MER NOIRE
Ljubljana
Tisa
R
Zagreb
Pécs
Dráva
Carpatii Meridionali
Trieste
Novi Sad
Padova
Rijeka
Constanţa
Verona
Venezia
BUCUREŞTI
Sava
BEOGRAD
Adige
Olt
Parma
Ruse
BLACK SEA
Dunărea
Ravenna
Dunáv
Drina
Varna
Bologna
YU
RSM
Sarajevo
Stara Planina
Veliko Târnovo
Firenze
Split
Dalmatska
2 376 Botev
Burgas
Pisa
MER ADRIATIQUE
A P P E N N I N I
SOFIA
BG
Siena
Kota
Perugia
Plovdiv
Titograd
Dubrovnik
Skopje
Edirne
Istanbul
ADRIATIC SEA
Gran Sasso
Pescara
Rodopi
Drin
2 764 Korab
Evros
TR
Marmara Denizi
V
ROMA
TIRANË
Durrës
Bursa
I
Bari
AL
Thessaloníki
MER TYRRHÉNIENNE
Napoli
1277 Vesuvio
Taranto
Ólimbos 2917
TYRRHENIAN SEA
AEGEAN SEA
Pindos
Lárissa
Vólos
Lésvos
Kérkira
Igoumenítsa
GR
Izmir
Évia
IONIAN SEA
MER ÉGÉE
Pátra
ATHÍNA
Ionia Nissiá
Kórinthos
Palermo
Messina
Peloponnisos
Kiklades
Dodekánissa
Reggio di Calabria
3 340 M. Etna
MER IONIENNE
Catania
Ródos
Katakolon
Sicilia
TUNIS
Iráklio
Valletta
M
MEDITERRANEAN SEA
Kriti

(IS) Iceland	1: 2 400 000	(P) Portugal	1: 1 000 000	(SU) Russia	1: 3 000 000
(L) Luxembourg	1: 1 000 000	(PL) Poland	1: 3 000 000	(TR) Turkey	1: 3 000 000
(M) Malta	1: 1 000 000	(R) Rumania	1: 3 000 000	(V) Vatican City	1: 140 000
(MC) Monaco	1: 1 000 000	(RSM) San Marino	1: 1 000 000	(YU) Yugoslavia	1: 1 000 000
(N) Norway	1: 1 500 000	(S) Sweden	1: 1 500 000		
(NL) Netherlands	1: 1 000 000	(SF) Finland	1: 1 500 000		

★ Germany: situation as at 1-9-90

Driving in Europe

Introduction

The information panels which follow give the principal motoring regulations for all the countries included in this atlas; an explanation of the symbols is given below, together with some additional notes.

- The name, address and telephone number of the national motoring organisation or organisations; the initials FIA and AIT indicate membership of the international touring associations, the Fédération Internationale de l'Automobile and the Alliance Internationale de Tourisme
- Speed restrictions in kilometres per hour applying to:
  - motorways
  - dual carriageways
  - single carriageways
  - urban areas

Where restrictions for 'trailers' or 'towing' are given, it may be assumed that these apply to both trailers and caravans

- The maximum permitted level of alcohol in the bloodstream. This should not be taken as an acceptable level; it is NEVER sensible to drink and drive
- Whether the wearing of seat belts is compulsory
- Restrictions applying to children
- Whether a warning triangle must be carried
- Whether a first aid kit must be carried
- Whether a spare bulb kit must be carried
- Whether crash helmets are compulsory for motorcyclists
- Whether tolls are payable on motorways and/or other parts of the road network
- Whether petrol concessions or restrictions apply
- The minimum age for drivers
- Documentation required; note that while insurance for driving at home usually provides the legally required minimum third party cover abroad, it will not provide cover against damage, fire, theft or personal accident; for this reason, an International Motoring Certificate (Green Card) is recommended for all countries and essential where 'Green Card required' is given
- ★ In this section are given any other regulations not falling into the categories above

Andorra

Automobil Club d'Andorra, FIA,
Babet Camp 4, Andorra-la-Vella Tel: 20-8-90

	70	70	40 km/h

0.08%
Compulsory if fitted for driver and front seat passengers
Children under 10 years of age not allowed in front seats
Recommended (compulsory if vehicle exceeds 3000 kg)
Recommended
Compulsory
Compulsory for motorcyclists and passengers
18
Valid driving licence; Vehicle registration document or Vehicle on hire certificate; Green Card recommended; National vehicle identification plate

Austria

Österreicher Automobil-, Motorrad- und Touring Club (ÖAMTC), FIA & AIT, Schubertring 1-3, 1010 Wien 1
Tel: (01) 711997

100-130		100	50 km/h
100		80	50 km/h
if towing trailer over 14.5 cwt			
100	100	100	50 km/h
if towing trailer under 14.5 cwt			

0.08%
Compulsory if fitted for driver and front and rear seat passengers
Children under 12 years of age not allowed in front seats
Compulsory
Compulsory
Compulsory
Compulsory for motorcyclists and passengers
Tolls payable on motorways for Brenner (A13), Tauern (part of the A10) and a section of the A9 north of Graz, as well as some roads (especially trans-alpine routes) and tunnels
18
Valid driving licence; Vehicle registration document or Vehicle on hire certificate; Green Card compulsory; National vehicle identification plate
★ Towing is forbidden on certain alpine routes

Belgium

Royal Automobile Club de Belgique (RACB), FIA,
53 rue d'Arlon, 1040 Bruxelles
Tel: (02) 2300810
Touring Club Royal de Belgique (TCB), AIT,
44 rue de la Loi, 1040 Bruxelles
Tel: (02) 2332211
Vlaamse Automobilistenbond (VTB-VAB),
Sint-Jacobs Markt 45, 2000 Antwerpen
Tel: (03) 2003211

120	90	90	60 km/h

0.08%
Compulsory if fitted for driver and front and rear seat passengers
Children under 12 years of age not allowed in front seats
Compulsory
Recommended
Compulsory for motorcyclists
18
Valid driving licence; Vehicle registration document or Vehicle on hire certificate; Green Card recommended; National vehicle identification plate

Bulgaria

Union of Bulgarian Motorists (SBA), FIA & AIT,
6 Sveta Sofia St., Sofia C
Tel: (02) 87 88 01/87 88 02

100	80	80	60 km/h

0.0%
Compulsory if fitted for driver and front seat passengers
Children under 10 years of age not allowed in front seats
Compulsory
Compulsory
Compulsory
Compulsory for motorcyclists
Foreign motorists must buy fuel with coupons available in unlimited quantities at border posts and within Bulgaria
18
Valid driving licence or International Driving Permit; Vehicle registration document or Vehicle on hire certificate; Green Card required; National vehicle identification plate

Czechoslovakia

Ustředni Automotoklub ČSSR, FIA & AIT,
Na strži 4, 14000 Praha 4 Tel: (02) 43 20 41

110	90	90	60 km/h

0.0% any alcohol found in the bloodstream may result in prosecution
Compulsory if fitted for driver and front seat passengers
Children under 12 years of age not allowed in front seats
Compulsory
Compulsory
Crash helmets and goggles compulsory for drivers of motorcycles over 50cc; crash helmets only for passengers
Petrol coupons can be purchased at frontier posts, Tuzex shops and banks; also from Czech Tourist Bureau Cedok (London) Ltd
18
Valid driving licence; Vehicle registration document or Vehicle on hire certificate; Green Card, valid for Czechoslovakia, required; National vehicle identification plate

Denmark

Forenede Danske Motorejere (FDM), AIT,
Firstovvej 32, 2800 Lyngby Tel: (45) 93 08 00

100	80	80	50 km/h
70	70	70	50 km/h if towing

0.08%
Compulsory if fitted for driver and front seat passengers over 15 years
Compulsory
Recommended
Compulsory for motorcyclists and passengers
17
Valid driving licence; Vehicle registration document or Vehicle on hire certificate; Green Card recommended; National vehicle identification plate

Finland

Autoliitto (Automobile and Touring Club of Finland) (ATCF),
FIA & AIT, Kansakoulukatu 10, 00101 Helsinki 10 Tel: (90) 6940022

120		80-100	50 km/h
80		80	50 km/h
towing if trailer has brakes			
60		60	50 km/h
towing if trailer unbraked			

0.05%
Compulsory if fitted for driver and front and rear seat passengers
Compulsory
Recommended
Recommended
Compulsory for motorcyclists and passengers
18
Valid driving licence; Vehicle registration document or Vehicle on hire certificate; Green Card recommended; National vehicle identification plate
★ Compulsory use of headlights at all times outside built-up areas

France

Automobile Club de France, FIA,
6-8 Place de la Concorde, 75008 Paris Tel: (01) 42 65 08 26
Association Française des Automobiles-Clubs (AFA),
FIA & AIT, 9 rue Anatole de la Forge, 75017 Paris
Tel: (01) 42 27 82 00

110-130	110	90	60 km/h
100-110	100	80	60 km/h if wet

0.08% or 0.40 mg per litre of air exhaled
Compulsory if fitted for driver and front and rear seat passengers
Children under 10 years of age not allowed in front seats
Compulsory unless hazard warning lights are fitted; triangle and lights compulsory for cars pulling caravans or trailers and for vehicles over 3.5 tons
Recommended
Recommended
Compulsory for motorcyclists and passengers
Tolls payable on most motorways although short urban sections of motorway around Paris and some other major cities are free; tolls also payable on some major bridges and in some tunnels
18
Valid driving licence; Vehicle registration document or Vehicle on hire certificate; Green Card recommended; National vehicle identification plate

FDR (West Germany)

Allgemeiner Deutscher Automobil-Club (ADAC), FIA & AIT,
Am Westpark 8, 8000 München 70 Tel: (089) 76760
Automobil-Club von Deutschland (AvD), FIA, Lyonerstraße
16, 6000 Frankfurt am Main 71 Tel: (069) 66060

130*	130*	100	50 km/h
80	80	80	50 km/h if towing

*recommended

0.08%
Compulsory if fitted for driver and front and rear seat passengers
Children under 12 years of age not allowed in front seats
Compulsory
Compulsory

Compulsory for motorcyclists and passengers

18

Valid driving licence; Vehicle registration document or Vehicle on hire certificate; Green Card recommended; National vehicle identification plate

Germany: situation as at 1 September 1990

DDR (East Germany)

Allgemeiner Deutscher Motorsport-Verband der DDR, FIA, 60 Charlottenstraße,108 Berlin (Ost) Tel: (02) 2071931/2071932

100	80	80	50 km/h
80	80	80	50 km/h if towing

0.0% any alcohol found in the bloodstream may result in prosecution

Compulsory if fitted for driver and front seat passengers

Children under 7 years of age not allowed in front seats

Compulsory

Compulsory

Compulsory

Compulsory for motorcyclists; smoking not allowed whilst driving

18

Valid driving licence; Vehicle registration document or Vehicle on hire certificate; Green Card recommended; National vehicle identification plate

Germany: situation as at 1 September 1990

Great Britain

Automobile Association (AA), FIA & AIT, Fanum House, Basingstoke, Hampshire RG21 2EA Tel: (0256) 20123

Royal Automobile Club (RAC), FIA & AIT, Lansdowne Road, Croydon CR9 2JA Tel: (081) 686 2525

112	112	96	48 km/h
96	96	80	48 km/h if towing

0.08%

Compulsory if fitted for driver and front seat passengers; compulsory if fitted in back seats for children under 14

Children under 1 year of age travelling in front seat must be strapped in or placed in a child's safety seat

Recommended

Compulsory for motorcyclists and passengers

Tolls payable on certain major bridges and tunnels

17

Valid driving licence; Vehicle registration document or Vehicle on hire certificate; Green Card recommended; National vehicle identification plate

★ Drive on the left!

Greece

The Automobile and Touring Club of Greece (ELPA), FIA & AIT, 2-4 Messagion, 115 27 Athina Tel: (01) 779 1615

Hellenic Touring Club, AIT, 12 Politehniou, 104 33 Athina Tel: (01) 524 0854

100	80	80	50 km/h

0.05%

Compulsory if fitted for driver and front seat passengers

Children under 10 years of age not allowed in front seats

Compulsory

Compulsory

Compulsory for motorcyclists and passengers

Tolls payable on most 'national' roads

17

Valid driving licence; Vehicle registration document or Vehicle on hire certificate; Green Card required; National vehicle identification plate

★ Fire extinguisher compulsory

Hungary

Magyar Autóklub (MAK), FIA & AIT, Rómer Flóris utca 4a, Budapest 11 Tel: (01) 152 040

120	100	100	50-60 km/h
80	70	70	50 km/h if towing

0.0% if the alcohol test changes colour, the driver is taken to a hospital for a blood test and his driving licence confiscated

Compulsory if fitted for driver and front seat passengers

Children under 6 years of age not allowed in front seats

Compulsory

Recommended

Compulsory

Compulsory for motorcyclists and passengers

Petrol can only be purchased with coupons obtainable at the border, at IBUSZ offices or in hotels; unused coupons not refundable

18

Valid driving licence; Vehicle registration document or Vehicle on hire certificate; Green Card strongly recommended; National vehicle identification plate

Iceland

Felag Islenskra Bifreidaeigenda (FIB), FIA & AIT, Borgatun 33, 105 Reykjavik Tel: (01) 29999

	70	70	50 km/h

0.05%

Compulsory for driver and front seat passengers; rear seat belts recommended

Children in rear seats must be strapped in or placed in a child's safety seat

Recommended

Recommended

Recommended

Compulsory for motorcyclists and passengers

17

Driver's passport; Valid driving licence; Vehicle registration document or Vehicle on hire certificate; Green Card, valid for Iceland, required; Temporary importation permit; National vehicle identification plate

★ Vehicle mud flaps compulsory; headlights compulsory at all times; vehicles with deisel engines are subject to a special charge on entry to Iceland

Ireland

Automobile Association (AA), FIA & AIT, 23 Suffolk Street, Dublin 2 Tel: (01) 779481

Royal Automobile Club (RAC), FIA & AIT, 34 Dawson Street, Dublin 2 Tel: (01) 775141

88	88	64-88	48 km/h
56	56	56	48 km/h if towing

0.10%

Compulsory if fitted for driver and front seat passengers

Children under 12 years of age not allowed in front seats unless strapped in or placed in a child's safety seat

Recommended

Recommended

Recommended

Compulsory for motorcyclists and passengers

Toll payable on two bridges over River Liffey in Dublin

17

Valid driving licence; Vehicle registration document or Vehicle on hire certificate; Green Card recommended; National vehicle identification plate

★ Drive on the left!

Italy

Automobile Club d'Italia (ACI), FIA & AIT, Via Marsala 8, 00185 Roma Tel: (06) 49981

Touring Club Italiano (TCI), AIT, Corso Italia 10, 20122 Milano Tel: (02) 85261

110*-130	110*-130	90	50 km/h
110*-130	110*-130	90	50 km/h if towing

* for vehicles up to 1100 cc

Severe penalties for drinking and driving

Compulsory in front (and in back if installed)

Children under 12 not allowed in front unless seat is fitted with child restraint system

Compulsory

Recommended

Compulsory

Compulsory for motorcyclists

Tolls payable on most motorways and passengers

Coupons at a discount available at RAC, AA, and Port Offices and frontier Automobile Clubs to personal callers; must be paid for in foreign currency

18

Valid driving licence (translation in Italian recommended); Vehicle registration document or Vehicle on hire certificate; Green Card recommended; Temporary importation document; National vehicle identification plate

Luxembourg

Automobile Club du Grand Duché de Luxembourg (ACL), FIA & AIT, 13 route de Longwy, 8007 Bertrange Tel: (012) 45 00 45

90	75	75	60 km/h

0.08%

Compulsory if fitted for driver and front seat passengers

Children under 10 years of age not allowed in front seats

Compulsory

Recommended

Compulsory

18

Valid driving licence; Vehicle registration document or Vehicle on hire certificate; Green Card recommended; National vehicle identification plate

Netherlands

Koninklijke Nederlandsche Automobiel Club (KNAC), FIA, Westvlietweg 118, Leidschendam Tel: (070) 399 74 51

Koninklijke Nederlandsche Toeristenbond (ANWB), AIT, Wassenaarseweg 220, Den Haag Tel: (070) 314 71 47

100-120	80	80	50 km/h
80	80	80	50 km/h if towing

0.05%

Compulsory if fitted for driver and front seat passengers

Children under 12 years of age not allowed in front seats unless child is under 4 years of age and using a child's safety seat

Compulsory

Recommended

Compulsory for motorcyclists and passengers

Tolls payable on: Zeeland Brug, Kiltunnel (from Dordrecht to Hoekse Waard), Prins Willem Alexander Brug

18

Valid driving licence; Vehicle registration document or Vehicle on hire certificate; Green Card recommended; National vehicle identification plate

Norway

Kongelig Norsk Automobilklub (KNA), FIA, Drammensveien 20c, 0255 Oslo 2 Tel: (02) 56 19 00

Norges Automobil-Forbund (NAF), AIT, Storgata 2, 0155 Oslo 1 Tel: (02) 34 15 00

80-90	80-90	80-90	50 km/h
80	80	80	50 km/h
if towing trailer with braking system			
60	60	60	50 km/h
if towing trailer without braking system			

0.05%

Compulsory if fitted for driver and front and rear seat passengers

Children are allowed in front if seat is fitted with child restraint system and seat and belt can be adapted to their size

Compulsory

Recommended

Recommended

Compulsory for motorcyclists and passengers

Tolls payable on most new major roads

18 or 20 depending on the type of vehicle

Valid driving licence; Vehicle registration document or Vehicle on hire certificate; Green Card recommended; National vehicle identification plate

★ Dipped headlights compulsory at all times

Poland

Polski Zwiazek Motorowy (PZM), FIA & AIT, Kazimierzowska 66, 02-518 Warszawa
Tel: (022) 499361/499212
Auto Assistance, Krucza 6-14, 00-537 Warszawa
Tel: (022) 293541/210467

110	100	90	50 km/h
70	70	70	50 km/h if towing

- 0.0%
- Compulsory, outside built-up areas, if fitted for driver and front seat passengers
- Children under 10 years of age not allowed in front seats
- △ Compulsory
- Recommended
- Recommended
- Compulsory for motorcyclists and passengers
- ⊖ 18
- Valid driving licence; International Driving Permit after 3 months; Vehicle registration document or Vehicle on hire certificate; Green Card, valid for Poland, required; National vehicle identification plate

Portugal

Automóvel Club de Portugal (ACP), FIA & AIT, Rua Rosa Araújo 24, 1200 Lisboa Tel: (01) 736121

120	90	90	60 km/h
100	70	70	50 km/h if towing

- 0.05%
- Compulsory, outside built-up areas, if fitted for driver and front seat passengers
- Children under 12 years of age not allowed in front seats
- △ Compulsory
- Recommended
- Compulsory
- Compulsory for motorcyclists
- Tolls payable on some motorways and bridges
- ⊖ 17
- Valid driving licence; Vehicle registration document or Vehicle on hire certificate; Green Card required; National vehicle identification plate
- ★ Vehicle mud flaps are compulsory

Romania

In the event of breakdown or accident contact **National Tourist Office Carpaţi-Bucureşti**, Bd Magheru 7, Bucureşti
Tel: (400) 145160
Automobile-Club romain, FIA & AIT, Strada Nikos Beloianis 27, Bucureşti Tel: (400) 155510

70-90*	60-90*	60-90*	60 km/h

*according to cylinder capacity

- 0.0% any alcohol found in the bloodstream may result in immediate imprisonment
- Compulsory if fitted
- Children under 12 years of age not allowed in front seats
- △ Compulsory
- Compulsory
- Recommended
- Compulsory for motorcyclists and passengers
- Tolls payable on some major routes
- Coupons obtainable with convertible currency only at frontier posts, tourist offices, the Automobile-Club and some hotels; for use at PECO filling stations
- ⊖ 18
- Valid driving licence; Vehicle registration document or Vehicle on hire certificate; Green Card, valid for Romania, required; National vehicle identification plate

Spain

Real Automóvil Club de España (RACE), FIA & AIT, José Abascal 10, 28003 Madrid Tel: (91) 447 3200

120	120	100	60 km/h
80	80	80	60 km/h if towing

these limits are increased by 20 km/h for overtaking

- 0.08%
- Compulsory, outside built-up areas, if fitted for driver and front seat passengers
- Children under 10 years of age not advised in front seats
- △ Two are compulsory for vehicles with 9 or more seats; recommended for other vehicles
- Recommended
- Compulsory
- Compulsory for motorcycles but not for mopeds
- Tolls payable on most motorways and Cadí tunnel
- ⊖ 18
- International Driving Permit required if 'pink' EEC licence not held; Vehicle registration document or Vehicle on hire certificate; Green Card required; Bail Bond strongly recommended; National vehicle identification plate

Sweden

Motormännens Riksförbund (M), AIT, Sturegatan 32, Stockholm Tel: (08) 7 82 38 00

110	70-110	70-110	50 km/h
90*	70-90*	70-90*	50 km/h
70	70	70	50 km/h if towing with braking device
40	40	40	40 km/h if towing with no braking device

*limit imposed 21 June - 19 August

- 0.02%
- Compulsory if fitted for driver and front and rear seat passengers
- △ Compulsory
- Recommended
- Compulsory
- Compulsory for motorcyclists and passengers
- ⊖ 18
- Valid driving licence; Vehicle registration document or Vehicle on hire certificate; Green Card required; National vehicle identification plate
- ★ Dipped headlights compulsory at all times

Switzerland

Automobile Club de Suisse (ACS), FIA, Wasserwerkgasse 39, 3000 Bern 13
Tel: (031) 22 47 22
Touring Club Suisse (TCS), AIT, 9 rue Pierre-Fatio, 1211 Genève 3 Tel: (022) 737 12 12

120	80	80	50 km/h
80	80	80	50 km/h if towing – up to 20 cwt trailer
60	60	60	50 km/h if towing – over 20 cwt trailer

- 0.08%
- Compulsory if fitted for driver and front seat passengers
- Children under 12 years of age not allowed in front seats
- △ Compulsory
- Compulsory
- Compulsory for motorcyclists and passengers
- Vignette compulsory: obtainable from frontier posts, post offices or garages; separate vignette required for trailer or caravan
- ⊖ 18
- Valid driving licence; Vehicle registration document or Vehicle on hire certificate; Green Card required; National vehicle identification plate

Turkey

Turkiye Turing ve Otomobil Kurumu (TTOK), FIA & AIT, Halaskargasi Cad. 364, 80222 Sisli, Istanbul Tel: (01) 1314631/6

	90	90	50 km/h
	70	70	40 km/h if towing

- 0.05%
- Compulsory if fitted for driver and front seat passengers
- Children under 12 years of age not allowed in front seats
- △ Two must be carried – one to place in front of the vehicle, one behind
- Compulsory
- Compulsory for motorcyclists
- Tolls payable on some roads
- ⊖ 18
- Passport; valid driving licence; International Driving Permit advised and compulsory if driving Turkish vehicle (obtainable at frontier with 2 photos and 54 000 Turkish Lire); Vehicle registration document or Vehicle on hire certificate; Green Card required – must cover European and Asian regions; National vehicle identification plate
- ★ Fire extinguisher, chock and towrope compulsory

USSR

In the event of breakdown or accident contact officer of State Automobile Inspection (Militia) or nearest office of Intourist (obliged to give tourists assistance)

90	90	90	60 km/h

- 0.0%
- Compulsory if fitted for driver and front seat passengers
- Children under 12 years of age not allowed in front seats
- △ Compulsory
- Compulsory
- Recommended
- Compulsory
- Road tax payable on entry to USSR though some foreign cars exempt
- Petrol coupons advised; obtainable at border posts
- ⊖ 18
- Valid driving licence meeting requirements of International Convention on Road Traffic; Vehicle registration document or Vehicle on hire certificate; Car insurance obtainable on entry to USSR at Ingosstrakh offices or at Intourist offices; Itinerary card, service coupons and motor routes map issued by Intourist; Customs obligation to take the car out of the country on departure; National vehicle identification plate
- ★ Fire extinguisher compulsory

Yugoslavia

Auto-Moto Savez Jugoslavija (AMSJ), FIA & AIT, Ruzveltova 18, 11001 Beograd Tel: (011) 401699

120	100	80	60 km/h
80	80	80	60 km/h if towing

- 0.05%
- Compulsory if fitted for driver and front and rear seat passengers
- Children under 12 years of age not allowed in front seats
- △ Compulsory – two are necessary if towing trailer or caravan
- Compulsory
- Compulsory
- Compulsory for motorcyclists and passengers
- Tolls payable on several major roads, Tito Bridge, Krk Island Bridge and Ucka Tunnel
- Concessionary petrol coupons available at frontier posts for purchase with convertible currency; unused coupons refundable at place of purchase
- ⊖ 18
- Valid driving licence; Vehicle registration document or Vehicle on hire certificate; Green Card required; National vehicle identification plate

Key to Symbols

Road classification

Motorway: dual carriageway – single carriageway
Dual carriageway with motorway characteristics
Interchange: complete – half – limited – unspecified
Interchange: number

International and national surfaced road network:
dual carriageway
four lanes – three lanes
two wide lanes – two lanes

Interregional surfaced road network:
dual carriageway
two lanes or more – two narrow lanes
surfaced, of doubtful quality : Greece
Unsurfaced: suitable for vehicles, macadam
Other surfaced road – unsurfaced
Surfaced, in bad condition: Portugal, Spain
Narrow road with passing places (Scotland)
Service road or cart track, footpath
10-1991 Road under construction – scheduled opening date

Distances in kilometres (total and intermediate)

12 / 5 7 — on motorway: toll section
12 / 5 7 — free section
12 / 5 7 — on other roads
14 10 / 24 39 — GB and IRL: in miles / in kilometres

Obstacles

Road and pass closed during the period shown
Gradient (ascent in the direction of the arrow)
Toll road

Road classification

E 10 — N 51 — International E-road – other roads
A 40 — A 68 — Primary route (GB) and National Primary route (IRL)
YORK — Wells — GB: signposting for places on primary route network

Eastern Europe

Checkpoint
For the nationals of bordering countries only
Transit road (GDR and USSR)

Transportation

Railway – Motorail
B — Ferry – Ferry (DK, N, S, SF)
Car ferry: all the year – seasonal
Airport

Administration – Facilities

International boundary
Administrative boundary
A ... L .. P — Capital of administrative area
Place with at least one hotel (GR, IS, N, S, SF, YU)
Spain: Parador, Portugal: Pousada
Refuge (IS) – Camp site (GR, IS, N, S, SF, YU)

Important isolated sights

Ecclesiastical building
Castle
Rune stone
Cave
Stave church
Ruins
Rock carving
Additional sights
Scenic road
Monastery (GR)
Antiquities (GR)
Megalithic monument
National Park

Symbols on town plans

H — Town Hall
POL — Police
Post office
Cemetery
Ecclesiastical building
Country park
Windmill
U — University
M — Museum
Tourist information centre
Castle
Monument or statue
Zoo
Car park
Covered market
Hospital
Ruins
Botanic gardens
Golf
Racecourse
Stadium
Station

Légende

Importance des itinéraires

Autoroute à chaussées séparées – à une seule chaussée
Double chaussée de type autoroutier
Échangeurs: complet – demi-échangeur – partiel – sans précision
Numéro d'échangeur

Route de liaison internationale ou nationale revêtue:
chaussées séparées
4 voies – 3 voies
2 voies larges – 2 voies

Route de liaison interrégionale revêtue:
chaussées séparées
2 voies et plus – 2 voies étroites
revêtue, en mauvais état : Grèce
Non revêtue: carrossable, en macadam
Autre route revêtue – non revêtue
Revêtue, en mauvaise condition: Portugal, Espagne
Route très étroite avec emplacement pour croisement (Écosse)
Chemin d'exploitation, sentier
10-1991 Route en construction – date de mise en service prévue

Distances en kilomètres (totalisées et partielles)

12 / 5 7 — sur autoroute: section à péage
12 / 5 7 — section libre
12 / 5 7 — sur route
14 10 / 24 39 — GB et IRL: en miles / en kilomètres

Obstacles

Routes et cols fermés pendant la période indiquée
Forte déclivité (montée dans le sens de la flèche)
Péage sur route

Numéros des routes

E 10 — N 51 — Européennes – Autres
A 40 — A 68 — Primary route (GB) et National Primary route (IRL)
YORK — Wells — GB: localités signalisées sur un itinéraire primary

Europe de l'Est

Point de passage contrôlé
Passage réservé aux ressortissants des pays limitrophes
Route de transit (RDA et URSS)

Transport

Voie ferrée – Train-auto
B — Bac – Bac (DK, N, S, SF)
Liaison maritime: permanente – saisonnière
Aéroport

Administration – Ressources

Frontière internationale
Limite administrative
A ... L .. P — Capitale de division administrative
Localité ayant des ressources hôtelières (GR, IS, N, S, SF, YU)
Espagne: Parador, Portugal: Pousada
Refuge (IS) – Camping (GR, IS, N, S, SF, YU)

Principales curiosités isolées

Édifice religieux
Château
Pierre runique
Grotte
Église en bois debout
Ruines
Gravure rupestre
Autres curiosités
Parcours pittoresque
Monastère (GR)
Site antique (GR)
Monument mégalithique
Parc national

Signes particuliers aux plans de villes

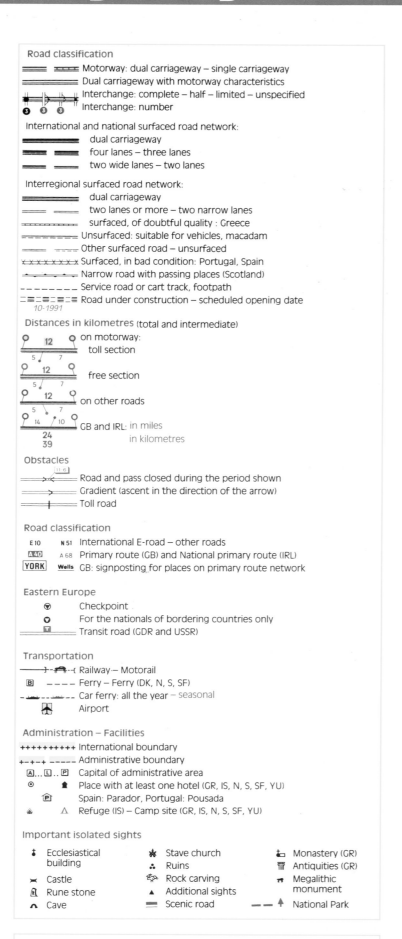

H — Hôtel de ville
POL — Police
Bureau de poste
Cimetière
Édifice religieux
Parc de loisirs
Moulin
U — Université
M — Musée
Office de tourisme
Château
Monument
Zoo
Parc de stationnement
Marché couvert
Hôpital
Ruines
Jardin botanique
Golf
Hippodrome
Stade
Gare

OUTER HEBRIDES
INNER HEBRIDES
WESTERN ISLES
SEA OF THE HEBRIDES
THE MINCH
The Little Minch
Butt of Lewis
Port of Ness
LEWIS
Flannan I.
Barvas
Carloway
Stornoway
Garynahine
Broad Bay
Portnaguran
Tiumpan Head
Eye Peninsula
Hushinish
Clisham
West Loch Tarbert
Tarbert
St. Kilda
Toe Head
Harris
Leverburgh
Rodel
Renish Point
Sound of Harris
Kebock Head
Rubha Còigeach
Rubha Réidh
North Uist
Tigharry
Lochmaddy
Sound of Monach
Balivanich
Benbecula
Creagorry
South Uist
Daliburgh
Lochboisdale
Sound of Barra
Barra
Castlebay
Bayhirivagh
Mingulay
Barra Head
Waternish Point
Dunvegan Head
Loch Snizort
Uig
Staffin
The Storr
Dunvegan
Portree
Bracadale
Idrigill Point
Loch Bracadale
Sligachan
Sconser
Scalpay
SKYE
The Cuillins
Broadford
Kyleakin
Kylerhea
Kyle of Lochalsh
Elgol
Isleornsay
Ardvasar
Sound of Sleat
Cuillin Sound
Canna
Rhum
Sound of Rhum
Eigg
Muck
Raasay
Sound of Raasay
Inner Sound
Rona
Mallaig
Loch Nevis
Loch Morar
Arisaig
Sound of Arisaig
Glenfinnan
Cape Wrath
Durness
Whiten Head
Kinlochbervie
Loch Eriboll
Kyle of Tongue
Bettyhill
Coldbackie
Tongue
Foinaven
Ben Hope
Scourie
Laxford Bridge
Eddrachillis Bay
Kylestrome
Syre
Altnaharra
L. Naver
Ben Klibreck
Ben Armine
Lochinver
Inchnadamph
Ben More Assynt
Ledmore
Loch Shin
Lairg
Coigach
Loch Broom
Ullapool
Gruinard Bay
Laide
Dundonnell
Beinn Dearg
Bonar Bridge
Gairloch
Loch Maree
Sgurr Mór
Loch Fannich
Wester Ross
Easter Ross
Torridon
Liathach
Kinlochewe
Achnasheen
Loch Torridon
Shieldaig
Lochcarron
Glen Carron
Garve
Ben Wyvis
Alness
Invergordon
Dingwall
Black Isle
Fortrose
Cromarty
Contin
Muir of Ord
Tore
Inverness
Stromeferry
Dornie
Eilean Donan Castle
Glenelg
Shiel Bridge
Carn Eige
Cannich
Drumnadrochit
Loch Ness
HIGHLAND
A' Chràlaig
Invermoriston
Glen Mòr
Foyers
White Bridge
Fort Augustus
Glen Albyn
Monadhliath Mountains
Carn Ban
Kingussie
Newtonmore
Loch Quoich
Sgurr na Ciche
Invergarry
Loch Lochy
Loch Arkaig
Caledonian Canal
Laggan
Creag Meagaidh
Spean Bridge
Loch Laggan
Dalwhinnie
Pass of Drumochter
Fort William
Ben Nevis
Ben Alder
Loch Ericht
GRAMPIAN
Kilchoan
Salen
Strontian
Corran
Inchree
Onich
Loch Shiel
Loch Sunart
Ballachulish
Glen Coe
Blackwater Resr.
Kinloch Rannoch
Loch Rannoch
Schiehallion
Coll
Arinagour
Tiree
Scarinish
Tobermory
Dervaig
Sound of Mull
Lochaline
Kentallen
Bidean nam Bian
Loch Linnhe
Portnacroish
L. Tuath
Ulva
L. na Keal
Staffa
MULL
Craignure
Ben More
Achnacroish
Lismore
Connel
Loch Etive
Ben Lawers
Killin
Loch Tay
Ben Chonzie
Iona
Fionnphort
Bunessan
Kerrera
Oban
Taynuilt
Ben Cruachan
Pass of Brander
Tyndrum
Dalmally
Crianlarich
Lochearnhead
Kilninver
Firth of Lorn
Seil
Luing
Loch Awe
Ben Vorlich
Crieff
Arduaine
CENTRAL
Toberonochy
Scarba
Inveraray
Argyll
Tarbet
Arrochar
The Trossachs
Callander
Ben Lomond
Queen Elizabeth Forest Park
Aberfoyle
Loch Lomond
Colonsay
Scalasaig
Crinan
Kilmartin
Furnace
Doune
Dunblane
Bridge of Allan
Alva
Drymen
Stirling
Ardlussa
JURA
Sound of Jura
Lochgilphead
Ardrishaig
Otter Ferry
Loch Fyne
Ardentinny
Kilcreggan
Helensburgh
Rubha a' Mhail
Beinn an Oir
Port Askaig
Feolin Ferry
Craighouse
ISLAY
Bridgend
Port Charlotte
Portnahaven
Beinn Bheigeir
Rinns Point
Ardbeg
Port Ellen
Mull of Oa
Knapdale
Tarbert
Tighnabruaich
Colintraive
Dunoon
Innellan
Gourock
Port Glasgow
Greenock
Dumbarton
Alexandria
Kirkintilloch
Kilsyth
Denny
Falkirk
Erskine Bridge
Clydebank
Cumbernauld
Coatbridge
Airdrie
Wemyss Bay
Rothesay
Bute
Kennacraig
Claonaig
Lochranza
Gigha I.
Kintyre
Largs
Johnstone
Paisley
Barrhead
GLASGOW
Hamilton
Motherwell
Wishaw
Carluke
Millport
Kilbirnie
Beith
Dalry
East Kilbride
W. Kilbride
Ardrossan
Saltcoats
Stewarton
Kilwinning
Irvine
Kilmarnock
Strathaven
Lanark
Galston
Tayinloan
Carradale
Kilbrannan Sound
Goat Fell
ARRAN
Brodick
Lamlash
Blackwaterfoot
Troon
Prestwick
Ayr
STRATHCLYDE
Mauchline
Douglas
Muirkirk
Machrihanish
Campbeltown
Southend
Mull of Kintyre
Firth of Clyde
Ailsa Craig
Cumnock
New Cumnock
Sanquhar
Elvanfoot
Turnberry
Maybole
Dalmellington
Girvan
Galloway
Ballantrae
DUMFRIES AND
Inishtrahull
Malin Head
Fanad Head
Culdaff
Carndonagh
Inishowen
Slieve Snaght
Portsalon
Buncrana
Moville
Inishowen Head
Carrigart
Rathmullan
Quigley's Point
Lough Swilly
Lough Foyle
Millford
Rathmelton
Letterkenny
Muff
Grianan of Aileach
Eglinton
Limavady
Portstewart
Portrush
Castlerock
Coleraine
Bushmills
Giant's Causeway
Antrim Coast
Rathlin Island
Fair Head
Ballycastle
Ballymoney
Cushendun
Cushendall
Red Bay
Trostan
Glenariff or Waterfoot
8
9
4

ORKNEY ISLANDS
Westray
Pierowall
North Ronaldsay
The North Sound
Kettletoft
Sanday
Rousay
Westray Firth
Eday
Brough Head
Stronsay Firth
Stronsay
Mainland
Shapinsay
Stromness
Stenness
Kirkwall
Scalloway
Skaill
Rora Head
Scapa Flow
Lyness
Hoy
Aberdeen
St. Margaret's Hope
South Ronaldsay
Pentland Firth
Burwick
Dunnet Head
Scrabster
Dunnet
Duncansby Head
John o'Groats
Thurso
Castletown
Roadside
Reiss
Noss Head
Wick
SHETLAND ISLANDS
Herma Ness
Haroldswick
Unst
Gutcher
Belmont
Fetlar
Isbister
Yell Sound
Mid Yell
Yell
Ulsta
Hillswick
Toft
St. Magnus Bay
Muckle Roe
Papa Stour
Laxo
Whalsay
Voe
Sandness
Mainland
Walls
Whiteness
Foula
Bressay
Scalloway
Lerwick
Tørshavn (Færøerne)
Seydisfjördur
Bergen
Aberdeen
Kirkwall
Sumburgh
Sumburgh Head
Fair I.
Latheron
Kinbrace
Morven
Helmsdale
Brora
Tarbat Ness
Moray Firth
Lossiemouth
Elgin
Buckie
Cullen
Banff
Macduff
Kinnairds Head
Fraserburgh
Forres
Fochabers
Rattray Head
Rothes
R. Spey
Keith
Deveron
Turriff
Craigellachie
Dufftown
New Deer
Mintlaw
Peterhead
Dava
Huntly
Buchan Ness
Grantown-on-Spey
Cruden Bay
Rhynie
Oldmeldrum
Ellon
Dulnain Bridge
Tomintoul
GRAMPIAN
Newburgh
Glen More Forest Park
Mossat
Inverurie
Stromness
Lerwick
Alford
Kintore
Craigievar Castle
Colnabaichin
Cairngorm Mountains
Ben Macdui
ABERDEEN
Aboyne
Crathes Castle
Braemar
Ballater
Balmoral Castle
Banchory
Dee
MOUNTAINS
Stonehaven
Devil's Elbow
Glas Maol
N. Esk
Laurencekirk
Inverbervie
TAYSIDE
Marykirk
S. Esk
Brechin
Pitlochry
Montrose
Kirriemuir
Alyth
Glamis Castle
Forfar
Rattray
Blairgowrie
Dunkeld
Glamis
Meigle
Coupar Angus
Sidlaw Hills
Arbroath
Tay
Monifieth
Carnoustie
Dundee
Perth
Buddon Ness
Newport-on-Tay
Tayport
Leuchars
Newburgh
St. Andrews
Auchtermuchty
Cupar
Fife Ness
FIFE
Falkland
Crail
Kinross
Anstruther
Pittenweem
Leven
Glenrothes
Methil
St. Monance
Elie
Buckhaven
Lochgelly
Cowdenbeath
Firth of Forth
Kirkcaldy
Burntisland
North Berwick
Hopetoun House
Inverkeithing
Forth Bridges
S. Queensferry
Aberlady
East Linton
Dunbar
Leith
Prestonpans
Haddington
Livingston
Musselburgh
Tranent
EDINBURGH
Dalkeith
Cockburnspath
St. Abb's Head
LOTHIAN
Lammermuir Hills
Eyemouth
Penicuik
Pentland Hills
West Linton
Duns
Berwick-upon-Tweed
Moorfoot Hills
Greenlaw
Lauder
Peebles
Tweed
Coldstream
Earlston
Holy Island
Innerleithen
Galashiels
Melrose
Mellerstain
Biggar
Kelso
Belford
Bamburgh
Newtown St. Boswells
Dryburgh
Selkirk
Wooler
Broad Law
BORDERS
The Cheviot
Hawick
Jedburgh
Alnwick
Moffat
Teviot
Cheviot Hills
Northumberland National Park
Carter Bar
Warkworth
Amble
Rothbury
Felton
GALLOWAY
NORTHUMBERLAND
The Border
5

A
B
C
IRISH SEA
NORTH CHANNEL
NORTHERN IRELAND
DONEGAL
LONDONDERRY
ANTRIM
TYRONE
FERMANAGH
ARMAGH
DOWN
MONAGHAN
CAVAN
LEITRIM
LONGFORD
LOUTH
MEATH
WESTMEATH
OFFALY
KILDARE
DUBLIN
WICKLOW
LAOIS
CARLOW
KILKENNY
BELFAST
Londonderry
DUBLIN/BAILE ÁTHA CLIATH
Dún Laoghaire
Bangor
Larne
Coleraine
Ballymena
Lisburn
Newry
Omagh
Strabane
Enniskillen
Newcastle
Dundalk
Dun Dealgan
Drogheda/
Droichead Átha
Armagh
Portadown
Dungannon
Carrickfergus
Newtownabbey
Newtownards
Downpatrick
Mullingar/
An Muileann gCearr
Tullamore/
Tulach Mhór
Navan/
An Uaimh
Kildare
Naas
Bray
Wicklow/Cill Mhantáin
Arklow/
An tInbhear Mór
Carlow
Kilkenny/
Cill Chainnigh
Athy
Portlaoise
Longford/
An Longfort
Cavan/An Cabhán
Monaghan/
Muineachán
Letterkenny/
Leitir Ceanainn
Donegal/
Dún na nGall
ISLE OF MAN
Douglas
Ramsey
Peel
Castletown
Point of Ayre
ISLAY
JURA
ARRAN
Kintyre
Campbeltown
GLASGOW
Greenock
Paisley
Kilmarnock
Ayr
Stranraer
Holyhead
Caergybi
Isle of Anglesey
Bangor
Caernarfon
Snowdonia
Lleyn Peninsula
Malin Head
Mull of Kintyre
Mull of Galloway
Giant's Causeway
Lough Neagh
Mourne Mts
Sperrin Mountains
Wicklow Mountains
Slieve Bloom Mts
Firth of Clyde
2
8
9
6

E
F
NORTH SEA
1
2
3
4
3
7
10
St. Andrews
Fife Ness
FIFE
Dunfermline
Kirkcaldy
Firth of Forth
North Berwick
Dunbar
Falkirk
EDINBURGH
LOTHIAN
Lammermuir Hills
St. Abb's Head
Eyemouth
Berwick-upon-Tweed
Holy Island
Bamburgh
Coldstream
Kelso
Jedburgh
Hawick
Galashiels
Peebles
BORDERS
CLYDE
SOUTHERN UPLANDS
DUMFRIES AND GALLOWAY
Dumfries
The Cheviot
Cheviot Hills
Northumberland National Park
NORTHUMBERLAND
Kielder Forest
Alnwick
Amble
Morpeth
Ashington
Newbiggin-by-the-Sea
Blyth
Whitley Bay
Kristiansand
Hirtshals
Oslo
Bergen
Stavanger
Göteborg
Esbjerg
NEWCASTLE-UPON-TYNE
Tynemouth
South Shields
SUNDERLAND
Gateshead
Hexham
Carlisle
Solway Firth
Workington
Whitehaven
Bees Head
CUMBRIA
Penrith
Keswick
Lake District National Park
Cumbrian Mountains
Kendal
Windermere
Barrow-in-Furness
Morecambe
Morecambe Bay
Lancaster
Fleetwood
BLACKPOOL
LANCASHIRE
Preston
Southport
LIVERPOOL
Liverpool Bay
Birkenhead
Wallasey
Chester
Wrexham
Warrington
St. Helens
Wigan
Bolton
Bury
Blackburn
Burnley
Rochdale
Oldham
MANCHESTER
Stockport
Macclesfield
CHESHIRE
Crewe
Stoke-on-Trent
Newcastle-under-Lyme
Durham
DURHAM
Hartlepool
Darlington
Stockton-on-Tees
Middlesbrough
Whitby
Scarborough
North York Moors National Park
Cleveland Hills
NORTH YORKSHIRE
Yorkshire Dales National Park
THE PENNINES
Harrogate
YORK
Ripon
Flamborough Head
Bridlington
HUMBERSIDE
KINGSTON-UPON-HULL
Humber Bridge
Scunthorpe
Great Grimsby
Cleethorpes
Spurn Head
Rotterdam
Zeebrugge
BRADFORD
LEEDS
Halifax
Huddersfield
Wakefield
Barnsley
Doncaster
Rotherham
SHEFFIELD
Peak District National Park
Chesterfield
Mansfield
NOTTS
NOTTINGHAM
DERBY
Derby
Lincoln
LINCOLN
Skegness
Boston
Grantham
Gainsborough
Louth
Hunstanton

DUBLIN/BAILE ÁTHA CLIATH
Malahide
Portmarnock
Howth
Dún Laoghaire
Dalkey
Bray
Greystones
Wicklow / Cill Mhantáin
Wicklow Head
Rathnew
Arklow / An tInbhear Mór
Cahore Point
LIVERPOOL
Liverpool Bay
Formby
Ormskirk
Skelmersdale
Wigan
Bolton
Bury
Bootle
Wallasey
St. Helens
Warrington
Widnes
Runcorn
Altrincham
Knutsford
Wilmslow
Birkenhead
Hoylake
Bebington
Ellesmere Port
Holywell
Flint/Fflint
Queensferry
Frodsham
Northwich
Winsford
Macclesfield
Middlewich
Congleton
Sandbach
Crewe
Little Moreton
Kidsgrove
Chester
Tarporley
Nantwich
Newcastle-under-Lyme
Audlem
Market Drayton
Wrexham
Wrecsam
Ruabon
Whitchurch
Ellesmere
Wem
Oswestry
Hodnet
Eccleshall
Llanfyllin
Llynclys
Crudgington
Newport
Shrewsbury
Telford
Iron-Bridge
Gailey
Welshpool
Y Trallwng
Minsterley
Montgomery
SHROPSHIRE
Much Wenlock
Church Stretton
WOLVERHAMPTON
Bridgnorth
Dudley
BIRMINGHAM
Stourbridge
Kidderminster
Bewdley
Stourport
Bromsgrove
Droitwich
Worcester
Tenbury Wells
Ludlow
Craven Arms
Clun
Bishop's Castle
Knighton
Presteigne
Kington
Leominster
Bromyard
HEREFORD
Hereford
Great Malvern
Upton
Ledbury
Newtown
Hay-on-Wye
Talgarth
Pontrilas
Ross-on-Wye
Tewkesbury
Gloucester
Abergavenny
Y Fenni
Monmouth/Trefynwy
Newnham
Coleford
Lydney
Stroud
Painswick
Raglan
Usk
Chepstow
Cas-gwent
Severn Bridge
Dursley
Nailsworth
Tetbury
Malmesbury
Chipping Sodbury
NEWPORT/CASNEWYDD
CARDIFF/CAERDYDD
Avonmouth
Portishead
Clevedon
Congresbury
BRISTOL
Keynsham
Corsham
Chippenham
Bath
Bradford-on-Avon
Melksham
Trowbridge
Radstock
AVON
Westbury
Warminster
Frome
Stonehenge
Wells
Cheddar gorge
Shepton Mallet
Longleat House
Glastonbury
Street
Bruton
Mere
Wincanton
Shaftesbury
Gillingham
Sherborne
Yeovil
Ilchester
Langport
Crewkerne
Ilminster
Chard
Beaminster
Sturminster Newton
Blandford Forum
Wimborne Minster
Bridport
Dorchester
Bere Regis
Poole
Wareham
Corfe Castle
Weymouth
Abbotsbury
Fortuneswell
Isle of Portland
Bill of Portland
St. Alban's Head
Cherbourg
DORSET
SOMERSET
Bridgwater
Taunton
Burnham
Weston-Super-Mare
Barry/Barri
Penarth
Cowbridge
Bridgend/Pen-y-bont
Porthcawl
Port Talbot
Maesteg
Neath/Castell-nedd
Swansea/Abertawe
The Mumbles
Rhossili
Worms Head
Port-Einon
Llanelli
Burry Port
Kidwelly
Pontarddulais
Ammanford
Pontardawe
Llandeilo
Llangadog
Llandovery/Llanymddyfri
Brecon/Aberhonddu
Brecon Beacons National Park
Black Mountain
Merthyr Tydfil
Hirwaun
Aberdare/Aberdar
Mountain Ash/Aberpennar
Rhondda
Pontypridd
Caerphilly
Bedwas
Tredegar
Ebbw Vale/Glyn Ebwy
Brynmawr
Crickhowell
Blaenavon
Abertillery
Pontypool
Cwmbran
Risca
Bargoed
GWENT
GLAMORGAN
BRISTOL CHANNEL
Carmarthen Bay
Pendine
Saundersfoot
Tenby/Dinbych-y-pysgod
Pembroke
Pembroke Dock/Doc Penfro
Neyland
Milford Haven/Aberdaugleddau
Haverfordwest/Hwlffordd
Narberth
Whitland
St. Clears/Sanclêr
Carmarthen/Caerfyrddin
St. Brides Bay
St. David's Head
St. David's
Fishguard/Abergwaun
Strumble Head
Pembrokeshire Coast National Park
Rosslare
St. Govan's Head
Cardigan/Aberteifi
Aberporth
Newcastle Emlyn
Crymmych
Llandysul
Lampeter
Synod Inn
New Quay
Aberaeron
Llanrhystud
Tregaron
Aberystwyth
Devil's Bridge
Cardigan Bay
DYFED
WALES
CAMBRIAN MOUNTAINS
POWYS
Llanwrtyd-Wells
Builth Wells/Llanfair-ym-Muallt
Llandrindod Wells
Rhayader/Rhaeadr
Llangurig
Llanidloes
Newtown/Drenewydd
Caersws
Machynlleth
Aberdovey
Tywyn
Cader Idris Park
Mallwyd
Dolgellau
Barmouth
Harlech
GWYNEDD and National
Bala
Berwyn
Corwen
Llangollen
Penrhyndeudraeth
Ffestiniog Forest
Blaenau Ffestiniog
Porthmadog
Criccieth
Pwllheli
Abersoch
Aberdaron
Lleyn Peninsula
Nefyn
Beddgelert
Snowdon
Snowdonia
Capel Curig
Betws-y-Coed
Llanrwst
Pentrefoelas
Cerrigydrudion
Ruthin/Rhuthun
Mold/Yr Wyddgrug
Denbigh/Dinbych
St. Asaph
Abergele
Colwyn Bay/Bae Colwyn
Rhyl
Prestatyn
Llandudno
Great Ormes Head
Conwy
Penmaenmawr
Llanfairfechan
Bangor
Bethesda
Carnedd Llewelyn
Llanberis
Caernarfon
Caernarfon Bay
Newborough
Menai Bridge
Beaumaris
Llangefni
Llanerchymedd
Amlwch
Holyhead
Caergybi
Holy Island
Rhosneigr
Isle of Anglesey
CLWYD
Lundy
Ilfracombe
Combe Martin
Lynton
Lynmouth
Porlock
Minehead
Dunster
Watchet
Williton
Exmoor
Simonsbath
Croyde
Braunton
Barnstaple
Northam
Bideford
Hartland Point
Clovelly
South Molton
Great Torrington
Kilkhampton
Bampton
Wellington
Tiverton
Cullompton
Honiton
Axminster
Lyme Regis
Seaton
Sidmouth
Budleigh Salterton
Ottery St. Mary
Exmouth
Lyme Bay
EXETER
Crediton
DEVON
Okehampton
High Willhays
Moretonhampstead
Dartmoor National Park
Bovey Tracey
Dawlish
Teignmouth
Newton Abbot
Torquay
Torbay
Paignton
Brixham
Kingswear
Dartmouth
Totnes
Buckfastleigh
Ashburton
Kingsbridge
Salcombe
Start Point
Modbury
Plympton
PLYMOUTH
Plymstock
Newton Ferrers
Saltash
Torpoint
Princetown
Tavistock
Callington
Launceston
Holsworthy
Hatherleigh
Winkleigh
Stratton
Bude
Tintagel
Camelford
Padstow
Wadebridge
Bodmin
CORNWALL
Liskeard
Lostwithiel
Fowey
Looe
Polperro
St. Austell
Mevagissey
Newquay
Fraddon
Tregony
Truro
St. Mawes
Falmouth
Penryn
Redruth
Camborne
Hayle
St. Ives
Penzance
St. Michael's Mount
St. Just
Sennen
Land's End
Mount's Bay
Helston
St. Keverne
Lizard
Lizard Point
Santander
Roscoff
Alderney
Jersey - Guernsey
Tresco
St. Martin's
Isles of Scilly
St. Mary's
ENGLAND

6
9
12

Huddersfield
Barnsley
Wakefield
Scunthorpe
Great Grimsby
Cleethorpes
Doncaster
Rotherham
SHEFFIELD
Peak District
Worksop
Gainsborough
Lincoln
Louth
Skegness
Chesterfield
Mansfield
Newark-on-Trent
NOTTS
NOTTINGHAM
DERBY
Derby
LINCOLN
Boston
Grantham
Burton-upon-Trent
Loughborough
LEICESTER
Melton Mowbray
Stamford
Spalding
King's Lynn
NORFOLK
Cromer
NORWICH
Great Yarmouth
Lowestoft
Peterborough
Hinckley
Nuneaton
COVENTRY
Rugby
Kettering
NORTHAMPTON
Wellingborough
CAMBRIDGE
Huntingdon
Ely
Thetford
Bury St. Edmunds
Cambridge
Bedford
SUFFOLK
IPSWICH
Felixstowe
Harwich
Colchester
OXFORD
BUCKINGHAM
Milton Keynes
Luton
Stevenage
HERTFORD
Aylesbury
St. Albans
Watford
High Wycombe
Chelmsford
ESSEX
Southend-on-Sea
LONDON
Reading
BERKSHIRE
Windsor
Newbury
Basingstoke
Guildford
SURREY
Maidstone
KENT
Canterbury
Margate
Ramsgate
Dover
Folkestone
Crawley
Winchester
HAMPSHIRE
SOUTHAMPTON
PORTSMOUTH
Chichester
W. SUSSEX
BRIGHTON
E. SUSSEX
Eastbourne
Hastings
ISLE OF WIGHT
Calais
Boulogne
Le Touquet-Paris-Plage
PAS DE CALAIS
STRAIT OF DOVER
MANCHE
CHANNEL
Channel tunnel under construction
Zeebrugge
Hoek van Holland
Vlissingen
Oostende
Dieppe
Le Havre
Caen
Cherbourg
St. Malo
5
10
13

A
B
C
1
2
3
4
Aran Island
4
Crolly
Dunglow
Errigal Mt. 752
Derryveagh Mountains
Millford
Rathmullan
Rathmelton
Buncrana
Quigley's Point
Muff
Letterkenny / Leitir Ceanainn
Gweebarra Bay
Fintown
DONEGAL
Glenties
Ardara
Glencolumbkille
Rossan Point
Killybegs
Blue Stack Mts.
Ballybofey
Stranorlar
Lifford
Strabane
Plumbridge
Castlederg
Newtownstewart
Gortin
Donegal / Dún na nGall
Lough Derg
Donegal Bay
Bundoran / Bun Dobhráin
Ballyshannon
Pettigoe
Belleek
Kesh
Omagh
Dromore
Fintona
Irvinestown
Lower Lough Erne
Ballygawley
Inishmurray
Erris Head
Broad Haven
Belmullet
Glenamoy
Ballycastle
Killala Bay
Easky
Rosses Point
Sligo Bay
Sligo / Sligeach
Strandhill
Manorhamilton
L. Melvin
FERMANAGH
Enniskillen
Fivemiletown
Belcoo
Lisnaskea
Inishkea
MAYO
Bangor
Inishcrone
The Ox Mountains
SLIGO
Ballysadare
Blacksod Bay
Ballycroy
Nephin Beg Range
Crossmolina
Ballina / Béal an Átha
L. Conn
Nephin
Keel
Achill Island
Mulrany
Corraun
Pontoon
Foxford
Tobercurry
Ballymote
Drumkeeran
Dowra
Swanlinbar
Rossiea
Newtownbutler
Clones
Monaghan
Lough Allen
Drumshanbo
Ballyconnell
Belturbet
Clare Island
Newport
Castlebar / Caisleán an Bharraigh
Swinford
Charlestown
Gorteen
Boyle / Mainistir na Búille
Keadew
Carrick-on-Shannon / Cora Droma Rúisc
LEITRIM
Ballinamore
Killashandra
Cootehill
Clew Bay
Kiltamagh
Ballaghaderreen
Louisburgh
Westport / Cathair na Mart
Croagh Patrick
Frenchpark
Elphin
Mohill
Cavan / An Cabhán
CAVAN
Inishturk
Inishbofin
Ballintober
Bailieborough
Inishshark
Mweelrea Mts.
Killary Harbour
Rinvyle Pt.
Claremorris
Ballyhaunis
ROSCOMMON
Castlerea
Tulsk
Strokestown
LONGFORD
Granard
Ballyjamesduff
Virginia
Letterfrack
Leenane
Partry Mountains
Lough Mask
Ballinrobe
Ballymoe
Longford / An Longfort
L. Sheelin
The Twelve Pins
Connemara
Maumturk Mts.
Clonbur
Cong
Kilmaing
Dunmore
Roscommon / Ros Comáin
Lanesborough
Mostrim (Edgeworthstown)
Oldcastle
Clifden / An Clochán
Slyne Head
Roundstone
Maam Cross
Lough Corrib
Headford
Tuam / Tuaim
Glennamaddy
IRELAND
L. Derravaragh
Castlepollard
Gortmore
Oughterard
Carna
Mount Bellew
Ballyforan
Lough Ree
Ballymahon
Royal Canal
Ballymore
Mullingar / An Muileann gCearr
Delvin
Kilkieran Bay
GALWAY
Athlone / Baile Átha Luain
WESTMEATH
L. Ennell
Lettermullan
Gorumna Island
Galway / Gaillimh
Spiddle
Barna
Oranmore
Athenry
Ballinasloe / Béal Átha na Sluaighe
Moate
Kinnegad
Aran Islands
Inishmore
Kilronan
Galway Bay
Black Head
Craughwell
Loughrea
Clonmacnoise
Kilbeggan
Tullamore / Tulach Mhór
Edenderry
Inishmaan
Inisheer
Ballyvaughan
Kinvarra
Ardrahan
Clonfert
Ferbane
Clara
Lisdoonvarna
Kilfenora
Gort
Banagher
Cloghan
Kilcormac
Grand Canal
OFFALY
Cliffs of Moher
Lahinch
Ennistimon
Corrofin
Portumna
Birr
Kinnitty
Portarlington
Monasterevin
Slieve Bloom Mts.
Mountmellick
Spanish Point
Milltown Malbay
CLARE
Ennis / Inis
Tulla
Scarriff
Lough Derg
Borrisokane
Portlaoise
Roscrea
Mountrath
LAOIS
Athy
Creegh
Knappogue Castle
Broadford
Newmarket on Fergus
Kilmurry
Killaloe
Nenagh / An tAonach
Moneygall
Abbeyleix
Kilkee
Kilrush
Killimer
Killadysert
Labasheeda
Shannon
Bunratty Castle
Dolla
Templemore
Rathdowney
Durrow
Carlow / Ceatharlach
Loop Head
Kilbaha
River Shannon
Mouth of the Shannon
LIMERICK / LUIMNEACH
Newport
TIPPERARY
Milestone
Thurles / Durlas
Castlecomer
Freshford
CARLOW
Tarbert
Askeaton
Ballybunnion
Holycross Abbey
Urlingford
KILKENNY
Adare
Rathkeale
Listowel
Ballyduff
Croom
Kilkenny / Cill Chainnigh
Muine Bheag (Bagenalstown)
Kerry Head
Ballyheigue
LIMERICK
Newcastle West
Ballingarry
Borris
Abbeyfeale
Cashel / Caiseal
Killenaule
Tralee Bay
Brandon Head
Brandon Mountain
Tralee / Trá Lí
Hospital
Tipperary / Tiobraid Árann
Fethard
Callan
Thomastown
Graiguenamanagh
Sybil Head
Dromcolliher
Kilmallock
Slievenamon
Jerpoint Abbey
Clogher Head
Dingle
Anascaul
Slieve Mish Mts.
Castleisland
Rath Luirc (Charleville)
Galty Mountains
Caher
Clonmel / Cluain Meala
Carrick-on-Suir / Carraig na Siúire
Great Blasket I.
Castlemaine
Newmarket
Buttevant
New Ross
Slea Head
Killorglin
KERRY
Kanturk
Kildorrery
Mitchelstown
Clogheen
R. Suir
Dingle Bay
Glenbeigh
L. Caragh
Killarney / Cill Airne
Boherboy
Knockmealdown Mts.
Comeragh Mts.
Waterford / Port Láirge
Doulus Head
Ring of Kerry
Carrantuohill
Muckross House
Rathmore
Mallow / Mala
Lismore
Knight's Town
Valencia Island
Cahersiveen
Iveragh
Macgillycuddy's Reeks
Mangerton Mountain
Millstreet
CORK
Fermoy
Cappoquin
WATERFORD
Arthurstown
Kilgarvan
Derrynasaggart Mts.
Tallow
Bunmahon
Tramore
Dunmore East
Waterville
L. Currane
St. Finan's Bay
Bolus Head
Skellig
Ring of Kerry
Sneem
Kenmare
Macroom
Coachford
Blarney
CORK / CORCAIGH
Dungarvan / Dún Garbhán
Dungarvan Harbour
Helvick Head
Waterford Harbour
Hook Head
Kenmare River
Lauragh
Beara
Caha Mts.
Glengarriff
Pass of Keimaneigh
Midleton
Youghal / Eochaill
Ardmore
Youghal Bay
Cobh / An Cóbh
Castletownbere
Dursey Island
Bere I.
Bantry / Beanntraí
Bantry Bay
Dunmanway
Bandon
Ringaskiddy
Crosshaven
Ballycotton
Sheep's Head
Dunmanus Bay
Skull
Timoleague
Kinsale
Rosscarbery
Clonakilty
Skibbereen
Roaringwater Bay
Old Head of Kinsale
Roscoff
le Havre
Mizen Head
Galley Head
Toe Head
Clear Island

NORTH CHANNEL
IRISH SEA
ST. GEORGE'S CHANNEL
ISLE OF MAN
Isle of Anglesey
Cardigan Bay
Liverpool Bay
Solway Firth
Luce Bay
Wigtown Bay
BELFAST
DUBLIN/BAILE ÁTHA CLIATH
LIVERPOOL
BLACKPOOL
Coleraine
Ballymena
Larne
Bangor
Newry
Newcastle
Dundalk/
Dun Dealgan
Drogheda/
Droichead Átha
Dún Laoghaire
Bray
Wicklow / Cill Mhantáin
Arklow /
An tInbhear Mór
Enniscorthy /
Inis Córthaidh
Wexford /
Loch Garman
Rosslare
Harbour /
Calafort
Ros Láir
Stranraer
Dumfries
Carlisle
Workington
Whitehaven
Barrow-
in-Furness
Morecambe
Lancaster
Fleetwood
Preston
Southport
Douglas
Ramsey
Peel
Castletown
Holyhead
Caergybi
Llandudno
Colwyn Bay /
Bae Colwyn
Rhyl
Birkenhead
Wallasey
Warrington
Bangor
Caernarfon
Chester
Wrexham
Shrewsbury
Telford
Welshpool /
Y Trallwng
Aberystwyth
Cardigan
Aberteifi
Fishguard /
Abergwaun
Carmarthen
Caerfyrddin
Haverfordwest /
Hwlffordd
Brecon /
Aberhonddu
Hereford
Leominster
Ludlow
Llangollen
Dolgellau
ANTRIM
DOWN
ARMAGH
LOUTH
MEATH
DUBLIN
WICKLOW
DUMFRIES AND GALLOWAY
GWYNEDD
CLWYD
POWYS
DYFED
WALES
SHROPSHIRE
HEREFORD AND WORCESTER
Snowdonia
Lake District National Park
Cambrian Mountains
Pembrokeshire Coast National Park
2
6
9
5
D
E
F

A
B
C
NORTH SEA
KINGSTON-UPON-HULL
Beverley
Hornsea
Hedon
Withernsea
Patrington
Kilnsea
Immingham Dock
Immingham
Great Grimsby
Cleethorpes
Spurn Head
Humberside
Brigg
Caistor
Rotterdam
Zeebrugge
Market Rasen
Louth
Mablethorpe
Sutton-on-Sea
Wragby
Lincoln
Horncastle
Alford
Partney
Spilsby
Skegness
Woodhall Spa
LINCOLN
Sleaford
Boston
The Wash
Hunstanton
Sutterton
Donington
Holbeach
Long Sutton
Spalding
Bourne
King's Lynn
Stamford
Crowland
Wisbech
Peterborough
Eye
Guyhirn
Outwell
Downham Market
Whittlesey
March
Chatteris
Ramsey
Littleport
Ely
CAMBRIDGE
Huntingdon
Earth
St. Ives
Soham
Godmanchester
St. Neots
Newmarket
Cambridge
Sandy
Potton
Biggleswade
Shefford
Royston
Saffron Walden
Haverhill
Clare
Sudbury
Letchworth
Hitchin
Baldock
Buntingford
Luton
Stevenage
Puckeridge
Stansted
Great Dunmow
Braintree
Finchingfield
Halstead
Harpenden
HERTFORD
Hertford
Bishop's Stortford
Welwyn Garden City
Ware
St Albans
Hatfield
Harlow
Sawbridgeworth
Hoddesdon
Cheshunt
Epping
Chelmsford
Witham
Potters Bar
Brentwood
Billericay
Wickford
Rayleigh
LONDON
Dagenham
Basildon
Benfleet
Southend-on-Sea
Canvey Island
Grays Thurrock
Tilbury
Gravesend
Dartford
Richmond
Kingston
Sutton
Croydon
Orpington
Swanley
Rochester
Gillingham
Chatham
Sheerness
Isle of Sheppey
Leysdown-on-Sea
Grain
R. Thames
Vlissingen
Whitstable
Herne Bay
Birchington
Margate
North Foreland
Broadstairs
Ramsgate
Sittingbourne
Faversham
Canterbury
Sandwich
Deal
South Foreland
Dover
Zeebrugge
Oostende
Folkestone
Hythe
Channel tunnel under construction
Ashford
Maidstone
KENT
Sevenoaks
Knole
Tonbridge
Southborough
Royal Tunbridge Wells
Reigate
Redhill
Horley
Gatwick
Crawley
East Grinstead
Crowborough
Hawkhurst
Tenterden
Biddenden
Horsham
Cuckfield
Haywards Heath
Heathfield
Uckfield
E. SUSSEX
Burgess Hill
Hailsham
Battle
Rye
Winchelsea
Lydd
New Romney
Dungeness
Lewes
Polegate
Hastings
Bexhill
Eastbourne
Seaford
Newhaven
Beachy Head
Dieppe
BRIGHTON
Shoreham
Hove
Worthing
Epsom
Hunstanton
Wells-next-the-Sea
Blakeney
Sheringham
Cromer
Holt
Mundesley
North Walsham
Sandringham House
Fakenham
Guist
Aylsham
Low Street
Acle
Great Yarmouth
NORFOLK
East Dereham
Swaffham
Stradsett
Watton
Wymondham
NORWICH
Gorleston-on-Sea
Mundford
Attleborough
Brandon
Thetford
Bungay
Beccles
Lowestoft
Harleston
Diss
Scole
Halesworth
Southwold
Ixworth
Bury St. Edmunds
Dennington
Yoxford
Saxmundham
Leiston
Aldeburgh
Stowmarket
SUFFOLK
Lavenham
IPSWICH
Woodbridge
Hadleigh
Felixstowe
Harwich
Göteborg
Esbjerg
Hamburg
Hoek van Holland
The Naze
Walton-on-the-Naze
Frinton-on-Sea
Colchester
Brightlingsea
Clacton-on-Sea
W. Mersea
ESSEX
Maldon
Bradwell-on-Sea
Burnham-on-Crouch
Foulness Point
PAS DE CALAIS
STRAIT OF DOVER
Kingston-upon-Hull
Felixstowe
Dover
Sheerness
Domburg
Walcheren
Middelburg
Vlissingen
Knokke-Heist
Zeebrugge
Blankenberge
Heist
Sluis
De Haan
Oostende
BRUGGE
(BRUGES)
Oostkamp
Jabbeke
Gistel
Middelkerke-Bad
Nieuwpoort
Koksijde-Bad
De Panne
Bray-Dunes
Malo-les-Bains
Dunkerque
Veurne
Diksmuide
Hondschoote
Tielt
Roeselare
(Roulers)
Ingelmunster
Kortrijk
(Courtrai)
Ieper
(Ypres)
Poperinge
Menen
Gravelines
Calais
Wissant
Cap Gris Nez
Guînes
Ardres
Audruicq
Bourbourg
Bergues
Wormhout
Steenvoorde
Cassel
Marquise
Wimereux
Boulogne
St Omer
Arques
Lumbres
Hazebrouck
Bailleul
Armentières
Tourcoing
Mouscron
Roubaix
LILLE
Hardelot
Desvres
Samer
Fauquembergues
Thérouanne
Aire
Lillers
Béthune
La Bassée
Seclin
Carvin
Orchies
Le Touquet-Paris-Plage
Étaples
Montreuil
Hucqueliers
Fruges
PAS-DE-
13
14
7

Ostfriesische Inseln
Waddeneilanden
NEDERLAND
GRONINGEN
FRIESLAND
DRENTHE
OVERIJSSEL
NOORD-HOLLAND
FLEVOLAND
GELDERLAND
UTRECHT
ZUID-HOLLAND
NOORD-BRABANT
LIMBURG
ANTWERPEN
BELGIQUE
HAINAUT
BRABANT
NORDRHEIN
IJsselmeer
Markermeer
Texel
Vlieland
Terschelling
Ameland
Schiermonnikoog
Borkum
Norderney
Juist
Baltrum
Langeoog
Spiekeroog
Den Helder
Alkmaar
Haarlem
AMSTERDAM
Leiden
DEN HAAG
('S-GRAVENHAGE)
Scheveningen
Delft
ROTTERDAM
Dordrecht
UTRECHT
Hilversum
Amersfoort
Apeldoorn
Zwolle
Deventer
ARNHEM
NIJMEGEN
's-Hertogenbosch
Tilburg
Breda
EINDHOVEN
Leeuwarden
GRONINGEN
Assen
Emmen
Emden
Enschede
Hengelo
Almelo
Nordhorn
Lingen
Rheine
Münster
Venlo
Roermond
Maastricht
AACHEN
Heerlen
KÖLN
BONN
DÜSSELDORF
DUISBURG
ESSEN
Krefeld
Mönchengladbach
WUPPERTAL
Hagen
Bochum
Gelsenkirchen
Leverkusen
Solingen
Neuss
Düren
ANTWERPEN
(ANVERS)
Mechelen
(Malines)
BRUSSEL
BRUXELLES
Leuven (Louvain)
Hasselt
Genk
LIEGE
(LUIK)
Namur
Spa
Verviers
Turnhout
Aalst
Lier
St. Niklaas

6

A
B
C
1
2
3
4
D E V O N
C O R N W A L L
D O R S E T
EXETER
PLYMOUTH
Torquay
Torbay
Paignton
Exmouth
Teignmouth
Dawlish
Sidmouth
Honiton
Tiverton
Crediton
Cullompton
Okehampton
Dartmoor
National
Park
High Willhays
Moretonhampstead
Bovey Tracey
Newton Abbot
Ashburton
Buckfastleigh
Totnes
Dartmouth
Kingswear
Brixham
Kingsbridge
Salcombe
Start Point
Modbury
Newton Ferrers
Plympton
Plymstock
Princetown
Tavistock
Callington
Liskeard
Saltash
Torpoint
Looe
Polperro
Fowey
Lostwithiel
St. Austell
Mevagissey
Bodmin
Wadebridge
Padstow
Camelford
Launceston
Tintagel
Bude
Stratton
Kilkhampton
Holsworthy
Hatherleigh
Winkleigh
Newquay
Fraddon
Truro
Tregony
Redruth
Camborne
Hayle
St. Ives
Penzance
St. Just
Sennen
Land's End
St. Michael's Mount
Mount's Bay
Helston
Penryn
St. Mawes
Falmouth
St. Keverne
Lizard
Lizard Point
Yeovil
Sherborne
Henstridge
Ilminster
Crewkerne
Chard
Axminster
Seaton
Ottery St. Mary
Budleigh Salterton
Beaminster
Bridport
Lyme Regis
Lyme Bay
Abbotsbury
Dorchester
Weymouth
Fortuneswell
Isle of Portland
Bill of Portland
Blandford Forum
Sturminster Newton
Bere Regis
Wareham
Santander
Roscoff
Alderney
Jersey - Guernsey
Cherbourg
M
A
N
Torquay
Alderney
Nez de Jobourg
Weymouth
Portsmouth
Guernsey
St. Peter Port
Sark
Jersey
St-Hélier
Cork
Plymouth
Batz
Roscoff
St Pol-de-Léon
Carantec
Brignogan
Plouescat
l'Aber-Wrac'h
Ploudalmézeau
Lannilis
Lesneven
le Folgoët
Landivisiau
Plouzévédé
Morlaix
St-Thégonnec
Guimiliau
Landerneau
Plabennec
Gulpavas
Ile d'Ouessant
Lampaul
Molène
le Conquet
St Renan
BREST
Plougastel-Daoulas
Daoulas
Pte de St Mathieu
Camaret
Pte de Penhir
Crozon
Morgat
Cap de la Chèvre
Landévennec
le Faou
Rumengol
Sizun
Monts d'Arrée
Huelgoat
Brennilis
Ménez-Hom
Châteaulin
Pleyben
F I N I S T È R E
Douarnenez
Tréboul
I. de Sein
Pte du Raz
Audierne
Pont-Croix
Locronan
Quimper
Briec
Coray
Châteauneuf-du-Faou
Montagnes Noires
Carhaix-Plougher
Gourin
Scaër
Rosporden
Bannalec
Quimperlé
Pont-Aven
Concarneau
Beg-Meil
Fouesnant
Bénodet
Pont-l'Abbé
Plonéour-Lanvern
St Guénolé
Pte de Penmarch
Guilvinec
Loctudy
Port-Manech
Moëlan
Riec
le Pouldu
Iles de Glénan
Lorient
Port-Louis
Larmor
Groix
I. de Groix
Hennebont
Pont-Scorff
Plouay
Arzano
le Faouët
Guémené
Kernascléden
Pontivy
Bubry
Baud
Locminé
St-Jean-Brévelay
Pluvigner
Grand Champ
Auray
Ste Anne-d'Auray
Vannes
Etel
Belz
Carnac
la Trinité
St Pierre
Quiberon
Locmariaquer
Port-Navalo
St Gildas-de-Rhuys
Sarzeau
Damgan
Muzillac
Pénestin
Questembert
Elven
Malestroit
Ploërmel
Josselin
Rohan
Loudéac
Mur-de-Bretagne
Gouarec
Rostrenen
Uzel
Plouguenast
Mauron
la Trinité-Porhoët
Merdrignac
Broons
Caulnes
Montfort
Montauban
Guer
Maure
Pipriac
Plélan-le-Grand
Rochefort-en-Terre
Allaire
Redon
la Roche-Bernard
St Gildas-des-Bois
Pontchâteau
Vilaine
M O R B I H A N
C Ô T E S   D U   N O R D
Perros-Guirec
Ploumanach
Trégastel
Pleumeur-Bodou
Trébeurden
Lannion
Tréguier
Lézardrieux
I. de Bréhat
Pte de l'Arcouest
Paimpol
Primel-Trégastel
Plougasnou
Locquirec
St Michel-en-Grève
Plestin
Lanmeur
Plouigneau
Plouaret
Belle-Isle-en-Terre
Bégard
Guingamp
Pontrieux
la Roche-Derrien
Plouha
Lanvollon
St Quay-Portrieux
Etables
Binic
Châtelaudren
Plouagat
St Brieuc
Bourbriac
Callac
Quintin
St Nicolas-du-Pélem
Maël-Carhaix
Corlay
Ploeuc
Moncontour
Collinée
Le Val-André
Erquy
Sables-d'Or
Cap Fréhel
Pléneuf
Lamballe
Matignon
St Cast
St Jacut
Plancoët
Jugon
Plélan-le-Pt
Ploubalay
Dinard
St Lunaire
St Briac
St Malo
Dinan
Evran

16

Folkestone
Channel tunnel under construction
Calais
Hythe
Tenterden
New Romney
Lydd
Rye
Winchelsea
Dungeness
Hastings
Bexhill
Battle
Hailsham
Eastbourne
Beachy Head
Seaford
Newhaven
Lewes
Polegate
BRIGHTON
Hove
Shoreham
Worthing
Littlehampton
Bognor Regis
Arundel
Chichester
Selsey
Selsey Bill
Havant
PORTSMOUTH
Southsea
Gosport
Fareham
Cosham
SOUTHAMPTON
Eastleigh
Romsey
Botley
Fawley
Beaulieu
Lyndhurst
Ringwood
Fordingbridge
Cranborne
Lymington
Christchurch
BOURNEMOUTH
Swanage
The Needles
Freshwater
Yarmouth
Cowes
Newport
Ryde
Brading
Sandown
Shanklin
Ventnor
Niton
St. Catherine's Point
ISLE OF WIGHT
Foreland
Crowborough
Uckfield
Heathfield
Hawkhurst
Cuckfield
Haywards Heath
Burgess Hill
Horsham
Billingshurst
Petworth
Pulborough
Midhurst
Petersfield
Cowfold
W. SUSSEX
E. SUSSEX
PAS DE CALAIS
Wissant
Cap Gris Nez
Marquise
Wimereux
Boulogne
Hardelot
Samer
Le Touquet-Paris-Plage
Etaples
Berck-s-Mer
Fort-Mahon
Rue
Le Crotoy
Nouvion
Cayeux
St. Valery
Abbeville
Ault
Mers
le Tréport
Eu
Criel
Gamaches
Dieppe
Envermeu
Arques
Offranville
Varengeville
Veules-les-Roses
St. Valery-en-Caux
Veulettes
Cany-Barville
Fécamp
Yport
Etretat
Cap d'Antifer
Criquetot-l'Esneval
Goderville
Bolbec
Yvetot
Doudeville
Tôtes
Clères
Neufchâtel-en-B.
Forges-les-Eaux
Aumale
Blangy
Gournay-en-B.
Buchy
Montivilliers
Ste. Adresse
LE HAVRE
Honfleur
Trouville
Deauville
Villers
Houlgate
Cabourg
Dives
Ouistreham
Luc
Langrune
St. Aubin
Courseulles
Arromanches
Port-en-Bessin
St. Laurent
Grandcamp-Maisy
Isigny
Carentan
Ste. Mère-Eglise
Montebourg
Valognes
Quettehou
St. Vaast-la-Hougue
Barfleur
St. Pierre-Eglise
Cap Lévy
Cherbourg
Hague
Bricquebec
Barneville
la Haye-du-Puits
Lessay
Périers
St. Sauveur-le-V.
Portbail
Coutances
Agon-Coutainville
St. Malo-de-la-Lande
Montmartin
Bréhal
Granville
St. Pair
Jullouville
Carolles
Sartilly
Avranches
Cancale
le Mont-St. Michel
Pontaubault
Pontorson
Dol-de-B.
St. Hilaire-du-Harcouët
St. James
Ducey
Mortain
Juvigny-le-T.
Sourdeval
Vire
Villedieu-les-Poêles
Percy
Gavray
Hambye
Cerisy-la-S.
St. Lô
Torigni
Caumont-l'Eventé
Balleroy
Bayeux
Tilly-s-S.
Creully
Villers-Bocage
Aunay-s-O.
CAEN
Evrecy
Thury-Harcourt
Troarn
Cambremer
Dozulé
Mézidon
Lisieux
Pont-l'Evêque
Pont-Audemer
Cormeilles
Beuzeville
Falaise
Condé-s-Noireau
Flers
Tinchebray
Vassy
Clécy
Pont-d'Ouilly
Trun
Livarot
Vimoutiers
Orbec
Argentan
Ecouché
Putanges
Briouze
la Ferté-Macé
Bagnoles-de-l'Orne
Domfront
Carrouges
Sées
Mortrée
Exmes
Gacé
Nonant-le-Pin
le Merlerault
Moulins-la-Marche
l'Aigle
Courtomer
Alençon
Mortagne-au-Perche
Bellême
Mamers
la Ferté-Vidame
Tourouvre
Longny
Verneuil
Breteuil
Conches
Evreux
Bernay
Brionne
Thiberville
Beaumont-le-Roger
le Neubourg
Elbeuf
Louviers
les Andelys
Vernon
Pacy
Gisors
Etrépagny
Lyons-la-F.
Boos
ROUEN
Duclair
Jumièges
Barentin
Pavilly
Caudebec
Lillebonne
Quillebeuf
Bourgtheroulde
Mantes
Houdan
Anet
Dreux
Nonancourt
Brezolles
Châteauneuf-en-Th.
Senonches
Chartres
Maintenon
Nogent-le-Roi
Rambouillet
Epernon
Auneau
Illiers
Courville
la Loupe
Nogent-le-Rotrou
Thiron-Gardais
Authon
Brou
Bonneval
Châteaudun
Cloyes
Orgères-en-B.
Patay
ORLÉANS
Vendôme
Morée
Ouzouer-le-Marché
Marchenoir
Beaugency
Blois
Chambord
Herbault
Château-Renault
St. Amand-Longpré
Montoire
la Chartre
Château-du-Loir
le Grand Lucé
St. Calais
Mondoubleau
Vibraye
Montmirail
la Ferté-Bernard
Bonnétable
Tuffé
Connerré
LE MANS
Bouloire
Ecommoy
la Suze
Sablé
Solesmes
Loué
Brûlon
Conlie
Sillé-le-Guillaume
Beaumont-s-S.
Fresnay-s-S.
Ballon
Marolles-les-Braults
Evron
Montsûrs
Bais
Villaines-la-Juhel
Mayenne
Lassay
Pré-en-Pail
Couptrain
Juvigny-s-A.
Passais
Gorron
Ambrières-les-Vallées
Landivy
Ernée
Chailland
Laval
Meslay
Vaiges
Ste. Suzanne
Château-Gontier
Craon
Cossé-le-Vivien
Loiron
Vitré
Châteaubourg
Argentré-du-Plessis
la Guerche-de-B.
Fougères
Louvigné-du-Désert
St. Brice-en-Coglès
St. Aubin-du-Cormier
Liffré
Combourg
Antrain
RENNES
Châteaugiron
Janzé
Retiers
Bain-de-Bretagne
Martigné-Ferchaud
Rougé
Châteaubriant
Pouancé
Segré
Derval
Nozay
Moisdon
St. Julien-de-Vouvantes
Candé
St. Mars-la-Jaille
Le Louroux
ANGERS
Seiches
Durtal
la Flèche
Baugé
le Lude
Château-la-Vallière
Neuillé-Pont-Pierre
Neuvy-le-Roi
Mayet
Pontvallain
Malicorne
Châteauneuf-s-S.
Grez-en-Bouère
Bierné
Renazé
MANCHE
CALVADOS
ORNE
EURE
SEINE-MARITIME
EURE-ET-LOIR
MAYENNE
SARTHE
LOIR
MAINE

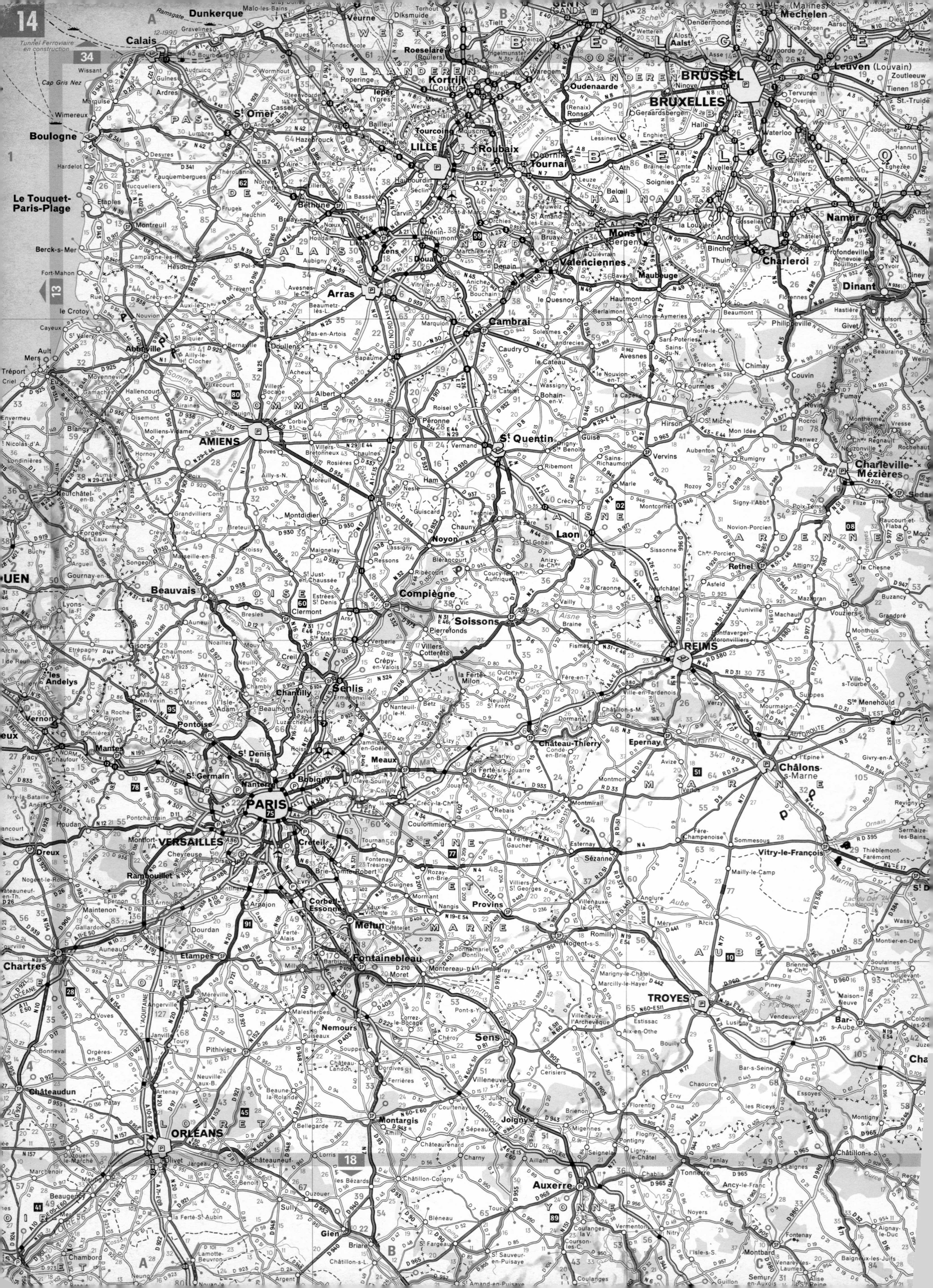
Dunkerque
Calais
Tunnel Ferroviaire en construction
Boulogne
Le Touquet-Paris-Plage
Berck-s-Mer
St. Omer
Lille
Roubaix
Tourcoing
Kortrijk
Brussel
Bruxelles
Mechelen
Leuven
Oudenaarde
Tournai
Mons
Charleroi
Namur
Dinant
Valenciennes
Maubeuge
Cambrai
Arras
Douai
Lens
Béthune
Abbeville
Amiens
St. Quentin
Laon
Soissons
Reims
Rethel
Charleville-Mézières
Compiègne
Beauvais
Noyon
Senlis
Chantilly
Pontoise
Mantes
Vernon
Les Andelys
St. Denis
St. Germain
Nanterre
Bobigny
PARIS
Versailles
Créteil
Evry
Meaux
Château-Thierry
Epernay
Châlons-s-Marne
Vitry-le-François
Rambouillet
Dreux
Chartres
Etampes
Melun
Fontainebleau
Provins
Nogent-s-S.
Troyes
Sens
Auxerre
Montargis
Nemours
Orléans
Châteaudun
Gien
Joigny
Tonnerre
Châtillon-s-S.
Bar-s-Aube
BELGIQUE
VLAANDEREN
BRABANT
HAINAUT
PAS-DE-CALAIS
NORD
SOMME
AISNE
OISE
ARDENNES
MARNE
SEINE-ET-MARNE
AUBE
YONNE
LOIRET
EURE-ET-LOIR

34
13
18

KÖLN
BONN
AACHEN
Maastricht
Hasselt
Genk
Heerlen
LIÈGE
Verviers
Spa
Siegen
Marburg
Gießen
Koblenz
WIESBADEN
FRANKFURT
MAINZ
Darmstadt
Offenbach
Bad Homburg
Bad Nauheim
Limburg
BUNDESREPUBLIK
DEUTSCHLAND
NORDRHEIN-WESTFALEN
RHEINLAND
PFALZ
HESSEN
SAARLAND
LUXEMBOURG
Trier
Bitburg
Bad Kreuznach
Worms
Ludwigshafen
MANNHEIM
HEIDELBERG
Kaiserslautern
Neustadt-a-d-W
Speyer
Landau
Pirmasens
Zweibrücken
SAARBRÜCKEN
Saarlouis
Völklingen
Merzig
Neunkirchen
Homburg
KARLSRUHE
Pforzheim
Baden-Baden
Rastatt
Wissembourg
Haguenau
STRASBOURG
Offenburg
Freudenstadt
Lahr/Schwarzwald
Sélestat
COLMAR
FREIBURG
MULHOUSE
BASEL
Villingen-
Schwenningen
Donaueschingen
Winterthur
Baden
Thionville
METZ
MOSELLE
Longwy
Verdun
MEUSE
Bar-le-Duc
Commercy
Toul
NANCY
Lunéville
MEURTHE-ET-MOSELLE
Pont-à-Mousson
Sarreguemines
Saverne
Sarrebourg
St Dié
Epinal
VOSGES
Vittel
Contrexéville
HAUTE-MARNE
Langres
Gérardmer
Remiremont
Plombières
Luxeuil
HAUTE-SAÔNE
Vesoul
Belfort
Montbéliard
Thann
Guebwiller
Arlon (Aarlen)
Bastogne
St Hubert
Neufchâteau
Huy
Waremme
Tongeren
Malmedy
Monschau
Düren
Euskirchen
Bad Godesberg
Mayen
Cochem
Wittlich
Bernkastel-Kues
Idar-Oberstein
Bingen
Bacharach
Boppard
Rüsselsheim
Weinheim
Bruchsal
Ettlingen
Saales
Obernai
Ribeauvillé
Kaysersberg
Neuf-Brisach
Lörrach
Rheinfelden
Bad Säckingen
Waldshut
Titisee
Schönau
Müllheim
Altkirch

Quimper
Concarneau
Quimperlé
Pontivy
Lorient
Hennebont
Auray
Vannes
Carnac
Quiberon
Belle-Ile
le Palais
Houat
Hœdic
Locmariaquer
Redon
la Baule
Guérande
le Croisic
St NAZAIRE
Pornic
Noirmoutier
Ile de Noirmoutier
Challans
St Jean-de-Monts
Ile d'Yeu
les Sables-d'Olonne
Bordeaux
MÉRIGNAC
CAUDÉRAN
LE BOUSCAT
BRUGES
LE VIGEAN
LA BASTIDE
BACALAN
LORMONT
CENON
FLOIRAC
BOULIAC
TALENCE
BÈGLES
PESSAC
GRADIGNAN
ARLAC
PONT-DE-LA-MAYE
CARBON-BLANC
GARONNE
Pont d'Aquitaine
12
20

RENNES
Vitré
Laval
LE MANS
ORLEANS
Châteaudun
Vendôme
Blois
Chambord
TOURS
Amboise
Romorantin
Chinon
Saumur
ANGERS
NANTES
Cholet
la Roche-s-Yon
Châteauroux
Châtellerault
POITIERS
Parthenay
Niort
LA ROCHELLE
Rochefort
Saintes
Cognac
Angoulême
LIMOGES
Royan
Périgueux
Brive-la-Gaillarde
Tulle
Bergerac
Libourne
BORDEAUX
Arcachon
Sarlat-la-Canéda
Rocamadour
Ile d'Oléron
GIRONDE
13
18
20
21

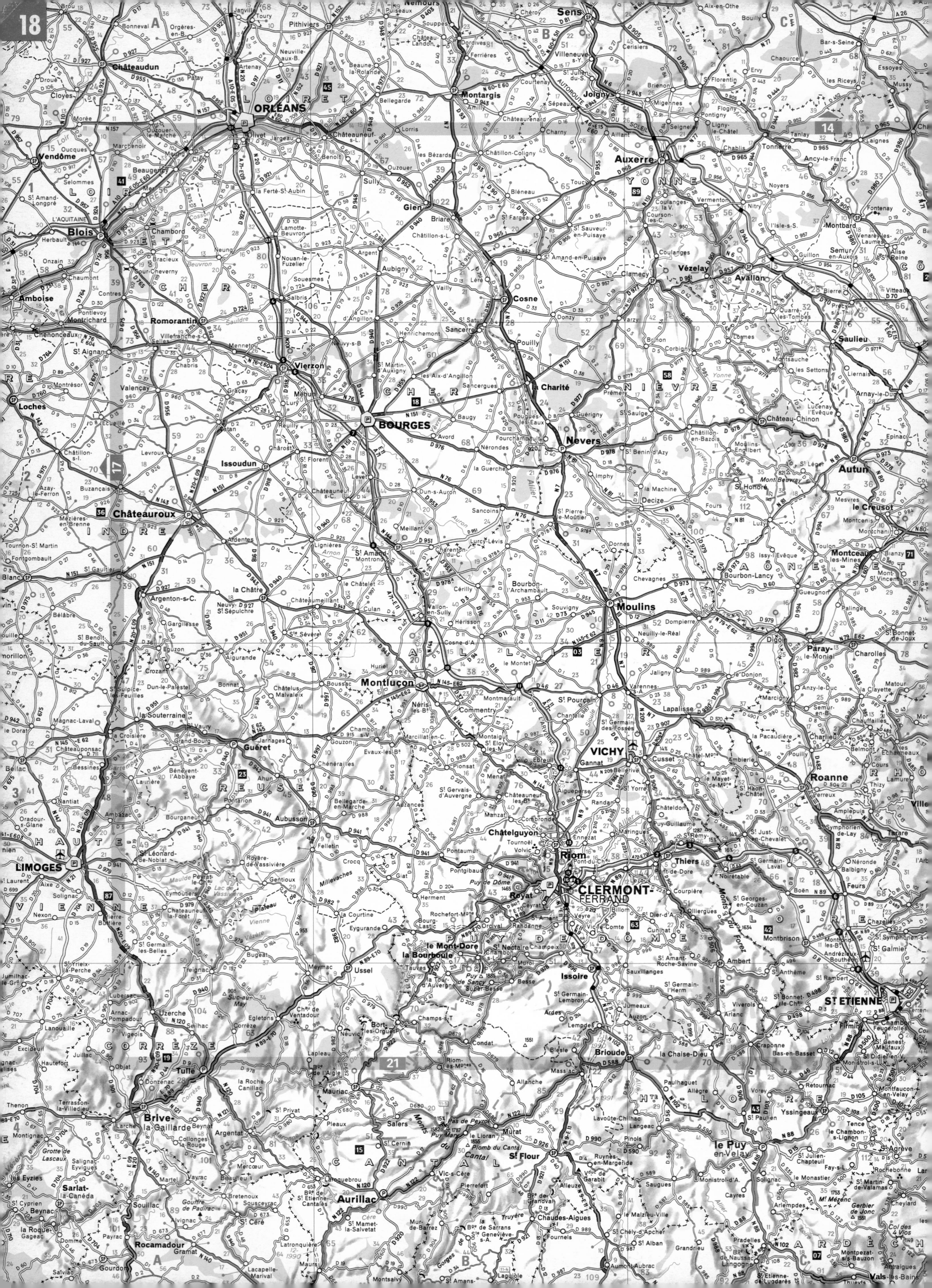
ORLÉANS
LOIRET
Châteaudun
Vendôme
Blois
Amboise
Loches
LOIR-ET-CHER
Romorantin
Vierzon
CHER
BOURGES
Issoudun
Châteauroux
INDRE
Argenton-s-C.
la Châtre
Montargis
Gien
Sens
Joigny
Auxerre
YONNE
Tonnerre
Avallon
Vézelay
Clamecy
Cosne
la Charité
Nevers
NIÈVRE
Château-Chinon
Autun
Saulieu
le Creusot
Montceau-les-Mines
SAÔNE-ET-LOIRE
Paray-le-Monial
Digoin
Moulins
ALLIER
Montluçon
VICHY
Roanne
Thiers
Riom
CLERMONT-FERRAND
PUY-DE-DÔME
Issoire
Brioude
St ÉTIENNE
LOIRE
Montbrison
Feurs
le Puy-en-Velay
HAUTE-LOIRE
ARDÈCHE
Guéret
CREUSE
Aubusson
LIMOGES
HAUTE-VIENNE
Tulle
CORRÈZE
Brive-la-Gaillarde
Ussel
Aurillac
CANTAL
St Flour
Sarlat-la-Canéda
Rocamadour
Mauriac

15
42
22
23
HAUTE-MARNE
VOSGES
HTE-SAÔNE
DOUBS
JURA
VAUD
SUISSE
VALAIS
SAVOIE
HAUTE-SAVOIE
ISÈRE
DRÔME
HTES-ALPES
AOSTA
PIEMONTE
ITALIA
AARGAU
SCHWEIZ
Chaumont
Langres
Contrexéville
Vittel
Epinal
Colmar
Freiburg
Gérardmer
Remiremont
Plombières
Guebwiller
Mulhouse
Luxeuil
Vesoul
Belfort
Montbéliard
Basel
Rheinfelden
Baden
Olten
Aarau
Delémont
Solothurn
Biel/Bienne
Luzern
Bern
Neuchâtel
La Chaux-de-Fonds
Le Locle
Pontarlier
Besançon
Dijon
Gray
Dole
Beaune
Chalon-s-S.
Lons-le-Saunier
Champagnole
Tournus
Mâcon
Bourg-en-Bresse
Lausanne
Montreux
Vevey
Fribourg
Thun
Interlaken
Grindelwald
Wengen
Jungfrau
Zermatt
Sion
Crans
Brig
Evian
Thonon
Genève
Annemasse
Annecy
Chamonix
Megève
St Gervais
Mont Blanc
Courmayeur
Aosta/Aoste
Biella
Ivrea
Torino
Lyon
Vienne
Aix-les-Bains
Chambéry
Albertville
Val d'Isère
Courchevel
Grenoble
Briançon
Valence
Romans
Sestriere
Pinerolo
Carmagnola

A
B
C
1
2
3
17
25
28
Ile d'Oléron
Marennes
Royan
Saintes
Cognac
Jarnac
Angoulême
Saujon
Pte de la Coubre
Pte de Grave
Soulac
le Verdon
Meschers
Cozes
Pons
Gémozac
Archiac
Barbezieux
Jonzac
Montendre
Mirambeau
Lesparre-Médoc
Montalivet
St Vivien-de-Médoc
G I R O N D E
Hourtin
Pauillac
Blaye
St Ciers
Montlieu
Montguyon
Chalais
Aubeterre
la Roche-Chalais
Coutras
Guitres
Bourg
St Savin
Carcans-Plage
Carcans
Maubuisson
Lacanau-Océan
Lacanau
Castelnau-de-Médoc
St André-de-Cubzac
Libourne
St Emilion
Castillon-la-Bataille
Blanquefort
St Médard-en-Jalles
Mérignac
BORDEAUX
Arès
Andernos
Audenge
Arcachon
Cap Ferret
Gujan-Mestras
Pyla
Pilat-Plage
la Teste
Facture
Cadillac
Podensac
St Macaire
la Réole
Langon
Marmande
Sauveterre-de-Guyenne
Monségur
Duras
Ste Foy-la-Grande
Pujols
Créon
la Brède
Cazaux
Sanguinet
Biscarrosse-Plage
Biscarrosse
Parentis-en-Born
Belin-Béliet
Villandraut
St Symphorien
Bazas
Grignols
Casteljaloux
Tonneins
Captieux
Sore
Pissos
Mimizan-Plage
Mimizan
Labouheyre
Sabres
Labrit
Houeillès
Lavardac
Nérac
L A N D E S
Morcenx
Onesse-et-Laharie
Lit-et-Mixe
St Girons-Plage
Roquefort
Gabarret
Barbotan
Mézin
Castets
Léon
Vieux-Boucau
Tartas
Mont-de-Marsan
Villeneuve-de-M.
Eauze
Soustons
Hossegor
Capbreton
Dax
Montfort-en-Chalosse
Mugron
Grenade
St Sever
Aire-s-l'Adour
Eugénie-les-Bains
Nogaro
Vic-Fezensac
GERS
Riscle
Plaisance
Marciac
G O L F E   D E   G A S C O G N E
St Vincent-de-Tyrosse
Hagetmau
Amou
Geaune
Garlin
Tarnos
Boucau
Anglet
BIARRITZ
Bayonne
Peyrehorade
Orthez
Arzacq-Arraziguet
Castelnau-Rivière-Basse
Maubourguet
Mirande
St Jean-de-Luz
Hendaye
Bidart
Guéthary
Ustaritz
Hasparren
la Bastide-Clairence
Salies-de-Béarn
Sauveterre-de-B.
Lacq
Mourenx
Lembeye
Vic-en-Bigorre
Morlaàs
Thèze
Cambo-les-Bains
St Pée
Ascain
Espelette
Ainhoa
St Palais
Navarrenx
Monein
Lescar
PAU
Tarbes
Rabastens-de-Bigorre
P Y R É N É E S
A T L A N T I Q U E S
Mauléon-Licharre
Oloron-Ste Marie
St Jean-Pied-de-Port
Tardets-Sorholus
Aramits
Arudy
Nay
Lestelle-Bétharram
LOURDES
Bagnères-de-Bigorre
Capvern
Tournay
Argelès-Gazost
Cauterets
Luz-St Sauveur
Barèges
C. du Tourmalet
la Mongie
Arreau
Vielle Aure
St Lary-Soulan
C. d'Aubisque
Laruns
Eaux Bonnes
Pic du Midi d'Ossau
Col du Somport
Pic d'Orhy
C. de la Pierre St Martin
Alto Laza
Lescun
Accous
Urdos
Gavarnie
Cirque de Gavarnie
Monte Perdido
Parque Nacional de Ordesa
Bielsa
Torla
Broto
Biescas
Sallent-de-Gállego
Canfranc
Hecho
Ansó
Jaca
Sabiñánigo
Puente la Reina de Jaca
Roncal
Isaba
Ochagavia
Burguete
Roncesvalles
Valcarlos
Errazu
Elizondo
Santesteban
Puerto de Velate
Pto Ibañeta
Irurzun
PAMPLONA
Noáin
Villava
Aoiz
Lumbier
Navascués
Burgui
Escároz
Yesa
Sangüesa
Sos del Rey Católico
Embalse de Yesa
S. Juan de la Peña
Peña de Oroel
Sierra de la Peña
E S P A Ñ A
N A V A R R A
Puente la Reina
Estella
Las Campanas
Artajona
Tafalla
Olite
Larraga
Lerín
Allo
Los Arcos
Sesma
Lodosa
Mendavia
Andosilla
Falces
Peralta
Carcastillo
Caparroso
Uncastillo
Logroño
Viana
Fuenmayor
Cenicero
Haro
Nájera
Navarrete
Laguardia
Labastida
L A   R I O J A
El Villar de Arnedo
DONOSTIA-S. SEBASTIÁN
Pasajes
Pasaia
Hondarribia
Fuenterrabia
Irún
Behobia
Hernani
Oyarzun
Andoain
Villabona
Tolosa
Zarautz
Zumaia
Zestoa
Azpeitia
Azkoitia
Deba
Ondárroa
Lekeitio
Eibar
Elgoibar
Markina
Durango
Amorebieta
Gernika-Lumo
Mungia
Bermeo
Bakio
Cabo Machichaco
Costa Vasca
BILBAO
Galdakao
Bergara
Arrasate-Mondragon
Oñati
Zumarraga
Beasain
Ordizia
Lecumberri
Leiza
Alsasua
Olazagutia
Etxarri-Aranaz
Salvatierra-Agurain
VITORIA-GASTEIZ
E U S K A D I
V A S C O
Treviño
Zambrana
Santa Cruz de Campezo
Acedo
Sierra de Urbasa
Pto de Urbasa
Pto de Echegárate
Pto de Arlaban
Pto Urquiola
Alto de Barazar
Peña Gorbea
Murguía
Legutiano
Sierra de Herrera

LIMOGES
CLERMONT-FERRAND
Riom
Châtelguyon
Thiers
Royat
Puy de Dôme
le Mont-Dore
la Bourboule
Issoire
Ussel
Tulle
Brive-la-Gaillarde
Périgueux
Brantôme
Uzerche
Égletons
Aurillac
St Flour
Brioude
le Puy-en-Velay
Sarlat-la-Canéda
Rocamadour
Figeac
Cahors
Villeneuve-s-Lot
Agen
Moissac
Montauban
Albi
Rodez
Millau
Mende
Marvejols
Florac
Meyrueis
le Vigan
Lodève
MONTPELLIER
Sète
Agde
Béziers
Narbonne
CARCASSONNE
Castres
Mazamet
TOULOUSE
Auch
Muret
St Gaudens
St Girons
Foix
Pamiers
Limoux
Quillan
PERPIGNAN
Canet-Plage
Argelès
Collioure
Port-Vendres
Banyuls
Cerbère
Céret
Prades
Font-Romeu
Andorra la Vella
Ax-les-Thermes
HAUTE-VIENNE
CORRÈZE
PUY-DE-DÔME
CANTAL
HAUTE-LOIRE
LOT
AVEYRON
LOZÈRE
TARN
TARN-ET-GARONNE
HAUTE-GARONNE
GARONNE
HÉRAULT
AUDE
ARIÈGE
PYRÉNÉES-OR
18
22
29

LYON
St ETIENNE
Vienne
GRENOBLE
Chambéry
AIX-LES-BAINS
Albertville
Valence
le Puy en-Velay
Privas
Montélimar
Gap
Briançon
Digne-les-Bains
Sisteron
Orange
Carpentras
AVIGNON
NÎMES
Alès
Arles
MONTPELLIER
Sète
Aix-en-Provence
MARSEILLE
TOULON
Draguignan
Fréjus
Hyères
Mende
Aubenas
Die
Nyons
Salon-de-P.
Istres
Martigues
Manosque
Apt
Cavaillon
Tarascon
GOLFE DU LION
MÉDITERRANÉE
Iles d'Hyères
A
B
C
21
18

Aosta/Aoste
Biella
Ivrea
Novara
Vercelli
Vigevano
MILANO
Monza
Gallarate
Busto Arsizio
Legnano
Lodi
Treviglio
BRESCIA
Cremona
Pavia
Piacenza
PARMA
Fidenza
Salsomaggiore
TORINO
Chivasso
Moncalieri
Chieri
Asti
Alessandria
Tortona
Voghera
Novi Ligure
Casale Monferrato
Valenza
Alba
Bra
Carmagnola
Pinerolo
Saluzzo
Savigliano
Fossano
Cuneo
Mondovì
Acqui-Terme
Ovada
GENOVA
Rapallo
S. Margherita Ligure
Chiavari
Sestri Levante
La Spezia
Portovenere
Lerici
Sarzana
Carrara
Massa
Viareggio
Pisa
LIVORNO
Savona
Varazze
Finale Ligure
Albenga
Alassio
Imperia
San Remo
Bordighera
Ventimiglia
Menton
Monte-Carlo-Monaco
NICE
Antibes
CANNES
Vence
CORSE
Bastia
Calvi
Corte
Ajaccio
Propriano
Sartène
Porto-Vecchio
Bonifacio
HAUTE-CORSE
CORSE-DU-SUD
Arcipelago della Maddalena
Bocche di Bonifacio
I. di Gorgona
I. di Capraia
I. Pianosa
19
42
44
D
E
F

A
B
C
1
2
3
4
Cabo Ortegal
Estaca de Bares
Cariño
Porto do Barqueiro
Cedeira
Ortigueira
Cabo Prior
Ferrol
Viveiro
Cervo
Burela
Costa Verde
Foz
Ribadeo
Tapia de Casariego
Navia
Luarca
Cabo Vidio
Cabo de S. Adrián
A CORUÑA/
LA CORUÑA
Malpica
Betanzos
Pontedeume
As Pontes de García Rodríguez
Mondoñedo
Vilanova
Castropol
Vegadeo
Coaña
Cabo Vilán
Camariñas
Laxe
Carballo
Villalba
Cabo Touriñan
Muxía
Corcubión
Fisterra
Cabo Fisterra
Cabo Finisterre
Carnota
Muros
Noia
Ordes
Curtis
Guitiriz
Baamonde
Rábade
Meira
Grandas
Pola de Allande
Tineo
Cangas de Narcea
Fonsagrada
Lugo
Castroverde
Nadela
Corgo
Baralla
Becerreá
Navia de Suarna
Degaña
Villablino
SANTIAGO DE COMPOSTELA
Padrón
Melide
Palas de Rei
Arzúa
A Estrada
Silleda
Lalín
Portomarín
Sarriá
Samos
Pedrafita do Cebreiro
Vega de Valcarce
Villafranca del Bierzo
Ponferrada
GALICIA
ASTURIAS
Caldas de Reis
Cambados
O Grove
Sanxenxo
Pontevedra
Marín
Chantada
Monforte de Lemos
Carballiño
Ribadavia
Ourense/
Orense
VIGO
Cangas
Islas Cíes
Baiona
Cabo Silleiro
Redondela
Porriño
Ponteareas
Tui
Valença do Minho
Monção
Melgaço
Celanova
Allariz
Xinzo de Limia
Verín
A Gudiña
Puebla de Trives
O Barco
A Rúa
Viana do Bolo
Puebla de Sanabria
Sierra de la Cabrera
Lago de Sanabria
Montes de León
Astorga
A Garda
Caminha
Moledo do Minho
Viana do Castelo
Ponte de Lima
Arcos de Valdevez
Ponte da Barca
MINHO
Parque Nacional da Peneda-Gerês
Sª do Gerês
Montalegre
Chaves
Bragança
Vinhais
Esposende
Barcelos
Braga
Póvoa de Varzim
Vila do Conde
Vila Nova de Famalicão
Guimarães
Fafe
Cabeceiras de Basto
Vila Real
Mirandela
Macedo de Cavaleiros
Vimioso
Miranda do Douro
Mogadouro
TRÁS-OS-MONTES
Matosinhos
PORTO
Vila Nova de Gaia
Valongo
Penafiel
Amarante
Peso da Régua
Lamego
Alijó
Vila Flor
Alfândega da Fé
Torre de Moncorvo
Vila Nova de Foz Côa
Freixo de Espada à Cinta
Espinho
Ovar
Oliveira de Azeméis
S. João da Madeira
Arouca
Castro Daire
Moimenta da Beira
Meda
Figueira de Castelo Rodrigo
Vitigudino
Ledesma
Aveiro
Ílhavo
Vagos
Agueda
Viseu
Mangualde
Sátão
Trancoso
Pinhel
Celorico da Beira
Guarda
Vilar Formoso
Fuentes de Oñoro
Ciudad Rodrigo
Mira
Cantanhede
Mealhada
Luso
Buçaco
Seia
Manteigas
Gouveia
ESTRELA
BEIRA ALTA
Sª da Estrela
Sª de Francia
Peña de Francia
26
27

M A R C A N T Á B R I C O
Costa Verde
Cabo de Peñas
Gijón
Avilés
OVIEDO
Mieres
Ribadesella
Llanes
SANTANDER
Torrelavega
Laredo
Castro Urdiales
BILBAO
VITORIA-GASTEIZ
PICOS DE EUROPA
C A N T A B R I A
LEÓN
Palencia
BURGOS
Miranda de Ebro
Haro
Nájera
VALLADOLID
C A S T I L L A Y L E Ó N
Benavente
Tordesillas
Medina del Campo
Aranda de Duero
El Burgo de Osma
Sierra de la Demanda
SALAMANCA
Segovia
Ávila
Sierra de Ávila
GUADARRAMA
E S P A Ñ A
Sigüenza
27
28
20

A
B
C
24
30
1
2
3
4
Viana do Castelo
Braga
Guimarães
Póvoa de Varzim
Vila do Conde
PORTO
Vila Nova de Gaia
Espinho
Aveiro
Viseu
Guarda
COIMBRA
Figueira da Foz
Leiria
Nazaré
Fátima
Tomar
Santarém
Castelo Branco
Covilhã
Portalegre
Elvas
Badajoz
Sintra
LISBOA
Estoril
Cascais
Chaves
Bragança
Vila Real
Mirandela
Amarante
Lamego
Pêso da Régua
Valença do Minho
Tui
Ponte de Lima
Barcelos
Penafiel
Matosinhos
Ovar
Estarreja
Agueda
Mangualde
Seia
Manteigas
Lousã
Pombal
Batalha
Alcobaça
Caldas da Rainha
Peniche
Óbidos
Torres Vedras
Abrantes
Entroncamento
Torres Novas
Nisa
Castelo de Vide
Marvão
Estremoz
Ponte de Sor
Coruche
Vila Franca de Xira
Mafra
Ericeira
Almada
Montijo
Alcochete
Sacavém
Amadora
Setúbal
Palmela
Vendas Novas
Montemor-o-Novo
Fundão
Belmonte
Sabugal
Penamacor
Alcántara
Valencia de Alcántara
Coria
Ciudad Rodrigo
Fuentes de Oñoro
Verín
Xinzo de Limia
Celanova
Porriño
Baiona
Ponteareas
Melgaço
Monção
Caminha
Esposende
Trás-os-Montes
MINHO
DOURO
BEIRA
BEIRA ALTA
BEIRA BAIXA
BEIRA LITORAL
ESTRELA
SERRA DA ESTRELA
RIBATEJO
ESTREMADURA
PORTUGAL
RIO TEJO
RIO TAJO
Rio Douro
Rio Mondego
Rio Zêzere
Rio Sorraia
Rio Vouga
Rio Côa
Rio Tâmega
Rio Minho
Rio Lima
Ilha Berlenga
Cabo Carvoeiro
Cabo da Roca
Cabo Mondego
Cabo Silleiro
Sª do Gerês
Sª do Marão
Sª da Peneda
Sª do Caramulo
Sª de Montemuro
Sª da Lousã
Sª dos Candeeiros
Sª da Gardunha
Sª de Alvelos
Sª de Malcata
Sª de S. Mamede
Sª de Montejunto
Parque Nacional da Peneda-Gerês

25
28
31
32
D
E
F
BURGOS
Palencia
VALLADOLID
Zamora
SALAMANCA
Segovia
Ávila
El Escorial
MADRID
Alcalá de Henares
Aranjuez
TOLEDO
Ciudad Real
Alcázar de S. Juan
Plasencia
Trujillo
Talavera de la Reina
Benavente
La Bañeza
Tordesillas
Medina del Campo
Aranda de Duero
Peñafiel
Arévalo
Béjar
Guadalupe
Sahagún
Osorno
Frómista
Lerma
Toro
Puebla de Sanabria
Miranda do Douro
Ledesma
Peñaranda de Bracamonte
Guadarrama
Getafe
Leganés
Móstoles
Ocaña
Consuegra
Madridejos
Daimiel
Almagro
Oropesa
Navalmoral de la Mata
CASTILLA LEÓN
ESPAÑA
MADRID
CASTILLA-LA MANCHA
SIERRA DE GREDOS
Sierra de Ávila
SIERRA DE GUADARRAMA
MONTES DE TOLEDO
Sierra de Guadalupe
Río Duero
Río Tajo
Río Tormes
Río Alberche
Río Tiétar
Río Esla
Río Guadiana
Embalse de Almendra
Embalse de Ricobayo
Embalse de Valdecañas
Embalse de Cíjara
Embalse de Orellana
Pto de Somosierra
Pto de Navacerrada
Pto del Pico
Pto de Béjar
Pto de Miravete
Pto Llano
Valdihuela
Villacastín
Cebreros
Arenas de S. Pedro
Candeleda
Jaraíz
Jarandilla de la Vera
Cuacos
Yuste
Hervás
Baños de Montemayor
La Alberca
Las Batuecas
Ciudad Rodrigo
Lozoyuela
Buitrago del Lozoya
Rascafría
Sepúlveda
Riaza
Ayllón
Cuéllar
Iscar
Olmedo
Coca
Simancas
Rueda
Medina de Rioseco
Villalpando
Dueñas
Baltanás
Roa
Covarrubias
Sto Domingo de Silos
Illescas
Torrijos
Maqueda
Escalona
Chinchón
Tembleque
Mora
Orgaz
Los Yébenes
Sonseca
Puerto Lápice
Herencia
Malagón
Fernancaballero
Piedrabuena
Luciana
Siruela
Herrera del Duque
Castilblanco
Logrosán
Zorita
Miajadas
Madrigalejo
Navalvillar de Pela
Orellana la Vieja
Villanueva de la Serena
Don Benito
Medellín
Campanario
Magacela
Guareña
Almoharín
Montánchez
Deleitosa
Jaraicejo
Almaraz
Casatejada
Talayuela
Lagartera
Velada
El Puente del Arzobispo
Belvis de la Jara
Sevilleja de la Jara
Anchuras
Cumbre Alta
Navahermosa
Menasalbas
Gálvez
Polán
Layos
Almonacid de Toledo
Mocejón
Bargas
Yepes
Villasequilla de Yepes
Dosbarrios
Noblejas
Villatobas
Lillo
La Guardia
Camuñas
Villafranca de los Caballeros
Campo de Criptana
Quero
Miguel Esteban
La Puebla de Almoradiel
Quintanar de la Orden
Villarrubia de los Ojos
Arenas de S. Juan
Villarta de S. Juan
Manzanares
Alcobendas
Barajas
Torrejón de Ardoz
San Sebastián de los Reyes
Colmenar Viejo
Torrelodones
Galapagar
El Pardo
Aravaca
Las Rozas
Majadahonda
Villaviciosa de Odón
Navalcarnero
Valdemoro
Pinto
Parla
Fuenlabrada
Griñón
Ciempozuelos
Seseña
Arganda
Vicálvaro
Loeches
Nuevo Baztán
Villarejo de Salvanés
Colmenar de Oreja
Morata de Tajuña
Perales de Tajuña
Torrelaguna
El Molar
Talamanca
Guadalix
Manzanares el Real
Navacerrada
Cercedilla
El Espinar
S. Rafael
Las Navas del Marqués
Valle de los Caídos
Robledo de Chavela
Valdemorillo
Chapinería
Aldea del Fresno
Villa del Prado
Cadalso de los Vidrios
Almorox
Méntrida
Valmojado
Camarena
Fuensalida
Sta Olalla
Cebolla
La Puebla de Montalbán
Escalonilla
El Carpio de Tajo
Navamorcuende
Sotillo de la Adrada
La Adrada
Piedralaves
Casavieja
Mombeltrán
Cuevas del Valle
S. Esteban del Valle
Navaluenga
Burgohondo
El Tiemblo
El Barraco
El Hoyo de Pinares
Navalperal de P.
Piedrahita
El Barco de Ávila
Navarredonda de la Sierra
Hoyos del Espino
Solosancho
Muñana
Muñogalindo
Cespedosa
Guijuelo
Alba de Tormes
Macotera
Fontiveros
Madrigal de las Altas Torres
Cantalapiedra
Fuentesaúco
Corrales
Mota del Marqués
Villanubla
Zaratán
Laguna de Duero
Tudela de Duero
Quintanilla de Onésimo
Portillo
Mojados
Valdestillas
Serrada
La Seca
Nava del Rey
Alaejos
Castronuño
Villalar de los Comuneros
Fuentelapeña
Castrejón
Cañizal
Villaflores
Villares de la Reina
Golpejas
Vitigudino
Villaseco de los Reyes
Villar de Peralonso
Almeida
Bermillo
Fermoselle
Moraleja del Vino
Coreses
Muelas del Pan
Carbajales de Alba
Fonfría
Alcañices
Trabazos
Tábara
Camarzana
Mombuey
Palacios de Sanabria
Castrocontrigo
Santibáñez de Vidriales
Morales de Rey
Villafáfila
Villalón de Campos
Paredes de Nava
Carrión de los Condes
Villasarracino
Melgar de Fernamental
Castrogeriz
Villadiego
Villasandino
Pampliega
Sta María del Campo
Quintana del Puente
Torquemada
Magaz
Baños de Cerrato
Cevico de la Torre
Tórtoles de E.
Esguevillas
Cabezón
Villafuerte
Olmedillo de Roa
Gumiel de Hizán
Caleruega
Huerta del Rey
Peñaranda de Duero
Langa de Duero
Fuentecén
Sacramenia
Fuentidueña
Olombrada
Campaspero
Hontalbilla
Cantalejo
Turégano
Carbonero el Mayor
Navas de Oro
Samboal
Nava de la Asunción
Sta María la Real de Nieva
Montuenga
Sangarcía
Abades
Madrona
San Ildefonso o la Granja
Torrecaballeros
Pedraza de la Sierra
Prádena
Cerezo de Abajo
La Pinilla
Boceguillas
Honrubia de la Cuesta
Maderuelo
Sarracín
Arlanzón
Rubena
Sotopalacios
Villahoz
Villafruela
Tamara
Astudillo
Amusco
Monzón de Campos
Villaumbrales
Villada
Cisneros
Frechilla
Mayorga
Valderas
Fuentes de Ropel
Villanueva del Campo
Castroverde de Campos
Villamayor de Campos
Villafrechós
Villabrágima
Montealegre
Ampudia
Mucientes
La Mudarra
Villardefrades
Vezdemarbán
Castronuevo
Montamarta
Fuentes de Nava
Villamartín
Villarramiel
Autillo de Campos
Becilla de Valderaduey
Melgar de Abajo
Villaquejida
Roperuelos del Páramo
Valencia de Don Juan
Sta María del Páramo
Villamañán
Castrotierra
Valdevimbre
Santas Martas
El Burgo Ranero
Riego de la Vega
Destriana
Truchas
Encinedo
Teleno

PAMPLONA
Logroño
Soria
ZARAGOZA
Huesca
Tudela
Teruel
Guadalajara
Cuenca
VALENCIA
Calatayud
Daroca
Sagunto
Alcalá de Henares
Alcázar de S. Juan
EUSKADI
NAVARRA
LA RIOJA
Sierra de la Demanda
Serranía de Cuenca
Montes Universales
Sierra de Urbión
Sierra de Gúdar
Miranda
Haro
Estella
Jaca
Calahorra
Alfaro
Tarazona
Almazán
Sigüenza
Medinaceli
Molina de Aragón
Alcañiz
Requena
Utiel
Motilla del Palancar
Tarancón
Belmonte
Segorbe
Onda
El Burgo de Osma
Aranda
Ejea de los Caballeros
Alagón
Caspe
Montalbán
Alcorisa
Calamocha
Albarracín
Mora de Rubielos
Sarrión
Torrijos
Priego
Pastrana
Huete
Taracena
Trillo
Cifuentes
Brihuega
Torija
Barbastro
Biescas
Sabiñánigo
Ayerbe
Lumbier
Sangüesa
Olite
Tafalla
Zuera
Borja
Mallén
Cortes
La Almunia de Doña Godina
Cariñena
Belchite
Híjar
Andorra
Utrillas
Aliaga
Cantavieja
Morella
Vilafranca del Cid
Vila-real
Nules
Vall de Uxó
Burjassot
Manises
Torrent
Chiva
Cheste
Llíria
Chelva
Ademuz
Cañete
Landete
Carboneras de Guadazaón
Valverde del Júcar
Almodóvar del Pinar
Minglanilla
Iniesta
Villanueva de la Jara
San Clemente
El Provencio
Las Pedroñeras
Mota del Cuervo
El Toboso
Quintanar de la Orden
Campo de Criptana

PERPIGNAN
B.-de-Luchon
Andorra la Vella
Font-Romeu
Puigcerdà
La Seu d'Urgell
Ripoll
Olot
Figueres/Figueras
Girona/Gerona
Vich/Vic
Manresa
Lleida/Lérida
Terrassa/Tarrasa
Sabadell
Granollers
Mataró
Badalona
BARCELONA
Genova
Reus
Tarragona
Tortosa
Vinaròs
Benicarló
Peñíscola
Benicasim
Castelló de la Plana/Castellón de la Plana
Costa Dorada
Costa del Azahar
MALLORCA
PALMA
Sóller
Inca
Manacor
Pollença
Alcudia
I. Columbretes
I. Dragonera
Golfo de Roses
Cabo de Tortosa
I. de Buda
Golfo de St. Jordi
Cap de Salou
Monte Perdido
Pico de Aneto
MALADETA
Serra del Cadí
CATALUNYA
PYRÉNÉES-OR
ARIÈGE
Pic du Canigou
S. Feliu de Guíxols
Blanes
Lloret de Mar
Palafrugell
Banyoles
Berga
Solsona
Cervera
Tàrrega
Balaguer
Monzón
Barbastro
Fraga
Valls
Vilafranca del Penedès
Sitges
Vilanova i la Geltrú
Amposta
Alcanar
20
21
32
33
D
E
F
1
2
3
4

PORTUGAL
LISBOA
Sintra
Estoril
Cascais
Setúbal
Sesimbra
Vila Franca de Xira
Montemor-o-Novo
Évora
Estremoz
Elvas
Badajoz
Olivenza
Alcácer do Sal
Grândola
Sines
Santiago do Cacém
Odemira
Beja
Serpa
Moura
Ferreira do Alentejo
Castro Verde
Ourique
Almodôvar
Mértola
ALENTEJO
ALGARVE
Lagos
Portimão
Silves
Albufeira
Loulé
Faro
Olhão
Tavira
Vila Real de Sto António
Ayamonte
Huelva
Moguer
Aracena
Zafra
Jerez de los Caballeros
Fregenal de la Sierra
Valverde del Camino
Nerva
Niebla
Almonte
El Rocío
Matalascañas
Parque Nacional de Doñana
Sanlúcar de Barrameda
Chipiona
Rota
Jerez de la Frontera
El Puerto de Sta María
CÁDIZ
S. Fernando
Chiclana de la Frontera
Conil de la Frontera
Cabo de Trafalgar
GOLFO DE CÁDIZ
Costa de la Luz
Cabo de S. Vicente
Ponta de Sagres
Cabo de Sines
Cabo Espichel
Cabo da Roca
Rio Guadiana
Rio Tejo
ILHA DE PORTO SANTO
Porto Santo
ARQUIPÉLAGO DA MADEIRA
Porto Moniz
Santana
Funchal
Pico Ruivo
Desertas
ILHA DA MADEIRA
1/2750000
1/2750000
OCEANO ATLANTICO
ISLAS CANARIAS
LANZAROTE
Haria
Teguise
Arrecife
Parque Nacional de Timanfaya
Playa Blanca
Corralejo
FUERTEVENTURA
La Oliva
Puerto del Rosario
Betancuria
Pájara
Tuineje
Gran Tarajal
Punta de Jandía
TENERIFE
La Laguna
Sta Cruz de Tenerife
Puerto de la Cruz
Icod de los Vinos
La Orotava
Güimar
Parque Nacional del Teide
Teide
Gula de Isora
Granadilla de Abona
Los Cristianos
LA PALMA
Barlovento
Puntagorda
Los Sauces
Parque Nacional de la Caldera de Taburiente
Sta Cruz de la Palma
Los Llanos de Aridane
Fuencaliente
GOMERA
Vallehermoso
Hermigua
Garajonay (Parque Nacional)
S. Sebastián
HIERRO
Valverde
Frontera
Puerto de la Estaca
GRAN CANARIA
LAS PALMAS DE GRAN CANARIA
Gáldar
Arucas
Telde
S. Nicolás de Tolentino
Cruz de Tejeda
Maspalomas
Cap Juby
Tarfaya
AFRIQUE
A
B
C
1
2
3
4

SEVILLA
CÓRDOBA
GRANADA
MÁLAGA
Ciudad Real
Jaén
Algeciras
Gibraltar
La Línea de la Concepción
Ceuta
Tarifa
Marbella
Torremolinos
Fuengirola
Estepona
Ronda
Antequera
Écija
Carmona
Utrera
Osuna
Lucena
Cabra
Baena
Montilla
Aguilar
Puente Genil
Andújar
Bailén
Linares
Úbeda
Baeza
La Carolina
Valdepeñas
Manzanares
Puertollano
Almadén
Daimiel
Alcázar de S. Juan
Vélez-Málaga
Nerja
Almuñécar
Motril
Loja
Alcalá la Real
Martos
Montoro
Peñarroya-Pueblonuevo
Pozoblanco
Villanueva de la Serena
Don Benito
Llerena
Castuera
Arcos de la Frontera
Medina-Sidonia
Villamartín
Olvera
Morón de la Frontera
Marchena
El Arahal
Dos Hermanas
Alcalá de Guadaira
Lebrija
Guadix
Lanjarón
Órgiva
Adra
SIERRA NEVADA
Pico Veleta
Mulhacén
Costa del Sol
MAR
ESTRECHO DE GIBRALTAR
Río Guadalquivir
Río Guadiana
Río Genil
CASTILLA
EXTREMADURA
ANDALUCÍA
D
E
F
1
2
3
4
27
32

VALENCIA
ALICANTE
MURCIA
Albacete
ALMERÍA
Cartagena
Lorca
Elx/Elche
Alcoy
Gandia
Requena
Utiel
Alarcón
Minglanilla
Iniesta
La Roda
Tomelloso
Alcázar de S. Juan
Socuéllamos
Villarrobledo
S. Clemente
Las Pedroñeras
Tarazona de la Mancha
Mahora
Casas Ibáñez
Almansa
Hellín
Tobarra
Yecla
Jumilla
Villena
Elda
Novelda
Ontinyent
Xàtiva
Alzira
Sueca
Cullera
Cieza
Archena
Mula
Molina de Segura
Orihuela
Alcantarilla
Totana
Torrevieja
S. Pedro del Pinatar
La Unión
Cabo de Palos
Mazarrón
Águilas
Puerto Lumbreras
Huércal-Overa
Vera
Garrucha
Mojácar
Carboneras
Níjar
Cabo de Gata
Roquetas de Mar
El Ejido
Adra
Berja
Baza
Huéscar
Caravaca de la Cruz
Calasparra
Moratalla
Cazorla
Villacarrillo
Alcaraz
Yeste
Chinchilla de Monte Aragón
LA MANCHA
MURCIA
VALENCIA
Sierra de Segura
Sierra de los Filabres
Sierra de Gádor
Golfo de Almería
Golfo de Mazarrón
Isla de Tabarca
Mar Menor
M E D I T E R R Á N E O
del Sol
Costa
A
B
C
1
2
3
4
28
31

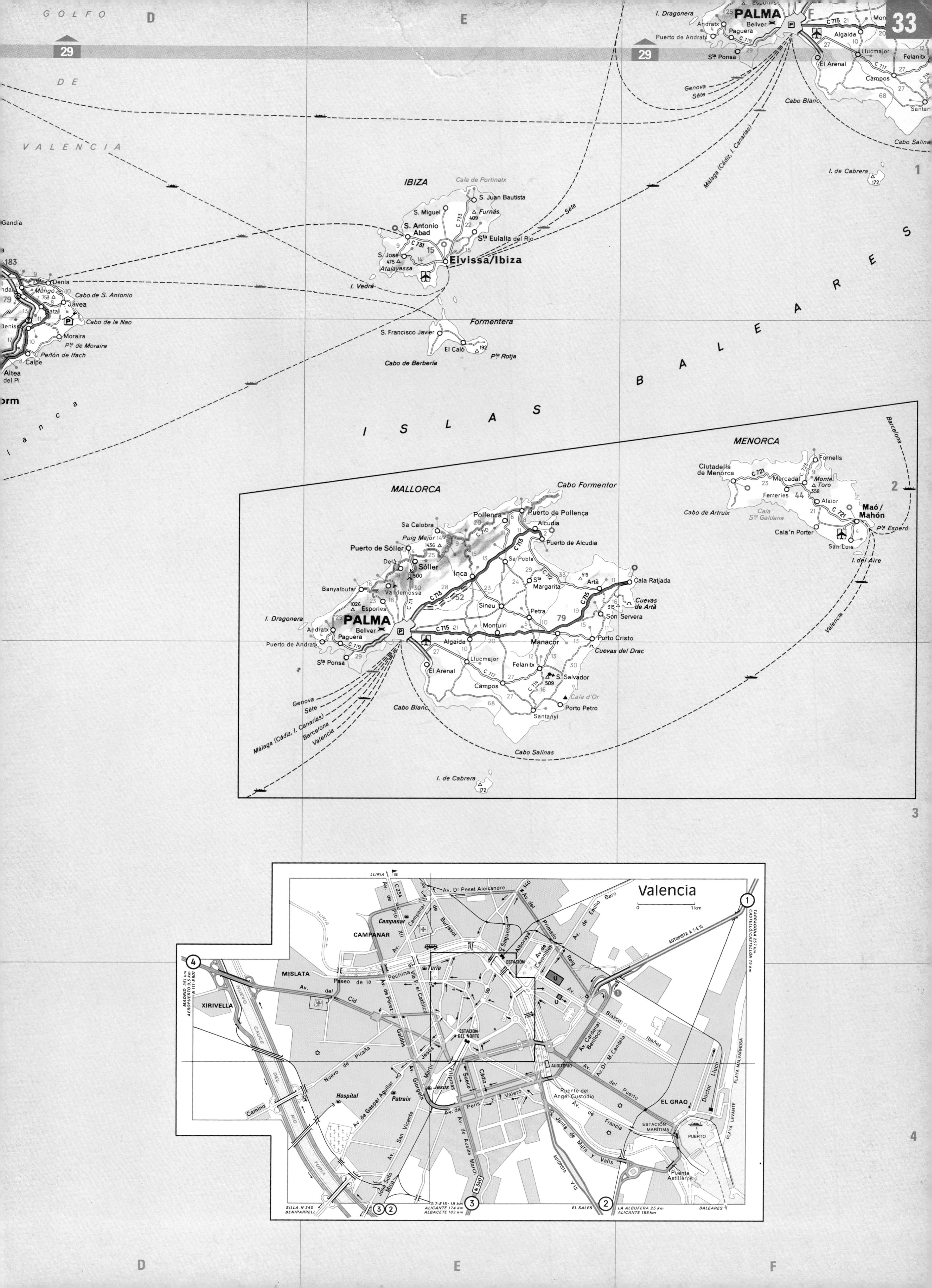
GOLFO
DE
VALENCIA
D
E
F
29
29
1
2
3
4
PALMA
I. Dragonera
Andratx
Paguera
Bellver
Puerto de Andratx
Sta Ponsa
C 715
Algaida
Llucmajor
Felanitx
El Arenal
Campos
Cabo Blanc
Santanyí
Cabo Salinas
Genova
Sète
Málaga (Cádiz, I. Canarias)
I. de Cabrera
172
IBIZA
Cala de Portinatx
S. Juan Bautista
S. Miguel
Furnás
409
C 733
S. Antonio Abad
Sta Eulalia del Río
C 731
S. José
475
Atalayassa
Eivissa/Ibiza
I. Vedrá
Formentera
S. Francisco Javier
El Caló
192
Pta Rotja
Cabo de Berbería
Gandía
183
Denia
Mongó
753
Cabo de S. Antonio
Jávea
Cabo de la Nao
Moraira
Pta de Moraira
Peñón de Ifach
Calpe
Altea
del Pi
ISLAS BALEARES
MENORCA
Fornells
Ciutadella de Menorca
C 721
Mercadal
C 723
Monte Toro
358
Ferreries
Alaior
Maó / Mahón
Cabo de Artruix
Cala Sta Galdana
Cala'n Porter
Pta Esperó
San Luis
I. del Aire
Barcelona
Valencia
MALLORCA
Cabo Formentor
Pollença
Puerto de Pollença
Alcudia
Puerto de Alcudia
Sa Calobra
Puig Major
1436
Puerto de Sóller
Deià
Sóller
500
Inca
C 713
Sa Pobla
Sta Margarita
519
Artà
Cala Ratjada
Banyalbufar
Valldemossa
1026
Esporles
Cuevas de Artà
315
Son Servera
C 715
Sineu
Petra
Montuïri
Manacor
Porto Cristo
Cuevas del Drac
Algaida
Llucmajor
Felanitx
S. Salvador
509
C 717
C 714
Campos
Cala d'Or
Porto Petro
Santanyí
Cabo Blanc
Cabo Salinas
I. de Cabrera
172
Genova
Sète
Málaga (Cádiz, I. Canarias)
Barcelona
Valencia
Valencia
0
1 km
LLIRIA
C 234
Av. Dr Peset Aleixandre
N 340
Av. del Primado Reig
Av. de Emilio Baro
Campanar
CAMPANAR
Av. de Pío XII
Av. Campanar
Av. de Burjasot
Av. de Saguntо
Alboraya
Av. de Cavanilles
ESTACIÓN
AUTOPISTA A 7-E15
TARRAGONA 257 km
CASTELLÓ/CASTELLÓN 75 km
MADRID 351 km
AEROPUERTO 9 km
N III-E 901
MISLATA
XIRIVELLA
NUEVO CAUCE DEL RIO TURIA
Paseo de la Pechina
Turia
Gran Vía F. el Católico
Av. de Pérez Galdós
Av. del Cid
Av. Blasco Ibáñez
Av. Cardenal Benlloch
Av. Dr. M. Candela
Av. del Puerto
ESTACIÓN DEL NORTE
Jesús
Nuevo de Picaña
Hospital
Patraix
Av. de Gaspar Aguilar
Av. Giorgeta
Av. San Vicente
José Soto Mico
Camino
Filipinas
Sueca
Cádiz
Av. de Peris y Valero
Av. de Ausias March
N 340
AUDITORIO
Puente del Angel Custodio
Av. de Francia
Junta de Murs y Valls
AUTOPISTA V 15
ESTACIÓN MARÍTIMA
PUERTO
Puente Astilleros
EL GRAO
Doctor Lluch
PLAYA MALVARROSA
PLAYA LEVANTE
SILLA, N 340
BENIPARRELL
A 7-E15: 18 km
ALICANTE 174 km
ALBACETE 183 km
EL SALER
LA ALBUFERA 25 km
ALICANTE 183 km
BALEARES
TURIA
D
E
F

Brugge
NOORD-HOLLAND
NEDERLAND
IJsselmeer
Markermeer
FLEVOLAND
OVERIJSSEL
GELDERLAND
UTRECHT
ZUID-HOLLAND
NOORD-BRABANT
ZEELAND
LIMBURG
ANTWERPEN
WEST-VLAANDEREN
OOST-VLAANDEREN
BRABANT
HAINAUT
NAMUR
LIÈGE
LUXEMBOURG
BELGIQUE
BELGIË
NORD
PAS-DE-CALAIS
SOMME
AISNE
ARDENNES
Den Helder
Alkmaar
Haarlem
AMSTERDAM
Hilversum
Zwolle
Apeldoorn
Deventer
Leiden
Scheveningen
DEN HAAG
('S-GRAVENHAGE)
Delft
Gouda
UTRECHT
Amersfoort
ARNHEM
NIJMEGEN
ROTTERDAM
Dordrecht
's-Hertogenbosch
Breda
Tilburg
EINDHOVEN
Roosendaal
Bergen op Zoom
Middelburg
Vlissingen
Venlo
Roermond
Mönchengladbach
Heerlen
Maastricht
AACHEN
Knokke-Heist
Blankenberge
Oostende
BRUGGE
GENT
St. Niklaas
ANTWERPEN
(ANVERS)
Turnhout
Lier
Mechelen
(Malines)
Leuven (Louvain)
Hasselt
Genk
BRUSSEL
BRUXELLES
Aalst
Oudenaarde
Kortrijk
(Courtrai)
Ieper
(Ypres)
Roeselare
(Roulers)
De Panne
Dunkerque
LILLE
Roubaix
Tourcoing
Tournai
Mons
Charleroi
Namur
Wavre
Liège
Verviers
Spa
Huy
Dinant
Bastogne
Arlon
LUXEMBOURG
Valenciennes
Maubeuge
Douai
Lens
Arras
Cambrai
St. Quentin
Laon
Charleville-Mézières
Sedan
Rethel
Noyon
14
11

NIEDERSACHSEN
NORDRHEIN-WESTFALEN
HESSEN
RHEINLAND-PFALZ
SAARLAND
BUNDESREPUBLIK
DRENTHE
Emmen
Coevorden
Almelo
Hengelo
Enschede
Lingen
Nordhorn
Rheine
Meppen
Cloppenburg
Vechta
Diepholz
Osnabrück
Minden
Nienburg
Celle
HANNOVER
BRAUNSCHWEIG
Hildesheim
Salzgitter-Lebenstedt
Hameln
Herford
Bielefeld
Detmold
Münster
Gütersloh
Paderborn
Lippstadt
Hamm
Soest
Göttingen
Kassel
Bocholt
Wesel
Recklinghsn
Gelsenkchn
Herne
Bottrop
Oberhsn
Bochum
ESSEN
DORTMUND
DUISBURG
Mülheim
Hagen
Iserlohn
Arnsberg
Krefeld
WUPPERTAL
DÜSSELDORF
Neuss
Solingen
Remscheid
Lüdenscheid
Leverkusen
KÖLN
Düren
BONN
Bad Godesberg
Siegen
Marburg
Gießen
Fulda
Bad Hersfeld
Koblenz
Limburg
Wetzlar
Bad Homburg
FRANKFURT A.M.
WIESBADEN
MAINZ
Offenbach
Hanau
Aschaffenburg
Darmstadt
Würzburg
Bad Kreuznach
Trier
Worms
Ludwigshafen
MANNHEIM
HEIDELBERG
Kaiserslautern
Bad Mergentheim
Tauberbischofsheim

Bremen
HAMBURG
BREMEN
HANNOVER
KIEL
Flensburg
Schleswig
Rendsburg
Neumünster
Itzehoe
Cuxhaven
Bremerhaven
Wilhelmshaven
Oldenburg
Delmenhorst
Emden
Groningen
Assen
Emmen
Zwolle
Almelo
Hengelo
Enschede
Deventer
Arnhem
Nordhorn
Lingen
Meppen
Osnabrück
Münster
Bielefeld
Herford
Minden
Hameln
Hildesheim
Paderborn
Detmold
Gütersloh
Hamm
Dortmund
Recklinghsn
Gelsenkchn
Celle
Stade
Harburg
Nordfriesische Inseln
Ostfriesische Inseln
Deutsche Bucht
Helgoland
SCHLESWIG
HOLSTEIN
NIEDERSACHSEN
NORDRHEIN
WESTFALEN
GRONINGEN
DRENTHE
OVERIJSSEL
76
11
34
38

76
77
78
39
LOLLAND
Fehmarn
Mecklenburger Bucht
Lübecker Bucht
Oderbucht
RÜGEN
DEUTSCHE DEMOKRATISCHE REPUBLIK
HARZ
Brocken
Stralsund
Greifswald
Wolgast
Anklam
Ueckermünde
Swinoujscie
SZCZECIN
ROSTOCK
Warnemünde
Bad Doberan
Kühlungsborn
Ribnitz-Damgarten
Barth
Bergen
Saßnitz
Binz
Demmin
Wismar
Grevesmühlen
LÜBECK
Travemünde
Oldenburg
Neustadt
Eutin
Ratzeburg
Mölln
Schwerin
Güstrow
Teterow
Malchin
Neubrandenburg
Waren
Neustrelitz
Prenzlau
Pasewalk
Parchim
Ludwigslust
Hagenow
Boizenburg
Lauenburg
Perleberg
Pritzwalk
Wittstock
Neuruppin
Oranienburg
Eberswalde
Schwedt
Templin
Zehdenick
Salzwedel
Uelzen
Wittenberge
Stendal
Tangermünde
Rathenow
Nauen
BERLIN
(WEST)
(OST)
Spandau
Köpenick
POTSDAM
Brandenburg
Genthin
Burg
Wolfsburg
Gifhorn
Gardelegen
Haldensleben
Helmstedt
BRAUNSCHWEIG
Wolfenbüttel
Salzgitter
MAGDEBURG
Schönebeck
Zerbst
Roßlau
Dessau
Wittenberg
Jüterbog
Luckenwalde
Zossen
Lübben
Lübbenau
Halberstadt
Wernigerode
Quedlinburg
Aschersleben
Bernburg
Köthen
Bitterfeld
Goslar
Bad Harzburg
Osterode
Nordhausen
Sangerhausen
Eisleben
HALLE
Halle-Neustadt
Merseburg
Delitzsch
Eilenburg
Torgau
LEIPZIG
Wurzen
Oschatz
Riesa
Großenhain
Meißen
DRESDEN
Finsterwalde
Weißenfels

36
37
34
15
42
WESTFALEN
HESSEN
BUNDESREPUBLIK
RHEINLAND-PFALZ
BADEN
DORTMUND
Paderborn
Göttingen
Nordhausen
KASSEL
Mühlhausen
Eisenach
Gotha
Bad Hersfeld
Marburg
Fulda
Siegen
Gießen
Bad Godesberg
Koblenz
Bad Nauheim
Bad Homburg
FRANKFURT A.M.
WIESBADEN
MAINZ
Darmstadt
Aschaffenburg
Würzburg
Schweinfurt
Bad Kissingen
Bad Kreuznach
Worms
Ludwigshafen
MANNHEIM
HEIDELBERG
Kaiserslautern
Speyer
Heilbronn
SAARBRÜCKEN
Zweibrücken
Pirmasens
Landau
KARLSRUHE
Pforzheim
Ludwigsburg
STUTTGART
Esslingen
Göppingen
Baden-Baden
STRASBOURG
Offenburg
Tübingen
Reutlingen
Ulm
Neu-Ulm
Heidenheim
Aalen
Ansbach
Crailsheim
Schwäbisch Hall
Wissembourg
Haguenau
Saverne
Sarreguemines
Hagen
Iserlohn
Lüdenscheid
Leverkusen
Bochum
Herne
Hamm
Soest
Lippstadt
Arnsberg
Brilon
Korbach
Frankenberg
Alsfeld
Lauterbach
Wetzlar
Limburg
Bad Ems
Boppard
Bingen
Alzey
Bensheim
Heppenheim
Weinheim
Mosbach
Bruchsal
Rastatt
Böblingen
Sindelfingen
Nürtingen
Kirchheim u. Teck
Geislingen
Günzburg
Hechingen
Balingen
Freudenstadt
Sélestat
Obernai
Erstein
Saint-Dié
Sarrebourg

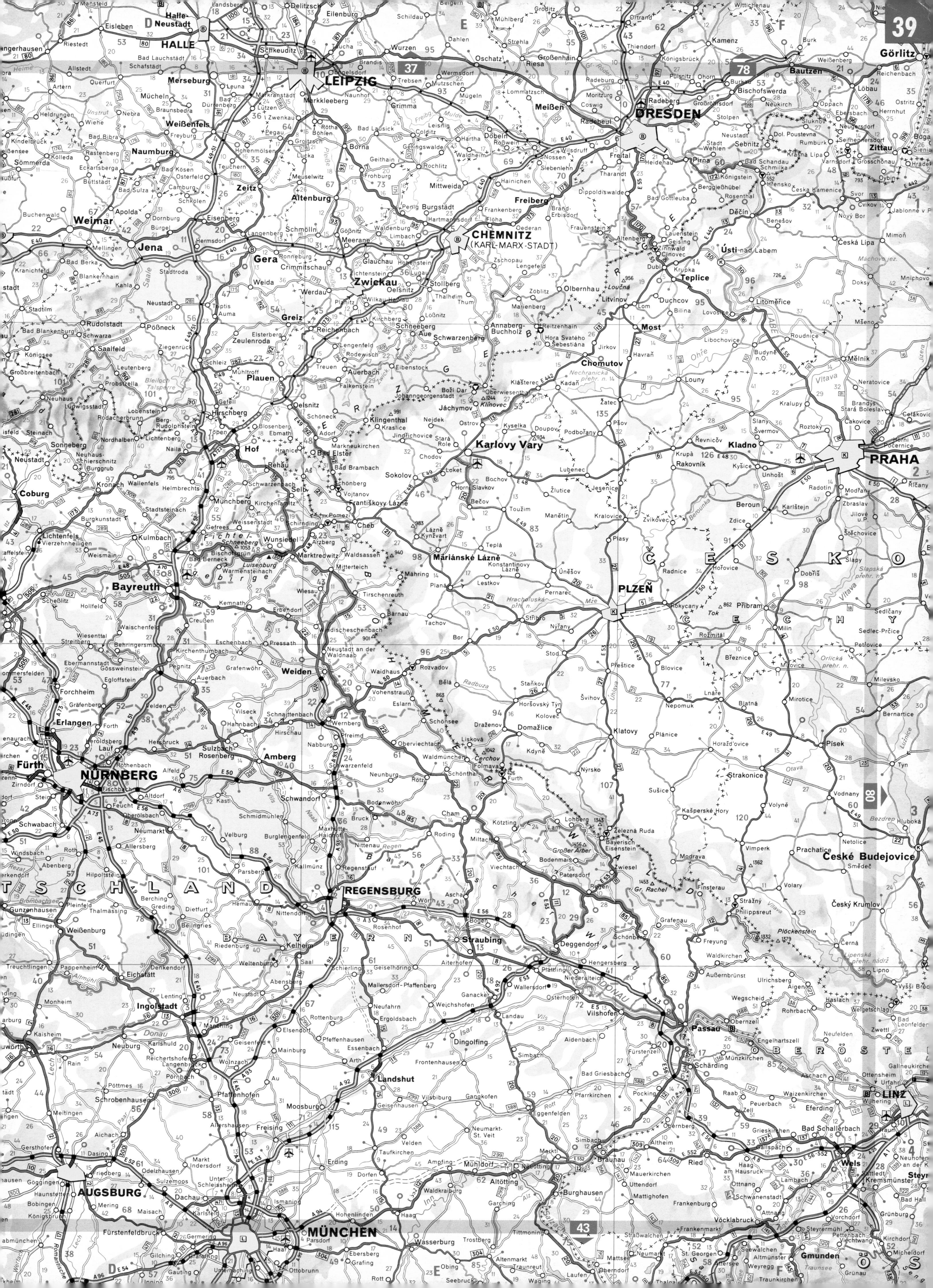
HALLE
LEIPZIG
DRESDEN
Görlitz
Bautzen
Meißen
Merseburg
Weißenfels
Naumburg
Weimar
Jena
Gera
Zeitz
Altenburg
Zwickau
CHEMNITZ
(KARL-MARX-STADT)
Freiberg
Plauen
Greiz
Hof
Coburg
Bayreuth
Erlangen
Fürth
NÜRNBERG
Amberg
Weiden
REGENSBURG
Ingolstadt
AUGSBURG
MÜNCHEN
Landshut
Straubing
Deggendorf
Passau
LINZ
Wels
Gmunden
Karlovy Vary
Cheb
Mariánské Lázně
PLZEŇ
PRAHA
Kladno
Teplice
Ústí nad Labem
Děčín
Most
Chomutov
Příbram
České Budějovice
Písek
Strakonice
ČESKO
ČECHY
BAYERN
DEUTSCHLAND
OBERÖSTERREICH
DONAU
37
78
80
43

Bad Kissingen
Schweinfurt
Bamberg
Würzburg
Bayreuth
Kulmbach
Lichtenfels
Münchberg
Cheb
Mariánské Lázně
Plzeň
Erlangen
Fürth
NÜRNBERG
Amberg
Weiden
Schwandorf
Ansbach
Schwabach
Rothenburg ob der Tauber
Crailsheim
Dinkelsbühl
DEUTSCHLAND
BAYERN
REGENSBURG
Straubing
Deggendorf
Passau
Weißenburg
Eichstätt
Ingolstadt
Nördlingen
Donauwörth
Heidenheim
Aalen
Schwäbisch Gmünd
Ulm
Neu-Ulm
Günzburg
AUGSBURG
Landshut
Freising
Dachau
MÜNCHEN
Erding
Mühldorf
Altötting
Burghausen
Memmingen
Kaufbeuren
Kempten
Landsberg
Starnberg
Weilheim
Rosenheim
Traunstein
SALZ
Bad Reichenhall
Berchtesgaden
Ravensburg
Friedrichshafen
Lindau
Bregenz
Dornbirn
Feldkirch
VORARLBERG
LIECHTENSTEIN
Vaduz
Bludenz
St. Anton
Landeck
Reutte
Füssen
Garmisch
Partenkirchen
Mittenwald
Seefeld
INNSBRUCK
Hall in Tirol
Schwaz
Kufstein
Kitzbühel
Wörgl
Zell am See
Mayrhofen
Brenner
Lienz
OSTTIROL
HOHE TAUERN
Großglockner
Davos
Chur
Klosters
Sölden
Brunico/Bruneck
Bressanone/Brixen
Vipiteno/Sterzing
Merano/Meran
Klatovy
Domažlice
Cham
Bad Tölz
Tegernsee
Schliersee
Zugspitze
Donau
Inn
38
39
42
43

ČESKOSLOVENSKO
ČECHY
MORAVA
NIEDERÖSTERREICH
OBERÖSTERREICH
ÖSTERREICH
STEIERMARK
BURGENLAND
KÄRNTEN
JUGOSLAVIJA
Olomouc
Prostějov
BRNO
Jihlava
Havlíčkův Brod
Tábor
Písek
Strakonice
České Budějovice
Český Krumlov
Jindřichuv Hradec
Znojmo
Břeclav
Hodonín
Mikulov
Mistelbach
Stockerau
Korneuburg
WIEN
BRATISLAVA
Krems
St. Pölten
Melk
LINZ
Wels
Steyr
Gmunden
Bad Ischl
Wiener Neustadt
Baden
Eisenstadt
Sopron
Szombathely
Mürzzuschlag
Bruck an der Mur
Leoben
GRAZ
Judenburg
Klagenfurt
Villach
Spittal
Maribor
Ptuj
Varaždin
Čakovec
Murska Sobota
Körmend
Fürstenfeld
Hartberg
Liezen
Schladming
Radstadt
Jesenice
Donau
Drava
Mur
Neusiedler See
Budapest 203
Győr 87
Beograd

WÜRTTEMBERG
SCHWEIZ
SVIZZERA
LIECHTENSTEIN
VORARLBERG
AARGAU
GRAUBÜNDEN
TICINO
VALAIS
VALLE D'AOSTA
PIEMONTE
LOMBARDIA
URI
UNTERWALDEN
COLMAR
FREIBURG
MULHOUSE
BASEL
Sélestat
Schaffhausen
Konstanz
Friedrichshafen
Ravensburg
Lindau
Bregenz
Kempten
Memmingen
Winterthur
ZÜRICH
St. Gallen
Zug
LUZERN
BERN
Solothurn
Thun
Interlaken
Einsiedeln
Schwyz
Glarus
Chur
Davos
St. Moritz
St. Anton
Feldkirch
Dornbirn
Landeck
Imst
Sion
Crans
Zermatt
Aosta/Aoste
TORINO
Biella
Novara
Vercelli
MILANO
Como
Varese
LUGANO
Bellinzona
Locarno
Stresa
Domodossola
Lecco
Bergamo
Sondrio
BRESCIA
Monza
Pavia
Piacenza
Cremona
PARMA
Alessandria
Asti
Vigevano
Tortona
Voghera
Bormio
Tirano
Landsberg
Schongau
Füssen
Oberstdorf
Villingen
Schwenningen
Tuttlingen
Sigmaringen
Riedlingen
Rottweil
Balingen
Waldshut
Lörrach
Arlbergpaß
Flexenpaß
Julierpass
Berninapass
Splügenpass
Sustenpass
Furkapass
Grimselpass
Simplonpass
Nufenenpass
Oberalppass
P. d. S. Gottardo
Klausenpass
Jungfrau
Finsteraarhorn
Aletschhorn
Säntis
Piz Bernina
Piz Buin
Piz Kesch
Rheinwaldhorn
M. Disgrazia
M. Adamello
Gran Paradiso
MONTE ROSA
CERVINO MATTERHORN
Lago Maggiore
Bodensee
Rhein
Po
Ticino
Adda
Oglio
38
19
23

MÜNCHEN
SALZBURG
INNSBRUCK
Partenkirchen
Rosenheim
Kitzbühel
Zell am See
Badgastein
Bad Ischl
Gmunden
Bad Reichenhall
Berchtesgaden
Lienz
Villach
Klagenfurt
Velden
Jesenice
Kranj
Udine
Gorizia
Nova Gorica
TRIESTE
Koper
Opatija
Pula
Poreč
Rovinj
Postojna
Cortina d'Ampezzo
Bolzano/Bozen
Merano/Meran
Trento
Belluno
Pordenone
Treviso
Vicenza
VERONA
PADOVA
VENEZIA
Mestre
Chioggia
Rovigo
FERRARA
MODENA
Carpi
GOLFO DI VENEZIA
Golfo di Trieste
HOHE TAUERN
SALZBURG
OSTTIROL
KÄRNTEN
FRIULI
VENEZIA GIULIA
VENETO
ITALIA
ÖSTERREICH
Großglockner
Großvenediger
Brenner
Dachsteingruppe
Hochgolling
Triglav
Lido di Jesolo
Lido di Venezia
Grado
Lignano Sabbiadoro
Bibione
Caorle
Comacchio
Dubrovnik
Kerkira (Corfou)
39
41
44
45
50
E
F

PARMA
Reggio nell'Emilia
MODENA
FERRARA
BOLOGNA
RAVENNA
Imola
Faenza
Forlì
Cesena
Rimini
Riccione
Cattolica
Pesaro
Fano
S. Marino
Comacchio
Argenta
Lugo
Cervia
Cesenatico
Salsomaggiore Terme
Fidenza
Sassuolo
Carpi
La Spezia
Sarzana
Carrara
Massa
Forte dei Marmi
Viareggio
Lucca
Pisa
LIVORNO
Pistoia
Prato
Montecatini-Terme
FIRENZE
Fiesole
Empoli
Pontedera
S. Miniato
Poggibonsi
S. Gimignano
Volterra
Siena
Arezzo
Cortona
Perugia
Assisi
Foligno
Spoleto
Terni
Gubbio
Città di Castello
Urbino
Montepulciano
Chianciano Terme
Chiusi
Orvieto
Viterbo
Grosseto
Follonica
Piombino
Portoferraio
Isola d'Elba
I. Pianosa
I. di Montecristo
I. d. Giglio
I. di Giannutri
I. di Gorgona
I. di Capraia
M. Argentario
Orbetello
Civitavecchia
ROMA
Fiumicino
Lido di Ostia
Tivoli
Frascati
Albano Laziale
Anzio
Nettuno
Rieti
Narni
Todi
Bolsena
L. di Bolsena
Lago Trasimeno
L. di Vico
L. di Bracciano
M. Amiata
Cecina
Rosignano Marittimo
Castiglioncello
M A R E   T I R R E N O
Arcipelago Toscano
T O S C A N A
U M B R I A
L A Z I O
M A R C H E
E M I L I A - R O M A G N A
42
43
23
46
A
B
C
1
2
3
4

MÜNCHEN
SALZBURG
Rosenheim
Bad Reichenhall
Berchtesgaden
Bad Ischl
Gmunden
Hallstatt
Bad Aussee
Liezen
Kufstein
Kitzbühel
Partenkirchen
INNSBRUCK
Schwaz
Wörgl
Zell am See
Saalfelden
Bischofshofen
Radstadt
Schladming
Badgastein
Bad Hofgastein
Tamsweg
Lienz
Spittal
Villach
Klagenfurt
Velden
Feldkirchen
St. Veit
Judenburg
Jesenice
Bled
Kranj
Merano/Meran
Bolzano/Bozen
Bressanone/Brixen
Brunico/Bruneck
Dobbiaco/Toblach
Cortina d'Ampezzo
Trento
Rovereto
Belluno
Feltre
Bassano d. Grappa
Treviso
Pordenone
Udine
Gorizia
Nova Gorica
Monfalcone
TRIESTE
Koper
Piran
Poreč
Rovinj
Pula
Opatija
Postojna
Vicenza
VERONA
PADOVA
VENEZIA
Mestre
Lido di Venezia
Chioggia
Rovigo
FERRARA
MODENA
Carpi
Comacchio
GOLFO DI VENEZIA
Golfo di Trieste
HOHE TAUERN
Großglockner
Großvenediger
OSTTIROL
SALZBURG
KÄRNTEN
Niedere Tauern
Dachsteingruppe
Karawanken
FRIULI
VENEZIA
VENETO
Lago di Garda
39
41
44
45
50

FERRARA
PARMA
Reggio nell' Emilia
MODENA
BOLOGNA
RAVENNA
Imola
Faenza
Forlì
Cesena
Rimini
Riccione
Cattolica
Pesaro
Fano
S. Marino
La Spezia
Carrara
Massa
Viareggio
Lucca
Pisa
Montecatini-Terme
Pistoia
Prato
FIRENZE
LIVORNO
S. Gimignano
Siena
Arezzo
Perugia
Assisi
Gubbio
Foligno
Spoleto
Terni
Orvieto
Chianciano Terme
Grosseto
Viterbo
Civitavecchia
ROMA
Piombino
Portoferraio
Isola d'Elba
I. di Capraia
I. di Gorgona
I. Pianosa
I. di Montecristo
I. d. Giglio
I. di Giannutri
M. Argentario
Orbetello
Arcipelago Toscano
Tarquinia
Fiumicino
Lido di Ostia
Anzio
Nettuno
Tivoli
Frascati
Albano Laziale
Salsomaggiore
Pontremoli
Aulla
Sarzana
Forte dei Marmi
Empoli
Volterra
Poggibonsi
Cecina
Follonica
Montepulciano
Cortona
Città di Castello
Sansepolcro
Urbino
Fabriano
Comacchio
Cervia
Cesenatico
Bagno di Romagna
Bibbiena
Rieti
Bracciano
Montalto di Castro
Tuscania
Bolsena
L. di Bolsena
Lago Trasimeno
Todi
Narni
Amelia
Sabaudia
M. Amiata
Porto S. Stefano
Ansedonia
Marina di Grosseto
Castiglione della Pescaia
Punta Ala
Rosignano Marittimo
Tirrenia
Marina di Pisa
Mare Tirreno
TOSCANA
UMBRIA
MARCHE
LAZIO
EMILIA-ROMAGNA
A
B
C
1
2
3
4
42
43
23
46

Roma
LA GIUSTINIANA
PRIMA PORTA
TOMBA DI NERONE
OTTAVIA
TORREVECCHIA
MONTE MARIO
CASALOTTI
MONTE SACRO
SETTECAMINI
TOR SAPIENZA
CENTOCELLE
TORRENOVA
TORRE MAURA
CORVIALE
CATACOMBE
S. PAOLO FUORI LE MURA
E.U.R.
CECCHIGNOLA
MORENA
COLOSSEO
TERMINI
STADIO OLIMPICO
CITTÀ DEL VATICANO
AEROPORTO DELL'URBE
VILLA ADA
DORIA PAMPHILI
CIAMPINO
TEVERE
VITERBO
RIETI
A 1: FIRENZE TERNI
TIVOLI
L'AQUILA AVEZZANO
PALESTRINA
A 1: NAPOLI
CASTELLI ROMANI
NAPOLI
OSTIA ANTICA LIDO DI ROMA
FIUMICINO
A 12: CIVITAVECCHIA
CIVITAVECCHIA
Grande Raccordo Anulare
Via Appia Nuova
Via Appia Antica
Via Aurelia
Via Cassia
Via Flaminia Nuova
Via Salaria
Via Nomentana
Via Tiburtina
Via Prenestina
Via Casilina
Via Tuscolana
Via Anagnina
Via Ardeatina
Via Laurentina
Via Pontina
Via Ostiense
Via del Mare
Via Portuense
Via della Magliana
Via Boccea
Ancona
Macerata
Civitanova Marche
Porto S. Giorgio
Fermo
Ascoli Piceno
S. Benedetto d. Tronto
Alba Adriatica
Giulianova
Teramo
Roseto d. Abruzzi
Pescara
Chieti
Francavilla al Mare
Ortona
Lanciano
Vasto
Termoli
L'Aquila
Gran Sasso d'Italia
Sulmona
Avezzano
Isernia
Campobasso
Foggia
Manfredonia
Vieste
Promontorio del Gargano
Golfo di Manfredonia
Cerignola
Lucera
Benevento
Caserta
Sora
Frosinone
Cassino
Formia
Gaeta
Terracina
Sabaudia
Golfo di Gaeta
Fiuggi
Alatri
Anagni
Subiaco
Colleferro
Canosa
Melfi
Ariano Irpino
Fondi
Sperlonga
Zadar
Split
Dubrovnik
Kérkira (Corfu)
Igoumenitsa
Pátra (Patrasso)
Lošinj
Mali Lošinj
Karlobag
Pag
Gospić
Titov Drvar
Sinj
Omiš
Hvar
I. Tremiti
I. Pianosa
Palagruža
A D R I A T
50
52
47
46

ROMA
Ostia Antica
Marino
Albano Laziale
Castel Gandolfo
Genzano di Roma
Frascati
Valmontone
Rocca di Papa
M. Cavo
Artena
Segni
Colleferro
Velletri
Cori
Fiuggi
Paliano
Anagni
Alatri
Ferentino
Frosinone
Veroli
Sora
Isola del Liri
Arce
Ceprano
Cassino
Abbazia di Montecassino
Atina
Pomezia
Aprilia
Cisterna di L.
Sermoneta
Sezze
Latina
Priverno
Abbazia di Fossanova
Lavinio Lido di Enea
Nettuno
Anzio
Foce Verde
Pontinia
Sabaudia
Terracina
Sperlonga
Fondi
Itri
M. Petrella
Gaeta
Formia
S. Felice Circeo
Golfo di Gaeta
I. Ponziane
I. Zannone
I. di Ponza
I. Ventotene
Isernia
Venafro
Campobasso
Vinchiaturo
Bojano
Campitello M.
M. Miletto
Monti del Matese
Alife
Piedimonte d'A.
Cerreto Sannita
Guardia Sanframondi
Telese
Benevento
Lucera
Ariano Irpino
Grottaminarda
Caianello
Teano
Sessa Aurunca
Roccamonfina
Carinola
Mondragone
Castel Volturno
Capua
Caserta
Maddaloni
S. Agata de' Goti
Montesarchio
Aversa
Giugliano in C.
Casoria
NAPOLI
Pozzuoli
Bacoli
Portici
Ercolano
Torre d. Greco
Torre Annunziata
VESUVIO
Pompei
Nola
Avellino
Sarno
Nocera
Castellammare di Stabia
Vico Equense
Sorrento
Positano
Amalfi
Ravello
Maiori
Salerno
Battipaglia
Eboli
Paestum
Agropoli
Capaccio
Ogliastro Cilento
Castellabate
Acciaroli
Pisciotta
CAMPANIA
Procida
Ischia
Casamicciola Terme
Forio
I. d'Ischia
Porto Vecchio
Golfo di Napoli
I. di Capri
Capri
Golfo di Salerno
Cagliari
Palermo
Catania-Siracusa
SARDEGNA
Isola Asinara
C. del Falcone
Stintino
Golfo dell' Asinara
Genova
Livorno
Toulon
Ajaccio
Porto Torres
Castelsardo
Sassari
Alghero
Fertilia
Grotta di Nettuno
Tramariglio
Olmedo
Palmadula
Sta Teresa Gallura
La Maddalena
I. Maddalena
I. Caprera
Palau
Baja Sardinia
Porto Cervo
Arzachena
Costa Smeralda
Porto Rotondo
Golfo Aranci
Olbia
I. Tavolara
Civitavecchia
Arbatax
Tempio Pausania
M. Limbara
Calangianus
Luogosanto
Trinità d'Agultu e V.
Aggius
Loiri
Monti
Padru
Oschiri
Lago del Coghinas
Ploaghe
Ozieri
Pattada
Buddusò
M. Nieddu
Posada
la Caletta
Siniscola
Lodè
Alà d. Sardi
Bitti
M. Albo
Orune
Nuoro
Orosei
Cala Gonone
Dorgali
Oliena
Golfo di Orosei
Orgosolo
Mores
Ittiri
Thiesi
Bonorva
Bono
Villanova Monteleone
Romana
Pozzomaggiore
Montresta
Bolotana
Bosa
Suni
Macomer
Ottana
Sarule
Orani
Gavoi
Fonni
Sedilo
Cuglieri
M. Ferru
Santu Lussurgiu
Abbasanta
Ghilarza
Lago Omodeo
Genna Cruxi
Sta Caterina Pittinuri
Narbolia
Milis
Tramatza
Riola Sardo
Cabras
Simaxis
Oristano
Torre Grande
S. Giovanni di Sinis
Sta Giusta
Golfo di Oristano
Arborea
Terralba
Uras
Ales
Sorgono
Tonara
Desulo
Aritzo
Monti del Gennargentu
P. La Marmora
Fordongianus
Samugheo
Laconi
Seulo
Seui
Lanusei
Tortolì
Jerzu
Nurallao
Isili
Barumini
Sardara
Mandas
Furtei
Sanluri
S. Gavino Monreale
Senorbì
S. Nicolò Gerrei
Ballao
Flumendosa
Guspini
Arbus
Gonnosfanadiga
Villacidro
M. Linas
Fluminimaggiore
Serramanna
Villasor
Monastir
Dolianova
P. Serpeddi
S. Andrea Frius
Villasalto
S. Vito
Muravera
Iglesias
Domusnovas
Siliqua
Assemini
Sestu
Selargius
Quartu S. Elena
CAGLIARI
Elmas
Castiadas
Villasimius
Capo Carbonara
Golfo di Cagliari
Villamassargia
Gonnesa
Portoscuso
Carbonia
Narcao
M. is Caravius
I. di S. Pietro
Carloforte
Calasetta
S. Antioco
I. di S. Antioco
S. Giovanni Suergiu
Giba
Sarroch
Pula
Teulada
Sta Margherita
Porto Pino
Capo Spartivento
Trapani-Palermo
Tunis
Isole Eolie
I. Filicudi
Capo d'Orlando
44
45
48
A
B
C
1
2
3
4

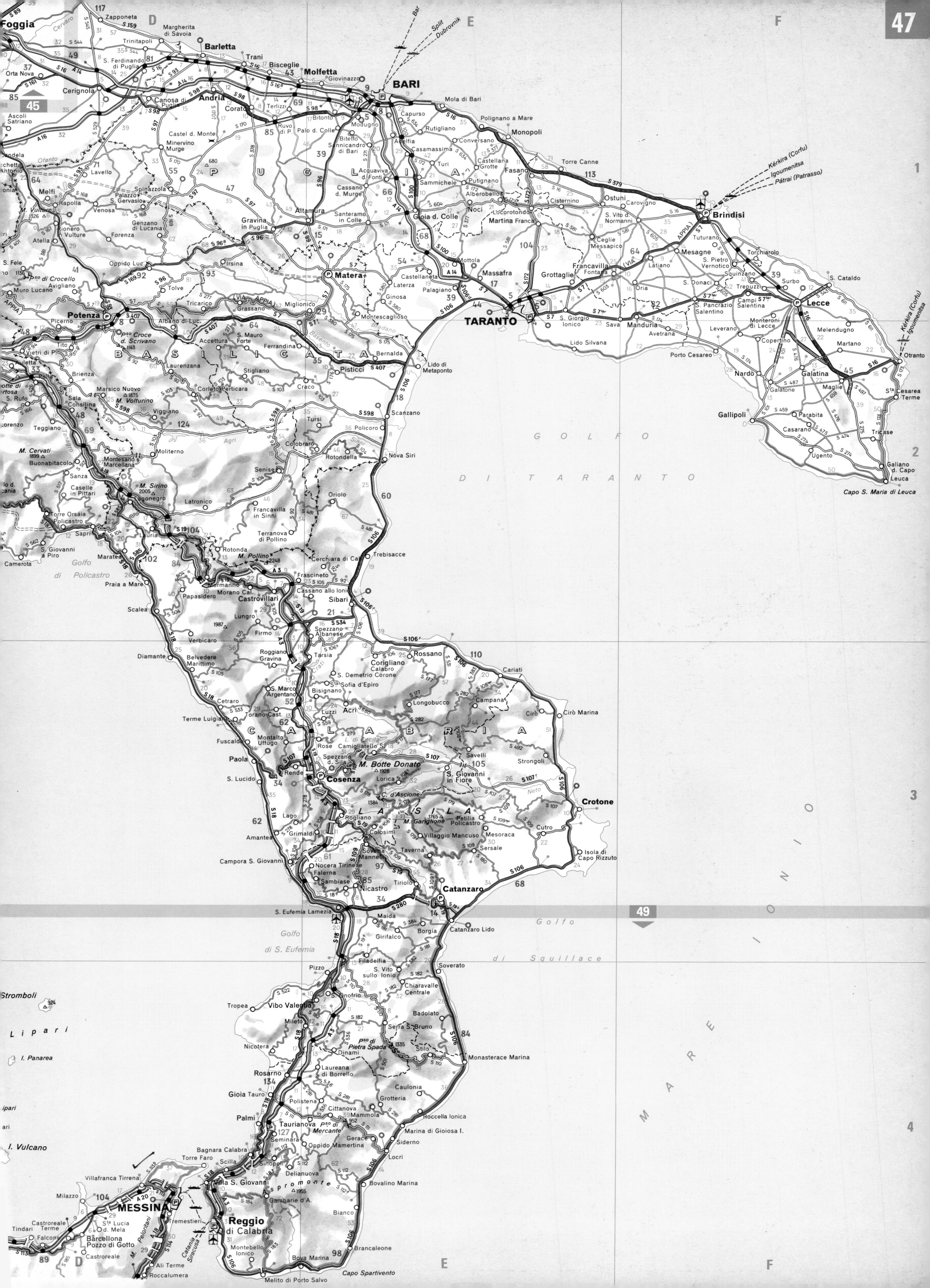
Foggia
Barletta
Trani
Bisceglie
Molfetta
BARI
Cerignola
Andria
Corato
Canosa di Puglia
Mola di Bari
Polignano a Mare
Monopoli
Conversano
Rutigliano
Altamura
Gravina in Puglia
Gioia d. Colle
Fasano
Torre Canne
Ostuni
Brindisi
Martina Franca
Matera
Massafra
TARANTO
Grottaglie
Manduria
Lecce
Nardò
Galatina
Maglie
Gallipoli
Otranto
Leuca
Capo S. Maria di Leuca
Melfi
Venosa
Potenza
Pisticci
Metaponto
Policoro
Nova Siri
Trebisacce
Sibari
Castrovilli
Scalea
Praia a Mare
Maratea
Sapri
Lauria
Rossano
Corigliano Calabro
Cariati
Cirò Marina
Crotone
Paola
Cosenza
Rende
San Giovanni in Fiore
Amantea
Nicastro
Catanzaro
Catanzaro Lido
S. Eufemia Lamezia
Pizzo
Vibo Valentia
Tropea
Soverato
Serra S. Bruno
Monasterace Marina
Rosarno
Gioia Tauro
Palmi
Taurianova
Siderno
Locri
Bovalino Marina
Villa S. Giovanni
Reggio di Calabria
MESSINA
Milazzo
Melito di Porto Salvo
Capo Spartivento
Brancaleone
GOLFO DI TARANTO
MARE IONIO
Golfo di Policastro
Golfo di S. Eufemia
Golfo di Squillace
P U G L I A
B A S I L I C A T A
C A L A B R I A
S I L A
Aspromonte
M. Pollino 2248
M. Botte Donato 1928
Stromboli
Lipari
I. Panarea
I. Vulcano
Kérkira (Corfu)
Igoumenitsa
Pátrai (Patrasso)
Split
Dubrovnik
Bar
45
49

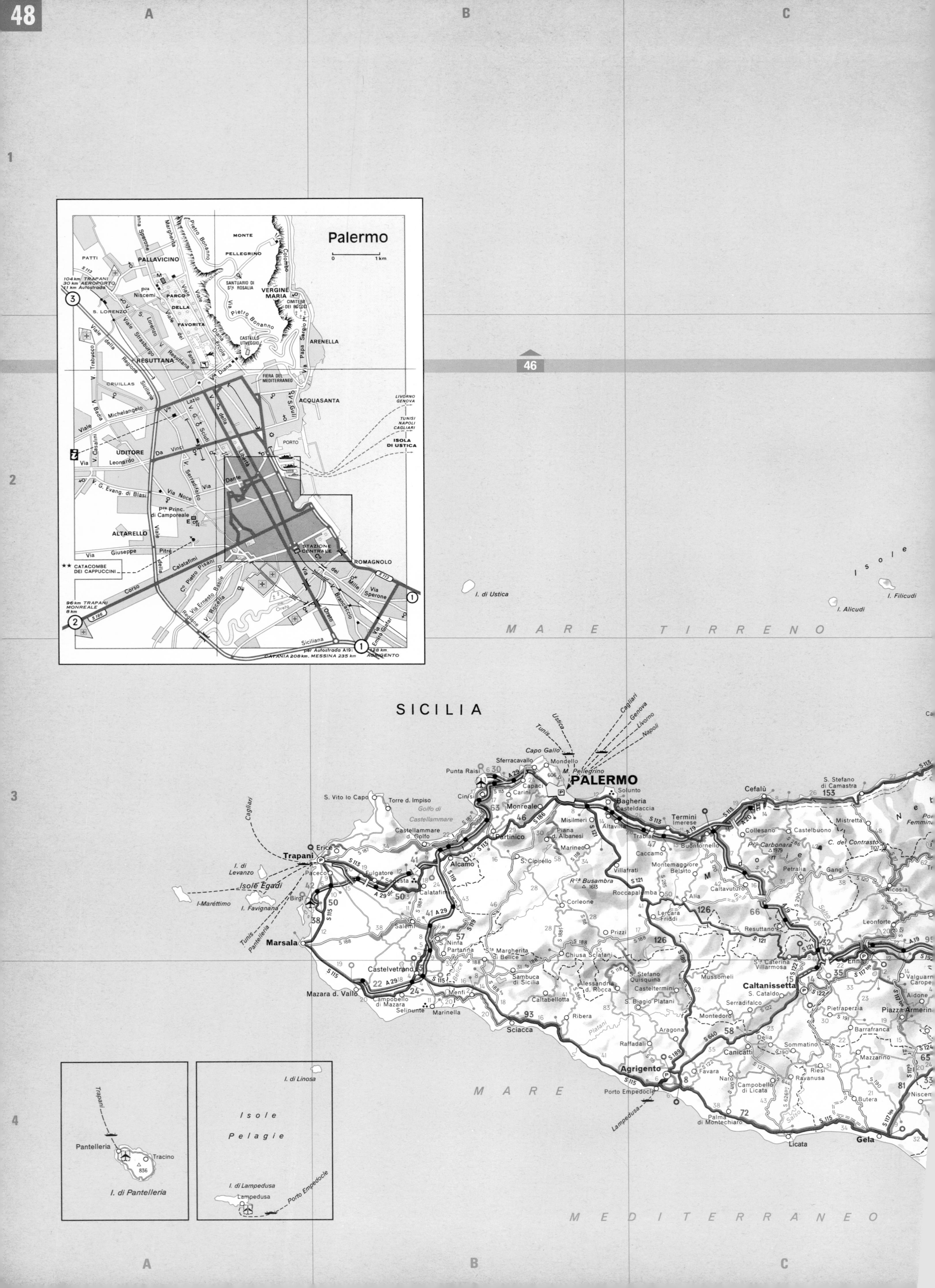
A
B
C
1
2
3
4
46
Palermo
0
1 km
MONTE
PELLEGRINO
PALLAVICINO
PATTI
SANTUARIO DI Sta ROSALIA
VERGINE MARIA
CIMITERO DEI ROTOLI
PARCO
DELLA
FAVORITA
S. LORENZO
ARENELLA
RESUTTANA
CASTELLO UTVEGGIO
FIERA DEL MEDITERRANEO
ACQUASANTA
CRUILLAS
UDITORE
PORTO
LIVORNO GENOVA
TUNISI NAPOLI CAGLIARI
ISOLA DI USTICA
ALTARELLO
STAZIONE CENTRALE
ROMAGNOLO
CATACOMBE DEI CAPPUCCINI
104 km TRAPANI
30 km AEROPORTO
11 km Autostrada
96 km TRAPANI
MONREALE 8 km
per Autostrada A19:
CATANIA 208 km, MESSINA 235 km
128 km AGRIGENTO
I. di Ustica
Isole
I. Filicudi
I. Alicudi
MARE TIRRENO
SICILIA
Ustica
Cagliari
Genova
Livorno
Napoli
Tunis
Capo Gallo
Mondello
M. Pellegrino
PALERMO
Sferracavallo
Punta Raisi
Capaci
Carini
Cinisi
Monreale
Solunto
Bagheria
Casteldaccia
Misilmeri
Altavilla
Termini Imerese
Trabia
Cefalù
S. Stefano di Camastra
Mistretta
Collesano
Castelbuono
P.zo Carbonara
C. del Contrasto
Petralia
Gangi
Nicosia
Leonforte
Enna
Valguarnera
Aidone
Piazza Armerina
S. Vito lo Capo
Torre d. Impiso
Golfo di Castellammare
Castellammare d. Golfo
Partinico
Piana d. Albanesi
Marineo
Caccamo
Montemaggiore Belsito
Erice
Trapani
Paceco
Fulgatore
Segesta
Calatafimi
Alcamo
S. Cipirello
R.ca Busambra
Villafrati
Roccapalumba
Alia
Caltavuturo
I. di Levanzo
Isole Egadi
I. Marettimo
I. Favignana
Pantelleria
Birgi
Marsala
Salemi
Corleone
Prizzi
Lercara Friddi
Resuttano
Ninfa
Partanna
S.ta Margherita di Belice
Chiusa Sclafani
S.ta Caterina Villarmosa
Castelvetrano
Mazara d. Vallo
Campobello di Mazara
Selinunte
Marinella
Menfi
Sambuca di Sicilia
Alessandria d. Rocca
S. Stefano Quisquina
Casteltermini
Mussomeli
Caltanissetta
S. Cataldo
Caltabellotta
Ribera
S. Biagio Platani
Serradifalco
Montedoro
Pietraperzia
Barrafranca
Sciacca
Aragona
Raffadali
Delia
Sommatino
Canicattì
Mazzarino
Agrigento
Porto Empedocle
Favara
Naro
Campobello di Licata
Ravanusa
Riesi
Butera
Palma di Montechiaro
Licata
Gela
Lampedusa
MARE
MEDITERRANEO
Trapani
Pantelleria
Tracino
836
I. di Pantelleria
I. di Linosa
Isole Pelagie
I. di Lampedusa
Lampedusa
Porto Empedocle

C A L A B R I A
S I L A
M A R E   I O N I O
Golfo di Policastro
Golfo di S. Eufemia
Golfo di Squillace
Golfo di Catania
Isole Lipari
I. Stromboli
I. Panarea
I. Salina
I. Lipari
I. Vulcano
Lipari
Policastro
Sapri
Maratea
Lauria
Praia a Mare
Scalea
Diamante
Belvedere Marittimo
Cetraro
Paola
Fuscaldo
Amantea
M. Pollino
Castrovillari
Morano Cal.
Mormanno
Trebisacce
Sibari
Cassano allo Ionio
Spezzano Albanese
Rossano
Corigliano Calabro
Cariati
Cirò
Cirò Marina
Acri
Longobucco
Bisignano
Cosenza
Rende
M. Botte Donato
S. Giovanni in Fiore
Savelli
Strongoli
Crotone
Isola di Capo Rizzuto
Cutro
Petilia Policastro
Mesoraca
Rogliano
Soveria Mannelli
Nicastro
Sambiase
S. Eufemia Lamezia
Catanzaro
Catanzaro Lido
Tiriolo
Maida
Girifalco
Borgia
Soverato
Pizzo
Vibo Valentia
Tropea
Nicotera
Mileto
Serra S. Bruno
Stilo
Monasterace Marina
Rosarno
Gioia Tauro
Palmi
Taurianova
Cittanova
Polistena
Caulonia
Roccella Ionica
Siderno
Locri
Gerace
Marina di Gioiosa I.
Bagnara Calabra
Scilla
Villa S. Giovanni
Reggio di Calabria
Aspromonte
Bovalino Marina
Bianco
Brancaleone
Bova Marina
Melito di Porto Salvo
Capo Spartivento
MESSINA
Milazzo
Villafranca Tirrena
Barcellona Pozzo di Gotto
Patti
Tindari
Castroreale
Novara di Sicilia
Taormina
Giardini
Mazzarò
Francavilla di Sicilia
Randazzo
Linguaglossa
M. ETNA
Bronte
Adrano
Giarre
Acireale
Aci Trezza
Aci Castello
Paternò
CATANIA
Misterbianco
Lentini
Augusta
Siracusa
Palagonia
Scordia
Francofonte
Grammichele
Caltagirone
Melilli
Sortino
Floridia
Palazzolo Acreide
Chiaramonte Gulfi
Giarratana
Comiso
Vittoria
Ragusa
Modica
Scicli
Rosolini
Ispica
Noto
Avola
Pachino
Pozzallo
Capo Passero
Malta
Napoli
Reggio di C.
Gozo
Victoria
Nadur
Mgarr
Comino
Mellieha
Mosta
Sliema
Valletta
Rabat
Dingli
Vittoriosa
Zejtun
Zurrieq
Birzebugga
Filfola
MALTA
47
D
E
F
1
2
3
4

Maribor
Nagykanizsa
Kaposvár
Varaždin
Čakovec
Celje
LJUBLJANA
ZAGREB
Karlovac
Sisak
Bjelovar
Koprivnica
Virovitica
Daruvar
Kutina
Novska
Nova Gradiška
Postojna
Novo mesto
Kočevje
Opatija
RIJEKA
Crikvenica
Senj
KRK
CRES
Lošinj
Mali Lošinj
RAB
PAG
Gospić
Otočac
Bihać
Prijedor
Banja Luka
Jajce
Bosanski Novi
Bosanska Krupa
Sanski Most
Titov Drvar
Knin
Zadar
Biograd
Šibenik
Trogir
SPLIT
Sinj
Omiš
Makarska
Livno
BRAČ
HVAR
Vis
Dugi Otok
Kornati
Plitvice
Slunj
Ogulin
Delnice
Jasenovac
Bosanska Dubica
Kostajnica
Glina
Petrinja
Velika Kladuša
Cazin
Drniš
Imotski
Hvar
Ancona
Pescara
Bari
Civitanova Marche
Porto S. Elpidio
Porto Recanati

PÉCS
Subotica
TIMIŞOARA
Osijek
NOVI SAD
Zrenjanin
Vukovar
Vinkovci
Slavonski Brod
Sremska Mitrovica
BEOGRAD
Pančevo
Smederevo
Šabac
Tuzla
Loznica
Valjevo
Kragujevac
Zenica
Čačak
Kraljevo
Titovo Užice
SARAJEVO
Mostar
Novi Pazar
Pljevlja
Bijelo Polje
Nikšić
Peć
Kikinda
Sombor
Bečej
Doboj
Brčko
Bijeljina
DUNAV
SAVA
TISA
80
52
53

Vinkovci
Đakovo
Slavonska Požega
Nova Gradiška
Slavonski Brod
Bosanski Brod
Bosanska Gradiška
Sremska Mitrovica
Ruma
Zemun
BEO
Šabac
Brčko
Bijeljina
Derventa
Doboj
Tuzla
Zvornik
Loznica
Valjevo
Banja Luka
Jajce
Zenica
Travnik
Bugojno
SARAJEVO
Ilidža
Visoko
Kakanj
Zavidovići
Olovo
Vlasenica
Rogatica
Višegrad
Goražde
Foča
Titovo Užice
Požega
Čačak
Priboj
Prijepolje
Nova Varoš
Pljevlja
Bijelo Polje
Žabljak
Nikšić
Titograd
Cetinje
Kotor
Budva
Bar
Ulcinj
Shkodër
Hercegnovi
DUBROVNIK
Cavtat
Trebinje
Bileća
Mostar
Konjic
Livno
Imotski
Makarska
Metković
Ploče
Korčula
PELJEŠAC
BRAČ
HVAR
KORČULA
Mljet
Lastovo
M O R E
Ivangrad
Kolašin
Mojkovac
Bari
Ancona
Venezia
Kérkira (Corfou)
Pátra
Pireás
Igoumenitsa
51
50
45
54
A
B
C
1
2
3
4

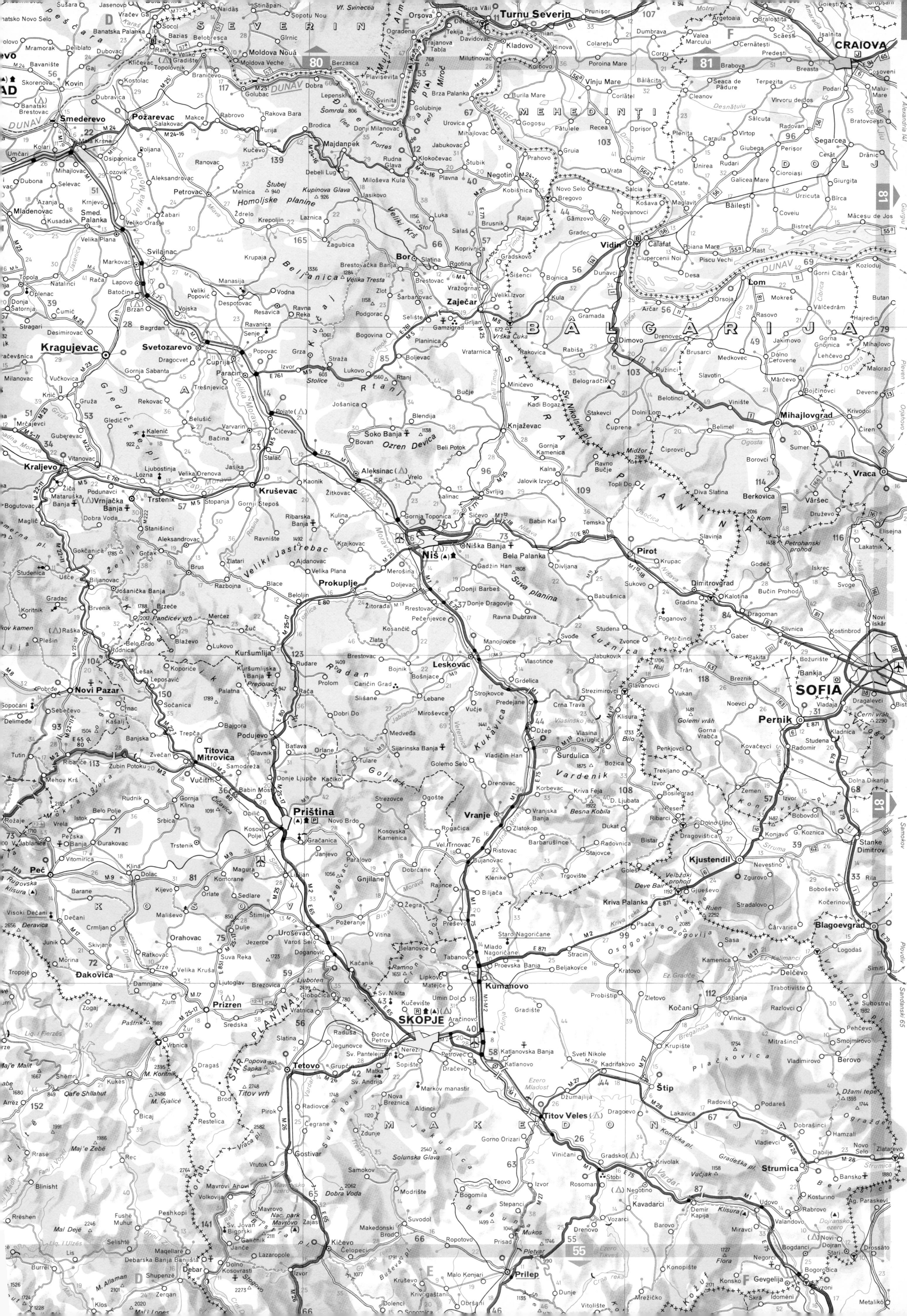
SEVERIN
MEHEDINTI
DOLJ
BĂLGARIJA
STARA PLANINA
KOSOVO
MAKEDONIJA
Turnu Severin
Craiova
Vidin
Calafat
Lom
Mihajlovgrad
Vraca
Smederevo
Požarevac
Kragujevac
Svetozarevo
Kraljevo
Kruševac
Zaječar
Bor
Niš
Pirot
Leskovac
Prokuplje
Novi Pazar
Titova Mitrovica
Priština
Vranje
Peć
Prizren
Kumanovo
SKOPJE
Tetovo
Titov Veles
Štip
Strumica
Kjustendil
Pernik
SOFIA
Blagoevgrad
Dimitrovgrad
Kičevo
Prilep
Gevgelija
Gostivar
Kočani
Berovo
DUNAV
DUNĂREA
80
81
55
1
2
3
4
D
E
F

52
53
58
TIRANË - DURRËS
ELBASAN - BERAT
SHQIPËRIA
KORÇË
VLORË
JUGOS
KASTORIÁ
FLÓRINA
GREVENÁ
IOÁNINA
THESPROTÍA
IPIROS
N. KÉRKIRA
N. KEPKYPA
TIRANË
Durrës
Elbasan
Berat
Fier
Vlorë
Korçë
Gjirokastër
Sarandë
Lushnjë
Kavajë
Krujë
Librazhd
Pogradec
Struga
Ohrid
Resen
Bitola
Kičevo
Debar
Ersekë
Përmet
Tepelenë
Delvinë
Buthrotum
Konispol
Kastoriá
Καστοριά
Flórina
Φλώρινα
Grevená
Γρεβενά
Métsovo
Μέτσοβο
Ioánina
Ιωάννινα
Kónitsa
Κόνιτσα
Igoumenítsa
Ηγουμενίτσα
Párga
Πάργα
Paramithiá
Παραμυθιά
Filiátes
Φιλιάτες
Dodóni
Δωδώνη
KÉRKIRA
KEPKYPA
Sidári
Paleokastrítsa
Mal i Dajt
Mali Shpat
Mali Tomorr
M. Ostrovice
Mallakastër
Kurvelesh
Ohridsko ezero
Prespansko ezero
Pelister
Baba
Óros Grámmos
Vório Píndos
Nótia Píndos
Zagória
Dubrovnik - Bar
Otranto, Venezia
Ancona
Brindisi
Othoni
N. Erikoússa
N. Mathráki
N. Paxí
Passage exceptionnel
A
B
C
1
2
3
4

MAKEDONIJA
MAKEDONIA
THESSALONÍKI
ΘΕΣΣΑΛΟΝΙΚΗ
LÁRISSA
ΛΑΡΙΣΑ
VÓLOS
ΒΟΛΟΣ
Kateríni
Κατερίνη
Véria
Βέροια
Édessa
Έδεσσα
Náoussa
Νάουσα
Kozáni
Κοζάνη
Ptolemaída
Πτολεμαΐδα
Kilkís
Κιλκίς
Séres
Σέρρες
Strumica
Gevgelija
Titov Veles
Štip
Tírnavos
Τύρναβος
Tríkala
Τρίκαλα
Kardítsa
Καρδίτσα
Elassóna
Ελασσόνα
Gianitsá
Γιαννιτσά
Polígiros
Πολύγυρος
N. Moudaniá
Ν. Μουδανιά
Langadás
Λαγκαδάς
PÉLA
IMATHIA
PIERIÁ
KOZÁNI
KILKÍS
THESSALONÍKI
HALKIDIKÍ
SÉRES
THESSALÍA
LÁRISSA
KARDÍTSA
ÓROS ÓLIMBOS
ΟΡΟΣ ΟΛΥΜΠΟΣ
Thermaïkós Kólpos
Θερμαϊκός Κόλπος
Kassándra
Sithonía
VARDAR
Strimónas
53
56
59

BÂLGARIJA
Zapadni Rodopi
DRÁMA
KAVÁLA
XÁNTHI
RODÓPI
THRÁKI
Dráma
Δράμα
Kavála
Καβάλα
Xánthi
Ξάνθη
Komotini
Κομοτηνή
Smoljan
Kârdžali
Goce Delčev
Eleftheroúpoli
Ελευθερούπολη
Hrissoúpoli
Χρυσούπολη
Filipi
Φίλιπποι
Sápes
Σάπες
Nea Zihni
Νέα Ζίχνη
Ierissós
Ιερισσός
Ouranópoli
Ουρανούπολη
Thássos
Θάσος
N. THÁSSOS
Ν. ΘΑΣΟΣ
Mírina
Μύρινα
N. LÍMNOS
Ν. ΛΗΜΝΟΣ
N. SAMOTH
Ν. ΣΑΜΟΘΡ
Samothráki
Σαμοθράκη
N. Ág. Efstrátios
Ν. Άγ. Ευστράτιος
N. Amoliani
Ν. Αμολιανή
Sithonia
Ágio Óros
Áthos
Άθως
THRAKIKÓ PÉLAGOS
ΘΡΑΚΙΚΟ ΠΕΛΑΓΟΣ
Strimonikós Kólpos
Στρυμονικός Κόλπος
Kólpos Agíou Órous
Κόλπος Αγίου Όρους
Kólpos Kaválas
Κόλπος Καβάλας
Kólpos Pournias
Κόλπος Πουρνιάς
Kassándras
Óros Falakró
Όρος Φαλακρό
Ditikí Rodópi
Δυτική Ροδόπη
Anatolikí Rodópi
Ανατολική Ροδόπη
Strimónas
Στρυμόνας
Néstos
Νέστος
Mesta
Arda
Iztočni Rodopi
Thessaloníki
E90
Akr. Pahis
Akr. Kefálas
Akr. Stavrós
Akr. Akrathos
Akr. Drépano
Akr. Makrívrahos
Akr. Kípos
Akr. Moúrdzeflos
Akr. Pláka
Akr. Ag. Irínis
Akr. Kalamáki
Akr. Tripití
Akr. Marónias
Akr. Gérakas
N. Gioúra
N. Kirá Panagiá
N. Pipéri
N. Psathoúra
Derekóy
Ayagalip
A
B
C
1
2
3
4
55
60
81

Edirne
Kırklareli
Svilengrad
Kapıkule
Orestiáda
Ορεστιάδα
Didimótiho
Διδυμότειχο
Soufli
Σουφλί
Férés
Φέρες
ÉVROS
MERİÇ
Uzunköprü
Havsa
Babaeski
Lüleburgaz
Alpullu
Pınarhisar
Vize
Saray
Çerkezköy
Çorlu
Muratlı
Hayrabolu
Malkara
Keşan
İpsala
Enez
Tekirdağ
Marmaraereğlisi
Barbaros
Şarköy
Mürefte
Ganosdağı
Kurudağı
Kavak
Bolayır
Saros Körfezi
Gelibolu
Gelibolu Yarımadası
Lâpseki
Eceabat
Çanakkale
Çanakkale Boğazı
Kilitbahir
Marmara Adası
Marmara
Avşa Ad.
Türkeli
Paşalimanı
Kapıdağı Yarımadası
Erdek
Erdek Körfezi
Bandırma
Karabiga
Biga
Gönen
Manyas
Kuş G.
Çan
Ezine
Bozcaada
Ayvacık
Küçükkuyu
Edremit
Edremit Körfezi
Burhaniye
Ayvalık
Balıkesir
Kazdağı 1767
Zeybek Dağı
Sakar Dağı
Armutçuk Dağı
Şapla Dağları
Madra Dağı
Mancınık Dağı
Balya
İvrindi
Havran
Akçay
Altınoluk
Mithimna
Μήθυμνα
MARMARA
TÜRKİYE
81
61

54
62
THESPROTÍA
PRÉVEZA
ÁRTA
EVRITANÍA
ETOLÍA AKARNANÍA
AHAÏA
ÍLIA
MESSINÍA
NISSIÁ
ΝΗΣΙΑ
N. Paxí
Ν. Παξοί
N. Andípaxi
Ν. Αντίπαξοι
N. LEFKÁDA
Ν. ΛΕΥΚΑΔΑ
N. KEFALONIÁ
Ν. ΚΕΦΑΛΛΩΝΙΑ
N. Itháki
Ν. Ιθάκη
N. ZÁKINTHOS
Ν. ΖΑΚΥΝΘΟΣ
N. Strofádes
Ν. Στροφάδες
N. Átokos
N. Kastós
N. Kálamos
N. Arkoúdi
N. Oxiá
Amvrakikós Kólpos
Αμβρακικός Κόλπος
Patraïkós Kólpos
Πατραϊκός Κόλπος
Kiparissiakós Kólpos
Κυπαρισσιακός Κόλπος
Párga
Πάργα
Préveza
Πρέβεζα
Árta
Άρτα
Lefkáda
Λευκάδα
Vónitsa
Βόνιτσα
Amfilohía
Αμφιλοχία
Agrínio
Αγρίνιο
Karpeníssi
Καρπενήσι
Kardítsa
Καρδίτσα
Astakós
Αστακός
Messolóngi
Μεσολόγγι
Náfpaktos
Ναύπακτος
PÁTRA
ΠΑΤΡΑ
Argostóli
Αργοστόλι
Sámi
Σάμη
Itháki
Ιθάκη
Zákinthos
Ζάκυνθος
Kalávrita
Amaliáda
Αμαλιάδα
Pírgos
Πύργος
Arhéa Olympía
Αρχ. Ολυμπία
Andrítsena
Ανδρίτσαινα
Kiparissía
Κυπαρισσία
Filiatrá
Φιλιατρά
Gargaliáni
Γαργαλιάνοι
Messíni
Μεσσήνη
Dimitsána
Ithómi
Vassés
Katákolo
Κατάκολο
Kilíni
Κυλλήνη
Fiskárdo
Φισκάρδο
Ássos
Άσσος
Lixoúri
Ληξούρι
Thérmo
Θέρμο
Etolikó
Αιτωλικό
Kalambáka
A
B
C
1
2
3
4

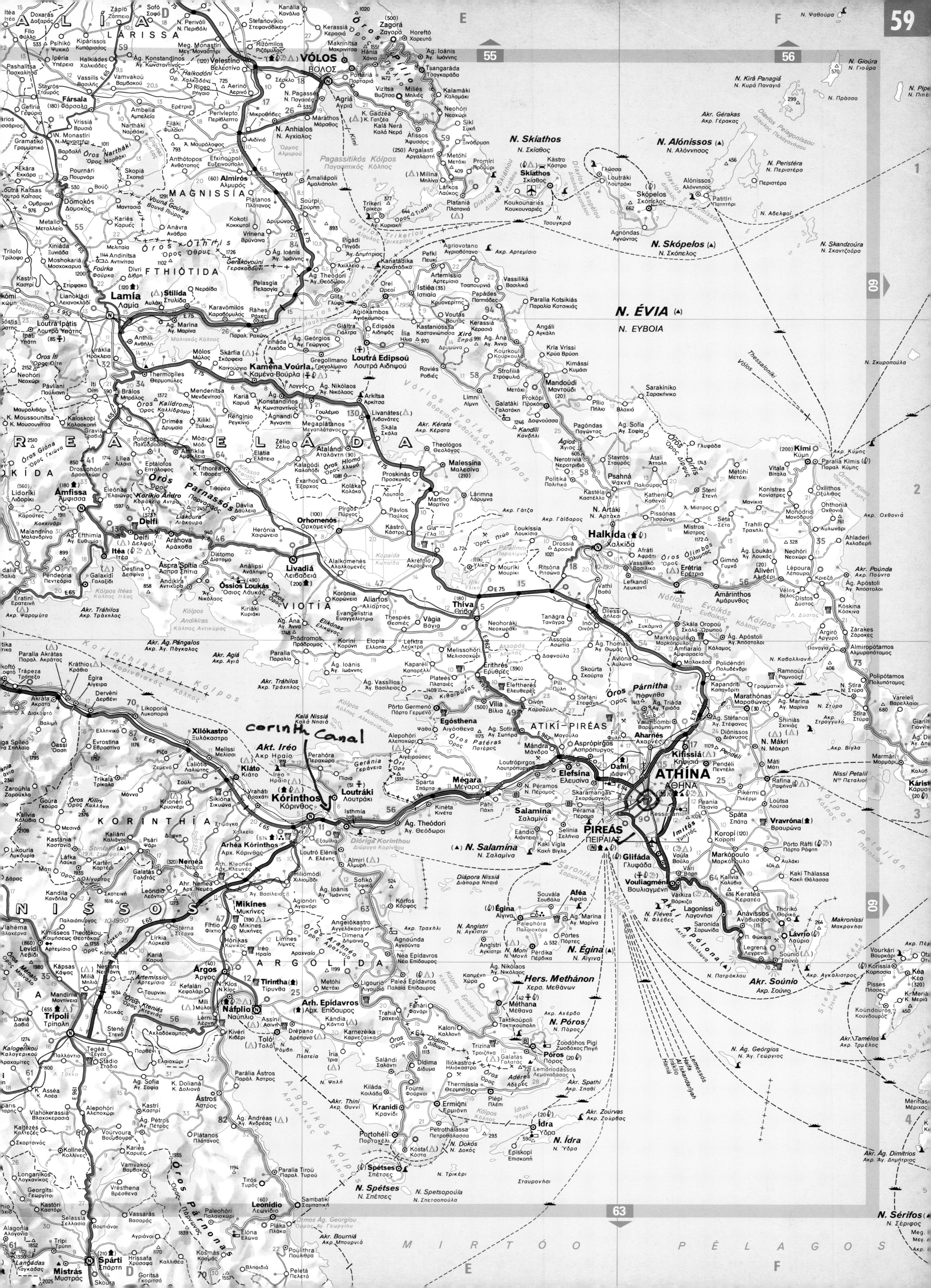
LÁRISSA
MAGNISSÍA
FTHIÓTIDA
VIOTÍA
ATIKÍ-PIREÁS
KORINTHÍA
ARGOLÍDA
ELLÁDA
PELOPÓNNISSOS
VÓLOS
ΒΟΛΟΣ
Lamía
Λαμία
Almirós
Stilída
Kaména Voúrla
Loutrá Edipsoú
Amfissa
Delfí
Itéa
Livadiá
Thíva
Halkída
Χαλκίδα
N. ÉVIA
N. ΕΥΒΟΙΑ
N. Skíathos
N. Σκίαθος
Skíathos
N. Alónissos
N. Αλόννησος
N. Skópelos
N. Σκόπελος
Skópelos
Kími
Erétria
Marathónas
Elefsína
Mégara
ATHÍNA
ΑΘΗΝΑ
PIREÁS
ΠΕΙΡΑΙΑΣ
Glifáda
Vouliagméni
Rafína
Lávrio
Akr. Soúnio
N. Salamína
Salamína
Égina
N. Égina
Hers. Methánon
Póros
N. Póros
Ídra
N. Ídra
Spétses
N. Spétses
Kranídi
Portohéli
Náfplio
Árgos
Tírintha
Mikínes
Neméa
Kórinthos
Κόρινθος
Loutráki
Kiáto
Xilókastro
Akt. Iréo
corinth Canal
Trípoli
Spárti
Mistrás
Leonídio
Arh. Epídavros
Saronikós Kólpos
Argolikós Kólpos
Korinthiakós Kólpos
Pagassitikós Kólpos
Vórios Evvoïkós Kólpos
Nótios Evvoïkós Kólpos
MIRTÓO PÉLAGOS
N. Sérifos
Kéa
55
56
60
63
E
F
1
2
3
4

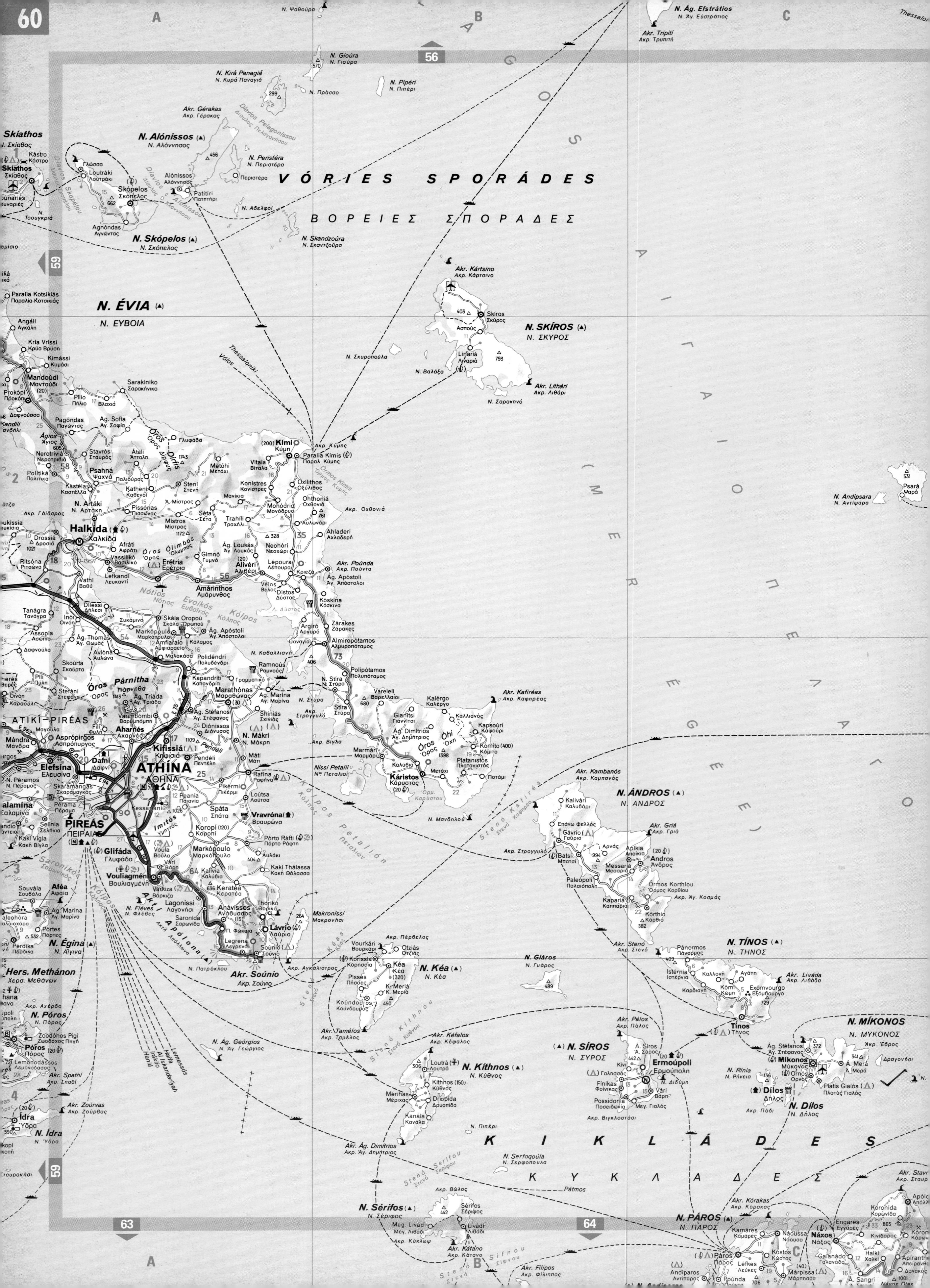
A
B
C
56
59
63
64
N. Ág. Efstrátios
N. Άγ. Ευστράτιος
Akr. Tripití
Ακρ. Τρυπητή
N. Gioúra
N. Γιούρα
N. Kirá Panagiá
N. Κυρά Παναγιά
N. Pipéri
N. Πιπέρι
N. Psathoúra
Akr. Gérakas
Ακρ. Γέρακας
Díavlos Pelagonísou
N. Alónissos
N. Αλόννησος
N. Peristéra
N. Περιστέρα
Skíathos
Skíathos
Σκίαθος
Kástro
Κάστρο
Loutráki
Λουτράκι
Glóssa
Γλώσσα
Skópelos
Σκόπελος
Alónissos
Αλόννησος
Patitíri
Πατητήρι
Agnóndas
Αγνώντας
N. Skópelos
N. Σκόπελος
N. Adelfoí
VÓRIES SPORÁDES
ΒΟΡΕΙΕΣ ΣΠΟΡΑΔΕΣ
N. Skandzoúra
N. Σκαντζούρα
AIGÉO PÉLAGOS
Akr. Kártsino
Ακρ. Κάρτσινο
Skíros
Σκύρος
N. SKÍROS
N. ΣΚΥΡΟΣ
Linariá
Λιναριά
N. Skiropoúla
N. Σκυροπούλα
N. Valáxa
N. Βαλάξα
Akr. Lithári
Ακρ. Λιθάρι
N. Sarakinó
N. ÉVIA
N. ΕΥΒΟΙΑ
Paralía Kotsikiás
Angáli
Kría Vríssi
Kimássi
Mandoúdi
Prokópi
Sarakíniko
Píllio
Vlahiá
Pagóndas
Ag. Sofía
Ágios
Glifáda
Neroriviá
Stavrós
Átali
Óros Dírfis
Kími
Κύμη
Paralía Kímis
Akr. Kímis
Psahná
Politiká
Kastélla
Metóhi
Vítala
Konístres
Oxílithos
Ohthoniá
Akr. Ohthoniá
Steni
Kathení
N. Artáki
Pissónas
Mistros
Séta
Trahíli
Monódrio
Ahladerí
Halkída
Χαλκίδα
Drossiá
Afráti
Óros Ólimbos
Gimnó
Ag. Loukás
Neohóri
Eretría
Ερέτρια
Vassilikó
Lefkandí
Alivéri
Αλιβέρι
Lépoura
Kriezá
Akr. Poúnda
Ag. Apóstoli
Ritsóna
Vathí
Amárinthos
Αμάρυνθος
Vélos
Dístos
Kóskina
Nótios Evoikós Kólpos
Tanágra
Dílessi
Inói
Skála Oropoú
Markópoulo
Ag. Apóstoli
Assopía
Ag. Thomás
Amfiaraío
Kálamos
Zárakes
Argiró
Almiropótamos
Avlóna
Malakássa
Polidéndri
Skoúrta
Ramnoús
N. Kavallianí
Polipótamos
Píli
Óros Párnitha
Kapandríti
Marathónas
Μαραθώνας
Ag. Marína
N. Stíra
Stíra
Vareléi
Kalérgo
Akr. Kafiréas
Ακρ. Καφηρέας
Stefáni
Ag. Triáda
Ag. Stéfanos
Shiniás
Akr. Strongilo
Gianítsi
Kallianós
ATIKÍ-PIREÁS
Varimbómbi
Dióníssos
Ág. Dimítrios
Kapsoúri
Fili
Aharnés
N. Mákri
Óros Óhi
Mándra
Aspropírgos
Kifissiá
Pendéli
Máti
Marmári
Kómito
Elefsína
Δafní
ATHÍNA
ΑΘΗΝΑ
Ráfina
Nissí Petalií
Kárístos
Κάρυστος
Platanistós
Potámi
N. Péramos
Skaramangás
Peania
Loútsa
Pérama
Spáta
Vravróna
Salamína
Kessarianí
Imittós
Koropí
Pórto Ráfti
PIREÁS
ΠΕΙΡΑΙΑΣ
Glifáda
Voúla
Vári
Markópoulo
Kalívia
Kaki Thálassa
Keratéa
Saronikós Kólpos
Vouliagméni
Várkiza
Lagoníssi
Saronída
Anávissos
Thorikó
Lávrio
Makroníssi
Afea
Ag. Marína
Pórtes
Perdika
N. Égina
N. Fléves
Aktí Apóllona
Legrená
Soúnio
Akr. Soúnio
Ακρ. Σούνιο
N. Patróklou
Hers. Methánon
N. Póros
Póros
Zoodóhos Pigí
Lemonodássos
Akr. Spathí
Akr. Zoúrvas
Ídra
N. Ídra
N. Ύδρα
Akr. Kambanós
N. ÁNDROS
N. ΑΝΔΡΟΣ
Kalivári
Gávrio
Akr. Griá
Batsí
Arnás
Apíkia
Andros
Messariá
Paleópoli
Ormos Korthíou
Kapariá
Kórthio
Stenó Kafiréa
N. Mandiloú
Akr. Strongilo
Akr. Ag. Kosmás
Akr. Pérvelos
Vourkári
Otziás
Korissía
Kéa
N. Kéa
N. Κέα
Píssés
Kato Meriá
Koúndouros
Akr. Tamélos
Stenó Kéas
Stenó Kíthnou
N. Giáros
N. Γύαρος
Akr. Stenó
Pánormos
N. TÍNOS
N. ΤΗΝΟΣ
Istérnia
Kardianí
Kóni
Exómvourgo
Akr. Livádа
Tínos
Τήνος
N. MÍKONOS
N. ΜΥΚΟΝΟΣ
Akr. Kéfalos
Loutrá
N. Kíthnos
N. Κύθνος
Kíthnos
Mérihas
Dríopída
Kanála
N. Ág. Geórgios
Lemessós
Haifa
Al Iskandarīyah
Iráklio
Haniá
Akr. Pálos
N. SÍROS
N. ΣΥΡΟΣ
Kíni
Galissás
Ermoúpoli
Ερμούπολη
Fínikas
Possidonía
Vári
Meg. Gialós
Akr. Viglostási
N. Rínia
Dílos
Δήλος
N. Dílos
Ag. Stéfanos
Mikonos
Μύκονος
Ornos
Platís Gialós
Á. Merá
Dragonísi
N. Pipéri
Akr. Ág. Dimítrios
KIKLÁDES
ΚΥΚΛΑΔΕΣ
N. Serfoqoúla
N. Σερφοπούλα
Stenó Serífou
Pátmos
Akr. Vólos
Sérifos
N. Sérifos
N. Σέριφος
Meg. Livádi
Livádi
Akr. Kíklops
Akr. Kátano
Stenó Sífnou
Akr. Fílipos
Akr. Kórakas
N. PÁROS
N. ΠΑΡΟΣ
Kamáres
Náoussa
Páros
Πάρος
Kostos
Léfkes
Márpissa
Andíparos
Poúnda
Náxos
Νάξος
Engarés
Kinídaros
Koronída
Apóllon
Galanádo
Halkí
Apíranthos
Sangrí
Akr. Stavrí
Psará
N. Andípsara
N. Αντίψαρα
Thessaloníki
Vólos

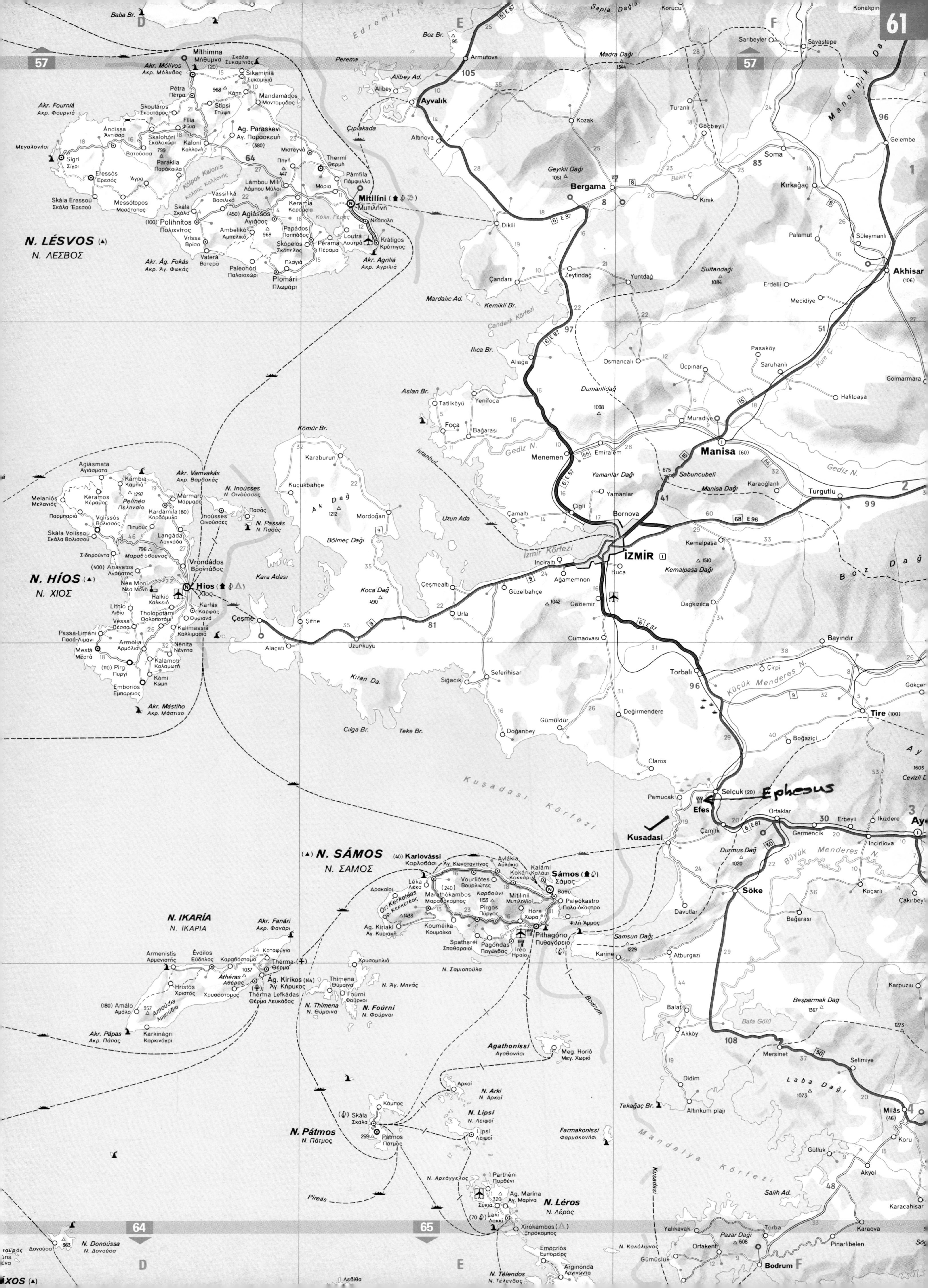
57
57
64
65
N. LÉSVOS
N. ΛΕΣΒΟΣ
Míthimna
Akr. Mólivos
Sikaminiá
Pétra
Stípsi
Mandamádos
Skoutáros
Fília
Ándissa
Skalohóri
Sígri
Kalloní
Ag. Paraskeví
Thermí
Pámfila
Eressós
Parákila
Kólpos Kalonís
Lámbou Míli
Mitilíni
Skála Eressoú
Messótopos
Vassiliká
Skála
Keramía
Polihnítos
Agiássos
Ambelikó
Papádos
Vrissa
Skópelos
Pérama
Loutrá
Krátigos
Akr. Ág. Fokás
Vaterá
Paleohóri
Plomári
Akr. Agriliá
Akr. Fourniá
Edremit
Perema
Alibey Ad.
Alibey
Ayvalık
Altınova
Çıplakada
Armutova
Boz Br.
Madra Dağı
Sarıbeyler
Savaştepe
Turanlı
Kozak
Göçbeyli
Soma
Gelembe
Geyikli Dağı
Bergama
Bakır Ç.
Kınık
Kırkağaç
Dikili
Palamut
Süleymanlı
Akhisar
Sultandağı
Çandarlı
Zeytindağ
Yuntdağ
Erdelli
Mecidiye
Mardalıç Ad.
Kemikli Br.
Çandarlı Körfezi
Ilıca Br.
Aliağa
Osmancalı
Üçpınar
Pasaköy
Saruhanlı
Gölmarmara
Dumanlıdağ
Halitpaşa
Aslan Br.
Tatlıköyü
Yenifoça
Foça
Bağarası
Muradiye
Manisa
Gediz N.
Menemen
Emiralem
Sabuncubeli
Yamanlar Dağı
Manisa Dağı
Karaoğlanlı
Turgutlu
Kömür Br.
Karaburun
Küçükbahçe
Ak Dağ
Mordoğan
Uzun Ada
Çiğli
Yamanlar
Bornova
Çamaltı
Kemalpaşa
Kemalpaşa Dağı
Bölmeç Dağı
İzmir Körfezi
İZMİR
Inciraltı
Ağamemnon
Buca
Boz Dağ
Kara Adası
Koca Dağ
Çeşmealtı
Güzelbahçe
Gaziemir
Dağkızılca
Çeşme
Şifne
Urla
Alaçatı
Uzunkuyu
Cumaovası
Bayındır
Torbalı
Çirpi
Küçük Menderes N.
Kiran Da.
Siğacık
Seferihisar
Tire
Değirmendere
Gümüldür
Doğanbey
Boğaziçi
Çılga Br.
Teke Br.
Claros
N. HÍOS
N. ΧΙΟΣ
Akr. Vamvakás
Agiásmata
Kambiá
Melaniós
Kéramos
Pelinéo
Mármaro
N. Inoússes
Volissós
Kardámila
Inoússes
N. Passás
Skála Volissoú
Langáda
Anavatos
Vrondádos
Néa Moní
Híos
Halkió
Karfás
Lithió
Thólopotámi
Véssa
Passá-Limáni
Kalimassiá
Armólia
Mestá
Nénita
Pirgí
Kalamotí
Kómi
Emboriós
Akr. Mástiho
Kuşadası Körfezi
Pamucak
Selçuk
Efes
Ephesus
Kuşadası
Ortaklar
Erbeyli
Germencik
Incirliova
Çamlık
Dumus Dağı
Büyük Menderes N.
Söke
Koçarlı
Çakırbeyli
N. SÁMOS
N. ΣΑΜΟΣ
Karlovássi
Avlákia
Kokári
Sámos
Vathí
Léka
Vourliótes
Marathókambos
Mitilíni
Or. Kerketéas
Pírgos
Paleókastro
Hóra
Ag. Kiriakí
Kouméika
Pithagório
Spatharéi
Pagóndas
Iréo
Samsun Dağı
Davutlar
Bağarası
Karine
Atburgazı
N. IKARÍA
N. IKAPIA
Akr. Fanári
Armenistís
Évdilos
Thérma
Athéras
Ag. Kírikos
Hristós
Thérma Lefkádas
Thímena
Foúrni
Amálo
N. Thímena
N. Foúrni
Akr. Pápas
Karkinágri
N. Samiopoúla
N. Agathonissí
Meg. Horió
Bodrum
Balat
Bafa Gölü
Akköy
Beşparmak Dag
Mersinet
Selimiye
Karpuzlu
Didim
Laba Dağı
Tekağaç Br.
Altınkum plajı
Milâs
N. Arkí
N. Lipsí
Lipsí
Skála
N. Pátmos
Pátmos
Farmakonissí
Mandalya Körfezi
Güllük
Akyol
Koru
Salih Ad.
Karacahisar
Pireás
Parthéni
Ag. Marína
N. Léros
Lakí
Xirókambos
Yalıkavak
Pazar Dağı
Torba
Karaova
Pinarlibelen
Ortakent
Gümüşlük
Bodrum
N. Kalólimnos
Emporiós
Argínonda
N. Télendos
N. Donoússa

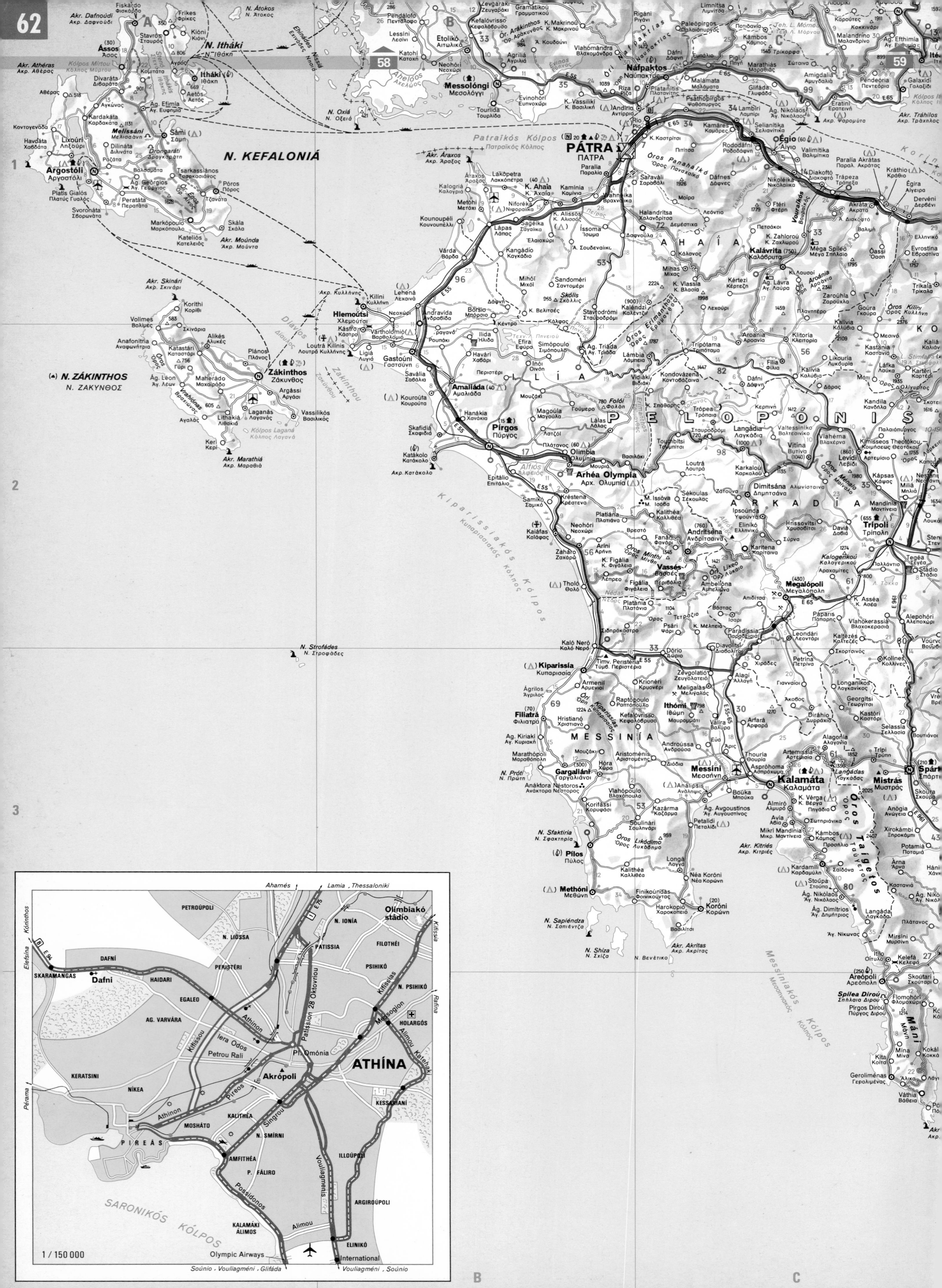
58
59
N. KEFALONIÁ
N. Itháki
N. Átokos
N. ZÁKINTHOS
N. ZAKYNΘOΣ
Argostóli
Lixoúri
Sámi
Ithákí
Zákinthos
Messolóngi
Náfpaktos
PÁTRA
ΠATPA
Patraïkós Kólpos
Égio
Kalávrita
Pírgos
Olimbía
Arhéa Olympía
Amaliáda
Gastoúni
Kilíni
Hlemoútsi
Kiparissiakós Kólpos
N. Strofádes
Kiparissía
Filiatrá
Gargaliáni
Pílos
Methóni
Koróni
Kalamáta
Messíni
Megalópoli
Trípoli
Mistrás
Areópoli
Messiniakós Kólpos
A H A Ï A
I L Í A
P E L O P O N I S
A R K A D Í A
M E S S I N Í A
Máni
Óros Taïgetos
E 55
E 65
ATHÍNA
PIREÁS
SARONIKÓS KÓLPOS
Akrópoli
Pl. Omónia
Dafni
Olimbiakó stádio
Olympic Airways
International
1 / 150 000
Soúnio , Vouliagméni , Glifáda
Vouliagméni , Soúnio
Lamia , Thessaloníki
Aharnés
Kifissiá
Rafína
Pérama
Elefsína
Kórinthos
A
B
C
1
2
3

ATHÍNA
ΑΘΗΝΑ
PIREÁS
ΠΕΙΡΑΙΑΣ
Halkída
Χαλκίδα
Thíva
Θήβα
Livadiá
Λεβαδειά
VIOTÍA
ATIKÍ-PIREÁS
ARGOLÍDA
LAKONÍA
Kórinthos
Κόρινθος
Loutráki
Λουτράκι
Mégara
Μέγαρα
Elefsína
Ελευσίνα
Salamína
Σαλαμίνα
Glifáda
Γλυφάδα
Vouliagméni
Βουλιαγμένη
Kifissiá
Κηφισιά
Rafína
Ραφήνα
Lávrio
Λαύριο
Akr. Soúnio
Ακρ. Σούνιο
Náfplio
Ναύπλιο
Árgos
Άργος
Mikínes
Μυκήνες
Arh. Epídavros
Póros
Πόρος
Ídra
Ύδρα
Spétses
Σπέτσες
N. Spétses
N. Égina
N. Salamína
Hers. Methánon
N. Kéa
N. Kíthnos
N. Sérifos
N. Sífnos
N. Kímolos
N. MÍLOS
N. ΜΗΛΟΣ
Kárístos
Κάρυστος
Eretria
Ερέτρια
Leonídio
Λεωνίδιο
Moláí
Μολάοι
Monemvassía
Μονεμβασία
Neápoli
Νεάπολη
Githio
Γύθειο
N. KÍTHIRA
N. ΚΥΘΗΡΑ
Kíthira
Κύθηρα
N. Andikíthira
N. KRÍTI
N. ΚΡΗΤΗ
Lakonikós Kólpos
Λακωνικός Κόλπος
Argolikós Kólpos
Saronikós Kólpos
Nótios Evoikós Kólpos
M I R T Ó O   P É L A G O S
Μ Υ Ρ Τ Ω Ο   Π Ε Λ Α Γ Ο Σ
N. Velopoúla
N. Falkonéra
N. Andímilos
N. Karávi
Akr. Maléas
Oros Párnitha
Oros Párnonas
59
60
64

A
B
C
63
60
61
1
2
3
4
N. Sérifos
Ν. Σέριφος
N. PÁROS
Ν. ΠΑΡΟΣ
Pátmos
Akr. Kórakas
Ακρ. Κόρακας
Apólonas
Απόλλωνας
Koronída
Κορωνίδα
Náxos
Νάξος
Naoússa
Νάουσα
Kamáres
Καμάρες
Páros
Πάρος
Léfkes
Λεύκες
Kóstos
Κώστος
Márpissa
Μάρπησσα
Aliki
Αλυκή
Driós
Δρυός
Roúnda
Andíparos
Αντίπαρος
N. Andíparos
Ν. Αντίπαρος
N. Despotikó
Ν. Δεσποτικό
N. Strongilí
Ν. Στρογγυλή
Akr. Petalída
Ακρ. Πεταλίδα
Engarés
Εγγαρές
Kóronos
Κόρωνος
Galanádo
Γαλανάδο
Hálki
Χαλκί
Apíranthos
Απείρανθος
Moutsoúna
Μουτσούνα
Kástro Staurós
Kastráki
Καστράκι
A. Sangrí
Α. Σαγκρί
Náxos Días
Νάξος Δίας
N. NÁXOS
Ν. ΝΑΞΟΣ
N. Donoússa
Ν. Δονούσα
Donoússa
Δονούσα
Akr. Kouroúnia
Ακρ. Κουρούνια
Koufoníssi
Κουφονήσι
Kéros
Κέρος
N. Kéros
Ν. Κέρος
N. Shinoússa
Ν. Σχοινούσα
N. Irákleia
Ν. Ηράκλεια
Akr. Katoméri
Ακρ. Κατωμέρι
Egiáli
Αιγιάλη
Hozoviótissa
Χοζοβιώτισσα
Katápola
Κατάπολα
Amorgós
Αμοργός
Arkessíni
Αρκεσίνη
N. AMORGÓS
Ν. ΑΜΟΡΓΟΣ
N. Nikouriá
Ν. Νικουριά
Akr. Kalotássi
Ακρ. Καλοτάσι
Meg. Livádi
Μεγ. Λιβάδι
Akr. Kíklops
Ακρ. Κύκλωψ
Akr. Kátano
Ακρ. Κάτανο
Steno Sífnou
Στενό Σίφνου
Akr. Filipos
Ακρ. Φίλιππος
Artemónas
Αρτεμώνας
Apolonía
Απολλωνία
Platís Gialós
Πλατύς Γιαλός
N. Sífnos
Ν. Σίφνος
Akr. Kondós
Ακρ. Κοντός
Akr. Kéndras
Ακρ. Κένδρας
N. Kímolos
Ν. Κίμωλος
Kímolos
Κίμωλος
Prássa
Πράσσα
N. Polígos
Ν. Πολύαιγος
Steno Kimólou - Sífnou
Steno Polégou - Folegándrou
N. Andímilos
Ν. Αντίμηλος
Akr. Spilás
Milos
Μήλος
Filakopí
Φυλακωπή
Psathi
Kánava
Κάνανα
Voúdia
Βούδια
Adámandas
Αδάμαντας
Zefíria
Ζεφύρια
Akr. Vani
Ακρ. Βάνη
Raláki Halakás
Akr. Psális
Ακρ. Ψάλης
Prof. Ilías
Προφ. Ηλίας
N. Paximádi
Ν. Παξιμάδι
N. MÍLOS
Ν. ΜΗΛΟΣ
Akr. Vígla
Ακρ. Βίγλα
N. Folégandros
Ν. Φολέγανδρος
Folégandros
Φολέγανδρος
Karavostássis
Καραβοστάσης
Akr. Vitzétzos
Ακρ. Βιτζέτζος
N. Kardiótissa
Ν. Καρδιώτισσα
Akr. Voreinó
Ακρ. Βορεινό
Síkinos
Σίκινος
N. Síkinos
Ν. Σίκινος
Akr. Géro Angelí
Ακρ. Γέρο Αγγελή
Íos
Ίος
N. Íos
Ν. Ίος
Pírgos
Πύργος
Akr. Poúntas
Ακρ. Πούντας
Manganári
Μαγγανάρι
Akr. Ahládes
Ακρ. Αχλάδες
N. Ánidros
Ν. Άνυδρος
N. Ofidoússa
Ν. Οφιδούσσα
N. Ananés
Ν. Ανανές
Irákliο
Ía
Οία
Akr. Mavrópetra
Ακρ. Μαυρόπετρα
N. THÍRA
Ν. ΘΗΡΑ
(N. SANTORÍNI)
N. Thirassía
Ν. Θηρασία
Thirasía
Θηρασία
Thíra
Θήρα
N. Kaméni
Ν. Καμένη
Mesariá
Μεσαριά
Kamári
Καμάρι
Arh. Thíra
Αρχ. Θήρα
Akrotíri
Ακρωτήρι
Períssa
Περίσσα
Akr. Exomítis
Ακρ. Εξωμύτης
Akr. Drépano
Ακρ. Δρέπανο
N. Anáfi
Ν. Ανάφη
Anáfi
Ανάφη
Kalamiótissa
Καλαμιώτισσα
Katelimátsa
Κατελιμάτσα
N. Makrá
Ν. Μακρά
N. Pahiá
Ν. Παχειά
N. Hristianí
Ν. Χριστιανή
N. Askanía
Ν. Ασκανία
Sitía
Ó P É L A G O S
(M E R D E C R È T E)
Κ Ρ Η Τ Ι Κ Ο Π Ε Λ Α Γ Ο
N. KRÍTI
Ν. ΚΡΗΤΗ
Potamós
Akr. Spánda
Ακρ. Σπάθα
Diktinéon
Δικτυναίον
Kólpos Kissámou
Κόλπος Κισσάμου
Kólpos Hanion
Κόλπος Χανίων
Akr. Voúxa
Ακρ. Βούξα
Gonía
Γωνιά
Rodopós
Ροδωπός
Kolimvári
Κολυμβάρι
Kastéli
Καστέλλι
Falássarna
Φαλάσαρνα
Plátanos
Πλάτανος
Polirinía
Πολυρρηνία
Topólia
Τοπόλια
Kámbos
Κάμπος
Strovlés
Στροβλές
Élos
Έλος
Hrissoskalítissa
Χρυσοσκαλίτισσα
Sklavopoúla
Σκλαβοπούλα
Akr. Kriós
Ακρ. Κριός
Paleohóra
Παλαιοχώρα
Kándanos
Κάντανος
Voukoliés
Βουκολιές
Kakópetros
Κακόπετρος
Omalós
Ομαλός
Xilóskalo
Ξυλόσκαλο
Lefká Óri
Farángi Samariás
Rodováni
Ροδοβάνι
Soúgia
Σούγια
Ag. Rouméli
Αγ. Ρουμέλη
Haniá
Χανιά
HANIÁ
Plataniás
Πλατανιάς
Máleme
Μάλεμε
Ag. Marina
Αγ. Μαρίνα
Alikianós
Αλικιανός
Fournés
Φουρνές
Láki
Λάκκοι
Mourniés
Μουρνιές
Soúda
Σούδα
Hers. Akrotíri
Χερσ. Ακρωτήρι
Stavrós
Σταυρός
Kounoupidianá
Κουνουπιδιανά
Pervolítsa
Περβολίτσα
Stérnes
Στέρνες
Akr. Drápano
Ακρ. Δρέπανο
Kalíves
Καλύβες
Áptera
Άπτερα
Vámos
Βάμος
Kefalás
Κεφαλάς
Ramní
Ραμνή
Vrísses
Βρύσες
Georgioúpoli
Γεωργιούπολη
Órmos Almiroú
Όρμος Αλμυρού
Askífou
Ασκύφου
Anópoli
Ανώπολη
Sfakiá
Σφακιά
Frangokástelo
Φραγκοκάστελλο
Pireás
Thessaloníki
Réthimno
Ρέθυμνο
RÉTHIMNO
Kournás
Κουρνάς
Argiroúpoli
Αργυρούπολη
Episkopí
Επισκοπή
Armeni
Αρμένοι
Spíli
Σπήλι
Plakiás
Πλακιάς
Préveli
Πρέβελη
Selía
Σελλιά
Á. Rodákino
Α. Ροδάκινο
Kissoú Kámbos
Κισσού Κάμπος
Mélambes
Μέλαμπες
Ag. Galíni
Αγ. Γαλήνη
N. Paximádia
Ν. Παξιμάδια
Órmos Messarás
Όρμος Μεσαράς
N. Gavdopoúla
Ν. Γαυδοπούλα
N. Gávdos
Ν. Γαύδος
Pánormos
Πάνορμος
Balí
Μπαλί
Akr. Stavrós
Ακρ. Σταυρός
Pérama
Πέραμα
Melidóni
Μελιδόνι
Fódele
Φόδελε
Margarítes
Μαργαρίτες
Arkádi
Αρκάδι
Assómaton
Axós
Αξός
Anógia
Ανώγεια
Zoniana
Ζωνιανά
Apóstoli
Αποστόλοι
Fourfourás
Φουρφουράς
Gerakári
Γεράκαρι
Óros Ídi
Idéo Ándro
Ιδαίο Άντρο
Kamáres
Καμάρες
Vrondíssi
Βρονδήσι
Zarós
Ζαρός
Timbáki
Τυμπάκι
Míres
Μοίρες
Górtis
Γόρτυς
Festós
Φαιστός
Mátala
Μάταλα
Pómbia
Πόμπια
Kalí Liménes
Καλοί Λιμένες
Léndas
Λέντας
Akr. Líthino
Ακρ. Λίθινο
Ag. Déka
Αγ. Δέκα
Vagioniá
Βαγιονιά
Gangáles
Γκαγκάλες
Ag. Varvára
Αγ. Βαρβάρα
Ag. Thomás
Αγ. Θωμάς
Ag. Pelagía
Αγ. Πελαγία
Rodiá
Ροδιά
Ammoudára
Αμμουδάρα
Tílissos
Τύλισος
Goniés
Γωνιές
Kroussónas
Κρουσώνας
Ag. Míronas
Αγ. Μύρωνας
IRÁKLIO
ΗΡΑΚΛΕΙΟ
IRÁKLIO
N. Día
Ν. Δία
Thíra
Sífnos
Knossós
Κνωσός
Arhánes
Αρχάνες
Vathípetro
Βαθύπετρο
Arkalohóri
Αρκαλοχώρι
Ag. Paraskiés
Αγ. Παρασκιές
Karterós
Καρτερός
N. Alikarnassós
Ν. Αλικαρνασσός
Episkopí
Επισκοπή
Goúrnes
Γούρνες
Gouves
Γούβες
Límani Hersonissou
Λιμάνι Χερσονήσου
Stalída
Σταλίδα
Mália
Μάλια
Potamiés
Ποταμιές
Kastéli
Καστέλλι
Psihró
Ψυχρό
Diktéo Ándro
Δικταίο Άντρο
Lassíthi
Tefélí
Τεφέλι
Garipa
Γαρίπα
Pírgos
Πύργος
Háraka
Χάρακας
Skiniás
Σκινιάς
A. Viános
Α. Βιάνος
Ahendriás
Αχεντριάς
Kapetaniana
Καπετανιανά
Keratókambos
Κερατόκαμπος
Árvi
Άρβη
Kárpathos
Ródos
Lemesós
Haifa
A
B
C

ATHÍNA
ΑΘΗΝΑ
PIREÁS
ΠΕΙΡΑΙΑΣ
ATIKÍ-PIRÉAS
ARGOLÍDA
VIOTÍA
LAKONÍA
Halkída
Χαλκίδα
Thíva
Θήβα
Livadiá
Λιβαδειά
Elefsína
Ελευσίνα
Mégara
Μέγαρα
Kórinthos
Κόρινθος
Loutráki
Λουτράκι
Árgos
Άργος
Náfplio
Ναύπλιο
Mikínes
Μυκήνες
Tirintha
Τίρυνθα
Arh. Epídavros
Αρχ. Επίδαυρος
Kranidi
Κρανίδι
Ermióni
Ερμιόνη
Portohéli
Πορτοχέλι
Leonídio
Λεωνίδιο
Geráki
Γεράκι
Molái
Μολάοι
Monemvassía
Μονεμβασία
Neápoli
Νεάπολη
Gíthio
Γύθειο
Lávrio
Λαύριο
Rafína
Ραφήνα
Kifissiá
Κηφισιά
Glifáda
Γλυφάδα
Vouliagméni
Βουλιαγμένη
Kárístos
Κάρυστος
N. Salamína
Ν. Σαλαμίνα
N. Égina
Ν. Αίγινα
N. Póros
Ν. Πόρος
Hers. Methánon
Χερσ. Μεθάνων
N. Ídra
Ν. Ύδρα
N. Spétses
Ν. Σπέτσες
N. Kéa
Ν. Κέα
N. Kíthnos
Ν. Κύθνος
N. Sérifos
Ν. Σέριφος
N. Sífnos
Ν. Σίφνος
N. Kímolos
Ν. Κίμωλος
N. MÍLOS
Ν. ΜΗΛΟΣ
N. KÍTHIRA
Ν. ΚΥΘΗΡΑ
N. Andikíthira
Ν. Αντικύθηρα
N. KRÍTI
Ν. ΚΡΗΤΗ
Akr. Soúnio
Ακρ. Σούνιο
Akr. Maléas
Ακρ. Μαλέας
Óros Párnitha
Όρος Πάρνηθα
Óros Párnonas
Όρος Πάρνωνας
MIRTÓO PÉLAGOS
ΜΥΡΤΩΟ ΠΕΛΑΓΟΣ
Saronikós Kólpos
Σαρωνικός Κόλπος
Argolikós Kólpos
Αργολικός Κόλπος
Lakonikós Kólpos
Λακωνικός Κόλπος
Nótios Evoïkós Kólpos
Νότιος Ευβοϊκός Κόλπος
Stenó Kéas
Stenó Kíthnou
Stenó Serífou
Stenó Sífnou
Stenó Kimólou
Porthmós Elafonissou
N. Velopoúla
Ν. Βελοπούλα
N. Falkonéra
Ν. Φαλκονέρα
N. Andímilos
Ν. Αντίμηλος
N. Karávi
Ν. Καράβι
N. Ananés
Ν. Ανανές
59
60
64
D
E
F
K
1
2
3
4

N. Sérifos
Ν. Σέριφος
N. PÁROS
Ν. ΠΑΡΟΣ
N. NÁXOS
Ν. ΝΑΞΟΣ
N. Donoússa
Ν. Δονούσα
N. Sífnos
Ν. Σίφνος
N. Andíparos
Ν. Αντίπαρος
N. Despotikó
Ν. Δεσποτικό
Koufoníssi
Κουφονήσι
N. Kéros
Ν. Κέρος
N. Shinoússa
Ν. Σχοινούσσα
N. Iráklia
Ν. Ηράκλεια
N. AMORGÓS
Ν. ΑΜΟΡΓΟΣ
N. Andímilos
Ν. Αντίμηλος
N. Kímolos
Ν. Κίμωλος
N. Políegos
Ν. Πολύαιγος
N. MÍLOS
Ν. ΜΗΛΟΣ
N. Folégandros
Ν. Φολέγανδρος
N. Síkinos
Ν. Σίκινος
N. Íos
Ν. Ίος
N. Anánes
Ν. Ανανές
N. THÍRA
Ν. ΘΗΡΑ
(N. SANTORÍNI)
N. Thirassía
Ν. Θηρασία
N. Kaméni
Ν. Καμένη
N. Anáfi
Ν. Ανάφη
N. Hristianí
Ν. Χριστιανή
N. Askanía
Ν. Ασκανία
N. Ofidoússa
N. Makrá
N. Paheiá
N. Ánidros
PÉLAGOS
ΚΡΗΤΙΚΟ ΠΕΛΑΓΟ
(MER DE CRÈTE)
N. KRÍTI
Ν. ΚΡΗΤΗ
Haniá
Χανιά
Hers. Akrotíri
Χερσ. Ακρωτήρι
Soúda
Kastéli
Kolimvári
Paleohóra
Sfakiá
Réthimno
Ρέθυμνο
RÉTHIMNO
HANIÁ
Órí
Lefká
Farángi Samariás
IRÁKLIO
ΗΡΑΚΛΕΙΟ
Knossós
Arhánes
Mália
Límáni Hersonissou
Anógia
Zarós
Míres
Festós
Mátala
Timbáki
Ag. Galíni
Spíli
Pérama
Fódele
Bali
Pánormos
Georgioúpoli
Vrisses
Ag. Déka
Górtis
Léndas
Kalí Liménes
Idéo Ándro
Ag. Triáda
Ag. Pelagía
N. Día
N. Gávdos
Ν. Γαύδος
N. Gavdopoúla
N. Paximádia
Ormos Mesarás
Akr. Líthino
Akr. Krios
Akr. Vouxa
Akr. Spánda
Kólpos Haníon
Kólpos Kissámou
Akr. Drápano
Órmos Almirou
Ag. Roúmeli
Omalós
Kándanos
Sougia
Plakiás
Frangokástelo
Ag. Nikólaos
Piréas
Thessaloníki
Thíra
Sífnos
Iráklio
Sitía
Pátmos
A
B
C
1
2
3
4
63
60
61

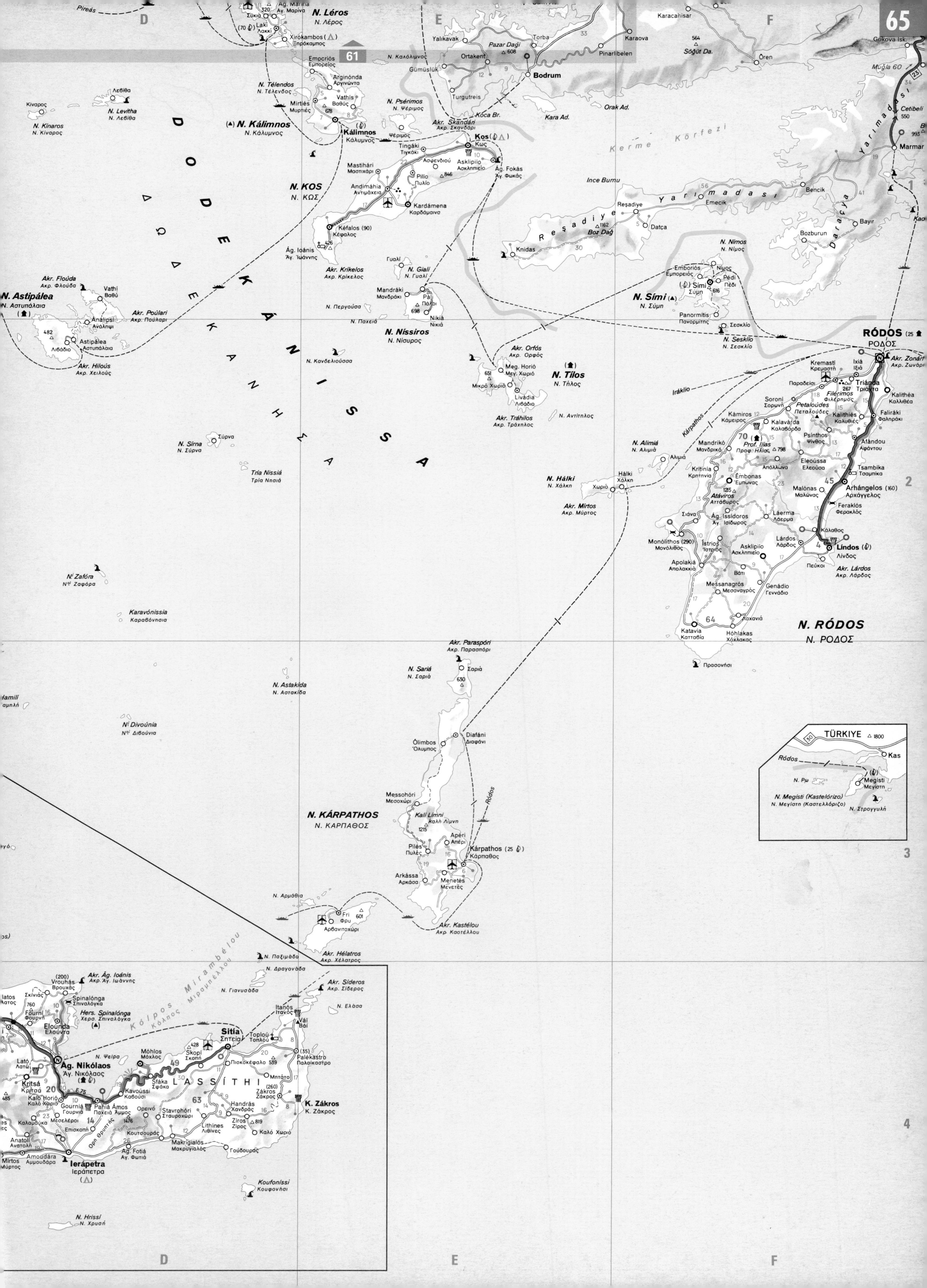
D
E
F
61
N. Léros
Ν. Λέρος
Laki
Λακκί
Xirókambos (△)
Ξηρόκαμπος
Emporiós
Εμπορειός
Arginónda
Αργινώντα
N. Télendos
Ν. Τέλενδος
Vathis
Βαθύς
Mirtiés
Μυρτιές
N. Kínaros
Ν. Κίναρος
N. Levítha
Ν. Λεβίθα
N. Kálimnos
Ν. Κάλυμνος
Kálimnos
Κάλυμνος
N. Psérimos
Ν. Ψέριμος
Ψέριμος
N. Kalólimnos
Yalıkavak
Pazar Daği
608
Ortakent
Gümüşlük
Turgutreis
Bodrum
Torba
Karaova
Pinarlibelen
Karacahisar
564
Söğüt Da.
Ören
Gökova Isk.
Muğla 60
23
Cetibeli
550
993
Marmar
Koca Br.
Kara Ad.
Orak Ad.
Kerme Körfezi
Akr. Skandári
Ακρ. Σκανδάρι
Kos
Κως
Tingáki
Τιγκάκι
Asfendioú
Ασφενδιού
Asklipiío
Ασκληπιείο
Ag. Fokás
Αγ. Φωκάς
Mastihári
Μαστιχάρι
Pilío
Πυλίο
846
N. KOS
Ν. ΚΩΣ
Andimáhia
Αντιμάχεια
Kardámena
Καρδάμαινα
Kéfalos (90)
Κέφαλος
426
Ág. Ioánis
Άγ. Ιωάννης
D O D E K Á N I S S A
Δ Ω Δ Ε Κ Α Ν Η Σ Α
Ince Burnu
Reşadiye
Reşadiye Yarımadası
Emecik
Bencik
Datça
1162
Boz Dağ
Knidas
Bozburun
Bayır
Daraçya
Yarımadası
N. Nimos
Ν. Νίμος
Emboriós
Εμπορειός
Sími
Σύμη
Pédi
Πέδι
616
N. Sími
Ν. Σύμη
Panormitis
Πανορμίτης
Σεσκλίο
N. Seskliό
Ν. Σεσκλίο
Akr. Krikelos
Ακρ. Κρίκελος
Γυαλί
N. Giali
Ν. Γυαλί
Mandráki
Μανδράκι
Páli
Πάλοι
698
Nikiá
Νικιά
N. Pergoúsa
Ν. Περγούσα
N. Pahiá
Ν. Παχειά
N. Nissiros
Ν. Νίσυρος
Akr. Floúda
Ακρ. Φλούδα
Vathí
Βαθύ
N. Astipálea
Ν. Αστυπάλαια
Akr. Poúlari
Ακρ. Πούλαρι
Análipsi
Ανάληψη
482
Livádio
Λιβάδιο
Astipálea
Αστυπάλαια
Akr. Hiloús
Ακρ. Χειλούς
N. Kandelioússa
Ν. Κανδελιούσσα
Akr. Orfós
Ακρ. Ορφός
Meg. Horió
Μεγ. Χωριό
651
Mikró Horió
Μικρό Χωριό
N. Tílos
Ν. Τήλος
Livádia
Λιβάδια
Akr. Tráhilos
Ακρ. Τράχηλος
N. Andítilos
Ν. Αντίτηλος
RÓDOS
ΡΟΔΟΣ
Akr. Zonári
Ακρ. Ζωνάρι
Kremastí
Κρεμαστή
Ixiá
Ιξιά
Paradísi
Παραδείσι
267
Triánda
Τριάντα
Iráklio
Kárpathos
Filérimos
Φιλέρημος
Soroní
Σορωνή
Petaloúdes
Πεταλούδες
Kalithéa
Καλλιθέα
Kámiros
Κάμειρος
Kalavárda
Καλαβάρδα
Kalithiés
Καλυθιές
Faliráki
Φαληράκι
Psínthos
Ψίνθος
70
Prof. Ilías
Προφ. Ηλίας
798
Afándou
Αφάντου
Mandrikó
Μανδρικό
N. Alimiá
Ν. Αλιμιά
Αλιμιά
Apóllona
Απόλλωνα
Eleoússa
Ελεούσα
Tsambíka
Τσαμπίκα
Kritinía
Κρητηνία
Émbonas
Έμπωνας
Hálki
Χάλκη
N. Hálki
Ν. Χάλκη
Horió
Χωριό
1215
Atáviros
Αττάβυρος
Malónas
Μαλώνας
Arhángelos (160)
Αρχάγγελος
Feraklós
Φεράκλος
Akr. Mírtos
Ακρ. Μύρτος
Siána
Σιάνα
Ág. Issidoros
Άγ. Ισίδωρος
Láerma
Λάερμα
Kálathos
Κάλαθος
Monólithos (290)
Μονόλιθος
Ístrios
Ίστριος
Asklipiío
Ασκληπιείο
Lárdos
Λάρδος
Líndos
Λίνδος
Apolakiá
Απολακκιά
Váti
Βάτι
Péfkoi
Πεύκοι
Akr. Lárdos
Ακρ. Λάρδος
Messanagrós
Μεσαναγρός
Genádio
Γεννάδιο
Lahaniá
Λαχανιά
64
Katavia
Κατταβία
Hóhlakas
Χόχλακας
N. RÓDOS
Ν. ΡΟΔΟΣ
Πρασονήσι
N. Sírna
Ν. Σύρνα
Σύρνα
Tría Nissiá
Τρία Νησιά
N. Zafóra
Ν. Ζαφόρα
Karavónissia
Καραβόνησια
Akr. Paraspóri
Ακρ. Παρασπόρι
N. Sariá
Ν. Σαριά
Σαριά
630
N. Astakída
Ν. Αστακίδα
N. Divoúnia
Ν. Διβούνια
Diafáni
Διαφάνι
Ólimbos
Όλυμπος
Messohóri
Μεσοχώρι
Kalí Límni
Καλή Λίμνη
1215
N. KÁRPATHOS
Ν. ΚΑΡΠΑΘΟΣ
Apéri
Απέρι
Piles
Πυλές
Kárpathos
Κάρπαθος
Ródos
Arkássa
Αρκάσα
Menetés
Μενετές
Akr. Kastélou
Ακρ. Καστέλλου
N. Armáthia
Ν. Αρμάθια
Fri
Φρυ
601
Arvanitohóri
Αρβανιτοχώρι
Akr. Hélatros
Ακρ. Χέλατρος
TÜRKIYE
1800
Kas
Ródos
N. Ro
Ν. Ρω
Megisti
Μεγίστη
N. Megísti (Kastelórizo)
Ν. Μεγίστη (Καστελλόριζο)
N. Strongilí
Ν. Στρογγυλή
1
2
3
4
Ν. Παξιμάδα
Ν. Δραγονάδα
Akr. Ág. Ioánis
Ακρ. Αγ. Ιωάννης
(200)
Vrouhás
Βρουχάς
Spinalónga
Σπιναλόγκα
Hers. Spinalónga
Χερσ. Σπιναλόγκα
Kólpos Mirambélou
Κόλπος Μιραμπέλλου
N. Gianissáda
Ν. Γιανυσάδα
Akr. Síderos
Ακρ. Σίδερος
N. Elása
Ν. Ελάσα
Itanos
Ιτανός
Vái
Βάι
760
Foúrni
Φουρνή
Elounda
Ελούντα
Sitía
Σητεία
Toploú
Τοπλού
428
Skopí
Σκοπή
Móhlos
Μόχλος
N. Psíra
Ν. Ψείρα
Piskokéfalo
Πισκοκέφαλο
539
Palékastro
Παλαίκαστρο
Latό
Λατώ
Ag. Nikólaos
Άγ. Νικόλαος
49
Mitáto
Μητάτο
Kritsá
Κριτσά
20
E 75
Kavoússi
Καβούσι
Sfáka
Σφάκα
LASSÍTHI
Zákros
Ζάκρος
(260)
K. Zákros
Κ. Ζάκρος
Kaló Horió
Καλό Χωριό
Gourniá
Γουρνιά
Pahiá Ámos
Παχειά Άμμος
Orinó
Ορεινό
Stavrohóri
Σταυροχώρι
63
Handrás
Χανδράς
Ziros
Ζίρος
819
Kaló Horió
Καλό Χωριό
1476
Lithines
Λιθίνες
14
Episkopí
Επισκοπή
Koutsourás
Κουτσουράς
Makrigialós
Μακρυγιαλός
Goúdouras
Γούδουρας
Anatolí
Ανατολή
Ag. Fotiá
Αγ. Φωτιά
Amoudára
Αμουδάρα
Ierápetra
Ιεράπετρα
(△)
Mírtos
Μύρτος
Koufonissi
Κουφονήσι
N. Hrissí
Ν. Χρυσή

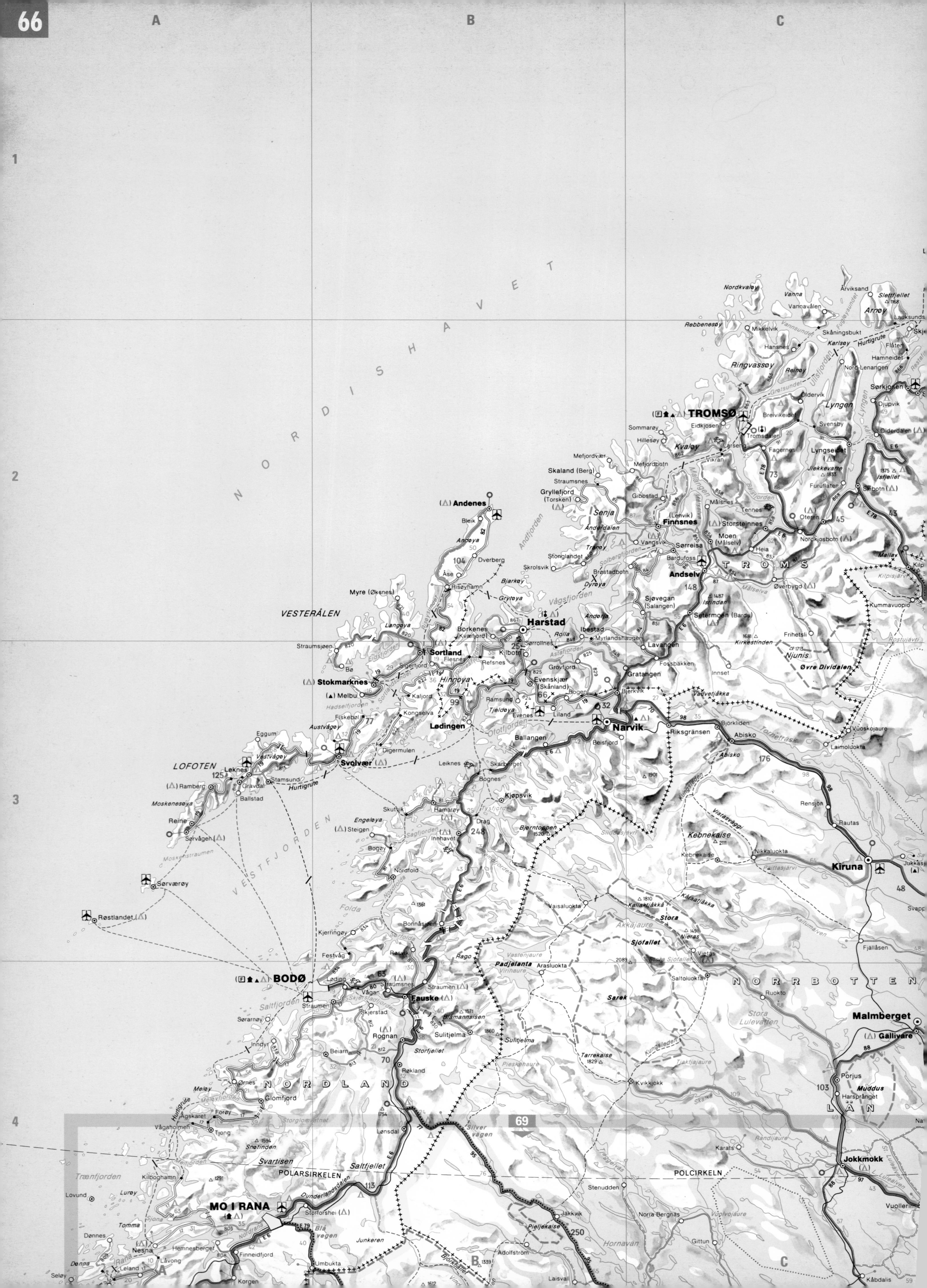
A
B
C
1
2
3
4
N O R D I S H A V E T
VESTERÅLEN
LOFOTEN
VESTFJORDEN
N O R D L A N D
T R O M S
N O R R B O T T E N
L Ä N
POLARSIRKELEN
POLCIRKELN
TROMSØ
Nordkvaløy
Vanna
Vannavålen
Årviksand
Slettfjellet
Arnøy
Lauksunds
Rebbenesøy
Mikkelvik
Hansnes
Skåningsbukt
Karlsøy
Hurtigrute
Fláten
Hamneidet
Nord-Lenangen
Ringvassøy
Reinøy
Sørkjosen
Djupvik
Olderdalen
Oldervik
Brevikeidet
Lyngen
Svensby
Sommarøy
Hillesøy
Eidkjosen
Tromsdalen
Kvaløy
Larseng
Fagernes
Lyngseidet
Jiekkevarre
Mefjordvær
Mefjordbotn
Skaland (Berg)
Straumsnes
Gryllefjord
(Torsken)
Senja
Gibostad
Finnsnes
(Lenvik)
Målsnes
Tennes
Storsteinnes
Moen
(Målselv)
Heia
Andørdalen
Vangsvik
Sørreisa
Bardufoss
Andselv
Nordkjosbotn
Oteren
Skibotn
Isfjellet
Furuflaten
Andenes
Bleik
Andøya
Dverberg
Åse
Risøyhamn
Bjarkøy
Grytøya
Vågsfjorden
Myre (Øksnes)
Skrolsvik
Stonglandet
Brøstadbotn
Dyrøya
Sjøvegan
(Salangen)
Setermoen (Bardu)
Istindan
Øverbygd
Kilpisjärvi
Kummavuopio
Langøya
Borkenes
(Kvæfjord)
Harstad
Rolla
Ibestad
Andørja
Myrlandshaugen
Lavangen
Straumsjøen
Bø
Sortland
Flesnes
Refsnes
Kilbotn
Sørrollnes
Grovfjord
Fossbakken
Gratangen
Innset
Frihetsli
Kirkestinden
Njunis
Øvre Dividalen
Stokmarknes
Melbu
Sigerfjord
Hinnøya
Kaljord
Evenskjær
(Skånland)
Bogen
Bjerkvik
Vadvetjåkka
Hadselfjorden
Kongselva
Ramsund
Tjeldøya
Liland
Evenes
Fiskebøl
Austvågøy
Lødingen
Ofotfjorden
Narvik
Riksgränsen
Bjørkliden
Abisko
Torneträsk
Vuoskojaure
Laimoluokta
Eggum
Digermulen
Ballangen
Beisfjord
Vestvågøy
Leknes
Svolvær
Stamsund
Gravdal
Ballstad
Ramberg
Hurtigrute
Leiknes
Skarberget
Bognes
Kjøpsvik
Moskenesøya
Reine
Sørvågen
Moskenstraumen
Skutvik
Hamarøy
Drag
Engeløya
Steigen
Innhavet
Bjørntoppen
Sørværøy
Bogøy
Nordfold
Kungsleden
Vistasvaggi
Kebnekaise
Nikkaluokta
Rensjön
Rautas
Kiruna
Jukkasjärvi
Svappavaara
Røstlandet
Folda
Vaisaluokta
Kallaktjåkkå
Kårsatjåkka
Stora
Akkajaure
Sjöfallet
Vietas
Fjällåsen
Kjerringøy
Bonnåsjøen
Festvåg
Rasvik
Rago
Padjelanta
Virihaure
Arasluokta
Saltoluokta
Ruokto
BODØ
Løding
Straumsnes
Vågan
Straumen
Fauske
Saltfjorden
Skjerstadfjorden
Skjerstad
Blåmannsisen
Sulitjelma
Sarek
Stora Lulevatten
Malmberget
Gällivare
Sørarnøy
Inndyr
Beiarn
Rognan
Storfjellet
Tarrekaise
Pieskehaure
Tjaktjajaure
Røkland
Kvikkjokk
Porjus
Muddus
Harsprånget
Meløy
Ørnes
Glomfjord
Forøy
Ågskaret
Vågaholmen
Tjong
Storglomvatnet
Snøtinden
Svartisen
Saltfjellet
Lønsdal
Silvervägen
Randijaure
Karats
Jokkmokk
Kilboghamn
Trænfjorden
Lurøy
Lovund
Stenudden
Dunderlandsdalen
MO I RANA
Storforshei
Jäkkvik
Pieljekaise
Norra Bergnas
Vuollerim
Tomma
Dønnes
Nesna
Hemnesberget
Lavong
Leland
Dønna
Seløy
Finneidfjord
Junkeren
Umbukta
Korgen
Adolfström
Hornavan
Gittun
Laisvall
Kåbdalis
Blåvegen
Bjørnfjellet

NORDKAPP
Knivskjelodden
Magerøya
Honningsvåg
Hjelmsøya
Havøysund
Rolvsøya
Måsøy
Kåfjord
Repvåg
Porsangerhalvøya
Sørøya
Hammerfest
Kvaløya
Seiland
Hasvik
Kvalsund
Russenes
Øksfjord
Alta
Talvik
Langfjord
Stabbursdalen
Lakselv
Porsangen
Børselv
Børselvfjellet
Kjøllefjord
Mehamn
Gamvik
Nordkinnhalvøya
Lebesby
Kalak
Ifjord
Ifjordfjellet
Berlevåg
Kongsfjord
Båtsfjord
Hamningberg
Vardø
Varangerhalvøya
Vadsø
Vestre Jakobselv
Nesseby
Varangerbotn
Tana
Skipagurra
Varangerfjorden
Bugøynes
Kirkenes
Bjørnevatn
Neiden
Grense Jakobselv
Petšenga
Nikel
Svanvik
AUSTHAVET
Hurtigrute
Utsjoki
Nuorgam
Sirma
Karasjok
Karigasniemi
Kevo
Paistunturit
FINNMARK
Finnmarksvidda
Kautokeino
Masi
Øvre Anarjokka
Lemmenjoki
Inari
Ivalo
INARIJÄRVI
Nellim
Akujärvi
Raja-Jooseppi
Saariselkä
Urho Kekkosen kansallispulsto
Vuotso
Sompio
Kaamanen
Sevettijärvi
Partakko
Enontekiö
Kaaresuvanto
Karesuando
Pallas-Ounastunturi
Muonio
Kittilä
Levi
Sodankylä
L A P I N
L Ä Ä N I
Pelkosenniemi
Savukoski
Salla
Kemijärvi
ARCTIC CIRCLE
Pello
NAPAPIIRI
ROVANIEMI
Ylitornio
Övertorneå
Pajala
Kolari
Kuusamo
Ranua
Tervola
Posio
Vittangi
Kovdor
Alakurtti
70
71

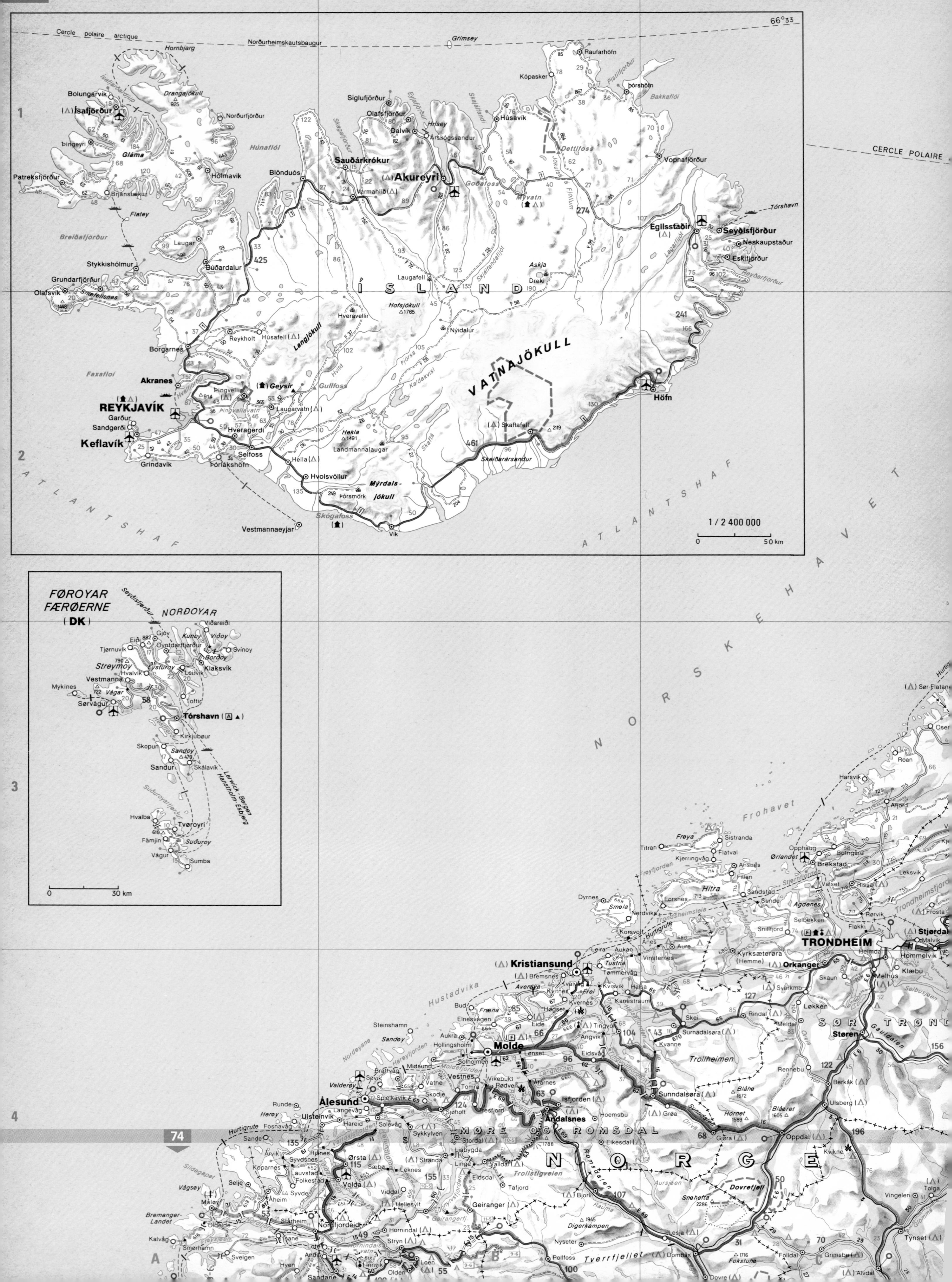
A
B
C
1
2
3
4
66°33
Cercle polaire arctique
Norðurheimskautsbaugur
Grímsey
CERCLE POLAIRE
Hornbjarg
Drangajökull
Bolungarvík
(△) Ísafjörður
Norðurfjörður
Þingeyri
Gláma
Húnaflói
Hólmavík
Patreksfjörður
Brjánslækur
Flatey
Breiðafjörður
Laugar
Búðardalur
Stykkishólmur
Grundarfjörður
Ólafsvík
Snæfellsnes
Siglufjörður
Ólafsfjörður
Hrísey
Dalvík
Árskógssandur
Húsavík
Kópasker
Raufarhöfn
Þórshöfn
Bakkaflói
Dettifoss
Vopnafjörður
Blönduós
Sauðárkrókur
(△) Akureyri
Varmahlíð (△)
Goðafoss
Mývatn
Egilsstaðir
Seyðisfjörður
Neskaupstaður
Eskifjörður
Reyðarfjörður
Tórshavn
Askja
Dreki
Laugafell
Í S L A N D
Hofsjökull
Hveravellir
Nýidalur
Langjökull
VATNAJÖKULL
Höfn
Borgarnes
Reykholt
Húsafell (△)
Faxaflói
Akranes
REYKJAVÍK
Garður
Sandgerði
Keflavík
Grindavík
Þingvellir
Geysir
Gullfoss
Laugarvatn (△)
Þingvallavatn
Hveragerði
Selfoss
Þorlákshöfn
Hekla
Landmannalaugar
Kaldakvísl
Skaftafell
Skeiðarársandur
Hella (△)
Hvolsvöllur
Mýrdals-jökull
Þórsmörk
Skógafoss
Vík
Vestmannaeyjar
ATLANTSHAF
1/2 400 000
0
50 km
FØROYAR
FÆRØERNE
(DK)
NORÐOYAR
Viðareiði
Viðoy
Kunoy
Borðoy
Klaksvík
Svínoy
Gjógv
Eiði
Tjørnuvík
Eysturoy
Streymoy
Leirvík
Hvalvík
Vestmanna
Mykines
Vágar
Sørvágur
Tórshavn
Kirkjubøur
Skopun
Sandoy
Sandur
Skálavík
Lerwick - Bergen
Hanstholm - Esbjerg
Hvalba
Tvøroyri
Fámjin
Suðuroy
Vágur
Sumba
0
30 km
NORSKEHAVET
Frohavet
Roan
Harsvik
Åfjord
Frøya
Sistranda
Titran
Flatval
Kjerringvåg
Hitra
Ørlandet
Brekstad
Botngård
Leksvik
Rissa
Agdenes
Trondheimsfjorden
Dyrnes
Smøla
Sandstad
Selbekken
Snillfjord
TRONDHEIM
Stjørdal
Hommelvik
Malvik
Heimdal
Klæbu
Melhus
Kyrksæterøra (Hemme)
Orkanger
(△) Kristiansund
Bremsnes
Tømmervåg
Averøya
Hustadvika
Bud
Elnesvågen
Aukra
Molde
Steinshamn
Sandøy
Hollingsholm
Ålesund
Runde
Herøy
Ulsteinvik
Fosnavåg
Åndalsnes
Isfjorden (△)
Sunndalsøra (△)
Surnadalsøra (△)
Rindal (△)
Løkken
Støren
SØR-TRØNDELAG
Trollheimen
Rennebu
Berkåk (△)
Oppdal (△)
Kvikne
MØRE OG ROMSDAL
N O R G E
Ørsta (△)
Volda (△)
Stranda
Geiranger (△)
Trollstigveien
Eikesdal (△)
Dovrefjell
Snøhetta
Tolga
Vingelen
Tynset (△)
Lesja (△)
Dombås
Digerkampen
Nordfjordeid
Stryn (△)
Loen
Olden
Hornindal (△)
Måløy
Selje
Bremanger-Landet
Kalvåg
Sandane
Hurtigrute
Tverrfjellet
Folldal
Alvdal

74

D
E
F
66
70
75
1
2
3
4
BODØ
Fauske
Rognan
Sulitjelma
Røkland
Glomfjord
NORDLAND
Meløy
Lønsdal
Svartisen
POLARSIRKELEN
Saltfjellet
MO I RANA
Nesna
Sandnessjøen
Mosjøen
Okstindan
Røssvatnet
Hattfjelldal
Trofors
Brønnøysund
Børgefjell
Namsskogan
Brekkvasselv
Høylandet
Namsos
Grong
NORD TRØNDELAG
Snåsa
Steinkjer
Verdalsøra
Levanger
Meråker
Storlien
Åre
Krokom
ÖSTERSUND
Sveg
Funäsdalen
Røros
Femundsmarka
Rogen
Hede
Vemdalen
Åsarna
Bräcke
Ånge
SUNDSVALL
Timrå
Härnösand
Kramfors
Sollefteå
Örnsköldsvik
Ramsele
Strömsund
Hammerdal
Dorotea
Åsele
Vilhelmina
Storuman
Tärnaby
Hemavan
Ammarnäs
Vindelfjällens N. R.
Arjeplog
Jäkkvik
Sorsele
Slagnäs
Arvidsjaur
Malå
Lycksele
Bjurholm
Fredrika
VÄSTERBOTTENS LÄN
VÄSTERNORRLANDS LÄN
JÄMTLANDS LÄN
SVERIGE
Kvikkjokk
Sarek
Padjelanta
Sjöfallet
Stora Lulevatten
Karats
POLCIRKELN
Hornavan
Uddjaure
Storavan
Gäddede
Frostviken
Hoting
Backe
Junsele
Näsåker
Kalkbyn
Borgafjäll
Saxnäs
Marsfjällen
Klimpfjäll
Fatmomakke
Kittelfjäll
Svenstavik
Berg
Hackås
Bispgården
Ragunda
Hammarstrand
Stugun
Liden
Indal
Nordingrå
Skuleskogen
Husum
Gideå
Nyåker
Trehörningsjö
Kilboghamn
Lovund
Vega
Leka
Rørvik
Vikna
Kolvereid

A
B
C
NORRBOTTENS LÄN
VÄSTERBOTTENS LÄN
VÄSTERNORRLANDS LÄN
SVERIGE
BOTTENVIKEN
PERÄMERI
POLCIRKELN
66
67
75
72
Fauske
Rognan
Sulitjelma
Padjelanta
Sarek
Sjöfallet
Stora Lulevatten
Malmberget
Gällivare
Porjus
Muddus
Harsprånget
Kvikkjokk
Jokkmokk
Vuollerim
Kåbdalis
Harads
Boden
LULEÅ
Gammelstaden
Bergnäset
Kalix
Haparanda
Pajala
Kolari
Junosuando
Övertorneå
Ylitornio
Karungi
Saltfjellet
Junkeren
Jäkkvik
Arjeplog
Laisvall
Ammarnäs
Hemavan
Tärnaby
Sorsele
Slagnäs
Arvidsjaur
Moskosel
Älvsbyn
Piteå
Storuman
Malå
Norsjö
Boliden
Skellefteå
Skelleftehamn
Lycksele
Vilhelmina
Dorotea
Åsele
Strömsund
Hoting
Vännäs
UMEÅ
Holmsund
Obbola
Nordmaling
Örnsköldsvik
Sollefteå
Kramfors
Härnösand
SUNDSVALL
Timrå
Ånge
Bräcke
Hammerdal
Kokkola
Karleby
Jakobstad
Pietersaari
Nykarleby
Uusikaarlepyy
VAASA
VASA
Seinäjoki
Lapua
Kurikka
Kaskinen
Kristinestad
Norra Kvarken
Merrenkurkku

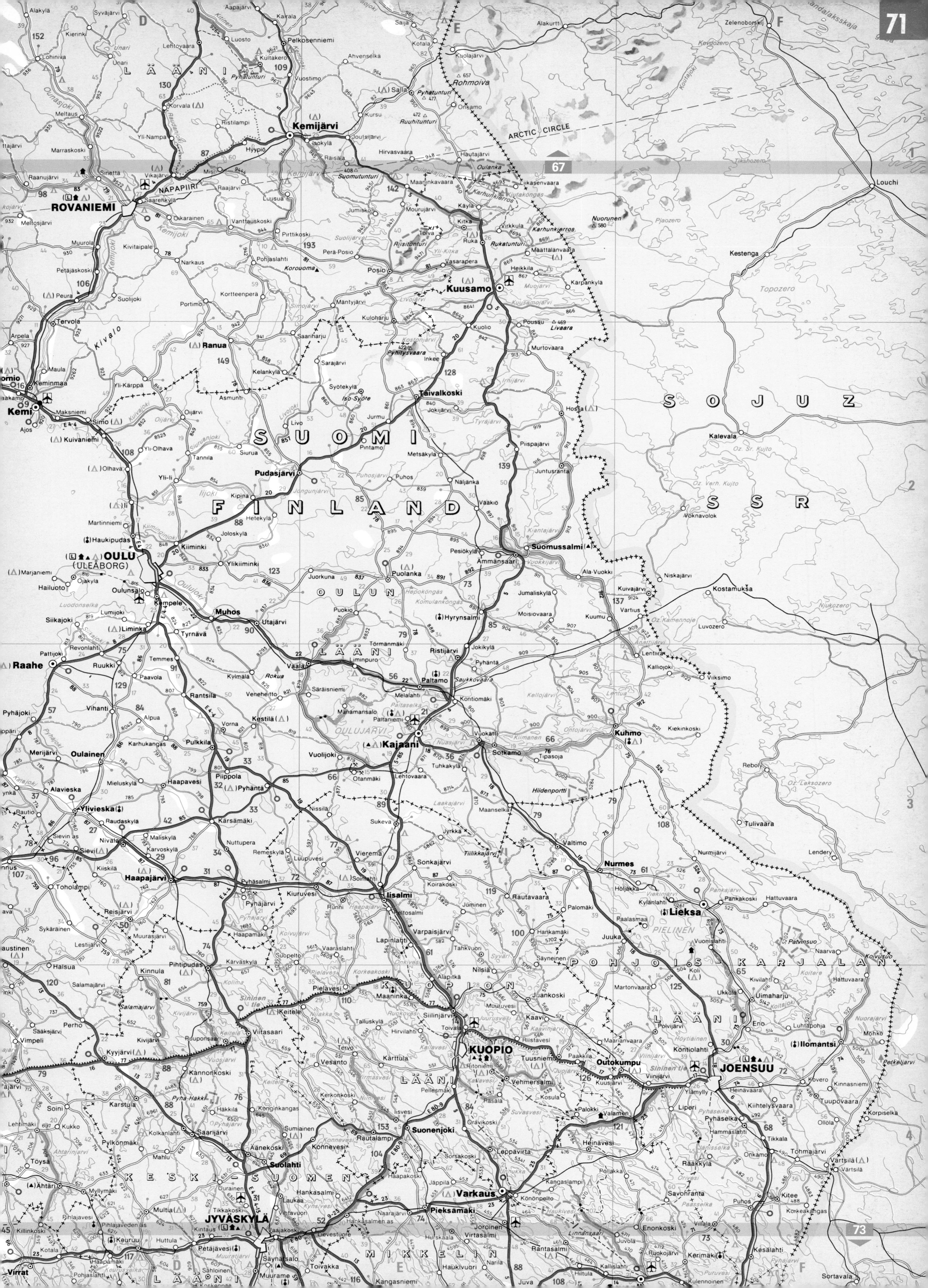
SUOMI
FINLAND
SOJUZ
SSR
OULUN LÄÄNI
LÄÄNI
POHJOIS-KARJALAN
LÄÄNI
KUOPION
LÄÄNI
KESKI-SUOMEN
MIKKELIN
LÄÄNI
ARCTIC CIRCLE
NAPAPIIRI
ROVANIEMI
Kemijärvi
Kuusamo
Ranua
Taivalkoski
Posio
Salla
Pelkosenniemi
Kemi
Simo
Tervola
OULU
(ULEÅBORG)
Pudasjärvi
Suomussalmi
Kuhmo
Puolanka
Hyrynsalmi
Kajaani
Vaala
Muhos
Raahe
Oulainen
Haapavesi
Ylivieska
Nivala
Haapajärvi
Iisalmi
Nurmes
Lieksa
Joensuu
JOENSUU
Outokumpu
KUOPIO
Suonenjoki
Varkaus
Pieksämäki
JYVÄSKYLÄ
Äänekoski
Suolahti
Viitasaari
Pihtipudas
Keitele
Kiuruvesi
Sotkamo
Valtimo
Ilomantsi
Kitee
Heinävesi
Sortavala
Värtsilä
Kostamuksa
Kalevala
Kestenga
Louchi
Topozero
Kuusamojärvi
Oulujärvi
Pielinen
Kallavesi
Juuka
Nilsiä
Siilinjärvi
Karttula
Pielavesi
Kannonkoski
Karstula
Saarijärvi
Keuruu
Virrat
Hailuoto
Kempele
Liminka
Utajärvi
Paltamo
Ristijärvi
Vuolijoki
Sievi
Kärsämäki
Pyhäjärvi
Rautavaara
Tuusniemi
Kaavi
Juankoski
Leppävirta
Rantasalmi
Enonkoski
Kerimäki
Rautalampi
Konnevesi
Hankasalmi
Joroinen
Juva
Kangasniemi
Ähtäri
Multia
Petäjävesi
Kinnula
Kivijärvi
Kyyjärvi
Perho
Vimpeli
Soini
Kokkola
Alavieska
Merijärvi
Pyhäjoki
Vihanti
Rantsila
Kestilä
Pulkkila
Piippola
Pyhäntä
Vieremä
Sonkajärvi
Lapinlahti
Varpaisjärvi
Maaninka
Vesanto
Tervo
Kontiolahti
Liperi
Polvijärvi
Eno
Tohmajärvi
Rääkkylä
Savonranta
Ylämylly
Tuupovaara
Kiihtelysvaara
Pyhäselkä
Hammaslahti
Hiidenportti
Rokua
Iso-Syöte
Rukatunturi
Pyhätunturi
Rohmoiva
Oulanka
Livaara
Nuorunen
Kiimingin
Haukipudas
Kiiminki
Ylikiiminki
Ii
Kuivaniemi
Pattijoki
Siikajoki
Lumijoki
Tyrnävä
Temmes
Ruukki
Paavola
Kemijoki
Ounasjoki
Kitinen
Iijoki
Oulujoki
Siikajoki
Pyhäjoki
Kalajoki
Ukkola
Koli
Vuonislahti
Patvinsuo
Uimaharju
Hattuvaara
Möhkö
Korpiselkä
Kalliojoki
Lentiira
Kuusamo
Ruka
Juntusranta
Hossa
Piispajärvi
Kuolio
Inkee
Kurenalus
Pintamo
Jurmu
Livo
Oijärvi
Yli-Olhava
Yli-Ii
Kipinä
Hetekylä
Joloskylä
Juorkuna
Ammänsaari
Vuokatti
Tipasoja
Maanselkä
Jyrkkä
Sukeva
Otanmäki
Lehtovaara
Manamansalo
Mieluskylä
Nuttupera
Karvoskylä
Tuhkakylä
Sortavala
Kulennoinen
Hirvensalmi
Haukivuori
Virtasalmi
Kinnasniemi
Kovero
Heinävaara
Onkamo
Tikkala
Ollola
Vartsilä
Kitee
Puhos
Korkeakangas
Vuokkijärvi
Ala-Vuokki
Vartius
Kuivajärvi
Niskajärvi
Viiksimo
Kiekinkoski
Reboly
Tulivaara
Lendery
Voknavolok
Luvozero
Oz. Kamennoje
Oz. Sr. Kujto
Oz. Verh. Kujto
Oz. Leksozero
Njukozero
Zelenoborskij
Alakurtti
Kuolajärvi
Onkamo
Vuostimo
Savukoski
Aapajärvi
Sodankylä
Luosto
Kairala
Saija
Kotala
Raanujärvi
Sinettä
Marraskoski
Meltaus
Lohiniva
Kierinki
Alakylä
Syväjärvi
Oikarainen
Vanttauskoski
Muurola
Petäjäskoski
Peura
Suolijoki
Portimo
Kortteenperä
Narkaus
Pohjaslahti
Kivitaipale
Arpela
Maula
Keminmaa
Maksniemi
Ajos
Olhava
Martinniemi
Marjaniemi
Ojakyla
Oulunsalo
Revonlahti
Mäntyjärvi
Kuloharju
Saariharju
Sarajärvi
Kelankylä
Syötekylä
Asmunti
Yli-Kärppä
Jokijärvi
Metsäkylä
Näljänkä
Puhos
Vääkiö
Pesiökylä
Jumaliskylä
Moisiovaara
Kuumu
Tormänmäki
Liminpuro
Melalahti
Paltaniemi
Säräisniemi
Veneheitto
Kylmälä
Vorna
Karhukangas
Alpua
Raudaskylä
Maliskylä
Kiiskilä
Toholampi
Lestijärvi
Halsua
Salamajärvi
Kärväskylä
Haapamäki
Pyhäsalmi
Runni
Peltosalmi
Jumiskoski
Koirakoski
Sulkava
Sorsakoski
Kangaslampi
Könönpelto
Haukivesi
Linnansaari
Paasselkä
Orivesi
Pyhäselkä
Viinijärvi
Kuusjärvi
Sysmäjärvi
Tohmajärvi
Raudanjoki
Ristilampi
Yli-Nampa
Hyypiö
Misi
Raajärvi
Lusua
Pirttikoski
Perä-Posio
Korouoma
Vasarapera
Heikkilä
Kärpänkylä
Murtovaara
Poussu
Kitka
Käylä
Mourujärvi
Jumisko
Suomutunturi
Raisala
Isokylä
Joutsijärvi
Hirvasvaara
Hautajärvi
Kursu
Ruuhitunturi
Kuktakero
Pyhätunturi
Kultakero
Ahvenselkä
Lehtovaara
Korvala
Vikajärvi
Saarenkylä
Meltosjärvi

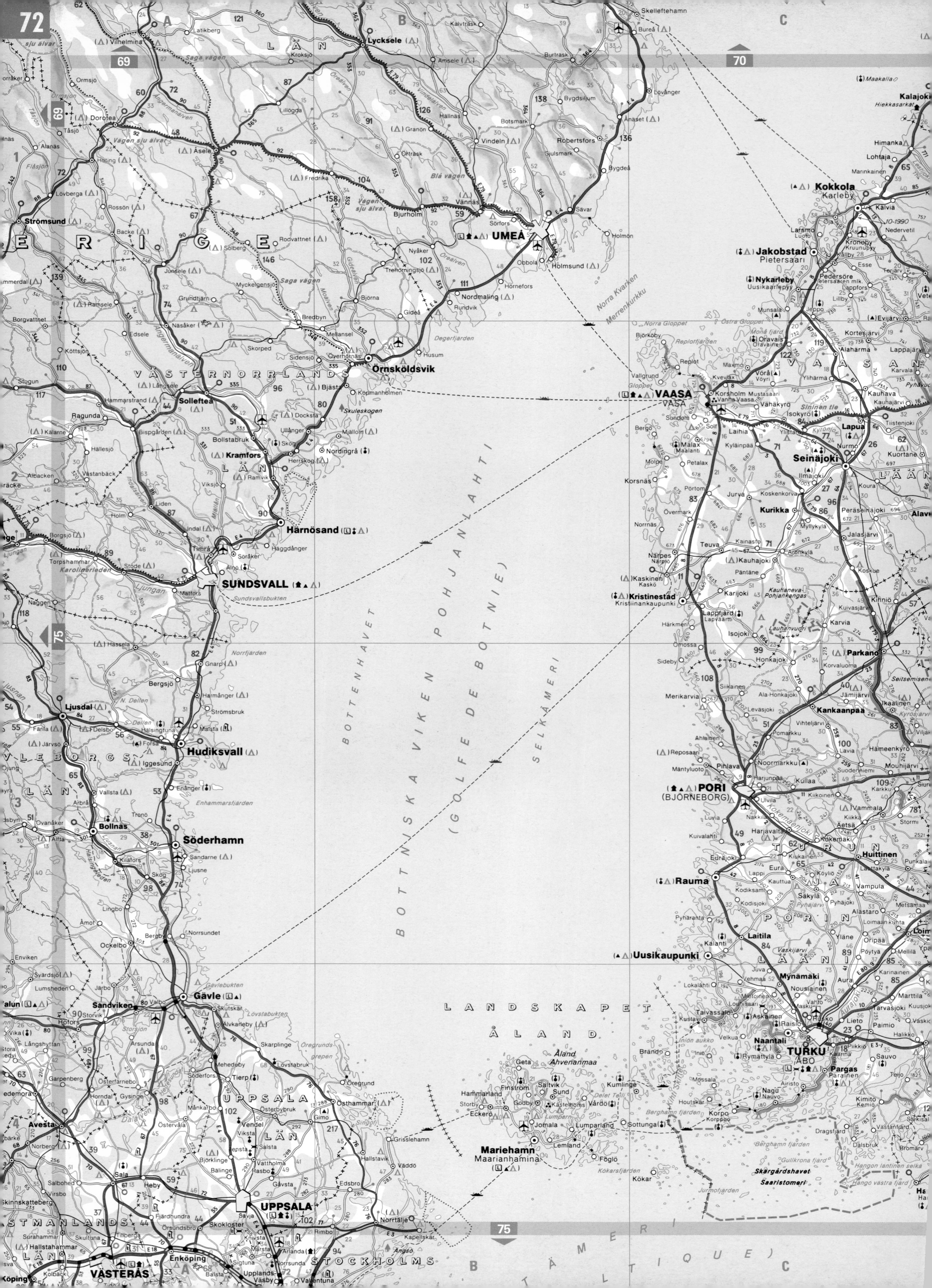
69
70
75
A
B
C
SVERIGE
VÄSTERNORRLANDS LÄN
UPPSALA LÄN
VÄSTMANLANDS LÄN
STOCKHOLMS
BOTTENHAVET
BOTTNISKA VIKEN POHJANLAHTI (GOLFE DE BOTNIE)
SELKÄMERI
LANDSKAPET ÅLAND
VAASAN LÄÄNI
TURUN JA PORIN LÄÄNI
Skellefteå
Lycksele
Vilhelmina
Dorotea
Åsele
Strömsund
Vännäs
UMEÅ
Holmsund
Örnsköldsvik
Sollefteå
Kramfors
Härnösand
SUNDSVALL
Timrå
Ljusdal
Hudiksvall
Bollnäs
Söderhamn
Gävle
Sandviken
Tierp
Östhammar
Avesta
UPPSALA
Norrtälje
Enköping
VÄSTERÅS
Kokkola
Karleby
Jakobstad
Pietersaari
Nykarleby
VAASA
VASA
Seinäjoki
Lapua
Kaskinen
Kristinestad
Kristiinankaupunki
Parkano
Kankaanpää
PORI
(BJÖRNEBORG)
Rauma
Uusikaupunki
Naantali
TURKU
ÅBO
Pargas
Mariehamn
Maarianhamina
Norra Kvarken
Merenkurkku
Skärgårdshavet
Saaristomeri

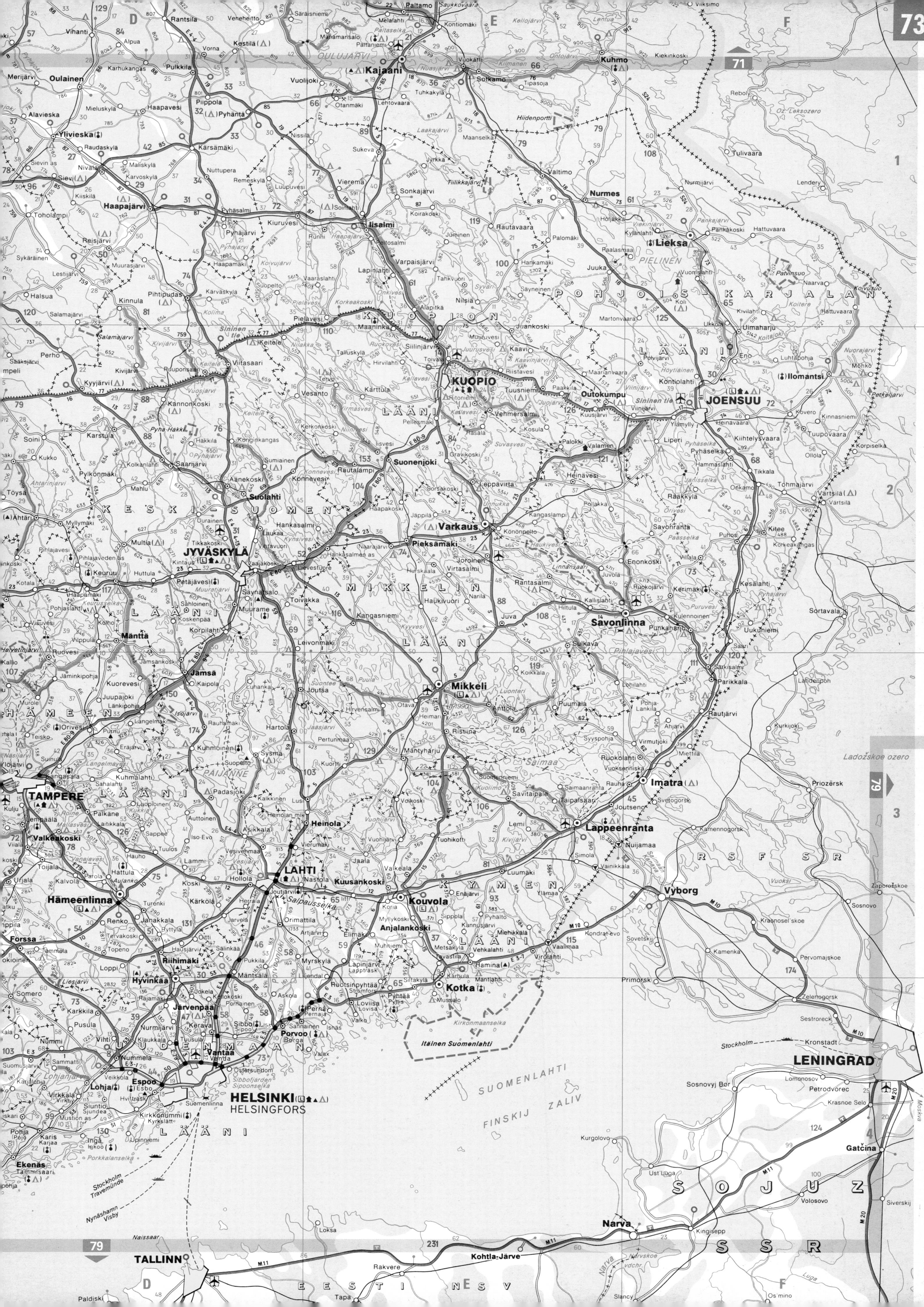
Kajaani
Kuhmo
Oulujärvi
Ylivieska
Haapajärvi
Iisalmi
Nurmes
Lieksa
Pielinen
Pohjois-Karjalan lääni
Kuopion lääni
KUOPIO
JOENSUU
Outokumpu
Ilomantsi
Varkaus
Pieksämäki
Savonlinna
JYVÄSKYLÄ
Keski-Suomen lääni
Mikkelin lääni
Mikkeli
Mänttä
Jämsä
TAMPERE
Hämeen lääni
Valkeakoski
Hämeenlinna
Forssa
Riihimäki
Hyvinkää
Järvenpää
Lahti
Heinola
Kouvola
Kuusankoski
Anjalankoski
Kymen lääni
Hamina
Kotka
Lappeenranta
Imatra
Porvoo
Vantaa
Espoo
HELSINKI
HELSINGFORS
Uudenmaan lääni
Lohja
Ekenäs
Tammisaari
Itäinen Suomenlahti
SUOMENLAHTI
FINSKIJ ZALIV
Vyborg
Ladožskoe ozero
Priozërsk
Sortavala
Zelenogorsk
Sestroreck
Kronstadt
LENINGRAD
Lomonosov
Petrodvorec
Gatčina
Kingisepp
Narva
Kohtla-Järve
Rakvere
TALLINN
Paldiski
Tapa
EESTI NSV
RSFSR
SOJUZ SSR
Stockholm
Travemünde
Nynäshamn
Visby
71
79

A
B
C
1
2
3
4
68
76
NORGE
MØRE OG ROMSDAL
SOGN OG FJORDANE
HORDALAND
ROGALAND
VEST-AGDER
AUST-AGDER
TELEMARK
BUSKERUD
OPPLAND
VESTFOLD
ØSTFOLD
AKERSHUS
SØR-TRØNDELAG
BOHUS
Molde
Ålesund
Åndalsnes
Sunndalsøra
Oppdal
Støren
Florø
Førde
Voss
BERGEN
Haugesund
STAVANGER
Sandnes
Egersund
Flekkefjord
Mandal
Kristiansand
Arendal
Grimstad
Skien
Porsgrunn
Larvik
Sandefjord
Tønsberg
Horten
Drammen
OSLO
Lillestrøm
Hønefoss
Lillehammer
Gjøvik
Hamar
Moss
Fredrikstad
Sarpsborg
Halden
Kongsberg
Notodden
Lyngdal
Jostedalsbreen
Jotunheimen
Hardangervidda
Dovrefjell
Rondane
Sognefjorden
Hardangerfjorden
Hurtigrute
Newcastle
Hanstholm
Hirtshals
Frederikshavn
Harwich
Lerwick
Tórshavn
Strömstad
Göteborg

ÖSTERSUND
Krokom
Frösön
Sunne
Brunflo
Storsjön
Åre
Undersåker
Duved
Enafors
Storlien
Snasahögarna
Sylene
Helagsfjället
Ljungdalen
Storsjö
Hackås
Berg
Svenstavik
Åsarna
Bräcke
Gällö
Ragunda
Hammarstrand
Sollefteå
Kramfors
Bollstabruk
Örnsköldsvik
Härnösand
Timrå
SUNDSVALL
Sundsvallsbukten
Alnö
Matfors
Stöde
Ånge
Torpshammar
VÄSTERNORRLANDS LÄN
Funäsdalen
Tännäs
Röros
Rogen
Femundsmarka
Hede
Vemdalen
Klövsjö
Sveg
Älvros
Ytterhogdal
Lillhärdal
Idre
Särna
Grövelsjön
Nipfjället
Fjätervålen
Ljusdal
Färila
Los
Hamra
Järvsö
Delsbo
Hudiksvall
Iggesund
Forsa
Enånger
GÄVLEBORGS LÄN
Bollnäs
Edsbyn
Alfta
Ovanåker
Söderhamn
Sandarne
Ljusne
Kilafors
Skog
Bergby
Norrsundet
Ockelbo
Gävle
Sandviken
Hofors
Storvik
Valbo
Skutskär
Älvkarleby
Mora
Orsa
Älvdalen
Sälen
Transtrand
Rättvik
Siljan
Leksand
Falun
Borlänge
Ludvika
Smedjebacken
Hedemora
Avesta
Säter
Fagersta
Norberg
Grängesberg
KOPPARBERGS LÄN
Malung
Vansbro
Torsby
Hagfors
Sunne
Munkfors
Arvika
Charlottenberg
Eda glasbruk
Karlstad
Kil
Forshaga
Deje
Filipstad
Grums
Säffle
Åmål
Kristinehamn
Karlskoga
VÄRMLANDS LÄN
Hällefors
Kopparberg
Lindesberg
Nora
Örebro
Kumla
Hallsberg
Laxå
Askersund
ÖREBRO LÄN
Gullspång
Vänern
Mariestad
Lidköping
Götene
Skara
Skövde
Falköping
Tibro
Vara
Vänersborg
Trollhättan
Mellerud
SKARABORGS LÄN
Motala
Vadstena
Mjölby
Linköping
NORRKÖPING
Söderköping
Finspång
Kolmården
ÖSTERGÖTLANDS LÄN
Nyköping
Oxelösund
Katrineholm
Flen
Vingåker
Eskilstuna
Strängnäs
Mariefred
Södertälje
SÖDERMANLANDS LÄN
Västerås
Köping
Arboga
Kungsör
Sala
Heby
Enköping
Hallstahammar
VÄSTMANLANDS LÄN
Uppsala
Tierp
Östhammar
Öregrund
Norrtälje
Sigtuna
Märsta
Arlanda
Upplands-Väsby
Vallentuna
Täby
Lidingö
Sollentuna
STOCKHOLM
Tumba
Nynäshamn
Drottningholm
Gnesta
Trosa
UPPSALA LÄN
STOCKHOLMS LÄN
BOTTENHAVET
BOTTNISKA VIKEN
Gotska Sandön
Helsinki
Gdansk
69
72
77
1
2
3
4
E
F
D

Egersund
Flekkefjord
Kristiansand
Mandal
Arendal
Grimstad
Lillesand
Risør
Kragerø
Strömstad
Uddevalla
GÖTEBORGS OCH BOHUS LÄN
Kungälv
GÖTEBORG
Kungsbacka
Varberg
Falkenberg
SKAGERRAK
Skagen
Hirtshals
Hjørring
Frederikshavn
Læsø
Hanstholm
Thisted
ÅLBORG
Brønderslev
Vendsyssel
Himmerland
Ålborg Bugt
KATTEGAT
Anholt
NORDSJØEN (NORDSJÖ)
Thyborøn
Lemvig
Struer
Skive
Viborg
Randers
Grenå
Holstebro
Ringkøbing
Herning
Silkeborg
DANMARK
JYLLAND
ÅRHUS
Ebeltoft
Skjern
Horsens
Vejle
Esbjerg
Fredericia
Ribe
Kolding
Haderslev
Åbenrå
Tønder
Sønderborg
Kalundborg
Holbæk
Hillerød
Helsingør
KØBENHAVN
Roskilde
Køge
SJÆLLAND
Ringsted
Slagelse
Sorø
Næstved
Vordingborg
ODENSE
Nyborg
FYN
Svendborg
Langeland
Lolland
Falster
Nakskov
Maribo
Nykøbing F
Møn
Sylt
Westerland
Flensburg
Schleswig
Husum
Rendsburg
KIEL
Neumünster
Itzehoe
Cuxhaven
Bremerhaven
Wilhelmshaven
LÜBECK
Travemünde
Wismar
ROSTOCK
Güstrow
Fehmarn
Kieler Bucht
Mecklenburger Bucht
Deutsche Bucht
Ostfriesische Inseln
Nordfriesische Inseln
Helgoland
Höganäs
74
36
1
2
3
4

Södertälje
Katrineholm
Nyköping
NORRKÖPING
LINKÖPING
Motala
Mariestad
Skövde
Falköping
Lidköping
Borås
JÖNKÖPING
Nässjö
Eksjö
Vetlanda
Tranås
Västervik
Visby
Gotska Sandön
Fårö
GOTLANDS LÄN
Gotland
Oskarshamn
Värnamo
Växjö
Ljungby
KRONOBERGS LÄN
KALMAR LÄN
Kalmar
Nybro
Öland
Borgholm
Karlskrona
Ronneby
Karlshamn
BLEKINGE LÄN
Kristianstad
Hässleholm
KRISTIANSTADS LÄN
MALMÖHUS LÄN
Lund
Ystad
Simrishamn
Hanöbukten
BORNHOLM (DK)
Rønne
ÖSTERSJÖN
Rügen
Greifswald
Kołobrzeg
Koszalin
Swinoujście
Helsinki
Gdansk
Travemünde
København
75
78
Uddevalla, Oslo
Trollhättan
GÖTEBORG
Hisingen
Mölndal
Mölnlycke
Lerum
Lindome
Landvetter
Angered
Partille
Kungälv
Örebro, Stockholm
Borås, Jönköping
Helsingborg, Malmö
0
5 km

Bottenhavet
SF
Turku
HELSINKI
Åland (SF)
Mariehamn
Vendel
Uppsala
Skokloster
STOCKHOLM
Drottningholm
Gripsholm
S
SVEALAND
TALLINN
ESTON
Saaremaa
Hiiumaa
Rižskij Zaliv
RĪGA
LATVIJ
LITVA
Visby
Gotland
Fårö
GÖTALAND
Kalmar
Öland
Linköping
Vadstena
Norrköping
Jönköping
BALTIC SEA
MER BALTIQUE
Bornholm (DK)
Kaliningrad
Klaipėda
Kaunas
Šiauliai
Liepāja
Gdynia
GDAŃSK
Sopot
Malbork
Toruń
Bydgoszcz
PL
WARSZAWA
Łódź
POZNAŃ
WROCŁAW
Częstochowa
Lublin
Radom
Białystok
Szczecin
Rügen
Stralsund
Rostock
BERLIN
Potsdam
DDR
DRESDEN
LEIPZIG
Meißen
KØBENHAVN
Malmö
Lund
Helsingborg
Halmstad
Kungsbacka
Borås
Trollhättan
Vänersborg
Karlstad
Örebro
Västerås
Gävle
Falun
Mora
Rättvik
Sundsvall
Kristianstad
Karlskrona
Ystad
Trelleborg
Simrishamn
Frankfurt a.d. Oder
Zielona Góra
Cottbus
Legnica
Kalisz
Gniezno
Koszalin
Słupsk
Elbląg
Olsztyn
Mazury
Grodno
Brest
Sochaczew
Płock
Włocławek
Inowrocław
Grudziądz
Piotrków Trybunalski
Kielce
Pabianice
Piła
Gorzów Wielkopolski
Stargard Szczeciński
Kołobrzeg
Neubrandenburg
Greifswald
Vilkaviškis
Panevėžys
Jelgava
Pärnu
Haapsalu
Tartu
Kärdla
Porvoo
Espoo
Hanko
Ekenäs
Rauma
Nynäshamn
Södertälje
Norrtälje
Kappelskär
Oskarshamn
Västervik
Vimmerby
Växjö
Ronneby
Karlshamn
Ljungby
Värnamo
Falköping
Skövde
Mariestad
Lidköping
Arvika
Kristinehamn
Karlskoga
Säffle
Åmål
Ängelholm
Landskrona
Falsterbo
Rønne
Allinge
Łeba
Władysławowo
Ustka
Darłowo
Lębork
Kartuzy
Tczew
Starogard Gdański
Chojnice
Szczecinek
Świnoujście
Wolgast
Anklam
Pasewalk
Prenzlau
Neustrelitz
Waren
Wittstock
Neuruppin
Oranienburg
Eberswalde
Bad Freienwalde
Fürstenwalde
Brandenburg
Rathenow
Nauen
Luckenwalde
Jüterbog
Wittenberg
Torgau
Bitterfeld
Halle
Wurzen
Riesa
Görlitz
Bautzen
Hoyerswerda
Senftenberg
Spremberg
Lübben
Guben
Eisenhüttenstadt
Kostrzyn
Świebodzin
Nowa Sól
Głogów
Żagań
Żary
Bolesławiec
Lubań
Jelenia Góra
Oleśnica
Brzeg
Kluczbork
Wieluń
Sieradz
Zduńska Wola
Bełchatów
Radomsko
Tomaszów Mazowiecki
Skierniewice
Żyrardów
Kutno
Konin
Koło
Września
Środa Wielkopolska
Jarocin
Kościan
Leszno
Gostyń
Krotoszyn
Ostrów Wielkopolski
Rawicz
Wolsztyn
Międzychód
Oborniki
Wągrowiec
Czarnków
Nakło n. Notecią
Chełmno
Świecie
Kwidzyn
Iława
Ostróda
Mława
Ciechanów
Pułtusk
Ostrołęka
Łomża
Ełk
Augustów
Suwałki
Giżycko
Mrągowo
Kętrzyn
Lidzbark Warmiński
Braniewo
Mamonovo
Baltijsk
Svetlogorsk
Sovetsk
Neman
Gusev
Černjachovsk
Pravdinsk
Polessk
Gvardejsk
Marijampolė
Alytus
Druskininkai
Prienai
Kapsukas
Jurbarkas
Tauragė
Šilutė
Palanga
Plungė
Telšiai
Mažeikiai
Skuodas
Kuršėnai
Radviliškis
Raseiniai
Kėdainiai
Joniškis
Biržai
Bauska
Dobele
Saldus
Kuldīga
Ventspils
Talsi
Tukums
Jūrmala
Ogre
Sigulda
Cēsis
Valmiera
Salacgrīva
Rūjiena
Kolka
Viljandi
Kilingi-Nõmme
Virtsu
Orissaare
Kingissepp
Paldiski
Paide
Türi
Tapa
Rakvere
Ostrów Mazowiecka
Siedlce
Mińsk Mazowiecki
Otwock
Międzyrzec Podlaski
Biała Podlaska
Terespol
Radzyń Podlaski
Włodawa
Chełm
Krasnystaw
Kraśnik
Puławy
Dęblin
Kazimierz Dolny
Zamość
Starachowice
Skarżysko-Kamienna
Ostrowiec Świętokrzyski
Sandomierz
Stalowa Wola
Biłgoraj
Hajnówka
Bielsk Podlaski
Sokołów Podlaski
Wisła
Odra
Narew
Bug
Pilica
Nemunas
Kurššiu Zaliv
Zatoka Gdańska
Zalew Wiślany
Puszcza Białowieska
Góry Świętokrzyskie
POMORZE
SKÅNE
SMÅLAND
MECKLENBURG
BRANDENBURG
SACHSEN

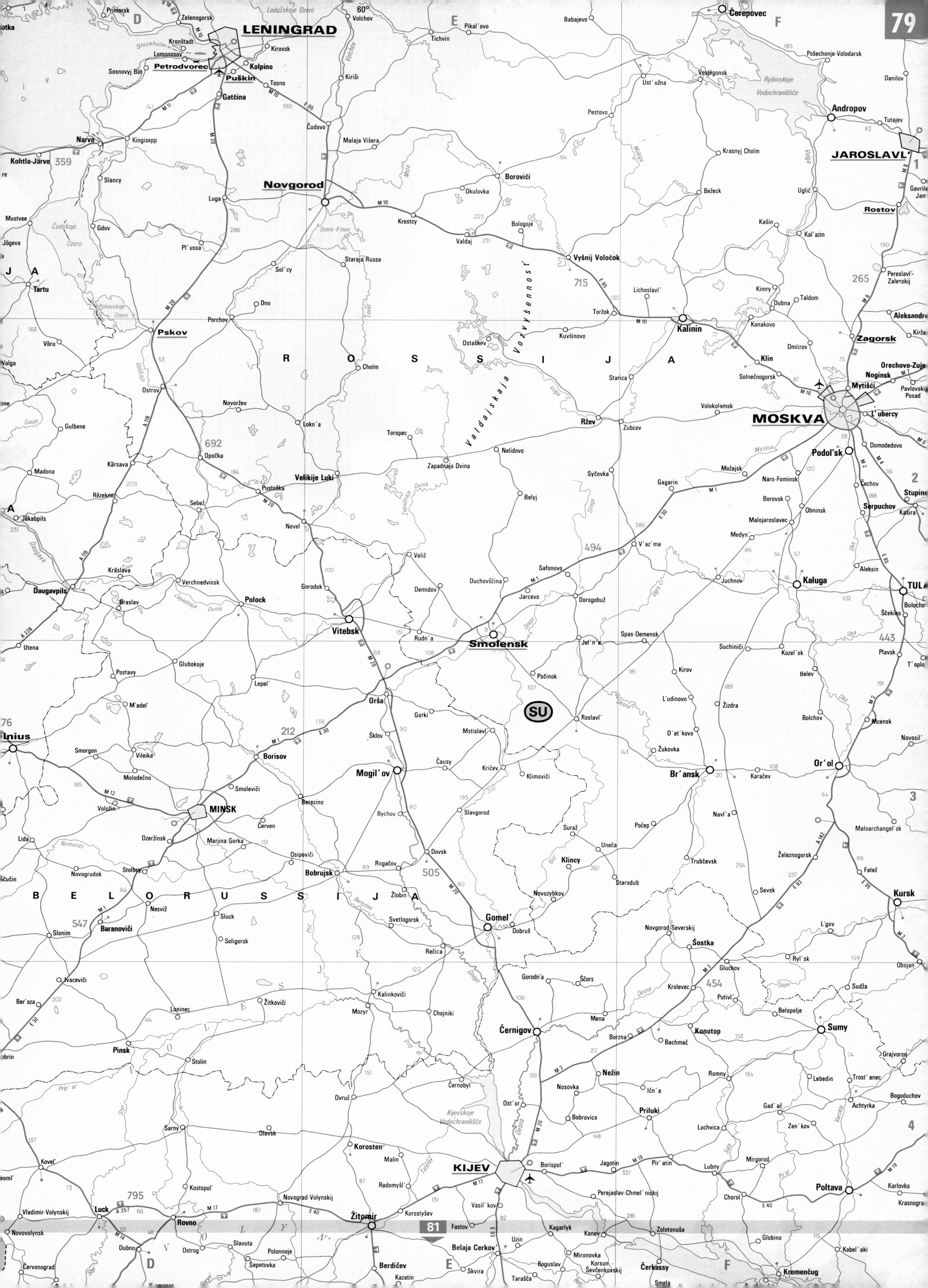
LENINGRAD
Primorsk
Zelenogorsk
Ladožskoje Ozero
60°
Volchov
Pikal'ovo
Babajevo
Čerepovec
Kronštadt
Kirovsk
Lomonosov
Tichvin
Petrodvorec
Kolpino
Puškin
Sosnovyj Bor
Tosno
Kiriši
Vesjegonsk
Ust'užna
Pošechonje-Volodarsk
Rybinskoje Vodochranilišče
Danilov
Gatčina
Pestovo
Andropov
Tutajev
Čudovo
Narva
Kingisepp
Malaja Višera
Kohtla-Järve
Krasnyj Cholm
JAROSLAVL'
Slancy
Luga
Novgorod
Borovići
Okulovka
Bežeck
Uglič
Gavrilov Jam
Rostov
Mustvee
Krestcy
Gdov
Bologoje
Kašin
Kal'azin
Jõgeva
Valdaj
Ozero Il'men
Pl'ussa
Vyšnij Voloček
Staraja Russa
Sol'cy
Pereslavl'-Zalesskij
Tartu
Lichoslavl'
Kimry
Taldom
Dubna
Dno
Porchov
Toržok
Kalinin
Konakovo
Aleksandrov
Pskov
Kuvšinovo
Zagorsk
Võru
Ostaškov
Dmitrov
Valdajskaja Vozvyšennost'
R O S S I J A
Cholm
Klin
Orechovo-Zujevo
Valga
Noginsk
Starica
Solnečnogorsk
Mytišči
Pavlovskij Posad
Ostrov
Novoržev
Volokolamsk
Rževv
Zubcov
MOSKVA
L'ubercy
Gulbene
Lokn'a
Toropec
Domodedovo
Podol'sk
Opočka
Nelidovo
Možajsk
Kārsava
Madona
Zapadnaja Dvina
Naro-Fominsk
Velikije Luki
Syčovka
Gagarin
Čechov
Stupino
Rēzekne
Pustoška
Belyj
Borovsk
Serpuchov
Kašira
Jēkabpils
Sebež
Obninsk
Nevel
Malojaroslavec
Medyn'
Daugava
V'az'ma
Veliž
Aleksin
Krāslava
Safonovo
Verchnedvinsk
Gorodok
Duchovščina
Juchnov
Kaluga
TULA
Daugavpils
Demidov
Polock
Jarcevo
Dorogobuž
Bolochovo
Braslav
Ščekino
Vitebsk
Rudn'a
Smolensk
Spas-Demensk
Utena
Jel'n'a
Suchiniči
Kozel'sk
Plavsk
T'oply
Glubokoje
Postavy
Počinok
Kirov
Lepel'
Belev
M'adel'
Orša
SU
Ľudinovo
Žizdra
Gorki
Roslavl'
Bolchov
Mcensk
Vilnius
Šklov
Mstislavl'
D'at'kovo
Novosil'
Smorgon
Vileika
Borisov
Žukovka
Molodečno
Mogil'ov
Čausy
Kričev
Br'ansk
Karačev
Or'ol
Klimoviči
Smoleviči
Voložin
MINSK
Berezino
Slavgorod
Bychov
Navl'a
Červen
Počep
Maloarchangel'sk
Lida
Dzeržinsk
Marjina Gorka
Suraž
Nemunas
Osipoviči
Dovsk
Unečа
Železnogorsk
Novogrudok
Stolbcy
Rogačov
Bobrujsk
Klincy
Trubčevsk
Fatež
Starodub
Ščučin
Žlobin
Sevsk
B E L O R U S S I J A
Nesviž
Novozybkov
Kursk
Sluck
Gomel'
Baranoviči
Svetlogorsk
Dobruš
Slonim
Soligorsk
Novgorod-Severskij
L'gov
Šostka
Rečica
Ryl'sk
Obojan'
Gluchov
Ivaceviči
Gorodn'a
Ščors
Kalinkoviči
Krolevec
Sudža
Ber'oza
Žitkoviči
Putivl'
Luninec
Mozyr
Chojniki
Mena
Belopolje
Černigov
Konotop
Sumy
Pinsk
Borzna
Bachmač
Grajvoron
Kobrin
Stolin
Nežin
Romny
Lebedin
Trost'anec
Pripjat
Černobyl'
Nosovka
Ičn'a
Bogoduchov
Ovruč
Ost'or
Kijevskoje Vodochranilišče
Priluki
Gad'ač
Achtyrka
Bobrovica
Sarny
Olevsk
Lochvica
Zen'kov
Korosten'
Malin
Desna
Kovel'
KIJEV
Borispol'
Jagotin
Pir'atin
Lubny
Mirgorod
Radomyšl'
Perejaslav-Chmel'nickij
Poltava
Karlovka
Krasnograd
Kostopol'
Chorol
Vladimir-Volynskij
Luck
Rovno
Novograd-Volynskij
Korostyšev
Vasil'kov
Žitomir
Fastov
Zolotonoša
Novovolynsk
81
Kagarlyk
Kanev
Globino
Dubno
Ostrog
Slavuta
Polonnoje
Berdičev
Belaja Cerkov'
Uzin
Mironovka
Kobel'aki
Šepetovka
Boguslav
Korsun-Ševčenkovskij
Čerkassy
Červonograd
Skvira
Kremenčug
Kazatin
Tarašča
Smela

DDR
CS
A
H
YU
I
AL
78
39
43
44
46
47
54
LEIPZIG
DRESDEN
Karl-Marx-Stadt
Cottbus
Görlitz
Zielona Góra
Legnica
WROCŁAW
Wałbrzych
Kalisz
ŁÓDŹ
Radom
Lublin
Częstochowa
Opole
Bytom
Sosnowiec
Katowice
Gliwice
KRAKÓW
Wieliczka
Tarnów
Rzeszów
Przemyśl
Kielce
PRAHA
Karlovy Vary
Plzeň
Karlštejn
Hradec Králové
Krkonoše
Ostrava
Olomouc
Brno
Macocha
Kroměříž
Gottwaldov
Telč
České Budějovice
Hluboká n. Vlt.
Regensburg
Šumava
Linz
Melk
Donautal
WIEN
Bratislava
Esztergom
SALZBURG
Salzkammergut
Graz
Großglockner
Klagenfurt
Sopron
Győr
BUDAPEST
Miskolc
Eger
Debrecen
Oradea
Košice
Zakopane
Dobšiná
Baradla
Banská Bystrica
Žilina
Nitra
Szombathely
Székesfehérvár
Veszprém
Kecskemét
Balaton
Szeged
Arad
Timişoara
Pécs
Subotica
Novi Sad
BEOGRAD
Osijek
ZAGREB
Ljubljana
SLOVENIJA
HRVATSKA
BOSNA I HERCEGOVINA
Sarajevo
Trebević
Mostar
Tuzla
Plitvička Jezera
Zadar
Split
Trogir
Dubrovnik
Boka Kotorska
CRNA GORA
Titograd
Shkodër
Tiranë
Durrës
SRBIJA
Studenica
Gračanica
Dečani
Peć
Priština
Skopje
Ohrid
Bitola
MAKED
Trieste
VENEZIA
Rijeka
Pula
Ravenna
Rimini
San Marino
Ancona
Perugia
Assisi
Pescara
ROMA
Vaticano
Tivoli
Montecassino
Foggia
Bari
MER ADRIATIQUE
ADRIATIC SEA
Dalmatska Kota

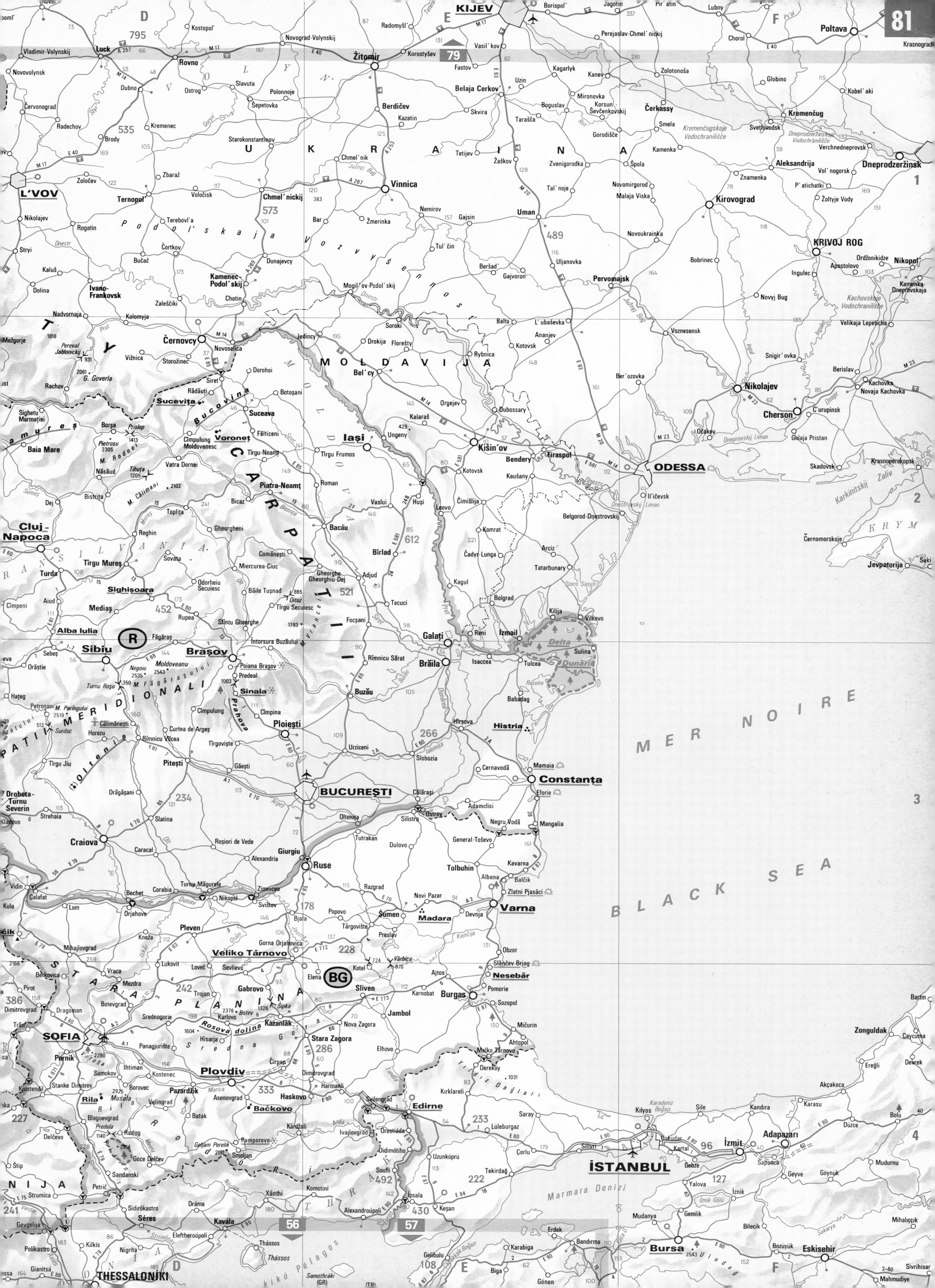
KIJEV
Žitomir
Luck
Rovno
Vladimir-Volynskij
L'VOV
Ternopol'
Chmel'nickij
Vinnica
Berdičev
Belaja Cerkov'
Uman
Čerkassy
Kremenčug
Poltava
Dneprodzeržinsk
Kirovograd
KRIVOJ ROG
Nikopol'
Pervomajsk
Nikolajev
Cherson
ODESSA
Kišin'ov
Bendery
Tiraspol
Bel'cy
Černovcy
Ivano-Frankovsk
Kamenec-Podol'skij
U K R A I N A
MOLDAVIJA
Podol'skaja vozvyšennost'
KRYM
Jevpatorija
Suceava
Iași
Bacău
Piatra-Neamț
Cluj-Napoca
Tîrgu Mureș
Sibiu
Brașov
Galați
Brăila
Tulcea
Constanța
Ploiești
BUCUREȘTI
Pitești
Craiova
Giurgiu
Ruse
CARPAȚII
CARPAȚII MERIDIONALI
TRANSILVANIA
R
BG
Delta Dunării
Varna
Burgas
Pleven
Veliko Tărnovo
SOFIA
Plovdiv
Stara Zagora
STARA PLANINA
Edirne
İSTANBUL
İzmit
Adapazarı
Bursa
Eskisehir
Zonguldak
Tekirdağ
Kavála
THESSALONÍKI
Marmara Denizi
MER NOIRE
BLACK SEA
79
56
57

Index

F Lorsqu'un nom figure plusieurs fois dans l'index, une précision est ajoutée entre parenthèses pour permettre de l'identifier plus facilement: pays, région ou ville la plus proche, élément géographique d'après les abréviations ci-dessous.

GB Where there are two or more identical place names, the name of the distinguishing country or region or nearest large town is given in brackets; geographical features are indicated by the abbreviations below.

Ákr	Ákra, Akrotírion
B	Bay, Baie, Bucht, Bahía, Baia, Bukt(en), Bugt, Bukhta
Bgem	Barragem
C	Cape, Cap, Cabo, Capo
Co	County
Ch	Chaîne
Chan	Channel
Dépt	Département
Emb	Embalse
Ez	Ezero
G	Gulf, Golfe, Golfo
Gges	Gorges
I(s), *I(s)*	Isle(s), Island(s), Ile(s), Ilha(s), Isla(s), Isola(e)
Jez	Jezero, Jezioro
K	Kanal, Kanaal
L, *L*	Lake, Loch, Lough, Llyn, Lac, Laguna, Lago, Limni
Liq	Liquen
Meg	Méga, Megál, -a, -i, -o
Mikr	Mikr-í, -ón
Mgne(s)	Montagne(s)
M, Mte(s)	Maj, Maj'e, Monte(s)
Mt(s), *Mt(s)*	Mount(s), Mountain(s), Mont(s)
Mti	Monti, Muntii
Nac	Nacional(e)
Nat	National
Naz	Nazionale
N	Nissí, Nissos
Ni	Nissiá, Nissi
Os	Ostrov(a)
Ot	Otok(i), Otoci
Oz	Ozero(a)
P	Pass
Pal	Paleós, á, ó
Pen	Peninsula, Penisola
Pk	Park
Pl	Planina
Pque	Parque
Prov	Province
Pso	Passo
Pt(e)	Point(e)
Rib	Ribeirão
R, *R*	River, Rivière, Rio, Ria, Rijeka
Reg	Region, Région
Res	Reservoir, Reservoire
Sa	Sierra, Serra
Sd	Sound, Sund
St	Saint, Sankt, Sint
Ste(s)	Sainte(s)
Teh L	Tehniti Limni
V	Valley, Vale, Vallée, Val, Valle, Vall

A

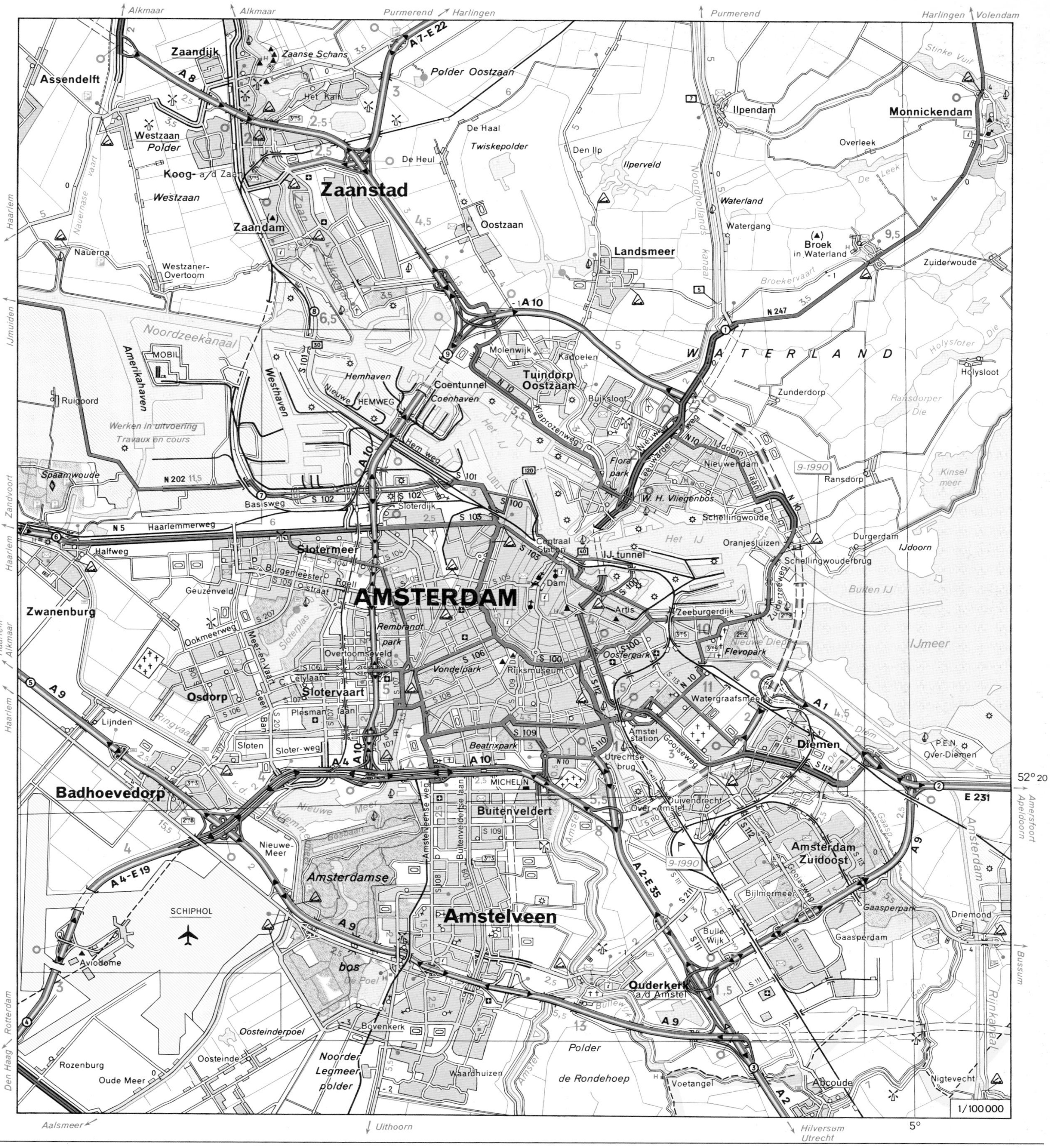
Alkmaar
Purmerend
Harlingen
Volendam
Zaandijk
Zaanse Schans
Assendelft
Polder Oostzaan
Westzaan Polder
Koog- a/d Zaan
Zaanstad
Zaandam
De Haal
Twiskepolder
De Heul
Den Ilp
Ilpendam
Monnickendam
Overleek
Ilperveld
Oostzaan
Waterland
Watergang
Broek in Waterland
Zuiderwoude
Landsmeer
Nauerna
Westzaner-Overtoom
Noordzeekanaal
A 10
N 247
W A T E R L A N D
Holysloot
Molenwijk
Kadoelen
Tuindorp Oostzaan
Amerikahaven
Westhaven
Hemhaven
Coentunnel
Coenhaven
Nieuwe HEMWEG
Buiksloot
Zunderdorp
Ransdorp
Ruigoord
Werken in uitvoering
Travaux en cours
Spaarnwoude
N 202
Basisweg
Sloterdijk
Nieuwendam
W. H. Vliegenbos
Schellingwoude
Oranjesluizen
Durgerdam
IJdoorn
Schellingwoudebrug
Buiten IJ
IJmeer
N 5
Haarlemmerweg
Halfweg
Slotermeer
Burgemeester Röell straat
Geuzenveld
AMSTERDAM
Centraal Station
IJ-tunnel
Dam
Artis
Zeeburgerdijk
Flevopark
Zwanenburg
Rembrandt park
Overtoomse veld
Vondelpark
Rijksmuseum
Oosterpark
Osdorp
Slotervaart
Lelylaan
Plesman laan
Watergraafsmeer
Lijnden
Sloten
Sloter-weg
Beatrixpark
Amstel station
Utrechtse brug
Diemen
P.E.N. Over-Diemen
A 10
A 4
A 9
A 1
Badhoevedorp
MICHELIN
Buitenveldert
Duivendrecht
Over-Amstel
E 231
52° 20
Amersfoort
Apeldoorn
Nieuwe-Meer
Bosbaan
Amsterdam Zuidoost
Amsterdamse bos
A4-E19
A2-E35
SCHIPHOL
Aviodome
Amstelveen
Bijlmermeer
Gaasperpark
Gaasperdam
Driemond
Bussum
De Poel
Bullewijk
Ouderkerk a/d Amstel
Rijnkanaal
Bovenkerk
Oosteinderpoel
Oosteinde
Noorder Legmeer polder
Waardhuizen
Polder
de Rondehoep
Voetangel
Abcoude
Nigtevecht
Rozenburg
Oude Meer
Den Haag
Rotterdam
Haarlem
IJmuiden
Zandvoort
Aalsmeer
Uithoorn
Hilversum
Utrecht
5°
1/100 000

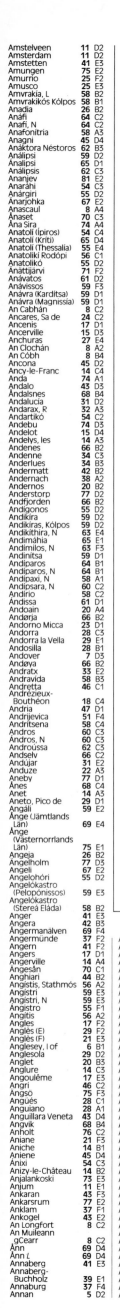

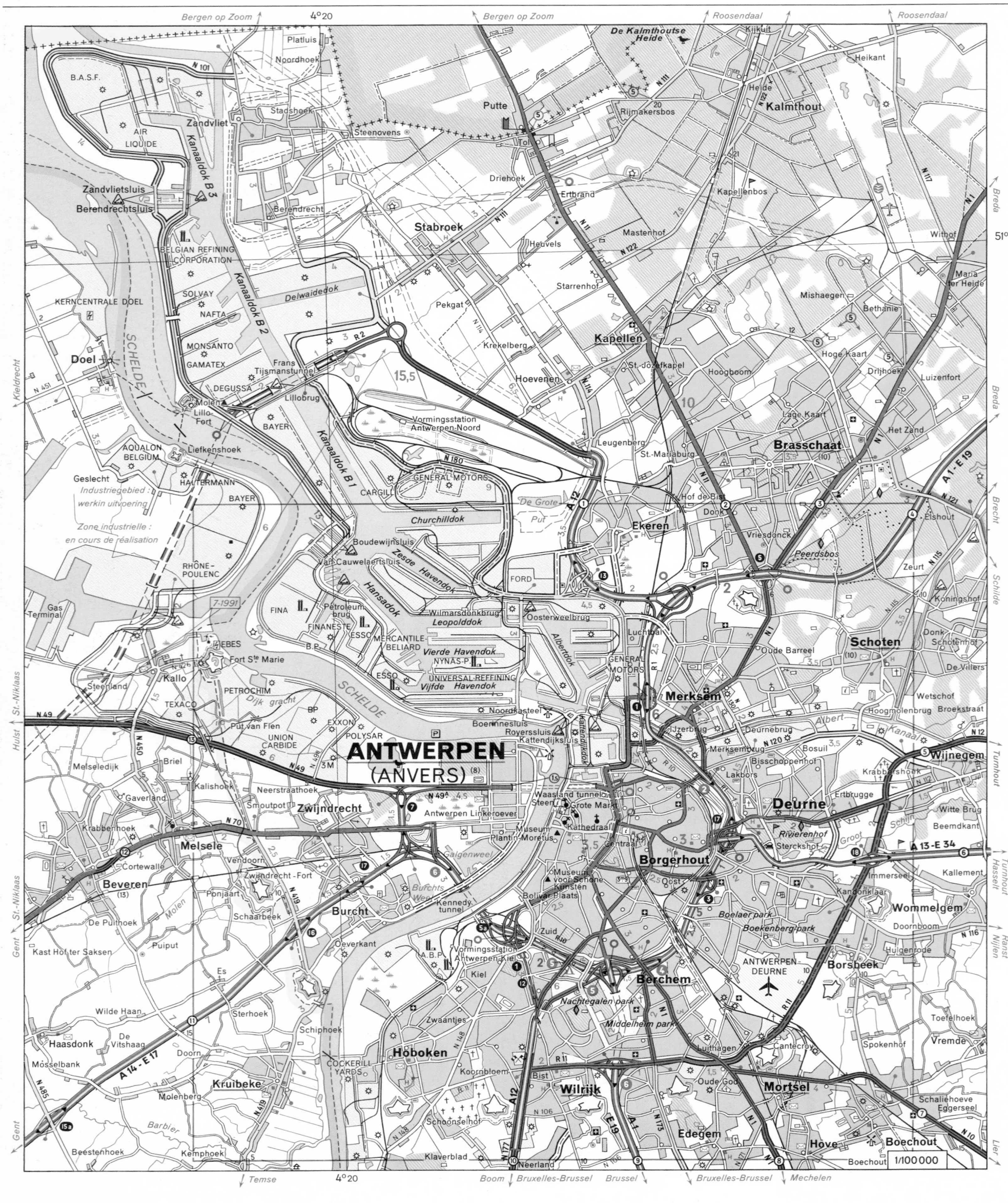

Bergen op Zoom
4°20
Roosendaal
De Kalmthoutse Heide
Kalmthout
Putte
Stabroek
Kapellen
Brasschaat
Ekeren
Schoten
Merksem
ANTWERPEN
(ANVERS)
Deurne
Borgerhout
Wommelgem
Zwijndrecht
Melsele
Beveren
Burcht
Berchem
Borsbeek
Hoboken
Wilrijk
Mortsel
Edegem
Hove
Boechout
Kruibeke
Doel
Kallo
Lillo
Zandvliet
Berendrecht
SCHELDE
Kanaaldok B 1
Kanaaldok B 2
Kanaaldok B 3
Delwaidedok
Churchilldok
Hansadok
Leopolddok
Vierde Havendok
Vijfde Havendok
Albertkanaal
51°20
Breda
Bergen op Zoom
Brecht
Schilde
Turnhout
Ranst
Lier
Mechelen
Bruxelles-Brussel
Boom
Temse
Gent
St.-Niklaas
Hulst
Kieldrecht
1/100 000

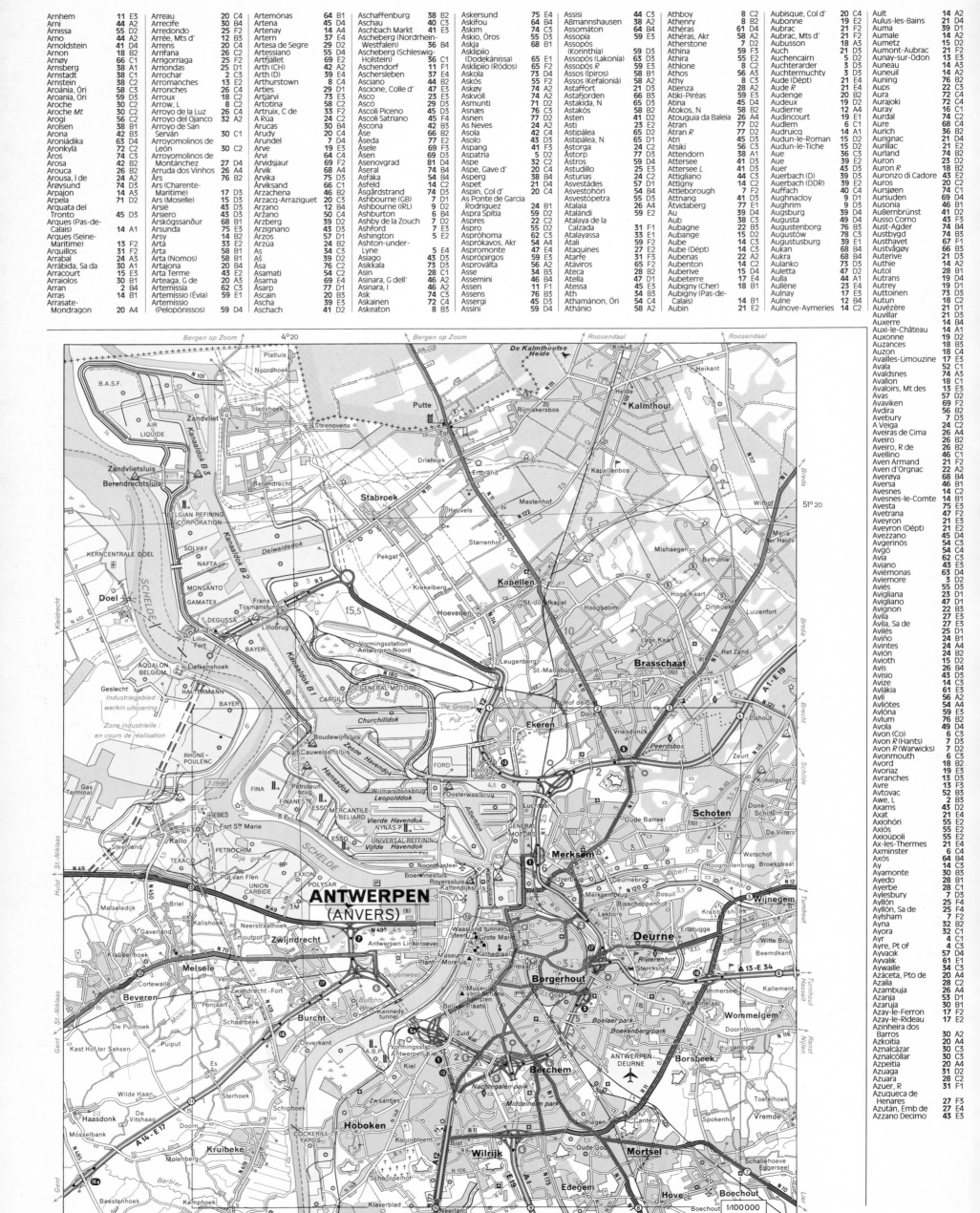

B

Baad 40 A4
Baal 11 E4
Baamonde 24 B1
Baarle-Nassau 11 D3
Baarn 11 E2
Baba 54 C2
Babadag 81 E3
Babajevo 79 E1
Babelsberg 37 F3
Babenhausen (Bayern) 40 A3
Babenhausen (Hessen) 38 B3
Babina Greda 51 D2
Babin Kal 53 E2
Babin Most 53 D3
Babino Polje 52 A4
Babin Potok 50 B3
Babljak 52 C3
Babuna 53 E4
Babušnica 53 E2
Bač 51 E1
Bacau 81 E2
Baccarat 15 E3
Baceno 42 A3
Bacharach 38 A2
Bächistock 42 B2
Bachmač 79 F4
Bačina 53 D2
Bačka Palanka 51 E1
Bäckaskog 77 D3
Bačka Topola 51 E1
Backe 69 E3
Bäckebo 77 E2
Bäckefors 75 D4
Bački Breg 51 D1
Bački Brestovac 51 E1
Bački Monoštor 51 D1
Bački Petrovac 51 E1
Backnang 38 C4
Bačko Gradište 51 E1
Bačko Novo Selo 51 E1
Bačko Petrovo Selo 51 E1
Bačkovo 81 D4
Bacoli 46 B2
Bacqueville 13 F2
Bad Aibling 40 B3
Badajoz 26 C4
Badalona 29 F2
Bad Aussee 41 D3
Bad Bentheim 11 F2
Bad Bergzabern 38 A4
Bad Berka 39 D1
Bad Berleburg 38 B1
Bad Berneck 39 D2
Bad Bertrich 38 A2
Bad Bevensen 37 D3
Bad Bibra 39 D1
Bad Blankenburg 39 D2
Bad Brambach 39 E2
Bad Bramstedt 36 C2
Bad Brückenau 38 C2
Bad Buchau 42 B1
Bad Camberg 38 B2
Bad Deutsch Altenburg 41 F2
Bad Doberan 37 D1
Bad Driburg 36 C4
Bad Düben 37 E4
Bad Dürkheim 38 A3
Bad Dürrenberg 37 E4
Bad Durrheim 42 A1
Bad Elster 39 E2
Bad Ems 38 A2
Baden (A) 41 F2
Baden (CH) 42 A2
Baden-Baden 38 B4
Bad Endorf 40 C3
Badenweiler 42 A1
Baden-Württemberg 42 B1
Baderna 43 F4
Bad Essen 36 B4
Bad Frankenhausen 37 D4
Bad Freienwalde 37 F3
Bad Friedrichshall 38 B3
Bad Gandersheim 36 C4
Badgastein 43 E2
Bad Gleichenberg 41 F4
Bad Godesberg 35 D3
Bad Goisern 41 D3
Bad Gottleuba 39 F1
Bad Griesbach 40 C2
Bad Grund 37 D4
Bad Hall 41 D3
Bad Harzburg 37 D4
Bad Herrenalb 38 B4
Bad Hersfeld 38 C1
Bad Hofgastein 40 C4
Bad Homburg 38 B2
Bad Honnef 35 D3
Bad Honnigen 38 A2
Badia Polesine 43 D4
Badia Tedalda 44 C2
Bad Iburg 36 B4
Badija 52 A3
Bad Ischl 41 D3
Bad Karlshafen 36 C4
Bad Kissingen 38 C2
Bad Kleinen 37 D2
Bad Kleinkirchheim 41 D4
Bad König 38 B3
Bad Königshofen 38 C2
Bad Kösen 39 D1
Bad Kreuznach 38 A3
Bad Krozingen 42 A1
Bad Laasphe 38 B1
Bad Langensalza 38 C1
Bad Lauchstädt 37 E4
Bad Lausick 39 E1
Bad Lauterberg 37 D4
Bad Leonfelden 41 D2
Bad Liebenstein 38 C1
Bad Liebenwerda 37 F4
Bad Liebenzell 38 B4
Bad Lippspringe 36 C4
Badljevina 50 C2
Bad Meinberg 36 C4
Bad Mergentheim 38 C3
Bad Mitterndorf 41 D3
Bad Münder 36 C4
Bad Münster am Stein-Ebernburg 38 A3
Bad Münstereifel 35 D3
Bad Nauheim 38 B2
Bad Nenndorf 36 C3
Bad Neuenahr-Ahrweiler 38 A2
Bad Neustadt 38 C2
Bad Oeynhausen 36 C4
Badolato 47 E4
Badalatosa 31 E3
Bad Oldesloe 37 D2
Badonviller 15 E3
Bad Orb 38 B2
Badovinci 51 E2
Bad Peterstal-Griesbach 38 B4
Bad Pyrmont 36 C4
Bad Ragaz 42 B2
Bad Rappenau 38 B3
Bad Reichenhall 40 C3
Bad Rippoldsau-Schapbach 38 B4
Bad Rothenfelde 36 B4
Bad Saarow-Pieskow 37 F3
Bad Sachsa 37 D4
Bad Säckingen 42 A1
Bad Salzdetfurth 36 C4
Bad Salzschlirf 38 B2
Bad Salzuflen 36 C4
Bad Salzungen 38 C1
Bad Schallerbach 41 D2
Bad Schandau 39 F1
Bad Schmiedeberg 37 E4
Bad Schönborn 38 B3
Bad Schussenried 42 B1
Bad Schwalbach 38 A2
Bad Schwartau 37 D2
Bad Segeberg 36 C2
Bad Soden 38 B2
Bad Soden 38 B2
Bad Sooden-Allendorf 38 C1
Bad St Leonhard 41 E4
Bad Sulza 39 D1
Bad Sülze 37 E1
Bad Tatzmannsdorf 41 F3
Bad Tennstedt 38 C1
Bad Tölz 40 B3
Badules 28 B3
Bad Urach 38 C4
Bad Vibel 38 B2
Bad Vöslau 41 F2
Bad Waldsee 42 B1
Bad Wiessee 40 B3
Bad Wildungen 38 B1
Bad Wilsnack 37 E3
Bad Wimpfen 38 B3
Bad Windsheim 38 C3
Bad Wörishofen 40 A3
Bad Wurzach 40 A3
Bad Zwischenahn 36 B2
Bæccegæhal'di 67 D2
Bae Colwyn 6 B1
Baena 31 E3
Bæskades 67 D2
Baeza 31 F2
Bagà 29 E1
Bâgé-le-Châtel 19 D3
Bagenalstown 8 C3
Bagenkop 76 B4
Bagheria 48 B3
Bagnacavallo 44 B1
Bagnara Calabra 47 D4
Bagnères-de-Bigorre 20 C4
Bagnères-de-Luchon 20 C4
Bagni del Masino 42 B3
Bagni di Lucca 44 A2
Bagno a Ripoli 44 B2
Bagno di Romagna 44 B2
Bagnoles-de-l'Orne 13 E3
Bagnoli del Trigno 45 E4
Bagnolo Mella 42 C4
Bagnols-les-Bains 21 F2
Bagnols-sur-Cèze 22 B3
Bagnoregio 44 C3
Bagolino 42 C3
Bagrationovsk 78 C3
Bagrdan 53 D1
Baia Mare 81 D2
Baiano 46 C1
Baião 24 B4
Baiersbronn 38 B4
Baignes-Ste-Radegonde 17 E4
Baigneux-les-Juifs 19 D1
Baile Átha Cliath 9 D3
Baile Átha Luain 8 C2
Băile Herculane 80 C3
Bailén 31 F2
Băile Tuşnad 81 D2
Bailieborough 8 C2
Bailleul 14 B1
Bain-de-Bretagne 13 D4
Bains-les-Bains 15 E4
Baio 24 A1
Baiona 24 A2
Bais 13 E4
Baïse 20 C3
Baïse-Darré 20 C3
Baja 80 B3
Baja Sardinia 46 B2
Bajgora 53 D3
Bajina Bašta 51 E3
Bajmok 51 E1
Bajram Curri 53 D4
Bajša 51 E1
Bajzë 52 C4
Bakar 50 A2
Bakarac 50 A2
Bakewell 7 D1
Bakio 25 F1
Bakkaflói 68 C1
Bakony 80 B2
Bakvattnet 69 E3
Bala 6 B1
Balaguer 29 D2
Balanegra 32 A4
Balaruc 21 F3
Balassagyarmat 80 B2
Balaton 80 B2
Balatonfüred 80 B2
Balatonkeresztúr 80 B2
Balazote 32 B1
Balbigny 18 C3
Balbriggan 9 D2
Balčik 81 E3
Balderschwang 40 A4
Baldock 7 E2
Baldo, Mte 43 D3
Bale 43 F4
Baleal 26 A4
Baleizão 30 B2
Balerma 32 A4
Balestrand 74 B2
Balí 64 B3
Balikesir 57 F4
Bälinge 75 F3
Balingen 42 B1
Balivanich 2 A2
Ballachulish 2 C3
Ballaghaderreen 8 B2
Ballangen 66 B3
Ballantrae 4 C2
Ballao 46 B4
Ballater 3 D2
Ballaugh 4 C3
Ballenstedt 37 D4
Balleroy 13 D3
Ballerup 76 C3
Ballina 8 B2
Ballinamore 8 C2
Ballinasloe 8 B2
Ballingarry 8 C3
Ballinrobe 8 B2
Ballintober 8 B2
Ballobar 29 D2
Ballon 13 F4
Ballon d'Alsace 15 E4
Ballstad 66 A3
Ballybay 9 D2
Ballybofey 8 C1
Ballybunnion 8 A3
Ballycastle (IRL) 4 B2
Ballycastle (N Ire) 8 B1
Ballyclare 9 D1
Ballyconnell 8 C2
Ballycotton 8 B4
Ballycroy 8 A2
Ballyduff 8 A3
Ballyforan 8 C2
Ballygawley 8 C1
Ballyhaunis 8 B2
Ballyheige 8 A3
Ballyjamesduff 8 C2
Ballymahon 8 C2
Ballymena 9 D1
Ballymoe 8 B2
Ballymoney 4 B2
Ballymore 8 C2
Ballymote 8 B2
Ballynahinch 9 D1
Ballysadare 8 B1
Ballyshannon 8 C1
Ballyvaughan 8 B3
Balmaseda 25 F2
Balme 23 D1
Balmoral Castle 3 D2
Balneario de Panticosa 20 C4
Balsareny 29 E2
Balsfjorden 66 C2
Balsicas 32 C2
Balsorano 45 D4
Bålsta 75 F4
Balsthal 19 F2
Balta 81 E2
Baltanás 25 E3
Baltar 24 B3
Baltic Sea 78 B2
Baltijsk 78 B3
Baltinglass 9 D3
Baltrum 36 A2
Bambalió 58 B2
Bamberg 39 D2
Bambíni 58 B2
Bamburgh 5 E1
Bampton 6 B3
Banagher 8 C3
Banat 80 C3
Banatska Palanka 53 D1
Banatska Topola 51 F1
Banatski Brestovac 53 D1
Banatski Dvor 51 F1
Banatski Karlovac 51 F1
Banatsko Karadđorđevo 51 F1
Banatsko Novo Selo 53 D1
Banbridge 9 D2
Banbury 7 D2
Banchory 3 D2
Bandak 74 B3
Bande 24 B3
Bandırma 81 E4
Bandol 22 C4
Bandon 8 B4
Bandon *R* 8 B4
Bañeres 32 C2
Banff 3 D2
Bangor (IRL) 8 B1
Bangor (N Ire) 9 D1
Bangor (Wales) 6 B1
Bangsund 69 D3
Banja Koviljača 51 E2
Banja Luka 50 C2
Banjani 52 C1
Banja (Srbija) 51 E3
Banja (Srbija) 53 D1
Banja Vrućica 51 D2
Banjska 53 D3
Bankeryd 77 D1
Bann (IRL) 9 D3
Bann (N Ire) 4 B2
Bannalec 12 B4
Banon 22 B3
Bañón 28 B3
Baños de Cerrato 25 E3
Baños de Fuensanta 25 D1
Baños de la Encina 31 F2
Baños de la Fuensanta 32 B3
Baños de Molgas 24 B2
Baños de Montemayor 27 D3
Banova Jaruga 50 C2
Banovići 51 D3
Banque de Fraiture 34 C4
Banque Michel 34 C3
Bansin 37 F1
Banská-Bystrica 80 B2
Banská-Štiavnica 80 B2
Bansko 53 F4
Bantry 8 A4
Bantry B 8 A4
Bañuela 31 E2
Banyalbufar 33 E2
Banyoles 29 F2
Banyuls 29 F2
Bao, Emb de 24 B2
Bapaume 14 B2
Bar (SU) 81 E1
Bar (YU) 52 C4
Baracaldo 25 F2
Baraći 50 C3
Baradla 80 C2
Barahona 28 A2
Barajas 27 F3
Barajas de Melo 28 A4
Barajevo 52 C1
Baralla 24 C2
Barane 53 D3
Baranoviči 79 D3
Baraqueville 21 E2
Barasona, Emb de 29 D1
Barbadillo del Mercado 25 F3
Barban 43 F4
Barbarano Vicentino 43 D4
Barbarušince 53 E3
Barbastro 29 D2
Barbat 50 A3
Barbate de Franco 31 D4
Barbate, Emb de 30 C4
Barbazan 21 D4
Barberino di Mugello 44 B2
Barbezieux 17 E4
Barbizon 14 B4
Barbotan 20 C3
Barby 37 E4
Barca de Alva 24 C4
Barca, Emb de la 24 C1
Barcarrota 30 C1
Barcellona Pozzo di Gotto 49 D3
Barcelona 29 F2
Barcelonnette 22 C2
Barcelos 24 A3
Barcena, Emb de 24 C2
Barchfeld 38 C1
Barcis 43 E3
Barcones 28 A2
Barcs 80 B3
Bardal 69 D3
Bardejov 80 C1
Bardi 23 F2
Bardineto 23 E2
Bardolino 42 C4
Bardonecchia 19 E4
Bardu 66 C2
Bardufoss 66 C2
Bare 51 F4
Barèges 20 C4
Barentin 13 F2
Barenton 13 D3
Bares, Estaca de 24 B1
Barfleur 13 D2
Barfleur, Pte de 13 D2
Bargas 27 F3
Bargoed 6 C3
Bargteheide 36 C2
Bari 47 E1
Barić Draga 50 B3
Barisciano 45 D3
Barjac 22 A2
Barjols 22 C3
Barlby 5 E3
Bar, le 23 D3
Bar-le-Duc 15 D3
Barletta 47 D1
Barlovento 30 A4
Barmouth 6 B1
Barmstedt 36 C2
Barna 8 B2
Barnard Castle 5 E3
Bärnau 39 D2
Barneveld 11 E2
Barneville 13 D2
Barnsley 5 E4
Barnstaple 6 B3
Barnstorf 36 B3
Barntrup 36 C4
Barovo 53 F4
Barqueiro 26 B3
Barr 15 E3
Barra 2 A2
Barracas 28 C4
Barrachina 28 B3
Barraco 27 E3
Barrafranca 48 C4
Barra Head 2 A2
Barrancos 30 C2
Barranco Velho 30 B3
Barranda 32 B2
Barra, Sd of 2 A2
Barrax 32 B1
Barrea 45 D4
Barre-des-Cévennes 21 F2
Barreiro 26 A4
Barrême 22 C3
Barrhead 2 C4
Barrhill 4 C2
Barri 6 C3
Barrow 8 C3
Barrow-in-Furness 5 D3
Barrow, R 8 C4
Barruecopardo 26 C2
Barruelo de Santullán 25 E2
Barry 6 C3
Barsinghausen 36 C3
Bar-sur-Aube 14 C4
Bar-sur-Seine 14 C4
Barth 37 E1
Barthe-de-Neste, la 20 C4
Barton-upon-Humber 5 F4
Barumini 46 A4
Baruth 37 F3
Barvas 2 B1
Barycz 78 B4
Barzio 42 B3
Bašaid 51 F1
Bàscara 29 F1
Baschi 44 C3
Basconcillos del Tozo 25 E2
Basel 19 F1
Baselga di Pinè 43 D3
Bas-en-Basset 18 C4
Basento 47 E2
Basildon 7 E3
Basilicata 47 D2
Basingstoke 7 D3
Baška 50 A2
Baška Voda 50 C4
Baške Oštarije 50 B3
Baslow 7 D1
Basovizza 43 F3
Bas-Rhin 15 E3
Bassano del Grappa 43 D3
Bassée, la 14 B1
Bassella 29 D2
Bassens 20 C2
Bassum 36 B3
Båstad 77 D2
Bastasi 50 C3
Bastelica 23 E4
Bas'tevarri 67 D2
Bastia 23 D3
Bastide-de-Sérou, la 21 D4
Bastogne 15 D2
Bastunäsfjället 69 E3
Bastuträsk 70 B3
Bataille, Col de la 22 B2
Batajnica 52 C1
Batak 81 D4
Batalha 26 A3
Batea 29 D3
Bath 6 C3
Bathgate 3 D4
Bâtie-Neuve, la 22 C2
Batina 51 D1
Batlava 53 D3
Batočina 53 D1
Båtsfjord 67 F1
Batsí 60 B3
Battaglia Terme 43 D4
Battenberg 38 B1
Battice 34 C3
Battipaglia 46 C2
Battle 7 E4
Batz (Finistère) 12 B3
Batz (Loire-Atlantique) 16 C2
Baud 12 C4
Baugé 17 E1
Baugy 18 B2
Baule, la 16 C2
Baume, Cirque de 19 D2
Baume-les-Dames 19 E1
Baumholder 38 A3
Bauska 78 C2
Bautzen 39 F1
Baux, les 22 B3
Bavanište 53 D1
Bavay 14 B1
Bavella, Col de 23 D4
Båven 75 F4
Baveno 42 B3
Bawtry 5 E4
Bayard, Col 22 C2
Bayerisch Eisenstein 39 F3
Bayerischer Wald 39 E3
Bayern 39 D3
Bayeux 13 D3
Bayhirivagh 2 A2
Bayındır 61 F2
Bayon 15 E3
Bayonne 20 B3
Bayreuth 39 D2
Bayrischzell 40 B3
Baza 32 A3
Bazas 20 C2
Baza, Sa de 32 A3
Bazoches-sur-Hoëne 13 E3
Bazzano 44 B1
Beachy Head 7 E4
Beaconsfield 7 D3
Béal an Átha 8 B2
Béal Átha na Sluaighe 8 B2
Beaminster 6 C4
Beanntraí 8 A4
Beara 8 A4
Beariz 24 B2
Beas 30 C3
Beasain 20 A4
Beas de Segura 32 A2
Beattock 5 D2
Beaucaire 22 B3
Beaufort (Jura) 19 D2
Beaufort (Savoie) 19 E3
Beaufort-en-Vallée 17 E1
Beaugency 18 A1
Beaujeu 18 C3
Beaulieu (Alpes-Maritime) 23 D3
Beaulieu (Corrèze) 21 E2
Beaulieu (GB) 7 D4
Beaumaris 6 B1
Beaumesnil 13 F3
Beaumetz-lès-Loges 14 B1
Beaumont (B) 34 B4
Beaumont (Dordogne) 21 D2
Beaumont (Manche) 13 D2
Beaumont (Val-d'Oise) 14 A3
Beaumont-de-Lomagne 21 D3
Beaumont-le-Roger 13 F3
Beaumont-sur-Sarthe 13 F4
Beaune 19 D2
Beaune-la-Rolande 14 A4
Beaupréau 17 D2
Beauraing 34 B4
Beaurepaire 19 D4
Beaurepaire-en-Bresse 19 D2
Beausset, le 22 C4
Beauvais 14 A2
Beauvoir (Deux-Sèvres) 17 E3
Beauvoir (Vendée) 16 C2
Bebington 5 D4
Bebra 38 C1
Beccles 7 F2
Becedas 27 D3
Beceite 29 D3
Bečej 51 E1
Becerreá 24 C2
Bec-Hellouin, le 13 F3
Bécherel 12 C4
Bechet 81 D3
Bechhofen 38 C3
Bečići 52 C4
Becilla de Valderaduey 25 D3
Beckenried 42 A2
Beckington 6 C3
Beckum 36 B4
Bečov 39 E2
Bedale 5 E3
Bédarieux 21 F3
Beddgelert 6 B1
Bederkesa 36 B2
Bedford 7 E2
Bedfordshire 7 D2
Bedlington 5 E2
Bedmar 31 F2
Bednja 50 B1
Bedonia 23 F2
Bedum 11 F1
Bedwas 6 C3
Bedworth 7 D2
Beeford 5 F3
Beelitz 37 F3
Beerfelden 38 B3
Beeskow 37 F3
Beetzendorf 37 D3
Bégard 12 B3
Begejci 51 F1
Begejski kanal 51 F1
Beg-Meil 12 B4
Begna 74 C2
Begov Han 51 D3
Bégude-de-Mazenc, la 22 B2
Begues 29 E2
Begur 29 F2
Behalúa de Guadix 32 A3
Behobia 20 B3
Behringersmühle 39 D3
Beiarn 69 E1
Beilen 11 F2
Beilingries 39 D3
Beinn a'Ghiò 3 D3
Beinn an Oir 2 B4
Beinn Bheigeir 2 B4
Beinn Dearg 2 C1
Beira Alta 26 B2
Beira Baixa 26 B3
Beira Litoral 26 B2
Beisfjord 66 B3
Beith 2 C4
Beitostølen 74 C2
Beitstadfjorden 69 D3
Beiuş 80 C2
Beja 30 B2
Béjar 27 D3
Béjar, Pto de 27 D3
Békés 80 C2
Békéscsaba 80 C2
Bel 29 D3
Bělá 39 E3
Bélâbre 17 F2
Bela Crkva (Srbija) 51 E2
Bela Crkva (Vojvodina) 53 D1
Belaja Cerkov' 81 E1
Belalcázar 31 D1
Belanovce 53 E3
Belanovica 52 C1
Bela Palanka 53 E2
Belasica 53 F4
Belcaire 21 E4
Belchen 42 A1
Belchite 28 C2
Belčište 54 C1
Belcoo 8 C1
Bel'cy 81 E2
Belec 50 B1
Belecke 38 A1
Belegiš 52 C1
Belej 50 A3
Beleña, Emb de 28 A3
Belesar, Emb de 24 B2
Belev 79 F3
Bele Vode 51 F3
Belfast 9 D1
Belfast L 9 D1
Belford 5 E1
Belfort 19 E1
Belforte all'Isauro 44 C2
Belgern 37 F4
België 34 B3
Belgique 34 B3
Belgodère 23 E3
Belgorod-Dnestrovskij 81 E2
Belianes 29 D2
Belice 48 B4
Beli Drim 53 D3
Beli Manastir 51 D1
Belin-Béliet 20 B2
Beli Potok 53 E2
Belišće 51 D1
Beli Timok 53 E2
Beljakovce 53 E3
Beljanica 53 D1
Beljina 52 C1
Bellac 17 F3
Bellagio 42 B3
Bellano 42 B3
Bellaria 44 C1
Bellcaire d'Urgell 29 D2
Belledonne, Chaîne de 19 E4
Belleek 8 C1
Bellegarde (Ain) 19 D3
Bellegarde (Gard) 22 A3
Bellegarde (Loiret) 14 A4
Bellegarde-en-Marche 18 B3
Belle-Ile 12 B4
Belle-Isle-en-Terre 12 B3
Bellême 13 F4
Bellencombre 14 A2
Bellerive 18 B3
Belleville 19 D3
Belley 19 D3
Bellinzona 42 B3
Bell-lloc d'Urgell 29 D2
Bello 28 B3
Bellpuig 29 D2
Belluno 43 E3
Bellver 33 E2
Bellver de Cerdanya 29 E1
Bélmez 31 D2
Belmont (F) 18 C3
Belmont (GB) 3 F1
Belmonte (Asturias) 24 C1
Belmonte (Castilla-la-Mancha) 28 A4
Belmonte (P) 26 C3
Belmont-sur-Rance 21 E3
Belmullet 8 A1
Belo Brdo 53 D2
Belœil 34 B3
Belogradčik 81 D3
Belo Jez 51 F1
Beloljin 53 D2
Belo Polje 53 D3
Belopolje 79 F4
Belorado 25 F3
Belorussija 79 D3
Belpech 21 E4
Belper 7 D1
Belsay 5 E2
Belsh 54 A2
Beltinci 41 F4
Belturbet 8 C2
Belušić 53 D2
Belvedere Marittimo 47 D3
Belver 29 D2
Belvès 21 D2
Belvis de la Jara 27 E4

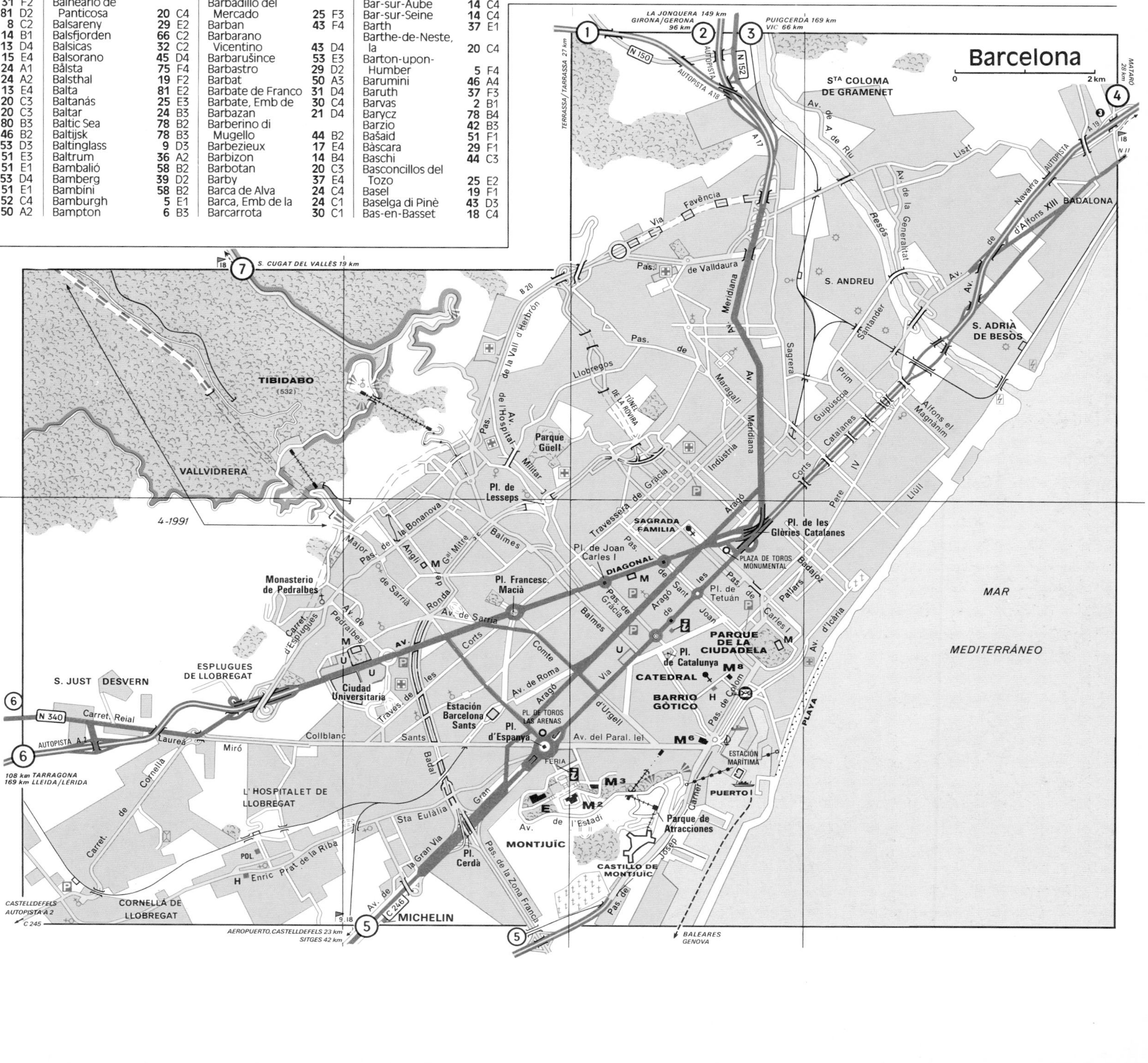

Barcelona
0
2 km
LA JONQUERA 149 km
GIRONA/GERONA 96 km
PUIGCERDA 169 km
VIC 66 km
MATARÓ 28 km
S. CUGAT DEL VALLÈS 19 km
TERRASSA/TARRASA 27 km
108 km TARRAGONA
169 km LLEIDA/LÉRIDA
CASTELLDEFELS AUTOPISTA A 2
AEROPUERTO, CASTELLDEFELS 23 km
SITGES 42 km
BALEARES GENOVA
STA COLOMA DE GRAMENET
BADALONA
S. ANDREU
S. ADRIÀ DE BESÒS
TIBIDABO (532)
VALLVIDRERA
Parque Güell
Pl. de Lesseps
SAGRADA FAMILIA
Pl. de les Glòries Catalanes
PLAZA DE TOROS MONUMENTAL
Monasterio de Pedralbes
Pl. Francesc. Macià
DIAGONAL
Pl. de Catalunya
PARQUE DE LA CIUDADELA
CATEDRAL
BARRIO GÓTICO
Ciudad Universitaria
S. JUST DESVERN
ESPLUGUES DE LLOBREGAT
Estación Barcelona Sants
Pl. d'Espanya
PL. DE TOROS LAS ARENAS
L'HOSPITALET DE LLOBREGAT
CORNELLÀ DE LLOBREGAT
MONTJUÏC
CASTILLO DE MONTJUÏC
Parque de Atracciones
FERIA
ESTACIÓN MARÍTIMA
PUERTO
Pl. Cerdà
MAR MEDITERRÁNEO
PLAYA
MICHELIN
4-1991

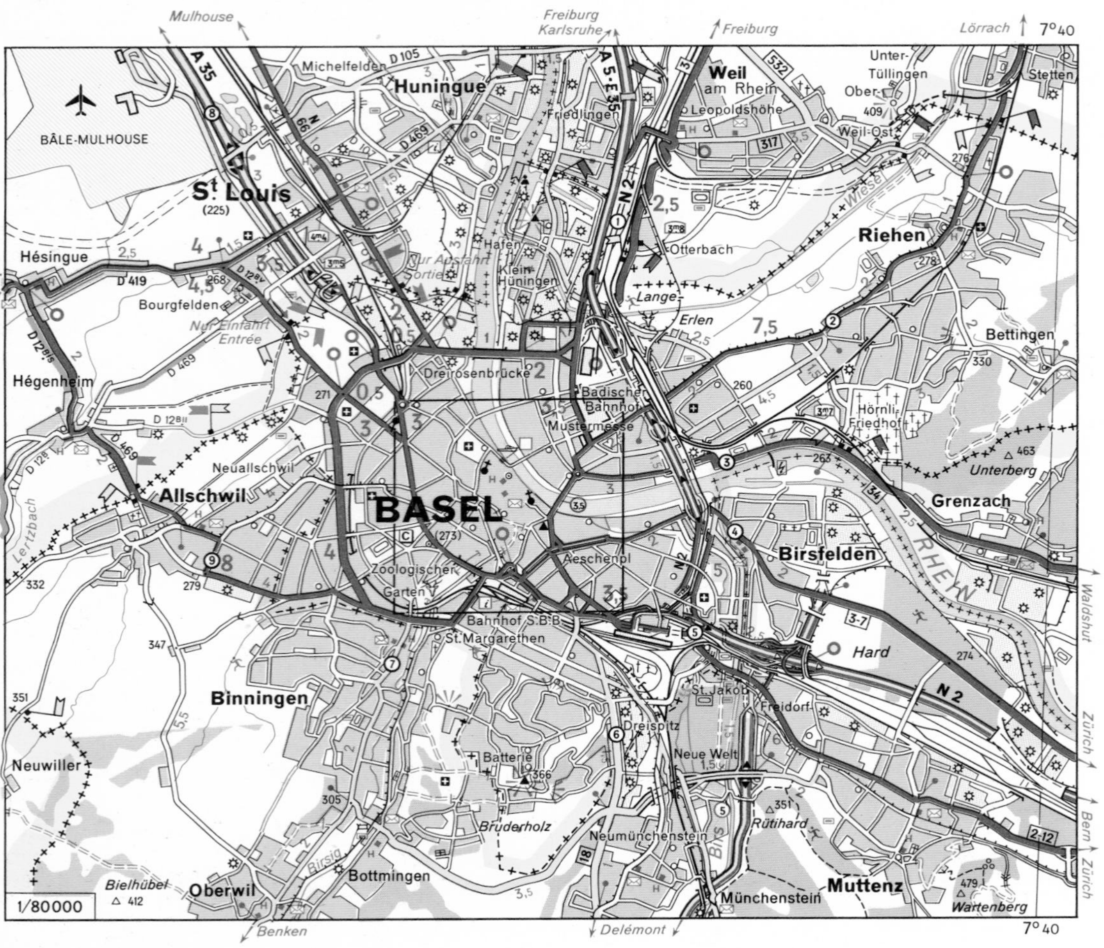
Mulhouse
Freiburg
Karlsruhe
Freiburg
Lörrach
7°40
BÂLE-MULHOUSE
Michelfelden
Huningue
Weil am Rhein
Leopoldshöhe
Unter-Tüllingen
Ober-
Stetten
St Louis
Hésingue
Bourgfelden
Hegenheim
Riehen
Otterbach
Lange
Erlen
Dreirosenbrücke
Badischer Bahnhof
Mustermesse
Bettingen
Hörnli Friedhof
Neuallschwil
Allschwil
BASEL
Zoologischer Garten
Aeschenpl
Birsfelden
Grenzach
Unterberg
RHEIN
Bahnhof S.B.B.
St.Margarethen
Hard
Binningen
Neuwiller
St.Jakob
Freidorf
Batterie
Neue Welt
Bruderholz
Neumünchenstein
Rütihard
Oberwil
Bottmingen
Muttenz
Münchenstein
Wartenberg
Bielhübel
1/80000
Benken
Delémont
Zürich
Bern
Waldshut
7°40

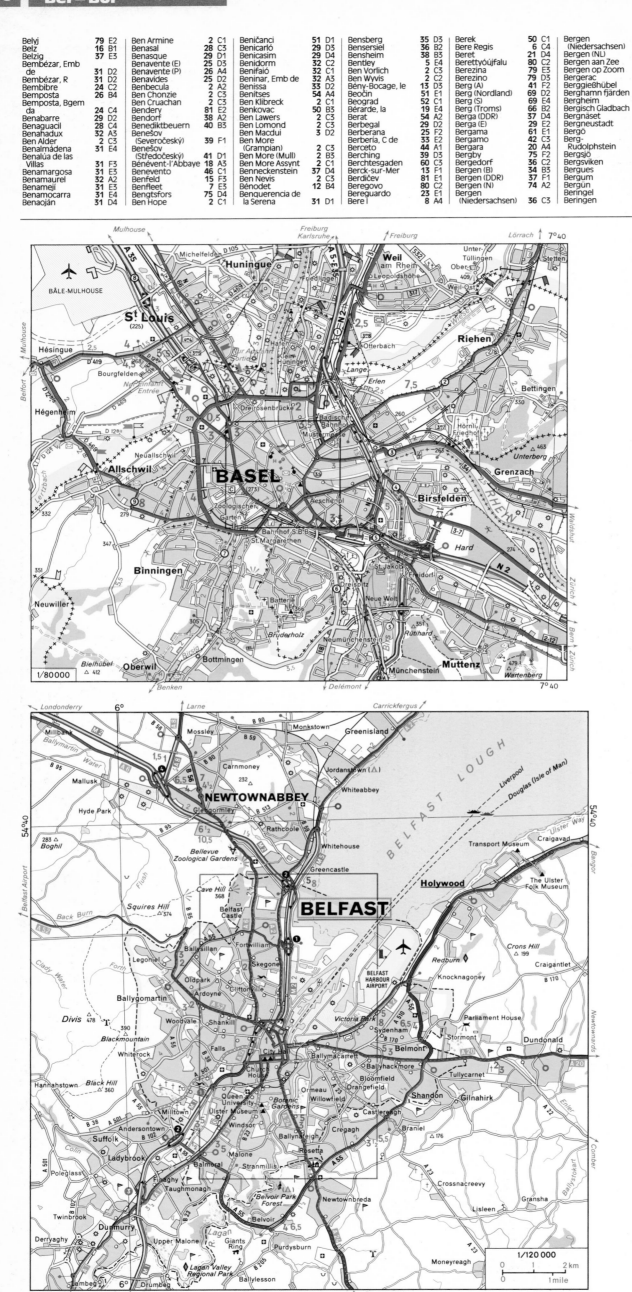

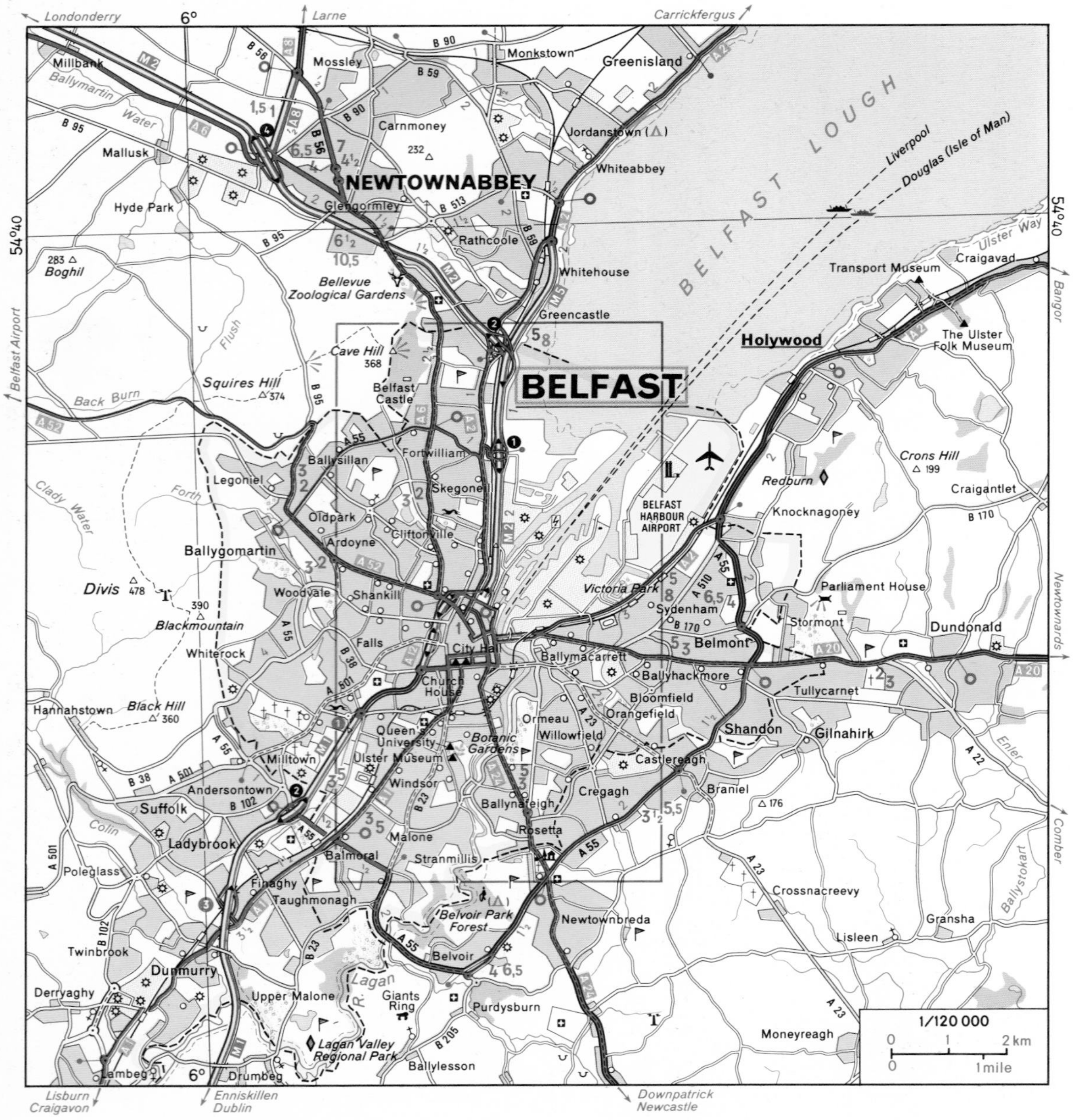
Londonderry
6°
Larne
Carrickfergus
Mossley
Monkstown
Greenisland
Millbank
Ballymartin Water
Carnmoney
Jordanstown
Mallusk
Whiteabbey
NEWTOWNABBEY
BELFAST LOUGH
Liverpool
Douglas (Isle of Man)
Hyde Park
Glengormley
Rathcoole
Whitehouse
Ulster Way
Transport Museum
Craigavad
54°40
Boghil
Bellevue Zoological Gardens
Greencastle
Holywood
The Ulster Folk Museum
Bangor
Cave Hill
Belfast Castle
BELFAST
Squires Hill
Back Burn
Belfast Airport
Ballysillan
Fortwilliam
Crons Hill
Legoniel
Skegoneill
Redburn
Craigantlet
BELFAST HARBOUR AIRPORT
Oldpark
Knocknagoney
Cliftonville
Ardoyne
Ballygomartin
Divis
Blackmountain
Woodvale
Shankill
Victoria Park
Sydenham
Parliament House
Stormont
Dundonald
Whiterock
Falls
City Hall
Belmont
Ballymacarrett
Ballyhackmore
Tullycarnet
Hannahstown
Black Hill
Bloomfield
Orangefield
Ormeau
Willowfield
Queen's University
Botanic Gardens
Shandon
Gilnahirk
Milltown
Ulster Museum
Castlereagh
Windsor
Andersonstown
Cregagh
Braniel
Suffolk
Ballynafeigh
Rosetta
Ladybrook
Malone
Balmoral
Stranmillis
Poleglass
Finaghy
Taughmonagh
Crossnacreevy
Belvoir Park Forest
Newtownbreda
Gransha
Twinbrook
Belvoir
Lisleen
Dunmurry
Derryaghy
Upper Malone
Lagan
Giants Ring
Purdysburn
Lagan Valley Regional Park
Moneyreagh
1/120 000
2 km
1 mile
Lambeg
Drumbeg
Ballylesson
Lisburn
Craigavon
Enniskillen
Dublin
Downpatrick
Newcastle
Newtownards
Comber
Ballygowan

Bojana 52 C4
Bøjden 76 B3
Bojnik 53 E3
Boka Kotorska 52 B4
Bøkfjorden 67 F1
Bokn 74 A3
Boknafjorden 74 A3
Bø (Telemark) 74 B3
Bø (Vesterålen) 66 B3
Bol 50 C4
Bøla 69 D3
Bolbec 13 E2
Bolchov 79 F3
Bolera, Emb de 32 A2
Bolesławiec 80 A1
Bolgrad 81 E2
Boliden 70 B3
Boliqueime 30 B3
Boljanići 51 E4
Boljevac 53 E2
Boljevci 52 C1
Boljkovci 51 F3
Boljuni 52 B3
Bolkesjø 74 B3
Bollebygd 77 D2
Bollène 22 B2
Bollnäs 75 E2
Bollstabruk 69 F4
Bollullos de la Mitación 30 C3
Bollullos par del Condado 30 C3
Bolmen 77 D2
Bolnãos de Calatrava 31 F1
Bologna 44 B1
Bologne 15 D4
Bologoje 79 E1
Bolos 32 A1
Bolotana 46 A3
Bolsena 44 C3
Bolsena, L di 44 C3
Bolsward 11 E1
Boltaña 29 D1
Boltenhagen 37 D1
Bolton 5 D4
Bolungarvik 68 A1
Bolus Head 8 A4
Bolzano 43 D2
Bombarral 26 A4
Bomenzien 37 D3
Bom Jesus 24 B3
Bømlo 74 A3
Bonaigua, Pto de la 21 D4
Boñar 25 D2
Bonar Bridge 2 C1
Bonares 30 C3
Bonassola 23 F2
Bondeno 43 D4
Bondone, Mte 43 D3
Bonefro 45 E4
Bo'-Ness 3 D4
Bonete 32 B1
Bonette, Col de la 22 C2
Bonhomme, Col du 15 E4
Bonifacio 23 D4
Bonn 35 D3
Bonnåsjøen 66 B3
Bonnat 18 A3
Bonndorf 42 A1
Bonnétable 13 F4
Bonneuil-Matours 17 E2
Bonneval (Eure-et-Loir) 14 A4
Bonneval (Savoie) 19 F4
Bonneville 19 E3
Bonneville, la 13 F3
Bonnières 14 A3
Bonnieux 22 B3
Bono 46 B3
Bonorva 46 A3
Bønsnes 74 C3
Boo 75 F4
Boom 34 B3
Boos 14 A2
Bootle 5 D4
Bopfingen 38 C4
Boppard 38 A2
Bor (CS) 39 E2
Bor (YU) 53 E1
Boračko jez 51 D4
Borås 77 D1
Borba 26 C4
Borbollón, Emb de 26 C3
Borbona 45 D3
Borča 52 C1
Borci 51 D4
Bordeaux 20 C2
Bordeira 30 A3
Bordères-Louron 20 C4
Border Forest Park, The 5 D2
Borders Region 5 D2
Bordesholm 36 C1
Bordighera 23 D3
Borðoy 68 A3
Bore 23 F2
Borello 44 B1
Borensberg 75 E4
Boréon, le 23 D2
Borga 73 D4
Borgafjäll 69 E3
Borga-fjällen 69 E3
Borgarnes 68 A2
Børgefjell 69 E2
Børgefjellet 69 E2
Borger 11 F2
Börger 36 B3
Borghetto 44 C3
Borghetto S.S. 23 E2
Borgholm 77 E2
Borgholzhausen 36 B4
Borghorst 36 B4
Borgia 47 E3
Borgomanero 42 B4
Borgone 23 D1
Borgonovo Val Tidone 42 C4
Borgorose 45 D3
Borgo San Dalmazzo 23 D2
Borgo San Lorenzo 44 B2
Borgosesia 42 A4
Borgo Tufico 44 C2
Borgo Val di Taro 23 F2
Borgo Valsugana 43 D3
Borgsjö 75 E1
Borgund 74 B2
Borgvattnet 69 E4
Boričje 51 E4
Borisov 79 D3
Borispol' 79 E4
Borja (E) 28 B2
Borja (YU) 51 D3
Borken 11 F3
Borkenes 66 B2
Børkop 76 B3
Borkum 36 A2
Borlänge 75 E3
Bormes-les-Mimosas 22 C4
Bormida 23 E2
Bormio 42 C3
Born 37 E1
Borna 39 E1
Bornes 24 C3
Bornes, Sa de 24 C3
Bornholm 77 E3
Bornhöved 36 C1
Börnicke 37 E3
Bornos 31 D3
Bornos, Emb de 31 D3
Boroughbridge 5 E3
Borovec 81 D4
Boroviči 79 E1
Borovnica 50 A1
Borovo 51 E1
Borovsk 79 F2
Borre 74 C3
Borriol 28 C4
Borris 8 C3
Borrisokane 8 C3
Borsa 81 D2
Børselv 67 E1
Børselva 67 E1
Børselvfjellet 67 E1
Borsio 58 B3
Bort-les-Orgues 18 B4
Börtnan 69 E4
Borzna 79 F4
Borzonasca 23 F2
Bosa 46 A3
Bosanci 50 B2
Bosanska Dubica 50 C2
Bosanska Gradiška 50 C2
Bosanska Kostajnica 50 C2
Bosanska Krupa 50 B2
Bosanska Rača 51 E2
Bosanski Brod 51 D2
Bosanski Kobaš 50 C2
Bosanski Novi 50 B2
Bosanski Petrovac 50 C3
Bosanski Šamac 51 D2
Bosansko Grahovo 50 C3
Bosansko Petrovo Selo 51 D2
Bosco 44 C2
Bosco Chiesanuova 43 D3
Bosilegrad 53 F3
Bosiljevo 50 B2
Bosjökloster 77 D3
Boskoop 11 D3
Bosna 51 D2
Bosna i Hercegovina 51 D3
Bošnjace 53 F3
Bošnjaci 51 D2
Bossòst 21 D4
Bostan 51 D4
Boštanj 50 A1
Boston 7 E1
Bosut 51 E2
Botev 81 D4
Botevgrad 81 D4
Bothel 5 D2
Botičas 24 B3
Botley 7 D4
Botngård 68 C3
Botnie, G de 72 B3
Botoš 51 F1
Botoşani 81 D2
Botrange 34 C3
Botsmark 70 B3
Botte Donato, Mte 47 E3
Bottenhavet 75 F2
Bottniska Viken Pohjanlahti 72 B3
Bottrop 11 F3
Botun 54 C1
Bouaye 17 D2
Boucau 20 B3
Bouchain 14 B1
Bouches-du-Rhône 22 A3
Boudry 19 E2
Bouillon 15 D2
Bouilly 14 C4
Bouka 62 C3
Boulay-Moselle 15 E3
Boulogne (Haute-Garonne) 21 D4
Boulogne (Pas-de-Calais) 14 A1
Boulogne R 17 D2
Bouloire 13 F4
Boulou, le 21 E4
Boumort 29 E1
Bourbon-Lancy 18 C2
Bourbon-l'Archambault 18 B2
Bourbonne-les-Bains 15 D4
Bourboule, la 18 B4
Bourbourg 14 A1
Bourbriac 12 B3
Bourdeaux 22 B2
Bourdeilles 17 E4
Bourg 20 C1
Bourg-Achard 13 F2
Bourganeuf 18 A3
Bourg-Argental 18 C4
Bourg-de-Péage 22 B2
Bourg-de-Visa 21 D2
Bourg-d'Oisans, le 19 E4
Bourg-en-Bresse 19 D3
Bourges 18 B2
Bourget, le 19 E3
Bourg-Lastic 18 B3
Bourg-Madame 29 E1
Bourgneuf-en-Retz 16 C2
Bourgogne 19 D2
Bourgoin-Jallieu 19 D3
Bourg-St-Andéol 22 B2
Bourg-St-Maurice 19 E3
Bourgtheroulde 13 F3
Bourgueil 17 E2
Bourmont 15 D4
Bourne 7 E2
Bourne, Gges de la 22 B2
Bournemouth 6 C4
Bourniá, Akr 59 E4
Bousquet-d'Orb, le 21 F3
Boussac 18 B3
Boussens 21 D4
Boutonne 17 E3
Bouxwiller 15 E3
Bouzonville 15 E2
Bovalino Marina 47 E4
Bova Marina 47 E4
Bovan 53 E2
Bovec 43 F2
Bóveda 24 B2
Bøverdal 74 B2
Boves 14 A2
Boves 23 D2
Bovey Tracy 6 B3
Bovolone 43 D4
Bowes 5 E3
Bowness 5 D3
Bowness-on-Solway 5 D2
Boxholm 77 E1
Boxmeer 11 E3
Boxtel 11 E3
Boyle 8 C2
Boyne 9 D2
Božaj 52 C4
Božava 50 A3
Bozel 19 E4
Bozen 43 D2
Božica 53 E3
Boži Dar 39 E2
Bozouls 21 E2
Bozüyük 81 F4
Bozzolo 42 C4

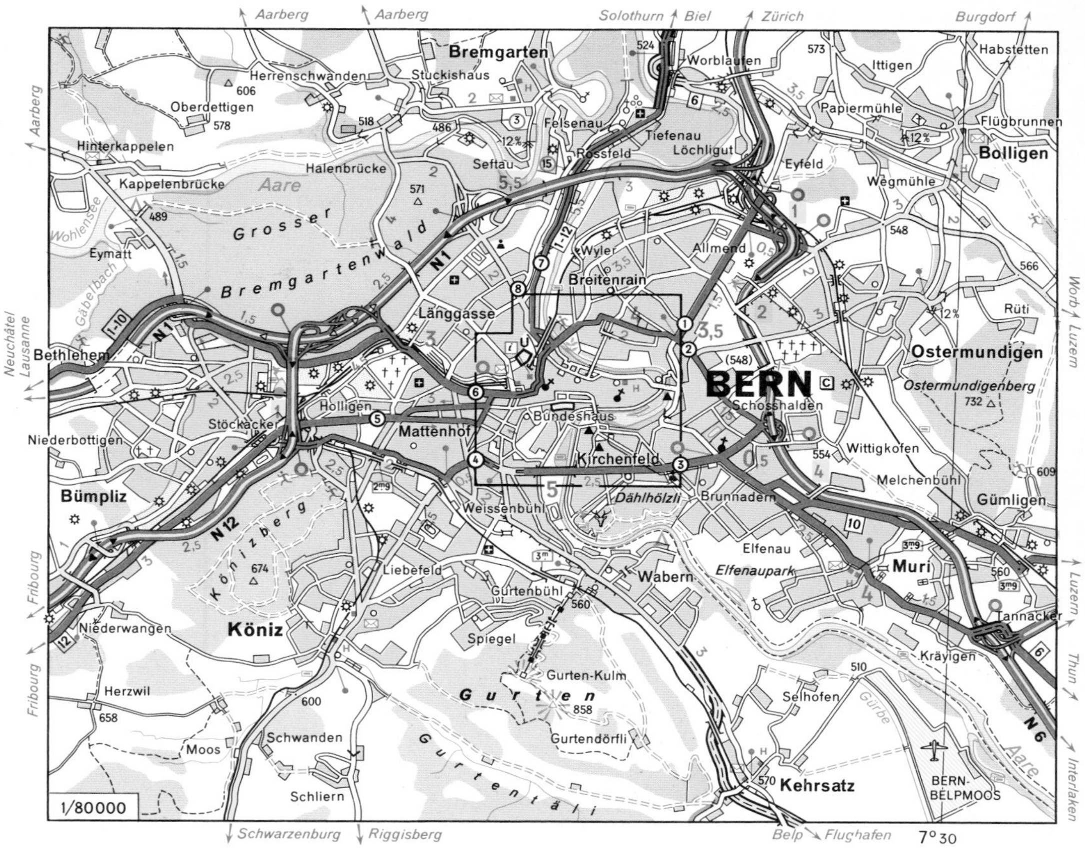

Bremgarten
Bolligen
Bremgartenwald
Bethlehem
BERN
Ostermundigen
Bümpliz
Wabern
Köniz
Gurten
Muri
Gümligen
Kehrsatz
Könizberg
1/80000
Aarberg
Solothurn
Biel
Zürich
Burgdorf
Schwarzenburg
Riggisberg
Belp
Flughafen

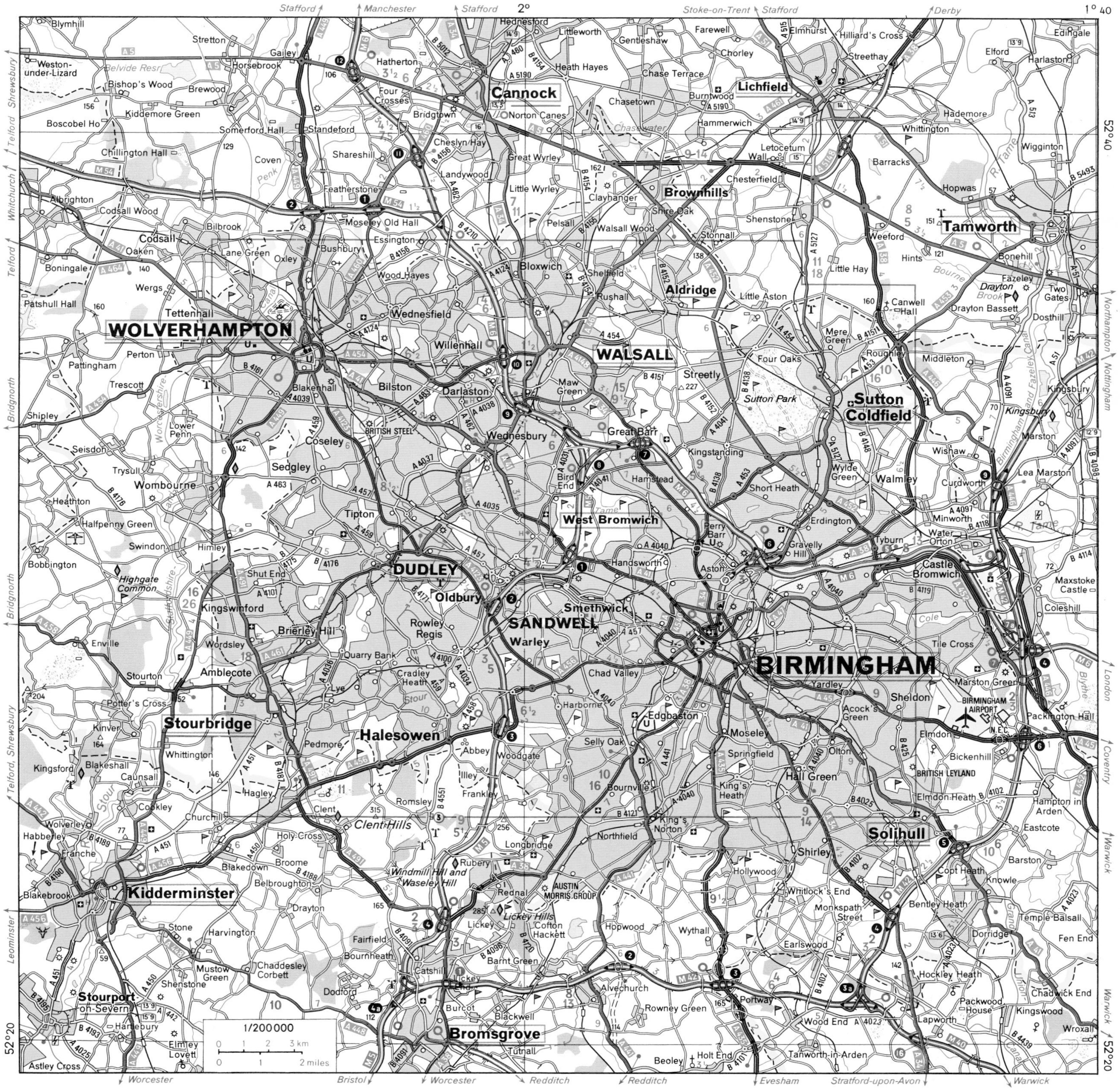

Cannock
Lichfield
Brownhills
Tamworth
WOLVERHAMPTON
WALSALL
Aldridge
Sutton Coldfield
West Bromwich
DUDLEY
Oldbury
SANDWELL
BIRMINGHAM
Stourbridge
Halesowen
Solihull
Kidderminster
Stourport-on-Severn
Bromsgrove
1/200000
Stafford
Manchester
Stoke-on-Trent
Derby
Worcester
Bristol
Redditch
Evesham
Stratford-upon-Avon
Warwick

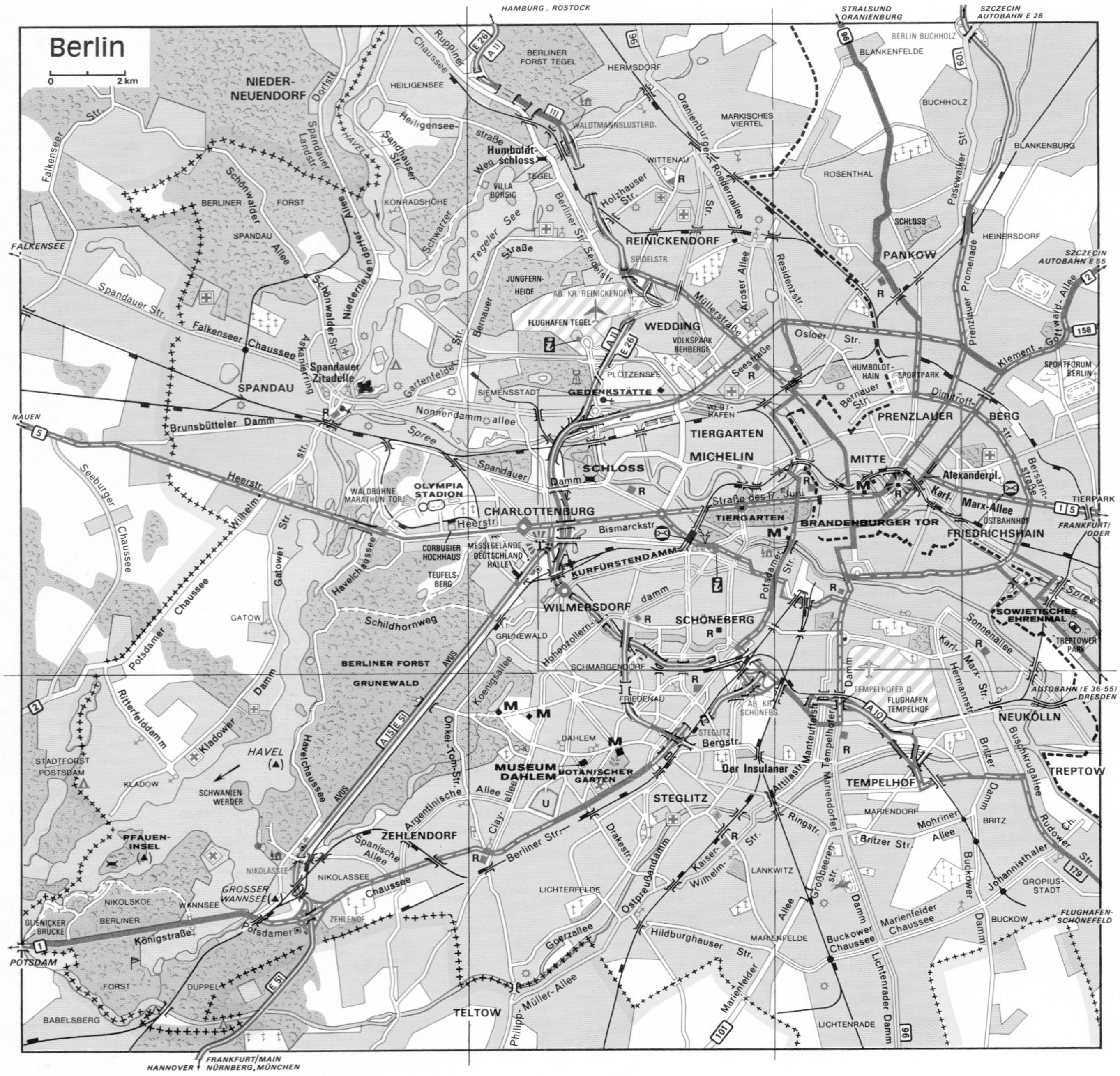
Berlin
0 2 km
HAMBURG . ROSTOCK
STRALSUND ORANIENBURG
SZCZECIN AUTOBAHN E 28
NIEDER-NEUENDORF
HERMSDORF
REINICKENDORF
PANKOW
WEDDING
SPANDAU
TIERGARTEN
MICHELIN
MITTE
PRENZLAUER
BERG
CHARLOTTENBURG
FRIEDRICHSHAIN
WILMERSDORF
SCHÖNEBERG
BRANDENBURGER TOR
NEUKÖLLN
TEMPELHOF
STEGLITZ
ZEHLENDORF
GRUNEWALD
BERLINER FORST
MUSEUM DAHLEM
TELTOW
POTSDAM
NAUEN
FALKENSEE
TREPTOW
HANNOVER
FRANKFURT/MAIN NÜRNBERG, MÜNCHEN

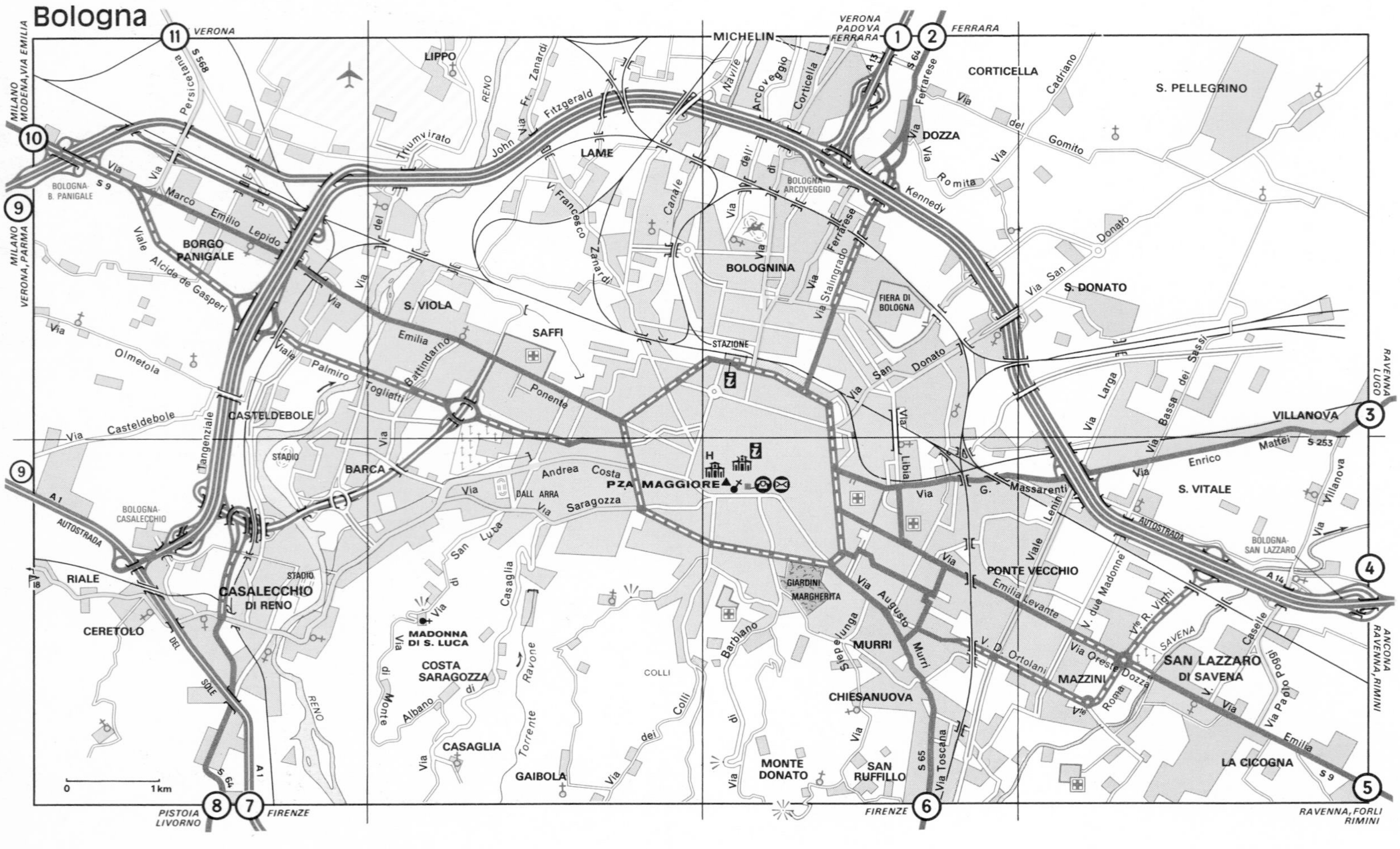
Bologna
VERONA
VERONA PADOVA FERRARA
FERRARA
MICHELIN
LIPPO
CORTICELLA
S. PELLEGRINO
LAME
DOZZA
BORGO PANIGALE
BOLOGNINA
S. VIOLA
SAFFI
S. DONATO
STAZIONE
CASTELDEBOLE
BARCA
PZA MAGGIORE
VILLANOVA
S. VITALE
CASALECCHIO DI RENO
RIALE
CERETOLO
PONTE VECCHIO
MURRI
SAN LAZZARO DI SAVENA
MAZZINI
CHIESANUOVA
COSTA SARAGOZZA
CASAGLIA
GAIBOLA
MONTE DONATO
SAN RUFFILLO
LA CICOGNA
0 1 km
PISTOIA LIVORNO
FIRENZE
RAVENNA, FORLI RIMINI
ANCONA RAVENNA, RIMINI
RAVENNA LUGO
MILANO MODENA, VIA EMILIA
MILANO VERONA, PARMA

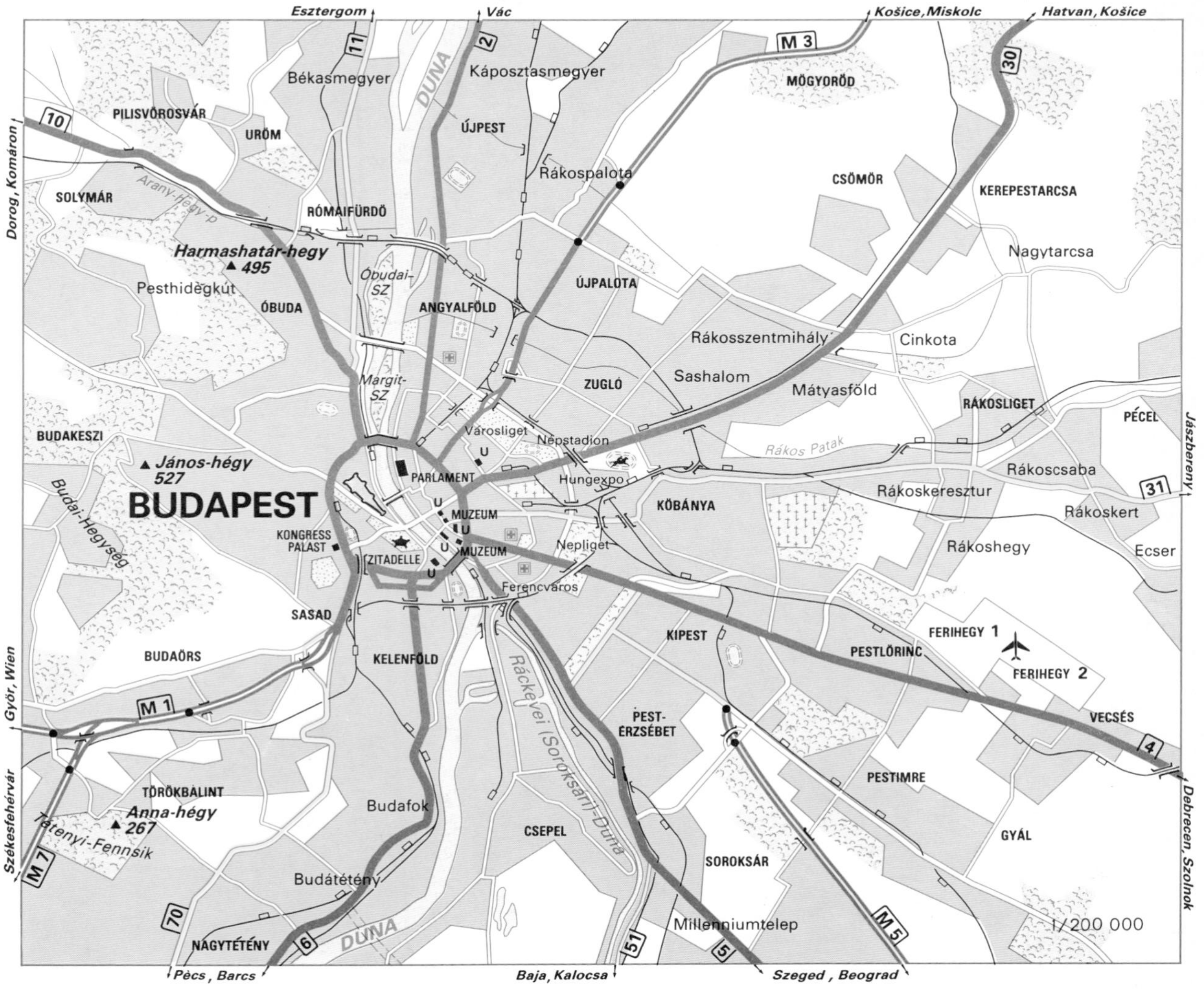
Esztergom
Vác
Košice, Miskolc
Hatvan, Košice
Dorog, Komárom
Győr, Wien
Székesfehérvár
Jászberény
Debrecen, Szolnok
Pécs, Barcs
Baja, Kalocsa
Szeged, Beograd
Békásmegyer
Káposztásmegyer
MÖGYORÓD
PILISVÖRÖSVÁR
ÚRÖM
ÚJPEST
Rákospalota
SOLYMÁR
RÓMAIFÜRDŐ
CSÖMÖR
KEREPESTARCSA
Harmashatár-hegy
495
Nagytarcsa
Pesthidegkút
Óbudai-SZ
ÓBUDA
ANGYALFÖLD
ÚJPALOTA
Rákosszentmihály
Cinkota
Margit-SZ
ZUGLÓ
Sashalom
Mátyásföld
RÁKOSLIGET
PÉCEL
BUDAKESZI
Városliget
Népstadion
János-hegy
527
PARLAMENT
Hungexpo
Rákoscsaba
Rákoskeresztúr
BUDAPEST
KŐBÁNYA
Rákoskert
KONGRESS PALAST
MUZEUM
Népliget
Rákoshegy
Ecser
ZITADELLE
Ferencváros
SASAD
KIPEST
FERIHEGY 1
FERIHEGY 2
BUDAÖRS
KELENFÖLD
PESTLŐRINC
PEST-ERZSÉBET
VECSÉS
TÖRÖKBÁLINT
Anna-hégy
267
PESTIMRE
Budafok
CSEPEL
GYÁL
SOROKSÁR
Budatétény
DUNA
NAGYTÉTÉNY
Millenniumtelep
1/200 000
M 1
M 3
M 5
M 7

C

91 km AACHEN
28 km KÖLN
FLUGHAFEN 25 km
0
400 m
DORTMUND 119 km
DÜSSELDORF 73 km
STADION
Lievelingsweg
KREUZ BONN NORD
AUTOBAHN
A 555
A 565
Lievelings- weg
Dorotheenstr.
Brühler Str.
Bornheimer Straße
Vorgebirgsstraße
BRÜHL
Ellerstraße
Bornheimer Str.
Bonn-West
Jägerstr.
Immenburg-
Endenicher Straße
Verdistr.
Kaufmann-
27 km EUSKIRCHEN
Auf dem Hügel
Endenicher Str.
Magdalenen-straße
Sebastianstr.
Endenicher Allee
Nußallee
POPPELSDORFER SCHLOSS
BOTANISCHER GARTEN
Clemens-August-Str.
Sternenburg-
Kirschallee
Trierer Str.
AHRTAL
NÜRBURGRING 56 km
COCHEM 97 km
VENUSBERG
Augustusring
Nordstr.
Kölnstraße
Graurheindorfer Straße
Römerstr.
Ellerstraße
Kaiser-
Adolfstr.
Heerstraße
Vorgebirgsstraße
KÜNSTHALLE
Dorotheenstr.
Breite Straße
Maxstraße
STADTHAUS
Stadthaus
Bornheimer Str.
ALTER FRIEDHOF
Viktoriabrücke
Hochstadenring
Thomastr.
Herwarthstr.
Mozartstr.
Wittelsbacherring
Haydnstr.
Bachstr.
Colmantstr.
Beethovenpl.
Baumschul-allee
Beethovenstr.
Meckenheimer Allee
Poppelsdorfer Allee
Bonner Talweg
Argelanderstr.
Weberstr.
Kurfürstenstr.
Reuterstr.
Argelanderstr.
Luisenstr.
Talweg
Hausdorffstr.
Schumannstr.
Lessingstr.
Bonner
Rosental
BEETHOVENHALLE
Theaterstr.
Sandkaule
Kölnstr.
Friedrichstr.
Beethovenhaus
STERNTOR
Am Hof
KURFÜRSTLICHE RESIDENZ
Universität
Markt
HAUPTBAHNHOF
Hbf
Quantiusstr.
Kaiserplatz
Am Hofgarten
HOFGARTEN
KOBLENZER TOR
STADTGARTEN
Adenauerallee
Juridicum
Lennéstr.
Kaiserstr.
Erzberger Ufer
Brassert-Ufer
Rathenau-Ufer
Auswärtiges Amt
Joachimstr.
Schedestr.
Kaiser-Friedrich-Str.
HAUS DES BUNDESPRÄSIDENTEN
Museum Koenig
HAUS DES BUNDESKANZLERS
Bundeskanzlerpl.
BUNDESKANZLERAMT
Buschstraße
Niebuhrstr.
BAD GODESBERG 7 km
KOBLENZ 63 km
Bonn
SCHWARZ-RHEINDORF-KIRCHE
AUTOBAHN (E 35 - A 3) 13 km
SIEGBURG 11 km
FLUGHAFEN 27 km
FRANKFURT 176 km
Rheinaustr.
Prof.-Neu-Allee
Rheindorfer Str.
Augustiner
KENNEDYBRÜCKE
Friedrich-Breuer-Str.
Hermann-
Rheinau
BEUEL
Goetheallee
16 km DRACHENFELS
11 km KÖNIGSWINTER
(KÖLN-DÜSSELDORFER)
RHEIN
Ringstraße
Wilhelm-Spiritus-Ufer
POL.

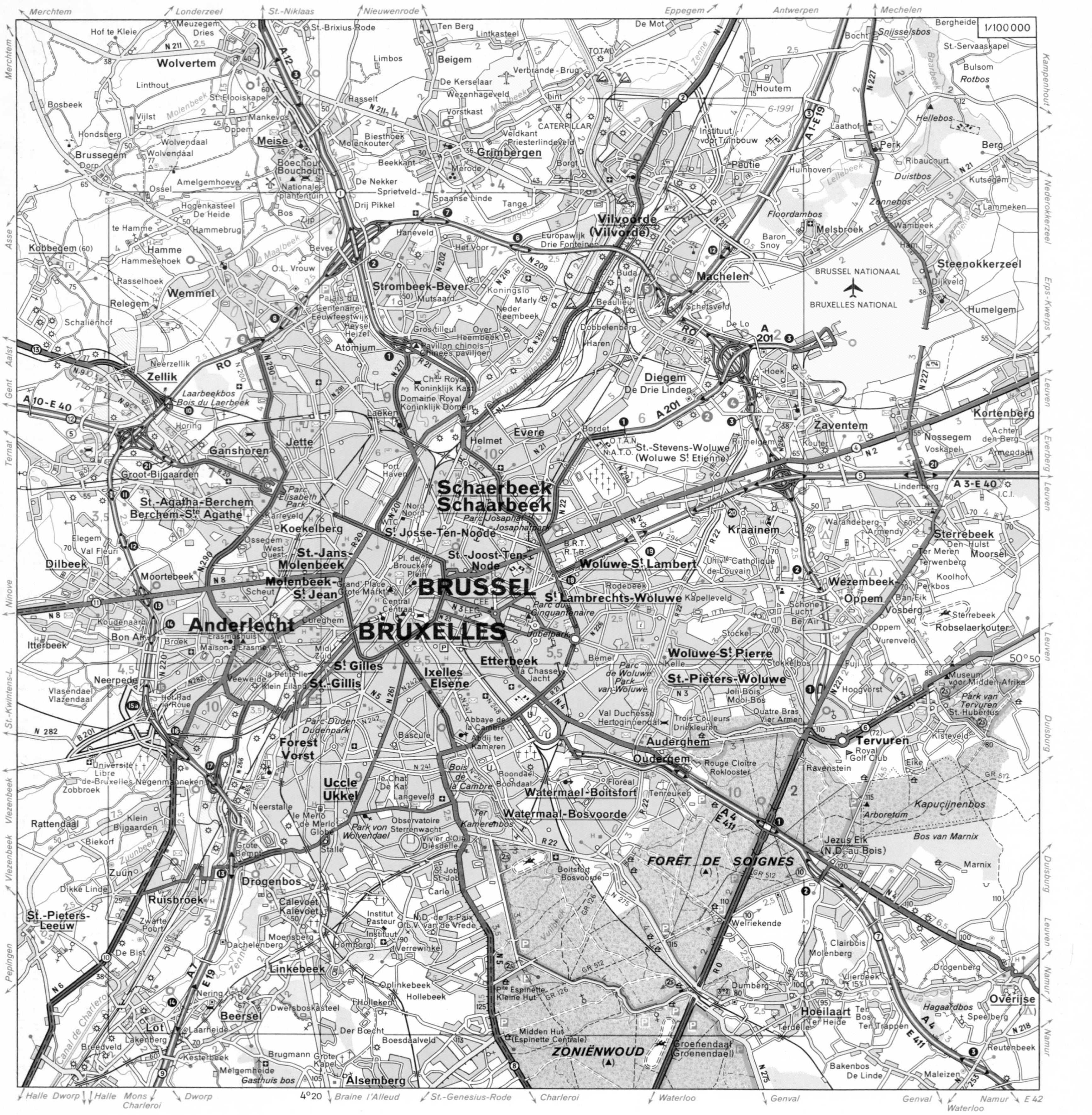
1/100 000
BRUSSEL
BRUXELLES
Schaerbeek
Schaarbeek
Anderlecht
Vilvoorde (Vilvorde)
Zaventem
Machelen
BRUSSEL NATIONAAL
BRUXELLES NATIONAL
Wolvertem
Grimbergen
Meise
Strombeek-Bever
Wemmel
Zellik
Jette
Ganshoren
Koekelberg
Evere
Diegem
Kortenberg
Steenokkerzeel
Humelgem
Sterrebeek
Kraainem
Woluwe-St Lambert
Wezembeek-Oppem
Etterbeek
Ixelles
Elsene
St Gilles
St-Gillis
Forest
Vorst
Uccle
Ukkel
Auderghem
Oudergem
Watermael-Boitsfort
Watermaal-Bosvoorde
Tervuren
FORÊT DE SOIGNES
ZONIËNWOUD
Drogenbos
Ruisbroek
St.-Pieters-Leeuw
Linkebeek
Beersel
Alsemberg
Hoeilaart
Overijse
Dilbeek
Itterbeek
Groenendaal
Merchtem
Londerzeel
St.-Niklaas
Nieuwenrode
Eppegem
Antwerpen
Mechelen
Halle
Mons
Charleroi
Braine l'Alleud
Waterloo
Genval
Namur
Leuven

Casa Branca (Ribatejo) 26 B4
Casacalenda 45 E4
Casalarreina 25 F2
Casalbordino 45 E3
Casalbuttano 42 C4
Casal di Principe 46 B1
Casalecchio di Reno 44 B1
Casale Monferrato 23 E1
Casale sul Sile 43 E3
Casalmaggiore 42 C4
Casalpusterlengo 42 C4
Casamassima 47 E1
Casamicciola Terme 46 B2
Casa Nuevas 32 B2
Casarabonela 31 E3
Casarano 47 F2
Casar de Cáceres 26 C4
Casares 31 D4
Casares de las Hurdes 27 D3
Casariche 31 E3
Casarsa 43 E3
Casas de Don Pedro 27 D4
Casas de Fernando Alonso 32 A1
Casas de Juan Núñez 32 B1
Casas del Puerto 32 B2
Casas de Luján 28 A4
Casas de Miravete 27 D4
Casas Ibáñez 32 B1
Casasimarro 32 B1
Casatejada 27 D3
Casavieja 27 E3
Cascais 26 A4
Cascante 28 B2
Cascia 44 C3
Casciana Terme 44 A2
Cascina 44 A2
Casei Gerola 23 E1
Caselle in Pittari 47 D2
Caselle Torinese 23 D1
Caserío del Puente 25 D3
Caserta 46 C1
Casetas 28 C2
Cas-gwent 6 C3
Cashel 8 C3
Casicas del Río Segura 32 A2
Casillas 26 C3
Casina 44 A1
Casinos 28 C4
Casnewydd 6 C3
Casoio 24 C2
Casola in Lunigiana 44 A1
Casoli 45 E3
Casoria 46 B1
Caspe 28 C2
Cassà de la Selva 29 F2
Cassagnes-Begonhès 21 E3
Cassano allo Ionio 47 E2
Cassano delle Murge 47 E1
Cassel 14 A1
Cassino 45 D4
Cassis 22 B4
Castalla 32 C2
Castanet-Tolosan 21 D3
Castanheira de Pêra 26 B3
Castaños, Pto de los 27 D3
Castasegna 42 B3
Casteggio 23 E1
Castejón 28 B1
Castejón de Monègros 28 C2
Castejón de Sos 29 D1
Castejón de Valdejasa 28 C2
Castelbuono 48 C3
Casteldaccia 48 B3
Casteldelfino 23 D2
Castel del Monte (Abruzzo) 45 D3
Castel del Monte (Puglia) 45 F4
Castel del Rio 44 B1
Castel di Sangro 45 E4
Castelfidardo 45 D2
Castelfiorentino 44 B2
Castelfranco Emilia 44 B1
Castelfranco in Miscano 45 F4
Castelfranco Veneto 43 D3
Castel Gandolfo 44 C4
Casteljaloux 20 C2
Castellabate 46 C2
Castellamare di Stabbia 46 C2
Castellammare, G di 48 B3
Castellamonte 23 D1
Castellana Grotte 47 E1
Castellane 22 C3
Castellaneta 47 E1
Castellar de la Muela 28 B3
Castellar del Vallès 29 E2
Castellar de Santiago 32 A2
Castellar de Santisteban 32 A2
Castell' Arquato 23 F1
Castelldans 29 D2
Castelldefels 29 E2
Castell de Ferro 31 F4
Castelleone 42 C4
Castellfollit de la Roca 29 F1
Castellina in Chianti 44 B2
Castell-nedd 6 B3
Castelló de la Plana 29 D4
Castello del Lago 46 C1
Castelló d'Empúries 29 F1
Castellolí 29 E2
Castellón de la Plana 29 D4
Castellón de Rugat 32 C1
Castellote 28 C3
Castello Tesino 43 D3
Castellterçol 29 E2
Castelluccio 45 D3
Castel Madama 45 D4
Castelmassa 43 D4
Castelmauro 45 E4
Castelmoron 20 C2
Castelnaudary 21 E3
Castelnau-de-Médoc 20 B2
Castelnau-de-Montmiral 21 E3
Castelnau-Magnoac 20 C4
Castelnau-Montratier 21 D2
Castelnau-Rivière-Basse 20 C3
Castelnovo ne' Monti 44 A1
Castelnuovo Berardenga 44 B2
Castelnuovo Bocca d'Adda 42 C4
Castelnuovo della Daunia 45 F4
Castelnuovo di Garfagnana 44 A2
Castelnuovo di Porto 44 C4
Castelnuovo Scrivia 23 E1
Castelo Branco 26 B3
Castelo de Bode, Bgem do 26 A4
Castelo de Paiva 24 A4
Castelo de Vide 26 B4
Castelraimondo 44 C2
Castelrotto 43 D2
Castel San Giovanni 23 E1
Castel San Lorenzo 46 C2
Castel San Pietro Terme 44 B1
Castelsardo 46 A2
Castelsarrasin 21 D3
Castelserás 28 C3
Casteltermini 48 C4
Castelvecchio Subequo 45 D3
Castelvetrano 48 B4
Castel Volturno 46 B1
Castets 20 B3
Castiadas 46 B4
Castiglioncello 44 A2
Castiglione d'Adda 42 C4
Castiglione dei Pepoli 44 B1
Castiglione del Lago 44 C2
Castiglione della Pescaia 44 B3
Castiglione delle Stiviere 42 C4
Castiglione in Teverina 44 C3
Castiglione Messer Marino 45 E4
Castiglione Olona 42 B3
Castiglion Fiorentino 44 B2
Castilblanco 31 E1
Castilblanco de los Arroyos 31 D2
Castilla, Canal de 25 E3
Castilla-La Mancha 31 F1
Castilla-León 25 E3
Castilla, Mar de 28 A3
Castilleja del Campo 30 C3
Castilléjar 32 A3
Castillejo 27 D2
Castillejo de Martin Viejo 26 C2
Castillo de Loarre 28 C1
Castillo de Locubín 31 E3
Castillon, Bge de 22 C3
Castillon-en-Couserans 21 D4
Castillon-la-Bataille 20 C2
Castillonnès 21 D2
Castillo, Pto del 31 F3
Castillo y Elejabeitia 20 A4
Castilruiz 28 B2
Castions di Strada 43 E3
Castlebar 8 B2
Castlebay 2 A2
Castlebellingham 9 D2
Castleblayney 9 D2
Castlecomer 8 C3
Castledawson 9 D1
Castlederg 8 C1
Castledermot 8 C3
Castle Douglas 4 C2
Castleford 5 E4
Castleisland 8 A4
Castlemaine 8 A4
Castlepollard 8 C2
Castlerea 8 B2
Castlerock 4 B2
Castleton 5 E4
Castletown (I of Man) 4 C3
Castletown (Scotland) 3 D1
Castletownbere 8 A4
Castlewellan 9 D2
Castocalbón 25 D3
Castrejón 25 D4
Castrejón, Emb de 27 E4
Castres 21 E3
Castries 22 A3
Castríl 32 A2
Castrillo de la Reina 25 F3
Castrillo de Villavega 25 E2
Castro 24 B1
Castro 24 B2
Castro Caldelas 24 B2
Castrocaro Terme 44 B1
Castrocontrigo 24 C3
Castro Daire 24 B4
Castro del Río 31 E2
Castrogeriz 25 E3
Castro Laboreiro 24 B3
Castro Marim 30 B3
Castromonte 25 D3
Castronuevo 25 D3
Castronuño 25 D4
Castropol 24 C1
Castrop-Rauxel 36 B4
Castroreale 49 D3
Castroreale Terme 49 D3
Castrotierra 25 D2
Castro Urdiales 25 F1
Castroverde 24 B2
Castro Verde 30 B2
Castroverde de Campos 25 D3
Castrovillari 47 D2
Castuera 31 D1
Cataluña 29 E1
Catalunya 29 D2
Catania 49 D3
Catania, G di 49 D4
Catanzaro 47 E3
Catanzaro Lido 47 E3
Catarroja 32 C1
Cateau, le 14 B2
Catelet, le 14 B2
Catenanuova 49 D3
Catež 50 B1
Cathair na Mart 8 B2
Čatići 51 D3
Catignano 45 D3
Catoira 24 A2
Catoute 24 C2
Catral 32 C2
Catria, Mte 44 C2
Cattenom 15 D2
Cattolica 44 C1
Catus 21 D2
Caudebec 13 F2
Caudete 32 C1
Caudiel 28 C4
Caudry 14 B2
Caulnes 12 C4
Caulonia 47 E4
Caumont-l'Eventé 13 D3
Caunes 21 E3
Caussade 21 D3
Čausy 79 E3
Cauterets 20 C4
Cava de' Tirreni 46 C2
Cávado, R 24 A3
Cavaglià 23 D1
Cavaillon 22 B3
Cavalaire 22 C4
Cavalerie, la 21 F3
Cavalese 43 D3
Cavalière 22 C4
Cavan 8 C2
Cavan (Co) 8 C2
Cavarzere 43 E4
Cavazzo 43 E2
Cavero, Pto de 28 B2
Cavezzo 43 D4
Cavo 44 A3
Cavo, Mte 44 C4
Cavour 23 D2
Cavtat 52 B4
Caya 26 C4
Cayeux 14 A2
Caylar, le 21 F3
Caylus 21 E2
Cayolle, Col de la 22 C2
Cayres 22 A2
Cazalla de la Sierra 31 D2
Cazals 21 D2
Cazaubon 20 C3
Cazaux 20 B2
Cazères 21 D4
Cazin 50 B2
Čazma 50 C1
Cazorla 32 A2
Cazorla, Sa de 32 A2
Cea 24 B2
Ceanannus Mor 8 C2
Cea, R 25 D2
Ceatharlach 8 C3
Cebolla 27 E3
Cebollera 28 A2
Cebreros 27 E3
Ceccano 45 D4
Cece 80 B2
Cechy 39 F2
Cecina 44 A2
Cecina R 44 A2
Cecita, L. di 47 E3
Ceclavín 26 C3
Cedeira 24 B1
Cedillo, Bgem de 26 B3
Cedrillas 28 C3
Cedrino 46 B3
Cedynia 37 F2
Cefalù 48 C3
Cega, R 25 E4
Cegléd 80 C2
Ceglie Messapico 47 E1
Čegrane 53 E4
Cehegín 32 B2
Čehotina 51 E4
Ceira, R 26 B3
Čejč 41 F1
Čelákovice 39 F2
Celano 45 D3
Celanova 24 B2
Čelavevo 51 E1
Čelebić 50 C3
Čelebići 51 E4
Celemín, Emb de 31 D4
Čelić 51 E2
Čelinac Donji 50 C2
Celje 50 A1
Cella 28 B3
Celle 36 C3
Celle Ligure 23 E2
Celles 17 E3
Čelopeci 53 E4
Celorico 24 B3
Celorico da Beira 26 C2
Čemerna pl 53 D2
Čemernica 50 C3
Čemerno 52 B3
Cenajo, Emb del 32 B2
Cencenighe 43 D2
Cenicero 28 A1
Čenta 51 F1
Centelles 29 F2
Cento 44 B1
Cento Croci, Pso 23 F2
Central Region 2 C3
Centre, Canal du 18 C2
Centuripe 49 D3
Cepagatti 45 D3
Čepin 51 D1
Ceppo 45 D3
Ceprano 45 D4
Čer 51 E2
Čeralije 50 C1
Cerbère 29 F2
Cercal (Alentejo) 30 A2
Cercal (Estremadura) 26 A4
Cercedilla 27 F3
Cerchiara di Calabria 47 E2
Cerchov 39 E3
Cerdedo 24 A2
Cerdeira 26 C3
Cère 21 E2
Cerea 43 D4
Cereda, Pso di 43 D3
Čerepovec 79 F1
Ceres 23 D1
Ceresole Reale 23 D1
Céret 29 F1
Cerezo de Abajo 27 F2
Cerezo de Riotirón 25 F2
Cerignola 45 F4
Cérilly 18 B2
Cerisiers 14 B4
Cerisy-la-Salle 13 D3
Cerizay 17 D2
Čerkassy 81 F1
Cerknica 50 A2
Cerkniško jez 50 A2
Cerkno 43 F3
Cerler 29 D1
Černá 41 D2
Cerna 51 D2
Cernache de Bonjardim 26 B3
Čern'achovsk 78 C3
Cernadilla, Emb de 24 C3
Cernavodă 81 E3
Cernay 15 E4
Černigov 79 E4
Cernik 50 C2
Cernobbio 42 B3
Černobyl' 79 E4
Černomorskoje 81 F2
Černovcy 81 D2
Cerreto, Pso del 44 A1
Cerreto Sannita 46 C1
Cerrigydrudion 6 B1
Cërrik 54 A2
Certaldo 44 B2
Certosa di Pavia 23 E1
Cervales 27 D4
Cervaro 45 F4
Cervati, Mte 47 D2
Cervatos 25 E2
Cervatos de la Cueza 25 E3
Červen' 79 D3
Cervera 29 E2
Cervera de la Cañada 28 B2
Cervera del Río Alhama 28 B2
Cervera de Pisuerga 25 E2
Cerveteri 44 C4
Cervia 44 C1
Cervialto, Mte 46 C1
Cervignano del Friuli 43 F3
Cervinara 46 C1
Cervino 19 F3
Cervione 23 D3
Cervo 24 B1
Červonograd 81 D1
Cesana Torinese 19 E4
Cesarica 50 A3
Cesarò 49 D3
Cesena 44 C1
Cesenatico 44 C1
Cēsis 78 C2
Česka Kamenice 39 F1
Česká Lípa 39 F1
České Budějovice 41 D2
České Velenice 41 E2
Český Krumlov 41 D2
Česma 50 C1
Çeşme 61 D2
Cespedosa 27 D3
Cessalto 43 E3
Cetina (E) 28 B2
Cetina R (YU) 50 C4
Cetinje 52 C4
Cetraro 47 D3
Ceutí 32 B2
Ceva 23 D2
Cevedale, Mte 42 C3
Cévennes, Parc Nat des 22 A2
Cevico de la Torre 25 E3
Čevo 52 C4
Ceyrat 18 B3
Ceyzériat 19 D3
Cèze 22 A2
Chabanais 17 E3
Chabeuil 22 B2
Chablis 14 C4
Chabris 18 A2
Chagny 19 D2
Chailland 13 D4
Chaillé 17 D3
Chaise-Dieu, la 18 C4
Chalabre 21 E4
Chalais 17 E4
Chalamont 19 D3
Chalampé 15 E4
Chalindrey 15 D4
Challans 16 C2
Challes 19 E3
Chalonnes 17 D1
Châlons-sur-Marne 14 C3
Chalon-sur-Saône 19 D2
Châlus 17 F3
Cham 39 E3
Chambéry 19 E3
Chambley 15 D3
Chambly 14 A3
Chambon, Bge du 19 E4
Chambon-Feugerolles, le 18 C4
Chambon-sur-Lac 18 B4
Chambon-sur-Lignon, le 22 A2
Chambon-sur-Voueize 18 B3
Chambord 18 A1
Chambre, la 19 E4
Chamonix 19 E3
Champagnac-de-Belair 17 E4
Champagne-Mouton 17 E3
Champagnole 19 E2
Champdeniers 17 E2
Champeaux 13 D4
Champéry 19 E3
Champex 19 F3
Champlitte 19 D1
Champlon, Bre de 34 C4
Champoluc 42 A3
Champorcher 23 D1
Champs-sur-Tarentaine 18 B4
Champtoceaux 17 D1
Chamrousse 19 E4
Chamusca 26 B4
Chanac 21 F2
Chanas 19 D4
Chança, R 30 B2
Chantada 24 B2
Chantelle 18 B3
Chantemerle 19 E4
Chantilly 14 A3
Chantonnay 17 D2
Chanza, Emb del 30 B2
Chaource 14 C4
Chapel-en-le-Frith 5 E4
Chapelle-d'Angillon, la 18 B2
Chapelle-de-Guinchay, la 19 D3
Chapelle-en-Valgaudemar, la 22 C2
Chapelle-en-Vercors, la 22 B2
Chapinería 27 F3
Charbonnières 19 D3
Charco Redondo, Emb de 31 D4
Chard 6 C4
Charente 17 D3
Charente (Dépt) 17 E3
Charente-Maritime 17 D3
Charenton-du-Cher 18 B2
Charité, la 18 B2
Charleroi 34 B3
Charlestown 8 B2
Charleville 8 B4
Charleville-Mézières 14 C2
Charlieu 18 C3
Charlottenberg 75 D3
Charly 14 B2
Charmes 15 E4
Charny (Meuse) 15 D3
Charny (Yonne) 14 B4
Charolles 18 C3
Chârost 18 A2
Charquemont 19 E2
Charroux 17 E3
Chartre, la 17 E1
Chartres 14 A4
Chãs 26 B2
Chasseneuil 17 E3
Chasseral la Neuveville 19 E2
Chasseron, le 19 E2
Châtaigneraie, la 17 D2
Château-Arnoux 22 C3
Châteaubourg 13 D4
Châteaubriant 17 D1
Château-Chinon 18 C2
Château-de-Bonaguil 21 D2
Château de Ventadour 18 A4
Château d'Oex 19 F2
Château-du-Loir 17 E1
Châteaudun 14 A4
Châteaugiron 13 D4
Château-Gontier 17 D1
Château-Landon 14 B4
Château-la-Vallière 17 E1
Château, le 17 D3
Châteaulin 12 B4
Châteaumeillant 18 B2
Châteauneuf (Charente) 17 E3
Châteauneuf (Ille-et-Vilaine) 12 C3
Châteauneuf-de-Randon 21 F2
Châteauneuf-du-Faou 12 B4
Châteauneuf-du-Pape 22 B3
Châteauneuf-en-Thymerais 14 A3
Châteauneuf-la-Forêt 18 A3
Châteauneuf-les-Bains 18 B3
Châteauneuf-sur-Cher 18 B2
Châteauneuf-sur-Loire 14 A4
Châteauneuf-sur-Sarthe 17 E1
Châteauponsac 17 F3
Château-Porcien 14 C2
Château-Queyras 19 E4
Château-Regnault 14 C2
Châteaurenard (Loiret) 14 B4
Châteaurenard (Vaucluse) 22 B3
Château-Renault 17 F1
Châteauroux 18 A2
Château-Salins 15 E3
Château-Thierry 14 B3
Châteauvillain 14 C4
Châtel 19 E3
Châtelaillon-Plage 17 D3
Châtelard, le 19 E3
Châtelaudren 12 C3
Châteldon 18 C3
Châtelet 34 B3
Châtelet, le (Cher) 18 B2
Châtelet, le (Seine-et-Marne) 14 B3
Châtelguyon 18 B3
Châtellerault 17 E2
Châtel-Montagne 18 C3
Châtel-St-Denis 19 E2
Châtel-sur-Moselle 15 E4
Châtelus-Malvaleix 18 A3
Châtenois 15 D4
Chatham 7 E3
Châtillon 42 A4
Châtillon-Coligny 14 B4
Châtillon-en-Bazois 18 C2
Châtillon-en-Diois 22 B2
Châtillon-sur-Chalaronne 19 D3
Châtillon-sur-Indre 17 F2
Châtillon-sur-Loire 18 B1
Châtillon-sur-Marne 14 B3
Châtillon-sur-Seine 14 C4
Châtre, la 18 A2
Chatsworth House 7 D1
Chatteris 7 E2
Chaudes-Aigues 21 F2
Chauffailles 18 C3
Chaufour 14 A3
Chaulnes 14 B2
Chaumergy 19 D2
Chaumont (Haute-Marne) 15 D4
Chaumont (Loir-et-Cher) 17 F1
Chaumont-en-Vexin 14 A3
Chauny 14 B2
Chausey, I 13 D3
Chaussin 19 D2
Chauvigny 17 E2
Chaux-de Fonds, la 19 E2
Chaves 24 B3
Chazelles 18 C3
Cheb 39 E2
Cheddar Gorge 6 C3
Chef-Boutonne 17 E3
Cheles 30 C1
Chełm 78 C4
Chełmno 78 B4
Chelmsford 7 E3
Cheltenham 6 C2
Chelva 28 C4
Chemillé 17 D2
Chemin 19 D2
Chénérailles 18 B3
Chenonceaux 17 F2
Chepstow 6 C3
Cher 18 B2
Cher (Dépt) 18 B2
Chera 28 C4
Cherbourg 13 D2
Chéroy 14 B4
Cherson 81 F2
Chert 29 D3
Cheshire 6 C1
Cheshunt 7 E3
Chesne, le 14 C2
Cheste 32 C1
Chester 6 C1
Chesterfield 7 D1
Chester-le-Street 5 E2
Chevagnes 18 C2
Chevillon 15 D3
Cheviot Hills, The 5 E2
Cheviot, The 5 E2
Chèvre, Cap de la 12 A4
Chevreuse 14 A3
Cheylard, le 22 A2
Chèze, la 12 C4
Chiampo 43 D3
Chianciano Terme 44 B3
Chianti 44 B2
Chiaramonte Gulfi 49 D4
Chiaravalle 45 D2
Chiaravalle Centrale 47 E4
Chiari 42 C4
Chiasso 42 B3
Chiavari 23 F2
Chiavenna 42 B3
Chichester 7 D4
Chiclana de la Frontera 30 C4
Chieming 40 C3
Chiemsee 40 C3
Chieri 23 D1
Chiers 15 D2
Chiesa in Valmalenco 42 C3
Chiesina Uzz. 44 A2
Chieti 45 E3
Chiltern Hills 7 D3
Chimay 34 B4
Chimorra 31 E2
Chinchilla de Monte Aragón 32 B1
Chinchón 27 F3
Chinon 17 E2
Chioggia 43 E4
Chioula, Col de 21 E4
Chipiona 30 C3
Chippenham 6 C3
Chipping Campden 7 D2
Chipping Norton 7 D2
Chipping Sodbury 6 C3
Chirivel 32 A3
Chișineu-Criș 80 C2
Chisone 23 D1
Chiusa 43 D2
Chiusa di Pesio 23 D2
Chiusa Sclafani 48 B3
Chiusatorte 43 E2
Chiusi 44 C3
Chiva 32 C1
Chivasso 23 D1
Chlum u Třeboně 41 E2
Chmel'nickij 81 D1
Chmel'nik 81 E1
Chodov 39 E2
Chojna 37 F2
Chojnice 78 B3
Chojniki 79 E4
Cholet 17 D2
Chollerford 5 E2
Cholm 79 E2
Chomutov 39 E2
Chorges 22 C2
Chorley 5 D4
Chorol 79 F4
Choszczno 78 A4
Chotin 81 D1
Chouto 26 B4
Chrastava 39 F1
Christchurch 7 D4
Christiansfeld 76 B3
Christiansø 77 D3
Chur 42 B2
Church Stretton 6 C2
Chust 81 D2
Ciamarella 23 D1
Cians, Gorges du 23 D3
Ćićarija 43 F3
Čičavica 53 D3
Cicciano 46 C1
Čićevac 53 D2
Čičevo 52 B3
Cidacos, R 28 B1
Cidade Nova de Santo André 30 A2
Cidones 28 A2
Ciechanów 78 C4
Ciechocinek 78 B4
Ciempozuelos 27 F3
Cíes, Is 24 A2
Cieszyn 80 B1
Cieza 32 B2
Cifuentes 28 A3
Cigliano 23 D1
Cigüela R 28 A4
Cijara, Emb de 31 E1
Cijevna 52 C4
Cilavegna 42 B4
Čilipi 52 B4
Cill Airne 8 A4
Cillas 28 B3
Cill Chainnigh 8 C3
Cilleros 26 C3
Cilleruelo de Bezana 25 E2
Cill Mhantáin 9 D3
Cima Brenta 43 D3
Cima d'Asta 43 D3
Cimadolmo 43 E3
Cima Presanella 42 C3
Cimišlija 81 E2
Cimone, Mte 44 A1
Cîmpeni 81 D2
Cîmpina 81 D3
Cîmpulung 81 D3
Cîmpulung Moldovenesc 81 D2
Cinca, R 29 D2
Cincar 50 C3
Cinctorres 28 C3
Ciney 34 C4
Cinfães 24 A4
Cingoli 45 D2
Cinigiano 44 B3
Cinisi 48 B3
Cinovec 39 F1
Cinque Terre 23 F2
Cintegabelle 21 D3
Cinto, M 23 E3
Cintruénigo 28 B1
Ciórraga 20 A4
Ciotat, la 22 B4
Čiovo 50 C4
Cirencester 7 D3
Cirey 15 E3
Ciria 28 B2
Ciriè 23 D1
Cirò 47 E3
Cirò Marina 47 E3
Čirpan 81 D4
Cisa, Pso della 23 F2
Cisneros 25 D3
Čista 50 B4
Cista Provo 50 C4
Cisterna di Latina 46 A1
Cisternino 47 E1
Cistierna 25 D2
Čitluk (Mostar) 52 A3
Čitluk (Posušje) 51 D4
Cittadella 43 D3
Città del Pieve 44 C3
Città di Castello 44 C2
Cittaducale 44 C3
Cittanova 47 E4
Cittareale 45 D3
Città Sant' Angelo 45 D3
Ciudad Encantada 28 B4
Ciudad Real 31 F1
Ciudad Rodrigo 26 C2
Ciutadella de Menorca 33 F2
Cividale del Friuli 43 F3
Civita Castellana 44 C3
Civitanova Marche 45 D2
Civitavecchia 44 B4
Civitella del Tronto 45 D3
Civitella Roveto 45 D4
Civray 17 E3
Clacton-on-Sea 7 F3
Clain 17 E3
Clairvaux 15 D2
Clairvaux-les-Lacs 19 D2
Clamecy 18 C1
Claonaig 2 B4
Clapham 5 D3
Clara 8 C3
Clare 7 E2
Clare (Co) 8 B3
Clare R 8 B2
Clare I 8 A2
Claremorris 8 B2
Claudy 4 A2
Clausthal-Zellerfeld 37 D4
Claut 43 E3
Claviere 19 E4
Clavín, Pto de 26 C4
Clay Cross 7 D1
Claye-Souilly 14 B3
Clayette, la 18 C3
Clear I 8 A4
Clécy 13 E3
Cleethorpes 5 F4
Clefmont 15 D4
Cléguérec 12 C4
Clelles 22 B2
Clères 13 F2
Clermont 14 A2
Clermont-en-Argonne 15 D3
Clermont-Ferrand 18 B3
Clermont-l'Hérault 21 F3
Cléry 18 A1
Cles 43 D3
Clevedon 6 C3
Cleveland Hills 5 E3
Cleveleys 5 D3
Clew B 8 A2
Clifden 8 A2
Clisham 2 B1
Clisson 17 D2
Clitheroe 5 D3
Cloghan 8 C3
Clogheen 8 B4
Clogher Head 8 A4
Clogherhead 9 D2
Clogh Mills 4 B2
Clonakilty 8 B4
Clonbur 8 B2
Clondalkin 9 D3
Clones 8 C2
Clonfert 8 C3
Clonmacnoise 8 C3
Clonmel 8 C4
Cloppenburg 36 B3
Clovelly 6 A3
Cloyes 14 A4
Cluain Meala 8 C4
Cluj-Napoca 81 D2
Clun 6 C2
Cluny 18 C3
Clusaz, la 19 E3
Cluse de Pontarlier 19 E2
Cluses 19 E3
Clusone 42 C3
Clwyd 6 C1
Clyde 5 D1
Clydebank 2 C4
Clyde, Firth of 4 C1
Coachford 8 B4
Coalisland 9 D1
Coalville 7 D2
Coaña 24 C1
Côa, R 26 C2
Coatbridge 2 C4
Cobeña 27 F3
Cobh 8 B4
Coburg 39 D2
Coca 25 E4
Coca, Pso di 42 C3
Cocentaina 32 C1
Cochem 38 A2
Cockburnspath 5 E1
Cockermouth 5 D2
Codevigo 43 E4
Codigoro 43 E4
Codogno 42 C4
Codos 28 B2
Codroipo 43 E3
Coesfeld 11 F3
Coevorden 11 F2
Cofrentes 32 C1
Coghinas, L del 46 A2
Cognac 17 E3
Cogne 23 D1
Cogolin 22 C3
Cogolludo 28 A3
Coigach 2 C1
Coimbra 26 B3
Coín 31 E4
Coina 26 A4
Čoka 51 E1
Col 43 F3
Colares 26 A4
Cölbe 38 B1
Colchester 7 F3
Coldbackie 2 C1
Colditz 39 E1
Coldstream 5 E1
Coleford 6 C3
Coleraine 4 B2
Colfiorito 44 C3
Colico 42 B3
Coligny 19 D3
Colindres 25 F1
Colintraive 2 C4
Coll 2 B3
Collado Bajo 28 B3
Coll de Nargó 29 E1
Collecchio 44 A1
Colle di Val d'Elsa 44 B2
Colleferro 45 D4
Colle Isarco 43 D2
Colle Salvetti 44 A2
Colle Sannita 45 E4
Collesano 48 C3
Colli a Volturno 46 B1
Collina, Pso della 44 B2
Collinée 12 C4
Colline Metallifere 44 A2
Collio 42 C3
Collioure 21 F4
Collobrières 22 C3
Collodi 44 A2
Collonges 19 E3
Collonges-la-Rouge 21 E2
Colmar 15 E4
Colmars 22 C2
Colmenar 31 E3
Colmenar de Oreja 27 F3
Colmenar Viejo 27 F3
Colnabaichin 3 D2
Colne 5 E3
Colobraro 47 D2
Cologna Veneta 43 D4
Cologne 21 D3
Colombey-les-Belles 15 D3
Colombey-les-Deux-Eglises 14 C4
Colombière, Col de la 19 E3
Colombres 25 E1
Colomera 31 F3
Colonsay 2 B3
Colorno 44 A1
Colosimi 47 E3
Columbretes, I 29 D4
Colunga 25 D1
Colwyn Bay 6 B1
Comacchio 44 B1
Comănești 81 D2
Coma-ruga 29 D3
Combarro 24 A2
Combeaufontaine 15 D4
Combe Laval 22 B2
Combe Martin 6 B3
Comber 9 D1
Combloux 19 E3
Combourg 13 D3
Combronde 18 B3
Comeglians 43 E2
Comeragh Mts 8 C4
Comillas 25 E1
Comines 14 B1
Comino 49 F4
Comiso 49 D4
Commentry 18 B3
Commercy 15 D3
Como 42 B3
Como, L di 42 B3
Cómpeta 31 E3
Compiègne 14 B2
Comporta 30 A1
Comps-sur-Artuby 22 C3
Comunanza 45 D3
Concarneau 12 B4
Conches 13 F3
Concordia sulla Secchia 43 D4
Condat 18 B4
Condé 14 B1
Conde, Emb del 31 E3
Condé-en-Brie 14 B3
Condeixa-a-Nova 26 B3
Condé-sur-Noireau 13 E3
Condom 20 C3
Condrieu 19 D4
Conegliano 43 E3
Conejeros, Pto de los 26 C4
Conflans 15 D3
Confolens 17 E3
Cong 8 B2
Congleton 6 C1
Congost de Tresponts 29 E1
Congosto de Valdavia 25 E2
Congresbury 6 C3
Conil de la Frontera 30 C4
Conisbrough 5 E4
Coniston 5 D3
Conlie 13 E4
Conliège 19 D2
Connaught 8 B2
Connel 2 B3
Connemara 8 A2
Connerré 13 E4
Conn, L 8 B2
Čonoplja 51 E1
Conques 21 E2
Conquet, le 12 A3
Conquista 31 E2
Conselice 44 B1
Conselve 43 D4
Consett 5 E2
Constância 26 B4
Constanța 81 E3
Constantina 31 D2
Consuegra 27 F4
Consuma 44 B2
Contamines, les 19 E3
Contarina 43 E4
Conthey 19 F3
Contigliano 44 C3
Contin 2 C2
Contrasto, C del 48 C3
Contraviesa, Sa de la 31 F4
Contreras, Emb de 28 B4
Contres 17 F1
Contrexéville 15 D4
Contursi 46 C2
Conty 14 A2
Convento de Calatrava 31 F1
Conversano 47 E1
Conwy 6 B1
Cookstown 9 D1
Cootehill 8 C2
Cop 80 C2
Cope 32 B3
Cope, C 32 B3
Copertino 47 F2
Copparo 43 D4
Corabia 81 D3
Cora Droma Rúisc 8 C2
Corato 47 D1
Coray 12 B4
Corbeil-Essonnes 14 B3
Corbie 14 A2
Corbigny 18 C2
Corbola 43 E4
Corbones, R 31 D3
Corbridge 5 E2
Corby 7 D2
Corcaigh 8 B4
Corcieux 15 E4
Córcoles, R 32 A1
Corconte 25 E2
Corcubión 24 A1
Cordes 21 E3
Córdoba 31 E2
Cordobilla de Lácara 26 C4
Cordobilla, Emb de 31 E3
Corduente 28 B3
Corella 28 B1
Coreses 25 D3
Corfe Castle 6 C4
Corgo 24 B2
Cori 45 D4
Coria 26 C3
Coria del Río 31 D3
Corias 24 C1
Corigliano Calabro 47 E3
Corinaldo 44 C2
Coripe 31 D3
Cork 8 B4
Cork (Co) 8 B4
Corlay 12 C3
Corleone 48 B3
Corleto Perticara 47 D2
Çorlu 81 E4
Cormatin 19 D2
Cormeilles 13 E3
Cormery 17 F2
Cormons 43 F3
Cornago 28 B1
Cornellana 25 D1
Corniche des Cévennes 21 F2
Corniglio 44 A1
Cornimont 15 E4
Cornuda 43 D3
Cornus 21 F3
Cornwall 6 A4
Corps 22 C2
Corraes 24 C3
Corral de Almaguer 28 A4
Corral de Cantos 27 E4
Corralejo 30 B4
Corrales 25 D4
Corran 2 C3
Corraun 8 A2
Corredoiras 24 B1
Correggio 44 A1
Corrèze 18 A4
Corrèze (Dépt) 17 F4
Corrèze R 21 E1
Corrib, L 8 B2
Corridonia 45 D2
Corrofin 8 B3
Corse 23 E3
Corse-du-Sud 23 E4
Corsham 6 C3
Čortanovci 51 E1
Corte 23 E3
Corte de Peleas 30 C1
Cortegada 24 B2
Cortegana 30 C2
Cortemaggiore 42 C4
Cortemilia 23 E2
Corteolona 23 E1
Cortes 28 B2
Cortes de Aragón 28 C3
Cortes de Baza 32 A3
Cortes de la Frontera 31 D4
Cortijos Nuevos 32 A2
Cortina d'Ampezzo 43 E2
Čortkov 81 D1
Cortona 44 C2
Coruche 26 A4
Corvara in Badia 43 D2
Corvera 32 B3
Corvera Toranzo 25 E2
Corwen 6 C1
Cosenza 47 E3
Cosham 7 D4
Cosne 18 B1
Cosne-d'Allier 18 B3
Cossato 23 D1
Cossé-le-Vivien 13 D4
Cosson 18 A1
Cossonay 19 E2
Costa Blanca 32 C2
Costa Brava 29 F2
Costa da Caparica 26 A4
Costa del Azahar 29 D4
Costa del Sol 31 F4
Costa de Santo André 30 A2
Costa Dorada 29 E3
Costalunga, Pso di 43 D2
Costa Smeralda 46 B2
Costa Vasca 20 A3
Costa Verde 24 C1
Costigliole d'Asti 23 E2
Coswig (Dresden) 39 E1
Coswig (Halle) 37 E4
Côte-d'Or 19 D1
Côtes-du-Nord 12 B3
Côte-St-André, la 19 D4
Cotignac 22 C3
Cottbus 78 A4
Coubet, Collado de 29 F1
Coubre, Pointe de la 17 D3
Couches 18 C2
Couço 26 B4
Coucy-le-Château-Auffrique 14 B2
Couesnon 13 D4
Couhé 17 E3
Couilly 14 B3
Couiza 21 E4
Coulanges 18 C1
Coulanges-la-Vineuse 18 C1
Coulommiers 14 B3
Coulon 17 D3
Coulonges 17 D2
Coupar Angus 3 D3
Couptrain 13 E3
Courchevel 19 E4
Cour-Cheverny 17 F1
Courçon 17 D3
Courmayeur 19 F3
Couronne, la 17 E3
Courpière 18 C3
Cours 18 C3
Coursan 21 F4
Coursegoules 23 D3
Courseulles 13 E2
Courson-les-Carrières 18 C1
Courtenay 14 B4
Courthézon 22 B3
Courtine, la 18 B3
Courtomer 13 E3
Courtown 9 D3
Courtrai 34 A3
Courville 14 A3
Cousin 18 C2
Coussey 15 D4
Coutances 13 D3
Coutras 20 C2
Couvertoirade, la 21 F3
Couvin 34 B4
Couze 17 F3
Cova da Iria 26 A3
Covadonga 25 D1
Covadonga, Pque Nac de la Sa de 25 D2
Covarrubias 25 F3
Coventry 7 D2
Covilhã 26 C3
Cowbridge 6 B3
Cowdenbeath 3 D3
Cowes 7 D4
Cowfold 7 E4
Cozes 17 D3
Craco 47 D2
Craigavon 9 D1
Craigellachie 3 D2
Craighouse 2 B4
Craigievar Castle 3 D2
Craignure 2 B3
Crail 3 D3
Crailsheim 38 C3
Craiova 81 D3
Cranborne 6 C4
Crans 19 F3
Craon 13 D4
Craonne 14 B2
Craponne 18 C4
Crathes Castle 3 D2
Crati 47 E3
Crato 26 B4
Craughwell 8 B3
Crau, la 22 C4
Craven Arms 6 C2
Crawinkel 38 C1
Crawley 7 E3
Creag Meagaidh 2 C2
Creagorry 2 A2
Crécy 14 B2
Crécy-en-Ponthieu 14 A1
Crécy-la-Chapelle 14 B3
Crediton 6 B4
Creegh 8 B3
Creeslough 4 A2
Creglingen 38 C3
Creil 14 A3
Crema 42 C4
Crémieu 19 D3
Cremona 42 C4
Créon 20 C2
Crepaja 52 C1
Crépy-en-Valois 14 B3
Cres 50 A3
Cres I 50 A3
Crescentino 23 D1
Crespino 43 D4
Crest 22 B2
Cresta 42 B3
Cresta del Gallo 32 C2
Créteil 14 B3
Crêtes, Route des 15 E4
Creully 13 E3
Creuse 18 A3
Creuse (Dépt) 18 A3
Creusot, le 18 C2
Creußen 39 D2
Creutzwald 15 E3
Creuzburg 38 C1
Crevacuore 42 A4
Crevalcore 44 B1
Crèvecœur-le-Grand 14 A2
Crevillente 32 C2
Crewe 6 C1
Crewkerne 6 C4
Crianlarich 2 C3
Criccieth 6 B1
Crickhowell 6 C2
Cricklade 7 D3
Crieff 2 C3
Criel 14 A2
Crikvenica 50 A2
Crimmitschau 39 D2
Crinan 2 B3
Criquetot-l'Esneval 13 E2
Crissolo 23 D2
Crișu Alb 80 C2
Crișu Negru 80 C2
Crișu Repede 80 C2
Crivitz 37 D2

Crkvice 52 B4
Çrmljan 53 D3
Çrmošnjice 50 A2
Črna 50 A1
Crna Bara (Srbija) 51 E2
Crna Bara (Vojvodina) 51 E1
Crnac (Hrvatska) 51 D1
Crnac (Srbija) 53 D3
Crna Gora 52 C3
Crna gora 53 E3
Crna reka 53 E4
Crna Trava 53 E3
Crnča 51 E3
Crni Drim 53 D4
Crni Guber 51 E3
Crni Lug (Bosna i Hercegovina) 50 C3
Crni Lug (Hrvatska) 50 A2
Crni Timok 53 E2
Çrnivec 50 A1
Crni vrh (Slovenija) 43 F3
Crni vrh *Mt* (Bosna i Hercegovina) 50 C3
Črni vrh *Mt* (Slovenija) 50 A1
Crni vrh *Mt* (Srbija) 51 E4
Çrnjelovo Donje 51 E2
Črnkovci 51 D1
Çrno jez 51 E4
Črnomelj 50 A2
Croagh Patrick 8 B2
Croce dello Scrivano, Pso 47 D2
Croce Domini, Pso di 42 C3
Crocello, Pso di 47 D1
Crocq 18 B3
Croisic, le 16 C2
Croisière, la 17 F3
Croix de Fer, Col de la 19 E4
Croix Haute, Col de la 22 B2
Croix-Valmer, la 22 C4
Crolly 8 C1
Cromarty 2 C2
Cromer 7 F1
Crook 5 E2
Croom 8 B3
Cross Fell 5 D2
Cross Hands 6 B3
Crosshaven 8 B4
Crossmaglen 9 D2
Crossmolina 8 B2
Crotone 47 E3
Crotoy, le 14 A1
Crowborough 7 E3
Crowland 7 E2
Crowle 5 F4
Croyde 6 B3
Croydon 7 E3
Crozant 18 A3
Crozon 12 A4
Cruden Bay 3 E2
Crudgington 6 C1
Crumlin 9 D1
Cruseilles 19 E3
Crussol 22 B2
Cruz 28 A4
Cruzamento de Pegões 26 A4
Cruz da Légua 26 A3
Cruz de Tejeda 30 B4
Crven Grm 51 D4
Crvenka 51 E1
Crymmych 6 B2
Csongrád 80 C2
Csorna 80 B2
Cuacos 27 D3
Cualedro 24 B3
Cuba 30 B2
Cubel 28 B3
Cucalón, Sa de 28 B3
Cuckfield 7 E3
Çudillero 25 D1
Čudovo 79 E1
Čudskoje Ozero 79 D1
Cuéllar 25 E4
Cuenca 28 B4
Cuenca, Serr de 28 B4
Cuerda 28 B4
Cuerda del Pozo, Emb de la 28 A2
Cuers 22 C4
Cuerva 27 E4
Cueva de la Pileta 31 D4
Cueva de la Vieja 32 B1
Cueva de Nerja 31 F4
Cueva Foradada, Emb de 28 C3
Cueva, Sa do 25 E1
Cuevas de Altamira 25 F1
Cuevas de Artà 33 F2
Cuevas de Canalobre 32 C2
Cuevas del Aguila 27 E3
Cuevas del Amanzora 32 B3
Cuevas del Becerro 31 D3
Cuevas del Campo 32 A3
Cuevas del Drac 33 E2
Cuevas del Valle 27 E3
Cuevas de San Clemente 25 F3
Cuevas de San Marcos 31 E3
Cuevas de Valporquero 25 D2
Cuevas de Vinromá 29 D3
Cuglieri 46 A3
Cuijk 11 E3
Cuillin Sd 2 B2
Cuillins, The 2 B2
Cuiseaux 19 D2
Cuisery 19 D2
Culan 18 B2
Culdaff 4 A1
Culebra, Sa de la 24 C3
Culemborg 11 E3
Cúllar Baza 32 A3
Cullen 3 D2
Cullera 32 C1
Cullompton 6 B4
Culoz 19 D3
Culross 3 D4
Cumbernauld 2 C4
Cumbre Alta 27 E4
Cumbres Mayores 30 C2
Cumbria 5 D2
Cumbrian Mts 5 D3
Çumiana 23 D2
Ćumić 53 D1
Cumnock 4 C1
Cunault 17 E2
Cuneo 23 D2
Çunlhat 18 C3
Čunski 50 A3
Cuorgnè 23 D1
Cupar 3 D3
Cupello 45 E3
Cupramontana 44 C2
Ćuprija 53 D2
Cure 18 C2
Cure, la 19 E2
Curia 26 B2
Currane, L 8 A4
Curtea de Argeș 81 D3
Çurtis 24 B1
Čurug 51 E1
C'urupinsk 81 F2
Cusano Mutri 46 C1
Cushendall 4 B2
Cushendun 4 B2
Cusna, Mte 44 A1
Cusset 18 C3
Cutro 47 E3
Cuxhaven 36 B2
Çvikov 39 F1
Čvrsnica 51 D4
Čvrstec 50 C1
Cwmbrân 6 C3
Cysoing 14 B1
Czarnków 78 B4
Czersk 78 B3
Częstochowa 80 B1
Człuchów 78 B3

D

Dabar 50 B2
Dabilje 53 F4
Dabo 15 E3
Dachau 40 B3
Dachsteingruppe 41 D3
Dačice 41 E1
Dadiá 57 D1
Dáfnes 58 C3
Dáfni (Límnos) 56 C3
Dáfni (Makedonía) 56 A3
Dáfni (Pelopónissos) 58 C3
Dáfni (Stereá Eláda) 58 C2
Dafní (Stereá Eláda) 59 E3
Dáfnio 63 D3
Dafnónas (Stereá Eláda) 58 C2
Dafnónas (Thráki) 56 B1
Dafnotí 54 C4
Dafnoúdi, Akr 58 A2
Dagali 74 B3
Dagebüll 36 B1
Dagenham 7 E3
Dahlen 37 F4
Dahlenburg 37 D2
Dahme (D) 37 D1
Dahme (DDR) 37 F4
Dahme *R* 37 F4
Dahn 38 A3
Daimiel 27 F4
Daimuz 32 C1
Dajt, Mal i 54 A1
Đakovica 53 D3
Đakovo 51 D2
Dalälven 75 E3
Dalane 74 A4
Dalbeattie 5 D2
Dalbosjön 75 D4
Dalby 77 D3
Dale (Hordaland) 74 A2
Dale (Sogn og Fjordane) 74 A2
Dalen 74 B3
Dalhem 77 F2
Dalías 32 A4
Daliburgh 2 A2
Dalj 51 E1
Dalkeith 3 D4
Dalkey 9 D3
Dalmally 2 C3
Dalmellington 4 C2
Dalmine 42 C3
Dalry 2 C4
Dalsbruk 72 C4
Dalsfjorden 74 A2
Dalsjöfors 77 D2
Dals Långed 75 D4
Dalton 5 D3
Daluis, Gorges de 22 C3
Dalvík 68 B1
Dalwhinnie 2 C3
Damaskiniá 54 C3
Damássi 55 D4
Damazan 20 C2
Damelevières 15 E3
Damgan 16 C1
Damianó 55 E2
Dammartin-en-Goële 14 B3
Damme 36 B3
Damnjane 53 D4
Dampierre 19 D2
Dampierre-sur-Salon 19 D1
Damville 13 F3
Damvillers 15 D2
Dangé 17 E2
Danilovgrad 52 C3
Dannemarie 19 E1
Dannenberg 37 D2
Dâo, R 26 B2
Daoulas 12 B3
Darda 51 D1
Dardesheim 37 D4
Darfo Boario Terme 42 C3
Dargilan, Grotte de 21 F3
Dargun 37 E1
Darlington 5 E3
Darłowo 78 B3
Darmstadt 38 B3
Darney 15 D4
Daroca 28 B3
Darque 24 A3
Darß 37 E1
Dartford 7 E3
Dartmoor Nat Pk 6 B4
Dartmouth 6 B4
Daruvar 50 C1
Darwen 5 D4
Dasburg 34 C4
Dasing 39 D4
Dassel 36 C4
Dassohóri 56 B2
Dassow 37 D2
D'at'kovo 79 F3
Datteln 36 B4
Daugava 79 D2
Daugavpils 79 D2
Daun 35 D4
Dava 3 D2
Đavat 54 C2
Daventry 7 D2
Davia 59 D4
Davidovac 53 E1
Dávlia 59 D2
Davor 50 C2
Davos 42 C2
Dawlish 6 B4
Dax 20 B3
Deädnu 67 E1
Deal 7 F3
Deauville 13 E2
Deba 20 A3
Debar 53 D4
Debarska Banja Banjišta 53 D4
Debeli Lug 53 E1
Debeli vrh 50 A2
Debeljača 51 F1
Dębica 80 C1
De Bilt 11 E3
Dęblin 78 C4
Debrc 51 E2
Debrecen 80 C2
Dečani 53 D3
Decazeville 21 E2
Děčín 39 F1
Decize 18 C2
Dedemsvaart 11 F2
Dee (Scotland) 3 D2
Dee (Wales/Eng) 6 C1
Degaña 24 C2
Degebe, R 30 B1
Degerfjärden 70 B4
Degerfors 75 E4
Degerndorf 40 C3
Deggendorf 39 E3
Dego 23 E2
Degracias 26 B3
De Haan 10 C4
Dehesa de Montejo 25 E2
Deià 33 E2
Deidesheim 38 B3
Deinze 34 A3
Deiva Marina 23 F2
Dej 81 D2
Deje 75 D3
Dejë, Mal 53 D4
De Koog 11 D1
Delčevo 53 F3
Delden 11 F2
Deleitosa 27 D4
Delémont 19 F1
Deléria 55 D4
Delet Teili 72 B4
Delfí 59 D2
Delft 11 D3
Delfzijl 11 F1
Delia 48 C4
Delianuova 47 D4
Deliblato 53 D1
Deliblatska Peščara 51 F1
Deliceto 45 F4
Delimedde 53 D3
Delitzsch 37 E4
Delle 19 E1
Dellen, N 75 F2
Dellen, S 75 F2
Delme 15 E3
Delmenhorst 36 B3
Delnice 50 A2
Delsbo 75 E2
Delta Dunării 81 E3
Delvin 8 C2
Delvináki 54 B4
Demanda, Sa de la 28 A1
Demer 34 B3
Demidov 79 E2
Demir Kapija 53 F4
Demmin 37 E1
Demoiselles, Grotte des 22 A3
Demonía 63 D4
Denain 14 B1
Denbigh 6 C1
Den Burg 11 D1
Dendermonde 34 B3
Dendre 34 B3
Dendrohóri 54 C2
Denekamp 11 F2
Den Haag 11 D3
Den Helder 11 D2
Denia 33 D1
Denkendorf 39 D4
Dennington 7 F2
Denny 2 C4
Den Oever 11 D2
Dent de Vaulion 19 E2
De Panne 34 A3
Đeravica 53 D3
Derby 7 D1
Derbyshire 7 D1
Der Chantecoq, L du 14 C3
Đerdap, Klisura 53 E1
Đerdap, H.E. 53 E1
Derekoy 81 E4
Derenburg 37 D4
Derg, L (Clare) 8 B3
Derg, L (Donegal) 8 C1
Der Grabow 37 E1
Dermatás, Akr 55 E4
Dermbach 38 C2
Derneburg 37 D4
Derravaragh, L 8 C2
Derrynasaggart Mts 8 B4
Derryveagh Mts 8 C1
Deruta 44 C3
Dervaig 2 B3
Derval 17 D1
Dervéni 59 D3
Derventa 51 D2
Derviziana 54 B4
Derwent (Derbys) 7 D1
Derwent (Durham) 5 E2
Derwent (Yorks) 5 F3
Derwent Water 5 D3
Desborough 7 D2
Descartes 17 E2
Desenzano 42 C4
Desertas 30 A3
Desfiladero de Despeñaperros 31 F2
Desfiladero de la Hermida 25 E2
Desfiladero de los Beyos 25 D2
Desfiladero del Teverga 25 D1
Desfina 59 D2
Desimirovac 53 D2
Desio 42 B4
Deskáti 55 D3
Desna 79 E3
Despotikó, N 64 B1
Despotovac 53 D1
Despotovo 51 E1
Dessau 37 E4
Destriana 24 C2
Desulo 46 B3
Desvres 14 A1
Deta 80 C3
Đetinja 51 F3
Detmold 36 C4
Dettelbach 38 C3
Dettifoss 68 B1
Deurne 11 E3
Deutsche Alpenstraße 40 A4
Deutsche Bucht 36 B2
Deutschkreutz 41 F3
Deutschlandsberg 50 A1
Deutsch-Wagram 41 F2
Deux-Alpes, les 19 E4
Deux-Sèvres 17 E2
Deva 81 D3
Deve Bair 53 F3
Deventer 11 E2
Deveron 3 D2
Devetak 51 E3
Devil's Bridge 6 B2
Devil's Elbow 3 D3
Devizes 6 C3
Devnja 81 E3
Dewsbury 5 E4
Deza 28 B2
Diablerets, les 19 F3
Diablerets, les *Mt* 19 F3
Diafáni 65 E3
Diakófti 63 D4
Diakoftó 59 D3
Diamante 47 D3
Día, N 64 C3
Diano Marina 23 E3
Diápora Nissiá 59 E3
Díavlos Alonissou 60 A1
Díavlos Oreón 59 E1
Díavlos Pelagonissou 60 A1
Díavlos Skiáthou 59 E1
Díavlos Skopélou 59 E1
Díavlos Trikeriou 59 E1
Díavlos Zákinthou 58 B3
Diavolítsi 58 C4
Diavolo, Pso del 45 D4
Diavolórema 57 D1
Dibbersen 36 C2
Dicmo 50 C4
Dicomano 44 B2
Dídima 59 E4
Dídimo, Óros 59 E4
Didimótiho 57 D1
Die 22 B2
Dieburg 38 B3
Diedorf 38 C1
Diego Alvaro 27 D3
Diekirch 15 D2
Diemel 36 C4
Diemelstadt 38 B1
Diepholz 36 B3
Dieppe 13 F2
Dierdorf 38 A2
Dieren 11 E3
Diesdorf 37 D3
Dießen 40 B3
Diest 34 B3
Dietenheim 40 A3
Dietfurt 39 D3
Dietikon 42 A2
Dietmannsried 40 A3
Dieulefit 22 B2
Dieulouard 15 D3
Dieuze 15 E3
Diez 38 A2
Diezma 31 F3
Differdange 15 D2
Digerkampen 74 B1
Digermulen 66 B3
Dignano 43 E3
Digne-les-Bains 22 C3
Digoin 18 C2
Dijle 34 B3
Dijon 19 D2
Dikanäs 69 E2
Díkea 57 D1
Díkela 56 C2
Diksmuide 34 A3
Diktéo Ándro 64 C4
Diktinéon 64 A3
Díkti, Óros 64 C4
Dílessi 59 E2
Dilináta 58 A3
Dilj 51 D2
Dillenburg 38 B2
Dillingen (Bayern) 38 C4
Dillingen (Saarland) 15 E2
Dílofos 57 D1
Dílos 60 C4
Dílos, N 60 C4
Dímena 59 E3
Dímitra 55 D4
Dimitrítsi 55 F2
Dimitrovgrad (BG) 81 E4
Dimitrovgrad (YU) 53 F2
Dimitsána 58 C4
Dinami 47 E4
Dinan 12 C3
Dinant 34 B4
Dinara *Mt* 50 C3
Dinara (Reg) 50 C3
Dinard 12 C3
Dinbych 6 C1
Dinbych-y-pysgod 6 B3
Dingelstädt 37 D4
Dingle 8 A4
Dingle 74 C4
Dingle B 8 A4
Dingle (Reg) 8 A4
Dingli 49 F4
Dinglingen 42 A1
Dingolfing 39 E4
Dingwall 2 C2
Dinjiška 50 B3
Dinkelsbühl 38 C3
Dinklage 36 B3
Dinslaken 11 F3
Dío 55 E3
Diónissos 59 F3
Dióriga Korinthou 59 E3
Dipótama 56 B1
Dippoldiswalde 39 E1
Diráhio 59 D4
Dírfis, Óros 59 F2
Disentis 42 B2
Disgrazia, Mte 42 C3
Dispílio 54 C3
Diss 7 F2
Dissen 36 B4
Dístomo 59 D2
Dístos 60 A2
Ditikí Rodópi 56 B1
Dittaino 49 D4
Ditzingen 38 B4
Divača 43 F3
Divaráta 58 A2
Divčibare 51 F3
Dives 13 E3
Dives *R* 13 E3
Divič 51 E3
Divjakë 54 A2
Divljana 53 E2
Divonne 19 E3
Divor, Bgem do 30 B1
Divor, Rib de 26 B4
Divoúnia, Ni 65 D3
Dívri 59 D1
Divuša 50 B2
Djupini 68 A3
Djupvik 66 C2
Djurås 75 E3
Djursland 76 C2
Dmitrov 79 F2
Dnepr 79 E2
Dneprodzeržinskoje Vodochranilišče 81 F1
Dneprovskij Liman 81 F2
Dnestr 81 D1
Dnestrovskij Liman 81 F2
Dno 79 D1
Dobanovci 52 C1
Dobbiaco 43 E2
Dobel 38 B4
Dobele 78 C2
Döbeln 39 E1
Doberlug-Kirchhain 37 F4
Dobersberg 41 E2
Dobieszczyn 37 F2
Doboj 51 D2
Dobošnica 51 D2
Dobra 53 E1
Dobra *R* 50 B2
Dobrašinci 53 F4
Dobratsch 41 D4
Dobra Voda 53 D2
Dobra Voda *Mt* 53 E4
Dobrčane 53 E3
Döbriach 41 D4
Dobrica 51 F1
Dobri Do 53 E3
Dobrinj 50 A2
Dobřiš 39 F2
Dobrljin 50 C2
Dobrna 50 A1
Dobromani 52 B3
Dobro Polje 51 E3
Dobrovnik 50 B1
Dobrun 51 E3
Dobruš 79 E3
Dobruševo 54 C1
Dobšiná 80 C2
Docksta 69 F4
Doc Penfro 6 A3
Dodekánissa 65 D1
Dodóni 54 B4
Doesburg 11 E3
Doetinchem 11 E3
Doganović 53 E3
Dogliani 23 D2
Doïráni 55 E1
Doïránis, L 55 E1
Doiras, Emb de 24 C1
Dojransko Ez 53 F4
Dokanj 51 D2
Dokka 74 C2
Dokkum 11 E1
Dokós, N 59 E4
Doksy 39 F1
Dolac 53 D3
Dol-de-Bretagne 13 D3
Dole 19 D2
Dôle, la 19 E3
Dølemo 74 B4
Dolenci 53 E4
Dolenja Vas 50 A2
Dolenjske Toplice 50 A2
Dolga Vas 41 F4
Dolgellau 6 B1
Dolianá 54 B3
Dolianova 46 B4
Dolíhi 55 D3
Dolina 81 D1
Doljani 50 B3
Doljevac 53 E2
Dolla 8 B3
Döllach 43 E2
Dollar 3 D3
Dolle 37 E3
Dolní Dvořiště 41 D2
Dolno Kosovrasti 53 D4
Dolo 43 E4
Dolomiti 43 D3
Dolores 32 C2
Dolovo 53 D1
Dol Poustevna 39 F1
Domaševo 52 B3
Domažlice 39 E3
Dombås 74 C1
Dombasle 15 E3
Dombóvár 80 B3
Domburg 10 C3
Domène 19 E4
Doméniko 55 D4
Domèvre-en-Haye 15 D3
Domfront 13 D3
Dömitz 37 D2
Domme 21 D2
Dommitzsch 37 E4
Domnísta 58 C2
Domodossola 42 A3
Domokós 59 D1
Dompaire 15 D4
Dompierre 18 C2
Domrémy 15 D3
Domusnovas 46 A4
Domžale 50 A1
Don (England) 5 E4
Don (Scotland) 3 D2
Donaghadee 9 E1
Doña María Ocaña 32 A3
Doña Mencía 31 E3
Doñana, Pque Nac de 30 C3
Donau 40 C2
Donaueschingen 42 A1
Donauwörth 39 D4
Donawitz 41 E3
Don Benito 31 D1
Doncaster 5 E4
Donegal 8 C1
Donegal (Co) 8 C1
Donegal B 8 C1
Dongen 11 D3
Donges 16 C1
Donington 7 E1
Donja Bebrina 51 D2
Donja Brela 50 C4
Donja Brezna 52 B3
Donja Bukovica 52 C3
Donja Kamenica 51 E2
Donja Šatornja 53 D1
Donje Crniljevo 51 E2
Donje Dragovlje 53 E2
Donje Ljupče 53 D3
Donji Andrijevci 51 D2
Donji Barbeš 53 E2
Donji Kazanci 50 C3
Donji Lapac 50 B3
Donji Malovan 50 C3
Donji Miholjac 51 D1
Donji Milanovac 53 E1
Donji Rujani 50 C3
Donji Seget 50 C4
Donji Vakuf 50 C3
Donji Vijačani 50 C2
Donji Zemunik 50 B3
Donjon, le 18 C3
Dønna 69 D2
Donnemarie-Dontilly 14 B3
Donnersbachwald 41 D3
Dønnes 69 D1
Donon 15 E3
Donon, Col du 15 E3
Donostia-San Sebastián 20 A3
Donoússa, N 64 C1
Donzenac 21 D1
Donzère 22 B2
Donzy 18 B1
Doorn 11 E3
Doornik 34 A3
Dora Baltéa 19 F3

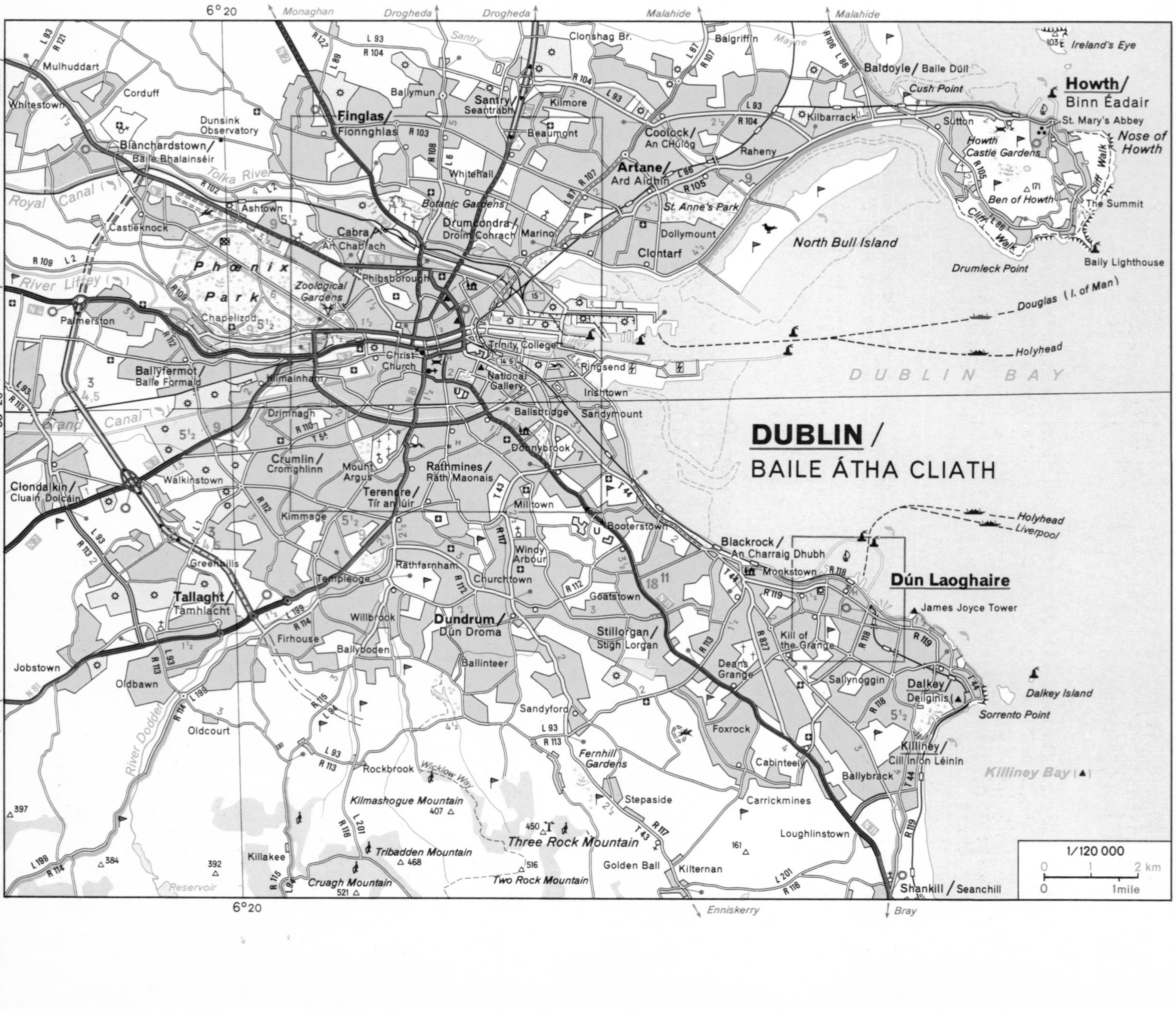

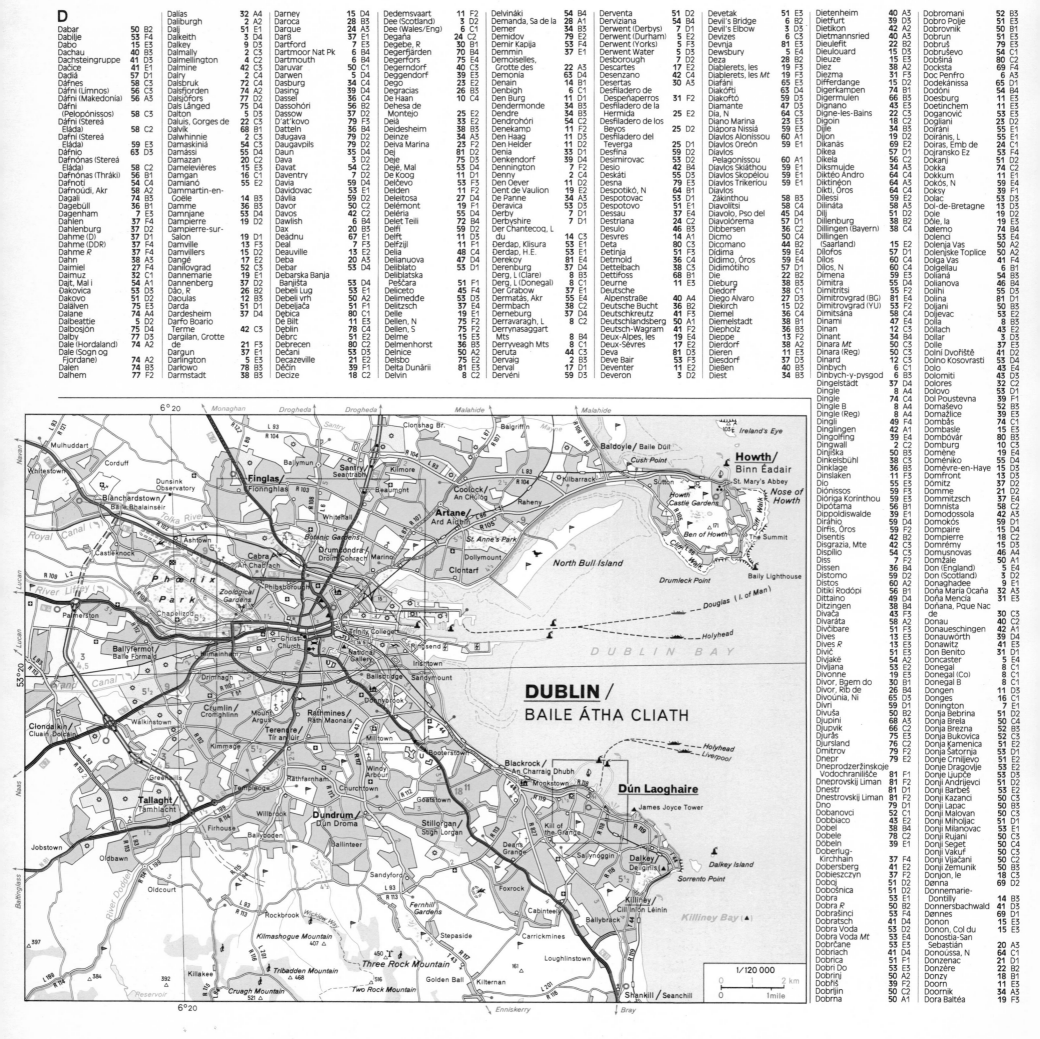

6°20
Monaghan
Drogheda
Drogheda
Malahide
Malahide
Navan
Lucan
Lucan
Naas
Baltinglass
Enniskerry
Bray
Santry
Mulhuddart
Corduff
Whitestown
Dunsink Observatory
Finglas / Fionnghlas
Ballymun
Santry / Seantrabh
Kilmore
Beaumont
Clonshag Br.
Balgriffin
Baldoyle / Baile Dúil
Ireland's Eye
Howth / Binn Éadair
Cush Point
Sutton
St. Mary's Abbey
Nose of Howth
Howth Castle Gardens
Ben of Howth
The Summit
Baily Lighthouse
Kilbarrack
Coolock / An Chúlóg
Raheny
Artane / Ard Aidhin
St. Anne's Park
Dollymount
Clontarf
North Bull Island
Drumleck Point
Douglas (I. of Man)
Holyhead
DUBLIN BAY
Blanchardstown / Baile Bhlainséir
Tolka River
Royal Canal
Whitehall
Botanic Gardens
Drumcondra / Droim Conrach
Marino
Ashtown
Castleknock
Cabra / An Chabrach
Phœnix Park
Zoological Gardens
Phibsborough
River Liffey
Palmerston
Chapelizod
Christ Church
Trinity College
Ringsend
National Gallery
Irishtown
Ballsbridge
Sandymount
Ballyfermot / Baile Formaid
Kilmainham
Grand Canal
Drimnagh
Crumlin / Cromghlinn
Mount Argus
Donnybrook
Rathmines / Ráth Maonais
Walkinstown
Terenure / Tír an Iúir
Milltown
Clondalkin / Cluain Dolcáin
Kimmage
Booterstown
Greenhills
Rathfarnham
Churchtown
Windy Arbour
Templeogue
Tallaght / Tamhlacht
Blackrock / An Charraig Dhubh
Monkstown
Dún Laoghaire
Holyhead
Liverpool
James Joyce Tower
Willbrook
Goatstown
Dundrum / Dún Droma
Stillorgan / Stigh Lorgan
Firhouse
Ballyboden
Ballinteer
Kill of the Grange
Deans Grange
Sallynoggin
Dalkey / Deilginis
Dalkey Island
Sorrento Point
Jobstown
Oldbawn
Oldcourt
River Dodder
Sandyford
Foxrock
Cabinteely
Killiney / Cill Inion Léinín
Killiney Bay
Ballybrack
Rockbrook
Wicklow Way
Fernhill Gardens
Kilmashogue Mountain 407
Stepaside
Carrickmines
Loughlinstown
Three Rock Mountain
Tibradden Mountain 468
Two Rock Mountain
Golden Ball
Kilternan
Killakee
Cruagh Mountain 521
Reservoir
Shankill / Seanchill
DUBLIN / BAILE ÁTHA CLIATH
1/120 000
0 1 2 km
0 1 mile

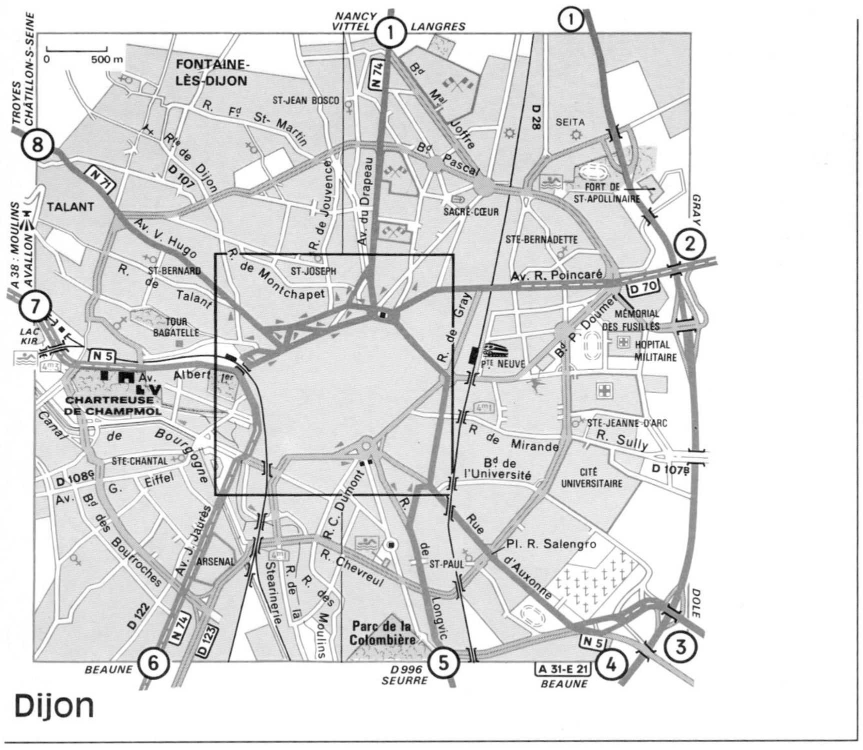
NANCY VITTEL
LANGRES
TROYES CHÂTILLON-S-SEINE
FONTAINE-LÈS-DIJON
TALANT
A 38 MOULINS AVALLON
GRAY
Av. R. Poincaré
SACRÉ-CŒUR
STE-BERNADETTE
FORT DE ST-APOLLINAIRE
SEITA
CHARTREUSE DE CHAMPMOL
TOUR SABATELLE
STE-CHANTAL
MÉMORIAL DES FUSILLÉS
HÔPITAL MILITAIRE
STE-JEANNE-D'ARC
CITÉ UNIVERSITAIRE
Pl. R. Salengro
ST-PAUL
ARSENAL
Parc de la Colombière
BEAUNE
D 996 SEURRE
A 31-E 21 BEAUNE
DOLE
Dijon

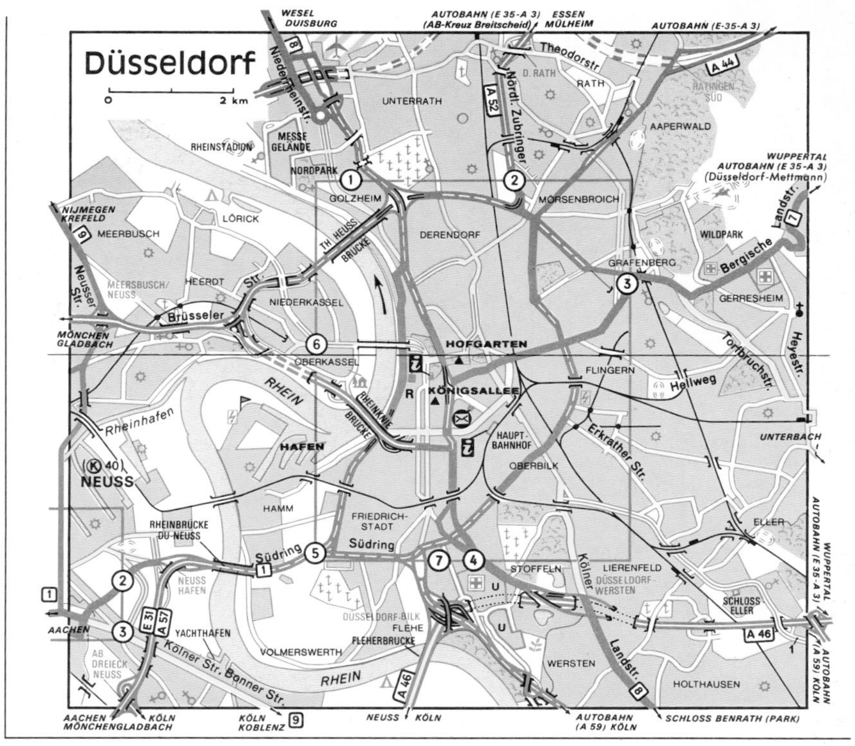
Düsseldorf
WESEL DUISBURG
AUTOBAHN (E 35-A 3) (AB-Kreuz Breitscheid)
ESSEN MÜLHEIM
AUTOBAHN (E 35-A 3)
WUPPERTAL AUTOBAHN (E 35-A 3) (Düsseldorf-Mettmann)
NIJMEGEN KREFELD
MEERBUSCH
LÖRICK
UNTERRATH
RATH
MESSE GELÄNDE
NORDPARK
GOLZHEIM
MÖRSENBROICH
AAPERWALD
WILDPARK
GRAFENBERG
GERRESHEIM
DERENDORF
NIEDERKASSEL
OBERKASSEL
HOFGARTEN
KÖNIGSALLEE
RHEIN
HAFEN
HAUPT-BAHNHOF
OBERBILK
FLINGERN
UNTERBACH
NEUSS
HAMM
FRIEDRICH-STADT
Südring
STOFFELN
LIERENFELD
ELLER
SCHLOSS ELLER
YACHTHAFEN
VOLMERSWERTH
FLEHE
FLEHERBRÜCKE
WERSTEN
HOLTHAUSEN
AACHEN
AACHEN MÖNCHENGLADBACH
KÖLN KOBLENZ
NEUSS KÖLN
AUTOBAHN (A 59) KÖLN
SCHLOSS BENRATH (PARK)
WUPPERTAL AUTOBAHN (E 35-A 3)
AUTOBAHN (A 59) KÖLN

E

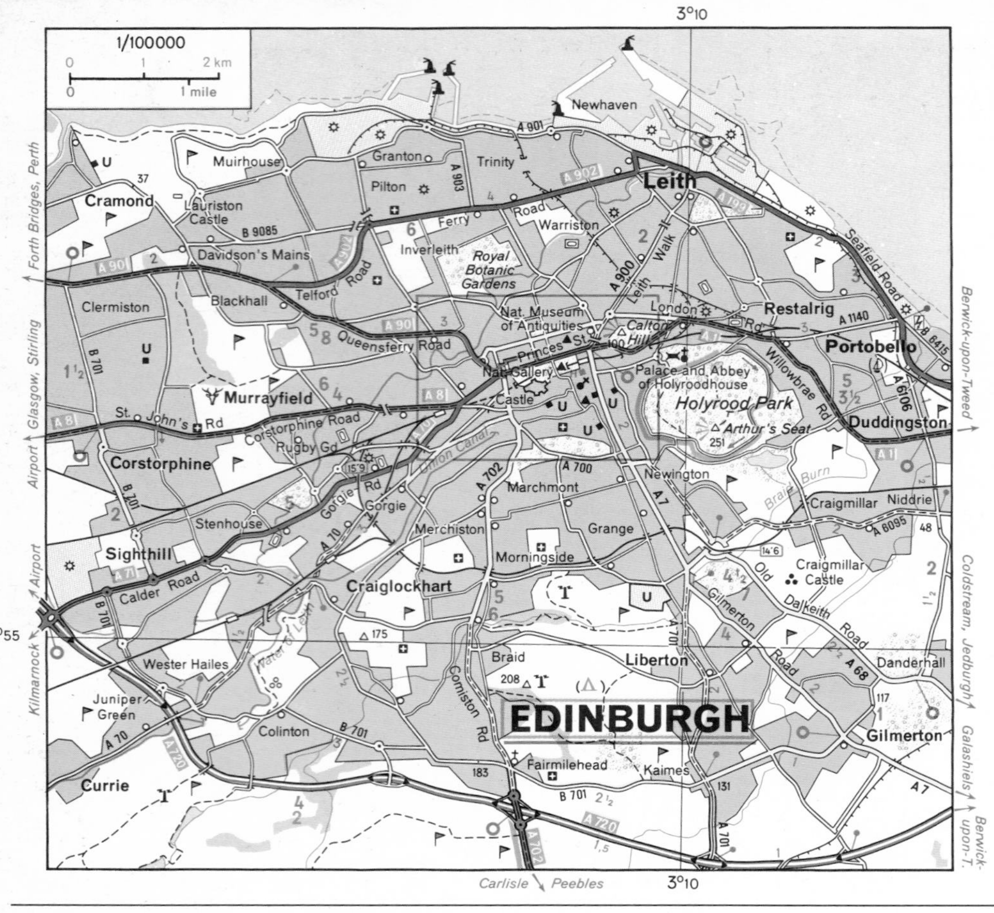
1/100000
EDINBURGH
Newhaven
Leith
Granton
Trinity
Cramond
Muirhouse
Pilton
Lauriston Castle
Davidson's Mains
Inverleith
Royal Botanic Gardens
Warriston
Restalrig
Portobello
Clermiston
Blackhall
Telford Road
Queensferry Road
Nat. Museum of Antiquities
Calton Hill
Princes St
Nat. Gallery
Castle
Palace and Abbey of Holyroodhouse
Holyrood Park
Arthur's Seat
Duddingston
Murrayfield
St. John's Rd
Corstorphine Road
Corstorphine
Marchmont
Newington
Craigmillar
Niddrie
Stenhouse
Gorgie
Merchiston
Grange
Morningside
Sighthill
Calder Road
Craiglockhart
Craigmillar Castle
Dalkeith Road
Gilmerton Road
Wester Hailes
Braid
Liberton
Danderhall
Juniper Green
Colinton
Comiston Rd
Gilmerton
Fairmilehead
Kaimes
Currie
Forth Bridges, Perth
Glasgow, Stirling
Airport
Kilmarnock
Carlisle
Peebles
Berwick-upon-Tweed
Coldstream, Jedburgh
Galashiels
Berwick-upon-T.
3°10
55°55

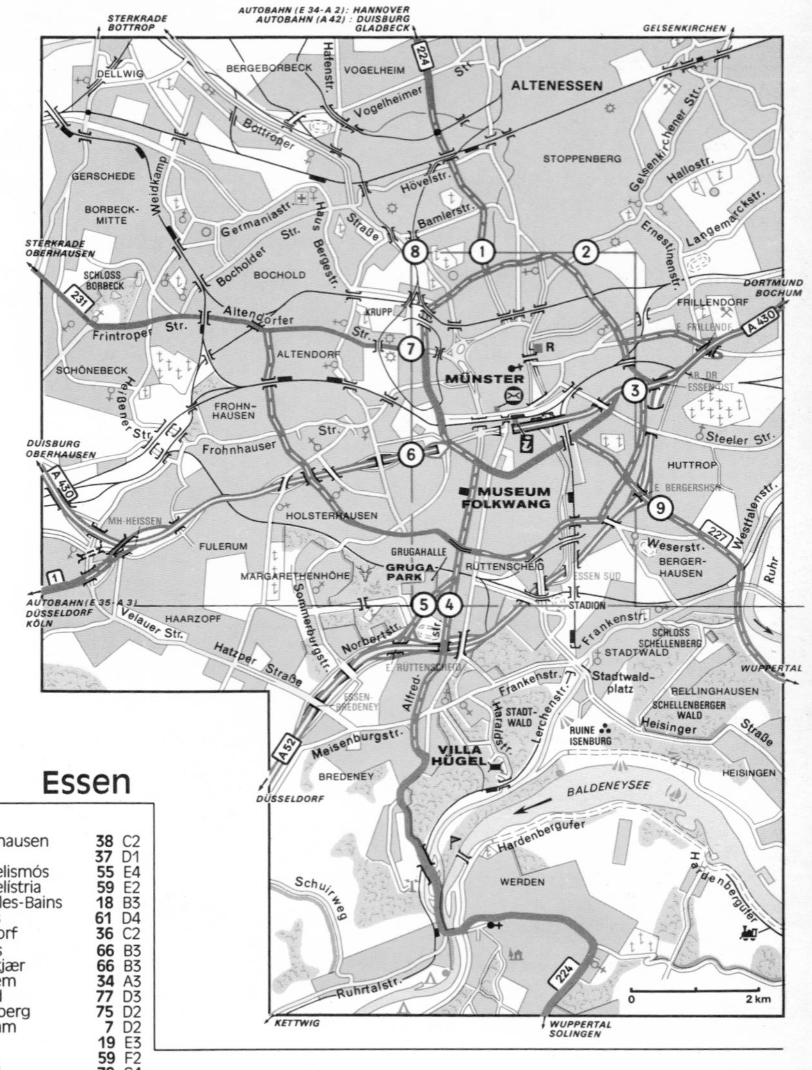
AUTOBAHN (E 34-A 2): HANNOVER
AUTOBAHN (A 42): DUISBURG GLADBECK
STERKRADE BOTTROP
GELSENKIRCHEN
DELLWIG
BERGEBORBECK
VOGELHEIM
ALTENESSEN
STOPPENBERG
GERSCHEDE
BORBECK-MITTE
STERKRADE OBERHAUSEN
SCHLOSS BORBECK
BOCHOLD
FRILLENDORF
DORTMUND BOCHUM
Frintroper Str.
ALTENDORF
SCHÖNEBECK
MÜNSTER
FROHN-HAUSEN
Frohnhauser Str.
DUISBURG OBERHAUSEN
HUTTROP
MUSEUM FOLKWANG
HOLSTERHAUSEN
FULERUM
MARGARETHENHÖHE
GRUGA-PARK
RÜTTENSCHEID
STADION
AUTOBAHN (E 35-A 3) DÜSSELDORF KÖLN
HAARZOPF
STADTWALD
WUPPERTAL
RELLINGHAUSEN
SCHELLENBERGER WALD
Heisinger Straße
RUINE ISENBURG
VILLA HÜGEL
BREDENEY
HEISINGEN
DÜSSELDORF
BALDENEYSEE
Hardenbergufer
WERDEN
Schuirweg
Ruhrtalstr.
KETTWIG
WUPPERTAL SOLINGEN
2 km

Essen

Eskifjörður 68 C1
Eskilstuna 75 E4
Eskisehir 81 F4
Eskoriatza 20 A4
Esla, R 25 D3
Eslarn 39 E3
Eslohe 38 A1
Eslöv 77 D3
Espa 74 C3
Espadañedo 24 C3
Espadán, Sa de 28 C4
Espalion 21 E2
Esparreguera 29 E2
Espedal 74 C2
Espejo 31 E2
Espelette 20 B3
Espelkamp 36 B3
Espenschied 38 A2
Espera 31 D3
Esperó, Pta 33 F2
Espichel, C 30 A1
Espiel 31 E2
Espigüete 25 E2
Espinama 25 E2
Espinho 24 A4
Espinilla 25 E2
Espinosa de Cerrato 25 E3
Espinosa de los Monteros 25 F2
Espoo 73 D4
Esporles 33 E2
Esposende 24 A3
Espot 29 E1
Espuña, Sa de 32 B2
Esquedas 28 C1
Esquivias 27 F3
Essarts, les 17 D2
Esse 70 C3
Essen (Niedersachsen) 36 B3
Essen (Nordrhein-Westfalen) 35 D2
Essenbach 39 E4
Essex 7 E3
Essími 57 D2
Esslingen 38 B4
Essonne 14 A4
Essoyes 14 C4
Estaca, Pto de la 30 A4
Estacas de Trueba, Pto de las 25 E2
Estadilla 29 D2
Estagel 21 E4
Estaires 14 B1
Estarreja 26 B2
Estats, Pic d' 21 D4
Estavayer 19 E2
Est, Canal de l' 15 D4
Este 43 D4
Estella 20 A4
Estepa 31 E3
Estepona 31 D4
Esteras de Medina 28 A3
Esterel 23 D3
Esternay 14 B3
Esterri d'Àneu 29 E1
Estissac 14 C4
Estói 30 B3
Estonija 78 C1
Estoril 26 A4
Estrées-St-Denis 14 B2
Estrela, Sa da 26 B3
Estrella 31 F2
Estremadura 26 A4
Estremoz 26 B4
Estret de Collegats 29 E1
Esztergom 80 B2
Etables 12 C3
Etain 15 D3
Etampes 14 A4
Etaples 14 A1
Etel 12 B4
Etelhem 77 F2
Etive, L 2 C3
Etna, M 49 D3
Etne 74 A3
Etolía-Akarnanía 58 B2
Etolikó 58 B2
Etrépagny 14 A3
Etretat 13 E2
Ettelbruck 15 D2
Etten 11 D3
Ettenheim 42 A1
Ettington 7 D2
Ettlingen 38 B4
Eugénie-les-Bains 20 C3
Eume, Emb del 24 B1
Eume, R 24 B1
Eupen 34 C3
Eura 72 C3
Eurajoki 72 C3
Euratsfeld 41 E3
Eure 14 A3
Eure (Dépt) 13 F3
Eure-et-Loir 14 A4
Europabrücke 43 D2
Europoort 11 D3
Euskadi 20 A4
Euskirchen 35 D3
Eußenhausen 38 C2
Eutin 37 D1
Evangelismós 55 E4
Evangelístria 59 E2
Evaux-les-Bains 18 B3
Évdilos 61 D4
Evendorf 36 C2
Evenes 66 B3
Evenskjær 66 B3
Evergem 34 A3
Everöd 77 D3
Evertsberg 75 D2
Evesham 7 D2
Evian 19 E3
Évia, N 59 F2
Evijärvi 70 C4
Evinohóri 58 C2
Évinos 58 C2
Evisa 23 E3
Evje 74 B4
Évlalo 56 B2
Evolène 19 F3
Évora 30 B1
Évoramonte 30 B1
Evran 12 C3
Evrecy 13 E3
Evreux 13 F3
Evritanía 58 C1
Evron 13 E4
Evropós 55 E2
Évros (Nomos) 57 D2
Évros *R* 57 D2
Evrostína 59 D3
Evrótas 63 D3
Evry 14 A3
Évzoni 55 E2
Exaplátanos 55 D2
Éxarhos 59 E2
Excideuil 17 F4
Exe 6 B4
Exeter 6 B4
Exmes 13 E3
Exmoor Nat Pk 6 B3
Exmouth 6 B4
Exohí (Ípiros) 54 B3
Exohí (Makedonía) 55 E3
Exohí (Makedonía) 56 A1
Exómvourgo 60 C4
Exter 36 C4
Extremadura 31 D1
Eydehavn 74 B4
Eye 7 E2
Eyemouth 5 E1
Eye Pen 2 B1
Eygues 22 B2
Eyguières 22 B3
Eygurande 18 B3
Eyjafjörður 68 B1
Eymet 20 C2
Eymoutiers 18 A3
Eyre 20 B2
Eyrieux 22 A2
Eysturoy 68 A3
Eyzies, les 21 D2
Ezcaray 28 A1
Eze 23 D3
Ezine 57 D4

F

Faak 41 D4
Fabara 29 D3
Fåberg 74 C2
Fabero 24 C2
Fåborg 76 B3
Fabriano 44 C2
Fábricas de Riópar 32 A2
Fabro 44 C3
Facinas 31 D4
Facture 20 B2
Faenza 44 B1
Færøerne 68 A3
Faeto 45 F4
Fafe 24 B3
Făgăras 81 D3
Făgărașului, M 81 D3
Fågelfors 77 E2
Fagernes (Oppland) 74 C2
Fagernes (Troms) 66 C2
Fagersta 75 E3
Fairford 7 D3
Fair Head 4 B2
Fair I 3 F2
Fakenham 7 F1
Fakovići 51 E3
Fakse 76 C3
Fakse Bugt 76 C3
Fakse Ladeplads 76 C3
Falaise 13 E3
Falakró, Óros 56 A1
Falássarna 64 A3
Falcade 43 D3
Falces 28 B1
Falconara Marittima 45 D2
Falcone 49 D3
Falcone, C del 46 A2
Falerna 47 E3
Faliráki 65 F2
Falkefjellet 67 F1
Falkenberg (DDR) 37 F4
Falkenberg (S) 76 C2
Falkensee 37 F3
Falkenstein 39 E2
Falkirk 2 C4
Falkland 3 D3
Falkonéra, N 63 E3
Falköping 77 D1
Fallersleben 37 D3
Fällfors 70 B2
Fallingbostel 36 C3
Falmouth 6 A4
Falset 29 D3
Falster 76 C4
Falterona Mte 44 B2
Fălticeni 81 D2
Falun 75 E3
Falzarego, Pso 43 D2
Fámjin 68 A3
Fanad Head 4 A1
Fanári (Pelopónissos) 58 C4
Fanári (Pelopónissos) 59 E4
Fanári (Thessalía) 55 D4
Fanári (Thráki) 56 C2
Fanári, Akr 61 D3
Fanefjord 76 C4
Fani i Madh 53 D4
Fani i Vogël 53 D4
Fanjeaux 21 E4
Fannich, L 2 C2
Fano 44 C2
Fanø 76 A3
Fanø Bugt 76 A3
Fanós 55 E2
Faouët, le 12 B4
Faou, le 12 B3
Farángi Samariás 64 A4
Farángi Víkou 54 B3
Fara Novarese 42 B4
Fårbo 77 E2
Fardes, R 31 F3
Fareham 7 D4
Fårevejle 76 C3
Färgelanda 74 C4
Färila 75 E2
Farindola 45 D3
Faringdon 7 D3
Farini d'Olmo 23 F2
Färjestaden 77 E2
Farkadóna 55 D4
Farkaždin 51 F1
Farlete 28 C2
Farmakoníssi 61 E4
Farnborough 7 D3
Farnese 44 B3
Farnham 7 D3
Faro 30 B3
Fårö 77 F1
Fårösund 77 F1
Farra d'Alpago 43 E3
Fársala 59 D1
Farsø 76 B2
Farsund 74 A4
Farum 76 C3
Fasano 47 E1
Fašku Vaskojoki 67 E2
Fastov 79 E4
Fátima 26 A3
Fatmomakke 69 E2
Faucille, Col de la 19 E3
Faucogney 15 E4
Faulquemont 15 E3
Fauquembergues 14 A1
Fauske 69 E1
Fauville 13 E2
Fåvang 74 C2
Favara 48 C4
Favareta 32 C1
Faverges 19 E3
Faverney 15 D4
Faversham 7 F3
Favignana, I 48 A3
Fawley 7 D4
Faxaflói 68 A2
Fayence 22 C3
Fayl-Billot 15 D4
Fayón 29 D2
Fay-sur-Lignon 22 A2
Fažana 43 F4
Feale 8 A3
Fécamp 13 E2
Feces 24 B3
Féclaz, la 19 E3
Feda 74 A4
Feggesund 76 B2
Fehmarn 37 D1
Fehmarnbelt 37 D1
Fehmarnsund 37 D1
Fehrbellin 37 E3
Fehring 41 F4
Fejø 76 C4
Feketić 51 E1
Felanitx 33 E3
Felbertauern-tunnel 43 E2
Feld 41 D4
Feldafing 40 B3
Feldbach 41 F4
Feldberg (D) 42 A1
Feldberg (DDR) 37 F2
Feldkirch 40 A4
Feldkirchen 41 D4
Felgueiras 24 A3
Felixstowe 7 F2
Fellbach 38 B4
Felletin 18 B3
Fellingsbro 75 E4
Felton 5 E2
Feltre 43 D3
Femer Bælt 76 C4
Femund 75 D1
Femundsmarka 75 D1
Fene 24 B1
Fener 43 D3
Fenestrelle 23 D1
Fénétrange 15 E3
Feolin Ferry 2 B4
Fer à Cheval, Cirque du 19 E3
Feraklós 65 F2
Ferbane 8 C3
Ferdinandovac 50 C1
Ferdinandshof 37 F2
Fère-Champenoise 14 C3
Fère-en-Tardenois 14 B3
Fère, la 14 B2
Ferentino 45 D4
Féres 57 D2
Feria 30 C1
Feričanci 51 D1
Ferlach 43 F2
Fermanagh 8 C1
Fermo 45 D2
Fermoselle 24 C4
Fermoy 8 B4
Fernancaballero 27 F4
Fernán Núñez 31 E2
Ferney-Voltaire 19 E3
Fernpaj 40 B4
Ferrandina 47 D2
Ferrara 43 D4
Ferreira 24 B1
Ferreira do Alentejo 30 B2
Ferreira do Zêzere 26 B3
Ferreiras 30 A3
Ferreras de Abajo 24 C3
Ferreries 33 F2
Ferreruela de Huerva 28 B3
Ferret, Cap 20 B2
Ferrette 19 F1
Ferriere 23 F2
Ferrières 14 B4
Ferrol 24 B1
Ferru, M 46 A3
Ferté-Alais, la 14 A3
Ferté-Bernard, la 13 E4
Ferté-Frênel, la 13 E3
Ferté-Gaucher, la 14 B3
Ferté-Macé, la 13 E3
Ferté-Milon, la 14 B3
Ferté-sous-Jouarre, la 14 B3
Ferté-St-Aubin, la 18 A1
Ferté-Vidame, la 13 F3
Fertilia 46 A3
Fervenza, Emb de 24 A1
Festós 64 B4
Festre, Col du 22 C2
Festvåg 66 B3
Fethard 8 C3
Fetlar 3 F1
Fetsund 74 C3
Feucht 39 D3
Feuchtwangen 38 C3
Feunte Dé 25 E2
Feurs 18 C3
Feyzin 19 D3
Ffestiniog 6 B1
Fflint 5 D4
Fiano R. 44 C4
Fiastra 44 C2
Ficarolo 43 D4
Fichtel-gebirge 39 D2
Fidenza 42 C4
Fieberbrunn 40 C3
Fier 54 A2
Fiera di Primiero 43 D3
Fierzës, Liq i 53 D4
Fiesole 44 B2
Fife 3 D3
Fife Ness 3 D3
Figália 58 C4
Figeac 21 E2
Figline Valdarno 44 B2
Figueira da Foz 26 A3
Figueira de Castelo Rodrigo 26 C2
Figueiró dos Vinhos 26 B3
Figueras 29 F1
Figueres 29 F1
Figueruela de Arriba 24 C3
Fíhtio 59 D3
Filabres, Sa de los 32 A3
Filadélfi 55 F2
Filadelfia 47 E4
Filáki 59 D1
Filákio 57 D1
Filakopí 64 A1
Filérimos 65 F2
Filey 5 F3
Filfola 49 F4
Filí 59 E3
Fília (Lésvos) 61 D1
Fília (Pelopónissos) 58 C3
Filiátes 54 B4
Filiatrá 62 B3
Filicudi, I 48 C2
Filiourí 56 C2
Fílipi 56 A2
Filipiáda 58 B1
Filipjakov 50 B3
Fílipos, Akr 63 F3
Filipstad 75 D3
Filíra 56 C1
Fillan 68 C3
Fille-fjell 74 B2
Fílo 55 D4
Filótas 55 D2
Filottrano 45 D2
Finale Emilia 43 D4
Finale Ligure 23 E2
Fiñana 32 A3
Finca de la Concepción 31 E3
Finchingfield 7 E2
Findhorn 2 C2
Fínikas 60 B4
Finikoúndas 62 C3
Finistère 12 B4
Finisterre, Emb de 27 F4
Finja 77 D3
Finn 8 C1
Finneidfjord 69 E2
Finnentrop 38 A1
Finnmark 67 D2
Finnmark 67 E1
Finnmarksvidda 67 D2
Finnøy 74 A3
Finnsnes 66 C2
Finow 37 F3
Finowfurt 37 F2
Finskij Zaliv 73 E4
Finspång 75 E4
Finsteraarhorn 42 A3
Finsterau 41 D2
Finsterwalde 37 F4
Finström 72 B4
Fintona 8 C1
Fintown 8 C1
Fionnphort 2 B3
Fiorenzuola d'Arda 42 C4
Firenze 44 B2
Firenzuola 44 B1
Firminy 18 C4
Firmo 47 D2
Fischamend Markt 41 F2
Fischbach 39 D3
Fischbeck 37 E3
Fischen 40 A4
Fishbourne 7 D4
Fishguard 6 A2
Fiskárdo 58 A2
Fiskari 73 D4
Fiskebøl 66 B3
Fismes 14 B3
Fissíni 56 C4
Fisterra 24 A2
Fisterra, C 24 A2
Fitero 28 B1
Fitíes 58 B2
Fitjar 74 A3
Fiuggi 45 D4
Fiumicino 44 C4
Fivemiletown 8 C1
Fivizzano 44 A1
Fjærland 74 B2
Fjällåsen 66 C3
Fjällbacka 74 C4
Fjällnäs 69 D4
Fjärdhundra 75 F3
Fjätervålen 75 D2
Fjelie 77 D3
Fjellerup 76 C2
Fjerritslev 76 B2
Fjerze 53 D4
Flå 74 C3
Fladså 76 B3
Fladungen 38 C2
Flaine 19 E3
Flakk 68 C3
Flåm 74 B2
Flamborough Head 5 F3
Flambourári 54 C4
Flámbouro (Makedonía) 54 C2
Flámbouro (Makedonía) 55 F2
Flamignano 45 D3
Flamouriá 55 D2
Flannan I 2 A1
Flåsjön 69 E3
Flåten 66 C2
Flatey 68 A1
Flatråker 74 A3
Flattnitz 41 D4
Flatval 68 C3
Flèche, la 17 E1
Fleetwood 5 D3
Flekkefjord 74 A4
Flen 75 E4
Flensborg Fjord 76 B4
Flensburg 36 C1
Flers 13 E3
Flesberg 74 C3
Flesnes 66 B3
Fleurance 21 D3
Fleurier 19 E2
Fleurus 34 B3
Fleury 14 B4
Fleury-sur-Andelle 14 A2
Fléves, N 59 F3
Flevoland 11 E2
Flexenpaß 40 A2
Flims Waldhaus 42 B2
Flint 5 D4
Flisa 75 D3
Flix 29 D2
Flixecourt 14 A2
Flize 14 C2
Floda 75 E3
Flogny 14 C4
Flöha 39 E1
Flomohóri 62 C4
Flora 53 F4
Florac 21 F2
Flor da Rosa 26 B4
Florennes 34 B4
Florensac 21 F3
Florenville 15 D2
Floreşty 81 E2
Floriáda 58 B1
Floridia 49 D4
Flórina 54 C2
Flórina (Nomos) 54 C2
Florø 74 A1
Flörsheim-Dalsheim 38 A3
Flötningen 75 D2
Floúda, Akr 65 D1
Flüelapass 42 C2
Flüelen 42 B2
Flühli 42 A2
Flumendosa 46 B4
Flumen, R 28 C2
Flumet 19 E3
Fluminimaggiore 46 A4
Flums 42 B2
Fluvià, R 29 F1
Foča 51 E4
Foça 61 E2
Foce Verde 46 A1
Fochabers 3 D2
Fockbek 36 C1
Focșani 81 E2
Fódele 64 C4
Foggia 45 F4
Föglö 72 B4
Fohnsdorf 41 E4
Föhr 36 B1
Foiano della Chiana 44 B2
Foinaven 2 C1
Foix 21 D4
Fojnica (Bosna i Hercegovina) 51 D3
Fojnica (Bosna i Hercegovina) 51 E4
Fokída 59 D2
Fokstuhø 74 C1
Folda 66 B3
Foldereid 69 D2
Foldfjorden 69 D3
Foleá 56 A2
Folégandros 64 B1
Folégandros, N 64 B1
Følen 74 A3
Folgaria 43 D3
Folgefonna 74 A3
Folgoët, le 12 B3
Folgoso de la Ribera 24 C2
Foligno 44 C3
Folkestad 74 A1
Folkestone 7 F3
Follafoss 69 D3
Folldal 74 C1
Follebu 74 C2
Follina 43 E3
Föllinge 69 E3
Follonica 44 A3
Folmava 39 E3
Folói 58 C3
Fombellida 25 E3
Fond-de-France, le 19 E4
Fondevila 24 B3
Fondi 45 D4
Fondo 43 D2
Fonfría (Aragón) 28 C3
Fonfría (Castilla-León) 24 C3
Fongen 69 D4
Fonn 74 B2
Fonni 46 B3
Fonollosa 29 E2
Fonsagrada 24 C1
Fontaine 15 E4
Fontainebleau 14 B4
Fontaine-de-Vaucluse 22 B3
Fontaine-Française 19 D1
Fontaine-Henry 13 E3
Fontaine-le-Dun 13 F2
Fontanigorda 23 E2
Fonte Longa 24 B4
Fontenay 18 C1
Fontenay-le-Comte 17 D2
Fontenay-Trésigny 14 B3
Fontevraud-l'Abbaye 17 E2
Fontfroide, Abbaye de 21 F4
Fontgombault 17 F2
Fontibre 25 E2
Fontiveros 27 E2
Fontoy 15 D2
Font-Romeu 29 E1
Fontvieille 22 B3
Fonz 29 D2
Fonzaso 43 D3
Foppolo 42 C3
Forata, Emb de 32 C1
Forbach 15 E3
Forca Canapine 45 D3
Forca Caruso 45 D3
Forca d'Acero 45 D4
Forcall 28 C3
Forcalquier 22 C3
Forcarei 24 A2
Forchheim 39 D3
Forclaz, Col de la 19 E3
Forcola di Mte Rest 43 E2
Førde 74 A2
Førdefjorden 74 A2
Förderstedt 37 E4
Fordingbridge 7 D4
Fordongianus 46 A3
Foreland 7 D4
Forenza 47 D1
Foresta di Burgos 46 A3
Føresvik 74 A3
Forêt d'Orient, Lac de la 14 C4
Forez, Monts du 18 C3
Forfar 3 D3
Forges-les-Eaux 14 A2
Forggensee 40 B3
Forio 46 B2
Forl 44 B1
Forli del Sannio 45 E4
Forlimpopoli 44 B1
Formazza 42 A3
Formby 5 D4
Formentera 33 E1
Formentor, C 33 E2
Formerie 14 A2
Formia 46 B1
Formigine 44 A1
Fornaci di Barga 44 A2
Fornells 33 F2
Forni Avoltri 43 E2
Forni di Sopra 43 E2
Forno di Zoldo 43 E3
Fornos de Algodres 26 C2
Fornovo di Taro 44 A1
Forøy 69 E1
Føroyar 68 A3
Forres 3 D2
Forsa 75 F2
Forserum 77 D2
Forshaga 75 D3
Forsnes 68 C3
Forssa 73 D3
Fort Augustus 2 C2
Forte dei Marmi 23 F2
Forth 39 D3
Forth *R* 2 C3
Forth Bridges 3 D4
Forth, Firth of 3 D3
Fort-Mahon 14 A1
Fortore 45 E4
Fortrose 2 C2
Fortuna 32 C2
Fortuneswell 6 C4
Fort William 2 C3
Forvik 69 D2
Fos (Ariège) 21 D4
Fos (Bouches-du-Rhône) 22 B3
Foscagno, Pso di 42 C2
Fosnavåg 68 A4
Fossacesia 45 E3
Fossano 23 D2
Fossat, le 21 D4
Fossbakken 66 C3
Fosses 34 B3
Fossli 74 B3
Fossombrone 44 C2
Fotiná 55 D3
Fotolívos 56 A2
Fouesnant 12 B4
Foug 15 D3
Fougères 13 D4
Fougerolles 15 E4
Foula 3 F2
Foulness Pt 7 F3
Fountains Abbey 5 E3
Fouras 17 D3
Fourchambault 18 B2
Fourfourás 64 B4
Foúrka 59 D1
Fourmies 14 C2
Fourná 58 C1
Fournels 21 F2
Fournés 64 A3
Foúrni (Dodekánissa) 61 E4
Fourní (Kríti) 65 D4
Foúrni (Pelopónissos) 59 E4
Fourniá, Akr 61 D1
Foúrni, N 61 E4
Fours 18 C2
Fousseret, le 21 D4
Foústani 55 D2
Fowey 6 A4
Foxford 8 B2
Foyers 2 C2
Foyle, L 4 A2
Foyle, R 4 A2
Foz 24 C1
Foz do Arelho 26 A3
Foz do Douro 24 A3
Foz Giraldo 26 B3
Frabosa Soprana 23 D2
Fraddon 6 A4
Fræna 68 B4
Fraga 29 D2
Frailes 31 F3
Fraize 15 E4
Fram 50 B1
Frammersbach 38 B2
Francavilla al Mare 45 E3
Francavilla di Sicilia 49 D3
Francavilla Fontana 47 E1
Francavilla in Sinni 47 D2
Francker 11 E1

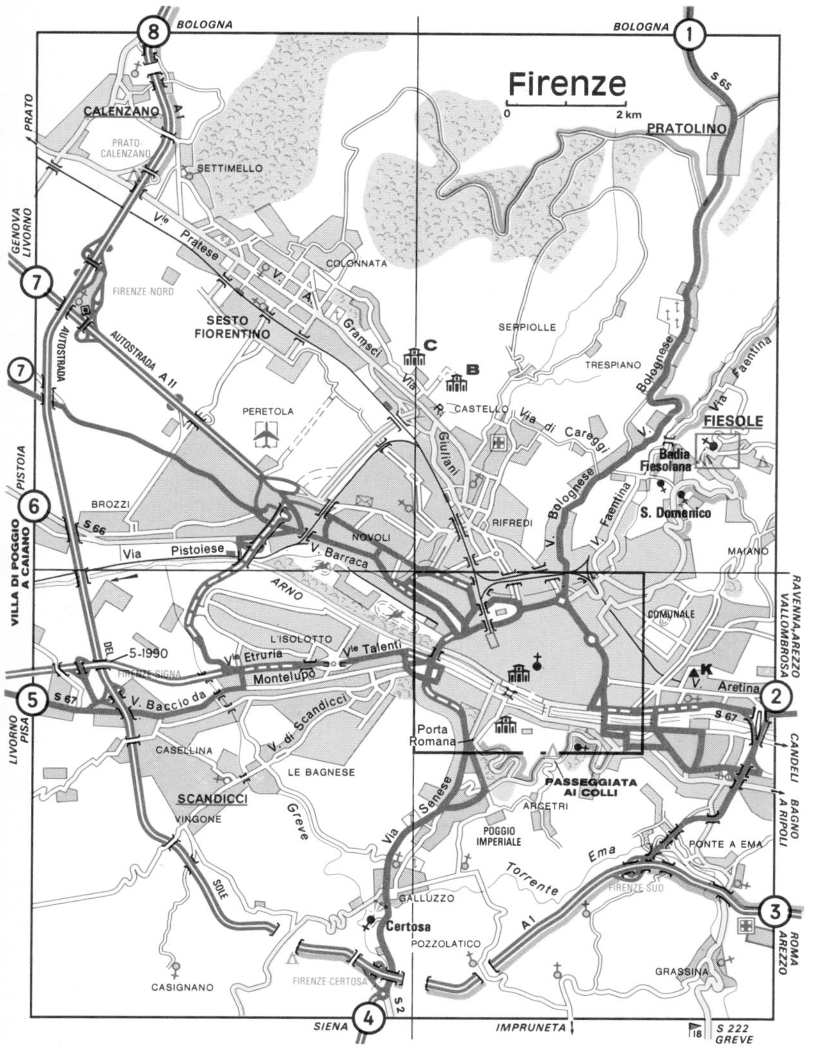
Firenze
0 2 km
BOLOGNA
PRATO
CALENZANO
PRATOLINO
SETTIMELLO
SESTO FIORENTINO
COLONNATA
PERETOLA
FIESOLE
S. Domenico
Badia Fiesolana
SERPIOLLE
TRESPIANO
RIFREDI
NOVOLI
BROZZI
Via Pistoiese
ARNO
L'ISOLOTTO
Monteluppo
CASELLINA
LE BAGNESE
SCANDICCI
VINGONE
Porta Romana
PASSEGGIATA AI COLLI
POGGIO IMPERIALE
ARCETRI
PONTE A EMA
GALLUZZO
Certosa
POZZOLATICO
GRASSINA
CASIGNANO
FIRENZE CERTOSA
SIENA
IMPRUNETA
S 222 GREVE
PISTOIA
GENOVA LIVORNO
LIVORNO PISA
VILLA DI POGGIO A CAIANO
RAVENNA, AREZZO VALLOMBROSA
CANDELI BAGNO A RIPOLI
ROMA AREZZO

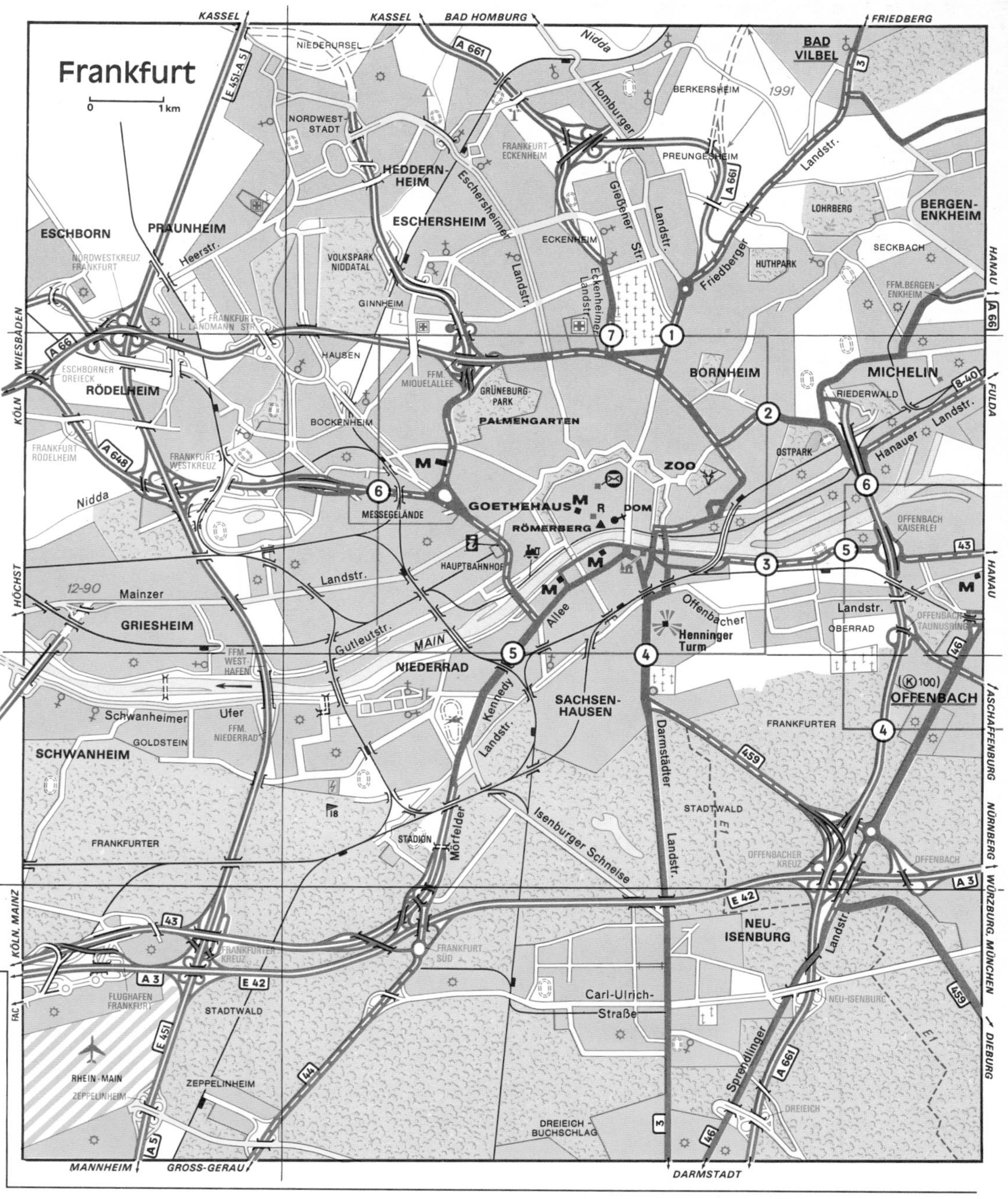
Frankfurt
0 1 km
KASSEL
BAD HOMBURG
FRIEDBERG
BAD VILBEL
NIEDERURSEL
NORDWEST-STADT
HEDDERN-HEIM
ESCHERSHEIM
PRAUNHEIM
ESCHBORN
BERGEN-ENKHEIM
RÖDELHEIM
BOCKENHEIM
PALMENGARTEN
BORNHEIM
MICHELIN
GOETHEHAUS
RÖMERBERG
DOM
ZOO
HAUPTBAHNHOF
MESSEGELÄNDE
GRIESHEIM
NIEDERRAD
SACHSEN-HAUSEN
Henninger Turm
OFFENBACH
SCHWANHEIM
STADTWALD
NEU-ISENBURG
Carl-Ulrich-Straße
ZEPPELINHEIM
DREIEICH-BUCHSCHLAG
MANNHEIM
GROSS-GERAU
DARMSTADT
HANAU
FULDA
KÖLN, WIESBADEN
HÖCHST
KÖLN, MAINZ
ASCHAFFENBURG
NÜRNBERG, WÜRZBURG, MÜNCHEN
DIEBURG

Francolí, R 29 E3
Francorchamps 34 C3
Frändefors 75 D4
Frangádes 54 C4
Frangísta 58 C1
Frangokástelo 64 B4
Frangy 19 E3
Frankenberg (D) 38 B1
Frankenberg (DDR) 39 E1
Frankenburg 41 D3
Frankenmarkt 41 D3
Frankenstein 38 A3
Frankenthal 38 B3
Frankfurt am Main 38 B2
Frankfurt an der Oder 78 A4
Fränk Rezat 39 D3
Fränk Saale 38 C2
Františkovy Lázně 39 E2
Franzburg 37 E1
Franz-Josephs-Höhe 43 E2
Frascati 44 C4
Frascineto 47 D2
Frasdorf 40 C3
Fraserburgh 3 E2
Frasno, Pto del 28 B2
Fratel 26 B3
Fratta Polesine 43 D4
Frauenfeld 42 B1
Frauenkirchen 41 F3
Frauenstein 39 E1
Frechen 35 D3
Frechilla 25 E3
Freckenhorst 36 B4
Fredensborg 76 C3
Fredericia 76 B3
Frederikshavn 76 C2
Frederikssund 76 C3
Frederiksværk 76 C3
Fredrika 69 F3
Fredriksberg 75 E3
Fredrikstad 74 C4
Fregenal de la Sierra 30 C2
Fregene 44 C4
Fréhel, Cap 12 C3
Frei 68 B4
Freiberg 39 E1
Freiberger Mulde 39 E1
Freiburg (Baden-Württemberg) 42 A1
Freiburg (Niedersachsen) 36 C2
Freienhufen 37 F4
Freilassing 40 C3
Freilingen 38 A2
Freising 39 D4
Freistadt 41 D2
Freital 39 F1
Freiwalde 37 F3
Freixedas 26 C2
Freixido 24 C2
Freixo de Espada à Cinta 24 C4
Fréjus 22 C3
Fréjus, Tunnel du 19 E4
Frenchpark 8 B2
Frêne, Col du 19 E3
Freren 36 B3
Freshford 8 C3
Freshwater 7 D4
Fresnay-sur-Sarthe 13 E4
Fresnes-en-Woëvre 15 D3
Fresne-St-Mamès 19 D1
Fresno Alhándiga 27 D2
Fresvikbreen 74 B2
Freudenberg (Baden-Württemberg) 38 B3
Freudenberg (Nordrhein-Westfalen) 38 A1
Freudenstadt 38 B4
Frévent 14 A1
Freyburg 37 E4
Freyenstein 37 E2
Freyung 39 F3
Frí 65 E3
Frias 25 F2
Frías de Albarracín 28 B3
Fribourg 19 F2
Fridingen 42 B1
Friedberg (A) 41 F3
Friedberg (Bayern) 39 D4
Friedberg (Hessen) 38 B2
Friedeburg 36 B2
Friedersdorf 37 F3
Friedland (D) 36 C4
Friedland (DDR) 37 F2
Friedrichroda 38 C1
Friedrichshafen 42 B1
Friedrichskoog 36 B2
Friedrichsort 36 C1
Friedrichstadt 36 C1
Friedrichsthal 15 E2
Friesach 41 D4
Friesack 37 E3
Friesland 11 E1
Friesoythe 36 B3
Frigiliana 31 F4
Frihetsli 66 C2
Fríkes 58 B2
Frilingiánika 63 D4
Frinton-on-Sea 7 F3
Friol 24 B1
Fristad 77 D1
Fritsla 77 D2
Fritzlar 38 B1
Friuli-Venezia Giulia 43 E3
Frizington 5 D3
Frodsham 5 D4
Frogner 74 C3
Frohavet 68 C3
Frohburg 39 E1
Frohnleiten 41 E3
Froissy 14 A2
Froitzheim 35 D3
Frome 6 C3
Fromentine 16 C2
Frómista 25 E3
Fronteira 26 B4
Frontenay-Rohan-Rohan 17 D3
Frontenhausen 39 E4
Frontera 30 A4
Frontignan 22 A3
Fronton 21 D3
Frosinone 45 D4
Frosolone 45 E4
Frösön 69 E4
Frosta 68 C3
Frostavallen 77 D3
Frøstrup 76 B2
Frouard 15 D3
Froússa 54 C4
Frövi 75 E4
Frøya 68 C3
Frøyfjorden 68 C3
Frøysjøen 74 A1
Fruges 14 A1
Fruška 51 E2
Frutigen 19 F2
Frýdek-Místek 80 B1
Fteliá 56 A2
Ftéri (Makedonía) 55 D3
Ftéri (Pelopónissos) 58 C3
Fthiótida 59 D1
Fucecchio 44 A2
Fuencaliente (Castilla-la-Mancha) 31 E2
Fuencaliente (Is Canarias) 30 A4
Fuendejalón 28 B2
Fuendetodos 28 C2
Fuengirola 31 E4
Fuenlabrada 27 F3
Fuenlabrada de los Montes 31 E1
Fuenmayor 28 A1
Fuensalida 27 E3
Fuensanta de Martos 31 F3
Fuensanta, Emb de la 32 A2
Fuente-Alamo 32 B1
Fuente Alamo 32 B3
Fuentecén 25 E3
Fuente de Cantos 30 C2
Fuente del Maestre 30 C1
Fuente de Pedro Naharro 28 A4
Fuente de Piedra 31 E3
Fuente el Fresno 27 F4
Fuenteguinaldo 26 C3
Fuente la Higuera 32 C1
Fuentelapeña 25 D4
Fuente Obéjuna 31 D2
Fuente Palmera 31 E2
Fuentepinilla 28 A2
Fuentesauco 25 D4
Fuentes de Andalucía 31 D3
Fuentes de Ayódar 28 C4
Fuentes de Ebro 28 C2
Fuentes de León 30 C2
Fuentes de Nava 25 E3
Fuentes de Oñoro 26 C2
Fuentes de Ropel 25 D3
Fuentes de Valdepero 25 E3
Fuentidueña 25 E4
Fuentidueña de Tajo 28 A4
Fuerte del Rey 31 F2
Fuerteventura 30 B4
Fügen 40 B4
Fuglebjerg 76 C3
Fugløysundet 66 C1
Fulda 38 C2
Fulda *R* 38 C2
Fulgatore 48 B3
Fulpmes 43 D2
Fulufjället 75 D2
Fumay 14 C2
Fumel 21 D2
Funäsdalen 69 D4
Funchal 30 A3
Fundão 26 B3
Funes 43 D2
Fuorn, Pso dal 42 C2
Furadouro 26 B2
Furci 45 E3
Furkapass 42 A3
Furnace 2 C3
Furnás 33 E1
Fürstenau 36 B3
Fürstenberg 37 F2
Fürstenfeld 41 F4
Fürstenfeldbruck 40 B3
Fürstenlager 38 B3
Fürstenwalde 37 F3
Fürstenwerder 37 F2
Fürstenzell 40 C2
Furtei 46 B4
Fürth 39 D3
Furth 39 E3
Furtwangen 42 A1
Furudal 75 E2
Furuflaten 66 C2
Fuscaldo 47 D3
Fusch 40 C4
Fuschl 40 C3
Fuseta 30 B3
Fushë Arrez 53 D4
Fushë Muhur 53 D4
Fusignano 44 B1
Füssen 40 A4
Fustiñana 28 B2
Futa, Pso della 44 B1
Futog 51 E1
Futrikelv 66 C2
Fyn 76 B3
Fyne, L 2 B3
Fynshav 76 B3
Fyresdal 74 B4
Fyresvatn 74 B4
Fyrkat 76 B2

G

Gaaldorf 41 E3
Gabarret 20 C3
Gabela 52 A3
Gaberl-Sattel 41 E4
Gabia la Grande 31 F3
Gabicce Mare 44 C1
Gabriel y Galán, Emb de 27 D3
Gabrovka 50 A1
Gabrovo 81 D4
Gacé 13 E3
Gacilly, la 16 C1
Gacko 52 B3
Gad'ač 79 F4
Gäddede 69 E3
Gadebusch 37 D2
Gádor 32 A3
Gádor, Sa de 32 A3
Gadžin Han 53 E2
Găești 81 D3
Gaeta 46 B1
Gaeta, G di 46 B1
Gagarin 79 F2
Gaggenau 38 B4
Gagnef 75 E3
Gail 43 E2
Gailbergsattel 43 E2
Gaildorf 38 C4
Gailey 6 C2
Gaillac 21 E3
Gaillimh 8 B2
Gaillon 14 A3
Gainsborough 7 D1
Gairloch 2 B2
Gaj 53 D1
Gajdobra 51 E1
Gajsin 81 E1
Gajvoron 81 E1
Gakovo 51 D1
Galan 20 C4
Galanádo 64 B1
Galanianá 63 E4
Galanta 80 B2
Galapagar 27 F3
Galarinós 55 F3
Galaroza 30 C2
Galashiels 5 D1
Galatádes 55 D2
Galatáki 59 E2
Galatás (Argolída) 59 E4
Galatás (Korinthía) 59 D3
Galați 81 E2
Galatina 47 F2
Galatiní 54 C3
Galátista 55 F3
Galatone 47 F2
Galaxídi 59 D2
Galdakao 20 A3
Galdhøpiggen 74 B2
Galeata 44 B2
Galegos 26 C4
Galende 24 C3
Galera 32 A2
Galiano del Capo 47 F2
Galibier, Col du 19 E4
Galicia 24 B2
Galičica 54 C2
Galičnik 53 D4
Galikós 55 E2
Galipsós 56 A2
Galisteo 27 D3
Galiz, Pto de 31 D4
Gallarate 42 B4
Gallardon 14 A3
Gallargues 22 A3
Gállego, R 28 C2
Galley Head 8 B4
Galliate 42 B4
Gallipoli 47 F2
Gällivare 66 C4
Gallneukirchen 41 D2
Gällö 69 E4
Gallo, C 48 B3
Gallocanta, L de 28 B3
Gallo, R 28 B3
Galloway Forest Park 4 C2
Gallspach 41 D3
Gallur 28 B2
Gälöfjärden 75 F4
Galston 2 C4
Galten 76 B3
Galtür 40 A4
Galty Mts 8 B4
Galveias 26 B4
Gálvez 27 E4
Galway 8 B2
Galway (Co) 8 B2
Galway B 8 B3
Gamaches 14 A2
Gambarie d'Aspromonte 47 D4

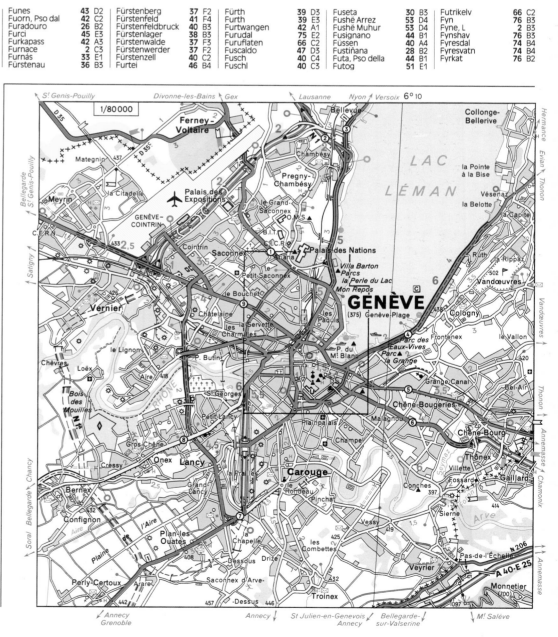

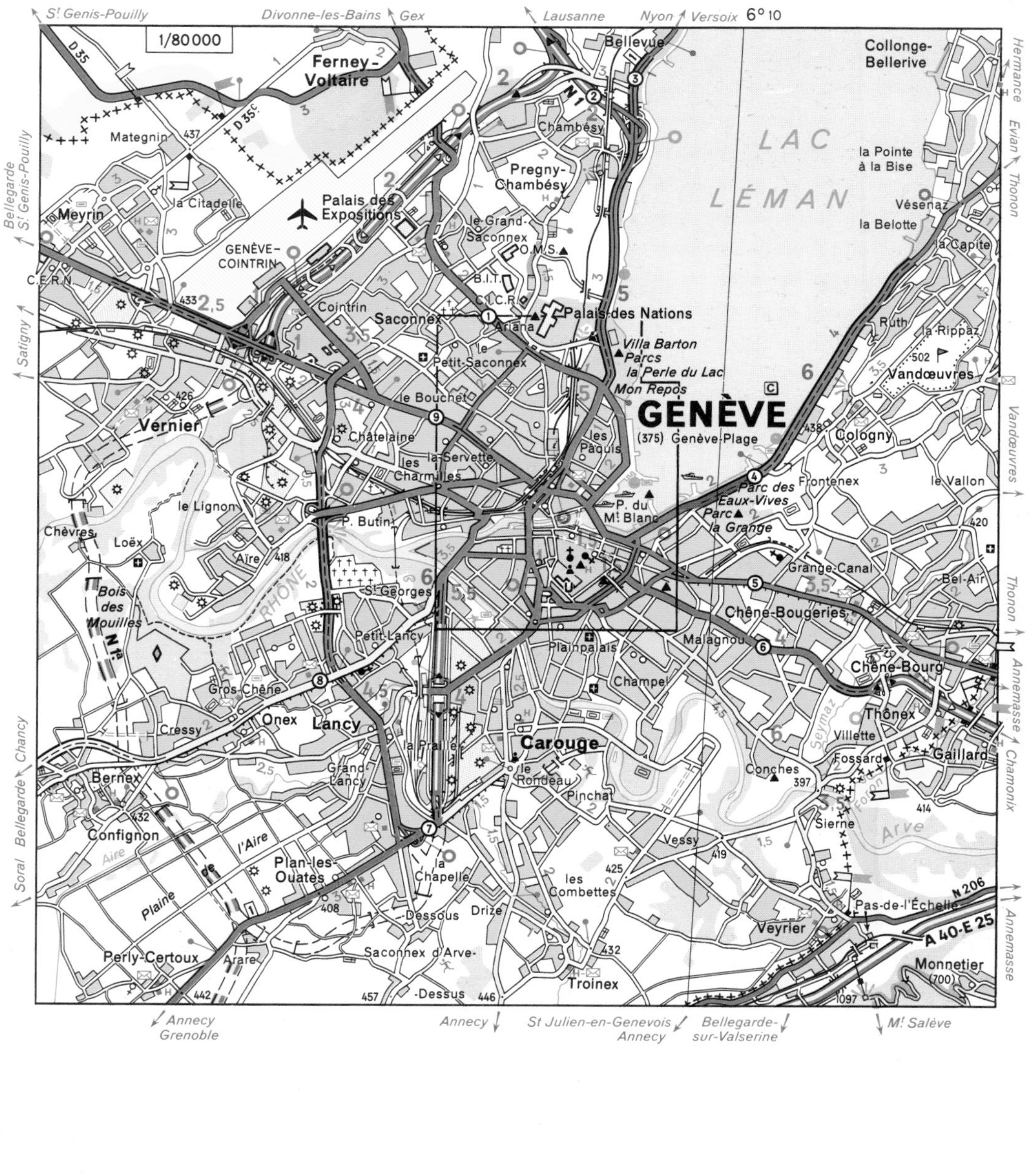
1/80 000
St Genis-Pouilly
Divonne-les-Bains
Gex
Lausanne
Nyon
Versoix
6° 10
Bellevue
Collonge-Bellerive
Ferney-Voltaire
Mategnin
Meyrin
Pregny-Chambésy
Chambésy
LAC LÉMAN
la Pointe à la Bise
Vésenaz
la Belotte
la Capite
Palais des Expositions
GENÈVE-COINTRIN
Cointrin
Saconnex
Palais des Nations
Villa Barton
Parcs la Perle du Lac Mon Repos
Petit-Saconnex
Vernier
Châtelaine
les Charmilles
GENÈVE
Genève-Plage
Cologny
Vandœuvres
le Lignon
Chèvres
Aïre
Parc des Eaux-Vives
Parc la Grange
Frontenex
le Vallon
Grange-Canal
Bel-Air
Chêne-Bougeries
Chêne-Bourg
Thônex
Onex
Lancy
Carouge
Plainpalais
Champel
Malagnou
Gaillard
Villette
Conches
Sierne
Bernex
Confignon
Plan-les-Ouates
Vessy
les Combettes
Troinex
Veyrier
Pas-de-l'Échelle
Perly-Certoux
Arare
Saconnex d'Arve-Dessus
Monnetier
A 40-E 25
N 206
Annecy Grenoble
Annecy
St Julien-en-Genevois Annecy
Bellegarde-sur-Valserine
Mt Salève
Hermance
Évian
Thonon
Chamonix
Annemasse
Bellegarde St Genis-Pouilly
Satigny
Soral
Chancy

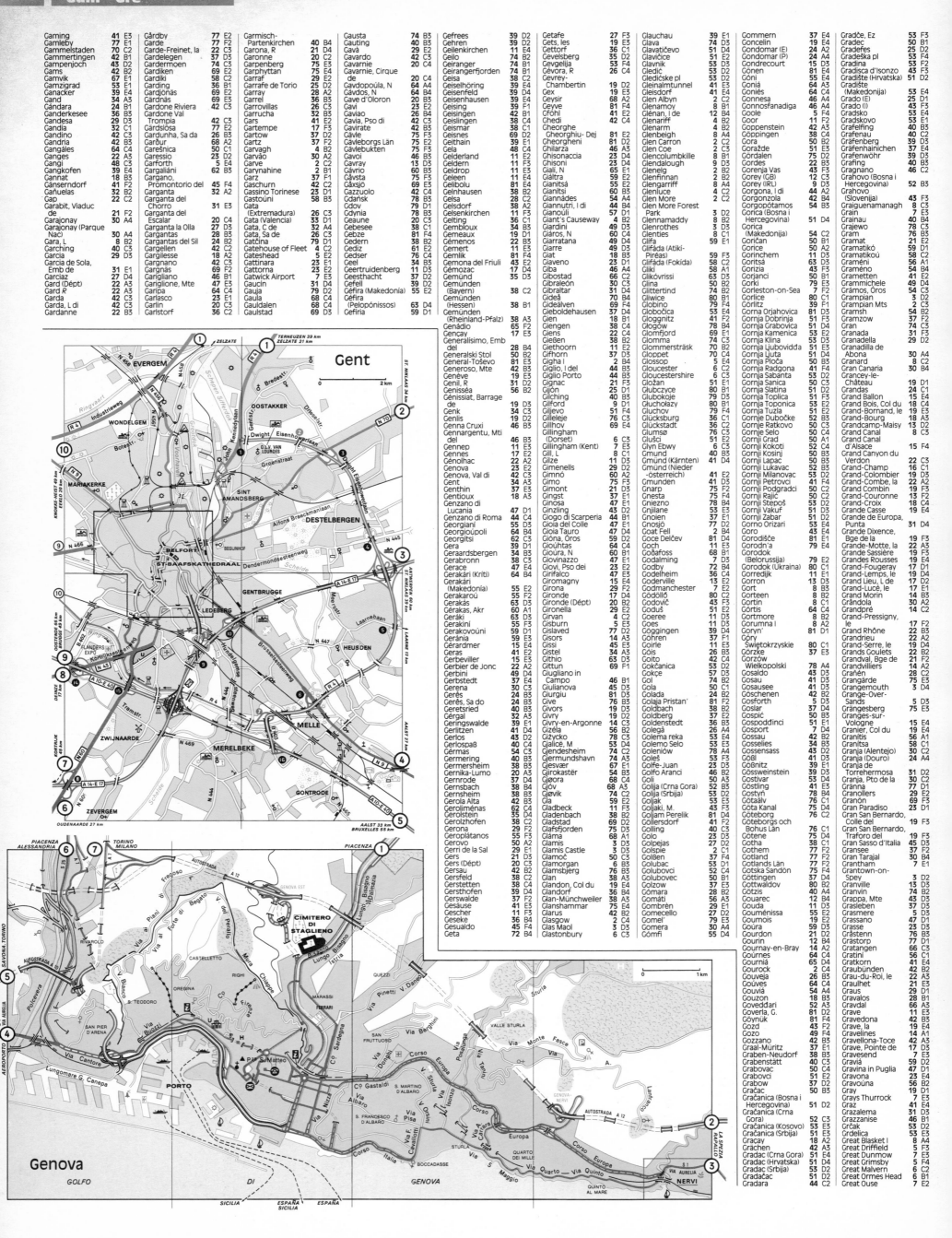

Gaming 41 E3
Gamleby 77 E1
Gammelstaden 70 C2
Gammertingen 42 B1
Gampenjoch 43 D2
Gams 42 B2
Gamvik 67 E1
Gamzigrad 53 E1
Ganacker 39 E4
Gand 34 A3
Gándara 24 B1
Ganderkesee 36 B3
Gandesa 29 D3
Gandía 32 C1
Gandino 42 C3
Gandria 42 B3
Gangáles 64 C4
Ganges 22 A3
Gangi 48 C3
Gangkofen 39 E4
Gannat 18 B3
Gänserndorf 41 F2
Gañuelas 32 B2
Gap 22 C2
Garabit, Viaduc de 21 F2
Garajonay 30 A4
Garajonay (Parque Nac) 30 A4
Gara, L 8 B2
Garching 40 C3
Garcia 29 D3
Garcia de Sola, Emb de 31 E1
Garciaz 27 D4
Gard (Dépt) 22 A3
Gard *R* 22 A3
Garda 42 C3
Garda, L di 42 C3
Gardanne 22 B3
Gårdby 77 E2
Garde 77 F2
Garde-Freinet, la 22 C3
Gardelegen 37 D3
Gardermoen 74 C3
Gardiken 69 E2
Gardíki 58 C2
Garding 36 B1
Gardjönäs 69 E2
Gärdnäs 69 E3
Gardone Riviera 42 C3
Gardone Val Trompia 42 C3
Gärdslösa 77 E2
Gardunha, Sa da 26 B3
Garður 68 A2
Garešnica 50 C1
Garessio 23 D2
Garforth 5 E4
Gargaliáni 62 B3
Gargano, Promontorio del 45 F4
Garganta 32 A2
Garganta del Chorro 31 E3
Garganta del Escalar 20 C4
Garganta la Olla 27 D3
Gargantas 28 B3
Gargantas del Sil 24 B2
Gargellen 42 C2
Gargilesse 18 A2
Gargnano 42 C3
Gargnäs 69 F2
Garigliano 46 B1
Gariglione, Mte 47 E3
Garípa 64 C4
Garlasco 23 E1
Garlin 20 C3
Garlstorf 36 C2
Garmisch-Partenkirchen 40 B4
Garona, R 21 D4
Garonne 20 C2
Garpenberg 75 E3
Garphyttan 75 E4
Garraf 29 E2
Garrafe de Torio 25 D2
Garray 28 A2
Garrel 36 B3
Garrovillas 26 C3
Garrucha 32 B3
Gars 41 E2
Gartempe 17 F3
Gartow 37 D2
Gartz 37 F2
Garvagh 4 B2
Garvão 30 A2
Garve 2 C2
Garynahine 2 B1
Garz 37 F1
Gaschurn 42 C2
Gassino Torinese 23 D1
Gastoúni 58 B3
Gata (Extremadura) 26 C3
Gata (Valencia) 33 D1
Gata, C de 32 A4
Gata, Sa de 26 C3
Gatčina 79 D1
Gatehouse of Fleet 4 C2
Gateshead 5 E2
Gattinara 23 E1
Gattorna 23 E2
Gatwick Airport 7 E3
Gaucín 31 D4
Gauja 79 D2
Gaula 68 C4
Gauldalen 68 C4
Gaulstad 69 D3
Gausta 74 B3
Gauting 40 B3
Gavà 29 E2
Gavardo 42 C3
Gavarnie 20 C4
Gavarnie, Cirque de 20 C4
Gavdopoúla, N 64 A4
Gávdos, N 64 B4
Gave d'Oloron 20 B3
Gavi 23 E2
Gaviao 26 B4
Gavia, Pso di 42 C3
Gavirate 42 B3
Gävle 75 F3
Gävleborgs Län 75 E2
Gävlebukten 75 F3
Gavoi 46 B3
Gavray 13 D3
Gávrio 60 B3
Gåvsta 75 F3
Gåxsjö 69 E3
Gazzuolo 42 C4
Gdańsk 78 B3
Gdov 79 D1
Gdynia 78 B3
Geaune 20 C3
Gebesee 38 C1
Gebze 81 F4
Gedern 38 B2
Gediz 61 E2
Gedser 76 C4
Geel 34 B3
Geertruidenberg 11 D3
Geesthacht 37 D2
Gefell 39 D2
Géfira (Makedonía) 55 E2
Géfira (Pelopónissos) 63 D4
Gefíria 59 D1
Gefrees 39 D2
Gehren 39 D2
Geilenkirchen 11 E4
Geilo 74 B2
Geiranger 74 B1
Geirangerfjorden 74 B1
Geisa 38 C2
Geiselhöring 39 E4
Geisenfeld 39 D4
Geisenhausen 39 E4
Geising 39 F1
Geisingen 42 B1
Geislingen 38 C4
Geismar 38 C1
Geisnes 69 D2
Geithain 39 E1
Gela 48 C4
Gelderland 11 E2
Geldern 11 F3
Geldrop 11 E3
Geleen 11 E4
Gelibolu 81 E4
Gelnhausen 38 B2
Gelsa 28 C2
Gelsdorf 38 A2
Gelsenkirchen 11 F3
Gelting 36 C1
Gembloux 34 B3
Gemeaux 19 D1
Gémenos 22 B3
Gemert 11 E3
Gemlik 81 F4
Gemona del Friuli 43 E2
Gémozac 17 D4
Gemünd 35 D3
Gemünden (Bayern) 38 C2
Gemünden (Hessen) 38 B1
Gemünden (Rheinland-Pfalz) 38 A3
Genádio 65 F2
Gençay 17 E3
Generalísimo, Emb del 28 B4
Generalski Stol 50 B2
General-Toševo 81 E3
Generoso, Mte 42 B3
Genève 19 E3
Genil, R 31 D2
Genisséa 56 B2
Génissiat, Barrage de 19 D3
Genk 34 C3
Genlis 19 D2
Genna Cruxi 46 B3
Gennargentu, Mti del 46 B3
Gennep 11 E3
Gennes 17 E2
Génolhac 22 A2
Genova 23 E2
Genova, Val di 42 C3
Gent 34 A3
Genthin 37 E3
Gentioux 18 A3
Genzano di Lucania 47 D1
Genzano di Roma 44 C4
Georgianí 55 D3
Georgioúpoli 64 B4
Georgítsi 62 C3
Gera 39 D1
Geraardsbergen 34 B3
Gerabronn 38 C3
Gerace 47 E4
Gerakári (Kríti) 64 B4
Gerakári (Makedonía) 55 E2
Gerakaroú 55 F2
Gerakás 63 D3
Gérakas, Akr 60 A1
Geráki 63 D3
Gerakiní 55 F3
Gerakovoúni 59 D1
Gerània 59 E3
Gérardmer 15 E4
Geras 41 E2
Gerbeviller 15 E3
Gerbier de Jonc 22 A2
Gerbini 49 D4
Gerbstedt 37 E4
Gerena 30 C3
Gerês 24 B3
Gerês, Sa do 24 B3
Geretsried 40 B3
Gérgal 32 A3
Geringswalde 39 E1
Gerlitzen 41 D4
Gerlos 43 D2
Gerlospaß 40 C4
Gérmas 54 C3
Germering 40 B3
Germersheim 38 B3
Gernika-Lumo 20 A3
Gernrode 37 D4
Gernsbach 38 B4
Gernsheim 38 B3
Gerola Alta 42 B3
Geroliménas 62 C4
Gerolstein 35 D4
Gerolzhofen 38 C2
Gerona 29 F2
Geroplátanos 55 F3
Gerovo 50 A2
Gerri de la Sal 29 E1
Gers 21 D3
Gers (Dépt) 20 C3
Gersau 42 B2
Gersfeld 38 C2
Gerstetten 38 C4
Gersthofen 39 D4
Gerswalde 37 F2
Gesäuse 41 E3
Gescher 11 F3
Geseke 36 B4
Gesualdo 45 F4
Geta 72 B4
Getafe 27 F3
Gets, les 19 E3
Gettorf 36 C1
Gevelsberg 35 D2
Gevgelija 53 F4
Gévora, R 26 C4
Gevrey-Chambertin 19 D2
Gex 19 E3
Geysir 68 A2
Geyve 81 F4
Gföhl 41 E2
Ghedi 42 C4
Gheorghe Gheorghiu-Dej 81 E2
Gheorgheni 81 D2
Ghilarza 46 A3
Ghisonaccia 23 D4
Ghisoni 23 D4
Gialí, N 65 E1
Giáltra 59 E2
Gianitsá 55 E2
Gianítsi 60 B3
Giannádes 54 A4
Giannutri, I di 44 B4
Gianoúli 57 D1
Giant's Causeway 4 B2
Giardini 49 D3
Giáros, N 60 C4
Giarratana 49 D4
Giarre 49 D3
Giat 18 B3
Giaveno 23 D1
Giba 46 A4
Gibostad 66 C2
Gibraleón 30 C3
Gibraltar 31 D4
Gideå 70 B4
Gideälven 69 F4
Gieboldehausen 37 D4
Gien 18 B1
Giengen 38 C4
Giens 22 C4
Gießen 38 B2
Giethoorn 11 E2
Gifhorn 37 D3
Gigha I 2 B4
Giglio, I del 44 B3
Giglio Porto 44 B3
Gignac 21 F3
Gijón 25 D1
Gilching 40 B3
Gilford 9 D1
Giljevo 51 F4
Gilleleje 76 C3
Gillhov 69 E4
Gillingham (Dorset) 6 C3
Gillingham (Kent) 7 E3
Gill, L 8 C1
Gilze 11 D3
Gimenells 29 D2
Gimnó 60 A2
Gimo 75 F3
Gimont 21 D3
Gingst 37 E1
Ginosa 47 E1
Ginzling 43 D2
Giogo di Scarperia 44 B1
Gioia del Colle 47 E1
Gioia Tauro 47 D4
Gióna, Óros 59 D2
Gioúhtas 64 C4
Gioúra, N 60 B1
Giovinazzo 47 E1
Giovi, Pso dei 23 E2
Girifalco 47 E3
Giromagny 15 E4
Girona 29 F2
Gironde 17 D4
Gironde (Dépt) 20 B2
Gironella 29 E2
Girvan 4 C2
Gisburn 5 E3
Gislaved 77 D2
Gisors 14 A3
Gissi 45 E3
Gistel 34 A3
Gíthio 63 D3
Gittun 69 F1
Giugliano in Campo 46 B1
Giulianova 45 D3
Giurgiu 81 D3
Give 76 B3
Givors 19 D3
Givry 19 D2
Givry-en-Argonne 14 C3
Gizéla 56 B2
Giżycko 78 C3
Gjalicë, M 53 D4
Gjendesheim 74 C2
Gjermundshavn 74 A3
Gjesvær 67 E1
Gjirokastër 54 B3
Gjøora 68 C4
Gjóv 68 A3
Gjøvik 74 C2
Gla 59 E2
Gladbeck 11 F3
Gladenbach 38 B2
Gladstad 69 D2
Glafsfjorden 75 D3
Gláma 68 A1
Glamis 3 D3
Glamis Castle 3 D3
Glamoč 50 C3
Glamorgan 6 B3
Glamsbjerg 76 B3
Glan 38 A3
Glandon, Col du 19 E4
Glandorf 36 B4
Glan-Münchweiler 38 A3
Glanshammar 75 E4
Glarus 42 B2
Glasgow 2 C4
Glas Maol 3 D3
Glastonbury 6 C3
Glauchau 39 E1
Glava 74 D3
Glavatičevo 51 D4
Glavičice 51 E2
Glavnik 53 D3
Gledić 53 D2
Gledićske pl 53 D2
Gleinalmtunnel 41 E3
Gleisdorf 41 E4
Glen Albyn 2 C2
Glenamoy 8 B1
Glénan, I de 12 B4
Glenariff 4 B2
Glenarm 4 B2
Glenbeigh 8 A4
Glen Carron 2 C2
Glen Coe 2 C3
Glencolumbkille 8 B1
Glendalough 9 D3
Glenelg 2 B2
Glenfinnan 2 B2
Glengarriff 8 A4
Glenluce 4 C2
Glen More 2 C2
Glen More Forest Park 3 D2
Glennamaddy 8 B2
Glenrothes 3 D3
Glenties 8 C1
Glífa 59 E1
Glifáda (Atikí-Piréas) 59 F3
Glifáda (Fokída) 58 C2
Glikí 58 A1
Glikóvrissi 63 D3
Glina 50 B2
Glittertind 74 B2
Gliwice 80 B1
Globino 79 F4
Globočica 53 E4
Gloggnitz 41 F2
Głogów 78 B4
Glomfjord 69 E1
Glomma 74 C3
Glommersträsk 70 B2
Gloppet 70 C4
Glossop 5 E4
Gloucester 6 C2
Gloucestershire 6 C3
Gložan 51 E1
Głubczyce 80 B1
Glubokoje 79 D3
Głuchołazy 80 B1
Gluchov 79 F4
Glücksburg 36 C1
Glückstadt 36 C2
Glumsø 76 C3
Glušci 51 E2
Glyn Ebwy 6 C3
Gmund 40 B3
Gmünd (Kärnten) 41 D4
Gmünd (Nieder-österreich) 41 E2
Gmunden 41 D3
Gnarp 75 F2
Gnesta 75 F4
Gniezno 78 B4
Gnjilane 53 E3
Gnoien 37 E1
Gnosjö 77 D2
Goat Fell 2 B4
Goce Delčev 81 D4
Goch 11 E3
Goðafoss 68 B1
Godalming 7 D3
Godby 72 B4
Godelheim 36 C4
Goderville 13 E2
Godmanchester 7 E2
Gödöllő 80 C2
Godovič 43 F3
Goduš 51 E2
Goeree 11 D3
Goes 11 D3
Göggingen 39 D4
Göhren 37 F1
Goirle 11 E3
Góis 26 B3
Goito 42 C4
Gokčanica 53 D2
Gokçe 57 D3
Gol 74 B2
Gola 50 C1
Golada 24 B2
Golaja Pristan' 81 F2
Goldbach 38 B2
Goldberg 37 E2
Goldenstedt 36 B3
Golegã 26 A4
Golema reka 53 E4
Golemo Selo 53 E3
Goleniów 78 A4
Goleš 53 F3
Golfe-Juan 23 D3
Golfo Aranci 46 B2
Goli 50 A3
Golija (Crna Gora) 52 B3
Golija (Srbija) 53 D2
Goljak 53 E3
Goljaki, M. 43 F3
Goljam Perelik 81 D4
Göllersdorf 41 F2
Golling 40 C3
Golo 23 D3
Golpejas 27 D2
Golspie 2 C1
Golßen 37 F4
Golubac 53 D1
Golubovci 52 C4
Golubovec 50 B1
Golzow 37 E3
Gómara 28 B2
Gomáti 56 A3
Gombrèn 29 E1
Gomecello 27 D2
Gomel' 79 E3
Gomera 30 A4
Gómfi 55 D4
Gommern 37 E4
Goncelin 19 E4
Gondomar (E) 24 A2
Gondomar (P) 24 A4
Gondrecourt 15 D3
Gönen 81 E4
Góni 55 E4
Goniá 64 A3
Goniés 64 C4
Gonnesa 46 A4
Gonnosfanadiga 46 A4
Goole 5 F4
Goor 11 F2
Goppenstein 42 A3
Göppingen 38 C4
Gora 50 B2
Goražde 51 E3
Gördalen 75 D2
Gordes 22 B3
Gorenja Vas 43 F3
Gorey (GB) 12 C3
Gorey (IRL) 9 D3
Gorgona, I di 44 A2
Gorgonzola 42 B4
Gorgopótamos 54 B3
Gorica (Bosna i Hercegovina) 51 D4
Gorica (Makedonija) 54 C2
Goričan 50 B1
Gorice 50 A2
Gorinchem 11 D3
Goritsá 63 D3
Gorizia 43 F3
Gorjanci 50 B1
Gorki 79 E3
Gorleston-on-Sea 7 F2
Gorlice 80 C1
Görlitz 39 F1
Gorna Orjahovica 81 D3
Gornja Dobrinja 51 F3
Gornja Grabovica 51 D4
Gornja Kamenica 53 E2
Gornja Klina 53 D3
Gornja Ljubovidđa 51 E3
Gornja Ljuta 51 D4
Gornja Ploča 50 B3
Gornja Radgona 41 F4
Gornja Sabanta 53 D2
Gornja Sanica 50 C3
Gornja Slatina 51 D2
Gornja Toplica 51 F3
Gornja Toponica 53 E2
Gornja Tuzla 51 E2
Gornje Dubočke 52 B3
Gornje Ratkovo 50 C3
Gornje Selo 50 C4
Gornji Grad 50 A1
Gornji Kokoti 52 C4
Gornji Kosinj 50 B3
Gornji Lapac 50 B3
Gornji Lukavac 52 B3
Gornji Milanovac 53 D2
Gornji Petrovci 41 F4
Gornji Podgradci 50 C2
Gornji Rajić 50 C2
Gornji Stepoš 53 D2
Gornji Vakuf 51 D3
Gornji Zabar 51 D2
Gorno Orizari 53 E4
Goro 43 E4
Gorodišče 81 E1
Gorodn'a 79 E4
Gorodok (Belorussija) 79 E2
Gorodok (Ukraina) 80 C1
Gorredijk 11 E1
Gorron 13 D3
Gort 8 B3
Gorteen 8 B2
Gortin 8 C1
Górtis 64 C4
Gortmore 8 B2
Gorumna I 8 A2
Goryn' 81 D1
Góry Świętokrzyskie 80 C1
Görzke 37 E3
Gorzów Wielkopolski 78 A4
Gosaldo 43 D3
Gosau 41 D3
Gosausee 41 D3
Göschenen 42 B2
Gosforth 5 D3
Goslar 37 D4
Gospić 50 B3
Gospođinci 51 E1
Gosport 7 D4
Gossau 42 B2
Gosselies 34 B3
Gossensass 43 D2
Gößl 41 D3
Gößnitz 39 E1
Gössweinstein 39 D3
Gostivar 53 D4
Göstling 41 E3
Gostyń 78 B4
Götaälv 76 C1
Göta Kanal 75 D4
Göteborg 76 C2
Göteborgs och Bohus Län 76 C1
Götene 75 D4
Gotha 38 C1
Gothem 77 F2
Gotland 77 F2
Gotlands Län 77 F2
Gotska Sandön 75 F4
Göttingen 37 D4
Gottwaldov 80 B2
Götzis 40 A4
Gouarec 12 B4
Gouda 11 D3
Gouménissa 55 E2
Goumois 19 E2
Goúra 59 D3
Gourdon 21 D2
Gourin 12 B4
Gournay-en-Bray 14 A2
Goúrnes 64 C4
Gourniá 65 D4
Gourock 2 C4
Gouveja 26 B3
Goúves 64 C4
Gouviá 54 A4
Gouzon 18 B3
Goveđari 52 A3
Goverla, G. 81 D2
Göynük 81 F4
Gozd 43 F2
Gozo 49 F4
Gozzano 42 B3
Graal-Müritz 37 E1
Graben-Neudorf 38 B3
Grabenstätt 40 C3
Grabovac 50 C4
Grabovci 51 E2
Grabow 37 D2
Gračac 50 B3
Gračanica (Bosna i Hercegovina) 51 D2
Gračanica (Crna Gora) 52 C3
Gračanica (Kosovo) 53 E3
Gračanica (Srbija) 51 E3
Graçay 18 A2
Grächen 42 A3
Gradac (Crna Gora) 51 E4
Gradac (Hrvatska) 51 D4
Gradac (Srbija) 53 D2
Gradačac 51 D2
Gradara 44 C2
Gradče, Ez 53 F3
Gradec 50 B1
Gradefes 25 D2
Gradeška pl 53 F4
Gradina 53 F2
Gradisca d'Isonzo 43 F3
Gradište (Hrvatska) 51 D2
Gradište (Makedonija) 53 E4
Grado (E) 25 D1
Grado (I) 43 F3
Gradsko 53 E4
Gradskovo 53 E1
Grafelfing 40 B3
Grafenau 40 C2
Gräfenberg 39 D3
Gräfenhainichen 37 E4
Grafenwöhr 39 D3
Grafing 40 B3
Gragnano 46 C2
Grahovo (Bosna i Hercegovina) 52 B3
Grahovo (Slovenija) 43 F3
Graiguenamanagh 8 C3
Grain 7 E3
Grainau 40 B4
Grajewo 78 C3
Gram 76 B3
Gramat 21 E2
Gramatikó 59 D1
Gramatikoú 58 C2
Graméni 56 A1
Graméno 54 B4
Grametten 41 E2
Grammichele 49 D4
Grámos, Óros 54 C3
Grampian 3 D2
Grampian Mts 2 C3
Gramsh 54 B2
Gramzow 37 F2
Gran 74 C3
Granada 31 F3
Granadella 29 D2
Granadilla de Abona 30 A4
Granard 8 C2
Gran Canaria 30 B4
Grancey-le-Château 19 D1
Grandas 24 C1
Grand Ballon 15 E4
Grand Bois, Col du 18 C4
Grand-Bornand, le 19 E3
Grand-Bourg 18 A3
Grandcamp-Maisy 13 D2
Grand Canal 8 C3
Grand Canal d'Alsace 15 F4
Grand Canyon du Verdon 22 C3
Grand-Champ 16 C1
Grand-Colombier 19 D3
Grand-Combe, la 22 A2
Grand Combin 19 F3
Grand-Couronne 13 F2
Grand-Croix 18 C4
Grande Casse 19 E4
Grande de Europa, Punta 31 D4
Grande Dixence, Bge de la 19 F3
Grande-Motte, la 22 A3
Grande Sassière 19 F3
Grandes Rousses 19 E4
Grand-Fougeray 17 D1
Grand-Lemps, le 19 D4
Grand Lieu, L de 17 D2
Grand-Lucé, le 17 E1
Grand Morin 14 B3
Grândola 30 A2
Grandpré 14 C2
Grand-Pressigny, le 17 F2
Grand Rhône 22 B3
Grandrieu 22 A2
Grand-Serre, le 19 D4
Grands Goulets 22 B2
Grandval, Bge de 21 F2
Grandvilliers 14 A2
Grañén 28 C2
Grangärde 75 E3
Grangemouth 3 D4
Grange-Over-Sands 5 D3
Grängesberg 75 E3
Granges-sur-Vologne 15 E4
Granier, Col du 19 E4
Granítis 56 A1
Granítsa 58 C1
Granja (Alentejo) 30 C2
Granja (Douro) 24 A4
Granja de Torrehermosa 31 D2
Granja, Pto de la 30 C2
Gränna 77 D1
Granollers 29 E2
Granön 69 F3
Gran Paradiso 23 D1
Gran San Bernardo, Colle del 19 F3
Gran San Bernardo, Traforo del 19 F3
Gran Sasso d'Italia 45 D3
Gransee 37 F2
Gran Tarajal 30 B4
Grantham 7 E1
Grantown-on-Spey 3 D2
Granville 13 D3
Granvin 74 B2
Grappa, Mte 43 D3
Grasleben 37 D3
Grasmere 5 D3
Grassano 47 D1
Grasse 23 D3
Gråstenn 76 B3
Grästorp 77 D1
Gratangen 66 C3
Gratiní 56 C1
Gratkorn 41 E4
Graubünden 42 B2
Grau-du-Roi, le 22 A3
Graulhet 21 E3
Graus 29 D1
Gravalos 28 B1
Gravdal 66 A3
Grave 11 E3
Gravedona 42 B3
Grave, la 19 E4
Gravelines 14 A1
Gravellona-Toce 42 A3
Grave, Pointe de 17 D3
Gravesend 7 E3
Graviá 59 D2
Gravina in Puglia 47 D1
Gravona 23 E4
Gravoúna 56 B2
Gray 19 D1
Grays Thurrock 7 E3
Graz 41 E4
Grazalema 31 D3
Grazzanise 46 B1
Grčak 53 D2
Grdelica 53 E3
Great Blasket I 8 A4
Great Driffield 5 F3
Great Dunmow 7 E3
Great Grimsby 5 F4
Great Malvern 6 C2
Great Ormes Head 6 B1
Great Ouse 7 E2

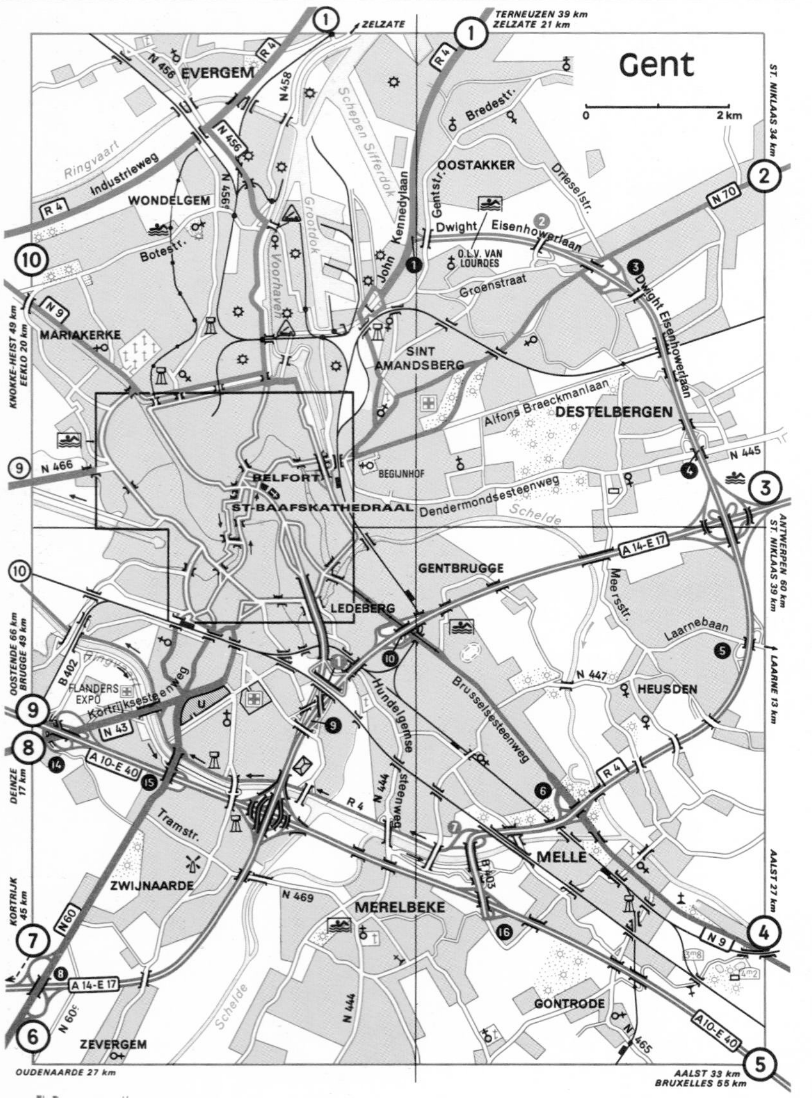

Gent
0
2 km
TERNEUZEN 39 km
ZELZATE 21 km
ZELZATE
EVERGEM
OOSTAKKER
WONDELGEM
MARIAKERKE
SINT AMANDSBERG
DESTELBERGEN
BELFORT
ST-BAAFSKATHEDRAAL
BEGIJNHOF
GENTBRUGGE
LEDEBERG
HEUSDEN
FLANDERS EXPO
ZWIJNAARDE
MERELBEKE
MELLE
GONTRODE
ZEVERGEM
OUDENAARDE 27 km
AALST 33 km
BRUXELLES 55 km

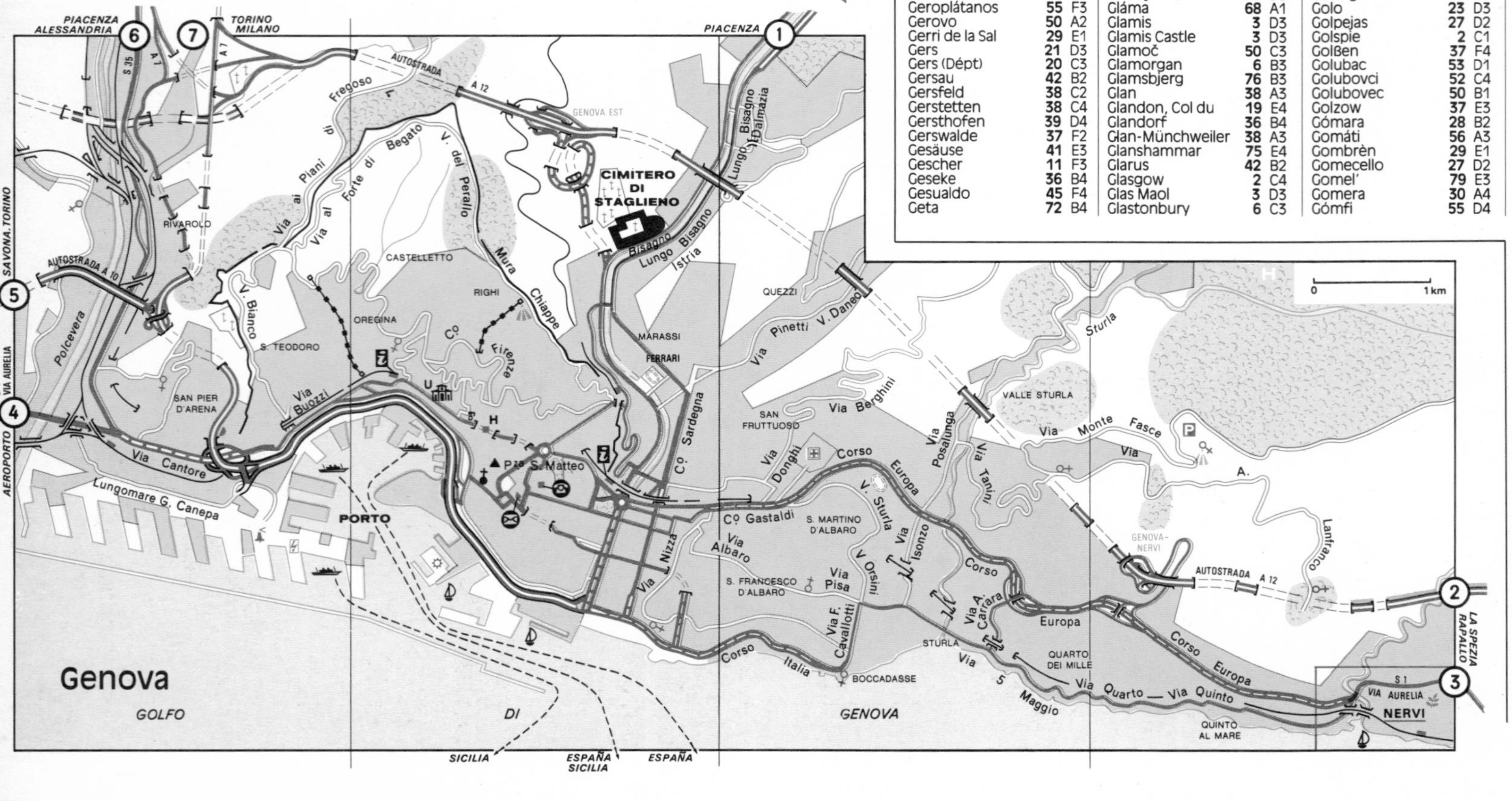

Genova
GOLFO
DI
GENOVA
PIACENZA
ALESSANDRIA
TORINO
MILANO
CIMITERO DI STAGLIENO
PORTO
NERVI
SICILIA
ESPAÑA
LA SPEZIA
0
1 km

Great Torrington 6 B3
Great Yarmouth 7 F2
Grebbestad 74 C4
Greccio 44 C3
Greding 39 D3
Gredos 27 E3
Gredos, Sa de 27 E3
Greenhead 5 D2
Greenlaw 5 E1
Greenock 2 C4
Greenodd 5 D3
Greggio 23 E1
Gregolímano 59 E2
Greifenburg 43 E2
Greiffenberg 37 F2
Greifswald 37 F1
Greifswalder Bodden 37 F1
Grein 41 E2
Greiz 39 D1
Grenå 76 C2
Grenade (Haute-Garonne) 21 D3
Grenade (Landes) 20 C3
Grenchen 19 F2
Grenoble 19 D4
Grense Jakobselv 67 F1
Gréoux-les-Bains 22 C3
Gressåmoen 69 D3
Gresse 22 B2
Gressoney-la-Trinite 42 A3
Gressoney-St Jean 42 A3
Gresten 41 E3
Grésy 19 E3
Greußen 38 C1
Greve 44 B2
Greven 36 B4
Grevená 54 C3
Grevená (Nomos) 54 C3
Grevenbroich 11 F4
Grevenbrück 38 A1
Grevenítio 54 C4
Grevesmühlen 37 D2
Greve Strand 76 C3
Greyabbey 9 D1
Greystones 9 D3
Grez-en-Bouère 13 D4
Grezzana 43 D4
Grgur 50 A3
Griá, Akr 60 C3
Grianan of Aileach 4 A2
Griebenow 37 E1
Gries 43 D2
Gries im Sellrain 40 B4
Grieskirchen 41 D2
Griffen 50 A1
Grignan 22 B2
Grigno 43 D3
Grignols 20 C2
Grimaldi 47 E3
Grimaud 22 C3
Grimma 37 E4
Grimmen 37 E1
Grimone, Col de 22 B2
Grimsbu 74 C1
Grimselpass 42 A3
Grímsey 68 B1
Grimstad 74 B4
Grindaheim 74 B2
Grindavík 68 A2
Grindelwald 42 A2
Grindsted 76 B3
Griñón 27 F3
Grintavec 50 A1
Gripsholm 75 F4
Grisignano 43 D4
Gris Nez, Cap 14 A1
Grisolles 21 D3
Grisslehamn 75 F3
Gríva 55 E2
Grizáno 55 D4
Grk 51 D2
Grljan 53 E1
Grmeč 50 B3
Grøa 68 C4
Gröbming 41 D3
Grocka 53 D1
Gröditz 37 F4
Grodno 78 C3
Groenlo 11 F3
Gröer Arber 39 E3
Groitzsch 39 D1
Groix 12 B4
Groix, I de 12 B4
Grömitz 37 D1
Gronau 11 F2
Grönenbach 40 A3
Grong 69 D3
Grönhögen 77 E3
Groningen 11 F1
Gröningen 37 D4
Groningen (Prov) 11 F1
Grönskåra 77 E2
Grønsund 76 C4
Gropello Cairoli 23 E1
Groscavallo 23 D1
Grosio 42 C3
Grosne 19 D2
Gross Beerberg 38 C2
Gross Bösenstein 41 D3
Großbreitenbach 39 D2
Großburgwedel 36 C3
Großenbrode 37 D1
Großenhain 37 F4
Großenzersdorf 41 F2

Glasgow
Paisley
Clydebank
Rutherglen
Coatbridge
Airdrie
Motherwell
Hamilton
East Kilbride
Kirkintilloch
Cumbernauld
Bearsden
Renfrew
Johnstone
Barrhead
Wishaw
1/200000
Kilmarnock
Strathaven
Dumfries, Carlisle
M 74, Kilmarnock
Stirling
Kincardine
Edinburgh
Peebles
Largs
Irvine
Greenock
Crianlarich

Grosse Pierre 15 E4
Grosse Röder 37 F4
Grosser Plöner See 37 D1
Grosseto 44 B3
Gross Feldberg 38 B2
Gross-Gerau 38 B3
Groß Gerungs 41 E2
Großglockner 43 E2
Großglockner Hochalpenstraße 43 E2
Großhabersdorf 38 C3
Groß Ötscher 41 E3
Großpetersdorf 41 F3
Gross Priel 41 D3
Gross Rachel 40 C2
Großraming 41 D3
Groß Reken 11 F3
Großröhrsdorf 39 F1
Groß Rosennock 41 D4
Grossschönau 39 F1
Groß-Schönebeck 37 F2
Groß Siegharts 41 E2
Gross-Umstadt 38 B3
Großvenediger 43 E2
Großweil 40 B3
Grostenquin 15 E3
Grosuplje 50 A1
Grötlingbo 77 F2
Grøtsundet 66 C2
Grotta di Nettuno 46 A3
Grottaglie 47 E1
Grottaminarda 46 C1
Grottammare 45 D2
Grotte di Pertosa 47 D2
Grotteria 47 E4
Grouin, Pte du 13 D3
Grove 24 A2
Grövelsjön 75 D1
Grovfjord 66 B3
Grubišno Polje 50 C1
Gruda 52 B4
Grude 51 D4
Grudziądz 78 B4
Gruinard B 2 C1
Gruissan 21 F4
Grums 75 D4
Grünau 41 D3
Grünberg 38 B2
Grünburg 41 D3
Grundarfjörður 68 A1
Grundforsen 75 D2
Grundlsee 41 D3
Grundlsee *L* 41 D3
Grundsund 76 C1
Grundtjärn 69 F4
Grünstadt 38 A3
Grünwald 40 B3
Grupčin 53 E4
Gruyères 19 E2
Gruža 53 D2
Gruža *R* 53 D2
Grycksbo 75 E3
Gryfice 78 A3
Gryllefjord 66 B2
Grythyttan 75 E3
Grytøya 66 B2
Grza 53 D2
Gschütt, Paß 41 D3
Gstaad 19 F2
Gstadt 40 C3
Guadahortuna 31 F3
Guadaira, R 31 D3
Guadajira, R 30 C1
Guadajoz, R 31 E2
Guadalajara 28 A3
Guadalaviar 28 B3
Guadalaviar, R 28 B3
Guadalcacín, Emb de 31 D3
Guadalcanal 31 D2
Guadalén, Emb de 31 F2
Guadalén, R 31 F2
Guadalete, R 31 D4
Guadalfeo, R 31 F4
Guadalhorce, R 31 E4
Guadalimar, R (Andalucía) 30 C3
Guadalimar, R (Andalucía) 32 A2
Guadalmellato, Emb del 31 E2
Guadalmena, Emb de 32 A2
Guadalmena, R 32 A2
Guadalmez, R 31 E1
Guadalope, R 28 C3
Guadalquivir, R 30 C3
Guadal, R 32 A2
Guadalteba-Guadalhorce, Emb del 31 E3
Guadalupe 27 D4
Guadalupe, Sa de 27 D4
Guadarrama 27 F3
Guadarrama, Pto de 27 F3
Guadarrama, R 27 F3
Guadarrama, Sa de 27 F2
Guadarranque, Emb del 31 D4
Guadasuar 32 C1
Guadazaón, R 28 B4
Guadiamar, R 30 C3
Guadiana Menor, R 32 A2
Guadiana, R 31 E1
Guadiaro 31 D4
Guadiaro, R 31 D4
Guadiato, R 31 E2
Guadiela, R 28 A3
Guadix 31 F3
Guajaraz, Emb de 27 F4
Gualdo Tadino 44 C2
Guara, Sa de 28 C1
Guarda 26 C2
Guardiagrele 45 E3
Guardia Sanframondi 46 C1
Guardias Viejas 32 A4
Guardo 25 E2
Guareña 31 D1
Guarrizas, R 31 F2
Guarromán 31 F2
Guastalla 43 D4
Gubbio 44 C2
Guben 78 A4
Guberevac 53 D2
Guča 51 F3
Guca Gora 51 D3
Gúdar, Sa de 28 C3
Gudavac 50 B2
Gudbrandsdalen 74 C2
Guderup 76 B3
Gudhjem 77 D3
Gudingen 77 E1
Gudow 37 D2
Gudvangen 74 B2
Guebwiller 15 E4
Guémené 12 B4
Guémené-Penfao 16 C1
Güeñes 25 F2
Guer 12 C4
Guérande 16 C1
Guerche-de-Bretagne, la 13 D4
Guerche, la 18 B2
Guéret 18 A3
Guérigny 18 B2
Guerlédan, L de 12 C4
Guernsey 12 C2
Guéthary 20 B3
Gueugnon 18 C2
Güglingen 38 B4
Guglionesi 45 E3
Guía 30 B4
Guía de Isora 30 A4
Guichen 13 D4
Guidonia 44 C4
Guignes 14 B3
Guijo de Granadilla 27 D3
Guijuelo 27 D3
Guildford 7 D3
Guillaumes 22 C3
Guillena 31 D2
Guillestre 22 C2
Guillon 18 C1
Guilvinec 12 B4
Güimar 30 A4
Guimarães 24 A3
Guimiliau 12 B3
Guînes 14 A1
Guingamp 12 B3
Guipavas 12 B3
Guisborough 5 F4
Guiscard 14 B2
Guise 14 B2
Guissona 29 E2
Guist 7 F2
Guitiriz 24 B1
Guîtres 20 C1
Gujan-Mestras 20 B2
Gulbene 79 D2
Guldborg Sund 76 C4
Gullesfjorden 66 B3
Gullfoss 68 B2
Gullkrona fjärd 72 C4
Gullspång 75 D4
Gumiel de Hizán 25 E3
Gummersbach 38 A1
Gundelfingen 38 C4
Gundelsheim 38 B3
Gunnarn 69 F2
Gunnarsbyn 70 C2
Gunnärsfjärden 70 C2
Gunnarskog 75 D3
Gunten 42 A2
Günterode 37 D4
Guntín de Pallares 24 B2
Günzburg 38 C4
Gunzenhausen 39 D3
Gurk 43 F2
Gurk *R* 41 D4
Gurrea de Gállego 28 C2
Gusev 78 C3
Gusinje 51 F4
Guspini 46 A4
Güssing 41 F4
Güsten 37 E4
Güstrow 37 E2
Gutcher 3 F1
Gutenstein 41 F2
Gütersloh 36 B4
Gutulia 75 D2
Gützkow 37 F1
Guyhirn 7 E2
Gvardejsk 78 C3
Gvarv 74 B3
Gvozd 52 C3
Gweebarra B 8 C1
Gwent 6 C3
Gwynedd 6 B1
Gy 19 D1
Gyöngyös 80 C2
Győr 80 B2
Gysinge 75 E3
Gyula 80 C2

H

Haag (A) 41 D3
Haag (D) 40 C3
Haag, Den 11 D3
Haag am Hausruck 41 D3
Haaksbergen 11 F2
Haamstede 11 D3
Haapajärvi 71 D3
Haapajärvi *L* 71 E3
Haapakoski 71 E4
Haapamäki (Keski-Suomen Lääni) 73 D2
Haapamäki (Oulun Lääni) 71 D3
Haapavesi 71 D3
Haapsalu 78 C1
Haar 40 B3
Haaren 36 C4
Haarlem 11 D2
Habay 15 D2
Habo 77 D1
Habsheim 15 E4
Hachenburg 38 A2
Hachmühlen 36 C4
Hackås 69 E4
Hadamar 38 A2
Haddington 3 D4
Hadersdorf 41 E2
Haderslev 76 B3
Hadleigh 7 F2
Hadmersleben 37 D4
Hadrian's Wall 5 E2
Hadselfjorden 66 B3
Hadsten 76 B2
Hadsund 76 B2
Hadžići 51 D3
Hægebostad 74 A4
Haganj 50 B1
Hagen (Niedersachsen) 36 B2
Hagen (Nordrhein-Westfalen) 35 D2
Hagenow 37 D2
Hagetmau 20 C3
Hagfors 75 D3
Häggdånger 75 F1
Haggenås 69 E4
Hagondange 15 D3
Hague, Cap de la 13 C2
Haguenau 15 F3
Hahn 36 B2
Hahnbach 39 D3
Haigerloch 38 B4
Hailsham 7 E4
Hailuoto 71 D2
Hainaut 34 B3
Hainburg 41 F2
Hainfeld 41 E3
Hainichen 39 E1
Hajdúböszörmény 80 C2
Hajdučica 51 F1
Hajdúszoboszló 80 C2
Hajla 53 D3
Hajnówka 78 C4
Hakarp 77 D1
Hakkas 70 C1
Häkkilä 71 D4
Halámky 41 E2
Halandrítsa 58 C3
Halbe 37 F3
Halberstadt 37 D4
Halden 74 C4
Haldensleben 37 D3
Halesowen 6 C2
Halesworth 7 F2
Halhjem 74 A3
Halifax 5 E4
Halikko 72 C4
Halju 67 D3
Halkeró 56 B2
Halkiádes 55 D4
Halkída 59 E2
Halkidikí 55 F3
Hálki (Dodekánissa) 65 F2
Halkí (Kikládes) 64 C1
Hálki (Thessalía) 55 E4
Halkidóna 55 E2
Hálki, N 65 E2
Halkío 59 D3
Halkió 61 D2
Halkodóni, Óros 55 E4
Hallands Län 77 D2
Halle (B) 34 B3
Halle (D) 36 B4
Halle (DDR) 37 E4
Hällefors 75 E3
Hälleforsnäs 75 E4
Hallein 40 C3
Hällekis 75 D4
Hallenberg 38 B1
Hallencourt 14 A2
Halle-Neustadt 37 E4
Hällesjö 69 E4
Hällevadsholm 74 C4
Halligen 36 B1
Hallingdal 74 C3

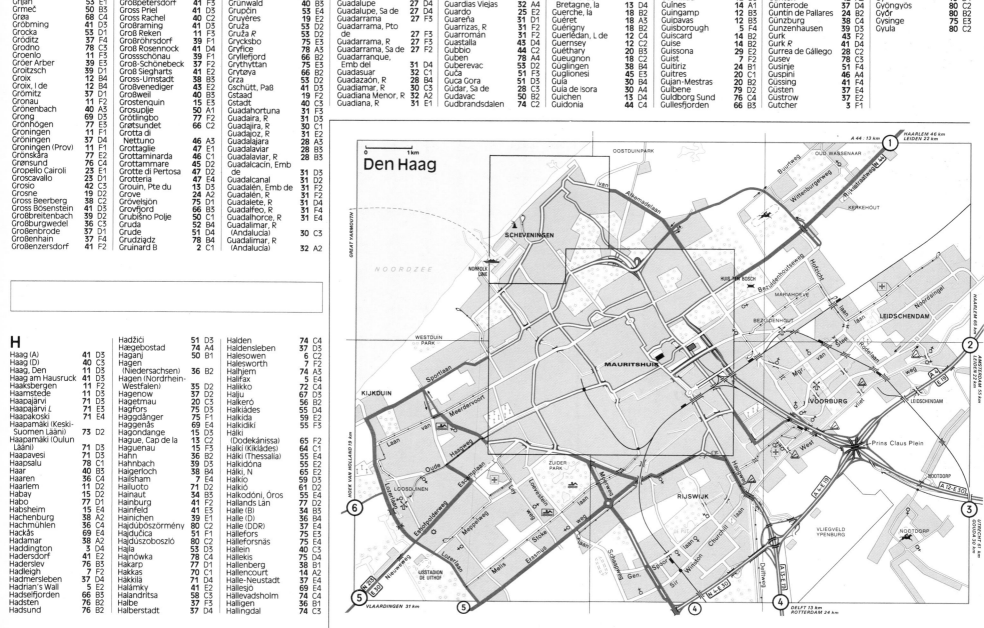

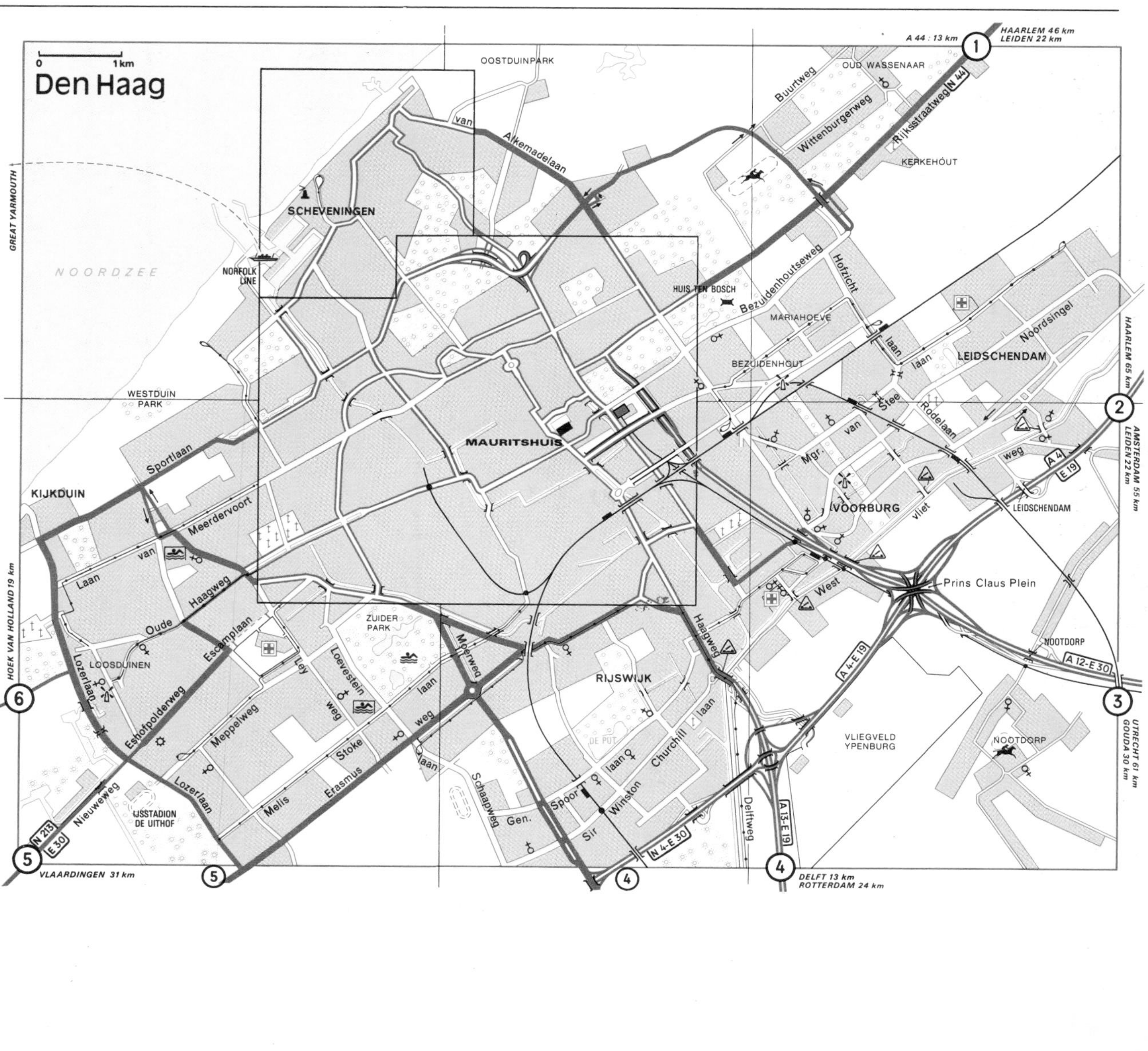
Den Haag
0 1 km
NOORDZEE
SCHEVENINGEN
MAURITSHUIS
KIJKDUIN
VOORBURG
RIJSWIJK
LEIDSCHENDAM
OOSTDUINPARK
OUD WASSENAAR
HUIS TEN BOSCH
Prins Claus Plein
HAARLEM 46 km
LEIDEN 22 km
A 44 : 13 km
DELFT 13 km
ROTTERDAM 24 km
VLAARDINGEN 31 km
HOEK VAN HOLLAND 19 km
GREAT YARMOUTH
VLIEGVELD YPENBURG
NOOTDORP

Hallingskarvet 74 B2
Hall in Tirol 40 B4
Hällnäs 70 B3
Hallsberg 75 E4
Hallstadt 39 D2
Hallstahammar 75 E3
Hallstatt 41 D3
Hallstavik 75 F3
Halluin 14 B1
Halmstad 77 D2
Hals 76 B2
Halsa 68 B4
Halsafjorden 68 B4
Hälsingtuna 75 F2
Halsskov 76 C3
Halstead 7 E2
Halsteren 11 D3
Halsua 71 D3
Haltdålen 69 D4
Haltern 11 F3
Halti-Haldi 67 D2
Halver 38 A1
Ham 14 B2
Hamar 74 C2
Hamarøy 66 B3
Hamburg 36 C2
Hambye 13 D3
Hamdorf 36 C1
Hämeenkyrö 72 C3
Hämeen Lääni 73 D3
Hämeenlinna 73 D3
Hämelerwald 37 D3
Hameln 36 C4
Hamersleben 37 D4
Hamilí, N 65 D3
Hamilton 2 C4
Hamina 73 E3
Hamm (Nordrhein-Westfalen) 36 B4
Hamm (Nordrhein-Westfalen) 36 A4
Hammarland 72 B4
Hammarstrand 69 E4
Hammaslahti 71 F4
Hammel 76 B2
Hammelburg 38 C2
Hammerdal 69 E4
Hammerfest 67 D1
Hammershus 77 D3
Hamneidet 66 C2
Hamningberg 67 F1
Hamoir 34 C3
Hampshire 7 D3
Hamra 75 E2
Hamra (Reg) 75 E2
Hamre 74 B4
Hamzali 53 F4
Hamzići 52 A3
Hanákia 58 B3
Hanau 38 B2
Handrás 65 D4
Hanerau-Hademarschen 36 C1
Hangö 72 C4
Hangon läntinen selkä 72 C4
Hangö västra fjärd 72 C4
Haniá (Kríti) 64 A3
Hánia (Lakonía) 62 C3
Haniá (Nomos) 64 A4
Hánia (Thessalía) 55 E4
Hani i Hotit 52 C4
Haníon, Kólpos 64 A3
Haniótis 55 F3
Hankamäki 71 E3
Hankasalmen as 73 E2
Hankasalmi 73 D2
Hankensbüttel 37 D3
Hanko 72 C4
Hannover 36 C3
Hannut 34 C3
Hanöbukten 77 D3
Han Pijesak 51 E3
Hansnes 66 C2
Han-sur-Lesse 34 C4
Hanstedt 36 C2
Hanstholm 76 B2
Haparanda 70 C2
Harads 70 B2
Harafjärden 70 C2
Haraldshaugen 74 A3
Haranes 69 D3
Haravgí 55 D3
Harburg (Bayern) 39 D4
Harburg (Hamburg) 36 C2
Hårby 76 B3
Hardangerfjorden 74 A3
Hardangerjøkulen 74 B2
Hardangervidda 74 B3
Hardbakke 74 A2
Hardegg 41 E2
Hardegsen 36 C4
Hardelot 14 A1
Hardenberg 11 F2
Harderwijk 11 E2
Hardheim 38 C3
Hardwick Hall 7 D1
Hareid 68 B4
Harelbeke 34 A3
Haren (D) 11 F2
Haren (NL) 11 F1
Harewood 5 E3
Haria 30 C4
Haringvlietdam 11 D3
Haritoméni 56 A1
Härjångsfjällen 69 D4
Harjavalta 72 C3
Harjunpää 72 C3
Hårkan 69 E4
Härkmeri 72 C2
Harlech 6 B1
Harlesiel 36 B2
Harleston 7 F2
Harlingen 11 E1
Harlow 7 E3
Harmånger 75 F2
Harmanli 81 E4
Härnösand 75 F1
Haro 20 A4
Harokopió 62 C3
Haroldswick 3 F1
Haroué 15 E3
Harøyfjorden 68 B4
Harpenden 7 E3
Harplinge 76 C2
Harpstedt 36 B3
Harris 2 B1
Harrislee 36 C1
Harris, Sd of 2 A1
Harrogate 5 E3
Härryda 76 C2
Harsefeld 36 C2
Harsprånget 66 C4
Harstad 66 B2
Harsvik 68 C3
Hartberg 41 F3
Hårteigen 74 B3
Hartha 39 E1
Hartkjölen 69 E3
Hartland Pt 6 A3
Hartlepool 5 E2
Hartmannsdorf 39 E1
Hartola 73 D3
Harwich 7 F3
Harz 37 D4
Harzgerode 37 D4
Hase 36 B3
Haselünne 36 B3
Haskovo 81 D4
Haslach (A) 41 D2
Haslach (D) 42 A1
Hasle 77 D3
Haslemere 7 D3
Haslev 76 C3
Hasparren 20 B3
Hassela 75 E2
Hasselfelde 37 D4
Hasselt 34 C3
Haßfurt 38 C2
Hássia, Óri 55 D3
Hässleholm 77 D3
Hastière 34 B4
Hastings 7 E4
Hasvik 67 D1
Hatě 41 E2
Haţeg 81 D3
Hatfield 7 E3
Hatherleigh 6 B4
Hattem 11 E2
Hattfjelldal 69 E2
Hattingen 11 F3
Hattula 73 D3
Hattuvaara (Ilomantsi) 71 F4
Hattuvaara (Lieksa) 71 F3
Hatvan 80 C2
Hatvik 74 A3
Hatzí 54 C4
Haubourdin 14 B1
Hauge 74 A4
Haugesund 74 A3
Hauho 73 D3
Haukelifjell 74 B3
Haukeligrend 74 B3
Haukipudas 71 D2
Haukivesi 73 E2
Haukivuori 73 E2
Haunstetten 39 D4
Haus 41 D3
Hausach 42 A1
Hausham 40 B3
Hausjärvi 73 D3
Hautajärvi 71 E1
Hautecombe 19 E3
Haute-Corse 23 E3
Hautefort 17 F4
Haute-Garonne 21 D3
Haute-Loire 21 F1
Haute-Marne 15 D4
Hautes-Alpes 22 C2
Haute-Saône 15 D4
Haute-Savoie 19 E3
Hautes-Pyrénées 20 C4
Haute-Vienne (Dépt) 17 F3
Hauteville-Lompnes 19 D3
Hautmont 14 C1
Haut-Rhin (Dépt) 15 E4
Havant 7 D4
Havári 58 B3
Havdalsfjellet 69 D3
Havdáta 58 A3
Havel 37 E3
Havelange 34 C3
Havelberg 37 E3
Haverfordwest 6 A2
Haverhill 7 E2
Haverö 75 E1
Havneby 76 A3
Havøysund 67 D1
Havraň 39 F2
Havre, Le 13 E2
Hawes 5 E3
Hawick 5 D2
Hawkhurst 7 E3
Hayange 15 D2
Haye-du-Puits, la 13 D2
Haye-Pesnel, la 13 D3
Hayle 6 A4
Hay-on-Wye 6 C2
Haywards Heath 7 E4
Hazebrouck 14 B1
Headford 8 B2
Heanor 7 D1
Héas 20 C4
Heathfield 7 E4
Heathrow Airport 7 E3
Hebrides, Outer 2 A1
Hebrides, Sea of the 2 B2
Heby 75 F3
Hechingen 38 B4
Hecho 20 B4
Hechtel 34 C3
Hecklingen 37 E4
Hedal 74 C3
Heddal 74 B3
Hédé 13 D4
Hede 75 D1
Hedemora 75 E3
Hedenäset 70 C1
Hedensted 76 B3
Hedesundafjärdarna 75 F3
Hedeviken 75 D1
Hedmark 74 C2
Hedon 5 F4
Heemstede 11 D2
Heerde 11 E2
Heerenveen 11 E2
Heerlen 34 C3
Heeze 11 E3
Hegge 74 C2
Hegra 69 D4
Heia 66 C2
Heide 36 C1
Heidelberg 38 B3
Heidenau 39 F1
Heidenheim 38 C4
Heidenreichstein 41 E2
Heikendorf 36 C1
Heikkila 71 E1
Heilbronn 38 B3
Heiligenberg 42 B1
Heiligenblut 43 E2
Heiligenhafen 37 D1
Heiligenkirchen 36 C4
Heiligenkreuz 41 F4
Heiligenstadt 38 C1
Heilsbronn 39 D3
Heimari 73 E3
Heimdal 68 C4
Heimertingen 40 A3
Heinävaara 71 F4
Heinävesi 71 E4
Heinola 73 E3
Heinolan mlk 73 D3
Heinsberg 11 E4
Heist 10 C3
Heist-op-den-Berg 34 B3
Hejde 77 F2
Hekla 68 B2
Hekuravë, Maj' e 53 D4
Helagsfjället 69 D4
Hélatros, Akr 65 E3
Heldburg 38 C2
Heldrungen 39 D1
Helechal 31 D1
Helensburgh 2 C4
Helgåa (N) 69 D3
Helgaå (S) 77 D3
Helgasjön 77 D2
Helgoland 36 B1
Hella *Is* 68 A2
Hella N 74 B2
Hellemofjorden 66 B3
Hellendoorn 11 F2
Hellesylt 74 B1
Hellevoetsluis 11 D3
Hellin 32 B2
Hellvik 74 A4
Helmbrechts 39 D2
Helme 37 D4
Helmond 11 E3
Helmsdale 3 D1
Helmsley 5 E3
Helmstadt 38 C3
Helmstedt 37 D3
Helpter Berge 37 F2
Helsa 38 C1
Helsingborg 76 C3
Helsinge 76 C3
Helsingfors 73 D4
Helsingør 76 C3
Helsinki 73 D4
Helston 6 A4
Helvetinjärvi 73 D2
Helvick Head 8 C4
Hemau 39 D3
Hemavan 69 E2
Hemel Hempstead 7 D3
Hemer 38 A1
Hemme 68 C4
Hemmoor 36 C2
Hemnefjorden 68 C3
Hemnes 74 C3
Hemnesberget 69 E1
Hemsedal 74 B2
Hemsedal *V* 74 B2
Henares, R 28 A3
Hendaye 20 B3
Hengelo 11 F2
Hengersberg 39 E4
Hengstpaß 41 D3
Hénin-Beaumont 14 B1
Henley 7 D2
Henley-on-Thames 7 D3
Henneberg 38 C2
Hennebont 12 B4
Hennef 35 D3
Hennigsdorf 37 F3
Henrichemont 18 B2
Henstedt-Ulzburg 36 C2
Henstridge 6 C3
Hepokongäs 71 E2
Heppenheim 38 B3
Hérault 21 F3
Hérault (Dépt) 21 F3
Herbault 17 F1
Herbertingen 42 B1
Herbiers, les 17 D2
Herbignac 16 C1
Herbolzheim 42 A1
Herborn 38 B2
Herbrechtingen 38 C4
Herbstein 38 B2
Herceg Novi 52 B4
Hercegovac 50 C1
Hercegov Goleša 51 E3
Hereford 6 C2
Hereford and Worcester 6 C2
Herencia 27 F4
Herentals 34 B3
Herford 36 B4
Héricourt 19 E1
Heringsdorf 37 F1
Herisau 42 B2
Hérisson 18 B2
Hérisson, Cascades du 19 D2
Herk 34 C3
Herleshausen 38 C1
Hermagor 41 D4
Herma Ness 3 F1
Hermannsburg 36 C3
Hermansverk 74 B2
Hermenault, l' 17 D2
Herment 18 B3
Hermeskeil 35 D4
Hermigua 30 A4
Hermsdorf 39 D1
Hernani 20 A3
Hernansancho 27 E2
Herne 11 F3
Herne Bay 7 F3
Herning 76 B3
Heroldsberg 39 D3
Herónia 59 D2
Herøy 68 A4
Herrala 73 D3
Herre 74 D3
Herrenberg 38 B4
Herrenchiemsee 40 C3
Herrera (Andalucía) 31 E3
Herrera (Aragón) 28 C2
Herrera *Mt* 28 C2
Herrera de Alcántara 26 C3
Herrera del Duque 31 E1
Herrera de Pisuerga 25 E2
Herrera, Pto de 20 A4
Herreruela 26 C4
Herrestad 76 C1
Herrieden 38 C3
Herrljunga 77 D1
Herrnburg 37 D2
Herrnhut 39 F1
Herrsching 40 B3
Herrskog 69 F4
Hersbruck 39 D3
Herselt 34 B3
Hérso 55 E2
Hersónissos Akrotíri 64 B3
Hersónissos Methánon 59 E4
Hersónissos Spinalónga 64 D4
Herstal 34 C3
Herten 11 F3
Hertford 7 E3
Hertfordshire 7 E3
Hervás 27 D3
Herzberg (D) 37 D4
Herzberg (DDR) 37 F4
Herzogenaurach 39 D3
Herzogenburg 41 E2
Herzsprung 37 E2
Hesdin 14 A1
Hesel 36 B2
Hessen 38 B2
Hesseng 67 F1
Hessisch-Lichtenau 38 C1
Hessisch Oldendorf 36 C4
Hestfjørður 68 A3
Hetekylä 71 D2
Hetin 51 F1
Hettange 15 D2
Hettstedt 37 E4
Heubach 38 C4
Heuchin 14 A1
Heukuppe 41 E3
Hevlin 41 F2
Hexham 5 E2
Heyrieux 19 D3
Heysham 5 D3
Hiddensee 37 E1
Hieflau 41 E3
Hiekkasarkät 70 C3
Hierbas 28 C4
Hierro 30 A4
Hiersac 17 E3
Hietaniemi 67 F3
Higham Ferrers 7 E2
Highland 2 C2
High Peak 5 E4
High Willhays 6 B4
High Wycombe 7 D3
Higuera de Arjona 31 F2
Higuera de la Serena 31 D1
Higuera de la Sierra 30 C2
Higuera de Vargas 30 C1
Higuera la Real 30 C2
Higueruela 32 B1
Hiidenportti 71 E3
Hiiumaa 78 C1
Híjar 28 C3
Hilchenbach 38 A1
Hildburghausen 38 C2
Hilden 35 D3
Hilders 38 C2
Hildesheim 36 C4
Hiliomódi 59 D3
Hillegom 11 D2
Hillerød 76 C3
Hillesøy 66 C2
Hillswick 3 F1
Hiloús, Akr 65 D2
Hilpoltstein 39 D3
Hiltula 73 E2
Hilvarenbeek 11 E3
Hilversum 11 E2
Himanka 70 C3
Hímaros 55 F2
Himmerland 76 B2
Hinckley 7 D2
Hindelang 40 A4
Hindhead 7 D3
Hindsholm 76 C3
Hinnøya 66 B3
Hinodejo 28 A2
Hinojares 32 A3
Hinojosa de Duero 26 C2
Hinojosa del Duque 31 D1
Hinterrhein 42 B2
Hintersee (D) 40 C3
Hintersee (DDR) 37 F2
Hinterstoder 41 D3
Hintertux 43 D2
Hinterweidenthal 38 A3
Híos 61 D2
Híos, N 61 D2
Hirschau 39 D3
Hirschberg 39 D2
Hirschegg 40 A4
Hirsingue 19 F1
Hirson 14 C2
Hirşova 81 E3
Hirtshals 76 B1
Hirvasvaara 71 E1
Hirvensalmi 73 E3
Hirvilahti 71 E4
Hirwaun 6 B3
Hisarja 81 D4
Histria 81 E3
Hitchin 7 E2
Hitra 68 C3
Hitzacker 37 D2
Hjalmare Kanal 75 E4
Hjälmaren 75 E4
Hjartdal 74 B3
Hjellestad 74 A2
Hjelmeland 74 A3
Hjelmsøya 67 D1
Hjo 77 D1
Hjørring 76 B2
Hjørundfjorden 68 B4
Hlebine 50 C1
Hlemoútsi 58 B3
Hlomó, Óros 59 E2
Hluboká 41 D2
Hobro 76 B2
Höchberg 38 C3
Hochdorf 42 A2
Hochfeiler 43 D2
Hochfelden 15 E3
Hochgolling 41 D4
Hochgrabe 43 E2
Hochosterwitz 50 A1
Hochreichart 41 E3
Hochschober 43 E2
Hochschwab 41 E3
Hochspeyer 38 A3
Höchst 38 B3
Höchstadt 38 C3
Höchstädt 38 C4
Hochtannbergpaß 40 A4
Hochtor (Osttirol) 43 E2
Hochtor (Steiermark) 41 E3
Hockenheim 38 B3
Hoddesdon 7 E3
Hodenhagen 36 C3
Hódmezővásárhely 80 C2
Hodnet 6 C1
Hodonín 41 F1
Hodoš 41 F4
Hodovo 52 B3
Hoedekenskerke 11 D3
Hœdic 16 C1
Hoek van Holland 11 D3
Hoemsbu 68 B4
Hof 39 D2
Hofgeismar 36 C4
Hofheim 38 C2
Hofles 69 D2
Höfn 68 C2
Hofolding 40 B3
Hofors 75 E3
Hofsjökull 68 B2
Höganäs 76 C3
Høgebru 74 B2
Höglekardalen 75 D1
Högsäter 75 D4
Högsby 77 E2
Høgset 68 B4
Hohe Acht 35 D3
Hohenau 41 F2
Hohenberg 41 E3
Hohenems 40 A4
Hohengandern 38 C1
Hohenlimburg 38 A1
Hohenlinden 40 B3
Hohenlockstedt 36 C2
Hohenmölsen 37 E4
Hohenpeißenberg 40 B3
Hohenseeden 37 E3
Hohenstein 39 E1
Hohentauern 41 D3
Hohenwestedt 36 C1
Hohenzollern 38 B4
Hoher Zinken 41 D3
Hohe Tauern 43 E2
Hohe Tauern, Nat Pk 43 E2
Hóhlakas 65 F2
Hohneck 15 E4
Hohwachter Bucht 37 D1
Hohwald, le 15 E3
Højer 76 B3
Hokksund 74 C3
Hol 74 B2
Holbæk 76 C3
Holbeach 7 E2
Holdorf 36 B3
Holíč 41 F1
Höljäkkä 71 F3
Höljes 75 D2
Hollabrunn 41 F2
Høllen 74 A4
Hollenstedt 36 C2
Höllental 41 E3
Holles 69 D2
Hollfeld 39 D2
Hollingsholm 68 B4
Hollola 73 D3
Hollum 11 E1
Hollywood 9 D3
Holm (N) 69 D2
Holm (S) 69 E4
Hólmavík 68 A1
Holmec 50 A1
Holmen 74 C3
Holmestrand 74 C3
Holmfirth 5 E4
Holmön 70 C3
Holmsjön 75 E1
Holmslands Klit 76 A3
Holmsund 70 B3
Holomóndas, Óros 55 F3
Holstebro 76 B2
Holsted 76 B3
Holsworthy 6 B4
Holt 7 F1
Holwerd 11 E1
Holycross Abbey 8 C3
Holyhead 6 B1
Holy I (Anglesey) 6 B1
Holy I (Northumberland) 5 E1
Holywell 5 D4
Holywood 9 D1
Holzappel 38 A2
Holzgau 40 A4
Holzkirchen 40 B3
Holzleitner Sattel 40 B4
Holzminden 36 C4
Homberg (Hessen) 38 B1
Homberg (Hessen) 38 B2
Homberg (Nordrhein-Westfalen) 11 F3
Homburg 15 E2
Hommelstø 69 D2
Hommelvik 68 C4
Hommersåk 74 A4
Homoljske planine 53 D1
Hondarribia Fuenterrabia 20 A3
Hondón de las Nieves 32 C2
Hönebach 38 C1
Hønefoss 74 C3
Honfleur 13 E2
Høng 76 C3
Hónikas 59 D3
Honiton 6 C4
Honkajoki 72 C3
Honningsvåg 67 E1
Honrubia 28 A4
Honrubia de la Cuesta 25 E4
Hontalbilla 25 E4
Hontoria del Pinar 25 F3
Hooge 36 B1
Hoogeveen 11 F2
Hoogezand 11 F1
Hoogstraten 34 B2
Hook Head 8 C4
Höör 77 D3
Hoorn 11 E2
Hopetoun House 3 D4
Hopfgarten 40 C4
Hopperstad 74 B2
Hóra (Dodekánissa) 61 E3
Hóra (Pelopónissos) 62 C3
Hora Svatého Šebestiána 39 E2
Horažd'ovice 39 F3
Horb 38 B4
Hörby 77 D3
Horcajo de los Montes 31 E1
Horcajo de Santiago 28 A4
Horcajo de Trevélez 31 F3
Horcajo-Medianero 27 D3
Horche 28 A3
Hordaland 74 A2
Horden 5 E2
Horeftó 55 E4
Horezu 81 D3
Horgen 42 B2
Horley 7 E3
Horn (A) 41 E2
Horn (Baden-Württemberg) 42 B1
Horn (N) 69 D2
Horn (Nordrhein-Westfalen) 36 C4
Hornachos 31 D1
Hornachuelos 31 D2
Hornavan 69 F1
Hornberg 42 A1
Hornbjarg 68 A1
Hornburg 37 D4
Horncastle 7 E1
Horndal 75 E3
Horneburg 36 C2
Hörnefors 70 B4
Hörnerkirchen 36 C2
Hornet 68 C4
Hornindal 74 B1
Hornindalsvatn 74 B1
Hørning 76 B3
Horni Počernice 39 F2
Hornisgrinde 38 B4
Horni Slavkov 39 E2
Hornos 32 A2
Hornoy 14 A2
Hornsea 5 F3
Hörnum 36 B1
Hořovice 39 F2
Horsens 76 B3
Horsham 7 E3
Hørsholm 76 C3
Horšovký Týn 39 E3
Horst 37 D2
Horstmar 11 F2
Hortafjorden 69 D2
Horten 74 C3
Hortezuela 28 A2
Hortiátis 55 E2
Hospental 42 B2
Hospital 8 B3
Hospital de Orbigo 25 D2
Hossa 71 E2
Hossegor 20 B3
Hostalric 29 F2
Hotagen 69 E3
Hotagen *L* 69 E3
Hotagsfjällen 69 E3
Hoting 69 E3
Hotton 34 C4
Houat 16 C1
Houches, les 19 E3
Houdain 14 B1
Houdan 14 A3
Houeillès 20 C2
Houffalize 34 C4
Houghton-le-Spring 5 E2
Houlgate 13 E2
Houmnikó 55 F2
Hoúni 58 C2
Hourtin 20 B1
Houtskår 72 C4
Hov 76 B3
Hovärken 75 D1
Hovden 74 B3
Hove 7 E4
Hovet 74 B2
Hovmantorp 77 E2
Høvringen 74 C2
Howden 5 F4
Howth 9 D3
Höxter 36 C4
Hoy 3 E1
Hoya 36 C3
Høyanger 74 A2
Hoyerswerda 78 A4
Hoylake 5 D4
Høylandet 69 D3
Hoym 37 D4
Hoyos 26 C3
Höytiainen 71 F4
Hoz de Beteta 28 B3
Hozoviótissa 64 C1
Hracholuská přehr nádrž 39 E2
Hradec-Králove 80 A1
Hrádek 41 F2
Hrádek nad Nisou 39 F1
Hranice (Severomoravský) 80 B1
Hranice (Západočeský) 39 D2
Hrasnica 51 D3
Hrastnik 50 A1
Hrastovlje 43 F3
Hřensko 39 F1
Hrísey 68 B1
Hríssafa 63 D3
Hrissí, N 65 D4
Hrissó 55 F2
Hrissoskalítissa 64 A4
Hrissoúpoli 56 B2
Hrissovítsi 58 C4
Hristianí, N 64 B2
Hristianó 58 C4
Hristós 61 D4
Hrómio 55 D3
Hrtkovci 51 E2
Hrušovany 41 F2
Hrvace 50 C4
Hrvatska 50 B2
Hückeswagen 38 A1
Hucknall 7 D1
Hucqueliers 14 A1
Huddersfield 5 E4
Hude 36 B3
Hudiksvall 75 F2

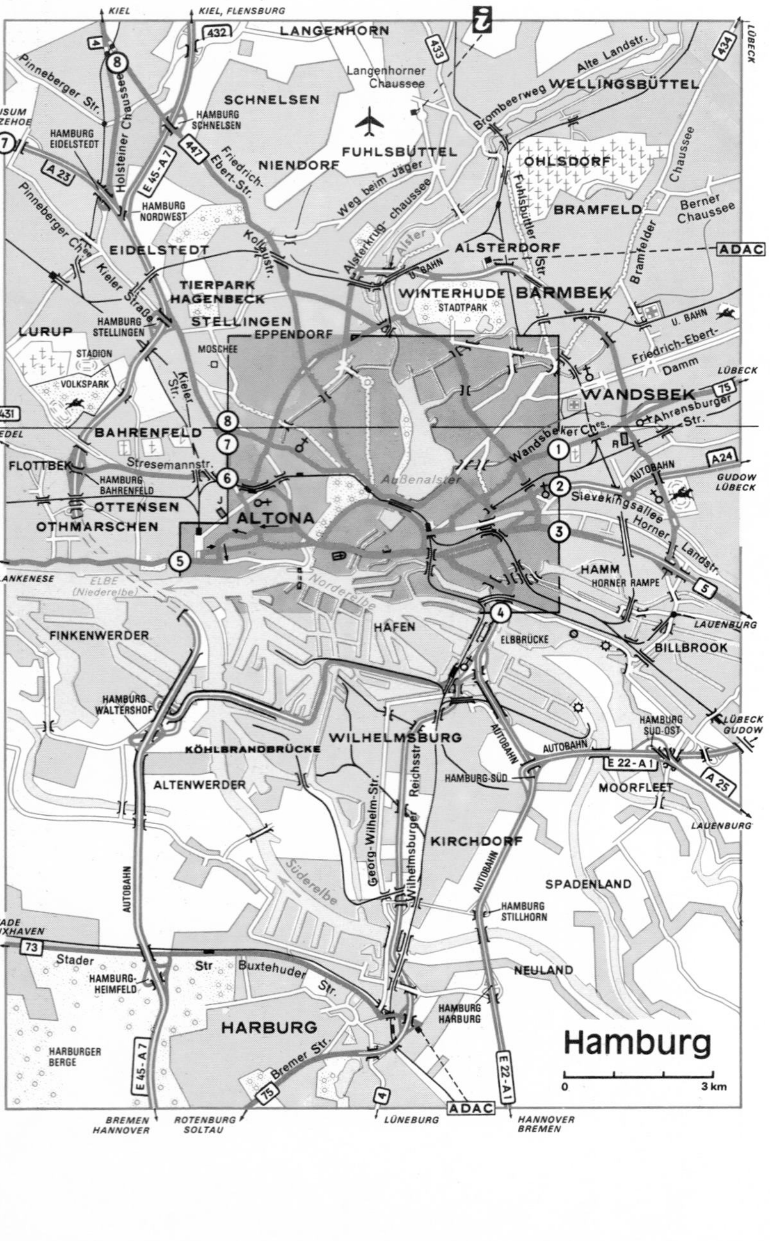

Hamburg
KIEL
KIEL, FLENSBURG
LANGENHORN
SCHNELSEN
FUHLSBÜTTEL
NIENDORF
WELLINGSBÜTTEL
OHLSDORF
BRAMFELD
EIDELSTEDT
ALSTERDORF
WINTERHUDE
BARMBEK
STELLINGEN
LURUP
WANDSBEK
BAHRENFELD
ALTONA
OTTENSEN
OTHMARSCHEN
HAMM
FINKENWERDER
HAFEN
BILLBROOK
WILHELMSBURG
ALTENWERDER
KIRCHDORF
SPADENLAND
NEULAND
HARBURG
LÜBECK
BREMEN HANNOVER
ROTENBURG SOLTAU
LÜNEBURG
HANNOVER BREMEN
0 3 km

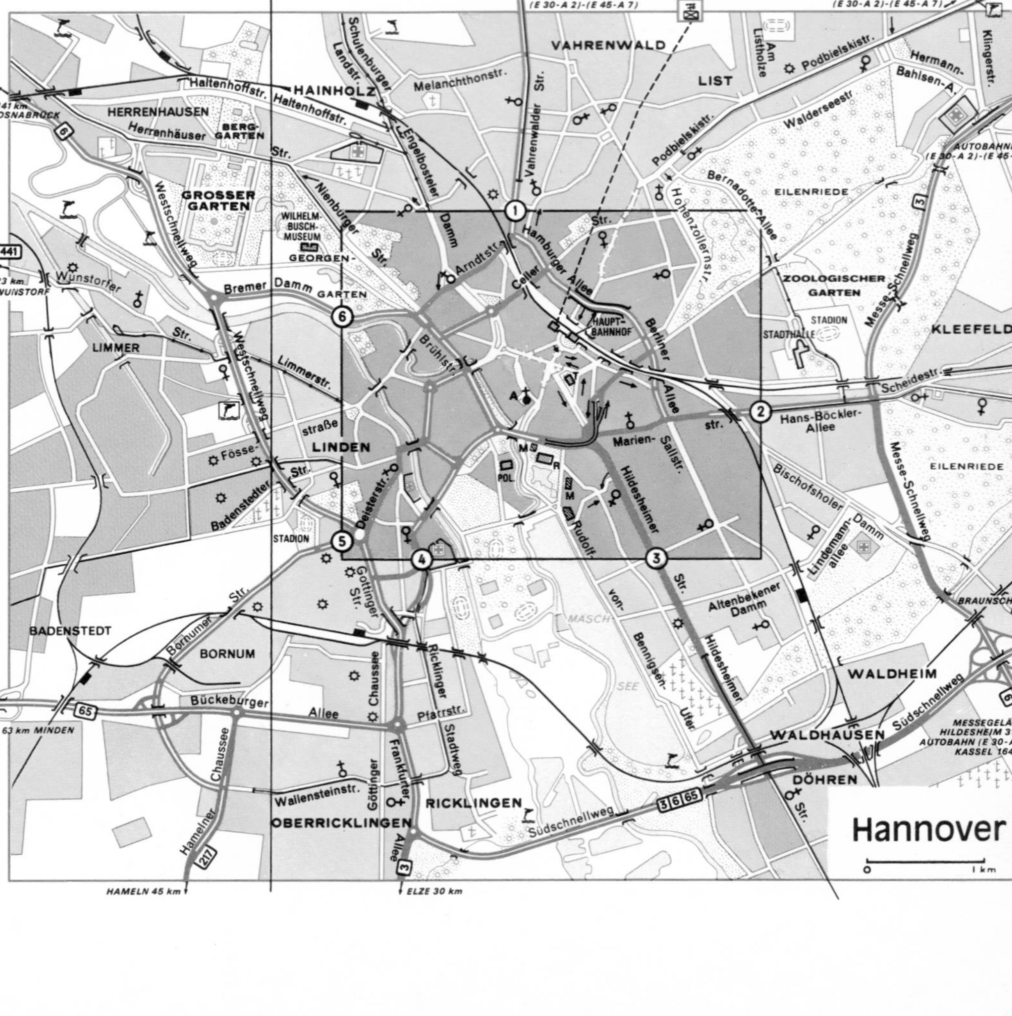

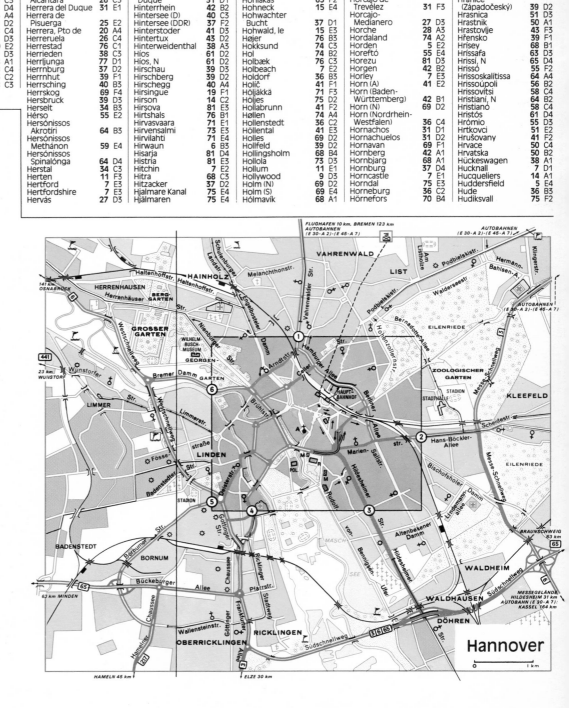

Hannover
FLUGHAFEN 10 km, BREMEN 123 km
AUTOBAHNEN (E 30-A 2)-(E 45-A 7)
VAHRENWALD
HAINHOLZ
LIST
HERRENHAUSEN
GROSSER GARTEN
LIMMER
LINDEN
KLEEFELD
WALDHEIM
BADENSTEDT
BORNUM
RICKLINGEN
OBERRICKLINGEN
WALDHAUSEN
DÖHREN
ZOOLOGISCHER GARTEN
HAMELN 45 km
ELZE 30 km
63 km MINDEN
BRAUNSCHWEIG 63 km
0 1 km

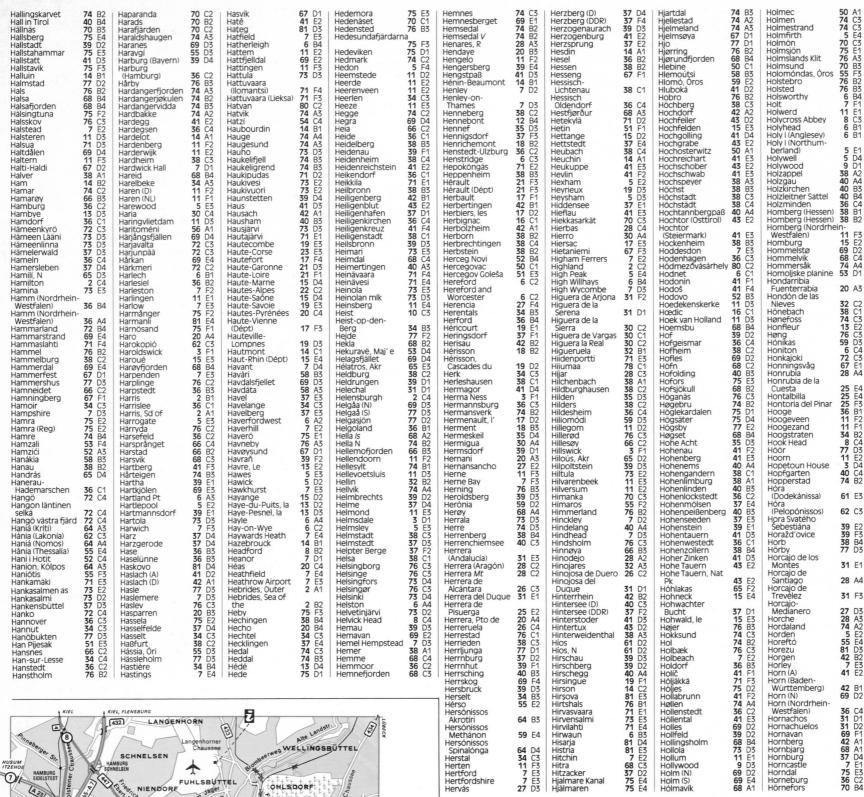

Huebra, R 27 D2
Huedin 81 D2
Huélago 31 F3
Huélamo 28 B3
Huelgoat 12 B3
Huelma 31 F3
Huelva 30 C3
Huelva, Riv de 30 C2
Huércal-Overa 32 B3
Huérguina 28 B4
Huerta del Rey 25 F3
Huerta de Valdecarábanos 27 F4
Huertahernando 28 B3
Huerto 28 C2
Huerva, R 28 C2
Huesa 32 A2
Huesca 28 C1
Huéscar 32 A2
Huesna, Emb de 31 D2
Huete 28 A4
Huétor-Santillán 31 F3
Huétor-Tájar 31 E3
Hüfingen 42 A1
Huftarøy 74 A3
Huisne 13 E4
Huittinen 72 C3
Huizen 11 E2
Hulst 11 D3
Hultsfred 77 E2
Humada 25 E2
Humanes 28 A3
Humber Bridge 5 F4
Humber, R 5 F4
Humberside 5 F3
Humberside (Airport) 5 F4
Humenné 80 C1
Humppila 73 D3
Hundested 76 C3
Hundorp 74 C2
Hunedoara 81 D3
Hünfeld 38 C2
Hungerford 7 D3
Hunnebostrand 74 C4
Húnsflói 68 A1
Hunspach 15 F3
Hunsrück 38 A3
Hunstanton 7 E1
Hunte 36 B3
Huntingdon 7 E2
Huntly 3 D2
Hurdal 74 C3
Huriel 18 B3
Hurones, Emb de los 31 D3
Hurskaala 73 E2
Hürth 35 D3
Hurum 74 B2
Hurup 76 B2
Husafell 68 A2
Húsavík *Is* 68 B1
Husavik (N) 74 A3
Husbands Bosworth 7 D2
Hushinish 2 B1
Huşi 81 E2
Huskvarna 77 D2
Husnes 74 A3
Hustadvika 68 B4
Hustopeče 41 F1
Husum (D) 36 C1
Husum (S) 70 B4
Hutovo 52 B3
Hutovo Blato 52 B3
Hüttenberg 41 E4
Hüttschlag 41 D4
Huttula 73 D2
Huttwil 42 A2
Huy 34 C3
Hvalba 68 A3
Hvalfjörður 68 A2
Hvalpsund 76 B2
Hvalvík 68 A3
Hvar 50 C4
Hvar / 50 C4
Hvarski kan 50 C4
Hveragerði 68 A2
Hveravellir 68 B2
Hvidbjerg 76 B2
Hvide Sande 76 A3
Hvítá 68 A2
Hvittingfoss 74 C3
Hvitträsk 73 D4
Hvolsvöllur 68 B2
Hwlffordd 6 A2
Hyde 5 E4
Hyen 74 A1
Hyères 22 C4
Hyères, Iles d' 22 C4
Hylsfjorden 74 A3
Hyltebruk 77 D2
Hyrynsalmi 71 E2
Hythe 7 F3
Hyvinkää 73 D4
Hyypiö 71 D1

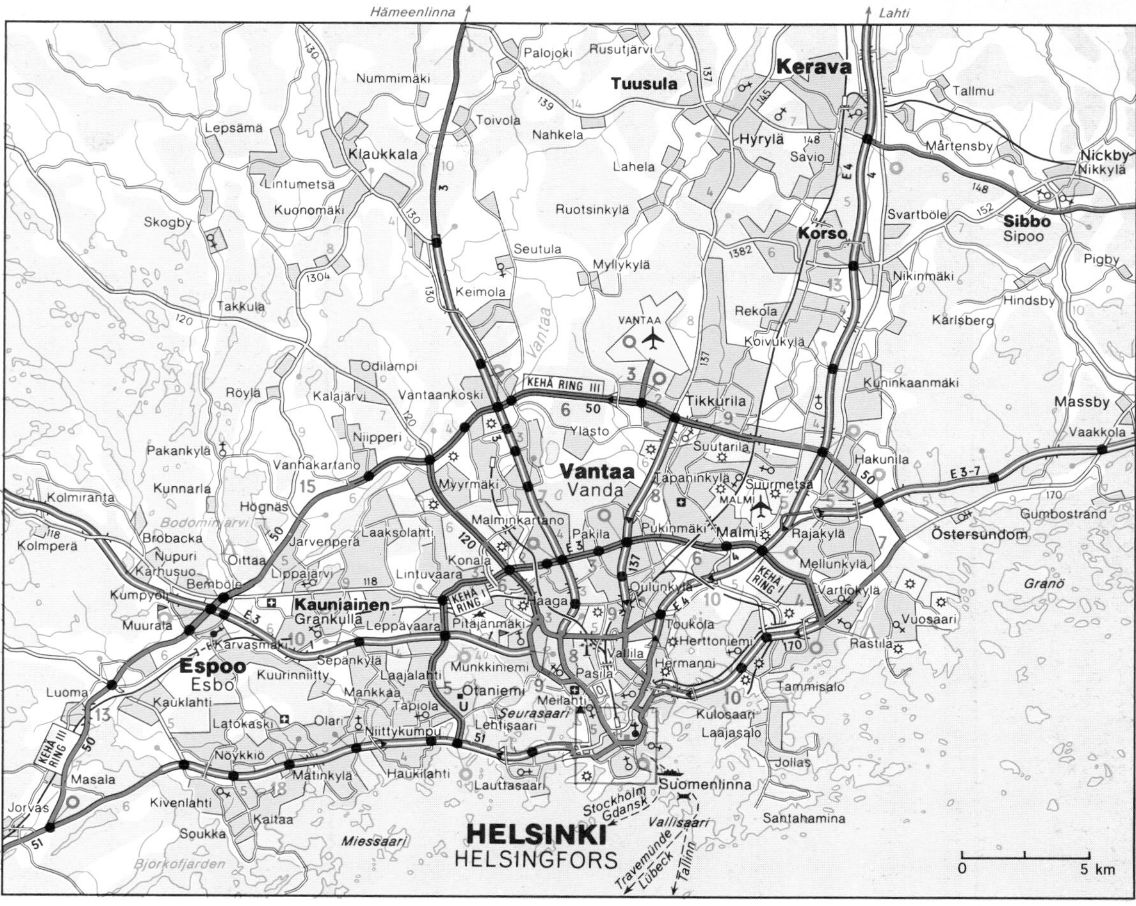

Hämeenlinna
Lahti
Kerava
Tuusula
Nummimäki
Palojoki
Rusutjärvi
Tallmu
Toivola
Nahkela
Lepsämä
Klaukkala
Hyrylä
Savio
Mårtensby
Nickby
Nikkylä
Kouvola, Kotka
Lahela
Lintumetsä
Kuonomäki
Ruotsinkylä
Skogby
Korso
Svartbole
Sibbo
Sipoo
Seutula
Myllykylä
Pigby
Nikinmäki
Hindsby
Keimola
Takkula
Rekola
Karlsberg
Vantaa
Koivukylä
Odilampi
Kuninkaanmäki
Royla
Kalajärvi
Vantaankoski
KEHÄ RING III
Tikkurila
Massby
Ylästö
Vaakkola
Niipperi
Suutarila
Pakankylä
Vanhakartano
Hakunila
Kunnarla
Vantaa
Vanda
Turku / Åbo
Kolmiranta
Myyrmäki
Malmi
Hognäs
Malminkartano
Gumbostrand
Bodominjärvi
Laaksolahti
Pukinmäki
Östersundom
Kolmperä
Bröbacka
Järvenperä
Pakila
Rajakylä
Nupuri
Karhusuo
Oittaa
Konala
Mellunkylä
Bemböle
Lippajärvi
Lintuvaara
Kumpyöri
Kauniainen
Grankulla
Haaga
Oulunkylä
Vartiokylä
Vuosaari
Muurala
Leppävaara
Pitäjänmäki
Karvasmäki
Vallila
Puotila
Herttoniemi
Rastila
Espoo
Esbo
Sepänkylä
Munkkiniemi
Hermanni
Kuurinniitty
Laajalahti
Pasila
Luoma
Kauklahti
Mankkaa
Otaniemi
Tammisalo
Tapiola
Meilahti
Latokaski
Olari
Seurasaari
Lehtisaari
Kulosaari
Niittykumpu
Laajasalo
Noykkiö
Jollas
Masala
Matinkylä
Haukilahti
Lauttasaari
Suomenlinna
Kivenlahti
Jorvas
Kaitaa
Santahamina
Soukka
Miessaari
Vallisaari
Hanko / Hangö
Björkofjärden
Stockholm
Gdansk
HELSINKI
HELSINGFORS
Travemünde
Lübeck
Tallinn
0
5 km

I

Ía 64 B2
Ialomiţa 81 E3
Iaşi 81 E2
Iasmos 56 C2
Ibañeta, Pto 20 B4
Ibar 53 D2
Ibbenbüren 36 B4
Ibestad 66 B2
Ibi 32 C2
Ibias, R 24 C2
Ibiza 33 E1
Ibiza / 33 E1
Iblei, Mti 49 D4
Ičn'a 79 F4
Icod de los Vinos 30 A4
Idanha a Nova 26 C3
Idar-Oberstein 38 A3
Idéo Ándro 64 B4
Ídi, Óros 64 C4
Idoméni 55 E2
Iđoš 51 E1
Ídra 59 E4
Ídra, N 59 E4
Ídras, Kólpos 59 E4
Idre 75 D2
Idrigill Pt 2 B2
Idrija 43 F3
Idrijca 43 F3
Idro 42 C3
Idstein 38 B2
Ielsi 45 E4
Ieper 34 A3
Ierápetra 65 D4
Ierissós 56 A3
Ieropigí 54 C2
If, Château d' 22 B3
Ifestía 56 C3
Ifjord 67 E1
Ifjordfjellet 67 E1
Igalo 52 B4
Iga Vas 50 A2
Iggesund 75 F2
Iglesias 46 A4
Igls 43 D2
Igoumenítsa 54 B4
Igrane 50 C4
Igualada 29 E2
Ihtiman 81 D4
Ii 71 D2
Iijarvi 67 E2
Iijoki 71 D2
Iisalmi 71 E3
Iisvesi 71 E4
Iitti 73 E3
IJmuiden 11 D2
IJssel 11 E3
IJsselmeer 11 E2
IJsselmuiden 11 E2
IJzendijke 11 D3
Ijzer 34 A3
Ikaalinen 72 C3
Ikaría, N 61 D4
Ikast 76 B3
Ilandža 51 F1
Ilanz 42 B2
Ilche 29 D2
Ilchester 6 C3
Ile-Bouchard, l' 17 E2
Ile-Rousse, l' 23 E3
Ilfracombe 6 B3
Ílhavo 26 B2
Ilía 58 C3
Ilia 59 E2
Il'ičevsk 81 F2
Ilida 58 B3
Ilidza 51 D3
Ilijas 51 D3
Ilíki 59 E2
Ilíki, L 59 E2
Iliókastro 59 E4
Ilirska Bistrica 50 A2
Ilkeston 7 D1
Ilkley 5 E3
Illana 28 A3
Illano 24 C1
Illar 32 A3
Ille 13 D4
Ille et Rance, Canal d' 13 D4
Ille-et-Vilaine 13 D4
Illertissen 40 A3
Illescas 27 F3
Ille-sur-Têt 21 E4
Illhæusern 15 E4
Illiers 14 A4
Illingen 38 B4
Illmitz 41 F3
Illora 31 F3
Illueca 28 B2
Ilm 39 D1
Ilmajoki 70 C4
Ilmenau *R* 37 D2
Ilmenau 38 C2
Il'men, Ozero 79 D1
Ilminster 6 C4
Ilok 51 E2
Ilomantsi 71 F4
Ilova 50 C1
Ilovik 50 A3
Ilsenburg 37 D4
Ilsfeld 38 B3
Imathía 55 D2
Ímeros 56 C2
Imitós 59 F3
Immenstaad 42 B1
Immenstadt 40 A4
Immingham 5 F4
Immingham Dock 5 F4
Imola 44 B1
Imotski 50 C4
Imperia 23 E3
Imphy 18 B2
Impruneta 44 B2
Imst 40 B4
Inari 67 E2
Inarijärvi 67 E2
Inarijoki 67 E2
Inca 33 E2
Inchnadamph 2 C1
Inchtree 2 C3
Incisa in Val d'Arno 44 B2
Incudine, M 23 D4
Indal 75 F1
Indalsälven 69 E4
Indija 51 E2
Indre 17 F1
Indre (Dépt) 17 F2
Indre-et-Loire 17 E1
Infiesto 25 D1
Ingå 73 D4
Ingelmunster 34 A3
Ingleton 5 D3
Ingolstadt 39 D4
Ingrandes 17 D1
Ingul 81 F2
Ingulec 81 F1
Ingulec *R* 81 F2
Ingwiller 15 E3
Iniesta 32 B1
Iniö 72 C4
Iniön aukko 72 C4
Inis 8 B3
Inis Córthaidh 9 D4
Inishbofin 8 A2
Inishcrone 8 B1
Inisheer 8 B3
Inishkea 8 A1
Inishmaan 8 B3
Inishmore 8 A3
Inishmurray 8 B1
Inishowen 4 A2
Inishowen Head 4 B2
Inishshark 8 A2
Inishtrahull 4 A1
Inishturk 8 A2
Inkee 71 E2
Inkoo 73 D4
Inn (CH) 42 C2
Inn (D) 40 C3
Innbygda 75 D2
Inndyr 69 E1
Innellan 2 C4
Inner Hebrides 2 A3
Innerleithen 5 D1
Inner Sd 2 B2
Innfield 8 C2
Innhavet 66 B3
Innichen 43 E2
Inning 40 B3
Innsbruck 40 B4
Innset 66 C3
Innvik 74 B1
Inói (Pelopónissos) 58 C3
Inói (Stereá Eláda) 59 E2
Inoússes 61 D2
Inoússes, N 61 D2
Inowrocław 78 B4
Ins 19 E2
Interlaken 42 A2
Întorsura Buzăului 81 D3
Inveraray 2 C3
Inverbervie 3 D3
Invergarry 2 C2
Invergordon 2 C2
Inverkeithing 3 D4
Invermoriston 2 C2
Inverness 2 C2
Inverurie 3 D2
Inzell 40 C3
Ioánina 54 B4
Ioánina (Nomos) 54 B4
Ioanínon, L 54 C4
Iona 2 B3
Ionia 55 E2
Íos 64 B1
Íos, N 64 B1
Ipáti 59 D2
Ipéria 55 D4
Iphofen 38 C3
Ípiros 54 B4
Ipsilí Ráhi 56 A1
Ípsos 54 A4
Ipsoúnda 58 C4
Ipswich 7 F2
Iput' 79 E3
Iráklia (Makedonía) 55 F1
Iráklia (Stereá Eláda) 59 D2
Iráklia, N 64 C1
Iráklio 64 C4
Iráklio (Nomos) 64 C4
Irati, R 20 B4
Irbes Šaurums 78 C2
Irdning 41 D3
Iregua, R 28 A1
Iréo (Argolída) 59 D3
Iréo (Dodekánissa) 61 E3
Iréo (Korinthía) 59 D3
Iréo, Akr 59 D3
Iria 59 E4
Irig 51 E2
Irish Sea 4 C3
Iriški venac 51 E2
Irixoa 24 B1
Irnijärvi 71 E2
Iron-Bridge 6 C2
Irschenberg 40 B3
Irsina 47 D1
Irún 20 B3
Irurzun 20 A4
Irvine 4 C1
Irvinestow 8 C1
Irxleben 37 E3
Isaba 20 B4
Isaccea 81 E3
Isafjarðardjúp 68 A1
Isafjörður 68 A1
Isala 81 E4
Isane 74 A1
Isar 39 E4
Isarco 43 D2
Isbister 3 F1
Iscar 25 E4
Ischgl 40 A4
Ischia 46 B2
Ischia, I d' 46 B2
Ise 74 C4
Isefjord 76 C3
Iselle 42 A3
Iselsberg 43 E2
Iseo 42 C3
Iseo, L d' 42 C3
Iseran, Col de l' 19 F4
Isère 19 D4
Isère (Dépt) 19 D4
Iserlohn 38 A1
Isernia 45 E4
Isfjellet 66 C2
Isfjorden 68 B4
Ishëm 54 A1
Ishëm *R* 54 A1
Isigny 13 D2
Isili 46 B3
Iskâr 81 D3
Is'kuras 67 E2
Isla 3 D3
Isla 25 F1
Isla Cristina 30 B3
Isla Mayor 30 C3
Island Magee 9 D1
Islay 2 B4
Isle 20 C2
Isle-Adam, l' 14 A3
Isle-de-Noé, l' 20 C3
Isle-en-Dodon, l' 21 D3
Isle-Jourdain, l' (Gers) 21 D3
Isle-Jourdain, l' (Vienne) 17 E3
Isle of Man 4 C3
Isle of Portland 6 C4
Isle of Whithorn 4 C2
Isle of Wight 7 D4
Isleornsay 2 B2
Isles of Scilly 6 A4
Isle-sur-la-Sorgue, l' 22 B3
Isle-sur-le-Doubs, l' 19 E1
Isle-sur-Serein, l' 18 C1
Ismaning 40 B3
Isnäs 73 E4
Isny 40 A3
Iso-Evo 73 D3
Isojärvi 73 D3
Isojoki 72 C2
Isokylä 71 E1
Isokyrö 70 C4
Isola 23 D2
Isola del Gran Sasso d'Italia 45 D3
Isola della Scala 43 D4
Isola del Liri 45 D4
Isola di Capo Rizzuto 47 E3
Isona 29 D1
Isonzo 43 F3
Isorella 42 C4
Iso-Syöte 71 E2
Ispica 49 D4
Issambres, les 22 C3
Issel 11 F3
Issigeac 21 D2
Issoire 18 B4
Issoma 58 C3
Issoudun 18 A2
Issóva, M. 58 C4
Is-sur-Tille 19 D1
Issy-l'Evêque 18 C2
Ist 50 A3
Istán 31 E4
Istanbul 81 F4
Istarske Toplice 43 F3
Istérnia 60 C4
Istha 38 B1
Isthmía 59 E3
Istibanja 53 F4
Istiéa 59 E1
Istindan 66 C2
Istok 53 D3
Istres 22 B3
Istrios 65 F2
Isturits et d'Oxocelhaya, Grottes d' 20 B3
Itä-Aure 72 C2
Itäinen Suomenlahti 73 E4
Itanós 65 D4
Itéa (Flórina) 54 C2
Itéa (Grevená) 55 D3
Itéa (Stereá Eláda) 59 D2
Itéa (Thessalía) 55 D4
Itéas, Kólpos 59 D2
Itháki 58 B2
Itháki, N 58 B2
Ithómi 58 C4
Iti 59 D2
Itilo 62 C3
Íti, Óros 59 D2
Iton 13 F3
Itri 46 B1
Itta 38 C1
Ittiri 46 A3
Itz 39 D2
Itzehoe 36 C2
Ivacevići 79 D4
Ivajlovgrad 81 E4
Ivalo 67 E2
Ivalojoki Ävvil 67 E3
Ivančice 41 F1
Ivančići 51 D3
Ivančna Gorica 50 A1
Ivanec 50 B1
Ivangrad 51 F4
Ivanić Grad 50 B1
Ivanjica 51 F3
Ivanjska 50 C2
Ivankovo 51 D2
Ivano-Frankovsk 81 D1
Ivanščica 50 B1
Ivan Sedlo 51 D3
Ivanska 50 C1
Iveland 74 B4
Iveragh 8 A4
Ivira 56 A2
Ivíron 56 A3
Ivrea 23 D1
Ivry-la-Bataille 14 A3
Ixiá 65 F2
Ixworth 7 F2
Iž 50 B3
Izeda 24 C3
Izegem 34 A3
Izernore 19 D3
Izlake 50 A1
Izmail 81 E2
Izmir 61 E2
Izmit 81 F4
Iznájar 31 E3
Iznájar, Emb de 31 E3
Iznallos 31 F3
Iznik 81 F4
Iznik Gölü 81 F4
Izoard, Col d' 22 C2
Izola 43 F3
Iz Veli 50 B3
Izvor (Makedonija) 53 D4
Izvor (Makedonija) 53 E4
Izvor (Srbija) 53 D2
Izvor (Srbija) 53 F3

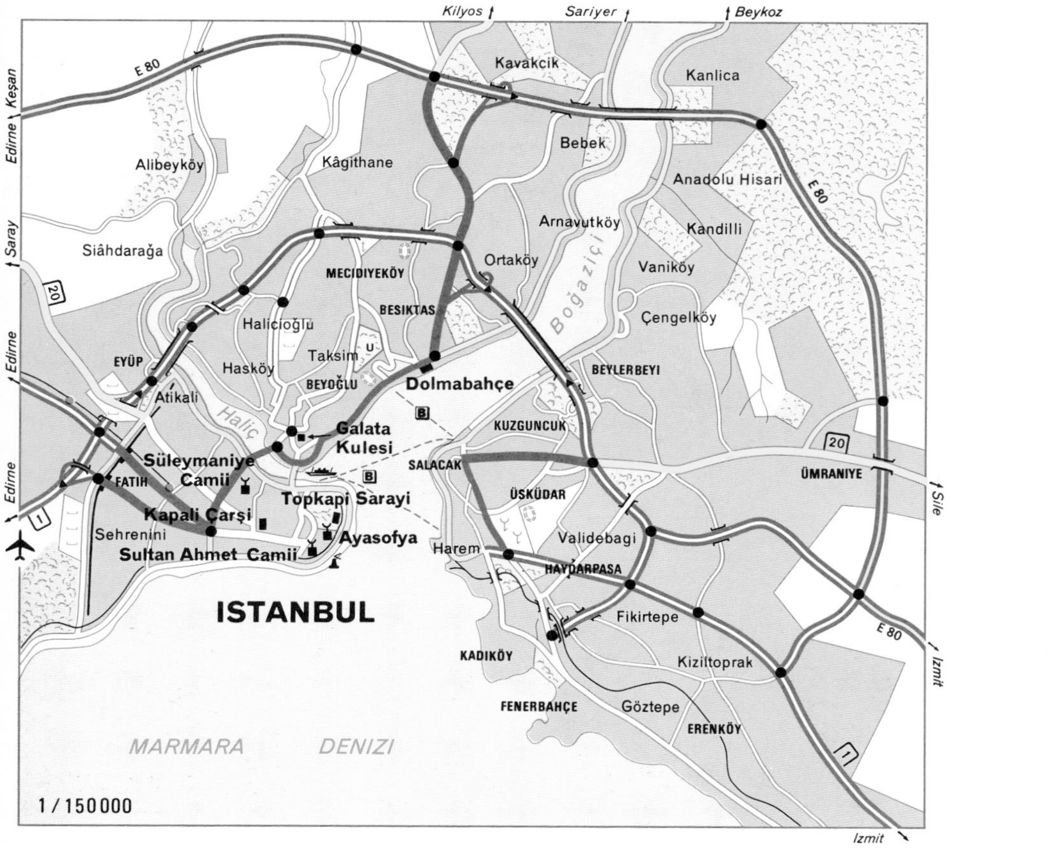

Kilyos
Sariyer
Beykoz
Edirne, Keşan
Kavakcık
Kanlıca
Bebek
Alibeyköy
Kâğıthane
Anadolu Hisarı
Arnavutköy
Kandilli
Saray
Siâhdarağa
Ortaköy
Vaniköy
MECIDIYEKÖY
BEŞIKTAŞ
Boğaziçi
Çengelköy
Edirne
Halıcıoğlu
EYÜP
Hasköy
Taksim
BEYOĞLU
BEYLERBEYI
Dolmabahçe
Atikali
Haliç
Galata Kulesi
KUZGUNCUK
Süleymaniye Camii
FATIH
SALACAK
ÜMRANIYE
Kapalı Çarşı
Topkapı Sarayı
ÜSKÜDAR
Şile
Sehrenini
Ayasofya
Sultan Ahmet Camii
Harem
Validebagi
HAYDARPAŞA
ISTANBUL
Fikirtepe
KADIKÖY
Kiziltoprak
Izmit
FENERBAHÇE
Göztepe
ERENKÖY
MARMARA
DENIZI
1/150000
Izmit

J

Jaala 73 E3
Jaäsjärvi 73 E3
Jabalón, R 31 F1
Jabbeke 34 A3
Jablanac 50 A3
Jablan Do 52 B4
Jablanica 51 D4
Jablanica *R* 53 E3
Jablanica (Reg) 54 B1
Jabláničko jez 51 D3
Jablonec nad Nisou 80 A1
Jablonné v Podještědí 39 F1
Jabugo 30 C2
Jabuka (Bosna i Hercegovina) 51 E3
Jabuka (Srbija) 51 E4
Jabuka (Vojvodina) 52 C1
Jabuka / 50 B4
Jabukovac (Hrvatska) 50 B2
Jabukovac (Srbija) 53 E1
Jabukovik 53 E2
Jaca 28 C1
Jáchymov 39 E2
Jadar (Bosna i Hercegovina) 51 E3
Jadar (Srbija) 51 E2
Jäder 75 E4
Jaderberg 36 B2
Jadovik 51 F4
Jadovnik 50 C3
Jadranska Lešnica 51 E2
Jadraque 28 A3
Jaén 31 F2
Jagodnjac 51 D1
Jagotin 79 E4
Jagst 38 C3
Jagsthausen 38 C3
Jahorina 51 E3
Jahorina (Reg) 51 E3
Jajce 50 C3
Jäkkvik 69 F1
Jakobselv 67 F1
Jakobstad 70 C3
Jakšić 50 C2
Jakupica 53 E4
Jalasjärvi 72 C2
Jaligny 18 C3
Jalón, R 28 B2
Jalovik Izvor 53 E2
Jambol 81 E4
Jamena 51 E2
Jämijärvi 72 C3
Jäminkipohja 73 D3
Jämjö 77 E3
Jammerbugten 76 B2
Jamnička Kiselica 50 B2
Jämsä 73 D3
Jämsänkoski 73 D3
Jämtlands Län 69 E4
Janakkala 73 D3
Janče 53 D4
Jandía, Pta de 30 B4
Jándula, Emb del 31 F2
Jandula, R 31 F2
Jänisselkä 71 F4
Janja 51 E2
Janjevo 53 E3
Janjina 51 D4
Jankov kamen 53 D2
Jañona 26 C3
Jantra 81 D3
Janville 14 A4
Janzé 13 D4
Japetić 50 B1
Jäppilä 71 E4
Jaraba 28 B2
Jarafuel 32 C1
Jaraicejo 27 D4
Jaráiz 27 D3
Jarak 51 E2
Jarama, R 27 F3
Jarandilla de la Vera 27 D3
Järbo 75 E3
Jarcevo 79 E2
Jard 17 D3
Jæren 74 A4
Jaren 74 C3
Jargeau 14 A4
Jarkovac 51 F1
Jarmen 37 F1
Jarmenovci 52 C1
Jarnac 17 E3
Jarnages 18 A3
Järna (Kopparbergs Län) 75 E3
Järna (Stockholms Län) 75 F4
Jarny 15 D3
Jarocin 78 B4
Jaroměřice 41 E1
Jarosław 78 C4
Järpen 69 D4
Jarrow 5 E2
Jarvelä 73 D3
Järvenpää 73 D4
Järvsö 75 E2
Jaša Tomić 51 F1
Jasenak 50 A2
Jasenica (Bosna i Hercegovina) 50 B2
Jasenica (Srbija) 53 D1
Jasenovac 50 C2
Jasenovo (Crna Gora) 52 C3
Jasenovo (Srbija) 51 F3
Jasenovo (Vojvodina) 53 D1
Jasika 53 D2
Jasikovo 53 E1
Jasło 80 C1
Jasmund 37 F1
Jastrebarsko 50 B2
Jastrowie 78 B4
Jászberény 80 C2
Jau, Col de 21 E4
Jaufenpass 43 D2
Jaunay-Clan 17 E2
Jaunpass 19 F2
Jausiers 22 C2
Javalambre 28 C4
Javalambre, Sa de 28 C4
Javalón 28 B4
Javea 33 D1
Jävenitz 37 D3
Javie, la 22 C2
Javor 51 F3
Javořice 41 E1
Javornjača 50 B3
Javorov 78 C4
Jävre 70 C2
Javron 13 E3
Jedburgh 5 D2
Jedincy 81 E2
Jędrzejów 80 C1
Jeesiö 67 E3
Jeetze 37 D3
Jegun 20 C3
Jegunovce 53 E4
Jekabpils 79 D2
Jektevik 74 A3
Jelah 51 D2
Jelašca 51 E4
Jelenia Góra 80 A1
Jelenje 50 A2
Jelgava 78 C2
Jelling 76 B3
Jel'n'a 79 E3
Jelsa (N) 74 A3
Jelsa (YU) 50 C4
Jemnice 41 E1
Jena 39 D1
Jenbach 40 B4
Jengejetneme 69 E3
Jennersdorf 41 F4
Jeppo 70 C4
Jerez de la Frontera 30 C3
Jerez de los Caballeros 30 C2
Jérica 28 C4
Jerichow 37 E3
Jerisjärvi 67 D3
Jerpoint Abbey 8 C4
Jersey 12 C3
Jerte 27 D3
Jerte, R 27 D3
Jerxheim 37 D4
Jerzu 46 B3
Jesenice (CS) 39 E2
Jesenice (YU) 43 F2
Jeseník 80 B1
Jesi 45 D2
Jesolo 43 E3
Jessen 37 E4
Jessheim 74 C3
Jeßnitz 37 E4
Jetzelsdorf 41 E2
Jeumont 14 C1
Jevenstedt 36 C1

Jever 36 B2
Jevišovice 41 E1
Jevnaker 74 C3
Jezerane 50 A2
Jezerce 53 D3
Jezercë, M 52 C4
Jezero 50 C3
Jezersko 50 A1
Ježevica 51 F3
Jičín 80 A1
Jiekkevarre 66 C2
Jihlava 41 E1
Jihlava *R* 41 E1
Jijona 32 C2
Jiloca, R 28 B3
Jílové u Prahy 39 F2
Jimbolia 80 C3
Jimena 31 F2
Jimena de la Frontera 31 D4
Jindřichovice 39 E2
Jindřichuv Hradec 41 E1
Jirkov 39 E2
Jiu 81 D3
Jizera 39 F2
Joachimsthal 37 F2
Jockfall 70 C1
Jódar 31 F2
Jodoigne 34 B3
Joensuu 71 F4
Jogeva 79 D1
Johanngeorgenstadt 39 E2
John o'Groats 3 D1
Johnstone 2 C4
Johovac 51 D2
Joigny 14 B4
Joinville 15 D3
Jokela 73 D4
Jokijärvi 71 E2
Jokikylä 71 E2
Jokioinen 73 D3
Jokkmokk 70 B1
Jökulsá á Fjöllum 68 B1
Joloskylä 71 D2
Jølstravatnet 74 B2
Jomala 72 B4
Jönåker 75 E4
Jondal 74 A3
Jongunjärvi 71 E2
Joniškis 78 C2
Jönköping 77 D1
Jönköpings Län 77 D2
Jonzac 17 E4
Jordbro 75 F4
Jordbruksveien 67 D2
Jormlien 69 E3
Jörn 70 B2
Joroinen 73 E2
Jørpeland 74 A3
Jørstadmoen 74 C2
Jošanica 53 E2
Jošanička Banja 53 D2
Jošavka 50 C2
Josenfjorden 74 A3
Jose Toran, Emb de 31 D2
Josipdol 50 B2
Josipovac 51 D1
Josselin 12 C4
Jostedalsbreen 74 B2
Jotunheimen 74 B2
Jou, Coll de 29 E1
Joué 17 E2
Jougne 19 E2
Joutjärvi 73 D3
Joutsa 73 E3
Joutseno 73 E3
Joutsijärvi 71 E1
Joyeuse 22 A2
Juankoski 71 E4
Juan-les-Pins 23 D3
Júcar, R 32 C1
Jüchen 11 F4
Juchnov 79 F2
Judaberg 74 A3
Judenau 41 E2
Judenburg 41 E4
Judio 31 E1
Juelsminde 76 B3
Jugenheim 38 B3
Jugon 12 C3
Jugorje 50 A2
Juillac 17 F4
Juist 36 A2
Jukkasjärvi 66 C3
Jülich 11 F4
Jullouville 13 D3
Jumaliskylä 71 E2
Jumeaux 18 B4
Jumièges 13 F2
Jumilhac-le-Grand 17 F4
Jumilla 32 B2
Jumilla, Pto de 32 B2
Juminen 71 E3
Jumisko 71 E1
Juneda 29 D2
Jungfrau 42 A3
Junik 53 D3
Juniville 14 C2
Junkeren 69 E1
Junosuando 67 D3
Junsele 69 F3
Juntusranta 71 E2
Juojärvi 71 E4
Juoksenki 70 C1
Juorkuna 71 E2
Jura 2 B3
Jura (Canton) 19 F1
Jura (Dépt) 19 D2
Jura, Sd of 2 B3
Jurbarkas 78 C3
Jurjevo 50 A3
Jurmala 78 C2
Jurmofjärden 72 C4
Jurmu 71 E2
Juromenha 30 C1
Jurva 70 C4
Jussey 15 D4
Justel 24 C3
Jüterbog 37 F4
Juuka 71 F4
Juupajoki 73 D3
Juurusvesi 71 E4
Juva (Mikkelin Lääni) 73 E2
Juva (Turun ja Porin Lääni) 72 C4
Juvigny-le-Tertre 13 D3
Juvigny-sous-Andaine 13 E3
Juvola 73 E2
Juzennecourt 14 C4
Južna Morava 53 E2
Južnyj Bug 81 F1
Jyderup 76 C3
Jylland 76 B2
Jyrkkä 71 E3
Jyväskylä 73 D2

K

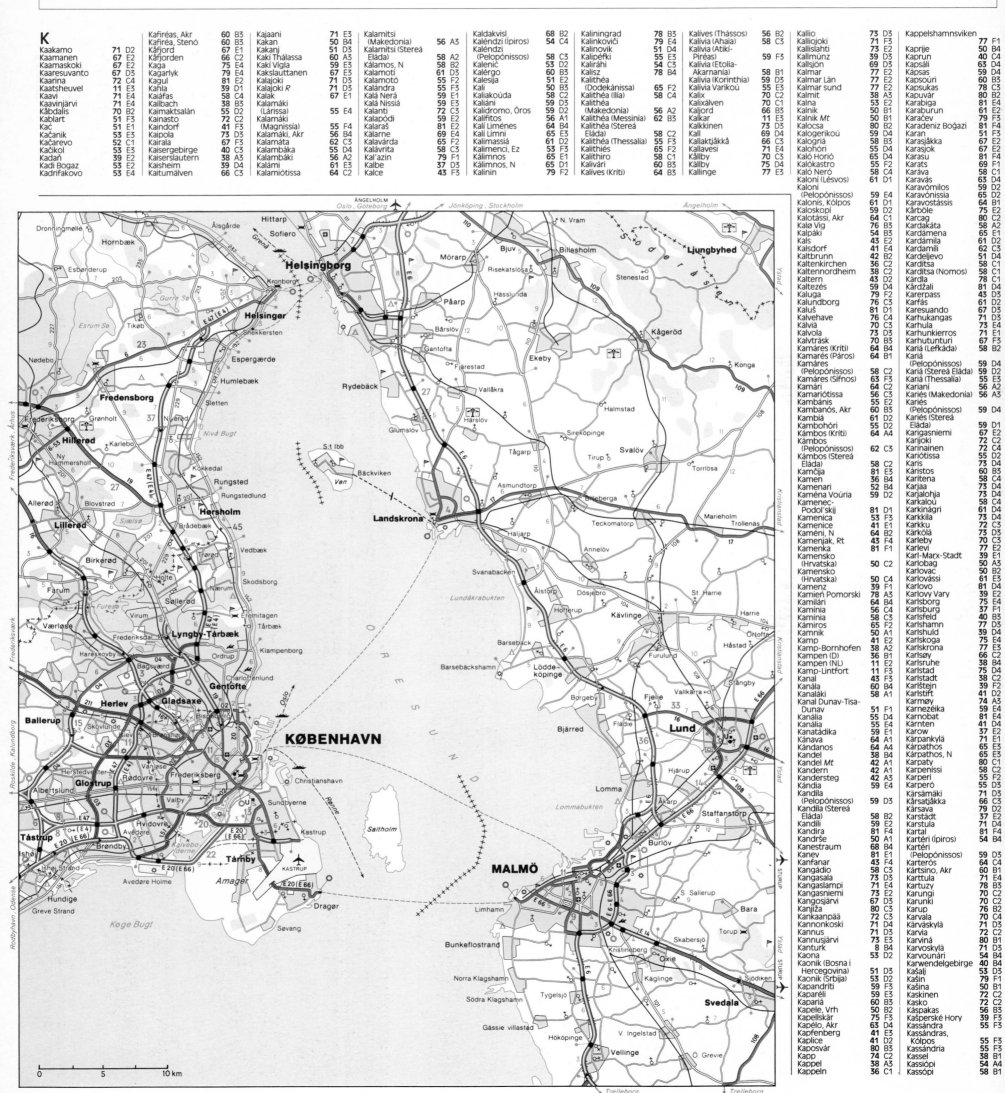

Kaakamo 71 D2
Kaamanen 67 E2
Kaamaskoki 67 E2
Kaaresuvanto 67 D3
Kaarina 72 C4
Kaatsheuvel 11 E3
Kaavi 71 E4
Kaavinjärvi 71 E4
Kåbdalis 70 B2
Kablart 51 F3
Kać 51 E1
Kačanik 53 E3
Kačarevo 52 C1
Kačikol 53 E3
Kadaň 39 E2
Kadi Bogaz 53 E2
Kadrifakovo 53 E4
Kafiréas, Akr 60 B3
Kafiréa, Stenó 60 B3
Kåfjord 67 E1
Kåfjorden 66 C2
Kaga 75 E4
Kagarlyk 79 E4
Kagul 81 E2
Kahla 39 D1
Kaiáfas 58 C4
Kailbach 38 B3
Kaimaktsalán 55 D2
Kainasto 72 C2
Kaindorf 41 F3
Kaipola 73 D3
Kairala 67 F3
Kaisergebirge 40 C3
Kaiserslautern 38 A3
Kaisheim 39 D4
Kaitumälven 66 C3
Kajaani 71 E3
Kakan 50 B4
Kakanj 51 D3
Kakí Thálassa 60 A3
Kakí Vígla 59 E3
Kakslauttanen 67 E3
Kalajoki 71 D3
Kalajoki *R* 71 D3
Kalak 67 E1
Kalamáki (Lárissa) 55 E4
Kalamáki (Magnissía) 55 F4
Kalamáki, Akr 56 B4
Kalamáta 62 C3
Kalambáka 55 D4
Kalambáki 56 A2
Kalámi 61 E3
Kalamiótissa 64 C2
Kalamítsi (Makedonía) 56 A3
Kalamítsi (Stereá Eláda) 58 A2
Kálamos, N 58 B2
Kalamotí 61 D3
Kalamotó 55 F2
Kalándra 55 F3
Kalá Nerá 59 E1
Kalá Nissiá 59 E3
Kalanti 72 C3
Kalapódi 59 E2
Kalaraš 81 E2
Kälarne 69 E4
Kalavárda 65 F2
Kalávrita 58 C3
Kal'azin 79 F1
Kalbe 37 D3
Kalce 43 F3
Kaldakvísl 68 B2
Kaléndzi (Ípiros) 54 C4
Kaléndzi (Pelopónissos) 58 C3
Kalenić 53 D2
Kalérgo 60 B3
Kalesija 51 E2
Kali 50 B3
Kaliakoúda 58 C2
Kaliáni 59 D3
Kalídromo, Óros 59 D2
Kalífitos 56 A1
Kalí Liménes 64 B4
Kalí Límni 65 E3
Kalimassiá 61 D2
Kalimenci, Ez 53 F3
Kálimnos 65 E1
Kálimnos, N 65 D1
Kalinin 79 F2
Kaliningrad 78 B3
Kalinkoviči 79 E4
Kalinovik 51 D4
Kalipéfki 55 E3
Kalirâhi 54 C3
Kalisz 78 B4
Kalithéa (Dodekánissa) 65 F2
Kalithéa (Ilía) 58 C4
Kalithéa (Makedonía) 56 A2
Kalithéa (Messinía) 62 B3
Kalithéa (Stereá Eláda) 58 C2
Kalithéa (Thessalía) 55 F3
Kalithiés 65 F2
Kalithiro 58 C1
Kalivári 60 B3
Kalíves (Kríti) 64 B3
Kalíves (Thássos) 56 B2
Kalívia (Ahaïa) 58 C3
Kalívia (Atikí-Piréas) 59 F3
Kalívia (Etolía-Akarnanía) 58 B1
Kalívia (Korinthía) 59 D3
Kalívia Varikoú 55 E3
Kalix 70 C2
Kalixälven 70 C1
Kaljord 66 B3
Kalkar 11 E3
Kalkkinen 73 D3
Kall 69 D4
Kallaktjåkkå 66 C3
Kallavesi 71 E4
Källby 70 C3
Källby 75 D4
Kallinge 77 E3
Kallio 73 D3
Kalliojoki 71 F3
Kallislahti 73 E2
Kallmünz 39 D3
Kallsjön 69 D3
Kalmar 77 E2
Kalmar Län 77 E2
Kalmar sund 77 E2
Kalmit 38 A3
Kalna 53 E2
Kalnik 50 B1
Kalnik *Mt* 50 B1
Kalocsa 80 B2
Kalogerikoú 59 D4
Kalogriá 58 B3
Kalohóri 55 D4
Kaló Horió 65 D4
Kalókastro 55 F2
Kaló Neró 58 C4
Kaloní (Lésvos) 61 D1
Kaloní (Pelopónissos) 59 E4
Kalonís, Kólpos 61 D1
Kaloskopí 59 D2
Kalotássi, Akr 64 C1
Kalø Vig 76 B3
Kalpáki 54 B3
Kals 43 E2
Kalsdorf 41 E4
Kaltbrunn 42 B2
Kaltenkirchen 36 C2
Kaltennordheim 38 C2
Kaltern 43 D2
Kaltezés 59 D4
Kaluga 79 F2
Kalundborg 76 C3
Kaluš 81 D1
Kalvehave 76 C4
Kälviä 70 C4
Kalvola 73 D3
Kalvträsk 70 B3
Kamáres (Kríti) 64 B4
Kamarés (Páros) 64 B1
Kamáres (Pelopónissos) 58 C2
Kamáres (Sífnos) 63 F3
Kamári 64 C2
Kamariótissa 56 C3
Kambánis 55 D3
Kambanós, Akr 60 B3
Kambiá 61 D2
Kambohóri 55 D2
Kámbos (Kríti) 64 A4
Kámbos (Pelopónissos) 62 C3
Kámbos (Stereá Eláda) 58 C2
Kamčija 81 E3
Kamen 36 B4
Kamenari 52 B4
Kaména Voúrla 59 D2
Kamenec-Podol'skij 81 D1
Kamenica 53 F3
Kamenice 41 E1
Kaméni, N 64 B2
Kamenjak, Rt 43 F4
Kamenka 81 F1
Kamensko (Hrvatska) 50 C2
Kamensko (Hrvatska) 50 C4
Kamenz 39 F1
Kamień Pomorski 78 A3
Kamilári 64 B4
Kamínia 56 C4
Kamínia 58 C3
Kámiros 65 F2
Kamnik 50 A1
Kamp 41 E2
Kamp-Bornhofen 38 A2
Kampen (D) 36 B1
Kampen (NL) 11 E2
Kamp-Lintfort 11 F3
Kanal 43 F3
Kanála 60 B4
Kanaláki 58 A1
Kanal Dunav-Tisa-Dunav 51 F1
Kanália 55 D4
Kanália 55 E4
Kanatádika 59 E1
Kánava 64 A1
Kándanos 64 A1
Kandel 38 B4
Kandel *Mt* 42 A1
Kandern 42 A1
Kandersteg 42 A3
Kándila 59 E4
Kandíla (Pelopónissos) 59 D3
Kandíla (Stereá Eláda) 58 B2
Kandíli 59 E2
Kandira 81 F4
Kandrše 50 A1
Kanestraum 68 B4
Kanev 81 E1
Kanfanar 43 F4
Kangádio 58 C3
Kangasala 73 D3
Kangaslampi 71 E4
Kangasniemi 73 E2
Kangosjärvi 67 D3
Kanjiža 80 C3
Kankaanpää 72 C3
Kannonkoski 71 D4
Kannus 71 D3
Kannusjärvi 73 E3
Kanturk 8 B4
Kaona 53 D2
Kaonik (Bosna i Hercegovina) 51 D3
Kaonik (Srbija) 53 D2
Kapandriti 59 F3
Kaparéli 59 E3
Kapariá 60 B3
Kapele, Vrh 50 B2
Kapellskär 75 F3
Kapélo, Akr 63 D4
Kapfenberg 41 E3
Kaplice 41 D2
Kaposvár 80 B3
Kapp 74 C2
Kappel 38 A3
Kappeln 36 C1
Kappelshamnsviken 77 F1
Kaprije 50 B4
Kaprun 40 C4
Kapsáli 63 D4
Kápsas 59 D4
Kapsoúri 60 B3
Kapsukas 78 C3
Kapuvár 80 B2
Karabiga 81 E4
Karaburun 61 E2
Karačev 79 F3
Karadeniz Boğazi 81 F4
Karan 51 F3
Karasjåkka 67 E2
Karasjok 67 E2
Karasu 81 F4
Karats 69 F1
Karáva 58 C1
Karavás 63 D4
Karavómilos 59 D2
Karavónissia 65 D2
Karavostássis 64 B1
Kårböle 75 E2
Karcag 80 C2
Kardakáta 58 A2
Kardámena 65 E1
Kardamíla 61 D2
Kardamíli 62 C3
Kardeljevo 51 D4
Karditsa 58 C1
Karditsa (Nomos) 58 C1
Kärdla 78 C1
Kărdžali 81 D4
Karerpass 43 D3
Karfás 61 D2
Karesuando 67 D3
Karhukangas 71 D3
Karhula 73 E4
Karhunkierros 71 E1
Karhutunturi 67 F3
Kariá (Lefkáda) 58 B2
Kariá (Pelopónissos) 59 D4
Kariá (Stereá Eláda) 59 D2
Kariá (Thessalía) 55 E3
Karianí 56 A2
Kariés (Makedonía) 56 A3
Kariés (Pelopónissos) 59 D4
Kariés (Stereá Eláda) 59 D1
Karigasniemi 67 E2
Karijoki 72 C2
Karinainen 72 C4
Kariótissa 55 D2
Karis 73 D4
Káristos 60 B3
Karítena 58 C4
Karjaa 73 D4
Karjalohja 73 D4
Karkalou 58 C4
Karkinágri 61 D4
Karkkila 73 D4
Karkku 72 C3
Kärkölä 73 D3
Karleby 70 C3
Karlevi 77 E2
Karl-Marx-Stadt 39 E1
Karlobag 50 A3
Karlovac 50 B2
Karlovássi 61 E3
Karlovo 81 D4
Karlovy Vary 39 E2
Karlsborg 75 E4
Karlsburg 37 F1
Karlsfeld 40 B3
Karlshamn 77 D3
Karlshuld 39 D4
Karlskoga 75 E4
Karlskrona 77 E3
Karlsøy 66 C2
Karlsruhe 38 B4
Karlstad 75 D4
Karlstadt 38 C2
Karlštejn 39 F2
Karlstift 41 D2
Karmøy 74 A3
Karnezéika 59 E4
Karnobat 81 E4
Kärnten 41 D4
Karow 37 E2
Kärpankylä 71 E1
Kárpathos 65 E3
Kárpathos, N 65 E3
Karpaty 80 C1
Karpenissi 58 C2
Karperí 55 F2
Karperó 55 D3
Kärsämäki 71 D3
Kårsatjåkka 66 C3
Kārsava 79 D2
Karstädt 37 E2
Karstula 71 D4
Kartal 81 F4
Kartéri (Ípiros) 54 B4
Kartéri (Pelopónissos) 59 D3
Karterós 64 C4
Kartsino, Akr 60 B1
Karttula 71 E4
Kartuzy 78 B3
Karungi 70 C2
Karunki 70 C2
Karup 76 B2
Karvala 70 C4
Karvaskylä 71 D3
Karvia 72 C2
Karviná 80 B1
Karvoskylä 71 D3
Karvounári 54 B4
Karwendelgebirge 40 B4
Kašalj 53 D3
Kašin 79 F1
Kašina 50 B1
Kaskinen 72 C2
Kasko 72 C2
Káspakas 56 B3
Kašperské Hory 39 F3
Kassándra 55 F3
Kassándras, Kólpos 55 F3
Kassándria 55 F3
Kassel 38 B1
Kassiópi 54 A4
Kassópi 58 B1

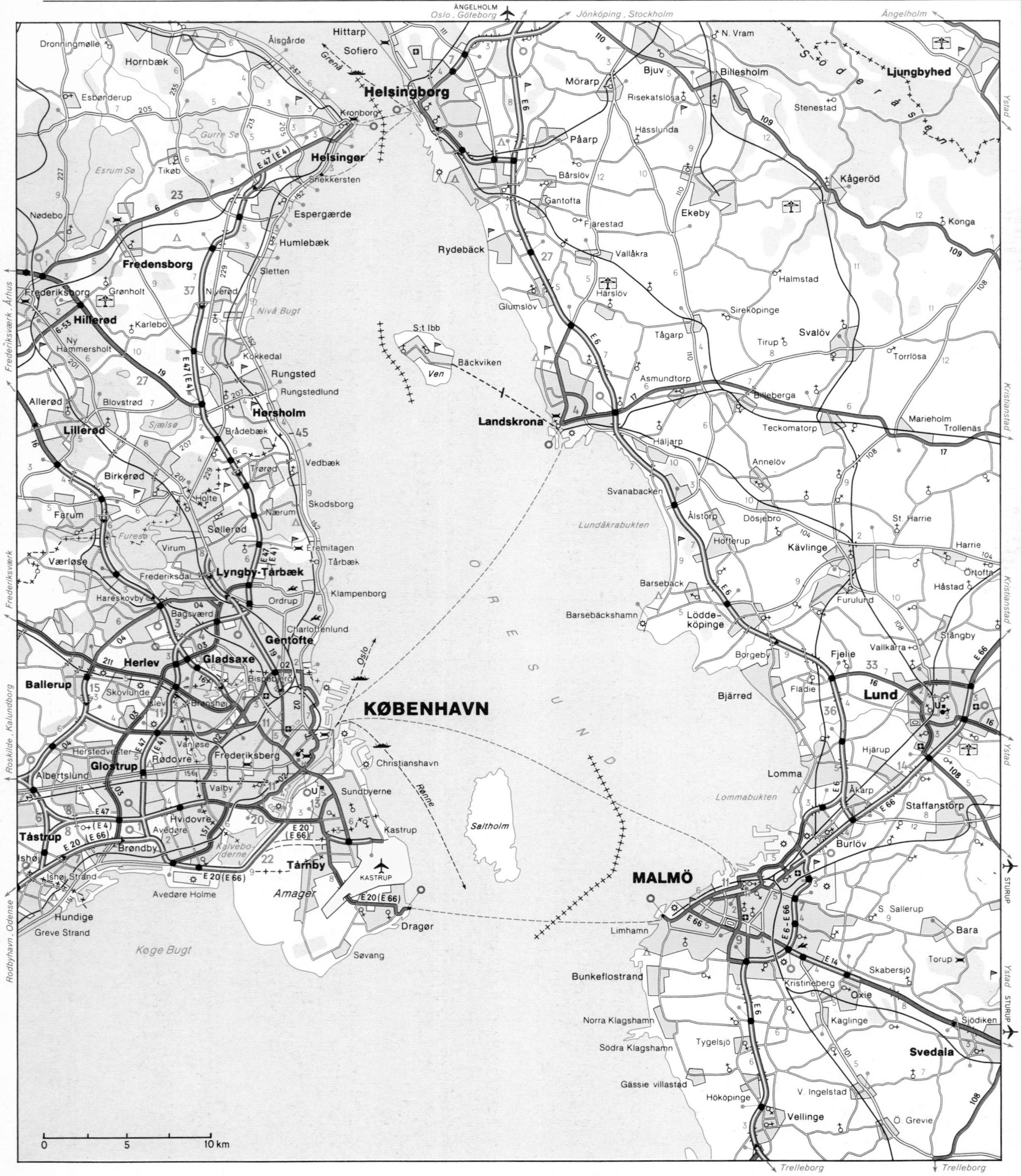
ÄNGELHOLM
Oslo, Göteborg
Jönköping, Stockholm
Helsingborg
Helsingør
Hillerød
Fredensborg
Hørsholm
Lyngby-Tårbæk
Gentofte
Gladsaxe
Herlev
Ballerup
Glostrup
Tåstrup
KØBENHAVN
Christianshavn
Tårnby
KASTRUP
Amager
Dragør
Saltholm
Ven
Landskrona
Lund
MALMÖ
Svedala
Lomma
Staffanstorp
Ljungbyhed
Kågeröd
Ekeby
Svalöv
Billesholm
Bjuv
Rydebäck
Trelleborg
Köge Bugt
Ø R E S U N D
Nivå Bugt
Lundåkrabukten
Lommabukten
0 5 10 km

Kássos, N 65 E3
Kastaniá (Makedonía) 55 D3
Kastaniá (Pelopónissos) 59 D3
Kastaniá (Thessalía) 54 C4
Kastaniá (Thessalía) 58 C1
Kastaniés 57 D1
Kastaniótissa 59 E2
Kastéla 59 E2
Kastelhoms 72 B4
Kastéli (Kríti) 64 A3
Kastéli (Kríti) 64 C4
Kastellaun 38 A2
Kastelórizo 65 F3
Kastélou, Akr 65 E3
Kastelruth 43 D2
Kaštel Stari 50 C4
Kaštel Žegarski 50 B3
Kasterlee 34 B2
Kastl 39 D3
Kastorf 37 D2
Kastóri 63 D3
Kastoriá 54 C2
Kastoriá (Nomos) 54 C3
Kastoriás, L 54 C2
Kastós, N 58 B2
Kastráki (Kiklådes) 64 B1
Kastráki (Stereá Eláda) 58 B2
Kastráki (Thessalía) 54 C4
Kastrakíou, Teh L 58 B2
Kastrí (Pelopónissos) 59 D4
Kastrí (Stereá Eláda) 59 D1
Kastrí (Thessalía) 55 E4
Kástro (Pelopónissos) 58 B3
Kástro (Skíathos) 59 E1
Kástro (Stereá Eláda) 59 E2
Kastrossikiá 58 A1
Katafígio 55 D3
Katáfito 55 F1
Katáfourko 58 B1
Katahás 55 E3
Katákolo 58 B3
Katálako 56 C3
Kátano, Akr 63 F3
Katápola 64 C1
Katára 54 C4
Katastári 58 B3
Katavía 65 F2
Katelimátsa 64 C2
Kateliós 58 B3
Kateríni 55 E3
Katerloch 41 E3
Katharó 64 C4
Katheni 60 A2
Katići 51 F3
Kätkäsuvanto 67 D3
Katlanovo 53 E4
Katlanovska Banja 53 E4
Katlenburg-Duhm 37 D4
Káto Ahaïa 58 C3
Káto Alissós 58 C3
Káto Asséa 59 D4
Káto Dolianá 59 D4
Káto Figália 58 C4
Káto Gadzéa 59 E1
Katohí 58 B2
Káto Kamíla 55 F2
Káto Klinés 54 C2
Káto Makrinoú 58 C2
Katoméri, Akr 64 B1
Káto Moussounítsa 59 D2
Káto Nevrokópi 56 A1
Káto Ólimbos 55 E3
Káto Tithoréa 59 D2
Katoúna (Lefkáda) 58 B2
Katoúna (Stereá Eláda) 58 B2
Káto Vassilikí 58 C2
Káto Vérga 62 C3
Káto Vérmio 55 D2
Káto Vlassía 58 C3
Katowice 80 B1
Káto Zahloroú 58 C3
Káto Zákros 65 D4
Katrineholm 75 E4
Katschberg 41 D4
Katschberg-tunnel 41 D4
Kattegat 76 C2
Katwijk aan Zee 11 D2
Kaub 38 A2
Kaufbeuren 40 A3
Kauhajärvi 70 C4
Kauhajoki 72 C2
Kauhaneva-Pohjankangas 72 C2
Kauhava 70 C4
Kaukonen 67 E3
Kaunas 78 C3
Kaupanger 74 B2
Kaušany 81 E2
Kaustinen 71 D3
Kautokeino 67 D2
Kautokeinoelva 67 D2
Kauttua 72 C3
Kavadarci 53 F4
Kavajë 54 A1
Kavála 56 B2
Kavála (Nomos) 56 B2
Kaválas, Kólpos 56 B2
Kavarna 81 E3
Kavíli 57 D1
Kavirio-Hlói 56 C3
Kävlinge 77 D3
Kávos 54 B4
Kavoússi 65 D4
Käylä 71 E1
Kaysersberg 15 E4
Kazan 53 E1
Kažani 54 C2
Kazanlâk 81 D4
Kazárma 62 C3
Kazatin 81 E1
Kazimierz Dolny 78 C4
Kazincbarcika 80 C2
Kdyně 39 E3
Kéa 60 B4
Keadew 8 C2
Keady 9 D2
Keähkkiljohka 67 D3
Keal, L na 2 B3
Kéa Meriá 60 B4
Kéa, N 60 B4
Kéas, Stenó 60 B3
Kebnekaise 66 C3
Kebnekaise *Mt* 66 C3
Kebock Head 2 B1
Kecskemét 80 C2
Kėdainiai 78 C3
Kédros 58 C1
Kędzierzyn-Koźle 80 C1
Keel 8 A2
Keerbergen 34 B3
Kefalári 59 D4
Kefalás, Akr 56 B2
Kefáli, Akr 63 E4
Kefaloniá, N 58 A2
Kéfalos 65 E1
Kéfalos, Akr 60 B4
Kefalóvrisso (Ípiros) 54 B3
Kefalóvrisso (Pelopónissos) 58 C4
Kefalóvrisso (Stereá Eláda) 58 B2
Kefalóvrisso (Thessalía) 55 D3
Keflavík 68 A2
Kehl 38 A4
Kehlstein 60 C3
Kehrókambos 56 B1
Kéhros 56 C1
Keighley 5 E3
Keimaneigh, Pass of 8 B4
Keitele 71 E4
Keitele *L* 71 D4
Keith 3 D2
Kéla 55 D2
Kelankylä 71 D2
Kelberg 35 D3
Kelbra 37 D4
Këlcyrë 54 B3
Kelefá 62 C3
Kelheim 39 D3
Kellinghusen 36 C2
Kellojärvi 71 E3
Kellokoski 73 D4
Kells 8 C2
Kelso 5 E1
Kelujärvi 67 E3
Kemberg 37 E3
Kembs 15 E4
Kemi 71 D2
Kemihaara 67 F3
Kemijärvi 71 F4
Kemijärvi *L* 71 F4
Kemijoki 71 D1
Keminmaa 71 D2
Kemiö 72 C4
Kemnath 39 D2
Kempele 71 D2
Kempen 11 F3
Kempenich 35 D3
Kempten 40 A3
Kendal 5 D3
Kéndras, Akr 64 A1
Kendrikó 55 E1
Kenilworth 7 D2
Kenmare 8 A4
Kenmare River 8 A4
Kennacraig 2 B4
Kenoúrgio 58 C2
Kent 7 E3
Kentallen 2 C3
Kenzingen 42 A1
Keramía 61 D1
Keramídi 55 E4
Keramítsa 54 B4
Kéramos 61 D2
Keramotí 56 B2
Kerassiá (Évia) 59 E2
Kerassiá (Thessalía) 55 E4
Kerassiés 55 D2
Kerassohóri 58 C1
Kerassóna 58 B1
Kérata, Akr 59 E2
Keratéa 59 F3
Kerava 73 D4
Kerdília, N. 56 A2
Kérēs 51 E1
Kerí 58 B3
Kerimäki 73 F2
Kerken 11 F3
Kerketéas, Óros 61 E3
Kerkétio, Óri 54 C4
Kerkíni, Óros 55 E1
Kerkínis, L 55 F1
Kérkira 54 A4
Kérkira, N 54 A4
Kerkonkoski 71 E4
Kerkrade 34 C3
Kernascléden 12 B4
Kéros, N 64 C1
Kerpen 11 F4
Kerrera 2 B3
Kerry 8 A4
Kerry Head 8 A3
Kerteminde 76 C3
Kértezi 58 C3
Kerzers 19 F2
Kesälahti 73 F2
Keşan 81 E4
Kesch, Piz 42 C2
Kesh 8 C1
Keski-Suomen Lääni 71 D4
Kessarianí 59 F3
Kestilä 71 D3
Keswick 5 D2
Keszthely 80 B2
Kętrzyn 78 C3
Kettering 7 D2
Kettletoft 3 E1
Kettwig 35 D2
Ketzin 37 E3
Keukenhof 11 D2
Keurusselkä 73 D2
Keuruu 73 D2
Kevelaer 11 E3
Kevo 67 E2
Kevo (Nat Pk) 67 E2
Key, L 8 C2
Keynsham 6 C3
Kežmarok 80 C1
Kianí 57 D1
Kiantajärvi 71 E2
Kiáto 59 D3
Kiberg 67 F1
Kičevo 53 E4
Kidderminster 6 C2
Kidlington 7 D3
Kidsgrove 6 C1
Kidwelly 6 B3
Kiefersfelden 40 C3
Kiekinkoski 71 F3
Kiel 36 C1
Kielce 80 C1
Kielder Reservoir 5 E2
Kieler Bucht 36 C1
Kiental 42 A3
Kierinki 67 E4
Kifissiá 59 F3
Kifíssos 59 D2
Kifjord 67 E1
Kihlanki 67 D3
Kihniö 72 C2
Kihti Skiftet 72 C4
Kiihtelysvaara 71 F4
Kiikala 73 D4
Kiikka 72 C3
Kiikoinen 72 C3
Kiimanen 71 E3
Kiiminginjoki 71 D2
Kiiminki 71 D2
Kiiskilä 71 D3
Kiistala 67 E3
Kijev 79 E4
Kijevo (Hrvatska) 50 C3
Kijevo (Kosovo) 53 D3
Kijevskoje Vodochranilišče 79 E4
Kikinda 51 F1
Kiklådes 60 C4
Kil 75 D3
Kíla 55 D3
Kiláda (Makedonía) 55 D3
Kiláda (Pelopónissos) 59 E4
Kilafors 75 E2
Kilbaha 8 A3
Kilbeggan 8 C3
Kilbirnie 2 C4
Kilboghamn 69 D1
Kilbotn 66 B3
Kilbrannan Sd 2 B4
Kilchoan 2 B3
Kilcock 9 D3
Kilcormac 8 C3
Kilcreggan 2 C4
Kilcullen 8 C3
Kildare 8 C3
Kildare (Co) 8 C3
Kildorrery 8 B4
Kilfenora 8 B3
Kilgarvan 8 A4
Kilija 81 E2
Kilingi-Nõmme 78 C2
Kilíni 58 B3
Kilíni, Óros 59 D3
Kilkee 8 A3
Kilkeel 9 D2
Kilkenny 8 C3
Kilkenny (Co) 8 C3
Kilkhampton 6 B3
Kilkieran B 8 A2
Kilkís 55 E2
Kilkís (Nomos) 55 E2
Killadysert 8 B3
Killala B 8 B1
Killaloe 8 B3
Killarney 8 A4
Killary Harbour 8 A2
Killashandra 8 C2
Killenaule 8 C3
Killimer 8 B3
Killin 2 C3
Killinkoski 73 D2
Killorglin 8 A4
Killybegs 8 C1
Killyleagh 9 D1
Kilmaing 8 B2
Kilmallock 8 B4
Kilmarnock 2 C4
Kilmartin 2 B3
Kilmore Quay 9 D4
Kilmurry 8 B3
Kilninver 2 B3
Kilnsea 5 F4
Kilpisjärvi 66 C2
Kilpisjärvi *L* 66 C2
Kilrea 4 B2
Kilronan 8 A3
Kilrush 8 A3
Kilsyth 2 C4
Kiltamagh 8 B2
Kiltealy 8 C3
Kilwinning 2 C4
Kilyos 81 F4
Kimássi 59 E2
Kiméria 56 B1
Kími 59 F2
Kímina 55 E2
Kimis, Órmos 60 B2
Kimísseos Theotókou 59 D3
Kimito 72 C4
Kímolos 63 F3
Kímolos, N 63 F3
Kimólou Sífnou, Stenó 64 A1
Kimry 79 F1
Kimstad 75 E4
Kínaros, N 65 D1
Kinbrace 3 D1
Kincardine 2 C3
Kindberg 41 E3
Kindelbrück 39 D1
Kinéta 59 E3
Kingisepp 79 D1
Kingissepp 78 C2
Kingsbridge 6 B4
Kingscourt 9 D2
King's Lynn 7 E2
Kingston 7 E3
Kingston-upon-Hull 5 F4
Kingswear 6 B4
Kington 6 C2
Kingussie 2 C2
Kínira 56 B2
Kinlochbervie 2 C1
Kinlochewe 2 C2
Kinloch Rannoch 2 C3
Kinna 77 D2
Kinnairds Head 3 E2
Kinnasniemi 71 F4
Kinnegad 8 C2
Kinnitty 8 C3
Kinnula 71 D4
Kinross 3 D3
Kinsale 8 B4
Kinsarvik 74 B3
Kintaus 73 D2
Kintore 3 D2
Kintyre 2 B4
Kinvarra 8 B3
Kinzig 42 A1
Kióni 58 B2
Kiparíssi 63 D3
Kiparissía 58 C4
Kiparissiakós Kólpos 58 C4
Kiparissías, Óri 58 C4
Kipárissos 55 D4
Kípi (Ípiros) 54 B3
Kípi (Thráki) 57 D2
Kipinä 71 D2
Kípos, Akr 56 C3
Kipourío 54 C3
Kippure 9 D3
Kipséli 55 E4
Kir 52 C4
Kirá Panagiá, N 60 A1
Kirchbach 41 F4
Kirchberg (D) 38 A3
Kirchberg (DDR) 39 E1
Kirchberg (Niederösterreich) 41 E2
Kirchberg (Tirol) 40 C4
Kirchberg an der Pielach 41 E3
Kirchdorf 41 D3
Kirchenlamitz 39 D2
Kirchenthumbach 39 D3
Kirchhain 38 B1
Kirchheim (Baden-Württemberg) 38 B4
Kirchheim (Hessen) 38 B1
Kirchheimbolanden 38 A3
Kirchheim unter Teck 38 C4
Kirchhundem 38 A1
Kirchlengern 36 B4
Kirchmöser 37 E3
Kirchschlag 41 F3
Kiriakí 57 D1
Kiriáki 59 D2
Kiriši 79 E1
Kirkağaç 61 F1
Kirkby Lonsdale 5 D3
Kirkby Stephen 5 E3
Kirkcaldy 3 D3
Kirkcolm 4 C2
Kirkcudbright 4 C2
Kirkenær 75 D3
Kirkenes 67 F1
Kirkeøy 74 C4
Kirkestinden 66 C2
Kirkham 5 D3
Kírki 56 C2
Kirkintilloch 2 C4
Kirkjubøur 68 A3
Kirkkonummi 73 D4
Kirklareli 81 E4
Kirkonmaanselkä 73 E4
Kirkwall 3 E1
Kirn 38 A3
Kirov 79 F3
Kirovograd 81 F1
Kirovsk 79 D1
Kirriemuir 3 D3
Kirtorf 38 B2
Kiruna 66 C3
Kisa 77 E1
Kisac 51 E1
Kiseljak (Loznica) 51 E2
Kiseljak (Sarajevo) 51 D3
Kiseljak (Tuzla) 51 D2
Kišin'ov 81 E2
Kisko 73 D4
Kiskőrös 80 C2
Kiskunfélegyháza 80 C2
Kiskunhalas 80 C2
Kissámou, Kólpos 64 A3
Kißlegg 40 A3
Kissoú Kámbos 64 B4
Kistanje 50 B3
Kisújszállás 80 C2
Kisvárda 80 C2
Kíta 62 C4
Kitee 73 F2
Kíthira 63 D4
Kíthira, N 63 D4
Kíthnos 60 B4
Kíthnos, N 60 B4
Kíthnou, Stenó 60 B4
Kitinen 67 E3
Kitka 71 E1
Kitriés, Akr 62 C3
Kittilä 67 E3
Kittsee 41 F2
Kitzbühel 40 C4
Kitzingen 38 C3
Kiukainen 72 C3
Kiuruvesi 71 E3
Kiutaköngäs 71 E1
Kivalo 71 D2
Kivéri 59 D4
Kívi 60 B4
Kivijärvi 71 D4
Kivijärvi *L* (Keski-Suomen Lääni) 71 D4
Kivijärvi *L* (Kymen Lääni) 73 E3
Kivilahti 71 F4
Kivitaipale 71 D1
Kivotós 54 C3
Kizário 56 C2
Kjellerup 76 B2
Kjerringøy 66 B3
Kjerringvåg 68 C3
Kjerringvik 69 D3
Kjølifjell 69 D4
Kjøllefjord 67 E1
Kjøpsvik 66 B3
Kjustendil 81 D4
Kladanj 51 E3
Kladnica 51 F3
Kladnice 50 C4
Kladno 39 F2
Kladovo 53 E1
Klæbu 68 C4
Klagenfurt 43 F2
Klaipėda 78 C3
Klaksvík 68 A3
Klana 50 A2
Klanac 50 B3
Klanxbüll 36 B1
Klarälven 75 D3
Klašnice 50 C2
Klässbol 75 D3
Klašterec 39 E2
Klatovy 39 F3
Klaukkala 73 D4
Klausen 43 D2
Klausenpass 42 B2
Klazienaveen 11 F2
Kleinhaugsdorf 41 E2
Kleinheubach 38 B3
Kleinwalsertal 40 A4
Klekovača 50 C3
Klenike 53 E3
Klenovica 50 A2
Kleppe 74 A4
Kleppestø 74 A2
Kleve 11 E3
Kličevac 53 D1
Klimoviči 79 E3
Klimpfjäll 69 E2
Klin 79 F2
Klina 53 D3
Klinča Selo 50 B2
Klincy 79 E3
Klingenbach 41 F3
Klingenthal 39 E2
Klinovec 39 E2
Klintehamn 77 F2
Klippan 77 D3
Klippen 69 E2
Klippitztörl 41 E4
Klis 50 C4
Klissoúra 54 C2
Klisura (Makedonija) 53 F4
Klisura (Srbija) 53 E3
Klitoría 58 C3
Klixbüll 36 B1
Kljajićevo 51 E1
Ključ 50 C3
Kłodzko 80 B1
Kløfta 74 C3
Klokkarvik 74 A3
Klokočevac 53 E1
Klos 53 D4
Kloštar 50 C1
Kloštar Ivanić 50 B1
Klösterle 40 A4
Klosterneuburg 41 F2
Klosters 42 C2
Kloten 42 B2
Klötze 37 D3
Klöverträsk 70 C2
Klövsjö 75 E1
Kluczbork 80 B1
Klupe 51 D2
Klütz 37 D1
Knapdale 2 B4
Knappogue Castle 8 B3
Knäred 77 D2
Knaresborough 5 E3
Knarvik 74 A2
Kneginec 50 B1
Kneža 81 D3
Knežak 50 A2
Kneževi Vinogradi 51 D1
Kneževo 51 D1
Knežica 50 C2
Knežina 51 E3
Knić 53 D2
Knídi 54 C3
Knighton 6 C2
Knight's Town 8 A4
Knin 50 B3
Knittelfeld 41 E4
Knivskjellodden 67 E1
Knivsta 75 F3
Knjaževac 53 E2
Knockmealdown Mts 8 B4
Knokke-Heist 10 C3
Knole House 7 E3
Knossós 64 C4
Knutsford 6 C1
Koarvikodds 67 E2
Kobarid 43 F2
Kobbfjorden 67 E1
Kobel'aki 81 F1
København 76 C3
Kobern-Gondorf 38 A2
Kobišnica 53 E1
Koblenz 38 A2
Kobrin 79 D4
Koca D 81 E4
Kočani 53 F4
Koceljevo 51 E2
Kočerin 51 D4
Kočevje 50 A2
Kočevski rog 50 A2
Kochel 40 B3
Kocher 38 C4
Kodiksami 72 C3
Kodisjoki 72 C3
Kœnigsbourg 15 E4
Köflach 41 E4
Køge 76 C3
Køge Bugt 76 C3
Kohtla-Järve 79 D1
Koikkala 73 E3
Koirakoski 71 E3
Koitajoki 71 F4
Koitelainen 67 E3
Koitere 71 F4
Koivujärvi 71 E3
Koivusuo 71 F4
Kokála 62 C4
Kökar 72 C4
Kokári 61 E3
Kökarsfjärden 72 B4
Kokemäenjoki 72 C3
Kokemäki 72 C3
Kokin Brod 51 F3
Kókino Neró 55 E4
Kokkola 70 C3
Kokotí 59 D1
Koksijde-Bad 34 A3
Kola 50 C2
Koláka 59 E2
Kolari (SF) 67 D4
Kolari (YU) 53 D1
Kolåsen 69 D3
Kolašin 52 C3
Kolbäck 75 E3
Kolbermoor 40 B3
Kolby Kås 76 B3
Kolding 76 B3
Kolho 73 D2
Koli 71 F3
Kolima 71 D4
Kolimvári 64 A3
Kolín 80 A1
Kolindrós 55 E3
Kolínes 59 D4
Kolka 78 C2
Kolkanlahti 71 D4
Kolkasrags 78 C2
Kölleda 39 D1
Kolmården 75 E4
Köln 35 D3
Koło 78 B4
Kołobrzeg 78 A3
Koločep 52 B4
Kolomyja 81 D2
Kolovec 39 E3
Kolovrat 51 E4
Kolpino 79 D1
Kolsva 75 E3
Kolubara 52 C1
Kolvereid 69 D2
Komagfjord 67 D1
Kómanos 55 D3
Komar 50 C3
Kómara 57 D1
Komarnica 52 B3
Komárno 80 B2
Kombóti 58 B1
Koméno 58 B1
Kómi (Híos) 61 D3
Kómi (Kiklådes) 60 C4
Komílio 58 A2
Komin 50 B1
Kómito 60 B3
Komiža 50 C4
Komló 80 B3
Komniná (Makedonía) 55 D2
Komniná (Thráki) 56 B1
Komninádes 54 C2
Komorane 53 D3
Komotiní 56 C2
Komovi 52 C3
Komrat 81 E2
Komulanköngäs 71 E3
Konak 51 F1
Konakovo 79 F2
Končanica 50 C1
Kondiás 56 C4
Kondopoúli 56 C3
Kondós, Akr 64 B1
Kondovázena 58 C3
Kondrić 51 D2
Konečka pl 53 F4
Køng 76 C3
Köngernheim 38 B3
Konginkangas 71 D4
Kongsberg 74 C3
Kongselva 66 B3
Kongsfjord 67 F1
Kongsvinger 75 D3
Königsbrück 39 F1
Königsbrunn 39 D4
Königsee 39 D2
Königsfeld 42 A1
Königslutter 37 D3
Königsschlösser 40 B4
Königssee 60 C3
Königssee *L* 60 C3
Königstein (D) 38 B2
Königstein (DDR) 39 F1
Königswiesen 41 E2
Königswinter 35 D3
Königs-Wusterhausen 37 F3
Konin 78 B4
Koniskós 55 D4
Konístres 60 A2
Kónitsa 54 B3
Konj 50 C4
Konjevrate 50 B4
Konjic 51 D4
Konjsko 52 B3
Konjuh 51 D3
Konkämäälven 67 D2
Könnern 37 E4
Konnevesi 71 E4
Konnevesi *L* 71 E4
Könönpelto 73 E2
Konopište 53 F4
Konotop 79 F4
Konsko 53 F4
Konsmo 74 B4
Konstantinovy Lázně 39 E2
Konstanz 42 B1
Kontich 34 B3
Kontiolahti 71 F4
Kontiomäki 71 E3
Konttajärvi 71 D1
Konz 35 D4
Kopaída 59 E2
Kopáni 54 C4
Kopanós 55 D2
Kopaonik 53 D2
Koparnes 68 A4
Kópasker 68 B1
Köpenick 37 F3
Koper 43 F3
Kopervik 74 A3
Köping 75 E4
Köpingsvik 77 E2
Koplik 52 C4
Köpmanholmen 69 F4
Koporiće 53 D3
Koppang 74 C2
Kopparberg 75 E3
Kopparbergs Län 75 E3
Kopparleden 69 E4
Kopperby 36 C1
Koprivna 51 D2
Koprivnica (Bosna i Hercegovina) 50 C1
Koprivnica (Srbija) 53 E1
Korab 53 D4
Kórakas, Akr 64 B1
Koralpe 50 A1
Korana 50 B2
Korbach 38 B1
Korbevac 53 E3
Korbovo 53 E1
Korçë 54 B2
Korčula 52 A3
Korčula *I* 52 A3
Korčulanski kan 50 C4
Korensko sedlo 43 F2
Kórfos 59 E3
Korgåsen 67 E1
Korgen 69 E2
Koria 73 E3
Korifássi 62 B3
Koríkio Ándro 59 D2
Kórimvos 57 D1
Koríni 59 E3
Korinós 55 E3
Korinthía 59 D3
Korinthiakós Kólpos 59 D3
Kórinthos 59 E3
Korissía 60 B4
Korissós 54 C2
Korita (Bosna i Hercegovina) 52 B3
Korita (Crna Gora) 52 C4
Korita (Mljet) 52 A4
Koríthi 58 B3
Koritnik 53 D2
Koritnik, M. 53 D4
Korkeakangas 73 F2
Korkeakoski 71 E4
Körmend 80 B2
Kornat 50 B4
Kornati 50 B4
Korneuburg 41 F2
Kornofoléa 57 D1
Kornwestheim 38 B4
Koromacno 50 A3
Koróna 55 E1
Koróni 62 C3
Korónia 59 E2
Korónia, L 55 F2
Koronída 64 C1
Koronissía 58 B1
Kóronos 64 C1
Koronoúda 55 E2
Koropí 59 F3
Körös 80 C2
Korosten' 79 E4
Korostyšev 79 E4
Korouoma 71 E1
Korpilahti 73 D2
Korpilombolo 70 C1
Korpo 72 C4
Korppoo 72 C4
Korsberga 77 E2
Korsfjorden 74 A3
Korsholm 70 C4
Korsnäs 70 C4
Korsør 76 C3
Korsun-Ševčenkovskij 81 E1
Korsvoll 68 B3
Kortesjärvi 70 C4
Kórthio 60 C3
Kortrijk 34 A3
Kortteenperä 71 D1
Korvala 71 D1
Korvaluoma 72 C3
Korvatunturi 67 F3
Kos 65 E1
Kosančić 53 E2
Kosanica 51 E4
Kościan 78 B4
Kościerzyna 78 B3
Kosel 54 C1
Koserow 37 F1
Košice 80 C2
Kosjerić 51 F3
Koška 51 D1
Koskenkorva 70 C4
Koskenpää 73 D2
Koski (Hameen Lääni) 73 D3
Koski (Turun ja Porin Lääni) 72 C4
Kóskina 60 B2
Koskue 72 C2
Kosmaj 52 C1
Kosmás 63 D3
Kósmio 56 C2
Kos, N 65 E1
Kosovo 53 D3
Kosovo Polje 53 D3
Kosovska Kamenica 53 E3
Kössen 40 C3
Kósta 59 E4
Kostajnica 50 C2
Kostanjevac 50 B1
Kostanjevica 50 B2
Kostenec 81 D4
Koster 74 C4
Kostolac 53 D1
Kostonjärvi 71 E2
Kostopol' 79 D4
Kóstos 64 B1
Kostrzyn 78 A4
Kosturino 53 F4
Kosula 71 E4
Koszalin 78 B3
Kőszeg 80 B2
Kotala (Keski-Suomen Lääni) 73 D2
Kotala (Lapin Lääni) 67 F4
Kótas 54 C2
Kotel 81 E4
Köthen 37 E4
Kotka 73 E4
Kotor 52 C4
Kotoriba 50 C1
Kotorsko 51 D2
Kotor Varoš 50 C3
Kotovsk (Moldavija) 81 E2
Kotovsk (Ukraina) 81 E2
Kotraža 51 F3
Kótronas 62 C4
Kotroniá 57 D1
Kötschach-Mauthen 43 E2
Köttsjön 69 E4
Kötzting 39 E3
Koufália 55 E2
Koufoníssi (Kiklådes) 64 C1
Koufoníssi (Kríti) 65 D4
Koufós 56 A3
Kouklií 54 B4
Koukounariés 59 E1
Koúla 56 B1
Kouméika 61 E3
Koúndouros 60 B4
Kounoupéli 58 B3
Koura 70 C4
Koúrenda 54 B4
Kourkoulí 59 E2
Kournás 64 B4
Kouroúta 58 B3
Koutselió 54 C4
Koutsó 56 B2
Koutsóhero 55 D4
Kouvola 73 E3
Kovačica 51 F1
Kovel' 79 D4
Kovero 71 F4
Kovin 53 D1
Köyliö 72 C3
Kozáni 55 D3
Kozáni (Nomos) 55 D3
Kozara 50 C2
Kozarac (Bosna i Hercegovina) 50 C2
Kozarac (Hrvatska) 51 D1
Kožel'sk 79 F3
Kozica 51 D4
Kozina 43 F3
Kozjak 55 D1
Kozluk 51 E2
Kožuf 53 F4
Kragenæs 76 C4
Kragerø 74 B4
Kragujevac 53 D2
Krajišnik 51 F1
Krajkovac 53 E2
Krajn 52 C4
Krakhella 74 A2
Krakow 37 E2
Kraków 80 C1
Kraljeva Sutjeska 51 D3
Kraljevica 50 A2
Kraljevo 53 D2
Kralovice 39 E2
Kralupy 39 F2
Kramfors 69 F4
Kranenburg 11 E3
Kraniá (Makedonía) 54 C3
Kraniá (Thessalía) 54 C4
Kraniá Elassónas 55 D3
Kranichfeld 39 D1
Kranídi 59 E4
Kranj 43 F2
Kranjska Gora 43 F2
Krapina 50 B1
Krapinske Toplice 50 B1
Krašić 50 B2
Krāslava 79 D2
Kraslice 39 E2
Krasná Lípa 39 F1
Kraśnik 78 C4
Krasno Polje 50 A3
Krasnyj Cholm 79 F1
Krasnystaw 78 C4
Kráthio 59 D3
Krátigos 61 E1
Kratovo 53 F3
Kratovska-Stena 51 F3
Krauchenwies 42 B1
Krautheim 38 C3
Kravarsko 50 B2
Krefeld 11 F3
Kremastí (Pelopónissos) 63 D3
Kremastí (Ródos) 65 F2
Kremastón, Teh L 58 C1
Kremenčug 81 F1
Kremenčugskoje Vodochranilišče 81 F1
Kremenec 81 D1
Kremídi, Akr 63 D3
Kremmen 37 F3
Kremna 51 E3
Kremnica 80 B2
Krems 41 E2
Kremsmünster 41 D3
Krepoljin 53 D1
Kreševo 51 D3
Krestcy 79 E1
Kréstena 58 C4
Kreuth 40 B3
Kreuzbergpass 43 E2
Kreuzlingen 42 B1
Kreuztal 38 A1
Kría Vríssi (Évia) 59 E2
Kría Vríssi (Makedonía) 55 D2
Kričev 79 E3
Krieglach 41 E3
Kriens 42 A2
Kríkelo 58 C2
Kríkelos 58 B1
Kríkelos, Akr 65 E1
Krimml 43 D2
Krimmler Wasserfälle 43 D2
Krimpen 11 D3
Krinídes 56 A2
Krionéri (Makedonía) 55 F2
Krionéri (Pelopónissos) 58 C4
Krionéri (Pelopónissos) 59 D3
Kriopigí 55 F3
Kriós, Akr 64 A4
Kristalopigí 54 C2
Kristdala 77 E2
Kristiansand 74 B4
Kristianstad 77 D3
Kristianstads Län 77 D3
Kristiansund 68 B4
Kristiinankaupunki 72 C2
Kristineberg 69 F2
Kristinehamn 75 D4
Kristinehov 77 D3
Kristinestad 72 C2
Krithéa 55 E2
Krithína, Óros 63 D4
Kríti, N 64 C3
Kritinía 65 F2
Kritsá 65 D4
Kriva Feja 53 E3
Krivaja (Bosna i Hercegovina) 51 D3
Krivaja (Vojvodina) 51 E1
Kriva Palanka 53 F3
Kriva reka 53 E3
Krivogaštani 53 E4
Krivoj Rog 81 F1
Krivolak 53 F4
Křižanov 41 E1
Križevci 50 B1
Krk 50 A2
Krk *I* 50 A2
Krka 50 A1
Krka *R* 50 B3
Krkonoše 80 A1
Krmčine 50 B3
Krn 43 F2
Krnjača 52 C1
Krnjak 50 B2
Krnjeuša 50 B3
Krnjevo 53 D1
Krnov 80 B1
Krnovo 52 C3
Krøderen 74 C3
Krokeés 63 D3
Krokeide 74 A3
Krokek 75 E4
Krokílio 58 C2
Krokom 69 E4
Krókos 55 D3
Kroksjö 69 F3
Krolevec 79 F4
Kröller Müller 11 E3
Kroměříž 80 B1
Kronach 39 D2
Kronobergs Län 77 D2
Kronoby 70 C3
Kronshagen 36 C1
Kronštadt 79 D1
Kröpelin 37 D1
Kropp 36 C1
Kroppenstedt 37 D4
Krosno 80 C1
Krosno Odrzańskie 78 A4
Krotoszyn 78 B4
Kroussónas 64 C4
Krovíli, Pal. 56 C2
Krrabe, M 53 D4
Krško 50 B1
Krstac 52 B3
Krstača 51 F4
Krstinja 50 B2
Kruë i Fushës 52 C4
Kruiningen 11 D3
Krujë 54 A1
Krumbach 40 A3
Krumpendorf 43 F2
Krün 40 B4
Krupà 39 F2
Krupac (Bosna i Hercegovina) 51 D3
Krupac (Crna Gora) 52 B3
Krupac (Srbija) 53 F2
Krupaja 53 D1
Krupa na Vrbasu 50 C3
Krupanj 51 E2
Krupište 53 F4
Krupka 39 F1
Kruså 76 B4
Kruščica 51 D3
Kruščica, Jezero 50 B3
Krušedol Selo 51 E2
Kruševac 53 D2
Kruševica 52 C1
Kruševo 53 E4
Krute 52 C4
Kruunupyy 70 C3
Krvavec 50 A1
Krynica 80 C1
Ktenías, Óros 59 D4
Ktísmata 54 B4
Kubitzer Bodden 37 E1
Küblis 42 C2
Kučaj 53 E1
Kučevište 53 E4
Kučevo 53 D1
Kuchl 40 C3
Kučina Kosa 50 B3
Kućište 51 F4
Kućište 52 A3
Kudowa-Zdrój 80 B1
Kufstein 40 C3
Kühlungsborn 37 D1
Kuhmalahti 73 D3
Kuhmo 71 F3
Kuhmoinen 73 D3
Kuivajärvi 71 F2
Kuivajoki 71 D2
Kuivalahti 72 C3
Kuivaniemi 71 D2
Kuivasjärvi 72 C2
Kuivi 67 E2
Kukavica 53 E3
Kukës 53 D4
Kukkia 73 D3
Kukko 71 D4
Kukujevci 51 E2
Kukulje 50 C2
Kula (BG) 81 D3
Kula (YU) 51 E1
Kuldīga 78 C2
Kulennoinen 73 F2
Kulen Vakuf 50 B3
Kulina 53 E2
Kulju 73 D3
Kulkjica 50 B3
Kullaa 72 C3
Kulm 42 A2
Kulmbach 39 D2
Kuloharju 71 E1

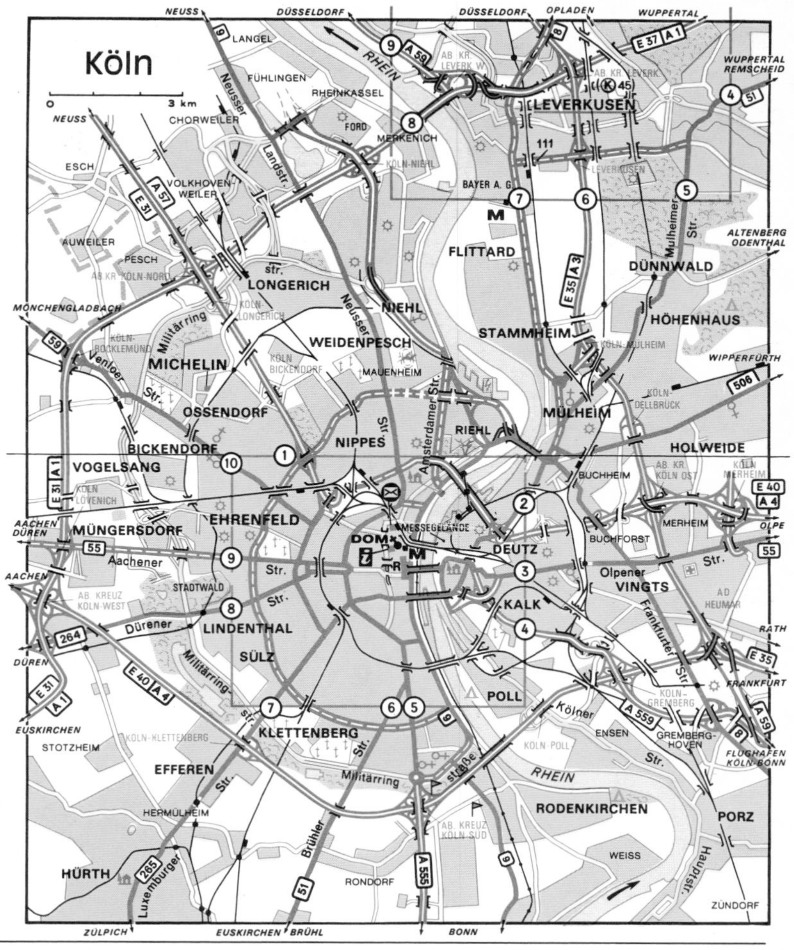

Köln
0
3 km
NEUSS
DÜSSELDORF
OPLADEN
WUPPERTAL
LANGEL
FÜHLINGEN
RHEINKASSEL
CHORWEILER
LEVERKUSEN
WUPPERTAL REMSCHEID
ESCH
AUWEILER
PESCH
VOLKHOVEN-WEILER
MERKENICH
FORD
BAYER A. G.
FLITTARD
DÜNNWALD
ALTENBERG ODENTHAL
LONGERICH
NIEHL
MÖNCHENGLADBACH
STAMMHEIM
HÖHENHAUS
WEIDENPESCH
MICHELIN
WIPPERFÜRTH
OSSENDORF
MÜLHEIM
BICKENDORF
NIPPES
RIEHL
HOLWEIDE
VOGELSANG
EHRENFELD
BUCHHEIM
MERHEIM
AACHEN DÜREN
MÜNGERSDORF
DEUTZ
BUCHFORST
OLPE
AACHEN
KALK
VINGTS
LINDENTHAL
SÜLZ
RATH
DÜREN
POLL
FRANKFURT
EUSKIRCHEN
STOTZHEIM
KLETTENBERG
ENSEN
GREMBERG-HOVEN
FLUGHAFEN KÖLN/BONN
EFFEREN
RHEIN
RODENKIRCHEN
HERMÜLHEIM
PORZ
WEISS
HÜRTH
RONDORF
ZÜNDORF
ZÜLPICH
EUSKIRCHEN
BRÜHL
BONN

Külsheim 38 C3
Kultakero 67 F4
Kultsjön 69 E2
Kum 50 A1
Kumane 51 E1
Kumanovo 53 E4
Kumla 75 E4
Kumlinge 72 C4
Kummavuopio 66 C2
Kummerower See 37 E1
Kumputunturi 67 E3
Kumrovec 50 B1
Kungälv 76 C1
Kungsbacka 76 C2
Kungshamn 74 C4
Kungsör 75 E4
Kunoy 68 A3
Kunrau 37 D3
Kunszentmárton 80 C2
Künzelsau 38 C3
Kuolimo 73 E3
Kuolio 71 E1
Kuopio 71 E4
Kuopion Lääni 71 E4
Kuorboaivi 67 E2
Kuorevesi 73 D3
Kuortane 72 C2
Kuortovare 67 D3
Kuortti 73 E3
Kupa 50 A2
Kupa 50 B2
Kupferzell 38 C3
Kupinova Glava 53 E1
Kupinovo 51 E2
Kupres 50 C3
Kupreška vrata 50 C3
Kurfar 43 D2
Kurikka 70 C4
Kuřim 41 F1
Kuršėnai 78 C2
Kuršskij Zaliv 78 C3
Kursu 71 E1
Kuršumlija 53 D2
Kuršumlijska Banja 53 D3
Kurtakko 67 E3
Kuru 73 D3
Kusadak 53 D1
Kuşadasi 61 F3
Kusel 38 A3
Küsnacht 42 B2
Küssnacht 42 A2
Kustavi 72 C4
Küstenkanal 36 B3
Kutina 50 C1
Kutjevo 51 D2
Kutná-Hora 80 A1
Kutno 78 B4
Kuttanen 67 D3
Kuttura 67 E3
Kúty 41 F2
Kuumu 71 E2
Kuusamo 71 E1
Kuusamojärvi 71 E1
Kuusankoski 73 E3
Kuusjärvi 71 F4
Kuusjoki 72 C4
Kuvšinovo 79 E2
Kuzma 41 F4
Kuzmin 51 E2
Kvæfjord 66 B2
Kvænangen 67 D2
Kvænangsbotn 67 D2
Kværndrup 76 B3
Kvaløy 66 C2
Kvaløya 67 D1
Kvalsund 67 D1
Kvalvøg 68 B4
Kvam 74 C2
Kvanndal 74 B2
Kvanne 68 C4
Kvarner 50 A3
Kvarnerič 50 A3
Kvernes 68 B4
Kvevlax 70 C4
Kvikkjokk 69 F1
Kvikne 68 C4
Kvina 74 A4
Kvinesdal 74 A4
Kvinesdal V 74 A4
Kvisvik 68 B4
Kviteseid 74 B3
Kvitnes 68 B4
Kvitsøy 74 A3
Kwidzyn 78 B3
Kyjov 41 F1
Kyläinpää 70 C4
Kylänlahti 71 F3
Kyleakin 2 B2
Kyle of Lochalsh 2 B2
Kyle of Tongue 2 C1
Kylerhea 2 B2
Kylestrome 2 C1
Kyll 35 D3
Kyllburg 35 D4
Kylmäkoski 73 D3
Kylmälä 71 D3
Kymen Lääni 73 E3
Kynsivesi 73 D2
Kyritz 37 E3
Kyrksæterøra 68 C4
Kyrkslätt 73 D4
Kyrönjoki 70 C4
Kyrösjärvi 72 C3
Kyselka 39 E2
Kyšice 39 F2
Kyyjärvi 71 D4
Kyyvesi 73 E2

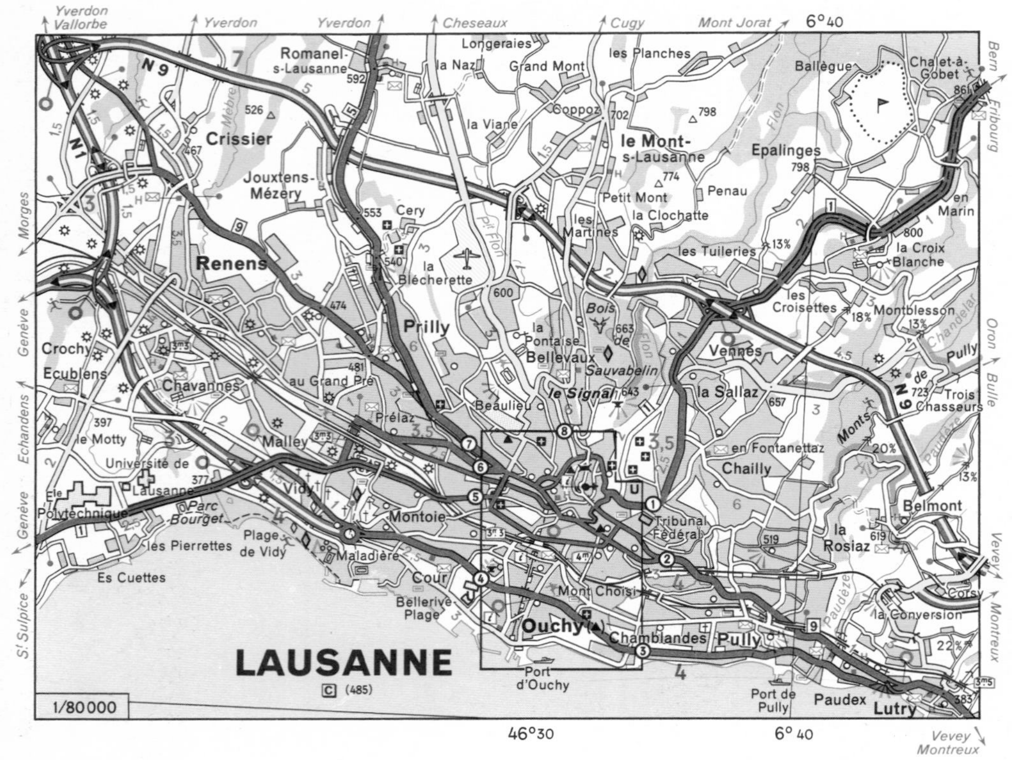

LAUSANNE
1/80000

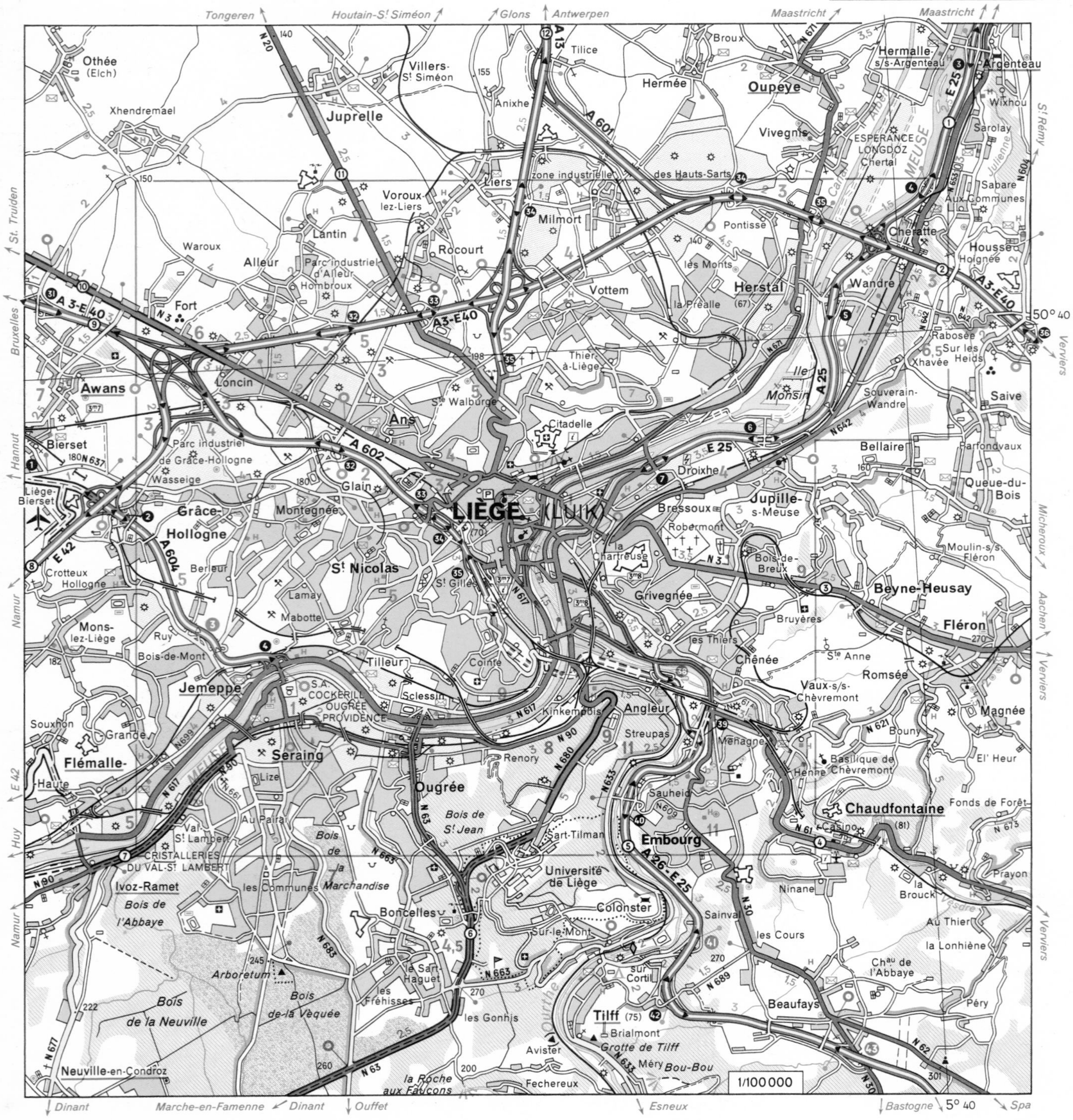

LIÈGE (LUIK)
1/100 000

L

Laa an der Thaya 41 F2
La Adrada 27 E3
Laage 37 E1
Laakajärvi 71 E3
La Alberca 27 D3
La Alberca de Záncara 28 A4
La Albuera 30 C1
La Albufera 32 C1
La Alcarria 28 A3
La Algaba 31 D3
La Almarcha 28 A4
La Almunia de Doña Godina 28 B2
La Antillas 30 B3
La Azohia 32 B3
Labacolla 24 A2
La Baells, Emb de 29 E1
Labajos 27 E2
La Bañeza 25 D2
La Barca de la Florida 31 D3
Labasheeda 8 B3
Labastida 20 A4
Labastide-Clairence 20 B3
Labastide-Murat 21 D2
Labastide-Rouairoux 21 E3
Labe 39 F1
Labin 43 F4
Labinot Fushë 54 B1
La Bisbal de Falset 29 D2
La Bisbal d'Empordà 29 F2
Laboe 36 C1
Labouheyre 20 B2
Labouret, Col du 22 C2
La Bóveda de Toro 25 D4
La Brède 20 C2
Labrit 20 C3
Labruguière 21 E3
Labudnjača 51 E1
Laç 52 C4
La Cabrera 27 F2
Lacalahorra 31 F3
La Campana 31 D3
Lacanau 20 B2
Lacanau-Océan 20 B2
Lacapelle-Marival 21 E2
Laćarak 51 E2
La Carlota 31 E2
La Carolina 31 F2
Lacaune 21 E3
Lacaune, Mts de 21 E3
La Cava 29 D3
La Cazada de Oropesa 27 D3
Lacedonia 46 C1
Läckö 75 D4
Lac Léman 19 E2
La Codosera 26 C4
Laconi 46 B3
La Coronada 31 D1
La Coruña 24 B1
Lacq 20 C3
La Cumbre 27 D4
Ladbergen 36 B4
Ládi 57 D1
Ladispoli 44 C4
Ladoeiro 26 C3
Ladožskoje Ozero 79 D1
Lærdalsøyri 74 B2
Láerma 65 F2
Læsø 76 C2
La Espina 24 C1
La Felguera 25 D1
Laferté 15 D4
Laffrey 22 C2
Láfka 59 D3
Láfkos 59 E1
Lafnitz 41 F3
La Franca, 25 E1
Lafrançaise 21 D3
La Fregeneda 26 C2
La Frontera 28 B3
La Fuente de San Esteban 27 D2
Lagan 77 D2
Lagan R 77 D2
Laganá, Kólpos 58 B3
Laganás 58 B3
Lagarfljót 68 C1
La Garganta 24 C1
La Garriga 29 F2
Lagartera 27 D3
Lagastrello, Pso di 44 A1
Lage 36 C4
Lågen (Buskerud) 74 C3
Lagen (Oppland) 74 C1
Laggan 2 C2
Laggan, L 2 C2
Laginá (Makedonía) 55 E2
Laginá (Thráki) 57 D2
La Gineta 32 B1
Lagnieu 19 D3
Lagny 14 B3
Lago 47 D3
Lagoa 30 A3
Lagoaça 24 C4
Lagonegro 47 D2
Lagoníssi 59 F3
Lagos 30 A3
Lágos 56 B2
La Granjuèla 31 D2
Lagrasse 21 E4
Laguardia 20 A4
La Guardia 27 F4
La Guardia de Jaén 31 F2
Laguarres 29 D1
Laguarta 28 C1
Laguiole 21 F2
Laguna de Duero 25 E3
Lahanás 55 F2
La Hermida 25 E2
La Herradura 31 F4
Lahinch 8 B3
Lahn 38 B1
Lahnstein 38 A2
Laholm 77 D2
Laholmsbukten 76 C2
La Horcajada 27 D3
La Horra 25 E3
Lahr Schwarzwald 38 A4
Lahti 73 D3
Laichingen 38 C4
Laide 2 B1
La Iglesuela del Cid 28 C3
Laignes 14 C4
Laigueglia 23 E3
Laihia 70 C4
Laïliás 55 F1
Laimbach 41 E2
Laimoluokta 66 C3
Lainate 42 B4
Lainioälven 67 D3
Lairg 2 C1
Laissac 21 E3
Laïsta 54 C3
Laisvall 69 F2
Laitikkala 73 D3
Laitila 72 C3
La Jana 29 D3
Lajkovac 52 C1
La Jonquera 29 F1
Laká 58 A1
Lakavica 53 F4
Lake District Nat Pk 5 D3
Lakí 61 E4
Láki 64 A3
Lákmos, Óri 54 C4
Lákoma 56 C3
Lákones 54 A4
Lakonía 63 D3
Lakonikós Kólpos 63 D4
Lakópetra 58 C3
Laksefjorden 67 E1
Lakselv 67 E1
Laktaši 50 C2
La Laguna 30 A4
La Lantejuela 31 D3
Lálas 58 C3
Lalbenque 21 D2
L'Alcudia 32 C1
L'Aldea 29 D3
Lalín 24 B2
Lalinac 53 E2
Lalinde 21 D2
La Línea de la Concepción 31 D4
Laliótis 59 D3
Lalm 74 C2
La Losa 32 A2
Lalouvesc 19 D4
Lalueza 28 C2
La Luisiana 31 D3
Lalzit, Gjiri i 54 A1
Lam 39 E3
Lama dei Peligni 45 E3
La Magdalena 25 D2
Lamalou 21 F3
La Manche 7 D4
La Manga del Mar Menor 32 C3
Lamarche 15 D4
La Marmora, P 46 B3
Lamarque 20 C1
Lamastre 22 B2
Lambach 41 D3
Lamballe 12 C3
Lambesc 22 B3
Lámbia 58 C3
Lambíri 58 C2
Lámbou Míli 61 D1
Lambrecht 38 A3
Lamego 24 B4
La Mesa Roldán 32 B3
L'Ametlla 29 D3
Lamía 59 D1
Lamlash 2 B4
Lammermuir Hills 3 D4
Lammhult 77 D2
Lammi 73 D3
La Molina 29 E1
Lamotte-Beuvron 18 A1
Lampaul 12 A3
Lampedusa 48 A4
Lampedusa, I di 48 A4
Lampertheim 38 B3
Lampeter 6 B2
L'Ampolla 29 D3
Lamstedt 36 C2
La Mudarra 25 D3
La Muela 28 C2
Lamure 18 C3
Lana 43 D2
Lanaja 28 C2
Lanaken 34 C3
Lanark 5 D1
La Nava de Ricomalillo 27 E4
La Nava de Santiago 26 C4
Lancashire 5 D3
Lancaster 5 D3
Lanchester 5 E2
Lanciano 45 E3
Landau (Bayern) 39 E4
Landau (Rheinland-Pfalz) 38 B3
Landeck 40 A4
Landerneau 12 B3
Landes 20 B3
Landes de Lanvaux 12 C4
Landete 28 B4
Landévennec 12 B3
Landivisiau 12 B3
Landivy 13 D3
Landmannalaugar 68 B2
Landquart 42 B2
Landrecies 14 B2
Landriano 42 B4
Landsberg 37 E4
Landsberg 40 B3
Land's End 6 A4
Landshut 39 E4
Landskapet Åland 72 B4
Landskrona 76 C3
Landstuhl 38 A3
Landverk 69 D4
Lanersbach 43 D2
Lanesborough 8 C2
Langáda (Híos) 61 D2
Langáda (Pelopónissos) 62 C3
Langadás 55 E2
Langádas 62 C3
Langa de Duero 25 F3
Langádia 58 C3
Langadíkia 55 F2
Langangen 74 C4
Langeac 21 F1
Langeais 17 E2
Langeland 76 C3
Langelandsbælt 76 C4
Langelmäki 73 D3
Langelmävesi 73 D3
Langelsheim 37 D4
Langen (Hessen) 38 B3
Langen (Niedersachsen) 36 B2
Langenargen 42 B1
Langenau 38 C4
Langenberg 39 D1
Langenbruck 39 D4
Langenburg 38 C3
Langeneß 36 B1
Langenfeld 35 D3
Längenfeld 40 B4
Langenhagen 36 C3
Langenhahn 38 A2
Langenlois 41 E2
Langenthal 42 A2
Langenwang 41 E3
Langenzenn 39 D3
Langeoog 36 B2
Långeserud 75 D4
Langeskov 76 B3
Langesund 74 C4
Langevåg 68 B4
Langevåg 74 A3
Långfjället 75 D1
Langfjord 67 D1
Langfjorden 67 E1
Langfjordjøkelen 67 D1
Langforden 68 B4
Langhirano 44 A1
Langholm 5 D2
Langjökull 68 B2
Langnau 42 A2
Langogne 22 A2
Langon 20 C2
Langøya 66 B2
Langport 6 C3
Langres 15 D4
Langrune 13 E2
Långsele 69 F4
Långshyttan 75 E3
Långträsk 70 B2
Lanjarón 31 F3
Lanke 37 F3
Länkipohja 73 D3
Lanmeur 12 B3
Lannemezan 20 C4
Lannilis 12 A3
Lannion 12 B3
Lanouaille 17 F4
Lans-en-Vercors 19 D4
Lanslebourg 19 E4
Lanta 21 D3
Lantosque 23 D3
La Nuez de Arriba 25 E2
Lanusei 46 B3
Lanvollon 12 C3
Lanzahita 27 E3
Lanzarote 30 B4
Lanzo Torinese 23 D1
Laois 8 C3
La Oliva (Is Canarias) 30 B4
La Oliva (Navarra) 28 B1
Laon 14 B2
La Orotava 30 A4
La Paca 32 B2
Lapalisse 18 C3
La Palma 30 A4
La Palma del Condado 30 C3
La Panadella 29 E2
Lápas 58 C3
Lapa, Sa da 26 C2
Laperdiguera 29 D2
La Pinilla 25 F4
Lapinjärvi 73 E3
Lapin Lääni 67 E3
Lapinlahti 71 E3

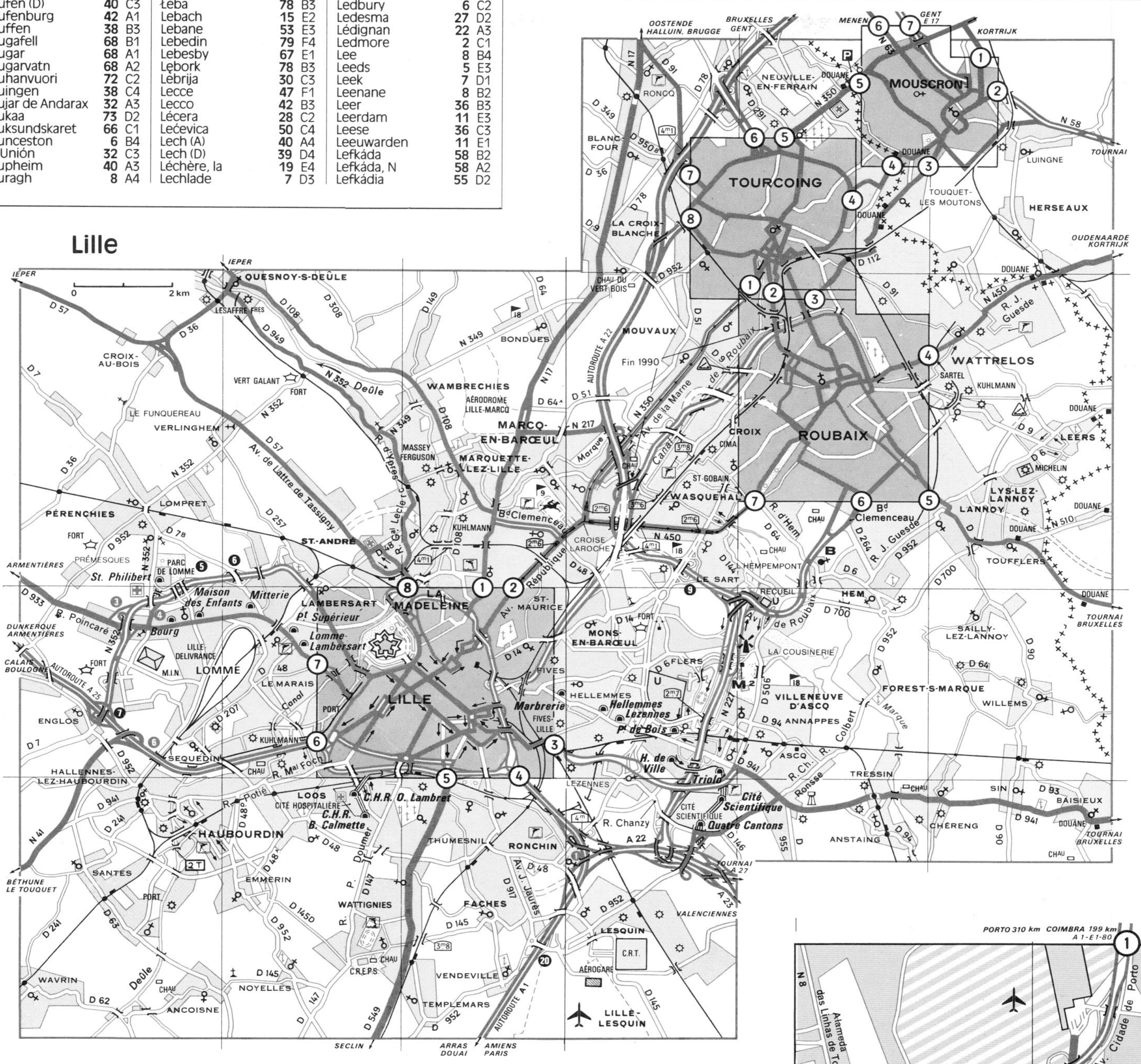
Lille
0
2 km
IEPER
QUESNOY-S-DEÛLE
OOSTENDE HALLUIN, BRUGGE
BRUXELLES GENT
MENEN
GENT E 17
KORTRIJK
NEUVILLE-EN-FERRAIN
MOUSCRON
RONCQ
TOURCOING
LUINGNE
HERSEAUX
TOUQUET-LES MOUTONS
OUDENAARDE KORTRIJK
LA CROIX-BLANCHE
BLANC FOUR
MOUVAUX
BONDUES
CROIX-AU-BOIS
VERT GALANT
WAMBRECHIES
MARCQ-EN-BARŒUL
MARQUETTE-LEZ-LILLE
WATTRELOS
ROUBAIX
CROIX
WASQUEHAL
LYS-LEZ-LANNOY
LANNOY
TOUFFLERS
PÉRENCHIES
VERLINGHEM
LOMPRET
ST-ANDRÉ
LA MADELEINE
LAMBERSART
St. Philibert
Maison des Enfants
Mitterie
LOMME
Bourg
DUNKERQUE ARMENTIÈRES
CALAIS BOULOGNE
ARMENTIÈRES
ENGLOS
SEQUEDIN
LILLE
MONS-EN-BARŒUL
HEM
SAILLY-LEZ-LANNOY
FOREST-S-MARQUE
WILLEMS
VILLENEUVE D'ASCQ
Hellemmes Lezennes
ANNAPPES
ASCQ
TRESSIN
Triolo
Cité Scientifique
Quatre Cantons
BAISIEUX
CHÉRENG
ANSTAING
TOURNAI BRUXELLES
HALLENNES-LEZ-HAUBOURDIN
HAUBOURDIN
LOOS
C.H.R. O. Lambret
C.H.R. B. Calmette
THUMESNIL
RONCHIN
EMMERIN
SANTES
WATTIGNIES
FACHES
LESQUIN
VENDEVILLE
TEMPLEMARS
LILLE-LESQUIN
NOYELLES
WAVRIN
ANCOISNE
BÉTHUNE LE TOUQUET
SECLIN
ARRAS DOUAI
AMIENS PARIS
VALENCIENNES
TOURNAI A 27
A 22
Deûle

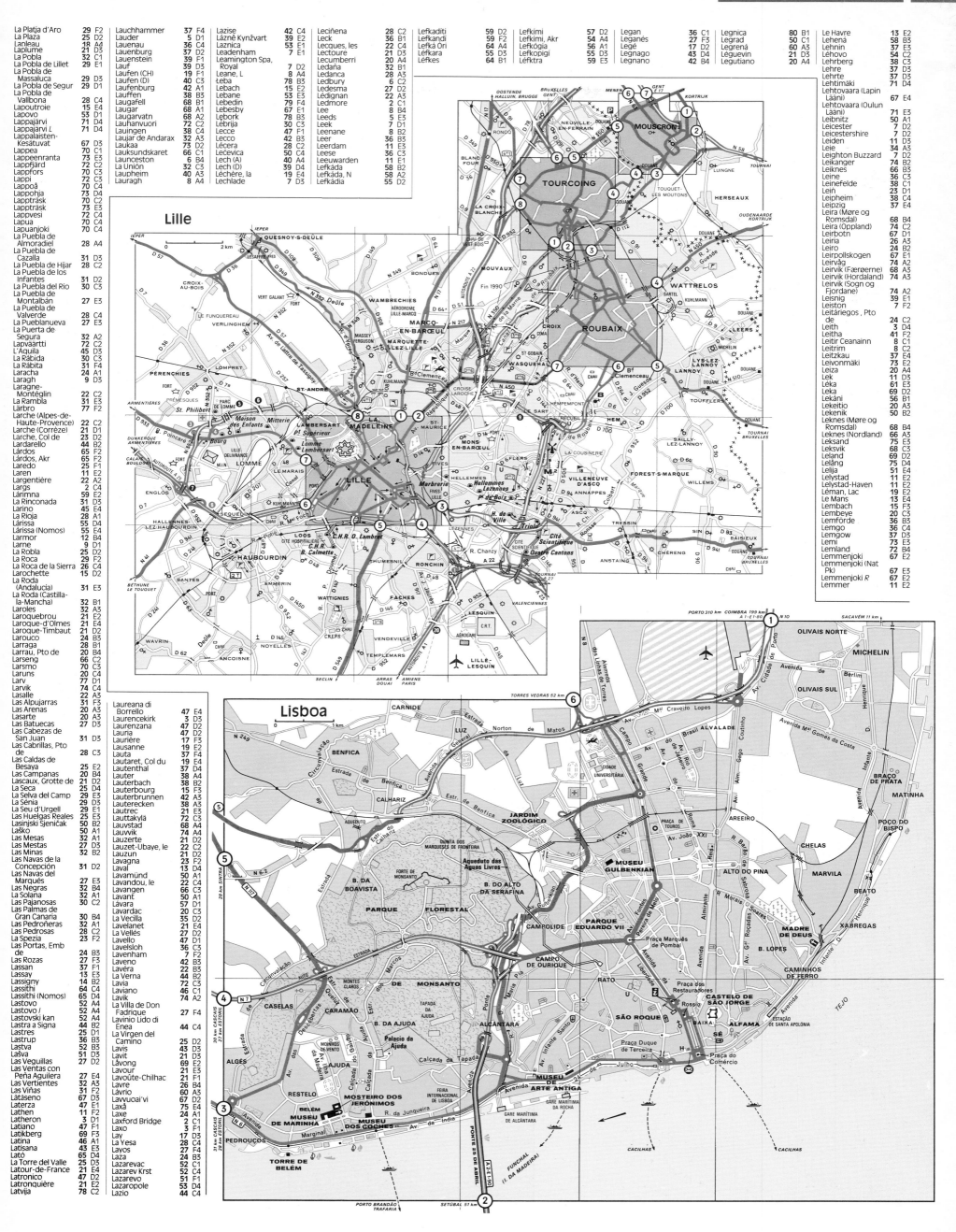

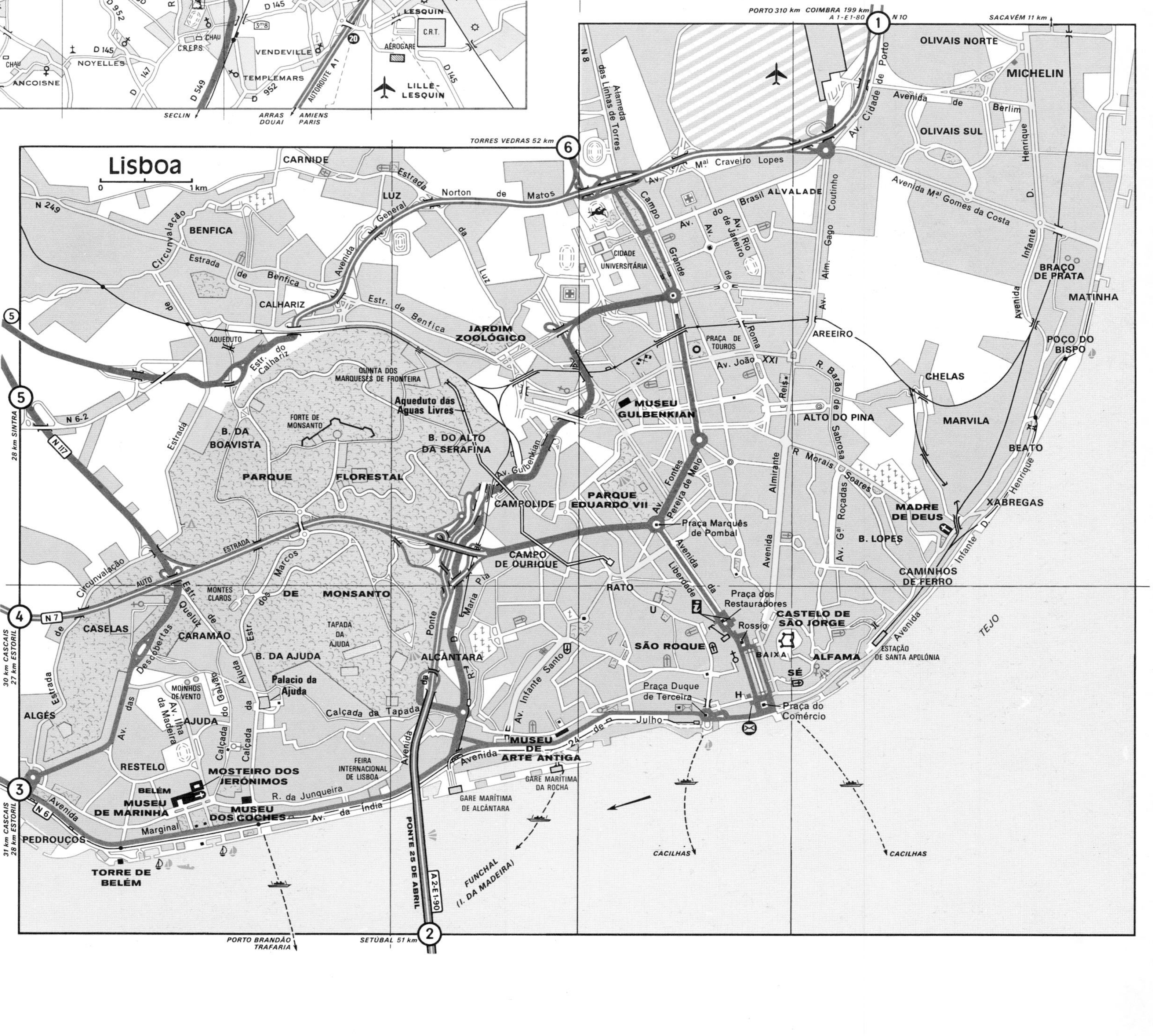
Lisboa
0
1 km
PORTO 310 km COIMBRA 199 km
SACAVÉM 11 km
TORRES VEDRAS 52 km
OLIVAIS NORTE
MICHELIN
OLIVAIS SUL
CARNIDE
LUZ
BENFICA
ALVALADE
CIDADE UNIVERSITÁRIA
CALHARIZ
JARDIM ZOOLÓGICO
PRAÇA DE TOUROS
AREEIRO
CHELAS
MARVILA
BRAÇO DE PRATA
MATINHA
POÇO DO BISPO
Aqueduto das Aguas Livres
MUSEU GULBENKIAN
ALTO DO PINA
B. DA BOAVISTA
B. DO ALTO DA SERAFINA
PARQUE FLORESTAL
PARQUE EDUARDO VII
CAMPOLIDE
Praça Marquês de Pombal
BEATO
XABREGAS
MADRE DE DEUS
B. LOPES
CAMINHOS DE FERRO
CAMPO DE OURIQUE
DE MONSANTO
RATO
Praça dos Restauradores
CASTELO DE SÃO JORGE
SÃO ROQUE
ALFAMA
BAIXA
SÉ
CASELAS
CARAMÃO
B. DA AJUDA
Palacio da Ajuda
ALCÂNTARA
AJUDA
ALGÉS
RESTELO
MOSTEIRO DOS JERÓNIMOS
MUSEU DE MARINHA
MUSEU DOS COCHES
MUSEU DE ARTE ANTIGA
FEIRA INTERNACIONAL DE LISBOA
GARE MARÍTIMA DA ROCHA
GARE MARÍTIMA DE ALCÂNTARA
TORRE DE BELÉM
PEDROUÇOS
BELÉM
PONTE 25 DE ABRIL
Praça do Comércio
Praça Duque de Terceira
ESTAÇÃO DE SANTA APOLÓNIA
TEJO
CACILHAS
FUNCHAL (I. DA MADEIRA)
PORTO BRANDÃO TRAFARIA
SETÚBAL 51 km
28 km SINTRA
30 km CASCAIS 27 km ESTORIL
31 km CASCAIS 28 km ESTORIL

Lemonodássos 59 E4
Lempäälä 73 D3
Lempdes 18 B4
Lemvig 76 B2
Lenart 50 B1
Lencloître 17 E2
Lend 40 C4
Léndas 64 C4
Lendava 41 F4
Lendava *R* 41 F4
Lendinara 43 D4
Lengefeld 39 E1
Lengenfeld 39 E2
Lengerich 36 B4
Lenggries 40 B3
Lenhovda 77 E2
Leningrad 79 D1
Lenk 19 E2
Lenne 38 A1
Lennestadt 38 A1
Lens 14 B1
Lensahn 37 D1
Lentföhrden 36 C2
Lenti 80 B2
Lentiira 71 F2
Lenting 39 D4
Lentini 49 D4
Lentua 71 F3
Lenvik 66 C2
Lenzburg 42 A2
Lenzen 37 D2
Lenzerheide Valbella 42 B2
Lenzkirch 42 A1
Leoben 41 E3
Leobersdorf 41 F3
Leogang 40 C3
Leominster 6 C2
Léon 20 B3
León 25 D2
Leonberg 38 B4
Léoncel 22 B2
Leondári (Pelopónissos) 58 C4
Leondári (Thessalía) 59 D1
Leóndio 59 D3
Leonessa 44 C3
Leonforte 48 C3
Leonídio 59 D4
León, Mtes de 24 C2
León, Pto del 31 E3
Leopoldsburg 34 C3
Leopoldsdorf 41 F2
Leopoldsteinersee 41 E3
Leovo 81 E2
Lepe 30 B3
Lepel' 79 D3
Lepenoú 58 B2
Lepenski vir 53 E1
Lepetane 52 B4
Lepoglava 50 B1
Leposavić 53 D3
Lépoura 60 A2
Leppäjärvi 67 D3
Leppävirta 71 E4
Leptokariá (Makedonía) 55 E3
Leptokariá (Thráki) 56 C2
Lercara Friddi 48 C3
Léré 18 B1
Lerici 23 F2
Lérida 29 D2
Lerín 28 B1
Lérins 23 D3
Lerma 25 E3
Lermoos 40 B4
Lérni 59 D4
Léros, N 61 E4
Lerum 76 C1
Lerwick 3 F2
Les 21 D4
Lešak 53 D3
Lešani 54 C1
Les Borges Blanques 29 D2
L'Escala 29 F2
Lescar 20 C3
Lesce 43 F2
Lešće 50 B2
Lescun 20 B4
Leshnicë 54 B2
Lesima, Mte 23 E2
Lesina 45 F3
Lesina, L di 45 F3
Lesja 74 C1
Lesjöfors 75 D3
Leskovac 53 E3
Les Llosses 29 E1
Lesneven 12 B3
Lešnica 51 E2
Lesparre-Médoc 20 B1
L'Espina 29 D3
L'Espluga de Francolí 29 E2
Les Portes de Fer 53 E1
L'Espunyola 29 E2
Lessay 13 D3
Lessebo 77 E2
Lessines 34 B3
Lessíni 58 B2
L'Estartit 29 F2
Lestelle-Bétharram 20 C4
Lestijärvi 71 D3
Lestijoki 71 D3
Lestkov 39 E2
Lésvos, N 61 D1
Leszno 78 B4
Letchworth 7 E2
Letenye 80 B3
Letino 46 B1
Letmathe 38 A1
Letterfrack 8 A2
Letterkenny 8 C1
Lettermullan 8 A2
Letur 32 B2
Letuš 50 A1
Letzlingen 37 D3
Leuca 47 F2
Leuchars 3 D3
Leuk 42 A3
Leukerbad 42 A3
Łeuna 37 E4
Leutenberg 39 D2
Leutershausen 38 C3
Leutkirch 40 A3
Leutschach 50 A1
Leuven 34 B3
Leuze 34 A3
Levajok 67 E1
Levanger 69 D3
Levanjska Varoš 51 D2
Levant, I du 22 C4
Levanto 23 F2
Levanzo, I di 48 A3
Levásjoki 72 C3
Leven (England) 5 F3
Leven (Scotland) 3 D3
Levene 77 D1
Levens 23 D3
Leverano 47 F2
Leverburgh 2 B1
Leverkusen 35 D3
Levet 18 F3
Levi 67 E3
Levice 80 B2
Levico Terme 43 D3
Levídi 59 D3
Levie 23 D4
Levier 19 E2
Levítha, N 65 D1
Levoča 80 C1
Levroux 18 A2
Lévy, Cap 13 D2
Lewes 7 E4
Lewis 2 B1
Leyburn 5 E3
Leyland 5 D4
Leyre 20 B4
Leysdown-on-Sea 7 F3
Leysin 19 E3
Lézardrieux 12 C3
Lézat 21 D4
Lezay 17 E3
Lezhë 52 C4
Lézignan-Corbières 21 E4
Ležimir 51 E2
Lezoux 18 C3
Lezuza 32 A1
L'gov 79 F3
L'Hospitalet de l'Infant 29 D3
Liabygda 68 B4
Liákoura 59 D2
Lianokládi 59 D1
Liathach 2 C2
Liberec 80 A1
Libochovice 39 F2
Libourne 20 C2
Librazhd 54 B1
Librilla 32 B2
Licata 48 C4
Licciana Nardi 44 A1
Lich 38 B2
Lichfield 7 D2
Lichoslavl' 79 F1
Lichtenberg 39 D2
Lichtenfels 39 D2
Lichtenstein 39 E1
Lichtenvoorde 11 F3
Lička Jesenica 50 B2
Lički Osik 50 B3
Ličko Lešće 50 B3
Lida 79 D3
Liddel Water 5 D2
Liden 69 F4
Lidhult 77 D2
Lidingö 75 F4
Lidköping 75 D4
Lido degli Estensi 44 C1
Lido delle Nazioni 44 C1
Lido di Camaiore 44 A2
Lido di Classe 44 C1
Lido di Jesolo 43 E3
Lido di Metaponto 47 E2
Lido di Ostia 44 C4
Lido di Savio 44 C1
Lido di Spina 44 C1
Lido di Venezia 43 E4
Lidoríki 59 D2
Lido Silvana 47 E2
Lidzbark Warmiński 78 B3
Liebenwalde 37 F3
Liège 34 C3
Liège (Prov) 34 C3
Lieksa 71 F3
Lienz 43 E2
Liepāja 78 C2
Lier 34 B3
Liérganes 25 F2
Liernais 18 C2
Lieser 41 D4
Liesjärvi 73 D4
Liestal 19 F1
Lieto 72 C4
Liétor 32 B2
Lieurey 13 E3
Lievestuore 73 E2
Liévin 14 B1
Liezen 41 D3
Liffey 9 D3
Liffol-le-Grand 15 D4
Lifford 8 C1
Liffré 13 D4
Lifjell 74 B3
Ligiá 58 B3
Lignano Sabbiadoro 43 E3
Ligné 17 D1
Lignières 18 F3
Ligny-en-Barrois 15 D3
Ligny-le-Châtel 14 C4
Ligourió 59 E4
Ligueil 17 F2
Liguria 23 E2
Lihàda 59 D2
Liikasenvaara 71 E1
Lijeva Rijeka 52 C3
Lijevi Dubravčak 50 B1
Lika 50 B3
Likenås 75 D3
Líkeo, Óri 58 C4
Likódimo, Óros 62 C3
Likófos 57 D2
Likoporiá 59 D3
Likórahi 54 C3
Likóstomo 56 B2
Likouría 59 D3
Liland 66 B3
Lílea 59 D2
Lilienfeld 41 E3
Liljendal 73 E4
Lilla Edet 76 C1
Lillby 70 C4
Lille 14 B1
Lille Bælt 76 B3
Lillebonne 13 E2
Lillehammer 74 C2
Lillerød 76 C3
Lillers 14 B1
Lillesand 74 B4
Lillestrøm 74 C3
Lillhärdal 75 D2
Lillo 27 F4
Lillögda 69 F3
Lillsholmsjön 69 E3
Lim 51 E3
Lima 75 D2
Limáni Hersonissou 64 C4
Limáni Litohórou 55 E3
Lima, R 24 A3
Limavady 4 A2
Limbach 39 E1
Limbara, M 46 B2
Limburg (B) 34 C3
Limburg (D) 38 A2
Limburg (NL) 11 E3
Limenária 56 B2
Limerick 8 B3
Limerick (Co) 8 B3
Limfjorden 76 B2
Limia, R 24 B3
Limingen 69 E3
Limingen *R* 69 D3
Liminka 71 D2
Liminpuro 71 E3
Limljani 52 C4
Límnes 59 D3
Límni 59 E2
Limniá 56 B2
Limnítsa 58 C2
Límnos, N 56 C4
Limoges 17 F3
Limogne 21 E2
Limone Piemonte 23 D2
Limonest 19 D3
Limours 14 A3
Limoux 21 E4
Lin 54 B2
Linares 31 F2
Linares del Arroyo, Emb de 25 F4

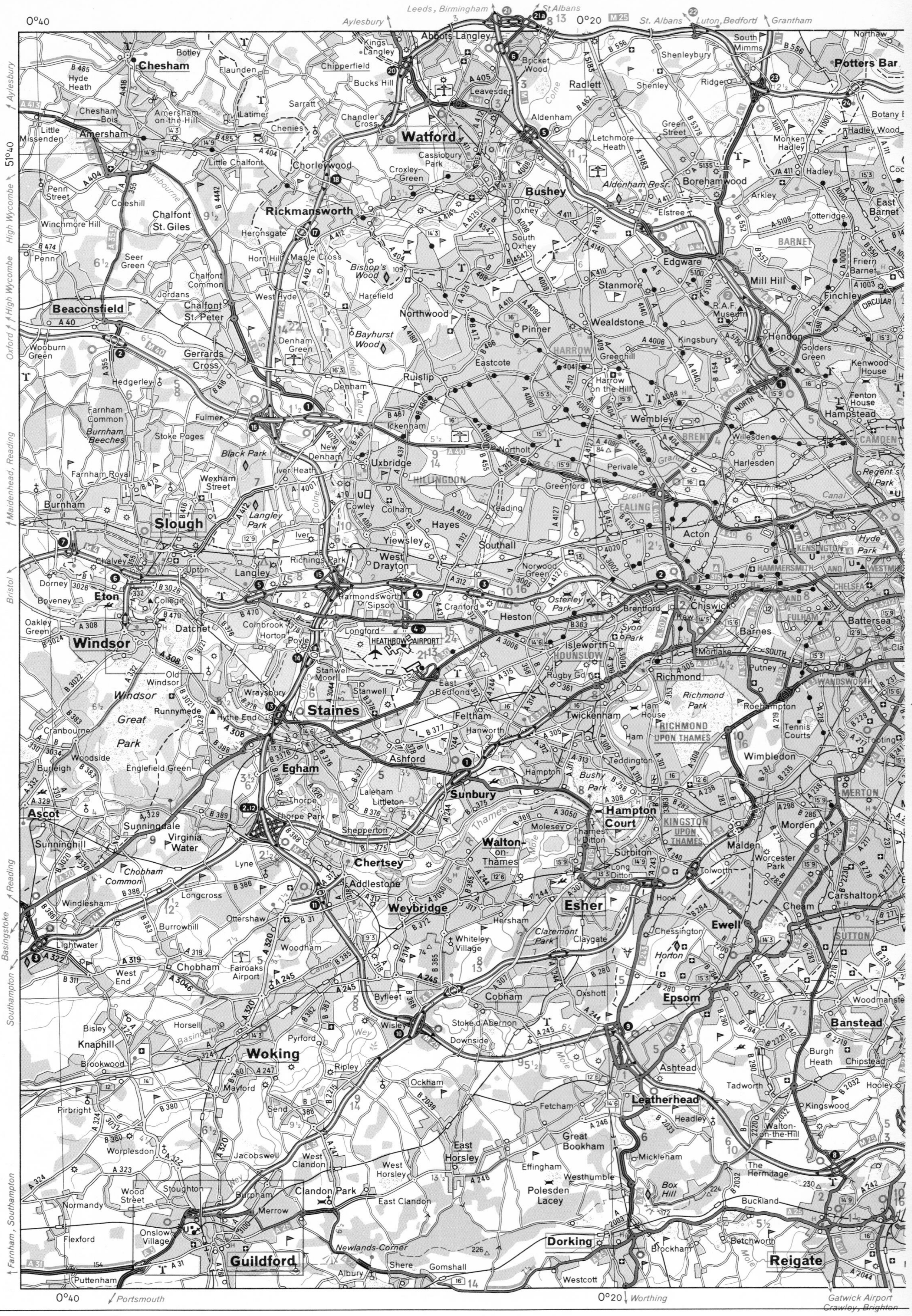

Aylesbury
Leeds, Birmingham
St. Albans
Luton, Bedford
Grantham
Chesham
Amersham
Watford
Rickmansworth
Bushey
Borehamwood
Potters Bar
Edgware
Beaconsfield
Gerrards Cross
Uxbridge
Ruislip
Harrow
Wembley
Slough
Eton
Windsor
Heathrow Airport
Staines
Egham
Hounslow
Richmond
Ascot
Chertsey
Weybridge
Walton-on-Thames
Esher
Hampton Court
Kingston upon Thames
Epsom
Sutton
Banstead
Woking
Guildford
Leatherhead
Dorking
Reigate
Portsmouth
Worthing
Gatwick Airport
Crawley, Brighton

Linares de Mora 28 C4
Linares de Riofrio 27 D3
Linariá 60 B2
Linas, M 46 A4
Lincoln 7 E1
Lincolnshire 7 E1
Lindås 74 A2
Lindau 42 B1
Linden 38 C2
Lindenberg 40 A4
Linderhof 40 B4
Lindesberg 75 E3
Lindesnes 74 A4
Lindhem 75 E4
Lindö 75 E4
Líndos 65 F2
Lindoso 24 B3
Lindow 37 F2
Lindsdal 77 E2
Lingbo 75 E3
Linge 68 B4
Lingen 11 F2
Linguaglossa 49 D3
Linken 37 F2
Linköping 75 E4
Linlithgow 3 D4
Linnansaari 73 E2
Linnhe, L 2 B3
Linosa, I di 48 A4
Linsell 75 D1
Linslade 7 D2
Linthal 42 B2
Linyola 29 D2
Linz 38 A2
Linz 41 D2
Lion 13 E2
Lion-d'Angers, le 17 D1
Lioni 46 C1
Lióprasso 55 D4
Lioran, le 21 E2
Lipar 51 E1
Lipari 49 D2
Lipari, I 49 D2
Lipenská přehr nádrž 41 D2
Liperi 71 F4
Lipica 43 F3
Lipik 50 C2
Lipkovo 53 E3
Lipljan 53 D3
Lipno 41 D2
Lipova 80 C3
Lipovac 51 E2
Lippe 36 B4
Lippstadt 36 B4
Lipsí 61 E4
Lipsí, N 61 E4
Liptovský Mikuláš 80 B1
Liqenas 54 C2
Lírkia 59 D3
Lis 53 D4
Lisac 50 C3
Lisboa 26 A4
Lisburn 9 D1
Liscia 46 B2
Lisdoonvarna 8 B3
Lisieux 13 E3
Lisina 50 C3
Liskeard 6 B4
Lisková 39 E3
Lisle 21 E3
Lismore (GB) 2 B3
Lismore (IRL) 8 B4
Lisnaskea 8 C2
Lišnja 50 C2
Lisovići 51 D2
Lisse 11 D2
List 76 A3
Listafjorden 74 A4
Lištica 51 D4
Listowel 8 A3
Lit 69 E4
Lit-et-Mixe 20 B3
Lithakiá 58 B3
Lithári, Akr 60 B2
Lithínes 65 D4
Líthino, Akr 64 B4
Lithío 61 D2
Lití 55 E2
Litija 50 A1
Litóhoro 55 E3
Litoměřice 39 F1
Litomyšl 80 B1
Litschau 41 E2
Littlehampton 7 E4
Little Minch, The 2 B2
Little Moreton Hall 6 C1
Littleport 7 E2
Litva 78 C3
Litvínov 39 E1
Livaara 71 E1
Liváda, Akr 60 C4
Livade 43 F3
Livaderó (Dráma) 56 A1
Livaderó (Kozáni) 55 D3
Livádi (Kíthira) 63 D4
Livádi (Makedonía) 55 F2
Livádi (Sérifos) 60 B4
Livádi (Thessalía) 55 D3
Livadiá (Makedonía) 55 E1
Livadiá (Stereá Eláda) 59 D2
Livádia (Tílos) 65 E2
Livadítis 56 B1
Livadohóri 56 C4
Livanátes 59 E2
Livari 52 C4
Livarot 13 E3
Livenza 43 E3
Liverá 55 D3
Liverdun 15 D3
Livernon 21 E2
Liverpool 5 D4
Liverpool B 5 D4
Livigno 42 C2
Livingston 3 D4
Livno 50 C3
Livo 71 D2
Livojärvi 71 E1
Livojoki 71 D2
Livold 50 A2
Livorno 44 A2
Livorno Ferraris 23 D1
Livron 22 B2
Lixoúri 58 A3
Lizard 6 A4
Lizard Pt 6 A4
Lizy 14 B3
Lizzano in Belvedere 44 A1
Ljeskove Vode 51 D2
Ljig 52 C1
Ljubaništá 54 C2
Ljubata, D. 53 E3
Ljubelj 43 F2
Ljubija 50 C2
Ljubinje 52 B3
Ljubiš 51 F3
Ljubišnja 51 E4
Ljubljana 50 A1
Ljubno 50 A1
Ljubojno 54 C2
Ljubostinja 53 D2
Ljuboten 53 E4
Ljubovija 51 E3
Ljubuša 50 C3
Ljubuški 51 D4
Ljugarn 77 F2
Ljungan 75 F1
Ljungby 77 D2
Ljungbyhed 77 D3
Ljungdalen 69 D4
Ljungsbro 75 E4
Ljungskile 76 C1
Ljusdal 75 E2
Ljusnan 75 D1
Ljusne 75 F2
Ljutići 51 E4
Ljutoglav 53 D4
Ljutomer 50 B1
Llagostera 29 F2
Llanberis 6 B1
Llanca 29 F2
Llandeilo 6 B2
Llandovery 6 B2
Llandrindod Wells 6 C2
Llandudno 6 B1
Llandysul 6 B2
Llanelli 6 B3
Llanerchymedd 6 B1
Llanes 25 E1
Llanfairfechan 6 B1
Llanfair-ym-Muallt 6 C2
Llanfyllin 6 C1
Llangadog 6 B2
Llangefni 6 B1
Llangollen 6 C1
Llangurig 6 B2
Llanidloes 6 B2
Llano, Pto 27 D4
Llanrhystud 6 B2
Llanrwst 6 B1
Llanwrtyd-Wells 6 B2
Llanymyddyfri 6 B2

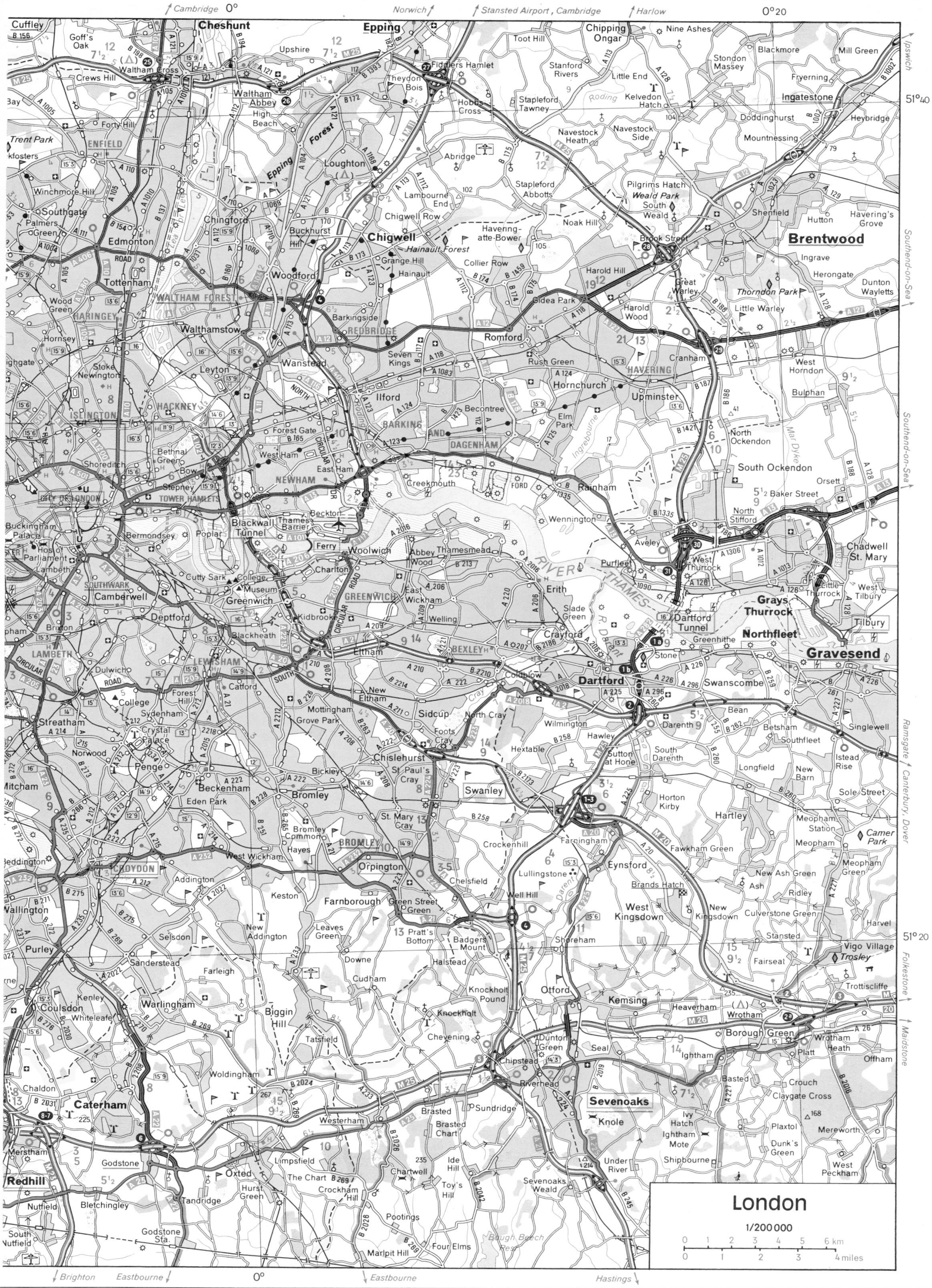
London
1/200 000
0 1 2 3 4 5 6 km
0 1 2 3 4 miles
Cambridge
Norwich
Stansted Airport, Cambridge
Harlow
Ipswich
Southend-on-Sea
Ramsgate, Canterbury, Dover
Folkestone
Maidstone
Brighton
Eastbourne
Hastings
Cheshunt
Epping
Chipping Ongar
Brentwood
Chigwell
Romford
Ilford
Woolwich
Dartford
Gravesend
Grays Thurrock
Northfleet
Bromley
Croydon
Sevenoaks
Caterham
Redhill
Swanley
Edmonton
Tottenham
Walthamstow
Greenwich
Orpington
Purley
Coulsdon
Westerham
Oxted

Llarga 32 C1
Llavorsi 29 E1
Lleida 29 D2
Llera 31 D1
Llerena 31 D2
Lles 29 E1
Llessui 29 E1
Lleyn Pen 6 B1
Lliria 28 C4
Llívia 29 E1
Llobregat, R 29 E2
Llodio 25 F2
Lloret de Mar 29 F2
Llucmajor 33 E3
Llynclys 6 C1
Lnáre 39 F3
Loanhead 3 D4
Loano 23 E2
Löbau 39 F1
Löbejün 37 E4
Lobenstein 39 D2
Löbnitz 37 E1
Lobo 25 F4
Lobón 30 C1
Loburg 37 E3
Locana 23 D1
Locarno 42 B3
Lochaline 2 B3
Lochboisdale 2 A2
Lochcarron 2 B2
Lochearnhead 2 C3
Lochem 11 F2
Loches 17 F2
Loch Garman 9 D4
Lochgelly 3 D3
Lochgilphead 2 B3
Lochinver 2 C1
Lochmaben 5 D2
Lochmaddy 2 A2
Loch Ness 2 C2
Lochranza 2 B4
Lochvica 79 F4
Lochy, L 2 C2
Lockenhaus 41 F3
Lockerbie 5 D2
Löcknitz 37 F2
Locle, le 19 E2
Locmariaquer 16 C1
Locminé 12 C4
Locorotondo 47 E1
Locquirec 12 B3
Locri 47 E4
Locronan 12 B4
Loctudy 12 B4
Lodè 46 B2
Lodève 21 F3
Lodi 42 C4
Løding 66 B4
Lødingen 66 B3
Lodosa 28 B1
Łódź 78 B4
Loeches 27 F3
Loen 74 B1
Løfallstrand 74 A3
Lofário 56 C2
Lofer 40 C3
Löffingen 42 A1
Lofoten 66 A3
Lofsdalen 75 D1
Lofthus 74 B3
Loftus 5 F3
Log 43 F2
Logarska dolina 50 A1
Logatec, D. 43 F3
Logroño 28 B1
Logrosán 27 D4
Løgstør 76 B2
Løgten 76 B2
Løgumkloster 76 B3
Lohals 76 C3
Lohberg 39 E3
Lohilahti 73 E3
Lohiniva 67 E4
Lohja 73 D4
Lohjanjärvi 73 D4
Lohne 36 B3
Löhne 36 C4
Lohr 38 C2
Lohtaja 70 C3
Loiano Rioveggio 44 B1
Loibltunnel 43 F2
Loimaa 72 C3
Loimaan kunta 72 C3
Loimijoki 72 C3
Loing 18 B1
Loir 14 A4
Loire 17 E1
Loire (Dépt) 18 C3
Loire-Atlantique 16 C1
Loir-et-Cher 17 F1
Loiret (Dépt) 14 A4
Loiri 46 B2
Loiron 13 D4
Loitz 37 E1
Loja 31 E3
Lojsta 77 F2
Lokalahti 72 C4
Lokan Tekojärvi 67 F3
Løken 74 C3
Lokeren 34 B3
Loket 39 E2
Lokka 67 F3
Løkken (N) 68 C4
Løkken (SF) 76 B2
Lokn'a 79 D2
Lokrum 52 B4
Lokve (Hrvatska) 50 A2
Lokve (Slovenija) 43 F3
Lokve (Vojvodina) 51 F1
Lolland 76 C4
L'Olleria 32 C1
Lom (BG) 81 D3
Lom (CS) 39 F1
Lom (N) 74 B2
Loma Negra 28 B1
Lomazzo 42 B3
Lombarde, Col de la 23 D2
Lombardia 42 C3
Lombez 21 D3
Lomello 23 E1
Lomen 74 C2
Lomma 77 D3
Lommatzsch 39 E1
Lommel 34 C2
Lomond, L 2 C3
Lomonosov 79 D1
Lomont, Mts du 19 E1
Lompolo 67 E3
Łomża 78 C4
Lonato 42 C4
Lončari 51 D2
Lončarica 50 C1
Londinières 14 A2
London 7 E3
Londonderry 4 A2
Londonderry (Co) 4 A2
Lonǵa 62 C3
Longádes 54 C4
Longaníkos 59 D4
Longares 28 C2
Longarone 43 E3
Long Eaton 7 D1
Longeau 15 D4
Longford 8 C2
Longford (Co) 8 C2
Longleat House 6 C3
Longny 13 F3
Longobucco 47 E3
Longós 58 A1
Long Preston 5 E3
Long Sutton 7 E2
Longtown 5 D2
Longué 17 E1
Longueville-sur-Scie 13 F2
Longuyon 15 D2
Longwy 15 D2
Lonigo 43 D4
Löningen 36 B3
Lonja 50 C2
Lonja *R* 50 B1
Lönsboda 77 D3
Lønsdal 69 E1
Lønset 68 B4
Lons-le-Saunier 19 D2
Looe 6 B4
Loop Head 8 A3
Loosdorf 41 E2
Lopar 50 A3
Lopare 51 E2
Lopcombe Corner 7 D3
Lopera 31 E2
Lopes, Mal i 54 B1
Loppa 67 D1
Loppi 73 D3
Lopud 52 B4
Lopud / 52 B4
Lora del Río 31 D2
Lorca 32 B3
Lorcé 34 C3
Lorch (Baden-Württemberg) 38 C4
Lorch (Hessen) 38 A2
Loreley 38 A2
Loreo 43 E4
Loreto 45 D2
Loreto Aprutino 45 D3
Lorgues 22 C3
Lorica 47 E3
Lorient 12 B4
Loriga 26 B3
Loriguilla, Emb de 28 C4
Loriol 22 B2
Lormes 18 C2
Lorn, Firth of 2 B3
Loro Ciuffenna 44 B2
Loroux-Bottereau, le 17 D2
Lorquin 15 E3
Lörrach 42 A1
Lorrez-le-Bocage 14 B4
Lorris 14 B4
Los 75 E2
Los Alcázares 32 C3
Losar 27 D3
Los Arcos 20 A4
Los Barreros 32 A1
Los Barrios 31 D4
Los Corrales de Buelna 25 E2
Los Cortijos 27 F4
Los Cristianos 30 A4
Los Dolores 32 C3
Losenstein 41 D3
Los Gallardos 32 B3
Losheim 35 D4
Los Hinojosos 28 A4
Lošinj 50 A3
Los Llanos de Aridane 30 A4
Los Lobos 32 B3
Los Navalmorales 27 E4
Los Navalucillos 27 E4
Los Palacios y Villafranca 31 D3
Los Santos 27 D3
Los Santos de Maimona 30 C1
Los Sauces 30 A4
Loßburg 38 B4
Lossiemouth 3 D2
Lossnen 75 D1
Lößnitz 39 E1
Lostwithiel 6 A4
Los Villares 31 F3
Los Yébenes 27 F4
Lot 21 E2
Lot (Dépt) 21 D2
Lote 74 A1
Løten 74 C2
Lot-et-Garonne 20 C2
Lothian 3 D4
Lötschbergtunnel 42 A3
Löttorp 77 E2
Loučná 39 E1
Loudéac 12 C4
Loudías 55 E2
Loudías *R* 55 E2
Loudun 17 E2
Loué 13 E4
Loue 19 D2
Loughborough 7 D2
Loughrea 8 B3
Louhans 19 D2
Louhisaari 72 C4
Louisburgh 8 A2
Loukinen 67 E3
Loukíssia 59 E2
Loulay 17 D3
Loulé 30 B3
Louny 39 F2
Loupe, la 13 F3
Loup, Gorge du (L) 15 D2
Loup, Gorges du (F) 23 D3
Lourdes 20 C4
Loures 26 A4
Louriçal 26 A3
Lourinha 26 A4
Loúros 58 B1
Loúros *R* 58 B1
Louroux, le 17 D1
Lousa 26 A4
Lousã 26 B3
Lousada 24 A3
Lousã, Sa da 26 B3
Louth 5 F4
Louth 9 D2
Loutrá (Kikládes) 60 B4
Loutrá (Lésvos) 61 E1
Loutrá (Makedonía) 56 A3
Loutrá (Pelopónissos) 58 C4
Loutrá Aridéas 55 D2
Loutrá Edipsoú 59 E2
Loutrá Eleftherón 56 A2
Loutrá Ipátis 59 D2
Loutrá Kaítsas 59 D1
Loutrá Kilínis 58 B3
Loutráki (Pelopónissos) 59 E3
Loutráki (Skópelos) 60 A1
Loutráki (Stereá Eláda) 58 B2
Loutrá Langadá 55 E2
Loutrá Smokóvou 58 C1
Loutrá Vólvis 55 F2
Loutró Elénis 59 E3
Loutropigí 58 C1
Loutrópirgos 59 E3
Loutrós 57 D2
Loútsa (Ípiros) 58 A1
Loútsa (Stereá Eláda) 60 A3
Louvain 34 B3
Louvain-la-Neuve 34 B3
Louvière, la 34 B3
Louviers 13 F3
Louvigné-du-Désert 13 D3
Lovag 51 F3
Lövånger 70 C3
Lövberga 69 E3
Lovćen 52 C4
Loveč 81 D4
Lovere 42 C3
Loviisa 73 E4
Lovisa 73 E4
Lovosice 39 F1
Lovran 50 A2
Lovrenc na Pohorju 50 A1
Lövstabruk 75 F3
Lövstabukten 75 F3
Lovund 69 D1
Löwenberg 37 F2
Lower L Erne 8 C1
Lowestoft 7 F2
Łowicz 78 C4
Low Street 7 F2
Lož 50 A2
Lozère 21 F2
Lozère, Mt 21 F2
Lozna 53 D2
Loznica 51 E2
Lozovac 50 B4
Lozovik 53 D1
Lozoyuela 27 F2
Luanco 25 D1
Luarca 24 C1
Lubań 80 A1
Lübars 37 E3
L'ubaševka 81 E2
Lübbecke 36 B3
Lübben 37 F4
Lübbenau 37 F4
Lübbow 37 D3
Lübeck 37 D2
Lübecker Bucht 37 D1
Lubenec 39 E2
Lubéron, Mgne du 22 B3
Lubersac 17 F4
Lubieszyn 37 F2
Lubin 78 B4
Lublin 78 C4
Lubliniec 80 B1
Lubmin 37 F1
Lubny 79 F4
L'uboml' 78 C4
Lubrín 32 B3
Lübtheen 37 D2
Lübz 37 E2
Luc 13 E2
Lucainena de las Torres 32 A3
Lucan 9 D3
Lučani 51 F3
Lúcar 32 A3
Lucca 44 A2
Luče 50 A1
Luce B 4 C2
Lucena 31 E3
Lucena del Cid 28 C4
Lucenay-l'Evêque 18 C2
Luc-en-Diois 22 B2
Lučenec 80 C2
Luceni 28 B2
Lucera 45 F4
Lüchow 37 D3
Luciana 31 E1
Lucito 45 E4
Luck 79 D4
Lucka 39 D1
Luckau 37 F4
Luckenwalde 37 F3
Luc, le 22 C3
Lucomagno, Pso del 42 B3
Luçon 17 D2
Ludbreg 50 B1
Lude, le 17 E1
Lüdenscheid 35 D2
Ludiente 28 C4
Lüdinghausen 36 B4
L'udinovo 79 F3
Ludlow 6 C2
Ludvika 75 E3
Ludwigsburg 38 B4
Ludwigsfelde 37 F3
Ludwigshafen (Baden-Württemberg) 42 B1
Ludwigshafen (Rheinland-Pfalz) 38 B3
Ludwigslust 37 D2
Ludwigstadt 39 D2
Luère, Col de la 19 D3
Lug 51 D3
Lug *R* 53 D1
Luga 79 D1
Luga *R* 79 D1
Lugagnano Val d'Arda 23 F2
Lugano 42 B3
Lugau 39 E1
Lügde 36 C4
Lugnano in Teverina 44 C3
Lugnaquillia Mt 9 D3
Lugo 24 B2
Lugo 44 B1
Lugoj 80 C3
Lugones 25 D1
Luhačovice 80 B2
Luhalahti 72 C3
Luhanka 73 D3
Luhtapohja 71 F4
Luik 34 C3
Luimneach 8 B3
Luing 2 B3
Luino 42 B3
Luiro 67 F3
Luisenburg 39 D2
Luka (Bosna i Hercegovina) 51 D4
Luka (Hrvatska) 50 B4
Luka (Srbija) 53 E1
Lukavac 51 D2
Lukavica 51 D2
Lukovica 50 A1
Lukovit 81 D4
Lukovo (Makedonija) 54 B1
Lukovo (Srbija) 53 D2
Lukovo (Srbija) 53 E2
Lukovo Šugarje 50 B3
Luleå 70 C2
Luleälven 70 C2
Lüleburgaz 81 E4
Lumbarda 52 A3
Lumbier 20 B4
Lumbrales 19 E4
Lumbrales 26 C2
Lumbres 14 A1
Lumezzane 42 C3
Lumi i Tiranës 54 A1
Lumijoki 71 D2
Lumparland 72 B4
Lumparn 72 B4
Lumsås 76 C3
Lumsheden 75 E3
Lun 50 A3
Luna 28 C1
Luna, Emb Barrios de 25 D2
Luna, R 25 D2
Lunas 21 F3
Lund 77 D3
Lunde (Sogn og Fjordane) 74 B2
Lunde (Telemark) 74 B3
Lunden 36 C1
Lundy 6 A3
Lune 5 D3
Lüneburg 37 D2
Lunel 22 A3
Lünen 36 B4
Lünersee 42 C2
Lunéville 15 E3
Lungern 42 A2
Lungro 47 D2
Luninec 79 D4
Lunz 41 E3
Luodonselkä 71 D2
Luogosanto 46 B2
Luonteri 73 E3
Luopioinen 73 D3
Luosto 67 E4
Luoto 70 C3
Lupoglav 50 B1
Luque 31 E3
Lurbe-St-Christau 20 C4
Lurcy-Lévis 18 B2
Lure 15 E4
Lure, Mgne de 22 C3
Lurgan 9 D1
Luri 23 D3
Lurisia 23 D2
Lurøy 69 D1
Lury 18 A2
Lušci Palanka 50 C3
Lushnjë 54 A2
Lusi 73 E3
Lusignan 17 E3
Lusigny 14 C4
Lusk 9 D2
Luso 26 B3
Lussac 20 C2
Lussac-les-Châteaux 17 F3
Lussan 22 A3

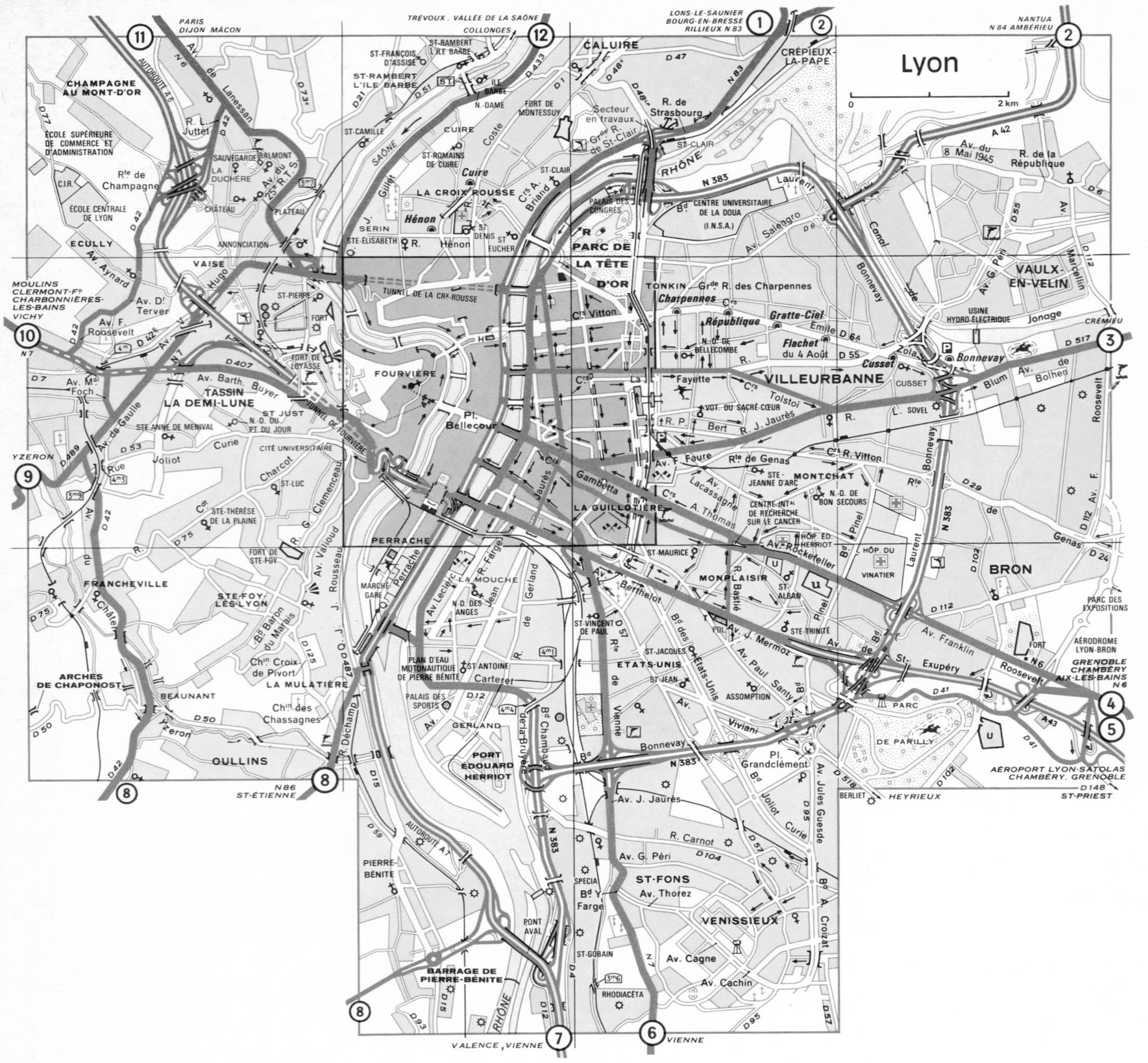
Lyon
0
2 km
CALUIRE
CRÉPIEUX-LA-PAPE
CHAMPAGNE AU MONT-D'OR
ECULLY
LA CROIX ROUSSE
PARC DE LA TÊTE D'OR
VAULX-EN-VELIN
VILLEURBANNE
TASSIN LA DEMI-LUNE
FOURVIÈRE
LA GUILLOTIÈRE
PERRACHE
MONTCHAT
BRON
FRANCHEVILLE
STE-FOY-LES-LYON
MONPLAISIR
ETATS-UNIS
ARCHES DE CHAPONOST
OULLINS
LA MULATIÈRE
PORT EDOUARD HERRIOT
ST-FONS
VENISSIEUX
PIERRE-BÉNITE
BARRAGE DE PIERRE-BÉNITE
RHÔNE
SAÔNE
AÉRODROME LYON-BRON
AÉROPORT LYON-SATOLAS CHAMBÉRY, GRENOBLE
VALENCE, VIENNE
VIENNE
ST-ÉTIENNE
HEYRIEUX
ST-PRIEST
PARIS DIJON MÂCON
TRÉVOUX, VALLÉE DE LA SAÔNE COLLONGES
LONS-LE-SAUNIER BOURG-EN-BRESSE RILLIEUX N 83
NANTUA N 84 AMBÉRIEU
YZERON
MOULINS CLERMONT-Fᵈ CHARBONNIÈRES-LES-BAINS VICHY

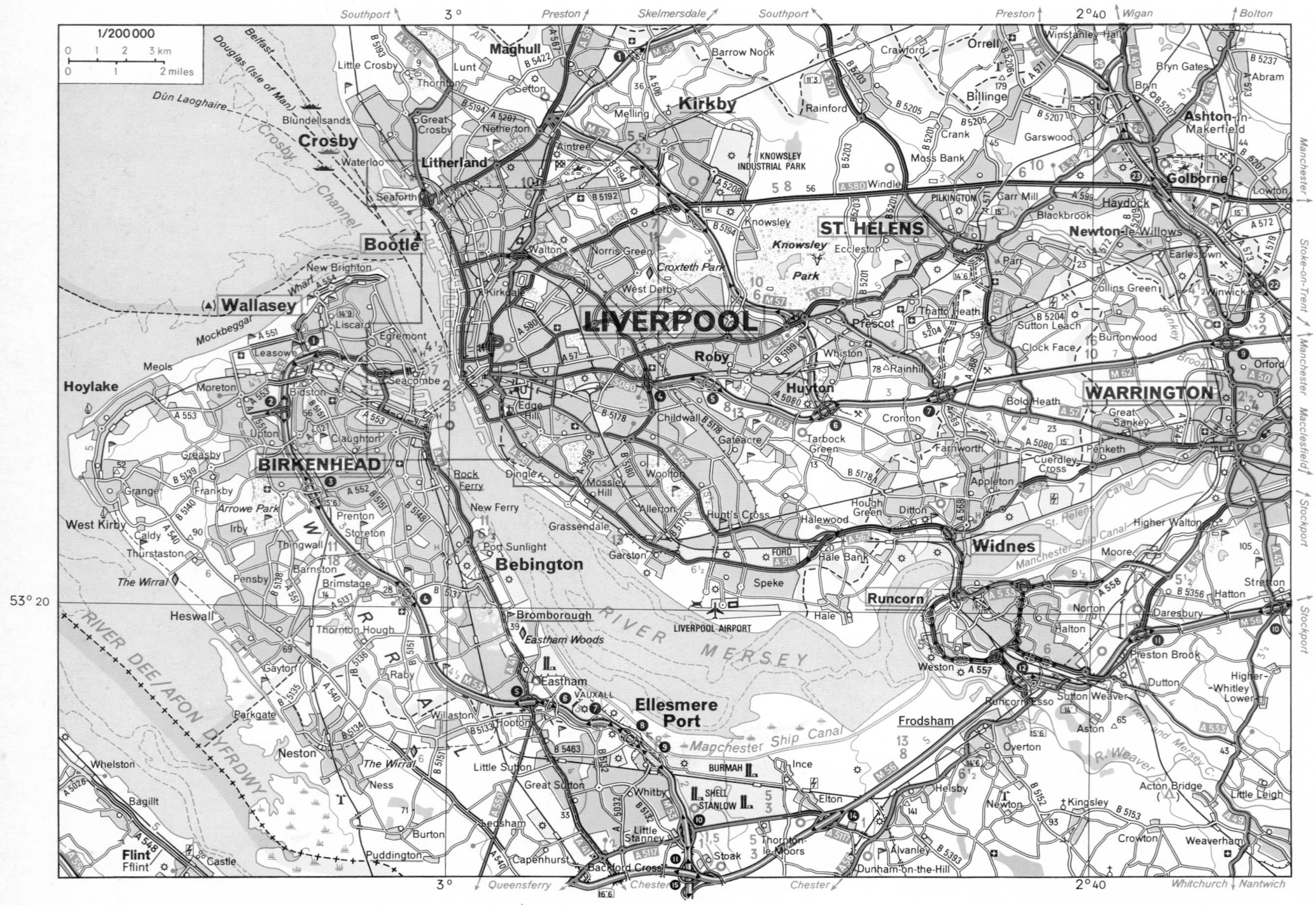
1/200 000
0 1 2 3 km
0 1 2 miles
Southport
Preston
Skelmersdale
Wigan
Bolton
3°
2° 40
53° 20
Crosby
Litherland
Bootle
Wallasey
Hoylake
Birkenhead
West Kirby
LIVERPOOL
Kirkby
Maghull
ST. HELENS
Knowsley
Prescot
Huyton
Roby
Widnes
Runcorn
WARRINGTON
Newton-le-Willows
Golborne
Ashton-in-Makerfield
Bebington
Ellesmere Port
Neston
Heswall
Flint
Fflint
Frodsham
LIVERPOOL AIRPORT
RIVER MERSEY
RIVER DEE/AFON DYFRDWY
Manchester Ship Canal
Manchester
Stoke-on-Trent
Macclesfield
Stockport
Queensferry
Chester
Whitchurch
Nantwich

M

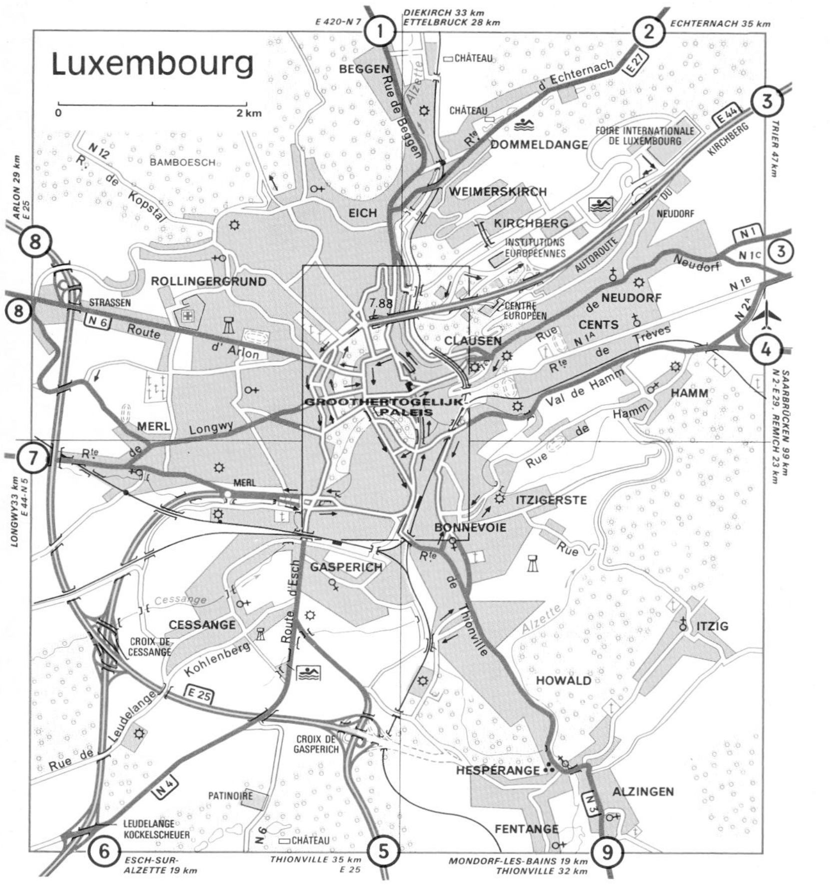
Luxembourg
0 2 km
DIEKIRCH 33 km
ETTELBRUCK 28 km
E 420-N 7
ECHTERNACH 35 km
TRIER 47 km
ARLON 29 km
E 25
LONGWY 33 km
E 44-N 5
SAARBRÜCKEN 99 km
N 2-E 29 REMICH 23 km
ESCH-SUR-ALZETTE 19 km
THIONVILLE 35 km
E 25
MONDORF-LES-BAINS 19 km
THIONVILLE 32 km
BEGGEN
CHÂTEAU
DOMMELDANGE
FOIRE INTERNATIONALE DE LUXEMBOURG
KIRCHBERG
BAMBOESCH
WEIMERSKIRCH
EICH
NEUDORF
INSTITUTIONS EUROPÉENNES
ROLLINGERGRUND
STRASSEN
CENTRE EUROPÉEN
CLAUSEN
CENTS
HAMM
MERL
GROOTHERTOGELIJK PALEIS
ITZIGERSTE
BONNEVOIE
GASPERICH
CESSANGE
CROIX DE CESSANGE
ITZIG
HOWALD
CROIX DE GASPERICH
HESPERANGE
ALZINGEN
PATINOIRE
LEUDELANGE-KOCKELSCHEUER
FENTANGE
Route d'Arlon
Longwy
Rue de Kopstal
Val de Hamm
Rue de Trèves
Route d'Esch
Route de Thionville
Kohlenberg
Rue de Leudelange
Rue de Beggen
Rue d'Echternach
Neudorf
Autoroute
Cessange
Alzette

Makarska 50 C4
Makce 53 D1
Makedonía 55 E2
Makedonija 53 F4
Makedonski Brod 53 E4
Makljen 51 D3
Makó 80 C3
Makovo 55 D2
Makrakómi 59 D1
Mákri 56 C2
Makríamos 56 B2
Makrígialos 55 E3
Makrigialós 65 D4
Makrihóri (Makedonía) 56 B2
Makrihóri (Thessalía) 55 E4
Makrinítsa 55 E4
Makrinóros 58 B1
Makriplágio 56 A1
Makriráhi 59 D1
Makrívrahos, Akr 56 C3
Makrohóri 55 D2
Makronissi 60 B3
Maksniemi 71 D2
Mala 8 B4
Malå 69 F2
Mala Bosna 51 E1
Malacky 41 F2
Maladeta 29 D1
Malaga 31 E4
Malagón 27 F4
Malahide 9 D3
Malaja Višera 79 E1
Malaja Viska 81 F1
Mala Kapela 50 B2
Mala Krsna 53 D1
Malalbergo 43 D4
Malámata 58 C2
Malandríno 59 D2
Malangen 66 C2
Mälaren 75 F4
Mala Subotica 50 B1
Malaucène 22 B2
Malax 70 C4
Malbork 78 B3
Malbuisson 19 E2
Malcata, Sa de 26 C3
Malcesine 43 D3
Malchin 37 E2
Malchiner See 37 E2
Malchow 37 E2
Maldegem 34 A3
Maldon 7 E3
Malé 43 D3
Maléas, Akr 63 D4
Máleme 64 A3
Malène, la 21 F2
Malente-Gremsmühlen 37 D1
Male Pijace 51 E1
Máles 65 D4
Malesherbes 14 A4
Malessína 59 E2
Malestroit 12 C4
Malgomaj 69 E3
Malgrat de Mar 29 F2
Mália 64 C4
Malicorne 17 E1
Mali Haian 50 B3
Mali Iđđos 51 E1
Mali kanal 51 E1
Mali Lošinj 50 A3
Malin 79 E4
Malines 34 B3
Malin Head 4 A1
Malinska 50 A2
Mali Požerevac 53 D1
Mališevo 53 D3
Maliskylä 71 D3
Malit, Maj'e 53 D4
Mali Zvornik 51 E3
Maljen 51 F3
Malko Târnovo 81 E4
Mallaig 2 B2
Mållejus 67 D2
Mallén 28 B2
Mallersdorf-Pfaffenberg 39 E4
Malles Venosta 42 C2
Mallnitz 43 E2
Mallorca 33 E2
Mallow 8 B4
Mallwyd 6 B2
Malm 69 D3
Malmberget 66 C4
Malmédy 34 C3
Malmesbury 6 C3
Malmköping 75 E4
Malmö 76 C3
Malmöhus Län 77 D3
Malmslätt 75 E4
Malo 43 D3
Maloja 42 C3
Malojaroslavec 79 F2
Malo Konjari 53 E4
Malo-les-Bains 14 A1
Malónas 65 F2
Malori 46 C2
Måløy 74 A1
Malpartida de Cáceres 26 C4
Malpartida de Plasencia 27 D3
Malpica (E) 24 A1
Malpica (P) 26 C3
Mals 42 C2
Målselv 66 C2
Målselva 66 C2
Målsnes 66 C2
Malsta 75 F2
Malta 41 D4
Malta / 49 F4
Maltby 5 E4
Maltiotunturi 67 F3
Malton 5 F3
Maluenda 28 B2
Malung 75 D3
Malungsfors 75 D3
Malveira 26 A4
Malvik 68 C4
Malzieu-Ville, le 21 F2
Mamaia 81 E3
Mamarrosa 26 B2
Mamers 13 E4
Mammola 47 E4
Mamonovo 78 B3
Mampodre 25 D2
Mamry, Jez 78 C3
Manacor 33 E2
Manacore 45 F3
Manamansalo 71 E3
Manasija 53 D1
Mancha Real 31 F2
Manche 13 D3
Manchester 5 E4
Manching 39 D4
Manciano 44 B3
Mandal 74 B4
Mandal selva 74 B4
Mandamádos 61 D1
Mandas 46 B4
Mandela 44 C4
Mandelieu 23 D3
Manderscheid 35 D4
Mandínia 59 D4
Mandoúdi 59 E2
Mándra (Stereá Eláda) 59 E3
Mándra (Thráki) 57 D1
Mandráki 65 E1
Mandre 50 A3
Mandrikó 65 F2
Mandrioli, Pso dei 44 B2
Manduria 47 F2
Måne 74 B3
Manerbio 42 C4
Manětín 39 E2
Manfredonia 45 F4
Manfredonia, G di 45 F4
Mangalia 81 E3
Mángana 56 B2
Manganári 64 B1
Manger 74 A2
Mangerton Mt 8 A4
Mangrt, Planica 43 F2
Mangualde 26 B2
Máni (Pelopónissos) 62 C4
Máni (Thráki) 57 D1
Maniago 43 E3
Manilva 31 D4
Man, I of 4 C3
Manisa 61 F2
Mánises 32 C1
Manjača 50 C3
Mank 41 E2
Månkarbo 75 F3
Manlleu 29 F2
Mannersdorf 41 F2
Mannheim 38 B3
Mannu 46 A4
Manojlovac slap 50 B3
Manojlovce 53 E2
Manoppello 45 D3
Manorhamilton 8 C1
Manosque 22 C3
Manresa 29 E2
Mansfeld 37 E4
Mansfield 7 D1
Mansilla de las Mulas 25 D2
Mansilla, Emb de 28 A1
Mansle 17 E3
Manteigas 26 B3
Mantes 14 A3
Mantiel 28 A3
Mäntlahti 73 E4
Mantorp 77 E1
Mantova 43 D4
Mäntsälä 73 D4
Mänttä 73 D2
Mäntyhariu 73 E3
Mäntyjärvi 71 E1
Mäntyluoto 72 C3
Manzanal, Pto del 24 C2
Manzanares 31 F1
Manzanares el Real 27 F3
Manzaneda 24 B2
Manzaneda *Mt* 24 B2
Manzanera 28 C4
Manzat 18 B3
Manziana 44 C4
Maó 33 F2
Maqellarë 53 D4
Maqueda 27 E3
Maramureș 81 D2
Maranchón 28 B3
Maranchón, Pto de 28 B3
Maranello 44 A1
Maranhão, Bgem do 26 B4
Marano 43 E3
Marano di Napoli 46 B1
Marano, L di 43 E3
Marans 17 D3
Marão, Sa do 24 B3
Marássia 57 D1
Maratea 47 D2
Marateca 30 A1
Marathéa 55 D4
Marathiá, Akr 58 B3
Marathiás 58 C2
Marathókambos 61 E3
Marathónas 59 F3
Marathópoli 62 B3
Márathos 59 E1
Marbach 38 B4
Mårbacka 75 D3
Marbella 31 E4
Marburg 38 B2
Marby 69 E4
Marčana 43 F4
March (A) 41 F2
March (GB) 7 E2
Marchamalo 28 A3
Marchaux 19 E2
Marche 44 C2
Marche-en-Famenne 34 C4
Marchegg 41 F2
Marchena 31 D3
Marchenoir 14 A4
Marchiennes 14 B1
Marciac 20 C3
Marciana Marina 44 A3
Marcianise 46 B1
Marcigny 18 C3
Marcilla 28 B1
Marcillac-Vallon 21 E2
Marcillat-en-Combraille 18 B3
Marcilly-le-Hayer 14 B4
Marckolsheim 15 F4
Marco de Canaveses 24 A4
Marcoule 22 B3
Maree, L 2 C2
Mare Ionico 47 F4
Marene 23 D2
Marennes 17 D3
Marentes 24 C2
Maréttimo, I- 48 A3
Mareuil (Dordogne) 17 E4
Mareuil (Vendée) 17 D2
Margarítes 64 B4
Margaríti 54 B4
Margate 7 F3
Margherita di Savoia 45 F4
Marguerittes 22 A3
María 32 A3
María Cristina, Emb de 28 C4
Mariannelund 77 E2
Máriánské Lázně 39 E2
Maria Saal 43 F2
Maria Taferl 41 E2
Mariazell 41 E3
Maribo 76 C4
Maribor 50 B1
Mariborsko Pohorje 50 B1
Marica 81 D4
Mariefred 75 F4
Mariehamn 72 B4
Marienberg 39 E1
Marienborn 37 D3
Marienburg 35 D4
Marienstedt 37 D2
Mariestad 75 D4
Marignane 22 B3
Marigny 13 D3
Marigny-le-Châtel 14 B4
Marija Bistrica 50 B1
Marikirk 3 D3
Marín 24 A2
Marina 50 C4
Marina di Camerota 47 D2
Marina di Campo 44 A3
Marina di Carrara 23 F2
Marina di Castagneto-Donoratico 44 A3
Marina di Gioiosa Ionica 47 E4
Marina di Grosseto 44 B3
Marina di Massa 23 F2
Marina di Pietrasanta 44 A2
Marina di Pisa 44 A2
Marina di Ragusa 49 D4
Marina di Ravenna 44 C1
Marinella 48 B4
Marineo 48 B3
Marines 14 A3
Maringues 18 B3
Marinha Grande 26 A3
Marinkainen 70 C3
Marino 44 C4
Marismas, Pto de las 30 C2
Marjaniemi 71 D2
Marjina Gorka 79 D3
Markaryd 77 D2
Markdorf 42 B1
Marken 11 E2
Markermeer 11 E2
Market Drayton 6 C1
Market Harborough 7 D2
Markethill 9 D2
Market Rasen 7 E1
Market Weighton 5 F3
Markgröningen 38 B4
Markina 20 A3
Märkisch Buchholz 37 F3
Markkleeberg 37 E4
Markneukirchen 39 E2
Markópoulo (Atikí-Piréas) 59 F3
Markópoulo (Atikí-Piréas) 59 F3
Markópoulo (Kefaloniá) 58 B3
Markovac 53 D1
Markov manastir 53 E4
Markranstädt 37 E4
Markstein, le 15 E4
Marktbreit 38 C3
Markt Erlbach 38 C3
Marktheidenfeld 38 C3
Markt Indersdorf 39 D4
Marktl 39 E4
Marktoberdorf 40 A3
Marktredwitz 39 D2
Markt St Florian 41 D3
Markušica 51 D1
Marl 11 F3
Marlborough 7 D3
Marle 14 B2
Marlow (DDR) 37 E1
Marlow (GB) 7 D3
Marmande 20 C2
Marmara Denizi 81 E4
Marmári 60 B3
Mármaro 61 D2
Marmolada, Mte 43 D2
Marmolejo 31 E2
Marmoutier 15 E3
Marnay 19 D2
Marne 36 C2
Marne (Dépt) 14 C3
Marne *R* 14 B3
Marne au Rhin, Canal de la 15 D3
Marnitz 37 E2
Marofa 26 C2
Marolles-les-Braults 13 E4
Marónia 56 C2
Maronías, Akr 56 C2
Maronne 21 E2
Maros 80 C3
Marostica 43 D3
Marotta 44 C2
Márpissa 64 B1
Marquartstein 40 C3
Marquion 14 B2
Marquise 14 A1
Marradi 44 B1
Marraskoski 71 D1
Marroquí o de Tarifa, Pta 31 D4
Marsaglia 23 F2
Marsala 48 A3
Marsberg 38 B1
Marsciano 44 C3
Marseillan 21 F3
Marseille 22 B4
Marseille-en-Beauvaisis 14 A2
Marsfjällen 69 E2
Marsico Nuovo 47 D2
Marske-by-the-Sea 5 E3
Mars-la-Tour 15 D3
Märsta 75 F3
Marstal 76 B4
Marstrand 76 C1
Marta 44 C3
Martano 47 F2
Martel 21 D2
Martelange 15 D2
Martes, Sa de 32 C1
Marthon 17 E3
Martignacco 43 E3
Martigné-Ferchaud 17 D1
Martigny 19 F3
Martigny-les-Bains 15 D4
Martigues 22 B3
Martim Longo 30 B2
Martin 80 B2
Martina 42 C2
Martina Franca 47 E1
Martin Brod 50 B3
Martinci Čepinski 51 D1
Martín de la Jara 31 E3
Martin de Yeltes 27 D2
Martinengo 42 C4
Martinet 29 E1
Martingança 26 A3
Martinniemi 71 D2
Martíno 59 E2
Martín, R 28 C3
Martinšćica 50 A3
Martis 46 A2
Martjanci 41 F4
Martofte 76 C3
Martonvaara 71 F4
Martorell 29 E2
Martos 31 F2
Martti 67 F3
Marttila 72 C4
Marvão 26 B4
Marvejols 21 F2
Marxwalde 37 F3
Maryport 5 D2
Mary, Puy 21 E2
Marzagran 14 C2
Mas-Cabardès 21 E3
Mas-d'Agenais, le 20 C2
Mas-d'Azil, le 21 D4
Mas de Barberans 29 D3
Mas de las Matas 28 C3
Masegoso 28 A3
Masevaux 15 E4
Masi 67 D2
Maside 24 B2
Mask, L 8 B2
Masku 72 C4
Maslenica 50 B3
Maslinica 50 C4
Maslovare 51 D3
Måsøy 67 D1
Maspalomas 30 B4
Massa 44 A2
Massa Fiscaglia 43 E4
Massafra 47 E1
Massamagrell 28 C4
Massa Marittima 44 B3
Massa Martana 44 C3
Massarosa 44 A2
Massat 21 D4
Massegros, le 21 F2
Masseube 21 D3
Massiac 18 B4
Mastihári 65 E1
Mástiho, Akr 61 D3
Masueco 24 C4
Mat 52 C4
Matachel, R 31 D1
Mátala 64 B4
Matalascañas 30 C3
Matalavilla, Emb de 24 C2
Matalebreras 28 B2
Matallana 25 D2
Mataránga 55 D4
Mataró 29 F2
Matarraña, R 29 D3
Mataruška Banja 53 D2
Matejče 53 E4
Matelica 44 C2
Matelles, les 22 A3
Matera 47 E1
Matese, Mti del 45 E4
Mateševo 52 C3
Mátészalka 80 C2
Mateus 24 B3
Matfors 75 F1
Matha 17 E3
Mathráki, N 54 A4
Máti 60 A3
Matignon 12 C3
Matka 53 E4
Matku 73 D3
Matlock 7 D1
Matosinhos 24 A3
Matour 18 C3
Mátra 80 C2
Matrei (Osttirol) 43 E2
Matrei (Tirol) 43 D2
Matterhorn 19 F3
Mattersburg 41 F3
Mattighofen 40 C3
Mattinata 45 F4
Mattsee 40 C3
Mattsmyra 75 E2
Matulji 50 A2
Matute 28 B2
Maubeuge 14 C1
Maubourguet 20 C3
Maubuisson 20 B1
Mauchline 4 C1
Mauerkirchen 40 C3
Mauguio 22 A3
Maula 71 D2
Maulbronn 38 B4
Maulde 18 A3
Mauléon 17 D2
Mauléon-Licharre 20 B4
Maumturk Mts 8 A2
Maun 50 A3
Maure 12 C4
Maure, Col de 22 C2
Maures, Massif des 22 C3
Mauriac 21 E1
Mauria, Pso 43 E2
Mauron 12 C4
Maurs 21 E2
Mautern 41 E3
Mauterndorf 41 D4
Mauthausen 41 D2
Mauvezin 21 D3
Mauvoisin, Bge de 19 F3
Mauzé 17 D3
Mavrohóri 54 C2
Mavroklíssio 57 D1
Mavroléfki 56 A2
Mavromáta 58 C1
Mavromáti 55 D4
Mavroúda 55 F2
Mavrovi Anovi 53 D4
Mavrovo 53 D4
Mavrovo, Nac park 53 D4
Mavrovoúni (Makedonía) 55 D2
Mavrovoúni (Thessalía) 55 D4
Mavrovoúni *Mt* 55 E4
Mavrovsko ezero 53 D4
Maxhütte-Haidof 39 E3
Maxmo 70 C4
Maybole 4 C2
Mayen 35 D3
Mayenne 13 D4
Mayenne (Dépt) 13 D4
Mayenne *R* 13 D4
Mayerling 41 F2
Mayet 17 E1
Mayet-de-Montagne, le 18 C3
Maynooth 9 D3
Mayo 8 B1
Mayor, C 25 F1
Mayorga 25 D3
Mayrhofen 43 D2
Maza, Emb Barrié de la 24 A2
Mazagón 30 C3
Mazamet 21 E3
Mazara d. Vallo 48 B4
Mazarakiá 54 B4
Mazarete 28 B3
Mazarrón 32 B3
Mazarrón, G de 32 B3
Mažeikiai 78 C2
Mazères 21 E4
Mázi 54 B3
Mazières-en-Gâtine 17 E2
Mazorra, Pto de la 25 F2
Mazury 78 C3
Mazzarino 48 C4
Mazzarò 49 D3
Mealhada 26 B3
Meath 9 D2
Meaux 14 B3
Mechelen 34 B3
Meckenbeuren 42 B1
Mecklenburger B 37 D1
Meda 24 B4
Međa 51 F1
Medak 50 B3
Mede 23 E1
Medebach 38 B1
Međeđa 51 E3
Medelim 26 C3
Medellín 31 D1
Medel, Piz 42 B2
Medemblik 11 E2
Medena Selišta 50 C3
Mediano, Emb de 29 D1
Mediaș 81 D2
Medicina 44 B1
Medina Azahara 31 E2
Medinaceli 28 A2
Medina del Campo 25 D4
Medina de Pomar 25 F2
Medina de Ríoseco 25 D3
Medina-Sidonia 31 D4
Médous, Grotte de 20 C4
Médoussa 56 B1
Medugorje 52 A3
Medulin 43 F4
Međumajdan 50 B2
Meduna 43 E3
Meduno 43 E3
Međurečje 51 F3
Medveđa 53 E3
Medvednica 50 B1
Medveja 50 A2
Medvida 50 B3
Medvode 50 A1
Medyn' 79 F2
Medžitlija 54 C2
Meerane 39 E1
Meersburg 42 B1
Mées, les 22 C3
Mefjordbotn 66 B2
Mefjordvær 66 C2
Méga Dério 57 D1
Mega Horió (Stereá Eláda) 58 C2
Megalohóri 55 D4
Megaló Horió (Agathoníssi) 61 E4
Megaló Horió (Tílos) 65 E2
Megalópoli 58 C4
Meganíssi 58 B2
Megaplátanos 59 E2
Mégara 59 E3
Megárhi 54 C4
Méga Spíleo 59 D3
Megève 19 E3
Megísti 65 F3
Megísti, N 65 F3
Megístis Lávras 56 B3
Meg. Livádi 63 F3
Meg. Panagía 56 A3
Meg. Vólvi 55 F2
Mehamn 67 E1
Mehedeby 75 F3
Mehov Krš 53 D3
Mehun 18 B2
Meigle 3 D3
Meijel 11 E3
Meije, la 19 E4
Meilen 42 B2
Meillant 18 F3
Meimoa 26 C3
Meina 42 B3
Meinerzhagen 38 A1
Meiningen 38 C2
Meira 24 C1
Meira, Sa de 24 C1
Meiringen 42 A2

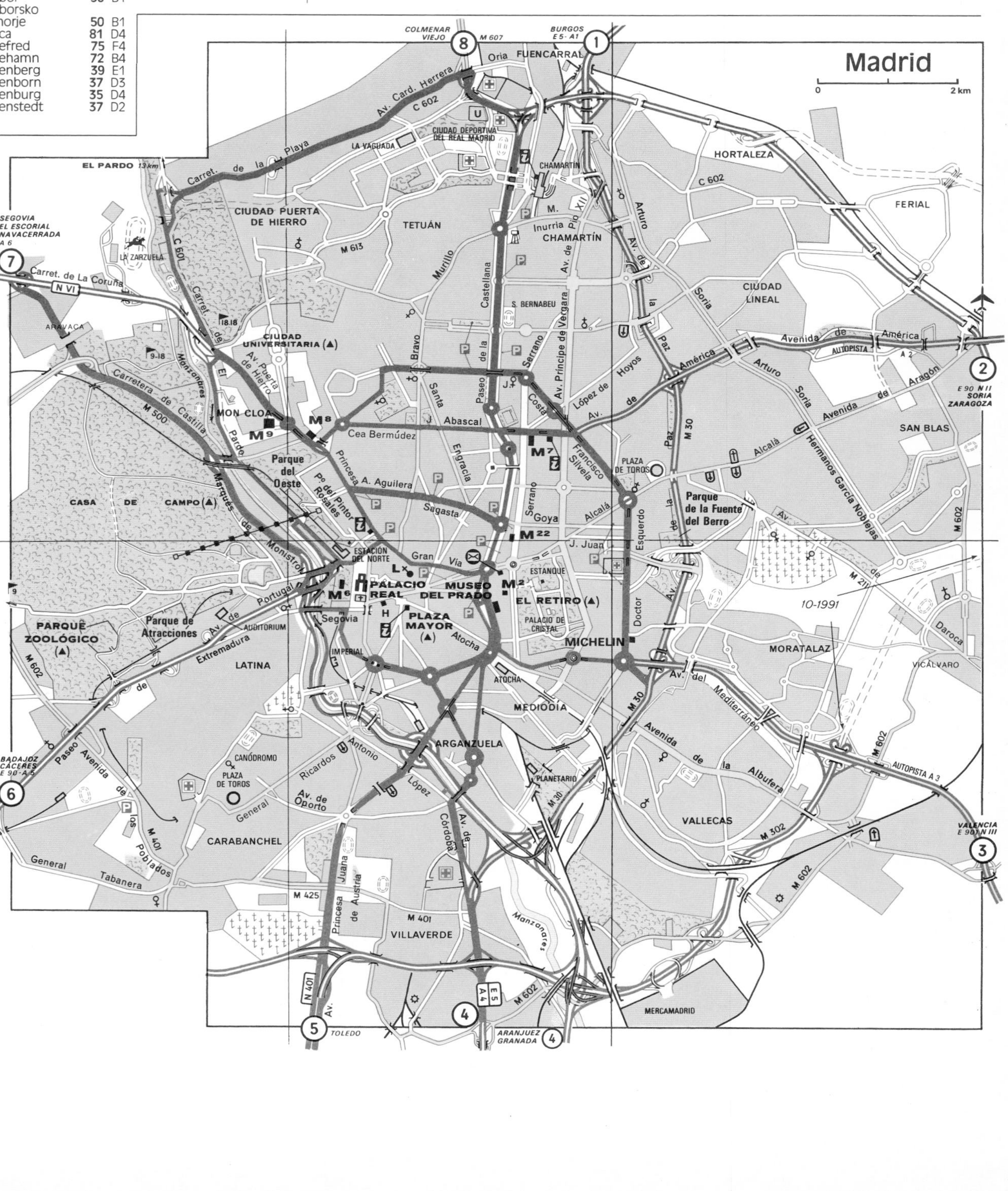
Madrid
0 2 km
COLMENAR VIEJO
M 607
BURGOS E 5 - A 1
Oria
FUENCARRAL
Av. Card. Herrera
C 602
LA VAGUADA
CIUDAD DEPORTIVA DEL REAL MADRID
EL PARDO 13 km
Carret. de la Playa
CHAMARTÍN
HORTALEZA
C 602
CIUDAD PUERTA DE HIERRO
TETUÁN
FERIAL
SEGOVIA
EL ESCORIAL
NAVACERRADA
A 6
LA ZARZUELA
Carret. de La Coruña
N VI
Inurria
CHAMARTÍN
Arturo
Soria
CIUDAD LINEAL
ARAVACA
CIUDAD UNIVERSITARIA (▲)
S. BERNABEU
Avenida de América
AUTOPISTA A 2
E 90 N II SORIA ZARAGOZA
Carretera de Castilla
M 500
MON-CLOA
Abascal
López de Hoyos
Avenida de Aragón
SAN BLAS
Cea Bermúdez
Francisco Silvela
Alcalá
Hermanos García Noblejas
Parque del Oeste
Princesa
A. Aguilera
PLAZA DE TOROS
Parque de la Fuente del Berro
CASA DE CAMPO (▲)
Sagasta
Goya
Gran Vía
J. Juan
ESTACIÓN DEL NORTE
PALACIO REAL
MUSEO DEL PRADO
EL RETIRO (▲)
ESTANQUE
PALACIO DE CRISTAL
PARQUE ZOOLÓGICO (▲)
Parque de Atracciones
AUDITORIUM
Segovia
PLAZA MAYOR
Atocha
MICHELIN
Doctor Esquerdo
10-1991
MORATALAZ
Daroca
VICÁLVARO
LATINA
Extremadura
IMPERIAL
ATOCHA
MEDIODÍA
Av. del Mediterráneo
Avenida de la Albufera
AUTOPISTA A 3
BADAJOZ CÁCERES E 90 - A 5
Paseo
Avenida de los Poblados
M 401
CANÓDROMO
PLAZA DE TOROS
General Ricardos
Antonio López
ARGANZUELA
PLANETARIO
M 30
Av. de Oporto
CARABANCHEL
VALLECAS
M 302
M 602
VALENCIA E 901 N III
General Tabanera
M 425
Princesa Juana de Austria
Córdoba
Manzanares
VILLAVERDE
M 401
MERCAMADRID
Av.
TOLEDO
ARANJUEZ GRANADA
E 5 A 4
M 602

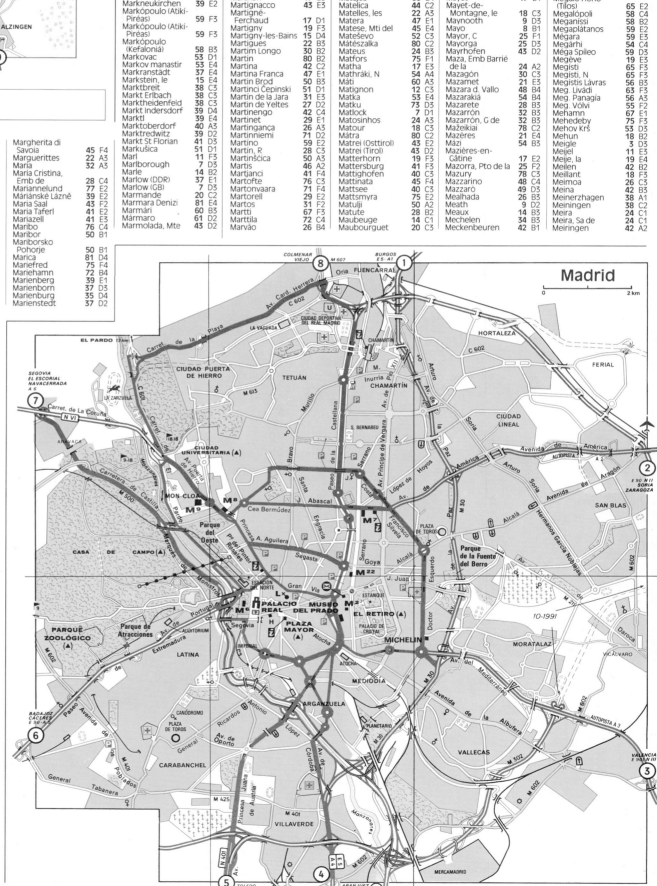

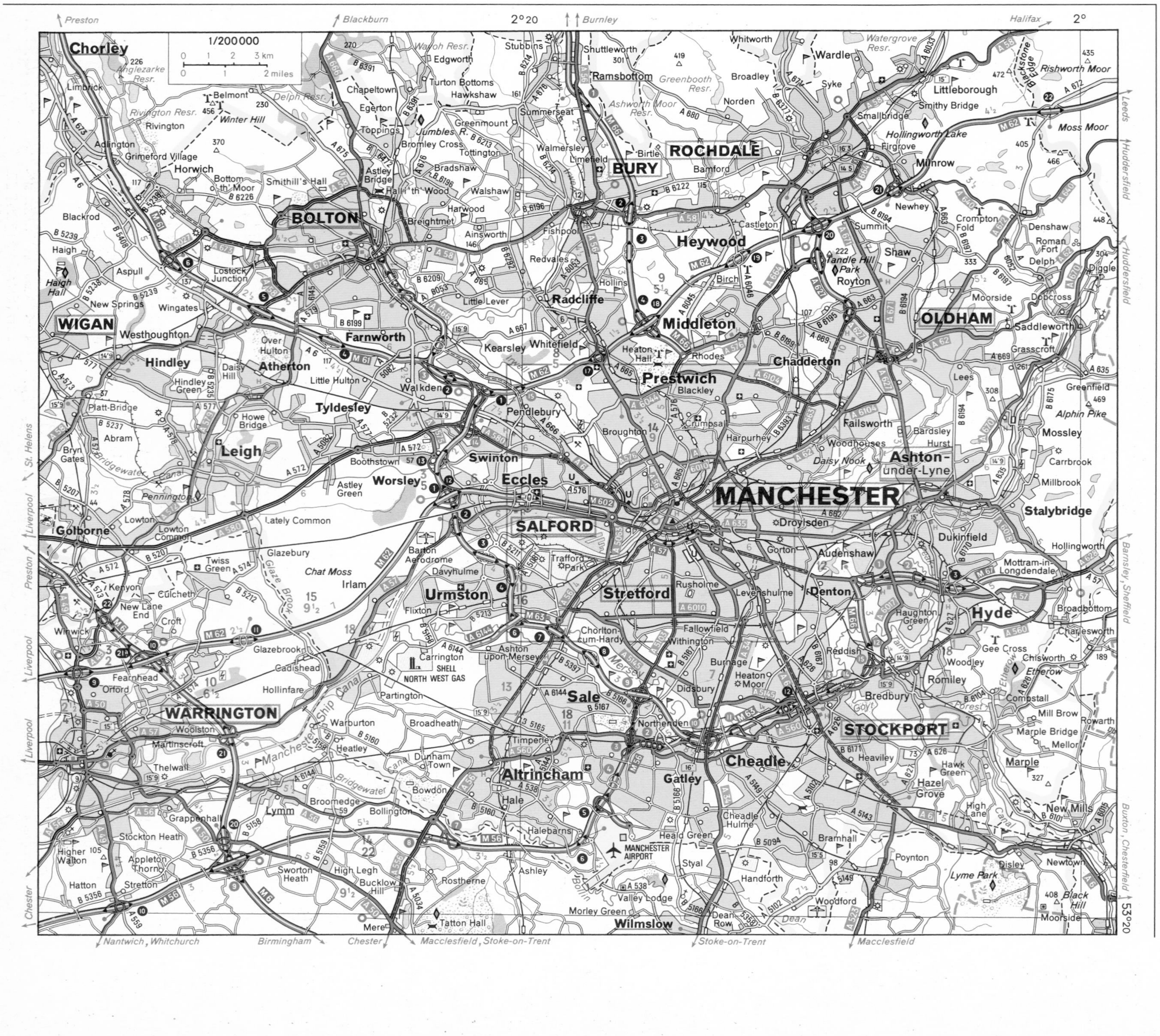

1/200 000
0 1 2 3 km
0 1 2 miles
Preston
Blackburn
2°20
Burnley
Halifax
2°
Chorley
BOLTON
BURY
ROCHDALE
WIGAN
Heywood
Middleton
OLDHAM
Radcliffe
Farnworth
Prestwich
Atherton
Hindley
Leigh
Tyldesley
Swinton
Eccles
Worsley
MANCHESTER
SALFORD
Ashton-under-Lyne
Stalybridge
Urmston
Stretford
Hyde
Denton
Sale
WARRINGTON
STOCKPORT
Cheadle
Altrincham
Gatley
Wilmslow
MANCHESTER AIRPORT
Nantwich, Whitchurch
Birmingham
Chester
Macclesfield, Stoke-on-Trent
Stoke-on-Trent
Macclesfield
Liverpool
St. Helens
Leeds
Huddersfield
Barnsley, Sheffield
Buxton, Chesterfield
53°20

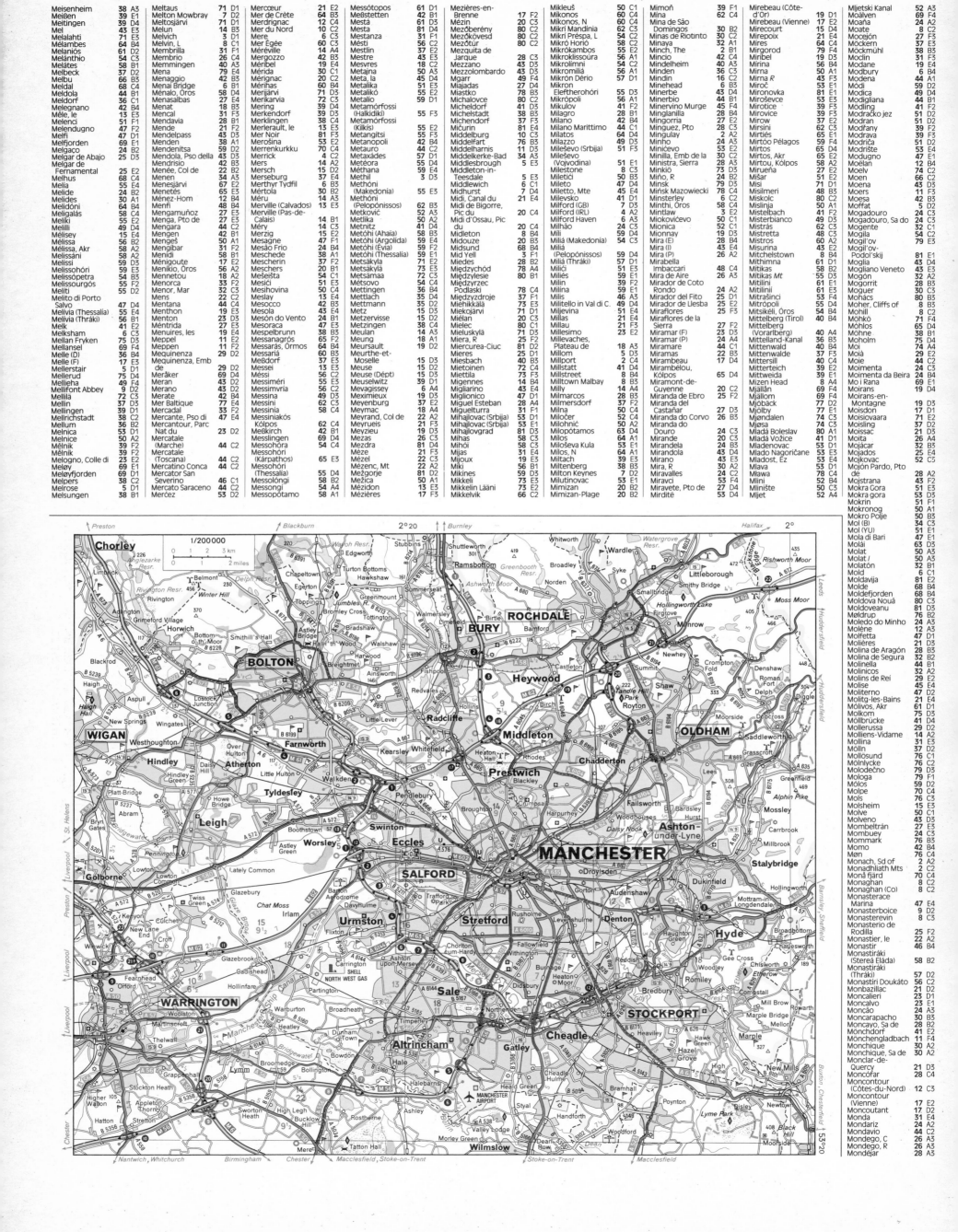

Mondello 48 B3
Mondim 24 B3
Mondolfo 44 C2
Mondoñedo 24 C1
Mondorf 15 D2
Mondoubleau 13 F4
Mondovì 23 D2
Mondragon 22 B2
Mondragone 46 B1
Mondsee 41 D3
Monein 20 C3
Monemvassia 63 D4
Monesi 23 D2
Monesterio 30 C2
Monestier-de-Clermont 22 B2
Monestiés 21 E3
Monêtier, le 19 E4
Moneygall 8 C3
Moneymore 9 D1
Monfalcone 43 F3
Monflanquin 21 D2
Monforte 26 B4
Monforte de Lemos 24 B2
Mongie, la 20 C4
Mongó 33 D1
Monguelfo 43 D2
Monheim 39 D4
Mönichkirchen 41 F3
Mon-Idée 14 C2
Monifieth 3 D3
Moní, N 59 E4
Monistrol 29 E2
Monistrol-d'Allier 21 F2
Monistrol-sur-Loire 18 C4
Mönkebude 37 F1
Monmouth 6 C3
Monnickendam 11 E2
Monodéndri 54 B3
Monódrio 60 A2
Monólithos 65 F2
Monopoli 47 E1
Monor 80 C2
Monóvar 32 C2
Monpazier 21 D2
Monreal 35 D3
Monreal del Campo 28 B3
Monreale 48 B3
Monrepós, Pto de 28 C1
Monroy 27 D4
Monroyo 28 C3
Mons 34 B3
Monsanto 26 C3
Monsaraz 30 B1
Monschau 34 C3
Monségur 20 C2
Monselice 43 D4
Monserrat 32 C1
Møns Klint 76 C4
Monsols 18 C3
Mönsterås 77 E2
Monsummano Terme 44 A2
Montabaur 38 A2
Montagnac 21 F3
Montagnana 43 D4
Montagne Noire 21 E3
Montagnes Noires 12 B4
Montagrier 17 D4
Montaigu 17 D2
Montaigu-de-Quercy 21 D2
Montaigut 18 B3
Montaione 44 A2
Montalbán 28 C3
Montalbo 28 A4
Montalcino 44 B3
Montalegre 24 B3
Montalieu 19 D3
Montalivet 20 B1
Montalto delle Marche 45 D2
Montalto di Castro 44 B3
Montalto Uffugo 47 D3
Montalvão 26 B4
Montamarta 25 D3
Montana 19 F3
Montañana 28 C2
Montánchez 27 D4
Montanejos 28 C4
Montargil 26 B4
Montargil, Bgem de 26 B4
Montargis 14 B4
Montastruc-la-Conseillère 21 D3
Montauban (Ille-et-Vilaine) 12 C4
Montauban (Tarn-et-Garonne) 21 D3
Montbard 18 C1
Montbazens 21 E2
Montbazon 17 E2
Montbéliard 19 E1
Montbenoît 19 E2
Mont Blanc 19 E3
Montblanc 29 E2
Mont Blanc, Tunnel du 19 E3
Montbozon 19 E1
Montbrió del Camp 29 D3
Montbrison 18 C3
Montbron 17 E3
Montceau-les-Mines 18 C2
Montcenis 18 C2
Mont Cenis, Col du 19 F4
Montchanin 18 C2
Montcornet 14 C2
Montcuq 21 D2
Mont-de-Marsan 20 C3
Montdidier 14 B2
Mont-Dore, le 18 B3
Monteagudo de las Vicarias 28 B2
Montealegre 25 D3
Montealegre del Castillo 32 B1
Montebello Ionico 47 D4
Montebello Vicentino 43 D4
Montebelluna 43 E3
Monte Bianco, Traforo di 19 E3
Montebourg 13 D2
Monte-Carlo-Monaco 23 D3
Montecarotto 44 C2
Montecatini-Terme 44 A2
Montecchio 44 C2
Montecchio Maggiore 43 D3
Montech 21 D3
Monte Citerna, Pso del 44 B2
Montecorvino Rovella 46 C2
Montecristo, I di 44 A4
Monte Croce Carnico, Pso di 43 E2
Monte Croce di Comelico, Pso 43 E2
Monte da Pedra 26 B4
Monte da Rocha, Bgem de 30 B2
Montedoro 48 C4
Montefalco 44 C3
Montefalcone di Val Fortore 46 C1
Montefalcone nel Sannio 45 E4
Montefeltro 44 C2
Montefiascone 44 C3
Montefiore dell' Aso 45 D2
Montefiorino 44 A1
Montefrío 31 E3
Montegallo 45 D3
Montegiorgio 45 D2
Monte Giovo, Pso di 43 D2
Montegranaro 45 D2
Montegrotto Terme 43 D4
Montehermoso 27 D3
Montejicar 31 F3
Montejo de Tiermes 25 F4
Montejunto, Sa de 26 A4
Monteleone di Spoleto 44 C3
Montélimar 22 B2
Montella 46 C1
Montellano 31 D3
Monteluco 44 C3
Montelupo Fiorentino 44 B2
Montemaggiore Belsito 48 C3
Montemagno 23 E1
Montemayor 31 E2
Montemayor de Pililla 25 E3
Montemor-o-Novo 30 B1
Montemor-o-Velho 26 A3
Montemuro, Sa do 24 B4
Montendre 17 E4
Montenegro de Cameros 28 A1
Montenero di Bisaccia 45 E3
Montenero Sabino 44 C3
Montepulciano 44 B3
Monte Real 26 A3
Montereale (Abruzzo) 45 D3
Montereale (Friuli-Venezia) 43 E3
Montereau 14 B4
Monte Redondo 26 A3
Monterenzio 44 B1
Monteriggioni 44 B2
Monteroni di Lecce 47 F2
Monte Rosa 42 A3
Monterosso al Mare 23 F2
Monterotondo 44 C4
Monterotondo Marittimo 44 B3
Monterroso 24 B2
Monterrubio de la Serena 31 D1
Monterubbiano 45 D2
Montesano sulla Marcellana 47 D2
Monte San Savino 44 B2
Monte Sant' Angelo 45 F4
Montesarchio 46 C1
Montescaglioso 47 E1
Montesilvano Marina 45 D3
Montesquieu-Volvestre 21 D4
Montesquiou 20 C3
Montet, le 18 B3
Montets, Col des 19 E3
Montevarchi 44 B2
Monteviejo, Pto de 25 D2
Montfaucon (Maine-et-Loire) 17 D2
Montfaucon (Meuse) 15 D3
Montfaucon-en-Velay 18 C4
Montfort 12 C4
Montfort-en-Chalosse 20 B3
Montfort-l'Amaury 14 A3
Montfort-sur-Risle 13 E3
Montgaillard 21 D4
Montgenèvre 19 E4
Montgenèvre, Col de 19 E4
Montgiscard 21 D3
Montgomery 6 C2
Montguyon 17 E4
Monthermé 14 C2
Monthey 19 E3
Monthois 14 C2
Monthureux 15 D4
Monti 46 B2
Montichiari 42 C4
Monticiano 44 B3
Montiel 32 A1
Montier-en-Der 14 C4
Montignac 21 D2
Montigny-le-Roi 15 D4
Montigny-sur-Aube 14 C4
Montijo (E) 30 C1
Montijo (P) 26 A4
Montilla 31 E2
Montioni 44 A3
Montivilliers 13 E2
Montjean 17 D1
Monthéry 14 A3
Montlieu 17 E4
Montlouis 17 F1
Mont-Louis 29 E1
Montluçon 18 B3
Montluel 19 D3
Montmarault 18 B3
Montmartin 13 D3
Montmédy 15 D2
Montmélian 19 E4
Montmirail (Marne) 14 B3
Montmirail (Sarthe) 13 F4
Montmirey-le-Château 19 D2
Montmoreau 17 E4
Montmorillon 17 F3
Montmort 14 B3
Montoggio 23 E2
Montoire 17 F1
Montoito 30 B1
Montone 44 B1
Montorio al Vomano 45 D3
Montoro 31 E2
Montoro, Emb de 31 E2
Montpellier 22 A3
Montpellier-le-Vieux, Chaos de 21 F3
Montpezat-de-Quercy 21 D2
Montpezat-sous-Bauzon 22 A2
Montpon-Ménestérol 20 C2
Montpont 19 D2
Montréal (Aude) 21 E4
Montréal (Gers) 20 C3
Montréal-la-Cluse 19 D3
Montredon-Labessonnie 21 E3
Montréjeau 20 C4
Montrésor 17 F2
Montresta 46 A3
Montreuil 14 A1
Montreuil-Bellay 17 E2
Montreux 19 E2
Montrevault 17 D2
Montrevel 19 D3
Montrichard 17 F2
Mont-roig del Camp 29 D3
Montrond-les-Bains 18 C3
Montrose 3 D3
Montsalvy 21 E2
Montsant, Sa del 29 D2
Montsauche 18 C2
Montsec, Serra de 29 D2
Montseny 29 F2
Montseny, Sa de 29 F2
Montserrat 29 E2
Mont-sous-Vaudrey 19 D2
Monts-sur-Guesnes 17 E2
Mont-St-Michel, le 13 D3
Mont-St-Vincent 18 C2
Montsûrs 13 E4
Montuenga 27 E2
Montuiri 33 E2
Monviso 23 D2
Monza 42 B4
Monzón 29 D2
Monzón de Campos 25 E3
Moordorf 36 A2
Moorfoot Hills 5 D1
Moosburg 39 D4
Mór 80 B2
Mora (E) 27 F4
Mora (P) 26 B4
Mora (S) 75 E2
Morača 52 C3
Morača R 52 C4
Morača klisura 52 C3
Móra d'Ebre 29 D3
Mora de Rubielos 28 C4
Moraira 33 D2
Moraira, Pta de 33 D2
Morais 24 C3
Moraitika 54 A4
Morakovo, G. 52 C3
Móra la Nova 29 D3
Moral de Calatrava 31 F1
Moraleda de Zafayona 31 F3
Moraleja 26 C3
Moraleja de Sayago 24 C4
Morales de Rey 25 D3
Morales de Toro 25 D3
Morano Calabro 47 D2
Mora, Pto de la 31 F3
Morar, L 2 B2
Morarp 77 D3
Morasverdes 27 D3
Morata de Jalón 28 B2
Morata de Tajuña 27 F3
Moratalla 32 B2
Morata, Pto de 28 B2
Morava 41 F1
Morava R 80 B1
Moravče 50 A1
Moravci 50 B1
Moravica 51 F3
Moravské Budějovice 41 E1
Moravske Toplice 41 F3
Moravský Krumlov 41 F1
Moray Firth 3 D2
Morbach 38 A3
Morbegno 42 B3
Morbihan 12 C4
Mörbisch 41 F3
Mörbylånga 77 E2
Morcenx 20 B3
Morciano di Romagna 44 C2
Morcone 46 C1
Morcote 42 B3
Morcuera, Pto de la 27 F2
Mordelles 12 C4
Morecambe 5 D3
Morecambe Bay 5 D3
Moreda 31 F3
Morée 14 A4
Moreleja del Vino 25 D3
Morella 28 C3
Møre og Romsdal 68 B3
Mores 46 A3
Morestel 19 D3
Moret 14 B4
Moreton 7 D2
Moretonhampstead 6 B4
Moreuil 14 B2
Morez 19 E2
Morfasso 23 F2
Mórfio 58 A1
Morgat 12 A4
Morges 19 E2
Morgex 19 E3
Morgins, Pas de 19 E3
Morhange 15 E3
Mori 43 D3
Morina 53 D3
Moritzburg 39 E1
Morjärv 70 C2
Morlaàs 20 C3
Morlaix 12 B3
Mormanno 47 D2
Mormant 14 B3
Mormoiron 22 B3
Mornant 19 D3
Mórnou, Teh L 58 C2
Morón de Almazán 28 A2
Morón de la Frontera 31 D3
Morosaglia 23 D3
Morović 51 E2
Morpeth 5 E2
Morrón 32 A3
Morrum 77 D3
Mors 76 B2
Morsbach 38 A2
Morsil 69 D4
Morsleben 37 D3
Mortagne 17 D4
Mortagne-au-Perche 13 E3
Mortagne-sur-Sèvre 17 D2
Mortágua 26 B3
Mortain 13 D3
Mortara 23 E1
Morteau 19 E2
Mortrée 13 E3
Morven 3 D1
Morzine 19 E3
Mosbach 38 B3
Mosby 74 B4
Moščenice 50 A2
Moščenička Draga 50 A2
Moschendorf 41 F3
Mosel 38 A2
Moselle (Dépt) 15 D3
Moselle R 15 D3
Moshokariá 59 D1
Moshopótamos 55 D3
Mosjøen 69 D2
Moskenesøya 66 A3
Moskenstraumen 66 A3
Mosko 52 B3
Moskosel 69 F2
Moskva 79 F2
Moskva R 79 F2
Moslavačka gora 50 C1
Mosonmagyaróvár 80 B2
Mosor 50 C4
Mosqueruela 28 C3
Moss 74 C3
Mossala 72 C4
Mossat 3 D2
Mosses, Col des 19 F2
Mössingen 38 B4
Most (CS) 39 F1
Most (YU) 43 F3
Mosta 49 F4
Mostar 52 B3
Mosteiro 24 A2
Mosterhamn 74 A3
Mostiska 80 C1
Móstoles 27 F3
Mostonga 51 E1
Mostrim 8 C2
Mosty 78 C3

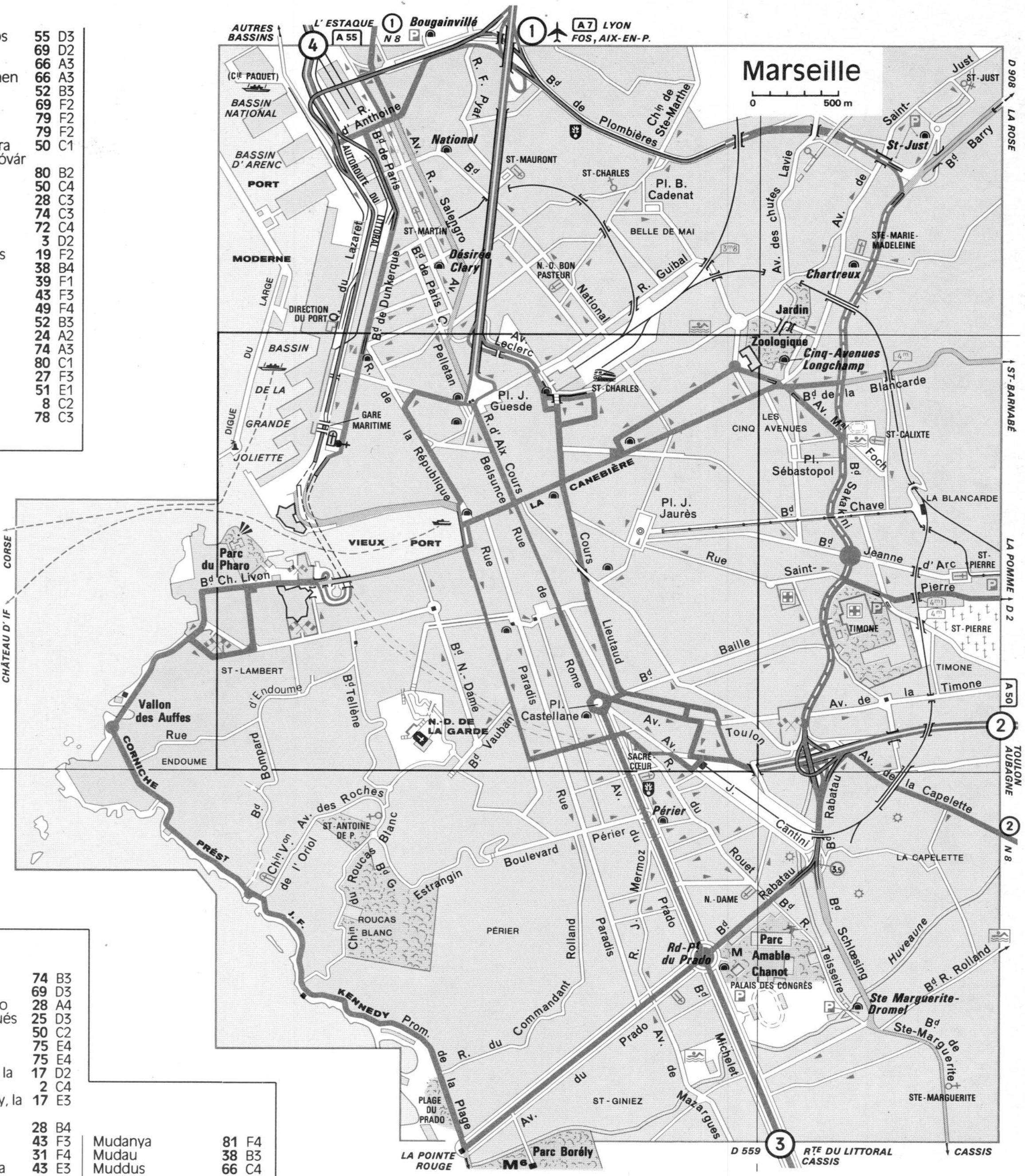
Marseille
500 m
AUTRES BASSINS
L' ESTAQUE
Bougainvillé
LYON
FOS, AIX-EN-P.
BASSIN NATIONAL
BASSIN D' ARENC
PORT
National
ST-MAURONT
ST-CHARLES
Pl. B. Cadenat
BELLE DE MAI
St-Just
STE-MARIE-MADELEINE
Chartreux
MODERNE
DIRECTION DU PORT
Désirée Clary
N.-D. BON PASTEUR
Jardin Zoologique
Cinq-Avenues Longchamp
BASSIN DE LA GRANDE JOLIETTE
GARE MARITIME
Pl. J. Guesde
CINQ AVENUES
ST-CALIXTE
Pl. Sébastopol
LA BLANCARDE
LA CANEBIÈRE
VIEUX PORT
Pl. J. Jaurès
CORSE
CHATEAU D'IF
Parc du Pharo
TIMONE
ST-PIERRE
ST-LAMBERT
Vallon des Auffes
ENDOUME
N.-D. DE LA GARDE
Pl. Castellane
SACRÉ CŒUR
Périer
CORNICHE
PRÉST
J.F. KENNEDY
ST-ANTOINE DE P.
ROUCAS BLANC
PÉRIER
LA CAPELETTE
N.-DAME
Rd-Pt du Prado
Parc Amable Chanot
PALAIS DES CONGRÈS
Ste Marguerite-Dromel
STE-MARGUERITE
ST-GINIEZ
PLAGE DU PRADO
LA POINTE ROUGE
Parc Borély
RTE DU LITTORAL CASSIS
CASSIS
TOULON AUBAGNE

Møsvatn 74 B3
Mosvik 69 D3
Mota del Cuervo 28 A4
Mota del Marqués 25 D3
Motajica 50 C2
Motala 75 E4
Motala S 75 E4
Mothe-Achard, la 17 D2
Motherwell 2 C4
Mothe-St-Héray, la 17 E3
Motilla del Palancar 28 B4
Motovun 43 F3
Motril 31 F4
Motta di Livenza 43 E3
Motta S.A. 49 D3
Motta Visconti 42 B4
Motte-Chalancon, la 22 B2
Motte, la 22 C2
Mottola 47 E1
Mouchard 19 D2
Moudon 19 E2
Moúdros 56 C4
Mougins 23 D3
Mouhijärvi 72 C3
Mouilleron-en-Pareds 17 D2
Moulins 18 B2
Moulins-Engilbert 18 C2
Moulins-la-Marche 13 E3
Moult 13 E3
Moúnda, Akr 58 B3
Mountain Ash 6 B3
Mount Bellew 8 B2
Mountmellick 8 C3
Mountrath 8 C3
Mount's B 6 A4
Mountsoúna 64 C1
Moura 30 B2
Mourão 30 B1
Mourdzeflos, Akr 56 B3
Mourenx 20 C3
Mouriki 59 E2
Mourmelon-le-Grand 14 C3
Mourne 8 C1
Mourne Mts 9 D2
Mourniés 64 A3
Mourujärvi 71 E1
Mouscron 34 A3
Moustiers-Ste Marie 22 C3
Mouthe 19 E2
Mouthier 19 E2
Mouthoumet 21 E4
Moutier 19 F2
Moûtiers 19 E4
Moutiers-les-Mauxfaits 17 D2
Mouy 14 A3
Mouzakéi 54 C4
Mouzáki 55 D4
Mouzon 14 C2
Moville 4 A2
Moy 8 B2
Moyenneville 14 A2
Moyeuvre 15 D3
Moyuela 28 C3
Možajsk 79 F2
Mozirje 50 A1
Mozyr' 79 E4
Mrągowo 78 C3
Mrakovica 50 C2
Mramorak 53 D1
Mratinje 51 E4
Mrazovac 50 B2
Mrčajevci 53 D2
Mrežičko 53 F4
Mrkonjić Grad 50 C3
Mrkopalj 50 A2
Mšeno 39 F1
Msta 79 E1
Mstislavl' 79 E3
Mú 30 B2
Muć 50 C4
Muccia 44 C2
Much 38 A2
Mucheln 37 E4
Much Wenlock 6 C2
Mucientes 25 E3
Muck 2 B2
Muckle Roe 3 F1
Muckross House 8 A4
Mudanya 81 F4
Mudau 38 B3
Muddus 66 C4
Muel 28 C2
Muelas del Pan 25 D3
Muff 4 A2
Muge 26 A4
Mügeln 39 E1
Muggia 43 F3
Mugron 20 B3
Mugueimes 24 B3
Mühlbach 40 C4
Mühlberg 37 F4
Mühldorf 39 E4
Mühlen-Eichsen 37 D2
Mühlhausen 38 C1
Mühltroff 39 D2
Muhniemi 73 E3
Muhos 71 D2
Muhu 78 C1
Muineachán 8 C2
Muine Bheag 8 C3
Muirkirk 4 C1
Muir of Ord 2 C2
Mukačevo 80 C2
Mukos 53 E4
Mula 32 B2
Mulacker 38 B4
Mula, R 32 B2
Mulargia, L 46 B4
Mulhacén 31 F3
Mülheim 11 F3
Mulhouse 15 E4
Mull 2 B3
Müllheim 42 A1
Mullingar 8 C2
Mull of Galloway 4 C2
Mull of Kintyre 4 B2
Mull of Oa 2 B4
Mull, Sd of 2 B3
Mullsjö 77 D1
Mulranny 8 B2
Multia 73 D2
Mumbles, The 6 B3
Muñana 27 E3
Münchberg 39 D2
Müncheberg 37 F3
München 40 B3
Münchhausen 38 B1
Münden 36 C4
Mundesley 7 F1
Mundford 7 E2
Mundo, R 32 B2
Munera 32 A1
Mungia 20 A3
Muñico 27 E3
Muniesa 28 C3
Munkebo 76 B3
Munkedal 74 C4
Munkfors 75 D3
Münnerstadt 38 C2
Muñogalindo 27 E3
Munsala 70 C4
Munsfjället 69 E3
Münsingen (CH) 19 F2
Münsingen (D) 38 C4
Münster (CH) 42 A3
Münster (F) 15 E4
Münster (Niedersachsen) 36 C3
Münster (Nordrhein-Westfalen) 36 B4
Münstertal 42 A1
Münzenberg 38 B2
Münzkirchen 41 D2
Muodoslompolo 67 D3
Muojärvi 71 E1
Muonio 67 D3
Muonioälven 67 D3
Muotkatonturit 67 E2
Mur 41 E3
Mura 50 B1
Muraglione, Pso del 44 B2
Murano 43 E3
Murat 21 F1
Murato 23 D3
Murat-sur-Vèbre 21 E3
Murau 41 D4
Muravera 46 B4
Murça 24 B3
Murchante 28 B2
Murcia 32 C2
Murcia (Reg) 32 B2
Mur-de-Barrez 21 E2
Mur-de-Bretagne 12 C4
Mureck 41 F3
Mure, la 22 C2
Mures 80 C3
Muret 21 D3
Murg 38 B4
Murguía 20 A4
Muri 42 A2
Murias de Paredes 24 C2
Murino 51 F4
Murigan 52 C4
Müritz See 37 E2
Murjek 70 B1
Murnau 40 B3
Muro 23 E3
Muro de Alcoy 32 C1
Murol 18 B4
Murole 73 D3
Muro Lucano 47 D1
Murovi 24 A2
Mürren 42 A3
Murrhardt 38 C4
Murska Sobota 41 F4
Mursko Središće 50 B1
Murten 19 E2
Murter 50 B4
Murter I 50 B4
Murtosa 26 B2
Murtovaara 71 E2
Murvica 50 B3
Murviel 21 F3
Mürz 41 E3
Mürzsteg 41 E3
Mürzzuschlag 41 E3
Musala 81 D4
Mussalo 73 E4
Musselburgh 3 D4
Musselkanaal 11 F2
Mussidan 20 C2
Mussomeli 48 C4
Mussy 14 C4
Mustair 42 C2
Mustasaari 70 C4
Müstér 42 B2
Mustion as 73 D4
Mustvee 79 D1
Muta 50 A1
Mutala 73 D3
Mutterstadt 38 B3
Mutzschen 39 E1
Muurame 73 D2
Muurasjärvi 71 D3
Muuratjärvi 73 D2
Muurla 73 D4
Muurola 71 D1

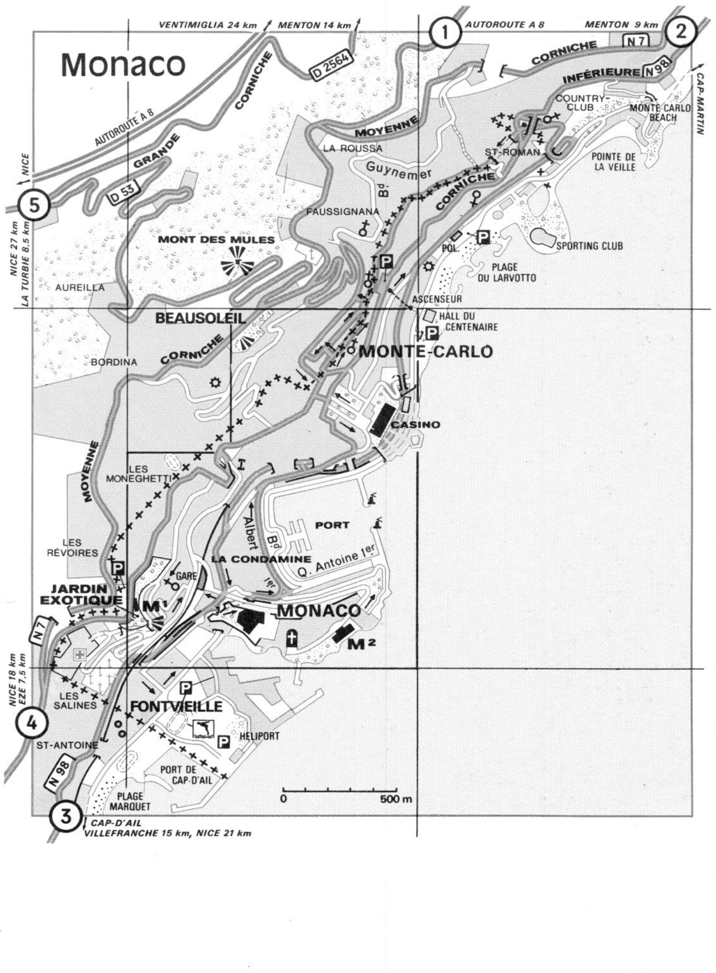
Monaco
VENTIMIGLIA 24 km
MENTON 14 km
AUTOROUTE A 8
MENTON 9 km
CORNICHE INFÉRIEURE
CAP-MARTIN
MONTE-CARLO BEACH
COUNTRY CLUB
POINTE DE LA VEILLE
MOYENNE CORNICHE
GRANDE CORNICHE
LA ROUSSA
ST-ROMAN
FAUSSIGNANA
MONT DES MULES
SPORTING CLUB
PLAGE DU LARVOTTO
AUREILLA
BEAUSOLEIL
ASCENSEUR
HALL DU CENTENAIRE
MONTE-CARLO
BORDINA
CASINO
LES MONEGHETTI
PORT
LES REVOIRES
LA CONDAMINE
JARDIN EXOTIQUE
MONACO
FONTVIEILLE
LES SALINES
HELIPORT
ST-ANTOINE
PORT DE CAP-D'AIL
PLAGE MARQUET
CAP-D'AIL
VILLEFRANCHE 15 km, NICE 21 km
500 m

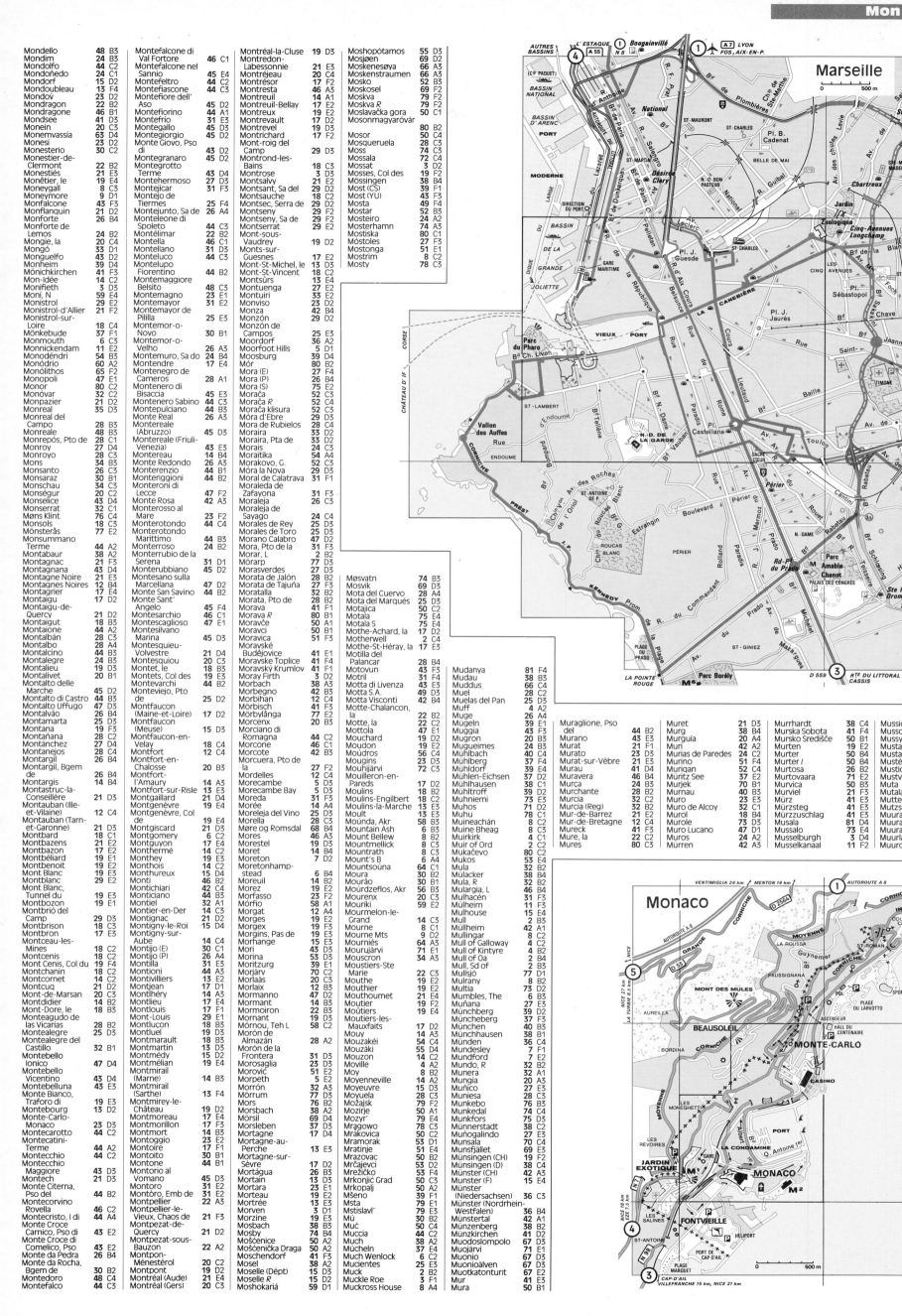

Muuruvesi 71 E4
Muxía 24 A1
Muy, le 22 C3
Muzillac 16 C1
Muzzana del Turgnano 43 E3
Mweelrea Mts 8 A2
Myckegensjö 69 F4
Mykines 68 A3
Myllykoski 73 E3
Myllykylä 72 C2
Myllymäki 71 D4
Mynämäki 72 C4
Mýrdalsjökull 68 B2
Myre 66 B2
Myrlandshaugen 66 C2
Myrskylä 73 E3
Myrviken 69 E4
Mysen 74 C3
Mysingen 75 F4
Myślibórz 78 A4
Mývatn 68 B1
Mže 39 E2

N

Naab 39 D3
Naamijoki 70 C1
Naantali 72 C4
Naarajärvi 73 E2
Naarva 71 F3
Naas 9 D3
Näätämöjoki 67 F2
Nabburg 39 E3
Načeradec 41 D1
Náchod 80 B1
Naddvik 74 B2
Nadela 24 B2
Nădlac 80 C3
Nadur 49 F4
Nadvornaja 81 D2
Nærbø 74 A4
Nærøy 69 D2
Næstved 76 C3
Näfels 42 B2
Nafpaktías, Óri 58 C2
Náfpaktos 58 C2
Náfplio 59 D4
Naggen 75 E1
Nagold 38 B4
Nagu 72 C4
Nagyatád 80 B3
Nagykálló 80 C2
Nagykanizsa 80 B3
Nagykőrös 80 C2
Nahe 36 C2
Nahe *R* 38 A3
Naila 39 D2
Nailloux 21 D3
Nailsworth 6 C3
Nairn 3 D2
Najac 21 E2
Nájera 28 A1
Najerilla, R 28 A1
Nakkila 72 C3
Nakło 78 B4
Nakovo 51 F1
Nakskov 76 C4
Näljänkä 71 E2
Na Logu 43 F2
Nalón, R 25 D2
Naltijärvi 67 E3
Namdalseid 69 D3
Nämdöfjärden 75 F4
Náměšt 41 E1
Namsen 69 D3
Namsos 69 D3
Namsskogan 69 D2
Namur 34 B3
Namur (Prov) 34 C3
Nancy 15 D3
Nangis 14 B3
Nannestad 74 C3
Nant 21 F3
Nanterre 14 A3
Nantes 17 D2
Nantes, Canal de 12 C4
Nanteuil-le-Haudouin 14 B3
Nantiat 17 F3
Nantua 19 D3
Nantwich 6 C1
Nao, C de la 33 D1
Náoussa (Kikládes) 64 B1
Náoussa (Makedonía) 55 D2
Napapiiri 71 D1
Napoli 46 B1
Napoli, G di 46 B2
Napoule, la 23 D3
Narberth 6 A2
Narbolia 46 A3
Narbonne 21 F4
Narbonne-Plage 21 F4
Narcao 46 A4
Narcea, R 24 C1
Nardò 47 F2
Narew 78 C3
Narila 73 E2
Narkaus 71 D1
Narni 44 C3
Naro 48 C4
Naro-Fominsk 79 F2
Närpes 72 C2
Närpio 72 C2
Narta 50 C1
Nartháki 59 D1
Nartháki, Óros 59 D1
Narva 79 D1
Narvik 66 C3
Nås 75 E3
Näsåker 69 F4
Năsăud 81 D2
Nasbinals 21 F2
Našice 51 D1
Näsijärvi 73 D3
Naso 49 D3
Nassau 38 A2
Nassereith 40 B4
Naßfeld-Paß 43 E2
Nässjö 77 D2
Nastola 73 E3
Natalinci 53 D1
Nattaset 67 E3
Nattavaara 70 B1
Nättraby 77 E3
Naucelle 21 E3
Nauders 40 A4
Nauen 37 E3
Naul 9 D2
Naumburg 39 D1
Naunhof 37 E4
Naussac, Bge de 22 A2
Naustdal 74 A2
Nauvo 72 C4
Nava 25 D1
Navacelles, Cirque de 21 F3
Navacepeda 27 E3
Navacerrada 27 F3
Navacerrada, Pto de 27 F2
Navachica 31 F3
Nava, Colle di 23 D2
Navaconcejo 27 D3
Nava de la Asunción 25 E4
Nava del Rey 25 D4
Navafria, Pto de 27 F2
Navahermosa 27 E4
Navalcán 27 E3
Navalcarnero 27 F3
Navaleno 28 A2
Navalmanzano 25 E4
Navalmoral de la Mata 27 D3
Navalperal de Pinares 27 E3
Navaluenga 27 E3
Navalvillar de Pela 31 D1
Navamorcuende 27 E3
Navan 9 D2
Navarra 20 B4
Navarredonda de la Sierra 27 E3
Navarrenx 20 B3
Navarrés 32 C1
Navarrete 28 A1
Navascués 20 B4
Navas del Madroño 26 C4
Navas de Oro 25 E4
Navas de San Juan 32 A2
Navasfrías 26 C3
Navatalgordo 27 E3
Nave 42 C3
Nävekvarn 75 E4
Navelli 45 D3
Naver, L 2 C1
Naveros 30 C4
Navia 24 C1
Navia de Suarna 24 C2
Navia, R 24 C1
Navl'a 79 F3
Náxos 64 B1
Náxos Días 64 B1
Náxos, N 64 C1
Nay 20 C4
Nazaré 26 A3
Naze, The 7 F3
Ndrejaj 52 C4
Ndroq 54 A1
Nea 69 D4
Néa Agathoúpoli 55 E3
Néa Alikarnassós 64 C4
Néa Anhíalos 59 D1
Néa Apolonía 55 F2
Néa Artáki 59 E2
Néa Éfessos 55 E3
Néa Epídavros 59 E4
Néa Fókea 55 F3
Neagh, L 9 D1
Néa Hilí 56 C2
Néa Iraklítsa 56 B2
Néa Kalikrátia 55 E3
Néa Kariá 56 B2
Néa Karváli 56 B2
Néa Kerassoús 58 B1
Néa Kíos 59 D4
Néa Koróni 62 C3
Néa Mákri 60 A3
Néa Messángala 55 E3
Néa Mihanióna 55 E3
Néa Moní 61 D2
Néa Moudaniá 55 F3
Néa Pagassés 59 E1
Néa Péla 55 E2
Néa Péramos (Makedonía) 56 A2
Néa Péramos (Stereá Eláda) 59 E3
Néa Perivóli 55 E4
Neápoli (Kríti) 65 D4
Neápoli (Makedonía) 54 C3
Neápoli (Pelopónissos) 63 D4
Néa Róda 56 A3
Néa Sánda (Makedonía) 55 E2
Néa Sánda (Thráki) 56 C2
Néa Sílata 55 E3
Néa Skióni 55 F3
Néa Stíra 60 B3
Neath 6 B3
Néa Tríglia 55 F3
Néa Víssa 57 D1
Néa Zíhni 56 A2
Néa Zoí 55 D2
Nebel 36 B1
Nebelhorn 40 A4
Nebljusi 50 B3
Nebra 39 D1
Nechranická přehr nádrž 39 E2
Neckar 38 B3
Neckarelz 38 B3
Neckargemünd 38 B3
Neckarsteinach 38 B3
Neckarsulm 38 B3
Nečujam 50 C4
Neda 24 B1
Nédas 58 C4
Nedelišće 50 B1
Nedervetil 70 C3
Nedstrand 74 A3
Neede 11 F2
Needles, The 7 D4
Neermoor 36 A2
Nefyn 6 B1
Negoiu 81 D3
Negorci 53 F4
Negotin 53 E1
Negotino 53 F4
Negra de Urbión, L 28 A1
Negrar 43 D3
Negratin, Emb del 32 A3
Negreira 24 A2
Nègrepelisse 21 D3
Negru Vodă 81 E3
Neheim-Hüsten 38 A1
Neiden 67 F2
Neige, Crêt de la 19 E3
Neila 28 A1
Nejdek 39 E2
Nekromandío Efíras 58 A1
Neksø 77 E4
Nela, R 25 F2
Nelas 26 B2
Nelidovo 79 E2
Nellim 67 F2
Nelson 5 E3
Neman 78 C3
Neméa 59 D3
Nemirov 81 E1

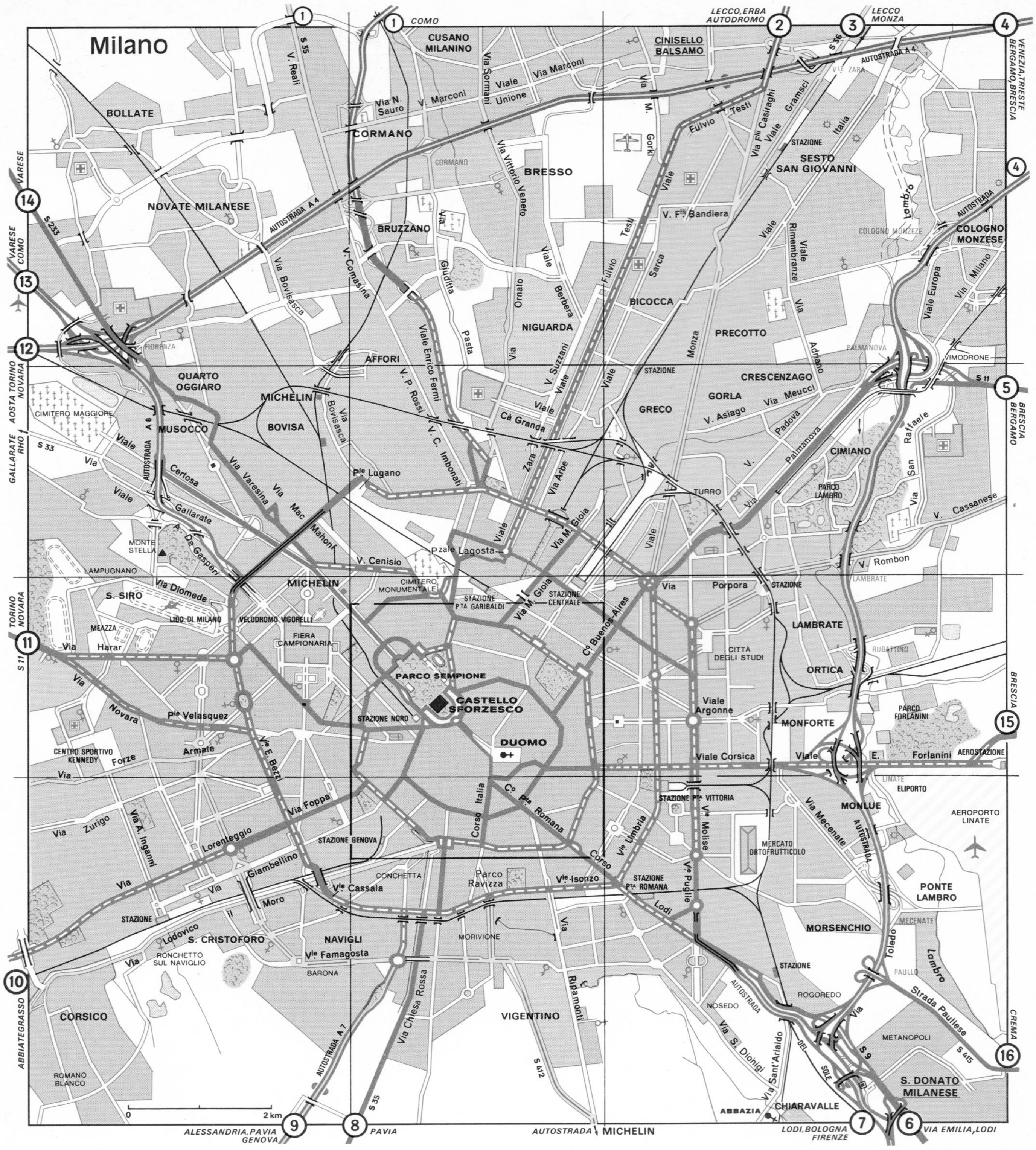
Milano
COMO
LECCO, ERBA AUTODROMO
LECCO MONZA
VENEZIA, TRIESTE BERGAMO, BRESCIA
CUSANO MILANINO
CINISELLO BALSAMO
BOLLATE
CORMANO
BRESSO
SESTO SAN GIOVANNI
NOVATE MILANESE
BRUZZANO
COLOGNO MONZESE
NIGUARDA
BICOCCA
PRECOTTO
AFFORI
QUARTO OGGIARO
CRESCENZAGO
GORLA
GRECO
MUSOCCO
BOVISA
CIMIANO
BRESCIA BERGAMO
GALLARATE RHO
AOSTA TORINO NOVARA
S. SIRO
MICHELIN
LAMBRATE
CITTÀ DEGLI STUDI
ORTICA
PARCO SEMPIONE
CASTELLO SFORZESCO
DUOMO
MONFORTE
BRESCIA
MONLUE
AEROPORTO LINATE
PONTE LAMBRO
MORSENCHIO
S. CRISTOFORO
NAVIGLI
CORSICO
VIGENTINO
ROGOREDO
S. DONATO MILANESE
CHIARAVALLE
ABBIATEGRASSO
CREMA
ALESSANDRIA, PAVIA GENOVA
PAVIA
AUTOSTRADA MICHELIN
LODI, BOLOGNA FIRENZE
VIA EMILIA, LODI

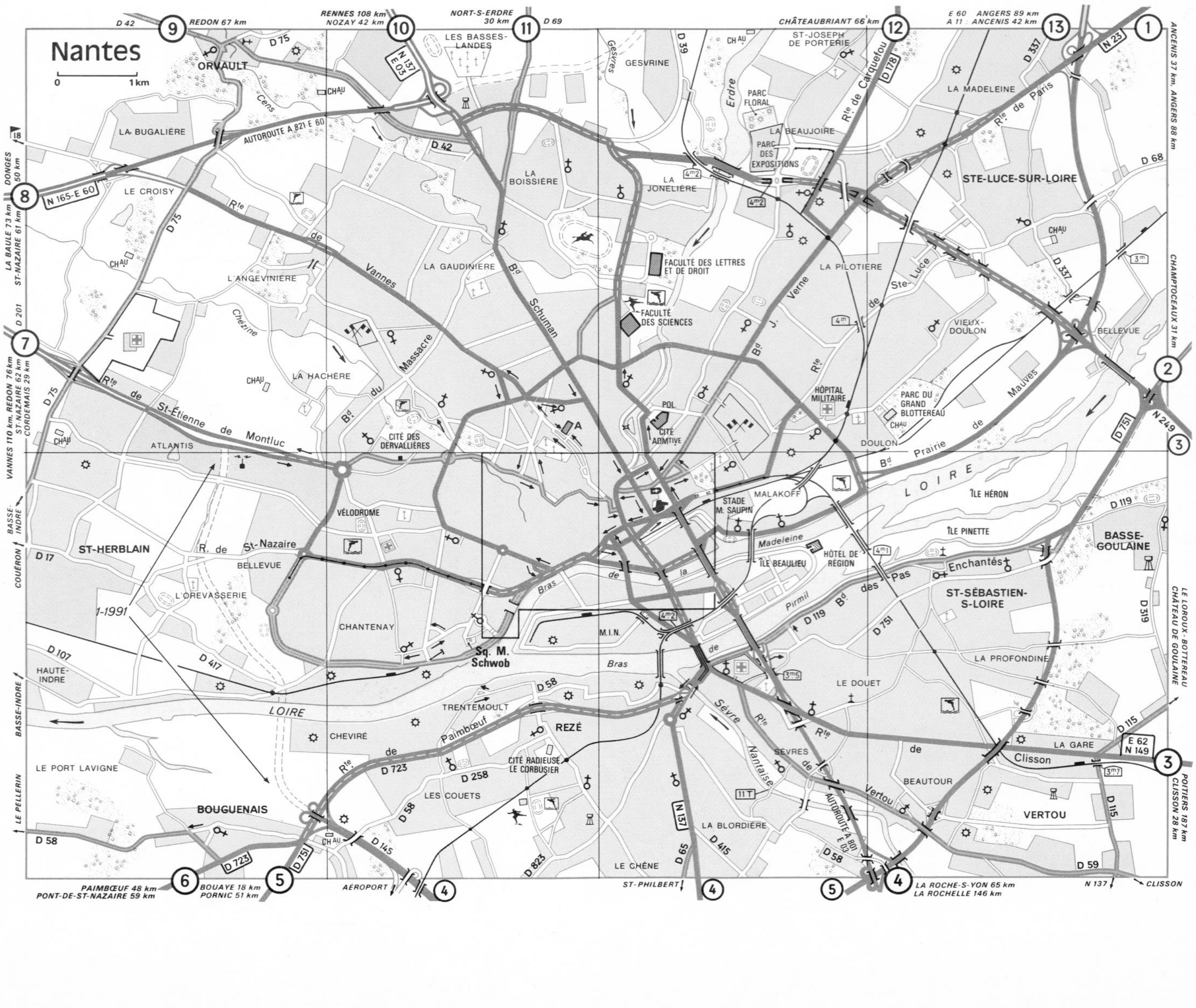
Nantes
REDON 67 km
RENNES 108 km NOZAY 42 km
NORT-S-ERDRE 30 km
CHÂTEAUBRIANT 66 km
ANGERS 89 km ANCENIS 42 km
ORVAULT
LA BUGALIÈRE
LA BOISSIÈRE
LA JONELIÈRE
LA MADELEINE
STE-LUCE-SUR-LOIRE
LE CROISY
LA GAUDINIÈRE
FACULTÉ DES LETTRES ET DE DROIT
FACULTÉ DES SCIENCES
LA PILOTIÈRE
BELLEVUE
L'ANGEVINIÈRE
LA HACHÈRE
ATLANTIS
CITÉ DES DERVALLIÈRES
LOIRE
ST-HERBLAIN
BELLEVUE
CHANTENAY
Sq. M. Schwob
BASSE-GOULAINE
ST-SÉBASTIEN-S-LOIRE
LA PROFONDINE
TRENTEMOULT
REZÉ
CHEVIRÉ
LE PORT LAVIGNE
BOUGUENAIS
LES COUETS
VERTOU
BEAUTOUR
LA BLORDIÈRE
LE CHÊNE
PAIMBŒUF 48 km PONT-DE-ST-NAZAIRE 59 km
BOUAYE 18 km PORNIC 51 km
AEROPORT
ST-PHILBERT
LA ROCHE-S-YON 65 km LA ROCHELLE 146 km
CLISSON

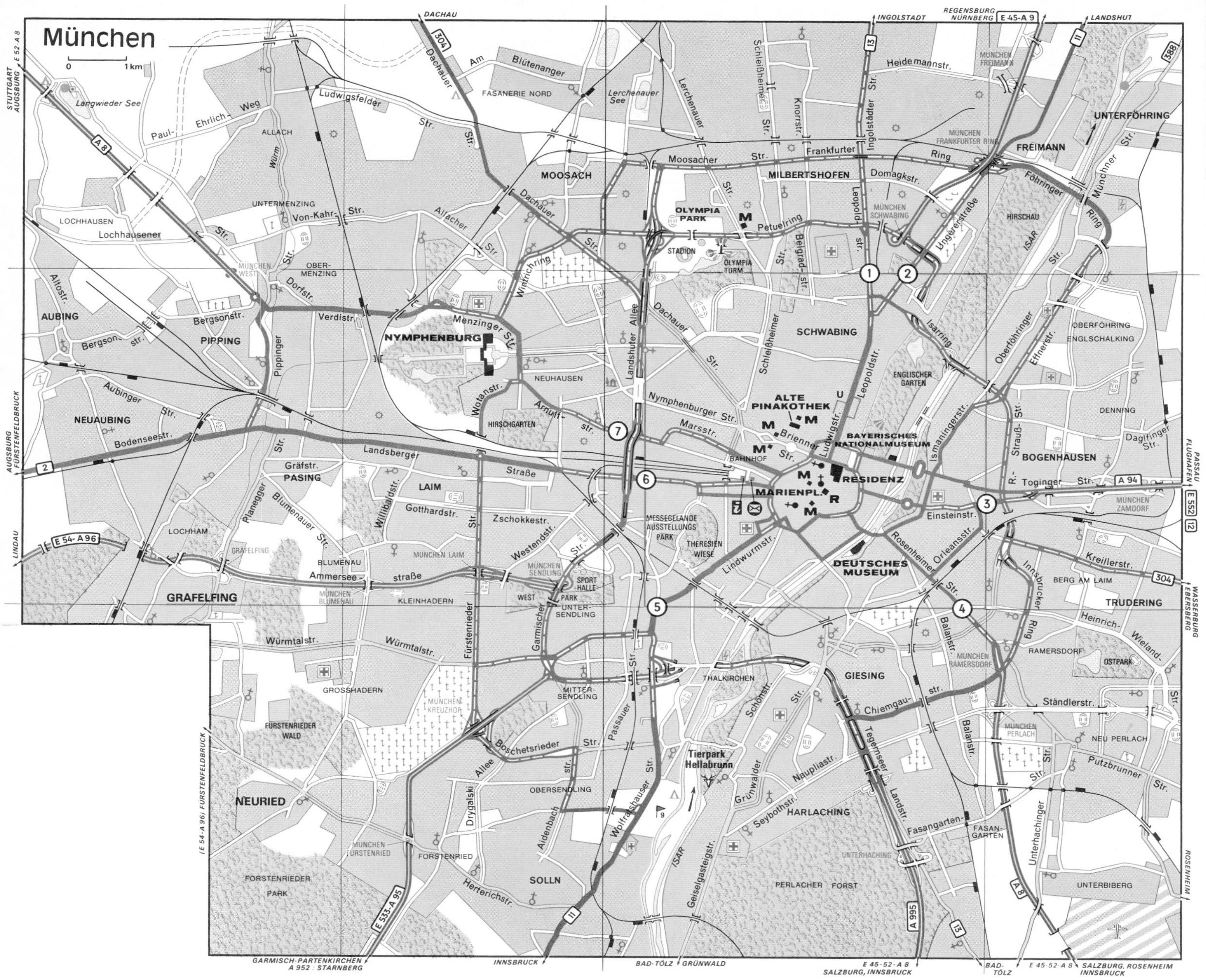
München
0
1 km
DACHAU
INGOLSTADT
REGENSBURG NÜRNBERG E 45-A 9
LANDSHUT
STUTTGART AUGSBURG E 52-A 8
Langwieder See
Paul-Ehrlich-Weg
Ludwigsfelder Str.
Blütenanger
FASANERIE NORD
Lerchenauer See
Heidemannstr.
UNTERFÖHRING
FREIMANN
MOOSACH
Moosacher Str.
Frankfurter Ring
MILBERTSHOFEN
Domagkstr.
ALLACH
UNTERMENZING
Von-Kahr-Str.
LOCHHAUSEN
Lochhausener Str.
OLYMPIA PARK
Petuelring
STADION
OLYMPIA TURM
HIRSCHAU
OBER-MENZING
AUBING
PIPPING
Bergsonstr.
Verdistr.
NYMPHENBURG
Menzinger Str.
SCHWABING
OBERFÖHRING
ENGLSCHALKING
ENGLISCHER GARTEN
NEUHAUSEN
HIRSCHGARTEN
NEUAUBING
Bodenseestr.
Landsberger Str.
Nymphenburger Str.
ALTE PINAKOTHEK
BAYERISCHES NATIONALMUSEUM
DENNING
BOGENHAUSEN
PASING
LAIM
MARIENPL.
RESIDENZ
BAHNHOF
Toginger Str.
Gotthardstr.
Zschokkestr.
MESSEGELÄNDE AUSSTELLUNGS PARK
THERESIEN WIESE
Einsteinstr.
MÜNCHEN ZAMDORF
LOCHHAM
BLUMENAU
Ammersee-straße
DEUTSCHES MUSEUM
Kreillerstr.
BERG AM LAIM
GRÄFELFING
KLEINHADERN
SPORT HALLE
WEST PARK
UNTER-SENDLING
TRUDERING
Würmtalstr.
RAMERSDORF
OSTPARK
GROSSHADERN
MITTER-SENDLING
THALKIRCHEN
GIESING
Ständlerstr.
FÜRSTENRIEDER WALD
Boschetsrieder Str.
Tierpark Hellabrunn
NEU PERLACH
Putzbrunner Str.
NEURIED
OBERSENDLING
HARLACHING
FORSTENRIED
SOLLN
PERLACHER FORST
UNTERBIBERG
FORSTENRIEDER PARK
GARMISCH-PARTENKIRCHEN A 952 : STARNBERG
INNSBRUCK
BAD-TÖLZ GRÜNWALD
E 45-52-A 8 SALZBURG, INNSBRUCK
BAD-TÖLZ
E 45-52-A 8 SALZBURG, ROSENHEIM INNSBRUCK
AUGSBURG FÜRSTENFELDBRUCK
LINDAU
PASSAU FLUGHAFEN
WASSERBURG EBERSBERG
ROSENHEIM

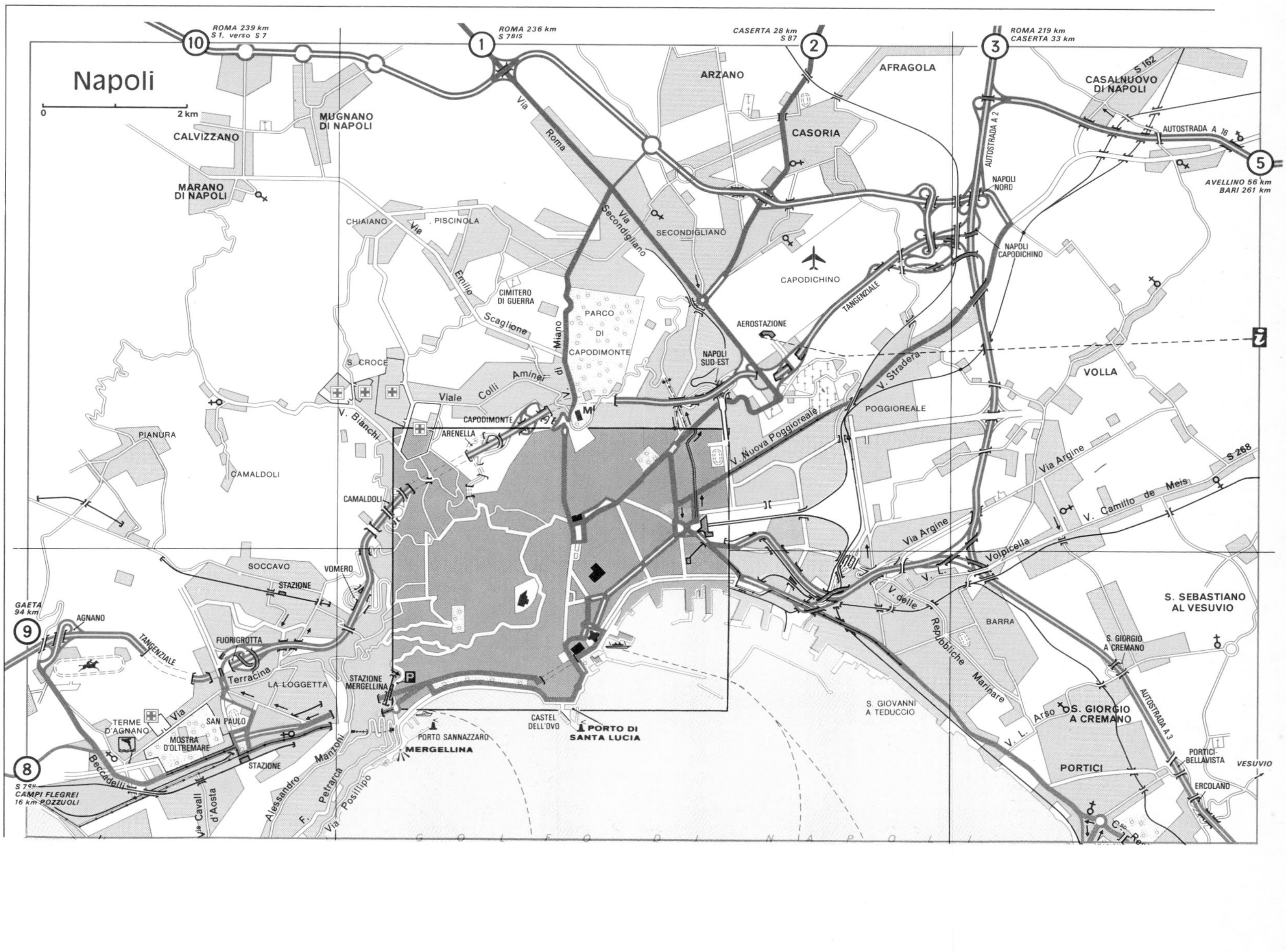
Napoli
0
2 km
ROMA 239 km S 1, verso S 7
ROMA 236 km S 7BIS
CASERTA 28 km S 87
ROMA 219 km CASERTA 33 km
ARZANO
AFRAGOLA
CASALNUOVO DI NAPOLI
MUGNANO DI NAPOLI
CALVIZZANO
CASORIA
AUTOSTRADA A 16
AVELLINO 56 km BARI 261 km
MARANO DI NAPOLI
NAPOLI NORD
CHIAIANO
PISCINOLA
SECONDIGLIANO
Via Roma
CIMITERO DI GUERRA
NAPOLI CAPODICHINO
CAPODICHINO
AEROSTAZIONE
PARCO DI CAPODIMONTE
NAPOLI SUD-EST
S. CROCE
TANGENZIALE
V. Stadera
VOLLA
Viale Colli Aminei
CAPODIMONTE
ARENELLA
POGGIOREALE
PIANURA
V. Nuova Poggioreale
CAMALDOLI
Via Argine
V. Camillo de Meis
S 268
SOCCAVO
VOMERO
STAZIONE
S. SEBASTIANO AL VESUVIO
GAETA 94 km
AGNANO
FUORIGROTTA
BARRA
S. GIORGIO A CREMANO
STAZIONE MERGELLINA
LA LOGGETTA
S. GIOVANNI A TEDUCCIO
TERME D'AGNANO
SAN PAOLO
MOSTRA D'OLTREMARE
CASTEL DELL'OVO
PORTO DI SANTA LUCIA
PORTO SANNAZZARO
MERGELLINA
PORTICI
PORTICI BELLAVISTA
VESUVIO
ERCOLANO
S 7qu CAMPI FLEGREI 16 km POZZUOLI
Via Posillipo
GOLFO DI NAPOLI
AUTOSTRADA A 3

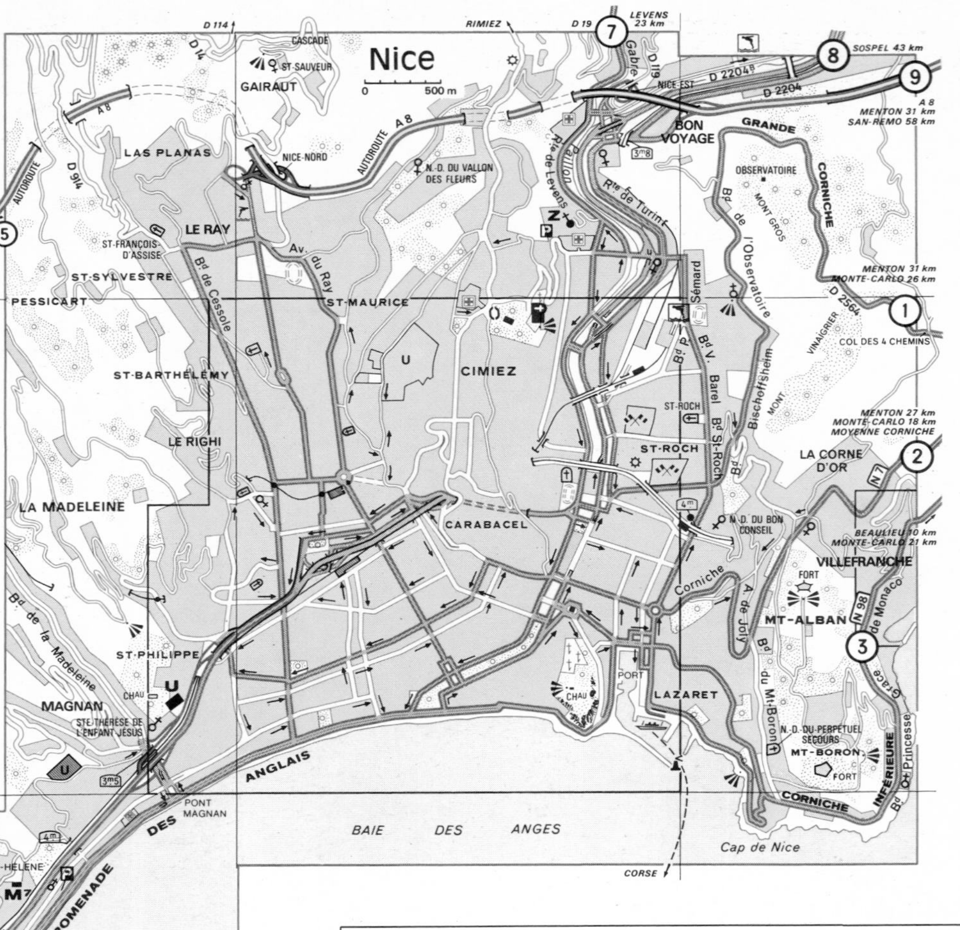

Nice
0 500 m
D 114
RIMIEZ
D 19
7
LEVENS 23 km
8
SOSPEL 43 km
9
MENTON 31 km
SAN-REMO 58 km
GAIRAUT
ST-SAUVEUR
CASCADE
LAS PLANAS
NICE-NORD
N.-D. DU VALLON DES FLEURS
BON VOYAGE
OBSERVATOIRE
GRANDE CORNICHE
MONT GROS
LE RAY
ST-FRANÇOIS-D'ASSISE
ST-SYLVESTRE
PESSICART
ST-MAURICE
CIMIEZ
MENTON 31 km
MONTE-CARLO 26 km
1
COL DES 4 CHEMINS
ST-BARTHÉLÉMY
LE RIGHI
ST-ROCH
MENTON 27 km
MONTE-CARLO 18 km
MOYENNE CORNICHE
2
LA CORNE D'OR
LA MADELEINE
CARABACEL
N.-D. DU BON CONSEIL
BEAULIEU 10 km
MONTE-CARLO 21 km
VILLEFRANCHE
FORT
MT-ALBAN
3
ST-PHILIPPE
PORT
LAZARET
MAGNAN
STE-THÉRÈSE DE L'ENFANT JÉSUS
N.-D. DU PERPÉTUEL SECOURS
MT-BORON
FORT
ANGLAIS
CORNICHE INFÉRIEURE
PONT MAGNAN
BAIE DES ANGES
Cap de Nice
CORSE

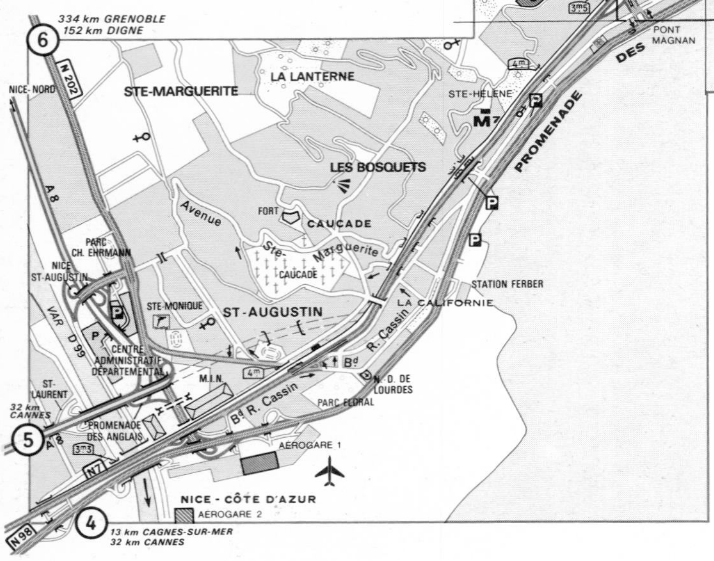

334 km GRENOBLE
152 km DIGNE
6
NICE-NORD
STE-MARGUERITE
LA LANTERNE
STE-HÉLÈNE
LES BOSQUETS
PROMENADE
CAUCADE
FORT
PARC CH. EHRMANN
NICE ST-AUGUSTIN
STE-MONIQUE
ST-AUGUSTIN
LA CALIFORNIE
STATION FERBER
CENTRE ADMINISTRATIF DÉPARTEMENTAL
ST-LAURENT
32 km CANNES
5
PROMENADE DES ANGLAIS
N.-D. DE LOURDES
PARC FLORAL
AÉROGARE 1
NICE - CÔTE D'AZUR
AÉROGARE 2
4
13 km CAGNES-SUR-MER
32 km CANNES

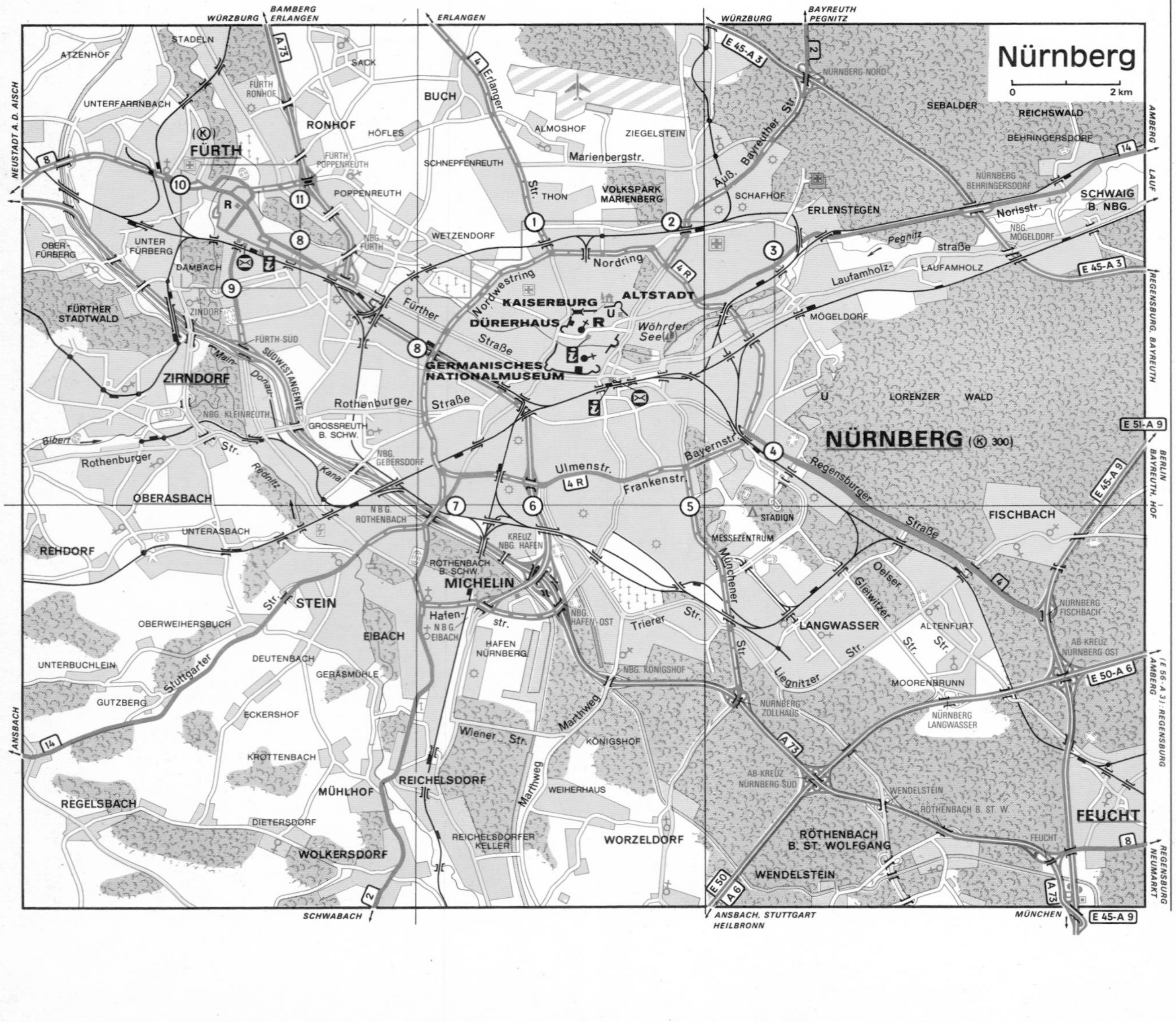

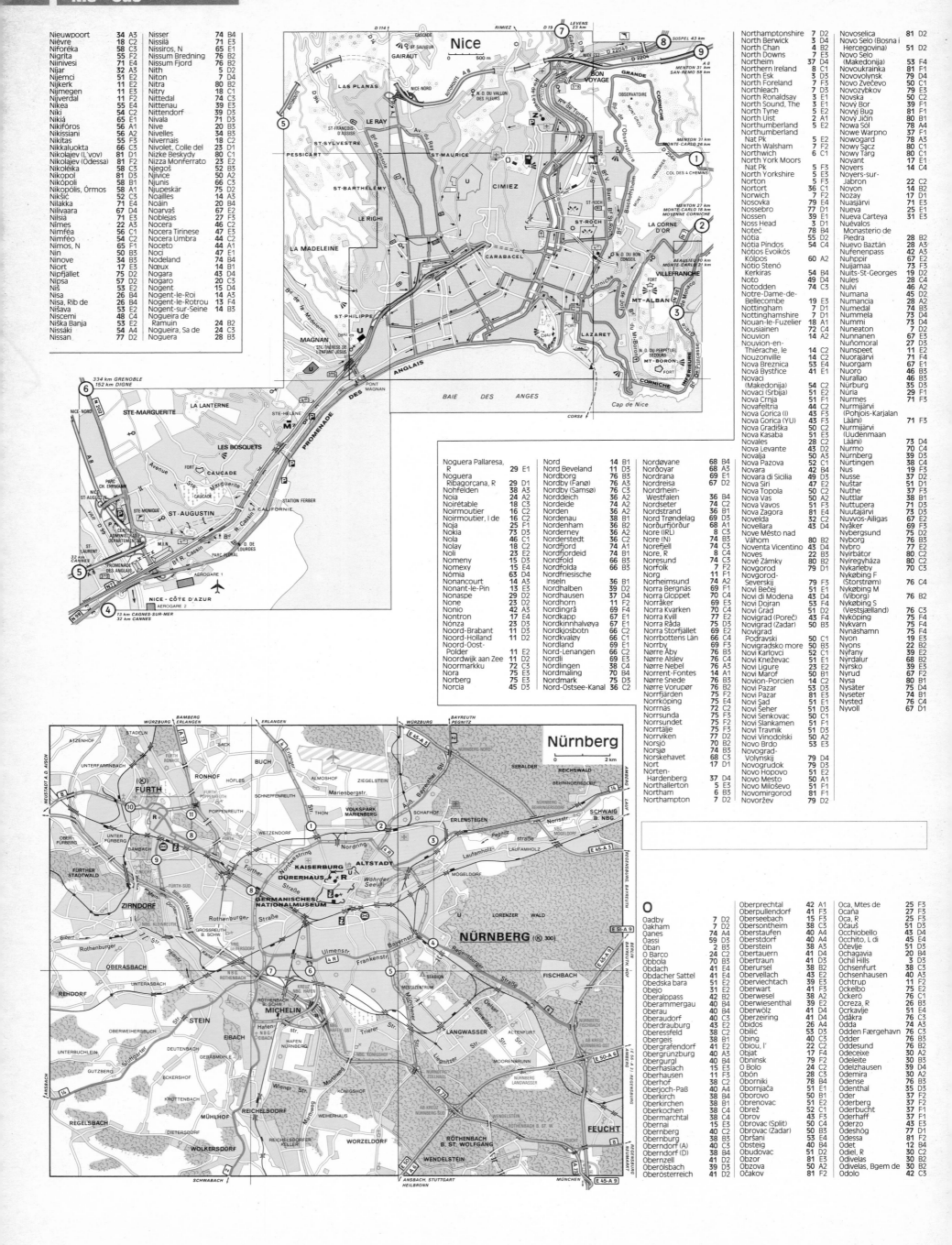

Nürnberg
0 2 km
WÜRZBURG
BAMBERG ERLANGEN
ERLANGEN
WÜRZBURG
BAYREUTH PEGNITZ
NEUSTADT A. D. AISCH
STADELN
ATZENHOF
SACK
UNTERFARRNBACH
FÜRTH
BUCH
RONHOF
NÜRNBERG-NORD
SEBALDER
REICHSWALD
AMBERG
SCHNEPFENREUTH
ZIEGELSTEIN
Marienbergstr.
POPPENREUTH
VOLKSPARK MARIENBERG
THON
SCHAFHOF
ERLENSTEGEN
SCHWAIG B. NBG.
LAUF
WETZENDORF
UNTER FÜRBERG
OBER-FÜRBERG
DAMBACH
Nordring
LAUFAMHOLZ
Laufamholz-
REGENSBURG, BAYREUTH
FÜRTHER STADTWALD
KAISERBURG
ALTSTADT
DÜRERHAUS
MÖGELDORF
ZIRNDORF
GERMANISCHES NATIONALMUSEUM
LORENZER WALD
Rothenburger Straße
NÜRNBERG (K) 300)
Ulmenstr.
Frankenstr.
Bayernstr.
Regensburger Straße
BERLIN BAYREUTH, HOF
OBERASBACH
UNTERASBACH
REHDORF
FISCHBACH
STADION
MESSEZENTRUM
STEIN
MICHELIN
ROTHENBACH B. SCHW.
OBERWEIHERSBACH
EIBACH
LANGWASSER
ALTENFURT
UNTERBUCHLEIN
DEUTENBACH
GERASMÜHLE
HAFEN NÜRNBERG
(E 56 - A 3): REGENSBURG AMBERG
GUTZBERG
ECKERSHOF
KRÖTTENBACH
MOORENBRUNN
ANSBACH
KÖNIGSHOF
WEIHERHAUS
MÜHLHOF
REICHELSDORF
REGELSBACH
DIETERSDORF
FEUCHT
RÖTHENBACH B. ST. WOLFGANG
WOLKERSDORF
WORZELDORF
WENDELSTEIN
REGENSBURG NEUMARKT
SCHWABACH
ANSBACH, STUTTGART HEILBRONN
MÜNCHEN

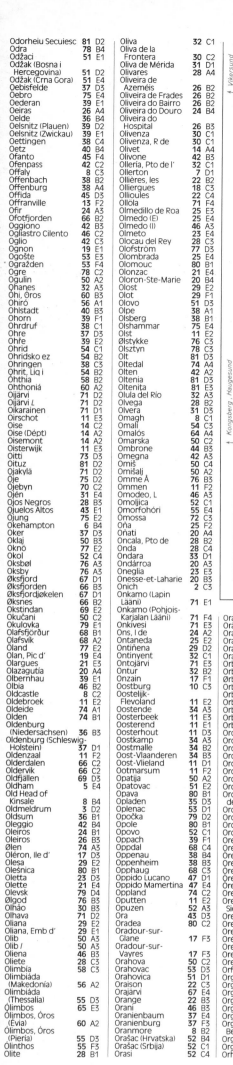

Odorheiu Secuiesc 81 D2
Odra 78 B4
Odžaci 51 E1
Odžak (Bosna i Hercegovina) 51 D2
Odžak (Crna Gora) 51 E4
Oebisfelde 37 D3
Oebro 75 E4
Oederan 39 E1
Oeiras 26 A4
Oelde 36 B4
Oelsnitz (Plauen) 39 D2
Oelsnitz (Zwickau) 39 E1
Oettingen 38 C4
Oetz 40 B4
Ofanto 45 F4
Ofenpass 42 C2
Offaly 8 C3
Offenbach 38 B2
Offenburg 38 A4
Offida 45 D3
Offranville 13 F2
Ofir 24 A3
Ofotfjorden 66 B2
Oggiono 42 B3
Ogliastro Cilento 46 C2
Oglio 42 C3
Ognon 19 E1
Ogošte 53 E3
Ogražden 53 F4
Ogre 78 C2
Ogulin 50 A2
Ohanes 32 A3
Ohi, Óros 60 B3
Ohiró 56 A1
Ohlstadt 40 B3
Ohorn 39 F1
Ohrdruf 38 C1
Ohre 37 D3
Ohře 39 E2
Ohrid 54 C1
Ohridsko ez 54 B2
Ohringen 38 C3
Ohrit, Liq i 54 B2
Ohthia 58 B2
Ohthoniá 60 A2
Oijärvi 71 D2
Oijärvi L 71 D2
Oikarainen 71 D1
Oirschot 11 E3
Oise 14 C2
Oise (Dépt) 14 A2
Oisemont 14 A2
Oisterwijk 11 E3
Oitti 73 D3
Oituz 81 D2
Ojakylä 71 D2
Oje 75 D2
Ojebyn 70 C2
Ojén 31 E4
Ojos Negros 28 B3
Ojuelos Altos 43 E1
Ojung 75 E2
Okehampton 6 B4
Oker 37 D3
Oklaj 50 B3
Oknö 77 E2
Okol 52 C4
Oksbøl 76 A3
Oksby 76 A3
Øksfjord 67 D1
Øksfjorden 66 B3
Øksfjordjøkelen 67 D1
Øksnes 66 B2
Okstindan 69 E2
Okučani 50 C2
Okulovka 79 E1
Olafsfjörður 68 B1
Olafsvík 68 A2
Öland 77 E2
Olan, Pic d' 19 E4
Olargues 21 E3
Olazagutía 20 A4
Olbernhau 39 E1
Olbia 46 B2
Oldcastle 8 C2
Oldebroek 11 E2
Oldeide 74 A1
Olden 74 B1
Oldenburg (Niedersachsen) 36 B3
Oldenburg (Schleswig-Holstein) 37 D1
Oldenzaal 11 F2
Olderdalen 66 C2
Oldervik 66 C2
Oldfjällen 69 D3
Oldham 5 E4
Old Head of Kinsale 8 B4
Oldmeldrum 3 D2
Oldsum 36 B1
Oleggio 42 B4
Oleiros 24 B1
Oleiros 26 B3
Ølen 74 A3
Oléron, Ile d' 17 D3
Olesa 29 E2
Oleśnica 80 B1
Oletta 23 D3
Olette 21 E4
Olevsk 79 D4
Ølgod 76 B3
Olhão 30 B3
Olhava 71 D2
Oliana 29 E2
Oliana, Emb d' 29 E1
Olib 50 A3
Olib I 50 A3
Oliena 46 B3
Oliete 28 C3
Olimbía 58 C3
Olimbiáda (Makedonía) 56 A2
Olimbiáda (Thessalía) 55 D3
Ólimbos 65 E3
Ólimbos, Óros (Évia) 60 A2
Ólimbos, Óros (Piería) 55 D3
Ólinthos 55 F3
Olite 28 B1
Oliva 32 C1
Oliva de la Frontera 30 C2
Oliva de Mérida 31 D1
Olivares 28 A4
Oliveira de Azeméis 26 B2
Oliveira de Frades 26 B2
Oliveira do Bairro 26 B2
Oliveira do Douro 24 B4
Oliveira do Hospital 26 B3
Olivenza 30 C1
Olivenza, R de 30 C1
Olivet 14 A4
Olivone 42 B3
Ollería, Pto de l' 32 C1
Ollerton 7 D1
Ollières, les 22 B2
Olliergues 18 C3
Ollioules 22 C4
Ollöla 71 F4
Olmedillo de Roa 25 E3
Olmedo (E) 25 E4
Olmedo (I) 46 A3
Olmeto 23 E4
Olocau del Rey 28 C3
Olofström 77 D3
Olombrada 25 E4
Olomouc 80 B1
Olonzac 21 E4
Oloron-Ste-Marie 20 B4
Olost 29 E2
Olot 29 F1
Olovo 51 D3
Olpe 38 A1
Olsberg 38 B1
Olshammar 75 E4
Olst 11 E2
Ølstykke 76 C3
Olsztyn 78 C3
Olt 81 D3
Oltedal 74 A4
Olten 42 A2
Oltenia 81 D3
Oltenița 81 E3
Olula del Río 32 A3
Olvega 28 B2
Olvera 31 D3
Omagh 8 C1
Omalí 54 C3
Omalós 64 A4
Omarska 50 C2
Ombrone 44 B3
Omegna 42 A3
Omiš 50 C4
Omišalj 50 A2
Omme Å 76 B3
Ommen 11 F2
Omodeo, L 46 A3
Omoljica 52 C1
Omorfohóri 55 E4
Ömossa 72 C3
Oña 25 F2
Oñati 20 A4
Oncala, Pto de 28 B2
Onda 28 C4
Ondara 33 D1
Ondárroa 20 A3
Oneglia 23 E3
Onesse-et-Laharie 20 B3
Onich 2 C3
Onkamo (Lapin Lääni) 71 E1
Onkamo (Pohjois-Karjalan Lääni) 71 F4
Onkivesi 71 E3
Ons, I de 24 A2
Ontaneda 25 E2
Ontiñena 29 D2
Ontinyent 32 C1
Ontojärvi 71 E3
Ontur 32 B2
Onzain 17 F1
Oostburg 10 C3
Oostelijk-Flevoland 11 E2
Oostende 34 A3
Oosterbeek 11 E3
Oosterend 11 E1
Oosterhout 11 D3
Oostkamp 34 A3
Oostmalle 34 B2
Oost-Vlaanderen 34 B3
Oost-Vlieland 11 D1
Ootmarsum 11 F2
Opatija 50 A2
Opatovac 51 E2
Opava 80 B1
Opladen 35 D3
Oplenac 53 D1
Opočka 79 D2
Opole 80 B1
Opovo 52 C1
Oppach 39 F1
Oppdal 68 C4
Oppenau 38 B4
Oppenheim 38 B3
Opphaug 68 C3
Oppido Lucano 47 D1
Oppido Mamertina 47 E4
Oppland 74 C2
Oputten 11 E2
Opuzen 52 A3
Ora 43 D3
Oradea 80 C2
Oradour-sur-Glane 17 F3
Oradour-sur-Vayres 17 F3
Orahova 50 C2
Orahovac 53 D3
Orahovica 51 D1
Oraison 22 C3
Orajärvi 67 E4
Orange 22 B3
Orani 46 B3
Oranienbaum 37 E4
Oranienburg 37 F3
Oranmore 8 B2
Orašac (Hrvatska) 52 B4
Orašac (Srbija) 52 C1
Orasi 52 C4
Orašje 51 D2
Orăştie 81 D3
Oravainen 70 C4
Oravais 70 C4
Oravikoski 71 E4
Oravița 80 C3
Orb 21 F3
Orba 32 C1
Ørbæk 76 B3
Orbassano 23 D1
Orbe 19 E2
Orbec 13 E3
Orbetello 44 B3
Orbey 15 E4
Orbigo, R 25 D2
Orce 32 A3
Orce, R 32 A3
Orcera 32 A2
Orchies 14 B1
Orcières 22 C2
Orcival 18 B3
Orco 23 D1
Ordes 24 B1
Ordesa, Pque Nac de 20 C4
Ordino 29 E1
Ordizia 20 A4
Orduña 25 F2
Orduña, Pto de 25 F2
Ore 75 E2
Orea 28 B3
Oreälven 69 F3
Orebić 51 D4
Örebro Län 75 E4
Öregrund 75 F3
Öregrundsgrepen 75 F3
Oreí 59 E1
Orellana de la Sierra 31 D1
Orellana, Emb de 31 D1
Orellana la Vieja 31 D1
Orense 24 B2
Oréo 56 B1
Oreókastro 55 E2
Orestiáda 57 D1
Oresund 76 C3
Orfós, Akr 65 E2
Orgáni 56 C1
Organyà 29 E1
Orgañyà 29 E1
Orgaz 27 F4
Orgejev 81 E2
Orgelet 19 D2
Orgères-en-Beauce 14 A4
Orgon 22 B3
Orgosolo 46 B3
Orhi, Pic d' 20 B4
Orhomenós 59 E2
Oria 32 A3
Oria 47 F1
Oria, R 20 A4
Origny-Ste-Benoîte 14 B2
Orihuela 32 C2
Orihuela del Tremedal 28 B3
Orimattila 73 D3
Oriní 55 F1
Oriolo 47 E2
Oripää 72 C3
Orissaare 78 C1
Oristano 46 A3
Oristano, G di 46 A3
Orivesi 73 D3
Orivesi L 71 F4
Orjahovo 81 D3
Ørjavik 68 B4
Ørje 74 C3
Orjen 52 B3
Orjiva 31 F3
Orkanger 68 C4
Örkelljunga 77 D3
Orkla 68 C4
Orkney Is 3 E1
Ørlandet 68 C3
Orlando, C d' 49 D3
Orlane 53 E3
Orlate 53 D3
Orléans 14 A4
Orlická přehr nádrž 39 F3
Orlovat 51 F1
Orly 14 A3
Orménio 57 D1
Ormília 55 F3
Órmos 55 E3
Órmos Korthíou 60 C3
Órmos Panagías 56 A3
Órmos Prínou 56 B2
Ormož 50 B1
Ormsjö 69 E3
Ormsjön 69 E3
Ormskirk 5 D4
Ormtjernkampen 74 C2
Ornain 14 C3
Ornans 19 E2
Orne (Calvados) 13 E3
Orne (Meuse) 15 D3
Orne (Dépt) 13 E3
Ørnes 69 E1
Ornós 60 C4
Örnsköldsvik 70 B4
Or'ol 79 F3
Orolik 51 E1
Orom 51 E1
Oron-la-Ville 19 E2
Oropesa (Castilla-la-Mancha) 27 E3
Oropesa (Valencia) 29 D4
Orosei 46 B3
Orosei, G di 46 B3
Orosháza 80 C2
Orpierre 22 B2
Orpington 7 E3
Orra 74 C2
Orsa 75 E2
Orša 79 E3
Orsajön 75 E2
Orsay 14 A3
Orsières 19 F3
Orsogna 45 E3
Orşova 80 C3
Ørsta 68 B4
Örsundsbro 75 F3
Orta Nova 45 F4
Orta San Giulio 42 B3
Orte 44 C3
Ortegal, C 24 B1
Orth 41 F2
Orthez 20 B3
Ortigueira 24 B1
Ortisei 43 D2
Ortnevik 74 A2
Orton 5 D3
Ortona 45 E3
Ortrand 37 F4
Örträsk 69 F3
Orubica 50 C2
Orune 46 B3
Orusco 28 A3
Orvalho 26 B3
Orvieto 44 C3
Órvilos, Óros 55 F1
Orvinio 44 C3
Orzinuovi 42 C4
Os 74 C1
Osa de la Vega 28 A4
Osâm 81 D3
Osby 77 D3
Oschatz 37 F4
Oschersleben 37 D4
Oschiri 46 B2
Osečina 51 E2
Oseja de Sajambre 25 D2
Osen 68 C3
Osera de Ebro 28 C2
Osijek 51 D1
Osilo 46 A2
Osimo 45 D2
Osinja 51 D2
Osipaonica 53 D1
Osipoviči 79 D3
Osječenica 50 B3
Oskarshamn 77 E2
Oskarström 77 D2
Oslava 41 E1
Oslo 74 C3
Oslo (Fylke) 74 C3
Oslofjorden 74 C3
Ösmo 75 F4
Osnabrück 36 B4
Osogovija 53 F3
Osogovske planine 53 F3
Osoppo 43 E3
Osor 50 A3
Osorno 25 E2
Osøyri 74 A3
Ospedaletti 23 D3
Ospitaletto 42 C4
Oss 11 E3
Óssa 55 F2
Ossa de Montiel 32 A1
Óssa, Óros 55 E4
Ossa, Sa de 26 B4
Ossiach 41 D4
Ossiacher See 41 D4
Óssios Loukás 59 D2
Ossun 20 C4
Ostaškov 79 E2
Østbirk 76 B3
Østby 75 D2
Oste 36 C2
Osted 76 C3
Osterburg 37 E3
Osterburken 38 B3
Österbybruk 75 F3
Østerby Havn 76 C2
Österbymo 77 E1
Österdalälven 75 D2
Østerdalen 74 C2
Österfärnebo 75 E3
Osterfeld 39 D1
Östergötlands Län 77 E1
Osterhofen 39 E4
Osterholz-Scharmbeck 36 C2
Osteria del Gatto 44 C2
Osterode 37 D4
Osterøya 74 A2
Östersjön 77 E4
Östersund 69 E4
Östersundom 73 D4
Östervåla 75 F3
Øster Vrå 76 B2
Osterwieck 37 D4
Østfold 74 C4
Ostfriesische Inseln 36 A2
Östhammar 75 F3
Ostheim 38 C2
Ostia Antica 44 C4
Ostiglia 43 D4
Östmark 75 D3
Ost'or 79 E4
Ostra 44 C2
Ostrach 42 B1
Östra Gloppet 70 C4
Östra Silen 75 D4
Ostrava 80 B1
Oštrelj 50 C3
Ostritz 39 F1
Ostróda 78 B3
Ostrog 81 D1
Ostrołęka 78 C4
Ostrov (CS) 39 E2
Ostrov (RO) 81 E3
Ostrov (SU) 79 D2
Ostrowiec-Świętokrzyski 80 C1
Ostrów Mazowiecki 78 C4
Ostrów Wielkopolski 78 B4
Ostrožac (Bosna i Hercegovina) 50 B2
Ostrožac (Bosna i Hercegovina) 51 D4
Ostsee 37 E1
Osttirol 43 E2
Ostuni 47 E1
Osuna 31 D3
Oswestry 6 C1
Oświęcim 80 B1
Otanmäki 71 E3
Otava (CS) 39 F3
Otava (SF) 73 E3
Oteren 66 C2
Oteševo 54 C2
Othem 77 F2
Othery 6 C3
Othoní, N 54 A3
Óthris, Óros 59 D1
Otívar 31 F3
Otley 5 E3
Otnes 74 C2
Otočac 50 B3
Otočec 50 A1
Otok 51 D2
Otoka 50 B2
Otra 74 B4
Otranto 47 F2
Otsamo 67 E2
Otta 74 C2
Ottana 46 B3
Ottaviano 46 C1
Ottenschlag 41 E2
Ottensheim 41 D2
Otterburn 5 E2
Otter Ferry 2 B3
Otterlo 11 E3
Otterndorf 36 B2
Otterøy 69 D3
Ottersberg 36 C3
Otterup 76 B3
Ottery St Mary 6 B4
Ottmarsheim 15 F4
Ottnang 41 D3
Ottobeuren 40 A3
Ottobrunn 40 B3
Ottsjö 69 D4
Ottweiler 15 E2
Otwock 78 C4
Otziás 60 B3
Ötztal 40 B4
Ötztaleralpen 40 B4
Ouchy 19 E2
Oucques 14 A4
Oud Beijerland 11 D3
Ouddorp 11 D3
Oude Maas 11 D3
Oudenaarde 34 A3
Oudenbosch 11 D3
Oude-Pekela 11 F1
Ouessant, Ile d' 12 A3
Oughterard 8 B2
Ouistreham 13 E2
Oul 35 D3
Oulainen 71 D3
Oulanka 71 E1
Oulankajoki 71 E1
Oulchy-le-Château 14 B3
Oulu 71 D2
Oulujärvi 71 E3
Oulujoki 71 D2
Oulun Lääni 71 E2
Oulunsalo 71 D2
Oulx 19 E4
Ounasjoki 71 D1
Oundle 7 E2
Our 34 C4
Ouranópoli 56 A3
Ource 14 C4
Ourcq 14 B3
Ourense 24 B2
Ourique 30 B2
Ourol 24 B1
Ourthe 34 C3
Ourville 13 E2
Ouse, R 5 E4
Oust 21 D4
Outes, Sa de 24 A2
Outokumpu 71 F4
Outomuro 24 B2
Outwell 7 E2
Ouvèze 22 B2
Ouzouer 18 B1
Ouzouer-le-Marché 14 A4
Ovada 23 E2
Ovanåker 75 E2
Ovar 26 B2
Ovčar Banja 51 F3
Ovedskloster 77 D3
Overath 38 A1
Øverbygd 66 C2
Overflakkee 16 B3
Overhalla 69 D3
Överhörnäs 69 F4
Overijssel 11 E2
Overjise 34 B3
Överkalix 70 C1
Övermark 70 C4
Översjuktan 69 E2
Övertorneå 70 C1
Överum 77 E1
Överuman 69 E2
Oviedo 25 D1
Ovindoli 45 D3
Øvre Anarjokka 67 E2
Øvre Årdal 74 B2
Øvre Dividalen 66 C3
Övre Fryken 75 D3
Øvre Pasvik 67 F2
Övre Soppero 67 D3
Ovruč 79 E4
Owel, L 8 C2
Oxelösund 75 F4
Oxford 7 D3
Oxfordshire 7 D2
Oxiá (Stereá Eláda) 58 C2
Oxiá (Thessalía) 54 C4
Oxiá, N 58 B2
Oxie 77 D3
Oxílithos 60 A2
Ox Mts, The 8 B2
Oyarzun 20 A3
Oybin 39 F1
Øye 74 B2
Øyer 74 C2
Øyeren 74 C3
Oy-Mittelberg 40 A3
Oyntdartfjørdur 68 A3
Oyón 20 A4
Oyonnax 19 D3
Øystese 74 A2
Oyten 36 C3
Ozalj 50 B2
Ožbalt 50 A1
Ózd 80 C2
Ozeblin 50 B3
Ozieri 46 A3
Ozren 51 D2
Ozren Devica 53 E2

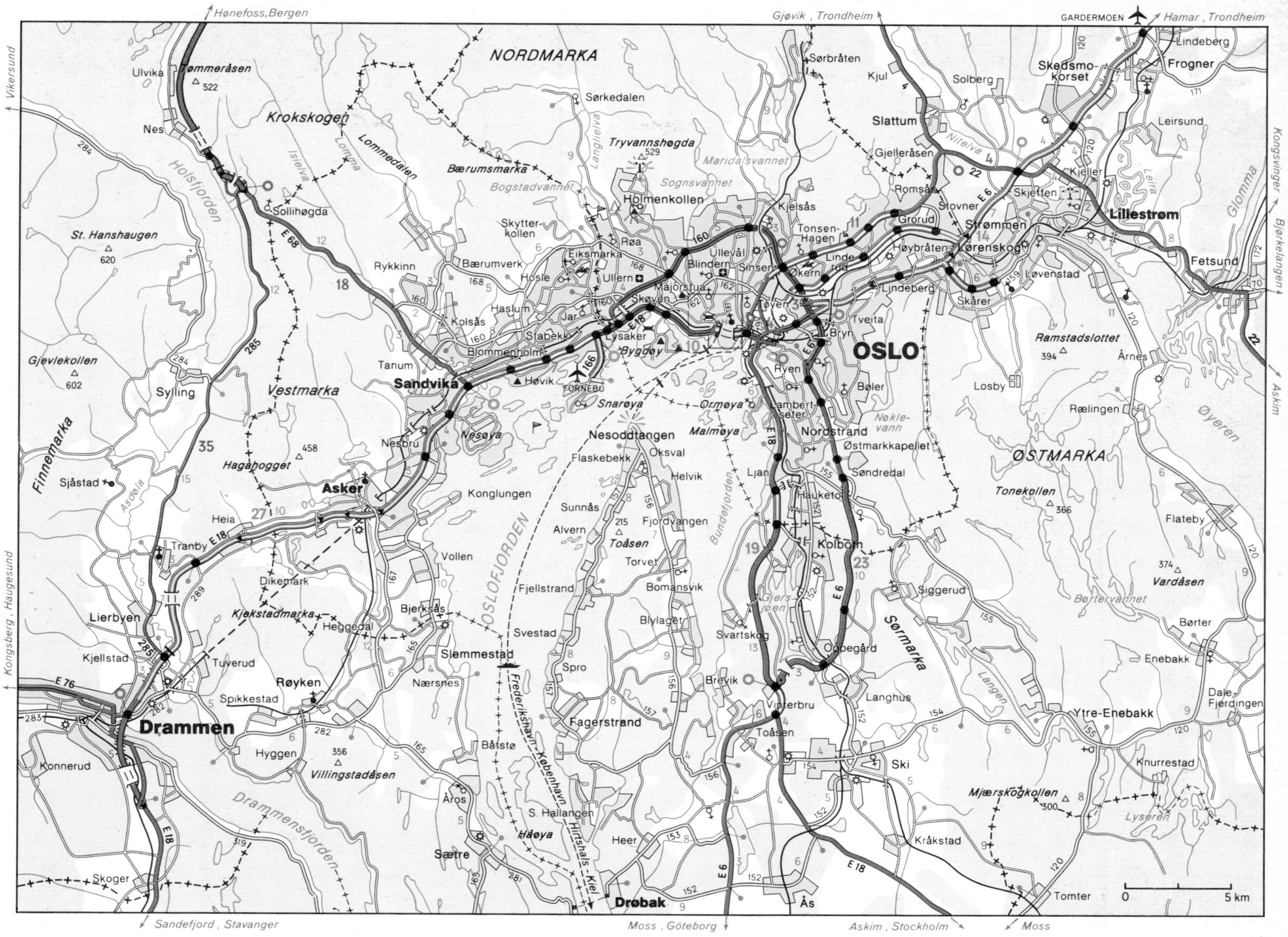

Hønefoss, Bergen
Gjøvik, Trondheim
GARDERMOEN
Hamar, Trondheim
NORDMARKA
Krokskogen
Holsfjorden
St. Hanshaugen
Vestmarka
Sandvika
Asker
Drammen
Drammensfjorden
OSLO
Oslofjorden
Lillestrøm
ØSTMARKA
Nesodden
Drøbak
Ski
Kolbotn
Lierbyen
Røyken
Slemmestad
Sandefjord, Stavanger
Moss, Göteborg
Askim, Stockholm
Moss
Kongsberg, Haugesund
Vikersund
Kongsvinger
Bjørkelangen
0
5 km

P

Paakkila 71 E4
Paalasmaa 71 F3
Páamo de Masa, Pto de 25 F2
Paar 39 D4
Paasselkä 73 F2
Paavola 71 D3
Pabianice 78 B4
Pacaudière, la 18 C3
Paceco 48 B3
Pachino 49 D4
Packsattel 41 E4
Paço de Sousa 24 A4
Paços de Ferreira 24 A3
Pacov 41 E1
Pacy 14 A3
Padasjoki 73 D3
Padej 51 E1
Pađene 50 B3
Paderborn 36 C4
Paderne 30 B3
Padiham 5 D3
Padina 51 F1
Padinska Skela 52 C1
Padirac, Gouffre de 21 E2
Padjelanta 66 B4
Padornelo 24 C3
Padova 43 D4
Padrela, Sa da 24 B3
Padrón 24 A2
Padru 46 B2
Padstow 6 A4
Padul 31 F3
Paesana 23 D2
Paestum 46 C2
Pag 50 A3
Pag I 50 A3
Paganico 44 B3
Pagassitikós Kólpos 59 E1
Paglia 44 C3
Pagny 15 D3
Pagóndas (Évia) 59 E2
Pagóndas (Sámos) 61 E3
Pagoúria 56 C2
Paguera 33 E2
Páhi 59 E3
Pahiá Ámos 65 D4
Pahís, Akr 56 B2
Paide 78 C1
Paignton 6 B4
Päijänne 73 D3
Páiko, Óros 55 D2
Paimbœuf 16 C2
Paimio 72 C4
Paimpol 12 C3
Painswick 6 C3
Paisley 2 C4
Paistunturit 67 E2
País Vasco 20 A4
Paittasjärvi 66 C3
Paiva, R 26 B2
Pajala 67 D4
Pájara 30 B4
Pajares, Pto de 25 D2
Paklenica Nac Park 50 B3
Pakoštane 50 B4
Pakrac 50 C2
Pakračka Poljana 50 C2
Paks 80 B2
Palacios de la Sierra 25 F3
Palacios del Sil 24 C2
Palacios de Sanabria 24 C3
Palade, Pso del 43 D2
Paládio 56 C2
Paladru 19 D4
Palafrugell 29 F2
Palagía 56 C2
Palagiano 47 E1
Palagonia 49 D4
Palaia 44 A2
Palaiseau 14 A3
Palais, le 16 B1
Palamás 55 D4
Palamós 29 F2
Palancia, R 28 C4
Palanga 78 C3
Pala, Pto del 24 C1
Palas de Rei 24 B2
Palata 45 E4
Palatitsía 55 D3
Palatna 53 D3
Palau 46 B2
Palavas 22 A3
Palazzo del Pero 44 B2
Palazzolo Acreide 49 D4
Palazzolo sull' Oglio 42 C4
Palazzo San Gervasio 47 D1
Palazzuolo sul Senio 44 B1
Paldiski 78 C1
Pale 51 E3
Paléa Epídavros 59 E4
Palékastro 65 D4
Palena 45 E4
Palencia 25 E3
Paleohóra (Égina) 59 E3
Paleohóri (Grevená) 55 D3
Paleohóri (Halkidikí) 55 F3
Paleohóri (Ípiros) 58 B1
Paleohóra (Kríti) 64 A4
Paleohóri (Lésvos) 61 D1
Paleohóri (Pelopónissos) 63 D3
Paleohóri (Thessalía) 54 C4
Paleokastrítsa 54 A4
Paleókastro (Halkidikí) 55 F3
Paleókastro (Kozáni) 55 D3
Paleókastro (Sámos) 61 E3
Paleókastro (Séres) 55 F1
Paleókastro (Stereá Eláda) 58 C1
Paleokómi 56 A2
Paleópirgos (Stereá Eláda) 58 C2
Paleópirgos Thessalía) 55 E3
Paleópoli (Ándros) 60 B3
Paleópoli (Samothráki) 56 C3
Paleós Kavála 56 B2
Paleós Xánthis 56 B1
Palermo 48 B3
Páleros 58 B2
Palérou, Órm 58 A2
Palestrina 45 D4
Palež 51 E3

CERGY-PONTOISE
Boisemont
Jouy-le-Moutier
Neuville-s-Oise
Eragny-s-Oise
Pierrelaye
Taverny
St Leu-la-Forêt
St Prix
DE MONTMORENCY
Beauchamp
le Plessis-Bouchard
Montlignon
Andilly
Margency
Montmorency
Soisy
Eaubonne
Ermont
Franconville
Herblay
Conflans-Ste H.
Maurecourt
Chennevières
Montigny-lès-Cormeilles
Sannois
St Gratien
Deuil
Enghien
Epinay
Andrésy
Triel-s-Seine
Chanteloup-les-Vignes
Achères
FORÊT DE ST GERMAIN
Maisons-Laffitte
la Frette-s-S.
Cormeilles-en-Parisis
ARGENTEUIL
Sartrouville
Villeneuve-la-Garenne
Médan
Carrières-s/s-Poissy
Villennes-s-Seine
Poissy
le Mesnil-le-Roi
Houilles
Bezons
Gennevilliers
Colombes
Bois-Colombes
Asnières-s-S.
Orgeval
Carrières-s-S.
la Garenne-Colombes
Clichy
St Ouen
Montesson
Chambourcy
Aigremont
ST-GERMAIN-EN-LAYE
le Vésinet
Chatou
NANTERRE
Courbevoie
Levallois-Perret
NEUILLY-s-S.
Fourqueux
le Pecq
la Défense
Puteaux
Mareil-Marly
Croissy-s-Seine
Rueil-Malmaison
Suresnes
Feucherolles
l'Étang-la-Ville
Marly-le-Roi
Bougival
Louveciennes
la Celle-St Cloud
St Nom-la-Bretèche
Noisy-le-Roi
Bailly
Vaucresson
Garches
St-Cloud
BOULOGNE-BILLANCOURT
Rocquencourt
Villepreux
Rennemoulin
Marnes-la-Coquette
Ville-d'Avray
Issy-les-Moulineaux
Vanves
Malakoff
Montrouge
Fontenay-le-Fleury
le Chesnay
Sèvres
Meudon
Clamart
Bois-d'Arcy
St Cyr-l'École
VERSAILLES
Chaville
Viroflay
Châtillon
Bagneux
Arcueil
Cachan
Trappes
Vélizy-Villacoublay
Fontenay-aux-Roses
le Plessis-Robinson
Bourg-la-Reine
Buc
Guyancourt
Montigny-le-Bretonneux
Jouy-en-Josas
Châtenay-Malabry
Sceaux
ST QUENTIN-EN-YVELINES
Voisins-le-Bretonneux
les Loges-en-Josas
Bièvres
Antony
Fresnes
Rungis
Abbe de Port-Royal-des-Champs
Toussus-le-Noble
Magny-les-Hameaux
St Lambert
Châteaufort
Saclay
Vauhallan
Igny
Verrières-le-Buisson
Massy
Milon-la-Chapelle
Villiers-le-Bâcle
PARC RÉGIONAL
Chevreuse
St Rémy-lès-Chevreuse
St Aubin
Palaiseau
Chilly-Mazarin
Dampierre-en-Yvelines
Gif-s-Yvette
Orsay
Bures-s-Yvette
Champlan
Villebon-s-Yvette
Longjumeau
Senlisse
Choisel
les Ulis
Saulx-les-Chartreux
VERSAILLES-Nord
VÉLIZY-Ouest
ARC DE TRIOMPHE
INVALIDES
MONTPARNASSE
OPÉRA
CONCORDE
MICHELIN

Paris
1/100 000
0 1 2 3 4km
Ecouen
Goussainville
Aéroport Charles de Gaulle
AÉROGARE Nº1
AÉROGARE Nº 2
le Mesnil-Amelot
Villiers-le-Bel
Sarcelles
Gonesse
Roissy-en-France
Vaudherland
Mitry-Mory
Tremblay-Vieux-Pays
Villepinte
Tremblay-lès-Gonesse
Pierrefitte
Garges-lès-Gonesse
Stains
Dugny
ST-DENIS
le Blanc-Mesnil
Aulnay-s/s-Bois
Sevran
Villeparisis
Claye-Souilly
le Bourget
la Courneuve
Drancy
Aubervilliers
BOBIGNY
Livry-Gargan
Vaujours
Coubron
Courtry
le Pin
Villevaudé
Bondy
les Pavillons-s/s-Bois
Clichy-s/s-B.
Montfermeil
le Raincy
Pantin
Noisy-le-Sec
Romainville
Villemomble
Gagny
Chelles
Brou-s-Chantereine
Pomponne
Thorigny-s-M.
les Lilas
Bagnolet
Rosny
Neuilly-Plaisance
Vaires-s-M.
Lagny-s-M.
St Thibault-des-Vignes
Montreuil
Vincennes
Fontenay-s/s-Bois
Neuilly-s-M.
Champs-s-Marne
Noisiel
Torcy
Gouvernes
Guermantes
Nogent-s-M.
le Perreux-s-M.
Bry-s-M.
Noisy-le-Grd
MARNE-LA-VALLÉE
Lognes
Bussy-St Martin
Bussy-St Georges
Collégien
St Mandé
Bois de Vincennes
Charenton
Villiers-s-M.
Croissy-Beaubourg
Ferrières
Joinville-le-Pont
St Maurice
Ivry-s-Seine
Maisons-Alfort
Champigny-s-M.
le Plessis-Trévise
Emerainville
Alfortville
St Maur-des-Fossés
Pontcarré
Chennevières-s-Marne
Pontault-Combault
Vitry-s-Seine
CRÉTEIL
Ormesson-sur-Marne
la Queue-en-Brie
Roissy-en-Brie
Noiseau
Ozoir-la-Ferrière
Choisy-le-Roi
Bonneuil-s-M.
Sucy-en-Brie
Thiais
Forêt Notre-Dame
Lésigny
Valenton
Limeil-Brévannes
Boissy-St Léger
Orly
Villeneuve-le-Roi
Gros Bois
Marolles-en-Brie
Santeny
Férolles-Attilly
Gretz-Armainvilliers
Villeneuve-St Georges
Ablon-s-Seine
Crosne
Yerres
Villecresnes
Servon
Chevry-Cossigny
Athis-Mons
Vigneux
Montgeron
Brunoy
Mandres-les-Roses
Périgny
Brie-Comte-Robert
Epinay-s-Sénart
Boussy-St Antoine
Moulin de Jarcy
Grisy-Suisnes

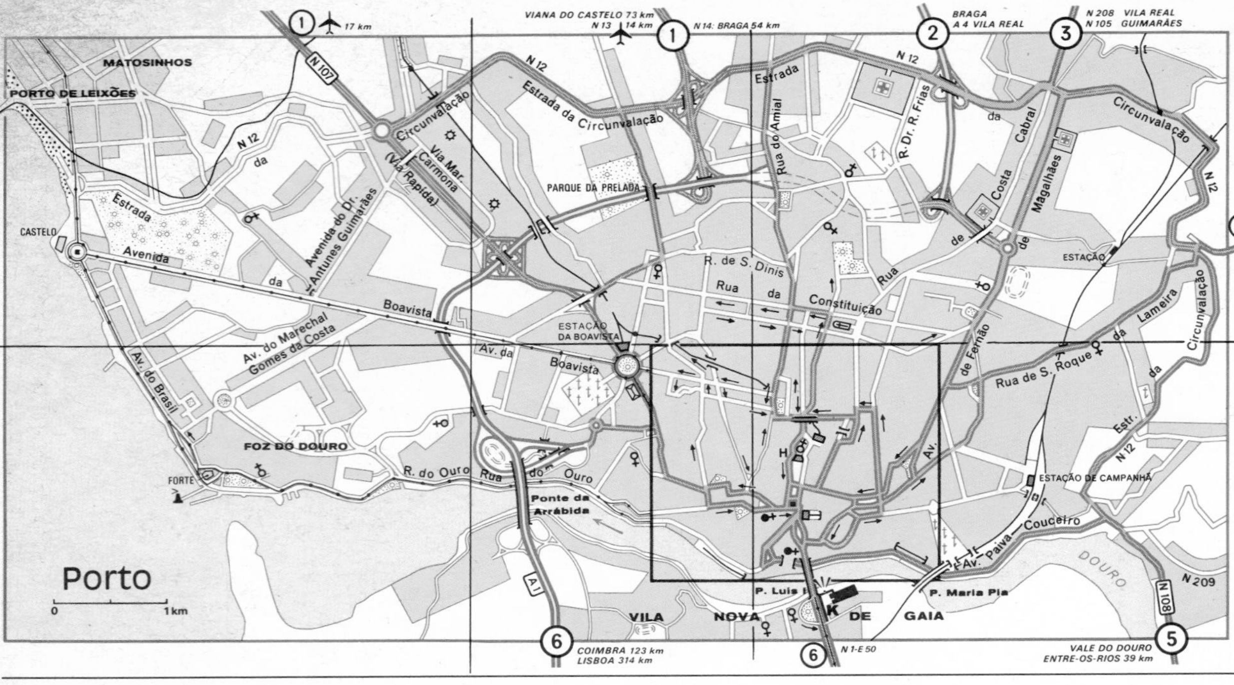
Porto
0
1 km
MATOSINHOS
PORTO DE LEIXÕES
CASTELO
FOZ DO DOURO
FORTE
VIANA DO CASTELO 73 km
N 13 14 km
N 14: BRAGA 54 km
BRAGA
A 4 VILA REAL
N 208 VILA REAL
N 105 GUIMARÃES
17 km
N 107
N 12
Estrada da Circunvalação
Circunvalação
Via Mar. Carmona (Via Rápida)
Avenida do Dr. Antunes Guimarães
Avenida da Boavista
Av. do Marechal Gomes da Costa
Av. do Brasil
R. do Ouro
Ponte da Arrábida
PARQUE DA PRELADA
ESTAÇÃO DA BOAVISTA
R. de S. Dinis
Rua da Constituição
Rua do Amial
R. Dr. R. Frias
Costa Cabral
Magalhães
Rua de S. Roque da Lameira
Av. de Fernão de
ESTAÇÃO
ESTAÇÃO DE CAMPANHÃ
Av. Paiva Couceiro
DOURO
P. Luís I
P. Maria Pia
VILA NOVA DE GAIA
COIMBRA 123 km
LISBOA 314 km
N 1-E 50
N 108
N 209
VALE DO DOURO
ENTRE-OS-RIOS 39 km
A1

Páli 65 E1
Paliano 45 D4
Palić 51 E1
Palidoro 44 C4
Palinges 18 C2
Palinuro 46 C2
Palioúri 55 F3
Paliouriá 55 D3
Paliseul 15 D2
Pälkäne 73 D3
Pålkem 70 C1
Pallas Ounastunturi 67 D3
Pallastunturi 67 D3
Pallice, la 17 D3
Palluau 17 D2
Palma 33 E2
Palmaces, Emb de 28 A2
Palma del Río 31 D2
Palma di Montechiaro 48 C4
Palmadula 46 A2
Palmanova 43 F3
Palmela 30 A1
Palmi 47 D4
Palo del Colle 47 E1
Palojoensuu 67 D3
Palojoki 67 D3
Palokki 71 E4
Palomäki 71 E3
Palomares del Campo 28 A4
Palomas 31 D1
Palomas, Pto de las 32 A2
Palombara Sabina 44 C4
Palombera, Pto de 25 E2
Palomera 28 B3
Pálos, Akr 60 C4
Palos, C de 32 C3
Palos de la Frontera 30 C3
Pals 29 F2
Pålsboda 75 E4
Paltamo 71 E3
Paltaselkä 71 E3
Paluzza 43 E2
Pámfila 61 E1
Pamhagen 41 F3
Pamiers 21 D4
Pampilhosa 26 B3
Pampilhosa da Serra 26 B3
Pampliega 25 E3
Pamplona 20 B4
Pamporovo 81 D4
Panagía (Ípiros) 54 C4
Panagía (Límnos) 56 C3
Panagía (Makedonía) 55 D3
Panagía (Thássos) 56 B2
Panagía (Thessalía) 54 C4
Panagjurište 81 D4
Panahaïkó, Óros 58 C3
Panarea, I 49 D2
Panaro 44 A1
Pancalieri 23 D2
Pančevo 52 C1
Pančicév vrh 53 D2
Pancorbo 25 F2
Pandánassa 63 D4
Pandeleimónas 55 E3
Pandino 42 C4
Pandokrátor 54 A4
Pandrup 76 B2
Panes 25 E1
Panetolikó, Óros 58 C2
Panetólio 58 C2
Panevėžys 78 C2
Pangbourne 7 D3
Pangéo, Óros 56 A2
Paniza, Pto de 28 B2
Pankajärvi 71 F3
Pankakoski 71 F3
Pankow 37 F3
Panórama (Dráma) 56 A1
Panórama (Thessaloníki) 55 E2
Panormítis 65 F1
Pánormos (Kikládes) 60 C4
Pánormos (Kríti) 64 B3
Päntäne 72 C2
Pantelleria 48 A4
Pantelleria, I di 48 A4
Paola 47 D3
Pápa 80 B2
Papádes 59 E1
Papádos 61 D1
Páparis 59 D4
Pápas, Akr 61 D4
Papasidero 47 D2
Papa Stour 3 F1
Papenburg 36 A2
Papíkio 56 C1
Pápingo 54 B3
Pappenheim 39 D4
Papuk *Mt* 50 C1
Papuk (Reg) 50 C1
Parabita 47 F2
Paracin 53 D2
Paracuellos de Jiloca 28 B2
Parada de Cunhos 24 B3
Paradas 31 D3
Paradela 24 B3
Paradíssia 58 C4
Parádissos 56 B2
Parainen 72 C4
Parajes 24 B1
Parakálamos 54 B3
Parákila 61 D1
Paralía (Ahaïa) 58 C3
Paralía (Lakonía) 63 D3
Paralía (Makedonía) 55 E3
Paralía (Stereá Eláda) 59 D3
Paralía Akrátas 59 D3
Parália Ástros 59 D4
Paralía Kímis 59 F2
Paralía Kotsikiás 59 E1
Paralía Skotínas 55 E3
Paralía Tiroú 59 D4
Paralímni 59 E2
Paralovo 53 E3
Paramé 12 C3
Paramera, Pto de 27 E3
Paramithía 54 B4
Páramo del Sil 24 C2
Paranésti 56 B1
Parapanda 31 F3
Parapótamos 54 B4
Paraspóri, Akr 65 E3
Paray-le-Monial 18 C3
Parchim 37 E2
Pardubice 80 A1
Paredes 24 A3
Paredes de Coura 24 A3
Paredes de Nava 25 E3
Pareja 28 A3
Pareloup, Lac de 21 E3
Parentis-en-Born 20 B2
Párga 58 A1
Pargas 72 C4
Parikkala 73 F3
Parîngului, M 81 D3
Paris 14 A3
Parkalompolo 67 D3
Parkano 72 C3
Parla 27 F3
Parlavà 29 F2
Parma 44 A1
Parnassós, Óros 59 D2
Parndorf 41 F2
Párnitha, Óros 59 F3
Párnonas, Óros 63 D3
Pärnu 78 C1
Parola 73 D3
Páros 64 B1
Páros, N 64 B1
Parrett 6 C3
Parsberg 39 D3
Parsdorf 40 B3
Parseierspitze 40 A4
Parsteiner See 37 F2
Partakko 67 E2
Partanna 48 B3
Partenen 42 C2
Partenkirchen 40 B4
Parthenay 17 E2
Parthéni 61 E4
Partille 76 C2
Partinico 48 B3
Partizani 52 C1
Partizanske Vode 51 F3
Partney 7 E1
Partry Mts 8 B2
Pasaia-Pasajes 20 A3
Pas de Calais 7 F3
Pas-de-Calais (Dépt) 14 A1
Pas de la Case 29 E1
Pas-en-Artois 14 B2
Pasewalk 37 F2
Pashalítsa 55 D4
Pasikovci 50 C2
Pašman 50 B4
Pašman / 50 B4
Passais 13 D3
Passá-Limáni 61 D2
Passás, N 61 D2
Passau 40 C2
Passavás 62 C3
Passero, C 49 D4
Passignano sul Trasimeno 44 C2
Passwang 19 F1
Pastrana 28 A3
Paštrik 53 D4
Pásztó 80 C2
Patay 14 A4
Pateley Bridge 5 E3
Patéras, Óros 59 E3
Paterna del Campo 30 C3
Paterna de Rivera 31 D4
Paternion 41 D4
Paternò 49 D3
Paternopoli 46 C1
Patersdorf 39 E3
P'atichatki 81 F1
Patiópoulo 58 B1
Patitíri 60 A1
Pátmos 61 E4
Pátmos, N 61 E4
Pátra 58 C3
Patraïkós Kólpos 58 C2
Patreksfjörður 68 A1
Patrington 5 F4
Pattada 46 B2
Patterdale 5 D3
Patti 49 D3
Pattijoki 71 D3
Patvinsuo 71 F3
Pau 20 C3
Pauillac 20 B1
Paúl 26 B3
Paularo 43 E2
Paulhaguet 21 F1
Paullo 42 B4
Pavia (I) 23 E1
Pavia (P) 26 B4
Pavilly 13 F2
Pavino Polje 51 F4
Pávliani 59 D2
Pávlos 59 E2
Pavullo nel Frignano 44 A1
Paxí 58 A1
Paxí, N 58 A1
Payerne 19 E2
Paymogo 30 B2
Payrac 21 D2
Pazardžik 81 D4
Pazin 43 F4
Pčinja 53 E3
Pčinja 53 E4
Péage-de-Roussillon, le 19 D4
Peak District Nat Pk 5 E4
Peal de Becerro 32 A2
Peanía 59 F3
Peares, Emb de los 24 B2
Peć 53 D3
Peča 50 A1
Peccioli 44 A2
Pečenjevce 53 E2
Pech-Merle, Grotte du 21 D2
Pećigrad 50 B2
Pećinci 51 E2
Pecka 51 E3
Peckelsheim 36 C4
Pécs 80 B3
Pećsa Banja 53 D3
Pečurice 52 C4
Pedaso 45 D2
Pedersker 77 D4
Pedersöre 70 C3
Pédi 65 F1
Pedrafita do Cebreiro 24 C2
Pedrafita do Cebreiro, Pto de 24 C2
Pedrajas de San Esteban 25 E4
Pedralba (Castilla-León) 24 C3
Pedralba (Valencia) 28 C4
Pedras Salgadas 24 B3
Pedraza de la Sierra 25 E4
Pedrera 31 E3
Pedrizas, Pto de las 31 E3
Pedro Abad 31 E2
Pedro Bernardo 27 E3
Pedrógão (Alentejo) 30 B2
Pedrógão (Estremadura) 26 A3
Pedrógão Grande 26 B3
Pedrola 28 B2
Pedro Muñoz 32 A1
Peebles 5 D1
Peel 4 C3
Peene 37 E1
Peenemünde 37 F1
Pefkári 56 B2
Pefkí 59 E1
Péfkos 54 C3
Pega 26 C3
Pegalajar 31 F2
Pegau 37 E4
Pegli 23 E2
Pegnitz 39 D3
Pego 32 C1
Pego do Altar, Bgem de 30 B1
Pegognaga 43 D4
Pegolotte 43 E4
Pehčevo 53 F4
Peine 37 D3
Peio Terme 42 C3
Peïra-Cava 23 D3
Peißenberg 40 B3
Peiting 40 B3
Pek 53 D1
Péla 55 E2
Péla (Nomos) 55 D2
Pelado 28 B4
Pelagie, Is 48 A4
Pelasgía 59 D1
Pelat, Mt 22 C2
Pelekános 54 C3
Pélekas 54 A4
Peletá 63 D3
Pelhřimov 41 E1
Pelinéo 61 D2
Pelister 54 C2
Pelješac 52 A3
Pelkosenniemi 67 F4
Pellegrino, M 48 B3
Pellegrino Parmense 23 F2
Pellegrue 20 C2
Pellerin, le 17 D2
Pellesmäki 71 E4
Pello 70 C1
Pellworm 36 B1
Pelopónissos 58 C3
Peloritani, M 49 D3
Peltosalmi 71 E3
Peltovuoma 67 D3
Pélussin 19 D4
Pelvoux, Mt 19 E4
Pembroke 6 A3
Pembroke Dock 6 A3
Pembrokeshire Coast Nat Pk 6 A2
Penacova 26 B3
Peña de Francia 27 D3
Peña de Francia, Sa de 27 D3
Peña de Oroel 28 C1
Penafiel 24 A3
Peñafiel 25 E3
Peñaflor 31 D2
Peñagolosa 28 C4
Peña Gorbea 20 A4
Peñalara 27 F2
Penalva do Castelo 26 B2
Penamacor 26 C3
Peña Mira 24 C3
Peña Nofre 24 B3
Peña Prieta 25 E2
Peñaranda de Bracamonte 27 E2
Peñaranda de Duero 25 F3
Peñarroya 28 C3
Peñarroya, Emb de 32 A1
Peñarroya-Pueblonuevo 31 D2
Penarth 6 C3
Peña, Sa de la 28 C1
Peña Sagra 25 E2
Peñas, C de 25 D1
Peñascosa 32 A1
Peñas de Cervera 25 F3
Peñas de San Pedro 32 B1
Peña Trevinca 24 C2
Peña Ubiña 25 D2
Peñausende 25 D4
Pendagií 58 C2
Pendálofo 58 B2
Pendálofos 54 C3
Pendéli 59 F3
Pendéli *Mt* 59 F3
Pendeória 59 D2
Pénde Vrísses 55 E2
Pendine 6 B3
Peneda-Gerês, Pque Nac da 24 A3
Peneda, Sa da 24 A3
Penedono 24 B4
Penela 26 B3
Pénestin 16 C1
Penha 24 A3
Penhas da Saude 26 B3
Penhas Juntas 24 C3
Penhir, Pte de 12 A3
Penice, Pso del 23 E2
Peniche 26 A4
Penicuik 3 D4
Penig 39 E1
Peñíscola 29 D3
Penkun 37 F2
Penmaenmawr 6 B1
Penmarch, Pte de 12 A4
Pennabilli 44 C2
Penne 45 D3
Penne-d'Agenais 21 D2
Pennes, Pso di 43 D2
Pennines, The 5 E3
Peñón de Ifach 33 D2
Penrhyndeudraeth 6 B1
Penrith 5 D2
Penryn 6 A4
Penserjoch 43 D2
Pentland Firth 3 D1
Pentland Hills 3 D4
Pentrefoelas 6 B1
Pen-y-bont 6 B3
Penzance 6 A4
Penzberg 40 B3
Penzlin 37 E2
Peqin 54 A2
Perahóra 59 E3
Peraleda de Zaucejo 31 D2
Peralejos de las Truchas 28 B3
Perales del Alfambra 28 C3
Perales del Puerto 26 C3
Perales de Tajuña 27 F3
Perales, Pto de 26 C3
Peralta 28 B1
Peralta de Alcofea 29 D2
Peralva 30 B3
Pérama (Ípiros) 54 C4
Pérama (Kérkira) 54 A4
Pérama (Kríti) 64 B4
Pérama (Lésvos) 61 E1
Pérama (Stereá Eláda) 59 E3
Peraméri 70 C2
Perä-Posio 71 E1
Peräseinäjoki 70 C4
Perast 52 B4
Peratáta 58 A3
Percy 13 D3
Perdido, M 20 C4
Pérdika (Égina) 59 E3
Pérdika (Ioánina) 54 C4
Pérdika (Thesprotía) 54 B4
Perdikáki 58 C1
Perdíkas 55 D2
Peréa (Péla) 55 D2
Peréa (Thessaloníki) 55 E3
Perejaslav-Chmel'nickij 79 E4
Pereruela 24 C3
Pereval Jablonickij 81 D2
Pereval Srednij Vereckij 80 C2
Pereval Užokskij 80 C1
Perg 41 D2
Pergine Valsugana 43 D3
Pergola 44 C2
Perho 71 D4
Perhonjoki 70 C3
Periana 31 E3
Périers 13 D3
Périgueux 21 D1
Períklia 55 D2
Perino 23 F2
Períssa 64 C2
Perísta 58 C2
Peristerá 55 F2
Peristéra, N 60 A1
Perithório 56 A1
Perívlepto 59 D1
Perivóli 54 C3
Perivólio 58 C2
Perjasica 50 B2
Perković 50 B4
Perleberg 37 E2
Perlez 51 F1
Përmet 54 B3
Pernå 73 E4
Pernaja 73 E4
Pernarec 39 E2
Pernes 22 B3
Pernik 81 D4
Perniö 72 C4
Pernitz 41 F2
Pernštejn 41 E1
Péronne 14 B2
Perosa Argentina 23 D1
Pérouges 19 D3
Perpignan 21 F4
Perrero 23 D2
Perreux 18 C3
Perros-Guirec 12 B3
Persenbeug 41 E2
Pershore 6 C2
Perstorp 77 D3
Perth 3 D3
Perthus, le 29 F1
Pertisau 40 B4
Pertoča 41 F4
Pertoúli 54 C4
Pertteli 73 D4
Pertuis 22 B3
Pertunmaa 73 E3
Pertusa 28 C2
Perućac Vrelo 51 E3
Peručko jez 50 C3
Perugia 44 C2
Perušić 50 B3
Péruwelz 34 A3
Pervenchères 13 E3
Pervomajsk 81 E1
Pesaro 44 C2
Pescara 45 E3
Pescasseroli 45 D4
Peschici 45 F3
Peschiera del Garda 42 C4
Pescia 44 A2
Pescina 45 D4
Pescocostanzo 45 D4
Pescolanciano 45 E4
Pescopagano 46 C1
Pescorocchiano 45 D3
Peshkopi 53 D4
Pesiökylä 71 E2
Pesmes 19 D2
Pesočani 54 C1
Pêso da Régua 24 B4
Pesoz 24 C1
Pessáni 57 D2
Peštani 54 C2
Pešter 51 F4
Pestovo 79 E1
Pešurići 51 E3
Petačinci 53 F2
Petäjäskoski 71 D1
Petäjäves 73 D2
Petalax 70 C4
Petalída, Akr 64 B1
Petalídi 62 C3
Petalií, Nissí 60 B3
Petalión, Kólpos 60 B3
Petaloúdes 65 F2
Pétange 15 D2
Pétas 58 B1
Petehovac 50 A2
Peterborough 7 E2
Peterhead 3 E2
Peterlee 5 E2
Petersfield 7 D3
Petershagen 36 C3
Pethelinós 55 F2
Petilia Policastro 47 E3
Petina 46 C2
Petite-Pierre, la 15 E3
Petit Morin 14 B3
Petit St Bernard, Col du 19 E3
Petkula 67 E3
Petlovača 52 C1
Petoússio 54 B4
Petra (E) 33 E2
Pétra (Lésvos) 61 D1
Pétra (Makedonía) 55 D3
Petralia 48 C3
Petrálona 55 F3
Petraná 55 D3
Petrčane 50 B3
Petrel 32 C2
Petrella, Mte 46 B1
Pétres 55 D2
Petreto-Bicchisano 23 E4
Petrič 81 D4
Petrijevki 51 D1
Petrína 58 C4
Petrinja 50 B2
Petrodvorec 79 D1
Petrohóri 58 C2
Pétrola 32 B1
Petróná 58 C1
Petroşani 81 D3
Petrotá 57 D1
Petrothálassa 59 E4
Petroússa 56 A1
Petrovac (Bosna i Hercegovina) 50 B2
Petrovac (Crna Gora) 52 C4
Petrovac (Srbija) 53 D1
Petrovaradin 51 E1
Petrovčić 51 E2
Petrovec 53 E4
Petrovice 39 F2
Petrovići 51 E3
Pettenbach 41 D3
Pettigoe 8 C1
Petworth 7 D4
Peuerbach 41 D2
Peura 71 D1
Pewsey 7 D3
Peyrat-le-Château 18 A3
Peyrehorade 20 B3
Peyresourde, C de 20 C4
Peyriac-Minervois 21 E4
Peyrolles 22 B3
Peyrol, Pas de 21 E1
Peyruis 22 C3
Pézenas 21 F3
Pezinok 80 B2
Pezoúla 56 B2
Pfaffenhofen 39 D4
Pfäffikon 42 B2
Pfalzgrafenweiler 38 B4
Pfarrkirchen 39 E4
Pfeffenhausen 39 E4
Pforzheim 38 B4
Pfreimd 39 E3
Pfronten 40 A4
Pfullendorf 42 B1
Pfullingen 38 B4
Pfunds 40 A4
Pfungstadt 38 B3
Phalsbourg 15 E3
Philippeville 34 B4
Philippsreut 41 D2
Piacenza 42 C4
Piadena 42 C4
Piana 23 E3
Piana d. Albanesi 48 B3
Piancastagnaio 44 B3
Piancavallo 43 E3
Piandelagotti 44 A1
Pian delle Fugazze, Pso 43 D3
Pian del Voglio 44 B1
Pianella 45 D3
Pianello 44 C2
Pianoro 44 B1
Pianosa, I (Mare Adriatico) 45 F3
Pianosa, I (Mare Tirreno) 44 A3
Piansano 44 B3
Piapaxaro, Pico 24 C2
Pias 30 B2
Piatra-Neamț 81 D2
Piave 43 E3
Piazza al Serchio 44 A1
Piazza Armerina 48 C4
Piazza Brembana 42 C3
Piazzola sul Brenta 43 D3
Piber 41 E4
Pibeste, P de 20 C4
Pićan 43 F4
Picassent 32 C1
Piccolo San Bernardo, Colle del 27 E3
Picerno 47 D2
Pickering 5 F3
Pico 45 D4
Pico, Pto del 27 E3
Pico Ruivo 30 A3
Picos de Europa 25 E2
Picote, Bgem de 24 C3
Picquigny 14 A2
Pídna 55 E3
Piedicavallo 42 A4
Piedicroce 23 D3
Piediluco 44 C3
Piedimonte d'A. 45 E4
Piedrabuena 31 E1
Piedrafita 24 C2
Piedrahita 27 E3
Piedralaves 27 E3
Piedra, R 28 B3
Piedras Albas 26 C3
Piedra San Martín, Collado de la 20 B4
Piedras, Emb de 30 B3
Piedrasluengas, Pto de 25 E2
Piedratajada 28 C1
Pieksämäki 73 E2
Pielavesi 71 E4
Pielavesi *L* 71 E4
Pielinen 71 F3
Pieljekaise 69 F1
Piemonte 23 D1
Piennes 15 D2
Pienza 44 B3
Pieriá 55 E3
Piéria, Óri 55 D3
Pierowall 3 E1
Pierre-Buffière 17 F3
Pierre-de-Bresse 19 D2
Pierrefitte 15 D3
Pierrefitte-Nestaias 20 C4
Pierrefonds 14 B2
Pierrefontaine-les-Varans 19 E2
Pierrefort 21 E2
Pierrelatte 22 B2
Pieskehaure 69 E1
Piešt'any 80 B2
Pietersaaren mlk 70 C3
Pietersaari 70 C3
Pietra Ligure 23 E2
Pietralunga 44 C2
Pietraperzia 48 C4
Pietrasanta 44 A2
Pietra Spada, Pso di 47 E4
Pietrosu 81 D2
Pieux, les 13 D2
Pieve de' Burgondi del Cairo 23 E1
Pieve di Bono 42 C3
Pieve di Cadore 43 E2
Pieve di Soligo 43 E3
Pieve di Teco 23 D3
Pievepelago 44 A1
Pieve Santo Stefano 44 B2
Pigádi 59 E1
Pigés 58 C1
Pigí 58 C2
Pigna 23 D3
Pigón, L 54 C4
Pihlajaveden as 73 D2
Pihlajavesi 73 D2
Pihlajavesi *L* 73 F3
Pihlava 72 C3
Pihtipudas 71 D3
Piikkiö 72 C4
Piippola 71 D3
Piispajärvi 71 E2
Pikal'ovo 79 E1
Pikérmi 59 F3
Piła 78 B4
Pilas 30 C3
Pila, Sa de la 32 B2
Pilat, Mt 19 D4
Pilat-Plage 20 B2
Pilatus 42 A2
Piléa 57 D2
Piles 32 C1
Pilés 65 E3
Píli (Makedonía) 54 C2
Píli (Stereá Eláda) 59 E3
Píli (Thessalía) 54 C4
Pilica 78 C4
Pílio 59 E2
Pilío 65 E1
Pílio, Óros 55 E4
Pillon, Col du 19 F3
Pilorí 55 D3
Pílos 62 C3
Pilštanj 50 B1
Pina 28 C2
Piña de Campos 25 E3
Pinar 31 D3
Pineda de la Sierra 25 F3
Pineda de Mar 29 F2
Pinerolo 23 D2
Pineto 45 D3
Piney 14 C4
Pinhal de Leiria 26 A3
Pinhal Novo 26 A4
Pinhão 24 B4
Pinheiro 24 A3
Pinhel 26 C2
Piniós (Pelopónissos) 58 C3
Piniós (Thessalía) 55 E4
Pinkafeld 41 F3
Pinneberg 36 C2
Pino 23 D3
Pinofranqueado 27 D3
Pinols 21 F2
Pinoso 32 C2
Pinos Puente 31 F3
Pinsk 79 D4
Pintado, Emb de 31 D2
Pintamo 71 E2
Pinto 27 F3
Pinzano al Tagliamento 43 E3
Pinzolo 42 C3
Piobbico 44 C2
Piombino 44 A3
Pione 23 F2
Pionsat 18 B3
Piotrków Trybunalski 78 B4
Piove di Sacco 43 E4
Piovene Rocchette 43 D3
Pipéri, N 60 B1
Pipriac 12 C4
Piqueras, Pto de 28 A1
Piran 43 F3
Pir'atin 79 F4
Pireás 59 E3
Pirgadíkia 56 A3
Pirgetós 55 E3
Pírgi (Dráma) 56 A1
Pirgí (Híos) 61 D3
Pirgí (Kérkira) 54 A4
Pírgi (Kozáni) 55 D2
Pírgos (Íos) 64 B1
Pírgos (Kríti) 64 C4
Pírgos (Makedonía) 55 E2
Pírgos (Pelopónissos) 58 C3
Pírgos (Sámos) 61 E3
Pírgos (Stereá Eláda) 59 E2
Pírgos Diroú 62 C4
Piriac 16 C1
Pirin 81 D4
Pirkkala 73 D3
Pirmasens 38 A3
Pirna 39 F1
Pirok 53 D4
Pirot 53 F2
Pirovac 50 B4
Pirsógiani 54 B3
Pirttikoski 71 D1
Pisa 44 A2
Pisciotta 46 C2
Pisek 39 F3
Piškorevci 51 D2
Pisogne 42 C3
Písses 60 B4
Pissodéri 54 C2
Pissónas 60 A2
Pissos 20 B2
Pisticci 47 E2
Pistoia 44 B2
Pisuerga, R 25 E3
Piteå 70 C2
Piteälven 70 B2
Pitești 81 D3
Pithagório 61 E3
Píthio (Thessalía) 55 D3
Píthio (Thráki) 57 D1
Pithiviers 14 A4
Pitigliano 44 B3
Pitlochry 3 D3
Pitomača 50 C1
Pittenweem 3 D3
Pivka 43 F3
Pivnica 50 C1
Pivnice 51 E1
Pivsko jezero 52 B3
Pizarra 31 E3
Piz Buin 42 C2
Pizzighettone 42 C4
Pizzo 47 E4
Pizzoli 45 D3
Plabennec 12 B3
Plaćenska pl 54 C1
Plačkovica 53 F4
Plagiá (Makedonía) 55 E2
Plagiá (Thráki) 56 C1
Plagne, la 19 E4
Plaisance 20 C3
Pláka (Límnos) 56 C3
Pláka (Pelopónissos) 59 D4
Pláka (Thráki) 56 C2
Pláka, Akr 56 C3
Pláka Litohórou 55 E3
Plakiás 64 B4
Planá 39 E2
Plana 52 B3
Planches-en-Montagne, les 19 E2
Plancoët 12 C3
Plandište 51 F1
Planica Mangrt 43 F2
Plánice 39 F3
Planina (Celje) 50 A1
Planina (Jesenice) 43 F2
Planina (Postojna) 43 F3
Planinica 53 E2
Planitz 39 E1
Plános 58 B3
Plansee 40 B4
Plasencia 27 D3
Plaški 50 B2
Plasy 39 E2
Platamona Lido 46 A2
Platamónas (Kavalá) 56 B2
Platamónas (Piería) 55 E3
Platanákia 55 E1
Platanés 64 B4
Platani 48 B4
Plataniá (Makedonía) 56 B1
Platánia (Pelopónissos) 58 C4
Plataniá (Thessalía) 59 E1
Platanistós 60 B3
Platanítis 58 C2
Plátanos (Kríti) 64 A3
Plátanos (Pelopónissos) 59 D4
Plátanos (Thessalía) 59 D1
Platariá 54 B4
Plateau-d'Assy 19 E3
Plateés 59 E3
Pláti 57 D1
Platiána 58 C4
Platičevo 51 E2
Platíkambos 55 E4
Platís Gialós (Kefaloniá) 58 A3
Platís Gialós (Míkonos) 60 C4
Platís Gialós (Sífnos) 64 B1
Platístomo 58 C1
Plattling 39 E4
Plau 37 E2
Plaue 37 E3
Plauen 39 D2
Plauer See (Potsdam) 37 E3
Plauer See (Schwerin) 37 E2
Plav 51 F4
Plavča 50 B2
Plavna 53 E1
Plavnica 52 C4
Plavnik / 50 A2
Plavnik *Mt* 50 A2
Playa Blanca 30 B4
Playa de Gandía 32 C1
Playa de San Juan 32 C2
Pleaux 21 E1
Pleine-Fougères 13 D3
Pleinfeld 39 D3
Pleiße 37 E4
Plélan-le-Grand 12 C4
Plélan-le-Petit 12 C3
Pléneuf 12 C3
Plentzia 25 F1
Plépi 59 E4
Plešin 53 D2
Plestin 12 B3
Pleternica 51 D2
Plettenberg 38 A1
Pletvar 53 E4
Pleumartin 17 F2
Pleumeur-Bodou 12 B3
Pleven 81 D3
Pleyben 12 B4
Pliego 32 B2
Plítra 63 D4
Plitvice 50 B2
Plitvička jezera 50 B2
Plitvički Ljeskovac 50 B3
Plješevica 50 B3
Pljevlja 51 E4
Ploaghe 46 A2
Ploče 51 D4
Plochingen 38 C4
Płock 78 B4
Plöckenpaß 43 E2
Plöckenstein 41 D2
Plоćno 51 D4
Ploërmel 12 C4
Plœuc 12 C3
Ploiești 81 D3
Plomári 61 D1
Plomb du Cantal 21 E2
Plombières 15 E4
Plomin 50 A2
Plön 37 D1
Plonéour-Lanvern 12 A4
Płońsk 78 C4
Plouagat 12 C3
Plouaret 12 B3
Plouay 12 B4
Ploubalay 12 C3
Ploudalmézeau 12 A3
Plouescat 12 B3
Plougasnou 12 B3
Plougastel-Daoulas 12 A3
Plougonven 12 B3
Plouguenast 12 C4
Plouha 12 C3
Plouigneau 12 B3
Ploumanach 12 B3
Plouzévédé 12 B3
Plovdiv 81 D4
Plumbridge 8 C1
Plungė 78 C3
Pl'ussa 79 D1
Pluvigner 12 C4
Plužine 52 B3
Plympton 6 B4
Plymstock 6 B4
Plzeň 39 F2
Po 43 D4
Poarta de Fier 80 C3
Poblet 29 D2
Pobrdđe 53 D3
Počep 79 F3
Pöchlarn 41 E2
Počinok 79 E3
Počitelj 51 D4
Pocking 40 C 2
Poćuta 51 E3
Pódareš 53 F4
Podbořany 39 E2
Podčetrtek 50 B1
Podensac 20 C2
Podersdorf 41 F3
Podgajci Posavski 51 D2
Podgarič 50 C1
Podgora 50 C4
Podgorač (Hrvatska) 51 D1
Podgorac (Srbija) 53 E1
Podgrad 43 F3
Podhum 50 C4
Podkoren 43 F2
Podlugovi 51 D3
Podnovlje 51 D2
Podogorá 58 B2
Podohóri 56 A2
Podol'sk 79 F2
Podol'skaja Vozvyšennost' 81 D1
Podpec 50 A1
Podrašnica 50 C3
Podravska Slatina 50 C1
Podromanija 51 E3
Podsreda 50 B1
Podsused 50 B1
Podturen 50 B1
Podujevo 53 D3
Podunavci 53 D2
Poel 37 D1
Poganovo 53 F2
Poggibonsi 44 B2
Poggio Imperiale 45 F4
Poggio Mirteto 44 C3
Poggio Renatico 43 D4
Poggio Rusco 43 D4
Pöggstall 41 E2
Pogoniani 54 B3
Pogradec 54 B2
Pohja 73 D4
Pohja-Lankila 73 F3
Pohjaslahti (Keski-Suomen Lääni) 73 D2
Pohjaslahti (Lapin Lääni) 71 D1
Pohjois-Karjalan Lääni 71 F3
Pohořelice 41 F1
Pohorje 50 A1
Poiana Brașov 81 D3
Poio 24 A2
Poiré, le 17 D2
Poirino 23 D2
Poissons 15 D3
Poitiers 17 E2
Põltsamaa 78 C1
Poix 14 A2
Poix-Terron 14 C2
Pojate 53 D2
Pojo 73 D4
Pokka 67 E3
Poklečani 51 D4
Pokljuka 43 F2
Pokupsko 50 B2
Polače 52 A3
Polacra, Pta de la 32 B4
Pola de Allande 24 C1
Pola de Gordón, la 25 D2
Pola de Laviana 25 D1
Pola de Lena 25 D2
Pola de Siero 25 D1
Polán 27 E4
Polcenigo 43 E3
Połczyn-Zdrój 78 A3
Polegate 7 E4
Poles 79 D4
Polesella 43 D4
Polessk 78 C3
Polhov Gradec 43 F3
Policastro 47 D2
Policastro, Golfo di 47 D2
Police 37 F2
Poličnik 50 B3
Policoro 47 E2
Polidéndri 59 F3
Polídrossos 59 D2
Políegos, N 64 B1
Poliégou-Folegándrou, Stenó 64 B1
Polígiros 55 F3
Polignano a Mare 47 E1
Poligny 19 D2
Polihnítos 61 D1
Polikárpi 55 D2
Polikástano 54 C3
Polikastro 55 E2
Polímilos 55 D3
Polinéri (Makedonía) 54 C3
Polinéri (Thessalía) 54 C4
Polióhni 56 C4
Polipótamo 54 C2
Polipótamos 60 B3
Políraho 55 D3
Polirinía 64 A3
Polis, M. 54 B1
Políssito 56 B2
Polistena 47 E4
Polithéa 54 C4
Politiká 59 E2
Poljana (Slovenija) 50 A1
Poljana (Srbija) 53 D1
Poljčane 50 B1
Polje 51 D2
Poljica 50 C4
Poljice 51 D3
Polla 47 D2
Pölläkkä 71 F4
Pöllau 41 F3
Polle 36 C4
Pollença 33 E2
Pollfoss 74 B1
Pollino, Mte 47 D2
Pollos 25 D4
Polmak 67 E1
Polock 79 D2
Polonnoje 81 D1
Polperro 6 A4
Poltava 79 F4
Polvijärvi 71 F4
Polzela 50 A1
Pomar 29 D2
Pomarance 44 A2
Pomarkku 72 C3
Pombal 26 A3
Pómbia 64 C4
Pomellen 37 F2
Pomezi 39 E2
Pomezia 44 C4
Pomigliano d'Arco 46 C1
Pommersfelden 39 D3
Pomokaira 67 E3
Pomorie 81 E4
Pomorze 78 B3
Pomovaara 67 E3
Pompei 46 C2
Pomposa 43 E4

Poncin 19 D3
Pondoiráklia 55 E2
Pondokómi 55 D3
Ponferrada 24 C2
Ponikovica 51 F3
Pons 17 D3
Ponsacco 44 A2
Pontacq 20 C4
Pontailler 19 D2
Pont-á-Marcq 14 B1
Pont-à-Mousson 15 D3
Pontão 26 B3
Pontardawe 6 B3
Pontarddulais 6 B3
Pontarion 18 A3
Pontarlier 19 E2
Pontassieve 44 B2
Pontaubault 13 D3
Pont-Audemer 13 E2
Pontaumur 18 B3
Pont-Aven 12 B4
Pont Canavese 23 D1
Pontcharra 19 E4
Pontchartrain 14 A3
Pontchâteau 16 C1
Pont-Croix 12 A4
Pont-d'Ain 19 D3
Pont-de-Beauvoisin, le 19 D3
Pont-de-Chéruy 19 D3
Pont-de-Claix, le 22 B2
Pont-de-Dore 18 C3
Pont-de-l'Arche 13 F3
Pont-de-Montvert, le 21 F2
Pont-de-Roide 19 E1
Pont-de-Salars 21 E2
Pont-d'Espagne 20 C4
Pont de Suert 29 D1
Pont-de-Vaux 19 D3
Pont-de-Veyle 19 D3
Pont-d'Oléron 17 D3
Pont-d'Ouilly 13 E3
Pont-du-Château 18 B3
Pont-du-Gard 22 A3
Ponte Arche 43 D3
Ponteareas 24 A2
Pontebba 43 E2
Pontecagnano 46 C2
Ponte Caldelas 24 A2
Ponteceno 23 F2
Ponte Ceso 24 A1
Pontecorvo 45 D4
Ponte da Barca 24 A3
Pontedecimo 23 E2
Ponte de Lima 24 A3
Pontedera 44 A2
Ponte de Sor 26 B4
Pontedeume 24 B1
Ponte di Legno 42 C3
Ponte di Piave 43 E3
Pontefract 5 E4
Pontelandolfo 46 C1
Ponte-Leccia 23 E3
Pontenelle Alpi 43 E3
Pont-en-Royans 19 D4
Ponte San Pietro 42 C3
Pontet, le 22 B3
Ponte Tresa 42 B3
Pontevico 42 C4
Pontfaverger-Moronvilliers 14 C3
Pontgibaud 18 B3
Pontigny 14 C4
Pontinia 46 A1
Pontinvrea 23 E2
Pontivy 12 C4
Pont-l'Abbé 12 B4
Pont-l'Evêque 13 E3
Pontlevoy 17 F1
Pontoise 14 A3
Pontones 32 A2
Pontón, Pto del 25 D2
Pontoon 8 B2
Pontorson 13 D3
Pontremoli 23 F2
Pontresina 42 C2
Pontrieux 12 C3
Pontrilas 6 C2
Ponts 29 E2
Pont-Scorff 12 B4
Ponts-de-Cé, les 17 D1
Pontsenni 6 B2
Pont-Ste-Maxence 14 B3
Pont-St-Esprit 22 B2
Pont St Martin 23 D1
Pont-St-Vincent 15 D3
Pont-sur-Yonne 14 B4
Pontvallain 17 E1
Pontypool 6 C3
Pontypridd 6 B3
Ponza, I de 46 A2
Ponziane, I 46 A2
Poole 6 C4
Poperinge 34 A3
Popinci 51 E2
Popoli 45 D3
Popovac 53 D2
Popovača 50 C2
Popova Šapka 53 D4
Popov Most 51 E4
Popovo 81 E3
Poppenhausen 38 C2
Poppi 44 B2
Poprad 80 C2
Porcari 44 A2
Porchov 79 D2
Porcuna 31 E2
Pordenone 43 E3
Poreč 43 F4
Pori 72 C3
Porjus 66 C4
Porkkalanselkä 73 D4
Porma, Emb del 25 D2
Porma, R 25 D2
Pornainen 73 D4
Pörnbach 39 D4
Pornic 16 C2
Pornichet 16 C2
Póros (Kefaloniá) 58 B3
Póros (Lefkáda) 58 A2
Póros (Póros) 59 E4
Póros, N 59 E4
Porozina 50 A2
Pórpi 56 C2
Porquerolles 22 C4
Porrentruy 19 E1
Porretta Terme 44 B1
Porriño 24 A2
Porsangen 67 E1
Porsangerhalvøya 67 D1
Porsgrunn 74 D3
Portadown 9 D1
Portaferry 9 D2
Portaje, Emb de 26 C3
Porta, la 23 D3
Portalegre 26 B4
Portalé, Pto del 20 C4
Portalrubio 28 C3
Portariá 55 E4
Portarlington 8 C3
Port Askaig 2 B4
Portavogie 9 E1
Porta Westfalica 35 E1
Port-Bacarès 21 F4
Portbail 13 D2
Portbou 29 F2
Port Charlotte 2 B4
Port, Col de 21 D4
Port-Cros 22 C4
Port-de-Bouc 22 B3
Porte, Col de 19 D4
Port-Einon 6 B3
Portel 30 B1
Portella Femmina Morta 49 D3
Port Ellen 2 B4
Portelo 24 C3
Port-en-Bessin 13 D2
Port Erin 4 C3
Pórtes 59 E3
Portet-d'Aspet, Col de 21 D4
Portezuelo 26 C3
Port Glasgow 2 C4
Portglenone 4 B2
Porthcawl 6 B3
Porthmadog 6 B1
Porthmós Elafoníssou 63 D4
Portici 46 C2
Porţile de Fier 81 D3
Portilla de la Reina 25 E2
Portillo 25 E4
Portillo de la Canda 24 C3
Portillo de Padornelo 24 C3
Portillo, Pto del 27 D3
Portimão 30 A3
Portimo 71 D1
Portinatx, Cala de 33 E1
Portinho 30 A1
Portishead 6 C3
Port-Joinville 16 C2
Port Láirge 8 C4
Portland, Bill of 6 C4
Port-la-Nouvelle 21 F4
Portlaoise 8 C3
Port-Leucate 21 F4
Port-Louis 12 B4
Portman 32 C3
Port-Manech 12 B4
Portmarnock 9 D3
Portnacroish 2 C3
Portnaguran 2 B1
ortnahaven 2 B4
Port-Navalo 16 C1
Porto (F) 23 E3
Porto (P) 24 A3
Porto Azzuro 44 A3
Pórto Carrás 56 A3
Porto Ceresio 42 B3
Porto Cervo 46 B2
Porto Cesareo 47 F2
Porto Cristo 33 E2
Porto de Lagos 30 A3
Porto de Mós 26 A3
Portodemouros, Emb de 24 B2
Porto do Barqueiro 24 B1
Porto do Son 24 A2
Porto Empedocle 48 C4
Porto Ercole 42 B3
Portoferraio 44 A3
Portofino 23 E2
Port of Ness 2 B1
Porto Garibaldi 44 C1
Porto, G de 23 E3
Pórto Germenó 59 E3
Portogruaro 43 E3
Portohéli 59 E4
Pórto Kágio 62 C4
Pörtom 70 C4
Portomaggiore 44 B1
Portomarín 24 B2
Porto-Maurizio 23 E3
Porto Moniz 30 A3
Portomouro 24 A1
Portonovo 24 A2
Porto Petro 33 E3
Porto Pino 46 A4
Pórto Ráfti 60 A3
Porto Recanati 45 D2
Porto Rotondo 46 B2
Portorož 43 F3
Porto San Giorgio 45 D2
Porto Sant' Elpidio 45 D2
Porto Santo 30 A3
Porto Santo, I de 30 A3
Porto Santo Stefano 44 B3
Portoscuso 46 A4
Porto Tolle 43 E4
Porto Torres 46 A2
Porto-Vecchio 23 D4
Portovenere 23 F2
Portpatrick 4 C2
Portree 2 B2
Portrush 4 B2
Portsalon 4 A2
Pörtschach 43 F2
Portsmouth 7 D4
Port-Ste-Marie 20 C2
Portstewart 4 B2
Port-St-Louis 22 B3
Port St Mary 4 C3
Port-sur-Saône 15 D4
Port Talbot 6 B3
Porttipahdan tekojärvi 67 E3
Portugalete 25 F2
Portumna 8 B3
Port-Vendres 21 F4
Port William 4 C2
Porvoo 73 D4
Porvoonjoki 73 E3
Porzuna 27 E4
Posada 46 B2
Posadas 31 D2
Pöschenhöhe 41 D3
Pošechonje-Volodarsk 79 F1
Posedarje 50 B3
Posets, Pico 20 C4
Posio 71 E1
Positano 46 C2
Possídi 55 F3
Possidonía 60 B4
Poßneck 39 D1
Posta 45 D3
Postavy 79 D3
Postira 50 C4
Postojna 50 A2
Postojnska jama 43 F3
Poštorná 41 F2
Posušje 51 D4
Potamí 56 A1
Potamiá 62 C3
Potamiés 64 C4
Potamós (Andikíthira) 63 E4
Potamós (Kíthira) 63 D4
Potamoúla 58 C2
Potenza 47 D1
Potenza *R* 44 C2
Potenza Picenza 45 D2
Potes 25 E2
Potídea, N. 55 F3
Potigny 13 E3
Potoci 51 D4
Potok 50 B2
Potós 56 B2
Potpećko jez 51 E3
Potsdam 37 F3
Pottenstein 41 F2
Potters Bar 7 E3
Pöttmes 39 D4
Potton 7 E2
Pouancé 17 D1
Pougues-les-Eaux 18 B2
Pouilly (Nièvre) 18 B2
Pouilly (Rhône) 18 C3
Pouilly-en-Auxois 19 D2
Poulaphouca Reservoir 9 D3
Poúlari, Akr 65 D1
Pouldu, le 12 B4
Pouliguen, le 16 C2
Poúlithra 59 D4
Poúnda 64 B1
Poúnda, Akr 60 B2
Pournári 59 D1
Pournári, Teh L 58 B1
Pourniás, Kólpos 56 C3
Pourri, Mt 19 E3
Poussu 71 E1
Pouyastruc 20 C4
Pouzauges 17 D2
Pouzin, le 22 B2
Považská Bystrica 80 B2
Poveda 28 B3
Povlja 50 C4
Povljana 50 A3
Povljen 51 E3
Povoa de Lanhoso 24 A3
Póvoa de Varzim 24 A3
Powerscourt 9 D3
Powys 6 B2
Poysdorf 41 F2
Pöytyä 72 C3
Poza de la Sal 25 F2
Požarevac 53 D1
Požega 51 F3
Požeranje 53 E3
Poznań 78 B4
Pozo Alcón 32 A3
Pozoblanco 31 E2
Pozo Cañada 32 B1
Pozo de Guadalajara 28 A3
Pozo Higuera 32 B3
Pozohondo 32 B1
Pozondón 28 B3
Pozozal, Pto 25 E2
Pozuelo (Castilla-la- Mancha) 32 B1
Pozuelo (Extremadura) 26 C3
Pozuelo de Calatrava 31 F1
Pozzallo 49 D4
Pozzomaggiore 46 A3
Pozzuoli 46 B2
Pozzuolo 43 E3
Präbichl 41 E3
Prača 51 E3
Prachatice 39 F3
Prada, Emb de 24 C2
Pradairo 24 B1
Pradarena, Pso di 44 A1
Pradelles 22 A2
Prádena 27 F2
Prades (E) 29 D2
Prades (F) 21 E4
Prado del Rey 31 D3
Pradoluengo 25 F3
Præstø 76 C3
Prägraten 43 E2
Praha 39 F2
Prahecq 17 E3
Prahova 81 D3
Prahovo 53 E1
Praia a Mare 47 D2
Praia da Barra 26 A2
Praia da Rocha 30 A3
Praia da Vieira 26 A3
Praia de Mira 26 A2
Praia de Santa Cruz 26 A4
Praia de Tocha 26 A3
Prali 23 D2
Pralognan 19 E4
Pra-Loup 22 C2
Prámanda 54 C4
Pramollo, Pso di 43 E2
Prangío 57 D1
Pranjani 51 F3
Prapatnica 50 C4
Prassiá 58 C1
Prassiés 64 B4
Prat de Compte 29 D3
Pratella 46 B1
Prati di Tivo 45 D3
Prato (Toscana) 44 B2
Prato (Umbria) 44 C3
Pratola Peligna 45 D3
Pratomagno 44 B2
Prato-Sornico 42 B3
Prats de Lluçanès 29 E2
Prats-de-Mollo 29 F1
Pravdinsk 78 C3
Pravia 25 D1
Praz 19 E3
Prebold 50 A1
Précy-sous-Thil 18 C1
Predappio 61 D3
Predazzo 43 D3
Preddvor 50 A1
Predeal 81 D3
Predejane 53 E3
Predel 43 F2
Predela 81 D4
Predil, Pso di 43 F2
Predjama 43 F3
Predoi 43 D2
Predošćica 50 A2
Pré-en-Pail 13 E3
Preetz 36 C1
Pregarten 41 D2
Preiner Gscheid 41 E3
Prekaja 50 C3
Prekestolen 74 A4
Preko 50 B3
Preljina 53 D2
Prelog 50 B1
Preloščica 50 B1
Premantura 43 F4
Prémery 18 B2
Premià de Mar 29 F2
Premilcuore 44 B2
Premnitz 37 E3
Premuda 50 A3
Premuda / 50 A3
Prenj 51 D4
Prenjas 54 B2
Prenzlau 37 F2
Prepolac 53 D3
Přerov 80 B1
Prerow 37 E1
Preševo 53 E3
Presjeka 52 B3
Preslav 81 E3
Presolana, Pso della 42 C3
Prešov 80 C1
Prespansko ez 54 C2
Pressath 39 D2
Pressbaum 41 F2
Prestatyn 5 D4
Pré-St Didier 19 E3
Presteigne 6 C2
Preste, la 29 F1
Prestfoss 74 C3
Přeštice 39 E3
Preston 5 D3
Prestonpans 3 D4
Prestwick 4 C1
Pretoro 45 E3
Prettau 43 D2
Prettin 37 F4
Pretzsch 37 F4
Preuilly 17 F2
Préveli 64 B4
Préveza 58 B1
Préveza (Nomos) 58 B1
Prevršac 50 B2
Prezid 50 A2
Pribini 51 D3
Priboj (Bosna i Hercegovina) 51 E2
Priboj (Srbija) 51 E3
Příbram 39 F2
Priego 28 A3
Priego de Córdoba 31 E3
Prien 40 C3
Prienai 78 C3
Prievidza 80 B2
Prigradica 52 A3
Prijeboj 50 B2
Prijedor 50 C2
Prijepolje 51 E3
Prilep 53 E4
Prilike 51 F3
Priluka 50 C3
Priluki 79 F4
Primaube, la 21 E2
Primel-Trégastel 12 B3
Primišlje 50 B2
Primolano 43 D3
Primorsk 79 D1
Primošten 50 B4
Primstal 35 D4
Princetown 6 B4
Prinés 64 B4
Prínos 56 B2
Prior, C 24 B1
Prip' at' 79 D4
Prisad 53 E4
Prislop 81 D2
Prisoje 50 C4
Priština 53 D3
Pritzerbe 37 E3
Pritzier 37 D2
Pritzwalk 37 E2
Privas 22 B2
Priverno 46 A1
Privlaka (Vincovci) 51 D2
Privlaka (Zadar) 50 B3
Prizren 53 D4
Prizzi 48 B3
Prnjavor (Bosna i Hercegovina) 51 D2
Prnjavor (Srbija) 51 E2
Proaza 25 D1
Probištip 53 E4
Probstzella 39 D2
Procida 46 B2
Pródromos 59 E3
Proenca-a-Nova 26 B3
Proevska Banja 53 E3
Profitis Ilías 65 F2
Profondeville 34 B3
Próhoma 55 E2
Prokletije 51 F4
Prokópi 59 E2
Prokuplje 53 E2
Prolom 53 E3
Prómahi 55 D2
Promahónas 55 F1
Promina, V. 50 B3
Promíri 59 E1
Pronsfeld 35 D4
Propriano 23 E4
Proskinás 59 E2
Prosna 78 B4
Prossedi 46 B1
Prossílio 56 B1
Prossotsáni 56 A1
Prostějov 80 B1
Próti 56 A2
Próti, N 62 B3
Protoklíssio 57 D1
Prötzel 37 F3
Proussós 58 C2
Provatónas 57 D2
Provence, Canal de 22 C3
Provenchères 15 E4
Provins 14 B3
Prozor 51 D3
Prudhoe 5 E2
Prukljansko jezero 50 C3
Prüm 35 D4
Pruna 31 D3
Prunetta 44 A2
Prut 81 D2
Prut 81 E2
Pružany 79 D4
Prvić 50 A2
Przasnysz 78 C4
Przełęcz Dukielska 80 C1
Przemyśl 80 C1
Psača 53 F3
Psahná 59 E2
Psáka 54 B4
Psális, Akr 64 A1
Psará 60 C2
Psarádes 54 C2
Psará, N 60 C2
Psári (Arkadía) 58 C4
Psári (Korinthía) 59 D3
Psári *Mt* 56 B2
Psáthi 63 F3
Psathópirgos 58 C2
Psathotópi 58 B1
Psérimos, N 65 E1
Psihikó 55 D4
Psihró 64 C4
Psínthos 65 F2
Pskov 79 D2
Pskovskoje Oz 79 D1
Ps'ol 79 F4
Pšov 39 E2
Psunj 50 C2
Pteléa 56 B1
Ptéri 58 C1
Ptolemaïda 55 D2
Ptóo 59 E2
Ptuj 50 B1
Puchberg 41 F2
Pučišća 50 C4
Puckeridge 7 E3
Puçol 28 C4
Pudasjärvi 71 D2
Puebla de Alcocer 31 E1
Puebla de Almenara 28 A4
Puebla de Beleña 28 A3
Puebla de Benifasar 29 D3
Puebla de Don Fadrique 32 A2
Puebla de D. Rodrigo 31 E1
Puebla de Guzmán 30 B2
Puebla de la Calzada 30 C1
Puebla de la Reina 31 D1
Puebla del Caramiñal 24 A2
Puebla de Obando 26 C4
Puebla de Sanabria 24 C3
Puebla de Trives 24 C3
Puebla do Lillo 25 D2
Puebla Tornesa 29 D4
Pueblica de V. 25 D3
Puente de Domingo Flórez 24 C2
Puente de Génave 32 A2
Puente de los Fierros 25 D2
Puente Genil 31 E3
Puente la Reina 20 A4
Puente la Reina de Jaca 28 C1
Puentenansa 25 E2
Puente Nuevo, Emb de 31 E2
Puentes, Emb de 32 B3
Puentes Viejas, Emb de 27 F2
Puente Viesgo 25 E2
Puerto Castilla 27 D3
Puerto de Alcudia 33 E2
Puerto de Andratx 33 E2
Puerto de la Cruz 30 A4
Puerto de la Encina 31 D3
Puerto del Rosario 30 B4
Puerto de Mazarrón 32 B3
Puerto de Pollença 33 E2
Puerto de San Vicente 27 E4
Puerto de Sóller 33 E2
Puerto Lápice 27 F4
Puertollano 31 F1
Puerto Lumbreras 32 B3
Puerto Real 30 C4
Puerto Serrano 31 D3
Pugets-Théniers 23 D3
Puglia 47 D1
Puhos (Oulun Lääni) 71 E2
Puhos (Pohjois-Karjalan Lääni) 73 F2
Puhosjärvi 71 E2
Puhovac 51 D3
Puigcerda 29 E1
Puig Major 33 E2
Puigmal 29 E1
Puig-reig 29 E2
Puigsacalm 29 F1
Puiseaux 14 A4
Puisserguier 21 F3
Pujols 20 C2
Pukë 53 D4
Pukiš 51 E2
Pukkila 73 E3
Pula (I) 46 B4
Pula (YU) 43 F4
Pulaj 52 C4
Puławy 78 C4
Pulborough 7 E4
Pulkau 41 E2
Pulkkila 71 D3
Pulpi 32 B3
Pulsnitz 39 F1
Pułtusk 78 C4
Punat 50 A2
Punkaharju 73 F2
Punkalaidun 72 C3
Punta Ala 44 A3
Punta di Penna 45 E3
Puntagorda 30 A4
Punta Križa 50 A3
Punta Raisi 48 B3
Punta Umbría 30 C3
Puokio 71 E3
Puolanka 71 E2
Purbach 41 F3
Purchena 32 A3
Purgstall 41 E3
Purkersdorf 41 F2
Purmerend 11 D2
Purnu 73 D3
Purullena 32 A3
Puruvesi 73 F2
Puškin 79 D1
Püspökladány 80 C2
Pustoška 79 D2
Pusula 73 D4
Puszcza 78 C4
Putanges 13 E3
Putbus 37 F1
Putignano 47 E1
Putinci 51 E2
Putivl' 79 F4
Putlitz 37 E2
Puttelange 15 E3
Puttgarden 37 D1
Puula 73 E3
Puumala 73 E3
Puy de Dôme 18 B3
Puy-de-Dôme (Dépt) 18 B3
Puy de Sancy 18 B4
Puy-en-Velay, le 22 A2
Puy-Guillaume 18 C3
Puylaurens 21 E3
Puy-l'Evêque 21 D2
Puymirol 21 D3
Puymorens, Col de 29 E1
Pwllheli 6 B1
Pyhä-Häkki 71 D4
Pyhäjärvi (Hameen Lääni) 73 D3
Pyhäjärvi (Oulun Lääni) 71 D3
Pyhäjärvi (Pohjois-Karjalan Lääni) 73 F2
Pyhäjärvi (Turun ja Porin Lääni) 72 C3
Pyhäjärvi *L* 71 D3
Pyhäjoki (Oulun Lääni) 71 D3
Pyhäjoki (Turun ja Porin Lääni) 72 C3
Pyhäjoki *R* 71 D3
Pyhälto 73 E3
Pyhäntä (Piipola) 71 D3
Pyhäntä (Ristijärvi) 71 E3
Pyhäranta 72 C3
Pyhäsalmi 71 D3
Pyhäselkä 71 F4
Pyhäselkä *L* 71 F4
Pyhätunturi 71 D1
Pyhatunturi 71 E1
Pyhävuori 71 D4
Pyhitysvaara 71 E2
Pyhrnpaß 41 D3
Pyhtää 73 E4
Pyla 20 B2
Pylkönmäki 71 D4
Pyrénées-Atlantiques 20 B3
Pyrénées-Orientales 21 E4
Pyrénées, Parc Nat des 20 C4
Pyrzyce 78 A4
Pyttis 73 E4

Q

Qaf'e Shllahut 53 D4
Qaf'e Shtamës 54 B1
Quakenbrück 36 B3
Quarré-les-Tombes 18 C1
Quarteira 30 B3
Quarto d'Altino 43 E3
Quartu San Elena 46 B4
Quatre Chemins, les 17 D2
Quatretonda 32 C1
Quedlinburg 37 D4
Queenborough 7 E3
Queen Elizabeth Forest Park 2 C3
Queensferry 5 D4
Quejigares, Pto de 27 F4
Queluz 26 A4
Queralbs 29 F1
Querfurt 37 E4
Quérigut 21 E4
Quero 27 F4
Quesada 32 A2
Quesnoy, le 14 B1
Questembert 16 C1
Quettehou 13 D2
Quiberon 16 B1
Quickborn 36 C2
Quiévrain 34 B3
Quigley's Point 4 A2
Quillan 21 E4
Quillane, Col de la 21 E4
Quillebeuf 13 E2
Quimper 12 B4
Quimperlé 12 B4
Quincinetto 23 D1
Quincoces de Yuso 25 F2
Quingey 19 D2
Quintana (Andalucía) 31 E2
Quintana (Extremadura) 31 D1
Quintana del Puente 25 E3
Quintana Martín Galíndez 25 F2
Quintanar de la Orden 28 A4
Quintanar de la Sierra 28 A1
Quintanar del Rey 32 B1
Quintana Redonda 28 A2
Quintanilha 24 C3
Quintanilla de Onésimo 25 E3
Quintin 12 C3
Quinto 28 C2
Quinzano d'Oglio 42 C4
Quipar, R 32 B2
Quiroga 24 B2
Quissac 22 A3
Qukës 54 B1
Quoich, L 2 C2

R

Raab 41 F4
Raabs 41 E2
Raahe 71 D3
Raajärvi 71 D1
Rääkkylä 71 F4
Raalte 11 E2
Raanujärvi 71 D1
Raasay 2 B2
Raasay, Sd of 2 B2
Raattama 67 D3
Rab 50 A3
Rab / 50 A3
Rába 80 B2
Rabac 50 A2
Rábade 24 B1
Rabastens 21 D3
Rabastens-de-Bigorre 20 C3
Rabat 49 F4
Rabka 80 C1
Rabrovo (Makedonija) 53 F4
Rabrovo (Srbija) 53 D1
Rača (Kragujevac) 53 D1
Rača (Radan) 53 D3
Racconigi 23 D2
Rače 50 B1
Rachov 81 D2
Racibórz 80 B1
Račinovci 51 E2
Račišće 52 A3
Radalj 51 E2
Radan 53 E3
Rădăuţi 81 D2
Radbuza 39 E3
Rade 36 C2
Råde 74 C4
Radeberg 39 F1
Radebeul 39 E1
Radeburg 37 F4
Radeče 50 A1
Radechov 81 D1
Radenci 41 F4
Radenthein 41 D4
Radevormwald 38 A1
Radici, Pso delle 44 A1
Radicondoli 44 B2
Radika 53 D4
Radimlje 52 B3
Radiovce 53 E4
Radlje 50 A1
Radljevo 52 C1
Radnice 39 F2
Radohinës, Maj'e 52 C4
Radojevo 51 F1
Radom 78 C4
Radomsko 78 B4
Radomyšl' 79 E4
Radotin 39 F2
Radovče 52 C3
Radovići 52 B4
Radoviš 53 F4
Radovljica 43 F2
Radovnica 53 E3
Radøy 74 A2
Radstadt 41 D4
Radstädter Tauernpaß 41 D4
Radstock 6 C3
Raduša 51 D3
Radusa 53 E4
Radviliškis 78 C2
Radzyn' Podlaski 78 C4
Raesfeld 11 F3
Raffadali 48 C4
Rafína 60 A3
Ragama 27 E2
Raglan 6 C3
Rago 66 B3
Ragua, Pto de la 32 A3
Raguhn 37 E4
Ragunda 69 E4
Ragusa 49 D4
Rahden 36 B3
Ráhes 59 D2
Rahlstedt 36 C2
Raia, Rib de 26 B4
Rain 39 D4
Räisälä 71 E1
Raisduoddarhal'di 67 D2
Raisio 72 C4
Raittijärvi 67 D2
Rajac 53 E1
Raja-Jooseppi 67 F2
Rajamäki 73 D4
Rajince 53 E3
Raka 50 B1
Rakalj 43 F4
Rakitna 50 A1
Rakitnica 50 C1
Rakkestad 74 C3
Rakova Bara 53 D1
Rakovac 50 C2
Rakovica 50 B2
Rakovnik 39 F2
Rakvere 78 C1
Ralja 52 C1
Ram 53 D1
Ramacca 49 D4
Ramales de la Victoria 25 F2
Ramallosa 24 A2
Ramberg 66 A3
Rambervillers 15 E4
Rambouillet 14 A3
Rambucourt 15 D3
Ramno 53 E3
Ramnoús 60 A3
Ramor, L 8 C2
Ramsau 40 C3
Ramsau 41 D3
Ramsele 69 E4
Ramsey (Cambridge) 7 E2
Ramsey (I of Man) 4 C3
Ramsgate 7 F3
Ramsjö 75 E1
Ramstein 38 A3
Ramsund 66 B3
Ramundberget 69 D4
Ramvik 69 F4
Rana 69 D2
Ranalt 43 D2
Rance 12 C4
Randaberg 74 A3
Randalstown 9 D1
Randan 18 B3
Randanne 18 B3
Randazzo 49 D3
Randers 76 B2
Randijaure 69 F1
Randow 37 F2
Randsfjorden 74 C3
Råneå 70 C2
Råneälven 70 C2
Rangsdorf 37 F3
Rankweil 40 A4
Rannoch, L 2 C3
Ranovac 53 D1
Rantasalmi 73 E2
Rantsila 71 D3
Ranua 71 D2
Raon-l'Etape 15 E3
Rapallo 23 E2
Rapolano Terme 44 B2
Rapolla 47 D1
Rapperswil 42 B2
Rapsáni 55 E3
Raptópoulo 58 C4
Raša 43 F4
Raša *R* 43 F4
Räsälä 71 E4
Rasbo 75 F3
Rascafría 27 F2
Rasdorf 38 C2
Raseiniai 78 C3
Rasimbegov Most 55 D1
Rasina 53 D2
Raška 53 D2
Rasno 51 D4
Raso, C 26 A4
Rasquera 29 D3
Rastatt 38 B4
Rastede 36 B2
Rastegai'sa 67 E1
Rastenberg 39 D1
Rastenfeld 41 E2
Rasueros 27 E2
Rätan 75 E1
Rateče 43 F2
Ratekau 37 D1
Rates 24 A3
Rathdowney 8 20C3
Rathdrum 9 D3
Rathenow 37 E3
Rathfriland 9 D2
Rathkeale 8 B3
Rathlin I 4 B2
Rath Luirc 8 B4
Rathmelton 4 A2
Rathmore 8 B4
Rathmullan 4 A2
Rathnew 9 D3
Raticosa, Pso della 44 B1
Ratingen 35 D2
Ratkovac 53 D3
Ratkovo 51 E1
Ratten 41 E3
Rattenberg 40 B4
Rattersdorf 41 F3
Rattray 3 D3
Rattray Head 3 E2
Rättvik 75 E2
Ratzeburg 37 D2
Raubling 40 C3
Raucourt-et-Flaba 14 C2
Raudanjoki 71 D1
Raudaskylä 71 D3
Raufarhöfn 68 B1
Raufoss 74 C2
Rauha 73 E3
Rauhamäki 73 D3
Rauland 74 B3
Rauma (N) 74 B1
Rauma (SF) 72 C3
Rauris 40 C4
Rautalampi 71 E4
Rautas 66 C3
Rautavaara 71 E3
Rautio 71 D3
Rautjärvi 73 F3
Ravan 51 D3
Ravanica 53 D1
Ravanjska 50 B3
Ravanusa 48 C4
Ravello 46 C2
Raven 50 B1
Ravenna 44 C1
Ravensbrück 37 F2
Ravensburg 42 B1
Ravna Dubrava 53 E2
Ravna Gora 50 A2
Ravna Reka 53 D1
Ravne na Koroškem 50 A1
Ravnište 53 D2
Ravnje 51 E2
Ravno 52 B3
Ravno Bučje 53 E2
Ravno, G. 50 C3
Rawicz 78 B4
Rawtenstall 5 D4
Rayleigh 7 E3
Rayol 22 C4
Räyrinki 71 D4
Ražana 51 F3
Ražanac 50 B3
Razboj 50 C2
Razbojna 53 D2
Raždaginja 51 F4
Razelm 81 E3
Razgrad 81 E3
Razlog 81 D4
Razlovci 53 F4
Raz, Pte du 12 A4
Reading 7 D3
Reales 31 D4
Réalmont 21 E3
Rebais 14 B3
Rebbenesøy 66 C2
Rebordelo 24 B3
Reç 53 D4
Recanati 45 D2
Recco 23 E2
Recey 14 C4
Rechnitz 41 F3
Rečica (SU) 79 E3
Rečica (YU) 50 B2
Recke 36 B3
Recklinghausen 11 F3
Recknitz 37 E1
Recoaro Terme 43 D3
Recuerda 25 F4
Redange 15 D2
Red B 4 B2
Redcar 5 E3
Redditch 7 D2
Redhill 7 E3
Redon 16 C1
Redondela 24 A2
Redondo 30 B1
Redruth 6 A4
Ree, L 8 C2
Rees 11 F3
Reeth 5 E3
Refsnes 66 B3
Reftele 77 D2
Regalbuto 49 D3
Regen 39 E3
Regensburg 39 E3
Regenstauf 39 E3
Reggello 44 B2
Reggio di Calabria 47 D4
Reggiolo 43 D4
Reggio nell' Emilia 44 A1
Reghin 81 D2
Regnitz 39 D3
Reguengos de Monsaraz 30 B1
Rehau 39 D2
Rehburg-Loccum 36 C3
Rehden 36 B3
Rehna 37 D2
Reichenau (A) 41 F2
Reichenau (CH) 42 B2
Reichenbach (Dresden) 39 F1
Reichenbach (Karl-Marx-Stadt) 39 E2
Reichertshofen 39 D4
Reichshoffen 15 F3
Reigate 7 E3
Reignier 19 E3
Ré, Ile de 17 D3
Reillanne 22 B3
Reims 14 C3
Reinach 42 A2
Reinbek 36 C2
Reinberg 37 E1
Reine 66 A3
Reinfeld 37 D2
Reinheim 38 B3
Reinli 74 C2
Reinosa 25 E2
Reinøy 66 C2
Reisaelva 67 D2
Reischenhart 40 C3
Reisjärvi 71 D3
Reiss 3 D1
Reit im Winkl 40 C3
Reitzenhain 39 E1
Reka 43 F3
Rekovac 53 D2
Remagen 38 A2
Rémalard 13 F3
Remeskylä 71 D3
Remich 15 D2
Remiremont 15 E4
Remolinos 28 B2
Remouchamps 34 C3
Remoulins 22 B3
Rempstone 7 D1
Remscheid 35 D2
Rémuzat 22 B2
Rena 74 C2
Renaix 34 A3
Renazé 17 D1
Renchen 38 A4
Rende 47 D3
Rendína (Makedonía) 55 F2
Rendína (Thessalía) 58 C1
Rendsburg 36 C1
Rengínio 59 D2
Rengsdorf 38 A2
Reni 81 E2
Renish Pt 2 B1
Renko 73 D3
Renkum 11 E3
Rennebu 68 C4
Rennerod 38 A2
Rennes 13 D4
Rennes-les-Bains 21 E4
Rennesøy 74 A3
Rennweg 41 D4
Reno 44 B1
Rensjön 66 C3
Renwez 14 C2
Réole, la 20 C2
Replot 70 C4
Replotfjärden 70 C4
Repojoki 67 E3
Reposaari 72 C3
République, Col de la 18 C4
Repvag 67 E1
Requena 32 C1
Réquista 21 E3
Rerik 37 D1
Resanovci 50 C3
Resavica 53 D1
Reschenpaß 40 A4
Resen (Makedonija) 54 C2
Resen (Srbija) 53 F3
Resende 24 B4
Resia, Pso di 42 C2
Reşiţa 80 C3
Resmo 77 E2
Resna 52 C4
Resnik 52 C1
Ressons 14 B2
Restafjorden 66 C2
Restelica 53 D4
Resuttano 48 C3
Retezatului, M 81 D3
Rethel 14 C2
Rethem 36 C3
Rethen 36 C3
Réthimno 64 B4
Réthimno (Nomos) 64 B4
Retiers 13 D4
Retortillo, Emb de 31 D2
Retuerta 28 C3
Retuerta del Bullaque 27 E4
Retuerta, Emb de 25 F3
Retz 41 E2
Reuilly 18 A2
Reus 29 E3
Reusel 11 E3
Reuss 42 A2
Reuterstadt-Stavenhagen 37 E2
Reutlingen 38 B4
Reutte 40 A4
Revard, Mt 19 E3
Revel 21 E3
Revesbotn 67 D1

Den Haag
Den Haag
Den Haag
Wateringen
Monster
Poeldijk
Kwintsheul
Honselersdijk
's-Gravenzande
Naaldwijk
Hoek van Holland
Hoekse Bosjes
Kingston upon Hull
Harwich
Felixstowe
NIEUWE
WATERWEG
Staelduinen
Heenweg
Nieuwe Tuinen
Oostbuurt
De Lier
Maasdijk
Westerlee
Rijnpoorthaven
Maasland
Maassluis
EUROPOORT
Maasvlakte
Europahaven
8e Petroleumhaven
6e Petroleumh.
4e Petroleumh.
5e Petroleumh.
7e Petroleumh.
Mississippihaven
Hartelkanaal
Calandkanaal
Oostvoornse Meer
Brielse Meer
Mildenburgbos
Oostvoorne
Stenenbaak
Kruiningergos
Brielle
Rozenburg
Zanddijk
Calandbrug
Heveringen
Helhoek
Strijpe
Rugge
Brielsebrug
Zwartewaal
Vierpolders
V O O R N E
Botlek
Rockanje
De Pinguin
Waterbos
Stuifakker
Heenvliet
Geervliet
Nieuwenhoorn
Abbenbroek
Ronde Weibos
Nieuw-Helvoet
Haringvlietdam
Hellevoetsluis
Oudenhoorn
Zuidland
Havenhoofd
H A R I N G V L I E T
G O E R E E
Brouwersdam
Gat Van de Hawk
Rak van Scheelhoek
Noord Pampus
E 30
A 20
N 218
N 57
A 15
N 15
52°
4°

S

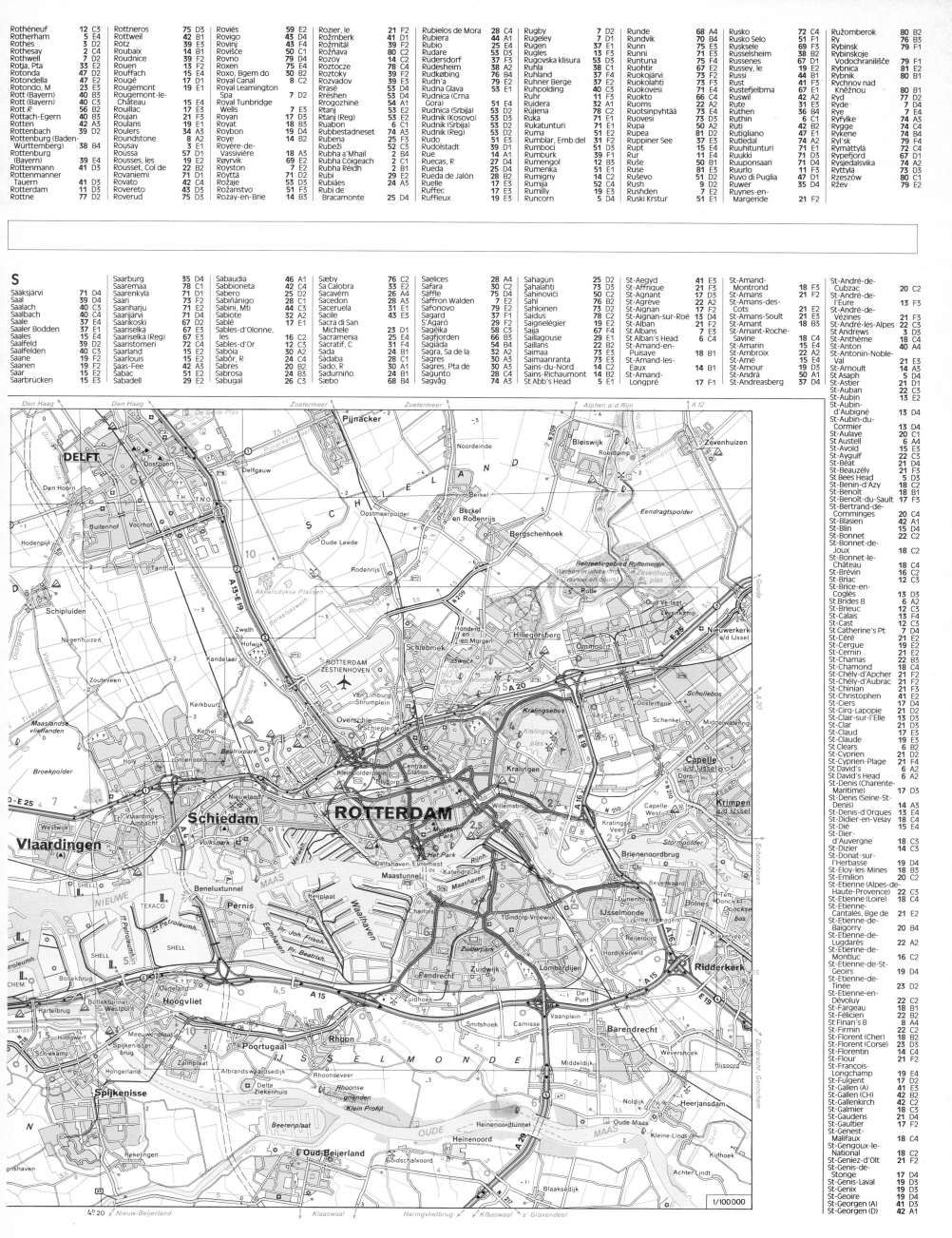

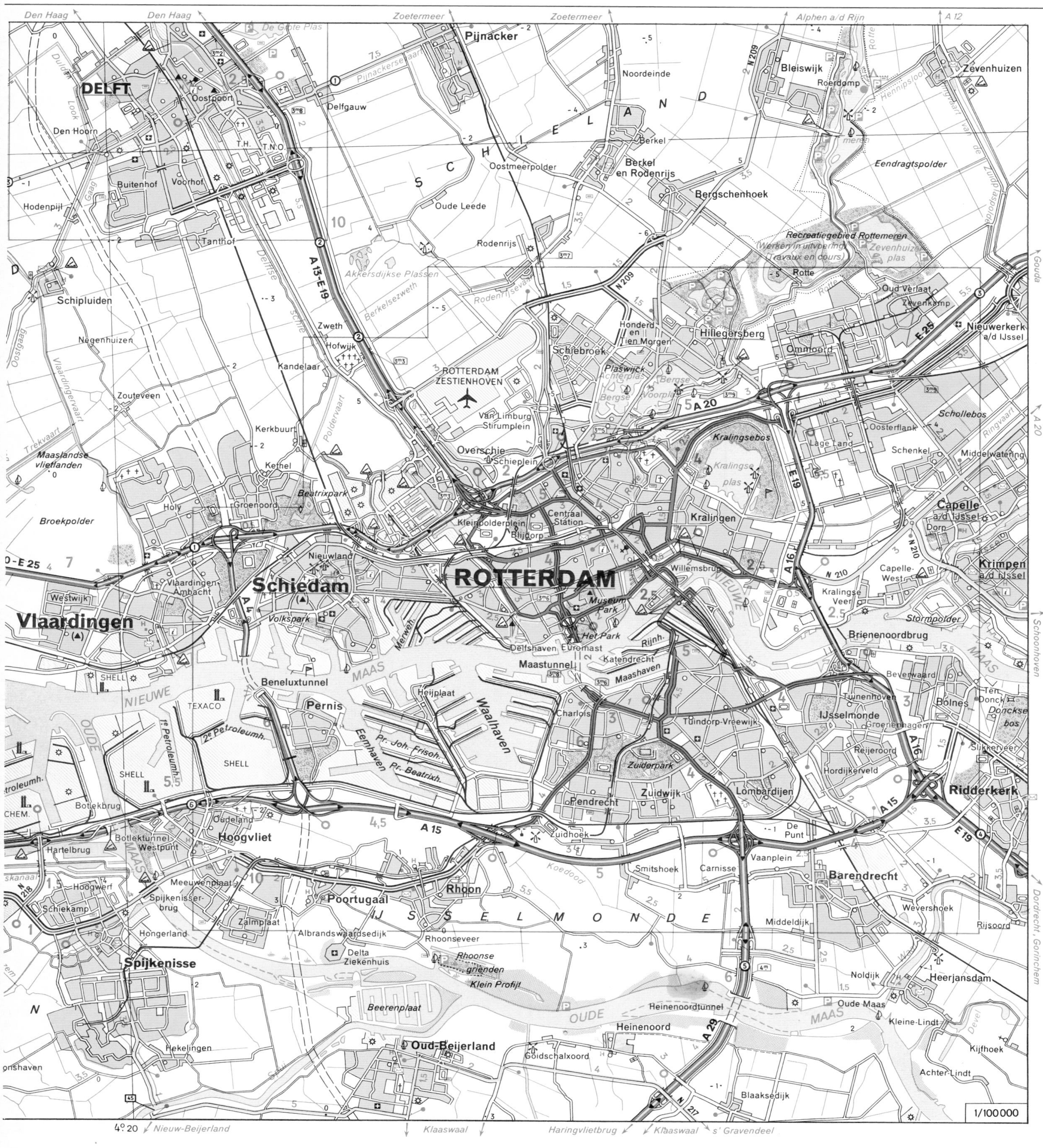
Den Haag
Zoetermeer
Alphen a/d Rijn
A 12
Pijnacker
DELFT
Den Hoorn
Delfgauw
Noordeinde
Bleiswijk
Zevenhuizen
Berkel en Rodenrijs
Bergschenhoek
Eendragtspolder
Hodenpijl
Schipluiden
Oude Leede
Rodenrijs
Recreatiegebied Rottemeren
Akkersdijkse Plassen
Zweth
Hofwijk
Negenhuizen
Kandelaar
ROTTERDAM ZESTIENHOVEN
Hillegersberg
Schiebroek
Ommoord
Nieuwerkerk a/d IJssel
Zouteveen
Kethel
Overschie
Kralingen
Capelle a/d IJssel
Krimpen a/d IJssel
Schiedam
Vlaardingen
ROTTERDAM
Broekpolder
Beneluxtunnel
Maastunnel
Pernis
Waalhaven
IJsselmonde
Ridderkerk
Hoogvliet
Poortugaal
Rhoon
Barendrecht
Heerjansdam
Spijkenisse
Oud-Beijerland
Heinenoordtunnel
Hekelingen
Kijfhoek
1/100 000
Nieuw-Beijerland
Klaaswaal
Haringvlietbrug
s' Gravendeel
Dordrecht, Gorinchem
Schoonhoven
Gouda

St-Georgen am Langsee 50 A1
St-Georges 17 D1
St Georges Channel 6 A2
St-Georges-de-Didonne 17 D3
St-Georges-en-Couzan 18 C3
St-Germain 14 A3
St-Germain-de-Calberte 22 A2
St-Germain-des-Fossés 18 C3
St-Germain-du-Bois 19 D2
St-Germain-du-Plain 19 D2
St-Germain-du-Teil 21 F2
St-Germain-Laval 18 C3
St-Germain-Lembron 18 B4
St-Germain-les-Belles 17 F3
St-Germain-l'Herm 18 C4
St-Gertraud 42 C2
St-Gervais 19 E3
St-Gervais-d'Auvergne 18 B3
St-Gervais-sur-Mare 21 F3
St-Géry 21 D2
St-Gildas-de-Rhuys 16 C1
St-Gildas-des-Bois 16 C1
St-Gildas, Pte de 16 C2
St-Gilgen 40 C3
St-Gilles 22 A3
St-Gilles-Croix-de-Vie 16 C2
St-Gingolph 19 E3
St-Girons 21 D4
St-Girons-Plage 20 B3
St-Goar 38 A2
St-Goarshausen 38 A2
St-Gobain 14 B2
St Govan's Head 6 A3
St-Guénolé 12 A4
St-Guilhem-le-Désert 21 F3
St-Haon-le-Châtel 18 C3
St Helens 5 D4
St-Hélier 12 C3
St-Hilaire 21 E4
St-Hilaire-des-Loges 17 D2
St-Hilaire-de-Villefranche 17 D3
St-Hilaire-du-Harcouet 13 D3
St-Hippolyte 19 E1
St-Hippolyte-du-Fort 22 A3
St-Honoré 18 C2
St-Hubert 15 D2
St-Imier 19 E2
St-Ingbert 15 E2
St Ives (Cambs) 7 E2
St Ives (Cornwall) 6 A4
St-Jacques 13 D4
St-Jacut 12 C3
St-Jakob 43 D2
St-Jakob im Rosental 43 F2
St-James 13 D3
St-Jean-Brévelay 12 C4
St-Jean-Cap-Ferrat 23 D3
St-Jean-d'Angély 17 D3
St-Jean-de-Bournay 19 D4
St-Jean-de-Daye 13 D3
St-Jean-de-Losne 19 D2
St-Jean-de-Luz 20 B3
St-Jean-de-Maurienne 19 E4
St-Jean-de-Monts 16 C2
St-Jean-du-Bruel 21 F3
St-Jean-du-Gard 22 A3
St-Jean-en-Royans 22 B2
St-Jean-Pied-de-Port 20 B4
St-Jeoire 19 E3
St-Johann im Pongau 40 C4
St-Johann in Tirol 40 C3
St John's Pt 9 D2
St-Jouin-de-Marnes 17 E2
St-Juéry 21 E3
St-Julien 19 D3
St-Julien-Chapteuil 22 A2
St-Julien-de-Vouvantes 17 D1
St-Julien-du-Sault 14 B4
St-Julien-en-Genevois 19 E3
St-Julien-l'Ars 17 E2
St-Junien 17 F3
St Just 6 A4
St-Just-en-Chaussée 14 A2
St-Just-en-Chevalet 18 C3
St-Justin 20 C3
St-Keverne 6 A4
St-Kilda 2 A1
St-Lambrecht 41 D4
St-Lary-Soulan 20 C4
St-Laurent (Calvados) 13 D2
St-Laurent (Vendée) 17 D2
St-Laurent (Vienne) 17 F3
St-Laurent-de-la-Salanque 21 F4
St-Laurent-du-Pont 19 D4
St-Laurent-en-Grandvaux 19 E2
St-Laurent-les-Bains 22 A2
St-Laurent-Médoc 20 B1
St-Léger 18 C2
St-Léonard-de-Noblat 17 F3
St-Leonhard (I) 43 D2
St-Leonhard (Niederösterreich) 41 E2
St-Leonhard (Tirol) 40 B4
St-Lô 13 D3
St-Lorenzen 43 E2
St-Louis 19 F1
St-Loup-Lamairé 17 E2
St-Loup-sur-Semouse 15 D4
St-Luc 42 A3
St-Lunaire 12 C3
St-Lys 21 D3
St-Macaire 20 C2
St Magnus B 3 F1
St-Maixent-l'Ecole 17 E3
St-Malo 12 C3
St-Malo-de-la-Lande 13 D3
St-Mamet-la-Salvetat 21 E2
St-Mandrier 22 C4
St-Marcellin 19 D4
St-Margarethen 36 C2
St Margaret's Hope 3 E1
St-Märgen 42 A1
St-Mars-la-Jaille 17 D1
St-Martin (Charente-Maritime) 17 D3
St-Martin (Pyrénées-Orientales) 21 E4
St-Martin-d'Auxigny 18 B2
St-Martin-de-Belleville 19 E4
St-Martin-de-Crau 22 B3
St-Martin-de-Londres 22 A3
St-Martin-de-Seignan 20 B3
St-Martin-de-Valamas 22 A2
St-Martin-en-Bresse 19 D2
St Martin's 6 A4
St-Martin-Vésubie 23 D3
St-Martory 21 D4
St Mary's 6 A4
St-Mathieu 17 F3
St-Mathieu, Pte de 12 A3
St-Maurice 19 E3
St Mawes 6 A4
St-Maximin-la-Ste-Baume 22 C3
St-Médard-en-Jalles 20 C2
St-Méen 12 C4
St-Michael (Salzburg) 41 D4
St-Michael (Steiermark) 41 D4
St-Michaelisdonn 36 C2
St Michael's Mount 6 A4
St-Michel 14 C2
St-Michel-de-Maurienne 19 E4
St-Michel-en-Grève 12 B3
St-Michel-en-l'Herm 17 D3
St-Michel-Mont-Mercure 17 D2
St-Mihiel 15 D3
St Monance 3 D3
St-Moritz 42 C2
St-Nazaire 16 C2
St-Nectaire 18 B3
St Neots 7 E2
St-Nicolas-d'Aliermont 14 A2
St-Nicolas-de-la-Grave 21 D3
St-Nicolas-de-Port 15 D3
St-Nicolas-du-Pélem 12 B3
St-Niklaas 34 B3
St-Niklaus 42 A3
St-Oedenrode 11 E3
St Olof 77 D3
St-Omer 14 A1
St-Oswald 41 D4
St-Pair 13 D3
St-Palais (Charente-Maritime) 17 D3
St-Palais (Pyrénées-Atlantiques) 20 B3
St-Pardoux-la-Rivière 17 F4
St-Paul (A) 50 A1
St-Paul (Alpes-de-Haute-Provence) 22 C2
St-Paul (Alpes-Maritimes) 23 D3
St-Paul-Cap-de-Joux 21 E3
St-Paul-de-Fenouillet 21 E4
St-Paulien 22 A1
St-Paul-Trois-Châteaux 22 B2
St-Pé-de-Bigorre 20 C4
St-Pée 20 B3
St-Péray 22 B2
St-Père-en-Retz 16 C2
St-Peter in der Au 41 D3
St-Peter-Ording 36 B1
St Peter Port 12 C2
St-Philbert 17 D2
St-Pierre (Charente-Maritime) 17 D3
St-Pierre (Morbihan) 16 B1
St-Pierre-d'Albigny 19 E3
St-Pierre-de-Chartreuse 19 E4
St-Pierre-de-Chignac 21 D1
St-Pierre-Eglise 13 D2
St-Pierre-le-Moûtier 18 B2
St-Pierre-sur-Dives 13 E3
St-Pois 13 D3
St-Pol-de-Léon 12 B3
St-Pol-sur-Ternoise 14 A1
St-Pölten 41 E2
St-Pons-de-Thomières 21 E3
St-Porchaire 17 D3
St-Pourçain 18 B3
St-Privat 21 E1
St-Quay-Portrieux 12 C3
St-Quentin 14 B2
St-Rambert 18 C4
St-Rambert-d'Albon 19 D4
St-Rambert-en-Bugey 19 D3
St-Raphaël 22 C3
St-Rémy-de-Provence 22 B3
St-Rémy-sur-Durolle 18 C3
St-Renan 12 A3
St-Riquier 14 A2
St-Romain-de-Colbosc 13 E2
St-Rome-de-Tarn 21 F3
St-Saëns 14 A2
St-Satur 18 B2
St-Saulge 18 C2
St-Sauveur-en-Puisaye 18 B1
St-Sauveur-Lendelin 13 D3
St-Sauveur-le-Vicomte 13 D2
St-Sauveur-sur-Tinée 23 D2
St-Savin (Gironde) 20 C1
St-Savin (Vienne) 17 F2
St-Savinien 17 D3
St-Seine-l'Abbaye 19 D1
St-Sernin-sur-Rance 21 E3
St-Sever (Calvados) 13 D3
St-Sever (Landes) 20 C3
St-Sulpice-les-Feuilles 17 F3
St-Symphorien 20 C2
St-Symphorien-de-Lay 18 C3
St-Symphorien-d'Ozon 19 D3
St-Symphorien-sur-Coise 18 C3
St-Trivier-de-Courtes 19 D3
St-Trivier-sur-Moignans 19 D3
St-Trojan 17 D3
St-Tropez 22 C3
St-Truiden 34 C3
St-Ulrich 43 D2
St-Vaast-la-Hougue 13 D2
St-Valentin 41 D3
St-Valentin an der Haide 42 C2
St-Valery 14 A2
St-Valery-en-Caux 13 E2
St-Valier 19 D4
St-Vallier-de-Thiey 22 C3
St-Varent 17 E2
St-Vaury 18 A3
St-Veit 43 F2
St-Véran 22 C2
St-Vincent 42 A4
St-Vincent-de-Tyrosse 20 B3
St-Vith 34 C4
St-Vivien-de-Médoc 20 B1
St-Wandrille 13 F2
St-Wendel 38 A3
St-Wolfgang 41 D3
St-Yorre 18 C3
St-Yrieix-la-Perche 17 F4
Ste Adresse 13 E2
Ste Anne-d'Auray 16 C1
Ste Baume, la 22 C3
Ste-Croix-Volvestre 21 D4
Ste Croix 19 E2
Ste Croix-du-Mont 20 C2
Ste Croix, Lac de 22 C3
Ste Enimie 21 F2
Ste Foy-la-Grande 20 C2
Ste Foy-l'Argentière 18 C3
Ste Geneviève-sur-Argence 21 E2
Ste Hélène 20 B2

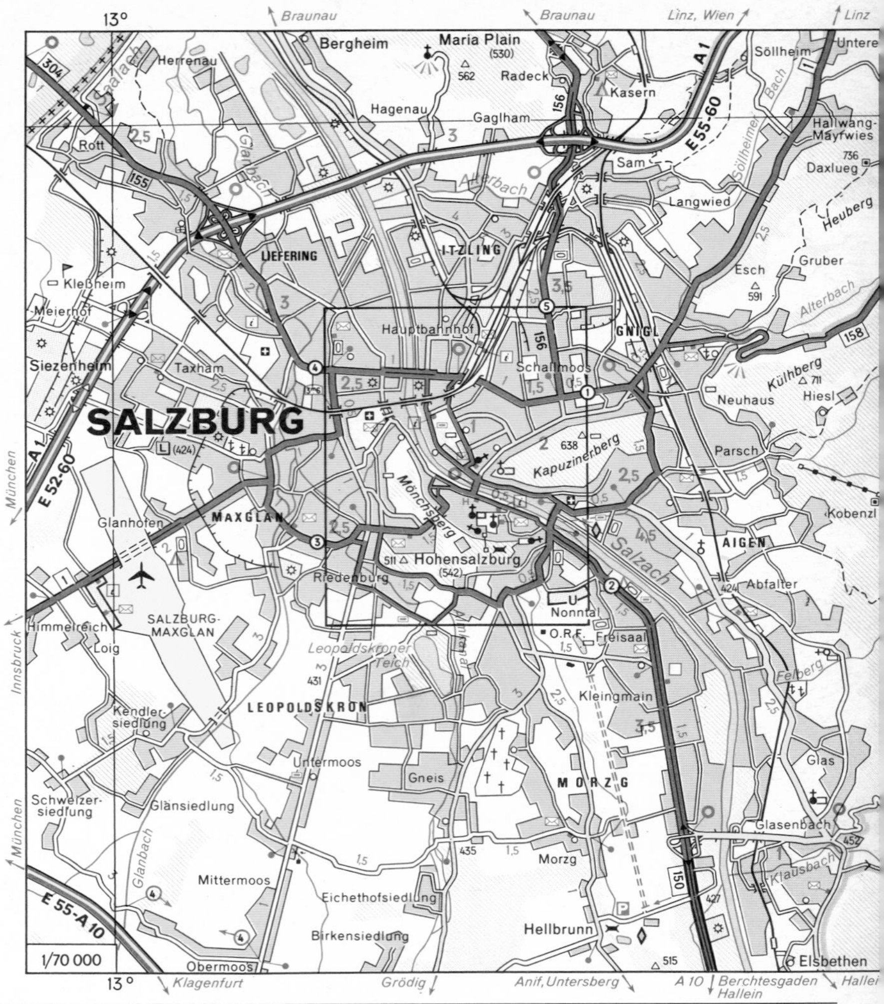
SALZBURG
Bergheim
Maria Plain
Liefering
Itzling
Gnigl
Hauptbahnhof
Schallmoos
Taxham
Siezenheim
Maxglan
Kapuzinerberg
Mönchsberg
Hohensalzburg
Riedenburg
Nonntal
Aigen
Parsch
Salzach
Leopoldskron
Morzg
Hellbrunn
Elsbethen
Salzburg-Maxglan
Gneis
Mittermoos
Eichethofsiedlung
Birkensiedlung
Obermoos
Himmelreich
Klagenfurt
Grödig
Anif, Untersberg
Berchtesgaden Hallein
Braunau
Linz, Wien
1/70 000

Ste Hermine 17 D2
Ste Livrade 21 D2
Ste Lucie-de-Tallano 23 E4
Ste Marie-aux-Mines 15 E4
Ste Maure-de-Touraine 17 E2
Ste Maxime 22 C3
Ste-Menehould 14 C3
Ste Mère-Eglise 13 D2
Ste Odile, Mt 15 E3
Ste Sévère 18 F3
Ste Suzanne 13 E4
Ste Tulle 22 C3
Saintes 17 D3
Stes Maries-de-la-Mer 22 A3
Saintfield 9 D1
Şaissac 21 E3
Šajkaš 51 E1
Sakarya 81 F4
Sakskøbing 76 C4
Sakule 51 F1
Säkylä 72 C3
Sala 75 E3
Salacgrīva 78 C2
Sala Consilina 47 D2
Salada 28 C4
Salakovac 53 D1
Salamajärvi 71 D4
Salamajärvi L 71 D4
Salamanca 27 D2
Salamína 59 E3
Salamína, N 59 E3
Salándi 59 E4
Salangen 66 C2
Salar 31 E3
Salardú 21 D4
Salas 24 C1
Salaš 53 E1
Salas de los Infantes 25 F3
Salazar, R 20 B4
Salbohed 75 E3
Salbris 18 A1
Salcombe 6 B4
Saldaña 25 E2
Sale 23 E1
Sålekinna 75 D1
Salem 42 B1
Salemi 48 B3
Sälen 75 D2
Salen (Highland) 2 B3
Salen (Mull) 2 B3
Salernes 22 C3
Salerno 46 C2
Salerno, G di 46 C2
Salers 21 E1
Salève, Mt 19 E3
Salgótarján 80 C2
Salgueiro do Campo 26 B3
Sali 50 B4
Salice Terme 23 E1
Salies-de-Béarn 20 B3
Salies-du-Salat 21 D4
Salignac-Eyvigues 21 D2
Salime, Emb de 24 C1
Salina, I 49 D2
Salinas (Andalucía) 31 E3
Salinas (Asturias) 25 D1
Salinas, C 33 E3
Salindres 22 A2
Sälinkää 73 D3
Salins 19 D2
Salisbury 7 D3
Salla 71 E1
Sallanches 19 E3
Sallent 29 E2
Sallent-de-Gállego 20 C4
Salles 21 E4
Salles-Curan 21 E3
Salling 76 B2
Salling Sund 76 B2
Salmerón 28 A3
Salmoral 27 E2
Salmünster 38 B2
Salò 42 C3
Salo 72 C4
Salobreña 31 F4
Salona 50 C4
Salon-de-Provence 22 C3
Salonta 80 C2
Salorino 26 C4
Salor, R 26 C4
Salou 29 E3
Salou, C de 29 E3
Salpausselkä 73 E3
Salsbruket 69 D2
Salses-le-Château 21 E4
Salso 48 C3
Salsomaggiore Terme 23 F2
Salsta 75 F3
Saltash 6 B4
Saltburn-by-the-Sea 5 F3
Saltcoats 4 C1
Saltee Is 9 D4
Saltfjellet 69 E1
Saltfjorden 69 E1
Salto 24 B3
Saltoluokta 66 C4
Saltvik 72 B4
Saluggia 23 D1
Saluzzo 23 D2
Salvacañete 28 B4
Salvagnac 21 D3
Salvan 19 E3
Salvaterra de Magos 26 A4
Salvatierra-Agurain 20 A4
Salvatierra de los Barros 30 C1
Salvattera de Miño 24 A3
Salvetat-Peyralès, la 21 E2
Salvetat-sur-Agout, la 21 E3
Salviac 21 D2
Sælvig 76 B3
Sálvora, I de 24 A2
Salza 41 E3
Salzach 56 B3
Salzburg 40 C3
Salzburg (Prov) 40 C4
Salzgitter-Bad 37 D4
Salzgitter-Lebenstedt 37 D4
Salzhausen 36 C2
Salzkammergut 41 D3
Salzkotten 36 B4
Şalzwedel 37 D3
Šamac Slavonski 51 D2
Sama de Langreo 25 D1
Samarína 54 C3
Samatan 21 D3
Sambatikí 59 D4
Sambiase 47 E3
Samboal 25 E4
Sambor 80 C1
Sambre 34 B4
Sambuca di Sicilia 48 B4
Samedan 42 C2
Sameiro, Mte 24 A3
Samer 14 A1
Sámi 58 B2
Samikó 58 C4
Sammatti 73 D4
Sammichele 47 E1
Samnanger 74 A2
Samobor 50 B1
Samodreža 53 D3
Samoëns 19 E3
Samokov (BG) 81 D4
Samokov (YU) 53 E4
Samora Correia 26 A4
Samos 24 B2
Samoš 51 F1
Sámos 61 E3
Sámos, N 61 E3
Samothráki 56 C3
Samothráki, N 56 C3
Samper de Calanda 28 C3
Sampeyre 23 D2
Samsø 76 C3
Samsø Bælt 76 C3
Samtens 37 E1
Samugheo 46 A3
San 78 C4
Sana 50 C3
Saná 55 F3
Sanabria, L de 24 C3
San Adrián 28 B1
San Adrián, C de 24 A1
San Agata de Goti 46 C1
San Agata di Militello 49 D3
San Agustín 27 F3
San Amaro 24 B2
San Andrea Frius 46 B4
San Andrés del Rabanedo 25 D2
San Antioco 46 A4
San Antioco, I di 46 A4
San Antonio 46 B2
San Antonio Abad 33 E1
San Antonio, C de 33 D1
San Bartolomé de las Abiertas 27 E3
San Bartolomé de la Torre 30 C3
San Bartolomeo in Galdo 45 E4
San Benedetto del Tronto 45 D2
San Benedetto in Alpe 44 B2
San Benedetto Po 43 D4
San Bernardino 42 B3
San Bernardino, Pso del 42 B3
San Biagio Platani 48 C4
San Bonifacio 43 D4
San Candido 43 E2
San Carlos de la Ràpita 29 D3
San Carlos del Valle 32 A1
San Casciano in Val di Pesa 44 B2
San Cataldo (Puglia) 47 F1
San Cataldo (Sicilia) 48 C4
San Cipirello 48 B3
San Clemente 32 A1
San Clemente, Emb de 32 A2
San Colombano al Lambro 42 C4
San Cosme 24 C1
San Cristóbal 30 C2
San Cristóbal de Entreviñas 25 D3
San Cristóbal de la Polantera 25 D2
San Cristóbal de la Vega 27 E2
San Damiano d'Asti 23 D2
San Daniele del Friuli 43 E3
San Daniele Po 42 C4
San Demetrio Corone 47 E3
San Donaci 47 F1
San Donà di Piave 43 E3
San Emiliano 25 D2
San Esteban de Gormaz 25 F4
San Esteban del Molar 25 D3
San Esteban del Valle 27 E3
San Esteban de Pravia 25 D1
San Fele 47 D1
San Felice a Cancello 46 C1
San Felice Circeo 46 A1
San Felices de Los Gallegos 26 C2
San Felice sul Panaro 43 D4
San Felipe 28 B3
San Feliu de Guíxols 29 F2
San Ferdinando di Puglia 45 F4
San Fernando 30 C4
San Francisco Javier 33 E2
San Fratello 49 D3
San Gavino Monreale 46 A4
San Gemini 44 C3
San Giacomo 43 D2
San Gimignano 44 B2
San Ginesio 45 D2
San Giorgio 23 D1
San Giorgio del Sannio 46 C1
San Giorgio di Nogaro 43 E3
San Giorgio Ionico 47 E2
San Giorgio Piacentino 42 C4
San Giovanni a Piro 47 D2
San Giovanni di Sinis 46 A3
San Giovanni in Fiore 47 E3
San Giovanni in Persiceto 44 B1
San Giovanni Lupatoto 43 D4
San Giovanni Rotondo 45 F4
San Giovanni Suergiu 46 A4

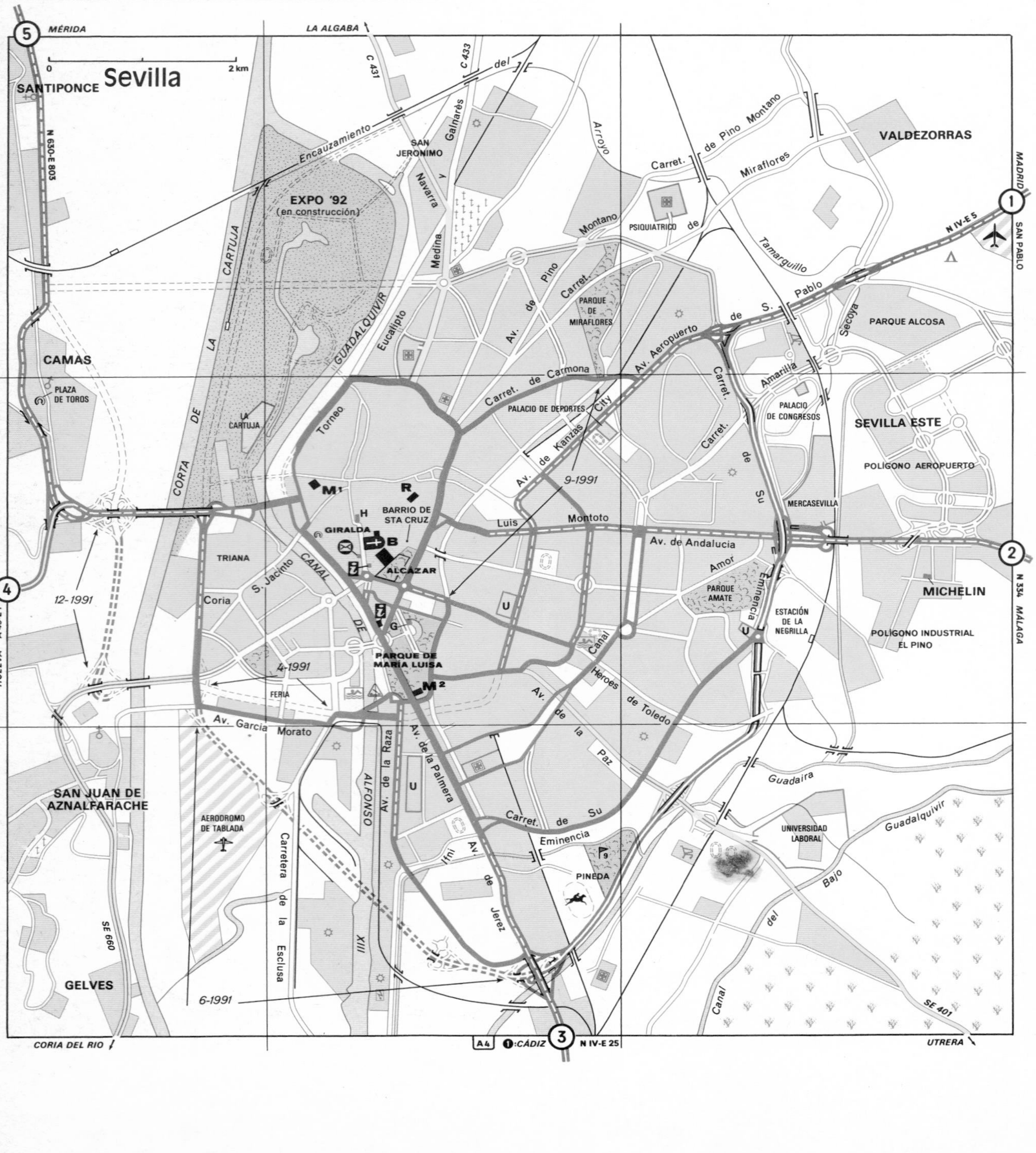
Sevilla
0 2 km
SANTIPONCE
CAMAS
SAN JUAN DE AZNALFARACHE
GELVES
VALDEZORRAS
SEVILLA ESTE
MICHELIN
EXPO '92 (en construcción)
GUADALQUIVIR
TRIANA
GIRALDA
ALCÁZAR
BARRIO DE STA CRUZ
PARQUE DE MARÍA LUISA
PARQUE ALCOSA
PARQUE DE MIRAFLORES
PALACIO DE DEPORTES
PALACIO DE CONGRESOS
POLÍGONO AEROPUERTO
POLÍGONO INDUSTRIAL EL PINO
MERCASEVILLA
ESTACIÓN DE LA NEGRILLA
UNIVERSIDAD LABORAL
AERÓDROMO DE TABLADA
PINEDA
MÉRIDA
LA ALGABA
MADRID
SAN PABLO
MÁLAGA
HUELVA
CORIA DEL RIO
UTRERA
CÁDIZ

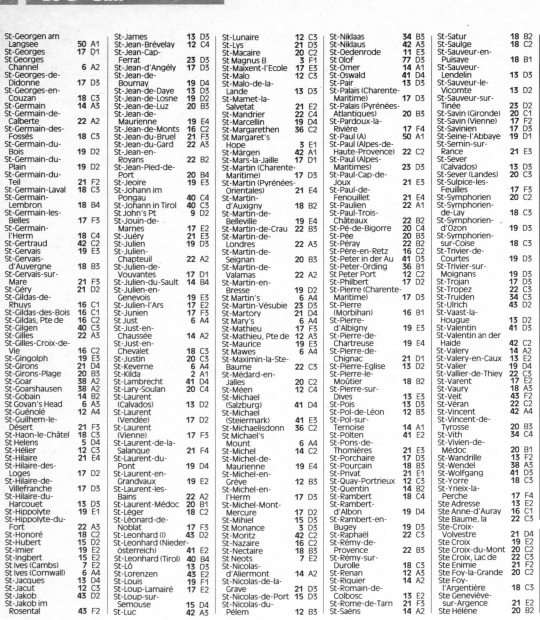

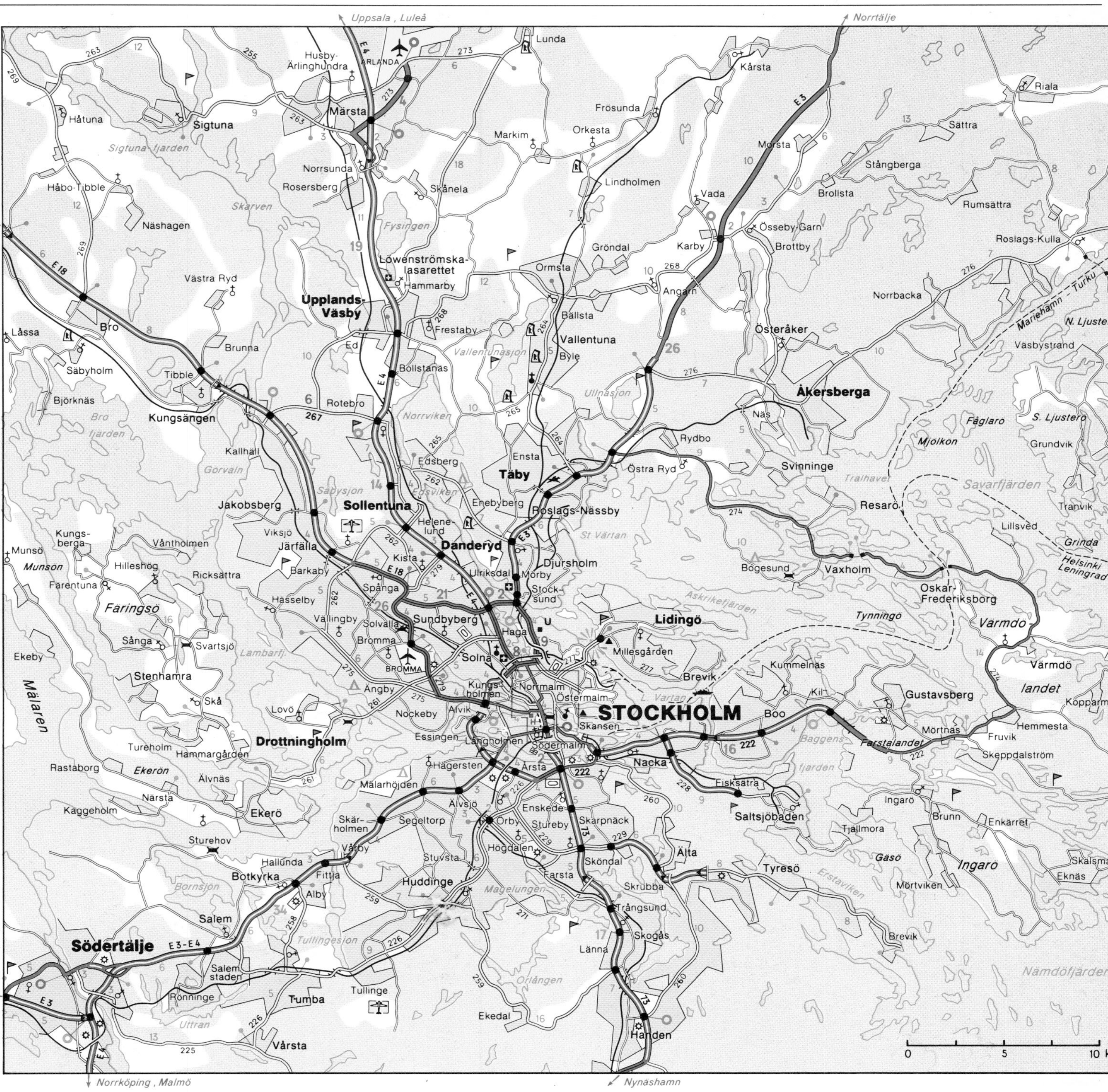
Uppsala, Luleå
Norrtälje
Lunda
ARLANDA
Husby-Ärlinghundra
Kårsta
Riala
Sigtuna
Märsta
Håtuna
Frösunda
Orkesta
Markim
Sättra
Sigtuna-fjärden
Norrsunda
Rosersberg
Skånela
Lindholmen
Vada
Stångberga
Brollsta
Rumsättra
Håbo-Tibble
Skarven
Näshagen
Fysingen
Össeby-Garn
Brottby
Roslags-Kulla
Löwenströmska-lasarettet
Hammarby
Gröndal
Karby
Ormsta
Vässby Ryd
Upplands-Väsby
Angarn
Norrbacka
Mariehamn - Turku
Västerås, Oslo
Bro
Frestaby
Ballsta
Vallentuna
Österåker
N. Ljusterö
Vasbystrand
Lässa
Brunna
Vallentunasjön
Byle
Sabyholm
Tibble
Bollstanäs
Ullnasjön
Åkersberga
Björknäs
Kungsängen
Rotebro
Norrviken
Nas
Fågelaro
S. Ljusterö
Kallhäll
Ensta
Rydbo
Mjölkön
Grundvik
Görvälln
Edsberg
Täby
Östra Ryd
Svinninge
Trälhavet
Savarfjärden
Jakobsberg
Sollentuna
Eneby berg
Roslags-Nässby
Resarö
Tranvik
Viksjö
Helenelund
Lillsved
Munsö
Kungsberga
Vånthoimen
Järfälla
Danderyd
St Värtan
Grinda
Munson
Hilleshög
Barkaby
Kista
Ulriksdal
Mörby
Djursholm
Bogesund
Vaxholm
Helsinki Leningrad
Färentuna
Ricksättra
Spånga
Stocksund
Oskar-Fredriksborg
Faringsö
Hässelby
Vällingby
Solvalla
Sundbyberg
Haga
Lidingö
Tynningö
Värmdö
Sånga
Svartsjö
Lambarfj.
Bromma
Solna
Millesgården
Värmdö
Ekeby
Stenhamra
Brevik
Kummelnäs
Mälaren
Skå
Angby
Kungsholmen
Normalm
Östermalm
STOCKHOLM
Boo
Gustavsberg
landet
Kopparmora
Lovö
Nockeby
Alvik
Skansen
Hemmesta
Drottningholm
Essingen
Langholmen
Mörtnäs
Farstalandet
Fruvik
Tureholm
Hammargården
Södermalm
Nacka
Baggens
Skeppdalström
Rastaborg
Ekeron
Alvnäs
Hägersten
Årsta
Fisksätra
Mälarhöjden
Enskede
Saltsjöbaden
Ingarö
Kaggeholm
Närsta
Ekerö
Älvsjö
Örby
Skarpnäck
Brunn
Enkarret
Skär-holmen
Segeltorp
Stureby
Tjallmora
Sturehov
Vårby
Högdalen
Ålta
Skalsmara
Hallunda
Stuvsta
Sköndal
Gaso
Ingarö
Ekn'as
Botkyrka
Fittja
Huddinge
Farsta
Tyresö
Mörtviken
Alby
Bornsjön
Magelungen
Ersta viken
Skrubba
Salem
Trångsund
Brevik
Södertälje
Tullingesjön
Skogås
Salem staden
Länna
Nämdöfjärden
Örebro, Göteborg
Orlången
Rönninge
Tumba
Tullinge
Uttran
Ekedal
Vårsta
Handen
Norrköping, Malmö
Nynäshamn
0 5 10 km

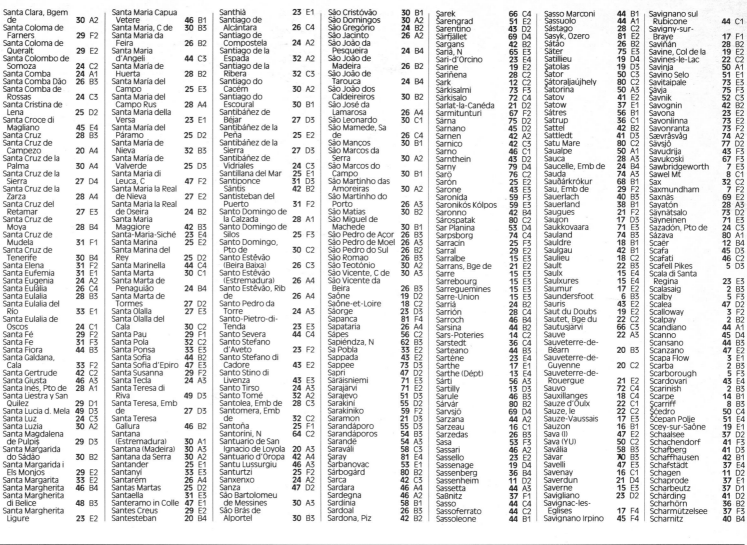

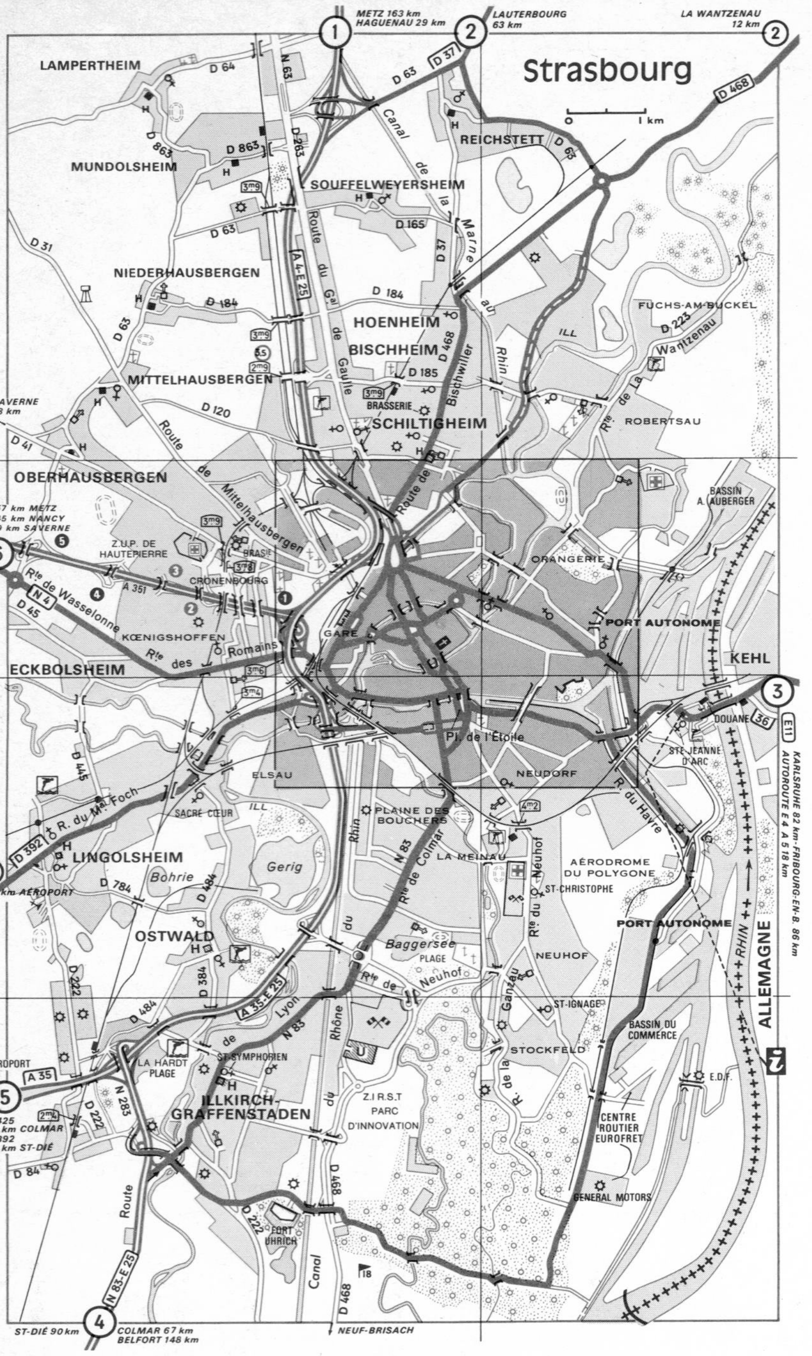
Strasbourg
0 1 km
METZ 163 km HAGUENAU 29 km
LAUTERBOURG 63 km
LA WANTZENAU 12 km
LAMPERTHEIM
MUNDOLSHEIM
REICHSTETT
SOUFFELWEYERSHEIM
NIEDERHAUSBERGEN
HOENHEIM
BISCHHEIM
FUCHS-AM-BUCKEL
MITTELHAUSBERGEN
SCHILTIGHEIM
ROBERTSAU
SAVERNE 38 km
OBERHAUSBERGEN
157 km METZ 145 km NANCY 39 km SAVERNE
Z.I.P. DE HAUTEPIERRE
CRONENBOURG
ORANGERIE
BASSIN A. AUBERGER
KOENIGSHOFFEN
PORT AUTONOME
ECKBOLSHEIM
KEHL
DOUANE
KARLSRUHE 82 km - FRIBOURG-EN-B. 86 km AUTOROUTE E 4 A 5 18 km
ELSAU
Pl. de l'Etoile
STE-JEANNE D'ARC
NEUDORF
SACRE COEUR
PLAINE DES BOUCHERS
LINGOLSHEIM
LA MEINAU
AÉRODROME DU POLYGONE
ST-CHRISTOPHE
15 km AÉROPORT
PORT AUTONOME
OSTWALD
Baggersee
NEUHOF
ST-IGNACE
BASSIN DU COMMERCE
ALLEMAGNE
RHIN
AÉROPORT
LA HARDT PLAGE
STOCKFELD
ILLKIRCH-GRAFFENSTADEN
Z.I.R.S.T PARC D'INNOVATION
CENTRE ROUTIER EUROFRET
N 425 72 km COLMAR N 392 90 km ST-DIÉ
GENERAL MOTORS
FORT UHRICH
ST-DIÉ 90 km
COLMAR 67 km BELFORT 148 km
NEUF-BRISACH

Schauinsland Feldberg 42 A1
Scheeßel 36 C2
Scheggia 44 C2
Scheibbs 41 E3
Scheifling 41 D4
Scheinfeld 38 C3
Schelde 34 B3
Schenefeld (Hamburg) 36 C2
Schenefeld (Itzehoe) 36 C1
Scherfede 38 B1
Schermbeck 11 F3
Scheßlitz 39 D2
Scheveningen 11 D3
Schia 44 A1
Schiedam 11 D3
Schieder 36 C4
Schiehallion 2 C3
Schierling 39 E4
Schiermonnikoog 11 E1
Schiermonnikoog / 11 E1
Schiers 42 B2
Schifferstadt 38 B3
Schildau 37 F4
Schilpario 42 C3
Schiltach 42 A1
Schio 43 D3
Schirmeck 15 E3
Schirnding 39 E2
Schkeuditz 37 E4
Schkölen 39 D1
Schladming 41 D4
Schlagsdorf 37 D2
Schlanders 42 C2
Schlangenbad 38 A2
Schleching 40 C3
Schlei 36 C1
Schleiden 35 D3
Schleiz 39 D2
Schleswig 36 C1
Schleswig-Holstein 36 C1
Schleusingen 38 C2
Schlieben 37 F4
Schliersee 40 B3
Schlitz 38 B2
Schlotheim 38 C1
Schluchsee 42 A1
Schlucht, Col de la 15 E4
Schlüchtern 38 C2
Schluderbach 43 E2
Schluderns 42 C2
Schlüsselfeld 38 C3
Schlutup 37 D2
Schmalkalden 38 C2
Schmallenberg 38 A1
Schmidmühlen 39 D3
Schmilka 39 F1
Schmölln (Leipzig) 39 D1
Schmölln (Neubrandenburg) 37 F2
Schnackenburg 37 D2
Schnaittenbach 39 D3
Schneeberg (A) 41 E3
Schneeberg (D) 39 D2
Schneeberg (DDR) 39 E1
Schneverdingen 36 C3
Schoberpaß 41 E3
Schöckl 41 E3
Schönau 42 A1
Schönberg (A) 43 D2
Schönberg (Bayern) 40 C2
Schönberg (Karl-Marx-Stadt) 39 E2
Schönberg (Rostock) 37 D2
Schönberg (Schleswig-Holstein) 36 C1
Schönbrunn 41 F2
Schönebeck 37 D4
Schöneck 39 E2
Schönecken 35 D4
Schönefeld 37 F3
Schönewalde 37 F4
Schongau 40 B3
Schöningen 37 D4
Schönmünzach 38 B4
Schönsee 39 E3
Schönthal 39 E3
Schönwald 42 A1
Schönwalde 37 D1
Schoonhoven 11 D3
Schopfheim 42 A1
Schöppenstedt 37 D4
Schoppernau 40 A4
Schorndorf 38 C4
Schortens 36 B2
Schotten 38 B2
Schouwen Duiveland 11 D3
Schramberg 42 A1
Schrems 41 E2
Schrobenhausen 39 D4
Schröcken 40 A4
Schrozberg 38 C3
Schruns 42 C2
Schuls 42 C2
Schüttorf 11 F2
Schwaan 37 E1
Schwabach 39 D3
Schwäbisch Gmünd 38 C4
Schwäbisch Hall 38 C3
Schwabmünchen 40 A3
Schwaigern 38 B3
Schwalenberg 36 C4
Schwalmstadt-Treysa 38 B1
Schwalmstadt-Ziegenhain 38 B1
Schwandorf 39 E3
Schwanebeck 37 D4
Schwanenstadt 41 D3
Schwanewede 36 B2
Schwarmstedt 36 C3
Schwarza (A) 41 E3
Schwarza (DDR) 39 D1
Schwarzach 40 C4
Schwarze Elster 37 F4
Schwarzenbach 39 D2
Schwarzenbek 37 D2
Schwarzenberg 39 E2
Schwarzenburg 19 F2
Schwarzenfeld 39 E3
Schwarzheide 39 E1
Schwarzsee 19 F2
Schwarzwald 38 B4
Schwaz 40 B4
Schwechat 41 F2
Schwedt 37 F2
Schweich 35 D4
Schweinfurt 38 C2
Schweinitz 37 F4
Schwelm 35 D2
Schwendi 40 A3
Schwenningen 42 A1
Schwerin 37 D2
Schweriner See 37 D2
Schwerte 38 A1
Schwetzingen 38 B3
Schwyz 42 B2
Sciacca 48 B4
Scicli 49 D4
Scilla 47 D4
Scilly, Is of 6 A4
Ščit, Jez 51 D3
Scole 7 F2
Sconser 2 B2
Scopello 42 A3
Scordia 49 D4
Scorff 12 B4
Ščors 79 E4
Scorzè 43 E3
Scotch Corner 5 E3
Scotland 2 C3
Scourie 2 C1
Scrabster 3 D1
Scridain, L 2 B3
Scrivia 23 E2
Ščučin 79 D3
Scunthorpe 5 F4
Scuol 42 C2
Seaford 7 E4
Seaham 5 E2
Seaton 6 C4
Seaton Delaval 5 E2
Sebečevo 53 D3
Sebeş 81 D3
Sebež 79 D2
Sebnitz 39 F1
Sečanj 51 F1
Secchia 44 A1
Seckau 41 E3
Seclin 14 B1
Secondigny 17 E2
Sedan 14 C2
Sedano 25 F2
Seda, Rib de 26 B4
Sedbergh 5 D3
Séderon 22 B2
Sedgefield 5 E3
Sedičany 39 F2
Sedico 43 E3
Sedilo 46 A3
Sedini 46 A2
Sedlare 53 D3
Sedlec-Prčice 39 F2
Sée 13 D3
Seebenau 37 D3
Seebergsattel 50 A1
Seeboden 41 D4
Seebruck 40 C3
Seefeld 40 B4
Seehaus 41 D3
Seehausen (Magdeburg) 37 D4
Seehausen (Stendal) 37 E3
Seeheim 38 B3
Seelisberg 42 B2
Sées 13 E3
Seesen 37 D4
Seevetal 36 C2
Seewalchen 41 D3
Seewiesen 41 E3
Sefkerin 52 C1
Segesta 48 B3
Segl 42 C3
Segni 45 D4
Segonzac 17 E3
Segorbe 28 C4
Segovia 27 F2
Segré 17 D1
Segre, R 29 D2
Segura 26 C3
Segura de la Sierra 32 A2
Segura de León 30 C2
Segura de los Baños 28 C3
Segura, R 32 C2
Segura, Sa de 32 A2
Sehnde 36 C3
Seia 26 B3
Seiches 17 E1
Seifhennersdorf 39 F1
Seignelay 14 B4
Seil 2 B3
Seiland 67 D1
Seilandsjøkelen 67 D1
Seilhac 18 A4
Seille (Meurthe-et-Moselle) 15 D3
Seille (Saône-et-Loire) 19 D2
Seinäjoki 70 C4
Seine 14 A3
Seine-et-Marne 14 B3
Seine-Maritime 13 E2
Sein, I de 12 A4
Seitenstetten 41 D3
Seitsemisen 72 C3
Seixal 26 A4
Seixo 24 B2
Sejerø 76 C3
Sejerø Bugt 76 C3
Sejm 79 F4
Sékoulas 58 C4
Šekovići 51 E3
Selargius 46 B4
Selassía 62 C3
Selb 39 D2
Selbekken 68 C3
Selbu 69 D4
Selbusjøen 68 C4
Selby 5 E4
Selce 50 A2
Selçuk 61 F3
Sele 46 C2
Selečka pl 55 D1
Selenter See 36 C1
Sélero 56 B2
Sélestat 15 E4
Selevac 53 D1
Selfoss 68 A2
Séli 55 D2
Selía 64 B4
Selianítika 58 C2
Seligenstadt 38 B2
Selínia 59 E3
Selinunte 48 B4
Selishtë 53 D4
Selište 53 E1
Selje 74 A1
Seljord 74 B3
Selkämeri 72 B3
Selkirk 5 D1
Sellajoch 43 D2
Sella Nevea 43 F2
Sella, Pso di 43 D2
Selles 18 A2
Sellières 19 D2
Sellin 37 F1
Selm 36 B4
Selmsdorf 37 D2
Selna 51 D2
Selommes 17 F1
Selongey 19 D1
Seløy 69 D2
Selsey 7 D4
Selsey Bill 7 D4
Selters 38 B2
Seltz 15 F3
Sélune 13 D3
Selva 43 D2
Selvino 42 C3
Seman 54 A2
Semeljci 51 D1
Semič 50 A2
Seminara 47 D4
Semizovac 51 D3
Semmering 41 F2
Semmering-Paß 41 F2
Semois 15 D2
Semproniano 44 B3
Semur-en-Auxois 18 C1
Semur-en-Brionnais 18 C3
Sena 29 D2
Sénas 22 B3
Sendim 24 C3
Senez 22 C3
Senftenberg 78 A4
Sengsengeb 41 D3
Senigallia 45 D2
Senise 47 D2
Senj 50 A2
Senja Ånderdalen 66 B2
Senje 53 D2
Senlis 14 B3
Sennecey-le-Grand 19 D2
Sennen 6 A4
Sennestadt 36 B4
Sennori 46 A2
Senonches 13 F3
Senones 15 E3
Senorbi 46 B4
Senožeče 43 F3
Sens 14 B4
Šenta 51 E1
Šentilj 41 F4
Šentjernej 50 A1
Šentjur 50 A1
Šentvid na Slemenu 50 A1
Sépeaux 14 B4
Šepetovka 81 D1
Sepino 45 E4
Sepúlveda 27 F2
Sequeros 27 D3
Sequillo, R 25 D3
Seraing 34 C3
Seravezza 44 A2
Seregno 42 B3
Serein 18 C1
Serena, Emb de la 31 D2
Séres 55 F2
Séres (Nomos) 55 F1
Serfaus 40 A4
Serfopoúla, N 60 B4
Seriate 42 C3
Sérifos 63 F3
Sérifos, N 63 F3
Serífou, Stenó 60 B4
Sermaize-les-Bains 14 C3
Sermide 43 D4
Sermoneta 46 A1
Sernancelhe 24 B4
Serón 32 A3
Serón de Nágima 28 B2
Seròs 29 D2
Serpa 30 B2
Serpeddì, P 46 B4
Serpis, R 32 C1
Serra 28 C4
Serracapriola 45 F4
Serrada 25 D4
Serradifalco 48 C4
Serradilla 27 D3
Serramanna 46 A4
Serrana, Pto de la 27 D3
Serra San Bruno 47 E4
Serravalle Scrivia 23 E2
Serre Chevalier 19 E4
Serre-Ponçon, Bge de 22 C2
Serres 22 C2
Serrières 19 D4
Serrota 27 E3
Sersale 47 E3
Sertã 26 B3
Servan 12 C3
Sérvia 55 D3
Servian 21 F3
Servigliano 45 D2
Servol, R 29 D3
Sesa 28 C2
Sesena 27 F3
Sesia 42 A3
Sesimbra 30 A1
Sesklío, N 65 F2
Sesma 28 B1
Sessa Aurunca 46 B1
Sesta Godano 23 F2
Šestanovac 50 C4
Sestino 44 C2
Sesto 43 E2
Sesto Calende 42 B3
Sesto Fiorentino 44 B2
Sestola 44 A1
Sesto San Giovanni 42 B4
Sestriere 22 C2
Sestri Levante 23 F2
Sestrunj 50 A3
Sestrunj / 50 A3
Sestu 46 B4
Sesvete 50 B1
Séta 60 A2
Setcases 29 F1
Sète 22 A3
Setenil 31 D3
Setermoen 66 C2
Setesdalen 74 B4
Setesdalsheiene 74 B3
Settebagni 44 C4
Settimo Torinese 23 D1
Settle 5 E3
Settons, les 18 C2
Setúbal 30 A1
Seudre 17 D3
Seui 46 B3
Seulo 46 B3
Seurre 19 D2
Sevastianá 55 D2
Sevenoaks 7 E3
Sévérac-le-Château 21 F2
Sever do Vouga 26 B2
Severn Bridge 6 C3
Severn, Mouth of the 6 C3
Severn,R 6 C3
Sever, R 26 B4
Seveso 42 B4
Sevettijärvi 67 F2
Sevilla 31 D3
Sevilleja de la Jara 27 E4
Sevlievo 81 D4
Sevnica 50 B1
Sevojno 51 F3
Sèvre Nantaise 17 D2
Sèvre Niortaise 17 D3
Sévrier 19 E3
Sevsk 79 F3
Sexten 43 E2
Seyches 20 C2
Seyda 37 F4
Seyðisfjörður 68 C1
Seyne 22 C2
Seyne, la 22 C4
Seyssel 19 E3
Sežana 43 F3
Sézanne 14 B3
Sezimovo-Ústí 41 D1
Sezze 46 A1
Sfáka 65 D4
Sfakiá 64 A4
Sfaktiría, N 62 B3
Sferracavallo 48 B3
Sfikiá, L 55 D3
Sfîntu Gheorghe 81 D2
Sforzacosta 45 D2
's Gravendeel 11 D3
's Gravenhage 11 D3
Sgùrr Mór 2 C2
Sgùrr na Ciche 2 B2
Shaftesbury 6 C3
Shanklin 7 D4
Shannon 8 B3
Shannon, Mouth of the 8 A3
Shannon, R 8 B3
Shap 5 D3
Shapinsay 3 E1
Shebenik, Mal i 54 B1
Sheelin, L 8 C2
Sheep Haven 4 A2
Sheep's Head 8 A4
's Heerenberg 11 E3
Sheerness 7 E3
Sheffield 5 E4
Shefford 7 E2
Shëmri (Shkodër) 53 D4
Shëmri (Tiranë) 54 B1
Shëngjin 52 C4
Sheppey, I of 7 F3
Shepshed 7 D2
Shepton Mallet 6 C3
Sherborne 6 C4
Shercock 8 C2
Sheringham 7 F1
's Hertogenbosch 11 E3
Shetland Is 3 F2
Shiel Bridge 2 C2
Shieldaig 2 B2
Shiel, L 2 B3
Shijak 54 A1
Shinás 55 E2
Shiniás 60 A3
Shin, L 2 C1
Shínos 58 C2
Shinoússa, N 64 C1
Shipston-on-Stour 7 D2
Shíza, N 62 B3
Shkodër 52 C4
Shkodrës, Liq i 52 C4
Shkumbin 54 A1
Sholári 55 F2
Shoreham 7 E4
Shpat, Mal i 54 B2
Shrewsbury 6 C1
Shrewton 7 D3
Shropshire 6 C2
Shupenzë 53 D4
Sía, Pto de la 25 F2
Siátista 54 C3
Šiauliai 78 C2
Sibari 47 E2
Sibbhult 77 D3
Sibbo 73 D4
Sibbofjärden 73 D4
Šibenik 50 B4
Šibenik Mt 51 D4
Sibinj 51 D2
Sibiu 81 D3
Sićevo 53 E2
Sichar, Emb de 28 C4
Sicié, Cap 22 C4
Sicignano degli Alburni 46 C2
Sicilia 48 B3
Sicó 26 B3
Šid 51 E2
Sidári 54 A4
Sideby 72 C3
Sidensjö 69 F4
Siderno 47 E4
Síderos, Akr 65 E4
Sidiró 57 D1
Sidirókastro 55 F1
Sidirónero 56 A1
Sidlaw Hills 3 D3
Sidmouth 6 C4
Siebenlehn 39 E1
Siedlce 78 C4
Sieg 35 D3
Siegburg 35 D3
Siegen 38 A1
Siegsdorf 40 C3
Siena 44 B2
Sieppijärvi 67 D4
Sieradz 78 B4
Sierck 15 D2
Sierentz 15 E4
Sierninghofen 41 D3
Sierpc 78 B4
Sierra Boyera, Emb de 31 D2
Sierra de Fuentes 27 D4
Sierra de Yeguas 31 E3
Sierre 19 F3
Sievi 71 D3
Sievin as 71 D3
Sífnos, N 63 F3
Sífnou, Stenó 63 F3
Sigean 21 F4
Sigerfjord 66 B3
Siggjarvåg 74 A3
Sighetu Marmaţiei 81 D2
Sighişoara 81 D2
Siglufjörður 68 B1
Sigmaringen 42 B1
Signy-l'Abbaye 14 C2
Sígri 61 D1
Sigtuna 75 F3
Sigüenza 28 A3
Sigulda 78 C2
Siiddasjávri 66 C3
Siikainen 72 C3
Siikajoki 71 D2
Siikajoki R 71 D2
Siilinjärvi 71 E4
Sijarinska Banja 53 E3
Sikaminiá 61 D1
Sikås 69 E3
Sikí 59 E1
Sikiá (Makedonía) 56 A3
Sikiá (Pelopónissos) 63 D3
Síkinos 64 B1
Síkinos, N 64 B1
Sikióna 59 D3
Sikoráhi 56 C2
Sikoúrio 55 E4
Sikovuono 67 E2
Sila, La 47 F3
Silandro 42 C2
Silba 50 A3
Silba / 50 A3
Silbaš 51 E1
Sildegapet 68 A4
Şile 81 F4
Siles 32 A2
Siliqua 46 A4
Silistra 81 E3
Silivri 81 E4
Siljan (N) 74 D3
Siljan (S) 75 E2
Siljansnäs 75 E3
Silkeborg 76 B3
Silla 32 C1
Silleda 24 B2
Silleiro, C 24 A2
Sillé-le-Guillaume 13 E4
Sillian 43 E2
Silloth 5 D2
Šilo 50 A2
Sílo 57 D1
Sil, R 24 C2
Sils 29 F2
Sils im Engadin 42 C3
Siltakylä 73 E4
Šilutė 78 C3
Silvalen 69 D2
Silvaplana 42 C3
Silvares 26 B3
Silves 30 A3
Silvi Marina 45 D3
Silvrettagruppe 42 C2
Silz 40 B4
Simancas 25 D3
Símandra 55 F3
Šimanovci 52 C1
Simaxis 46 A3
Simbach (Inn) 39 E4
Simbach (Isar) 39 E4
Simbruini, Mti 45 D4
Simeto 49 D4
Şimi 65 F1
Šimići 50 C2
Sími, N 65 F1
Simlångsdalen 77 D2
Simmerath 34 C4
Simmern 38 A3
Simo 71 D2
Simojärvi 71 E1
Simojoki 71 D2
Simola 73 E3
Símonos Pétras 56 A3
Simonsbath 6 B3
Simonswald 42 A1
Simópoulo 58 C3
Simplonpass 42 A3
Simrishamn 77 D3
Sinaia 81 D3
Sinalunga 44 B2
Sinarádes 54 A4
Sinarcas 28 B4
Sindelfingen 38 B4
Síndos 55 E2
Sines 30 A2
Sines, C de 30 A2
Sinettä 71 D1
Sineu 33 E2
Singen 42 B1
Singöfjärden 75 F3
Singra, Pto de 28 B3
Siniscola 46 B2
Sinj 50 C4
Sinjajevina 51 E4
Sinni 47 E2
Sinnicolau Mare 80 C3
Sinopoli 47 D4
Sinsheim 38 B3
Sintra 26 A4
Sinzig 38 A2
Siófok 80 B2
Sion 19 F3
Sioule 18 B3
Šipan 52 B4
Šipanska Luka 52 B3
Šipka 81 D4
Sipoo 73 D4
Sipoonselkä 73 D4
Šipovo 50 C3
Sippola 73 E3
Šiprage 51 D3
Sira 74 A4
Sira R 74 A4
Siracusa 49 D4
Sirdalen 74 A4
Sirdalvatn 74 A4
Siret 81 D2
Siret R 81 E2
Sirevåg 74 A4
Sirig 51 E1
Şirino, Mte 47 D2
Širitovci 50 B4
Sirkka 67 E3
Sirma 67 E1
Sirmione 42 C4
Şírna, N 65 D2
Široko Polje 51 D1
Sirolo 45 D2
Síros, N 60 C4
Siruela 31 E1
Şisak 50 B2
Šišan 43 F4
Şisante 32 B1
Šišljavić 70 C3
Sissa 42 C4
Sissach 42 A2
Sissonne 14 C2
Sisteron 22 C2
Sistiana 43 F3
Sistranda 68 C3
Sitges 29 E2
Sithonía 56 A3
Sitía 65 D4
Sitnica 53 D3
Sittard 11 E4
Sittensen 36 C2
Sittingbourne 7 E3
Siuntio 73 D4
Siuro 72 C3
Siurua 71 D2
Siuruanjoki 71 D2
Siusi 43 D2
Sivac 51 E1
Síviri 55 F3
Sívota 54 B4
Sívros 58 B2
Siziano 42 B4
Sizun 12 B3
Sjælland 76 C3
Sjællands Odde 76 C3
Sjenica 51 F4
Sjeništa 51 E3
Sjøåsen 69 D3
Sjöbo 77 D3
Sjøholt 68 B4
Sjona 69 D1
Sjötorp 75 D4
Sjoutnäset 69 E3
Sjøvegan 66 C2
Sjulsmark 70 B3
Sjundea 73 D4
Sjusjøen 74 C2
Skåbu 74 C2
Skäckerfjällen 69 D3
Skadarsko jez 52 C4
Skadovsk 81 F2
Skafidiá 58 B3
Skaftá 68 B2
Skaftafell 68 B2
Skagafjörður 68 B1
Skage 69 D3
Skagen 76 C1
Skagern 75 D4
Skagerrak 76 B1
Skaill 3 E1
Skajálfandi 68 B1
Skála (Kefaloniá) 58 B3
Skála (Lésvos) 61 D1
Skála (Pátmos) 61 E4
Skála (Pelopónissos) 63 D3
Skála (Stereá Eláda) 59 E2
Skála Eressoú 61 D1
Skála Kaliráhis 56 B2
Skaland 66 C2
Skála Oropoú 60 A2
Skála Potamiás 56 B2
Skála Rahoníou 56 B2
Skálavík 68 A3
Skála Volissoú 61 D2
Skälderviken 76 C3
Skålevik 74 B4
Skálfandafljót 68 B1
Skalka 69 F1
Skalohóri (Lésvos) 61 D1
Skalohóri (Makedonía) 54 C3
Skaloti 56 A1
Skælskør 76 C3
Skamnéli 54 C3
Skandáli 56 C4
Skandári, Akr 65 E1
Skanderborg 76 B3
Skandzoúra, N 60 A1
Skåne 77 D3
Skånevik 74 A3
Skåningsbukt 66 C2
Skånland 66 B3
Skänninge 75 E4
Skanör Falsterbo 76 C3
Skara 77 D1
Skaraborgs Län 77 D1
Skaramangás 59 E3
Skærbæk 76 B3
Skarberget 66 B3
Škarda 50 A3
Skåre 75 D4
Skárfia 59 D2
Skärgårdshavet 72 C4
Skärhamn 76 C1
Skarnes 75 D3
Skarplinge 75 F3
Skarsvåg 67 E1
Skärvången 69 E3
Skarżysko-Kamienna 78 C4
Skattungbyn 75 E2
Skatval 68 C3
Skaulo 67 D4
Skaun 68 C4
Skee 74 C4
Skegness 7 E1
Skei (Møre og Romsdal) 68 C4
Skei (Sogn og Fjordane) 74 B2
Skeiðarársandur 68 B2
Skela 52 C1
Skellefteå 70 C3
Skellefteälven 70 B2
Skelleftehamn 70 B2
Skellig 8 A4
Skelmersdale 5 D4
Skenderbeut, M i 53 D4
Skender Vakuf 50 C3
Skepastó 55 F2
Skerries 9 D2
Ski 74 C3
Skíathos 59 E1
Skiáthos, N 59 E1
Skibbereen 8 A4
Skibby 76 C3
Skibotn 66 C2
Skiddaw 5 D2
Skídra 55 D2
Skien 74 D3
Skierniewice 78 C4
Skillingaryd 77 D2
Skiloundía 58 C4
Skinári, Akr 58 B3
Skiniás 64 C4
Skinnarbu 74 B3
Skinnskatteberg 75 E3
Skipagurra 67 E1
Skipton 5 E3
Skíros 60 B2
Skíros, N 60 B2
Skíti 55 E4
Skive 76 B2
Skivjane 53 D3
Skjeberg 74 C4
Skjern 76 B3
Skjersholmane 74 A3
Skjerstad 69 E1
Skjerstadfjorden 69 E1
Skjervøy 66 C2
Skjønhaug 74 C3
Sklavopoúla 64 A4
Sklíthro 55 E4
Šklov 79 E3
Škočivir 55 D2
Škocjanske jame 43 F3
Skodje 68 B4
Škofja Loka 43 F2
Škofljica 50 A1
Skog (Gävleborgs Län) 75 F2
Skog (Västernorrlands Län) 69 F4
Skógafoss 68 B2
Skogerøya 67 F1
Skoghall 75 D4
Skogstorp 75 E4
Skokloster 75 F3
Skólis 58 C3
Skópelos (Lésvos) 61 D1
Skópelos (Skópelos) 60 A1
Skópelos, N 60 A1
Skopí 65 D4
Skopiá 59 D1
Skopje 53 E4
Skopós 55 D2
Skopun 68 A3
Skorenovac 53 D1
Skorovatn 69 D3
Skorped 69 F4
Skotína 55 E3
Skotterud 75 D3
Skoulikariá 58 B1
Skoúra 62 C3
Skoúrta 59 E3
Skoútari (Makedonía) 55 F2
Skoútari (Pelopónissos) 62 C4
Skoutáros 61 D1
Skövde 77 D1
Skrá 55 E2
Skrad 50 A2
Skradin 50 B4
Skradinski buk 50 B4
Skreia 74 C3
Skrim 74 C3
Skrolsvik 66 B2
Skrydstrup 76 B3
Skudeneshavn 74 A3
Skuleskogen 69 F4
Skull 8 A4
Skultuna 75 E3
Skuodas 78 C2
Skuov'gilraš'ša 67 D1
Skurup 77 D3
Skutskär 75 F3
Skutvik 66 B3
Skvira 81 E1
Skye 2 B2
Slagelse 76 C3
Slagnäs 69 F2
Slănčev Brjag 81 E4
Slancy 79 D1
Slane 9 D2
Slaney 9 D4
Slangerup 76 C3
Slano 52 B3
Slany 39 F2
Šlapanice 41 F1
Slapská přehr nádrž 39 F2
Slapy 39 F2
Śląsk 80 B1
Slatina (Bor) 53 E1
Slatina (Bosna i Hercegovina) 50 C2
Slatina (Kraljevo) 53 D2
Slatina (Makedonija) 53 D4
Slatina R 81 D3
Slatine 50 C4
Slatinski Drenovac 50 C1
Slavgorod 79 E3
Slavinja 53 F2
Slavkovica 51 F3
Slavkov u Brna 41 F1
Slavnik 43 F3
Slavonice 41 E1
Slavonska Požega 50 C2
Slavonski Brod 51 D2
Slavonski Kobaš 51 D2
Slavuta 81 D1
Sławno 78 B3
Sleaford 7 E1
Slea Head 8 A4
Sleat, Sd of 2 B2
Slettfjellet 66 C1
Sliedrecht 11 D3
Sliema 49 F4
Slieve Bloom Mts 8 C3
Slieve Donard 9 D2
Slieve Mish Mts 8 A4
Slievenamon 8 C4
Slieve Snaght 4 A2
Sligachan 2 B2
Sligeach 8 C1
Sligo 8 C1
Sligo (Co) 8 B2
Sligo B 8 B1
Slišane 53 E3
Slite 77 F2
Sliven 81 E4
Sljeme 50 A1
Šljivovica 51 E3
Slobozia 81 E3
Slonim 79 D3
Sloten 11 E2
Slough 7 D3
Slovac 52 C1
Slovenska Bistrica 50 B1
Slovenija 50 A1
Slovenj Gradec 50 A1
Slovenske Konjice 50 B1
Slovenské Rudohorie 80 C2
Slovinci 50 C2
Sluck 79 D3
Sluderno 42 C2
Sluis 10 C3
Sluknov 39 F1
Slunj 50 B2
Słupsk 78 B3
Slyne Head 8 A2
Småland 77 D2
Smålandsfarvandet 76 C3
Smålands-stenar 77 D2
Šmarje 50 B1
Šmarješke Toplice 50 A1
Šmartin 50 A1
Smedby 77 E2
Smědeč 39 F3
Smederevo 53 D1
Smedjebacken 75 E3
Smederevska Palanka 53 D1
Smela 81 F1
Smigáda 56 C1
Smilčić 50 B3
Smilde 11 F2
Smiltene 79 D2
Smojmirovo 53 F4
Smokovec 50 A2
Smokovljan 52 B3
Smøla 68 B3
Smolensk 79 E3
Smoleviči 79 D3
Smólikas, Óros 54 C3
Smoljan 81 D4
Smorgon 79 D3
Smørhamn 74 A1
Smygehamn 77 D3
Snaefell 4 C3
Snæfellsnes 68 A2
Snaith 5 E4
Snåsa 69 D3
Snasahögarna 69 D4
Snåsavatnet 69 D3
Sneek 11 E1
Sneem 8 A4
Sněžnik 50 A2
Śniardwy, Jez 78 C3
Snigir'ovka 81 F2
Snillfjord 68 C3
Snizort, L 2 B2
Šnjegotina Velika 51 D2
Snøfjord 67 D1
Snøhefta 74 C1
Snøtinden 69 E1
Snowdon 6 B1
Snowdonia Forest and Nat Pk 6 B1
Soave 43 D4
Soběslav 41 D1
Sobra 52 A4
Sobrado 24 B1
Sobral da Adiça 30 C2
Sobral de Monte Agraço 26 A4
Sobreira Formosa 26 B3
Sobrón, Emb de 25 F2
Søby 76 B4
Soča 43 F2
Soča R 43 F2
Sočanica 53 D3
Soccia 23 E3
Sochaczew 78 C4
Sochaux 19 E1
Socol 51 F1
Socovos 32 B2
Socuéllamos 32 A1
Sodankylä 67 E3
Söderåkra 77 E3
Söderbärke 75 E3
Söderfors 75 F3
Söderhamn 75 F2
Söderköping 75 E4
Södermanlands Län 75 E4
Söderskog 77 D3
Södertälje 75 F4
Sodražica 50 A2
Sodupe 25 F2
Soest-(D) 36 B4
Soest-(NL) 11 E2
Soestdijk 11 E2
Sofádes 55 D4
Sofia 81 D4
Sofiero 76 C3
Sofikó 59 E3
Sofó 55 E4
Sögel 11 F2
Sogliano al Rubicone 44 C1
Soglio 42 B3
Sogndal 74 B2
Søgne 74 B4
Sognefjell 74 B2
Sognefjorden 74 A2
Sognesjøen 74 A2
Sogn og Fjordane 74 B2
Soham 7 E2

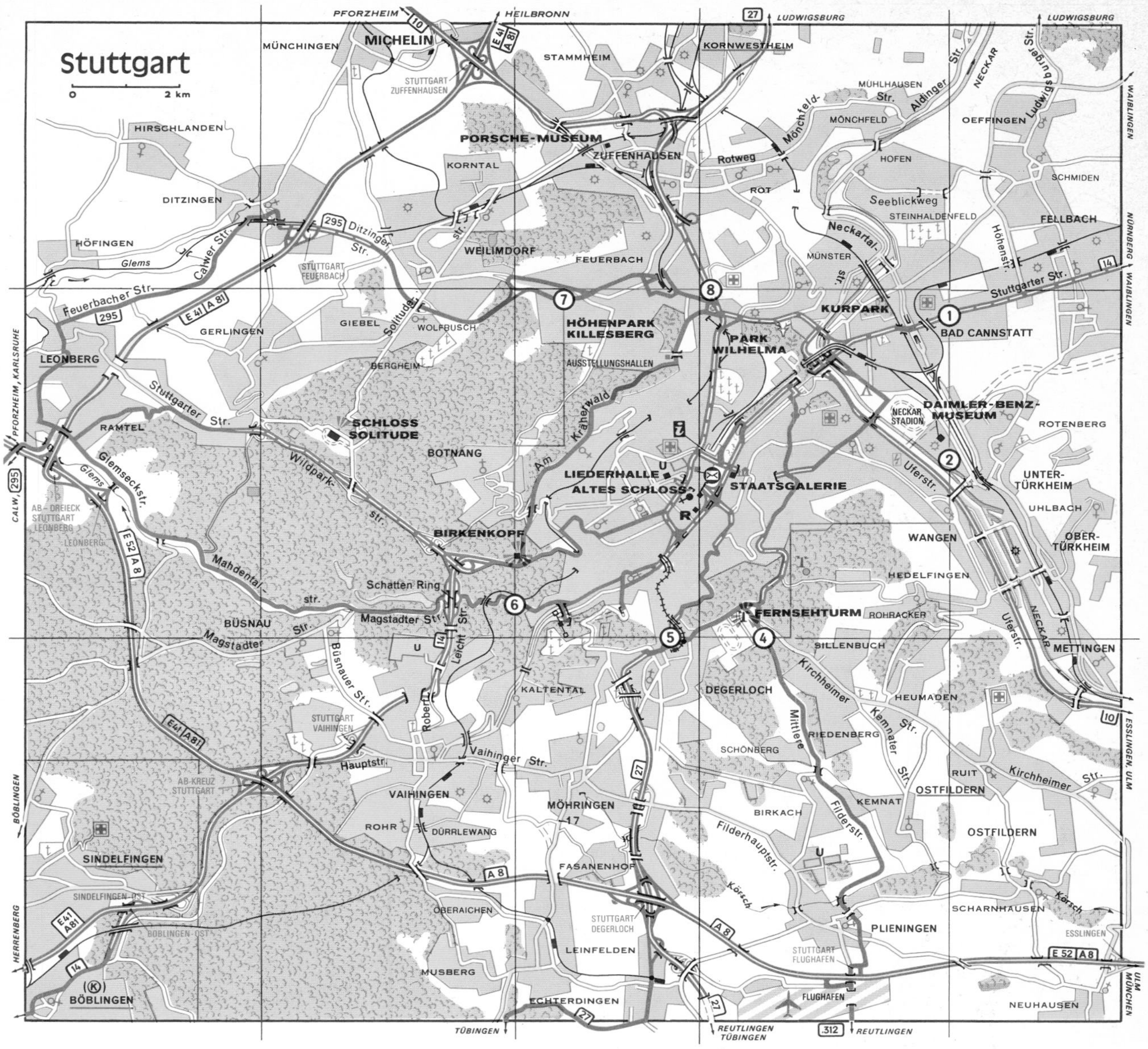
Stuttgart
0
2 km
PFORZHEIM
HEILBRONN
LUDWIGSBURG
MÜNCHINGEN
MICHELIN
STAMMHEIM
KORNWESTHEIM
STUTTGART ZUFFENHAUSEN
MÜHLHAUSEN
MÖNCHFELD
OEFFINGEN
HIRSCHLANDEN
PORSCHE-MUSEUM
ZUFFENHAUSEN
KORNTAL
Rotweg
HOFEN
SCHMIDEN
DITZINGEN
Seeblickweg
STEINHALDENFELD
FELLBACH
HÖFINGEN
WEILIMDORF
FEUERBACH
MÜNSTER
STUTTGART FEUERBACH
KURPARK
BAD CANNSTATT
GERLINGEN
GIEBEL
WOLFBUSCH
HÖHENPARK KILLESBERG
PARK WILHELMA
LEONBERG
BERGHEIM
AUSSTELLUNGSHALLEN
DAIMLER-BENZ-MUSEUM
NECKAR STADION
RAMTEL
SCHLOSS SOLITUDE
BOTNANG
ROTENBERG
LIEDERHALLE
ALTES SCHLOSS
STAATSGALERIE
UNTER-TÜRKHEIM
UHLBACH
AB.-DREIECK STUTTGART LEONBERG
BIRKENKOPF
WANGEN
OBER-TÜRKHEIM
HEDELFINGEN
Schatten Ring
BÜSNAU
Magstadter Str.
FERNSEHTURM
ROHRACKER
SILLENBUCH
METTINGEN
KALTENTAL
DEGERLOCH
HEUMADEN
STUTTGART VAIHINGEN
RIEDENBERG
SCHÖNBERG
AB.-KREUZ STUTTGART
VAIHINGEN
MÖHRINGEN
KEMNAT
OSTFILDERN
RUIT
ROHR
DÜRRLEWANG
BIRKACH
SINDELFINGEN
FASANENHOF
OBERAICHEN
STUTTGART DEGERLOCH
PLIENINGEN
SCHARNHAUSEN
ESSLINGEN
BÖBLINGEN-OST
LEINFELDEN
STUTTGART FLUGHAFEN
MUSBERG
BÖBLINGEN
ECHTERDINGEN
FLUGHAFEN
NEUHAUSEN
TÜBINGEN
REUTLINGEN TÜBINGEN
REUTLINGEN
CALW
PFORZHEIM, KARLSRUHE
HERRENBERG
WAIBLINGEN
NÜRNBERG
ESSLINGEN, ULM
ULM MÜNCHEN

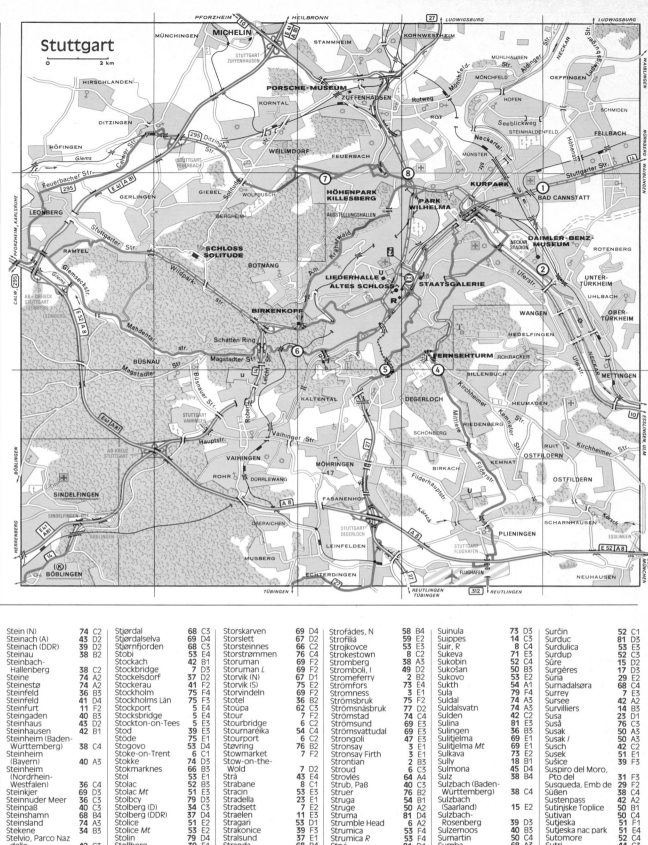

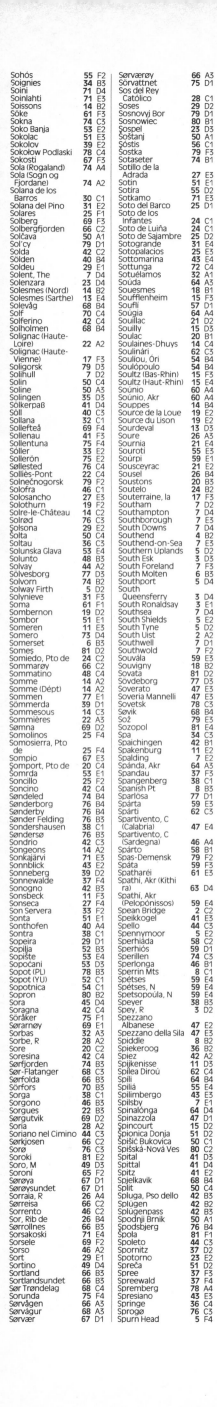

Svetozarevo 53 D2
Svetozar Miletić 51 E1
Svidník 80 C1
Švihov 39 E3
Svilaja 50 C4
Svilajnac 53 D1
Svilengrad 81 E4
Svingvoll 74 C2
Svinjar 51 D2
Svinoy 68 A3
Svištov 81 D3
Svitavy 80 B1
Svodde 53 E2
Svolvær 66 B3
Svor 39 F1
Svorkmo 68 C4
Svoronáta 58 A3
Svorónos 55 E3
Svrljig 53 E2
Swadlincote 7 D2
Swaffham 7 E2
Swale 7 E3
Swalmen 11 E3
Swanage 6 C4
Swanley 7 E3
Swanlinbar 8 C2
Swansea 6 B3
Świdnica 80 B1
Świebodzin 78 B4
Świecie 78 B4
Swilly, L 4 A2
Swindon 7 D3
Swinford 8 B2
Świnoujście 37 F1
Swords 9 D2
Sybil Head 8 A4
Syčovka 79 E2
Sykäräinen 71 D3
Syke 36 B3
Sykkylven 68 B4
Sylene 69 D4
Sylling 74 C3
Sylt 76 A3
Sylt Ost 36 B1
Sylvenstein-Stausee 40 B4
Synod Inn 6 B2
Syötekylä 71 E2
Syre 2 C1
Sysmä 73 D3
Sysslebäck 75 D3
Syväjärvi 67 E3
Syväri 71 E3
Syvde 74 A1
Syvdsnes 68 A4
Syyspohja 73 E3
Szarvas 80 C2
Szczecin 37 F2
Szczecinek 78 B3
Szczeciński, Zalew 37 F1
Szczytno 78 C3
Szécsény 80 C2
Szeged 80 C3
Székesfehérvár 80 B2
Szekszárd 80 B3
Szentendre 80 B2
Szentes 80 C2
Szigetvár 80 B3
Szolnok 80 C2
Szombathely 80 B2

T

Tabanovce 53 E3
Tábara 24 C3
Tabarca, I de 33 C2
Taberg 77 D2
Tabernas 32 A3
Tabernes de Valldigna 32 C1
Taboada 24 B2
Tábor 41 D1
Tábua 26 B3
Tabuaço 24 B4
Tabuenca 28 B2
Täby 75 F4
Tachov 39 E2
Tadcaster 5 E3
Tafalla 28 B1
Tafjord 74 B1
Taganheira 30 A2
Taggia 23 D3
Tagliacozzo 45 D4
Tagliamento 43 E2
Taglio di Po 43 E4
Tahal 32 A3
Tahkvuori 71 E3
Taibilla, Sa de 32 A2
Taígetos, Óros 62 C3
Tain 2 C2
Tain-l'Hermitage 22 B2
Taipadas 26 A4
Taipalsaari 73 E3
Taivalkoski 71 E2
Taivassalo 72 C4
Tajera, Emb de la 28 A3
Tajo, R 27 E4
Tajuña, R 28 A3
Takovo 51 F3
Taktikoúpoli 59 E4
Tálanda 63 D4
Talarrubias 31 E1
Talaván 27 D3
Talave, Emb de 32 B2
Talavera de la Reina 27 E3
Talavera la Real 30 C1
Talayuela 27 D3
Talayuelas 28 B4
Taldom 79 F1
Talgarth 6 C2
Talkkunapää 67 F3
Talla 44 B2
Tallante 32 B3
Tallard 22 C2
Tällberg 75 E3
Tallinn 78 C1
Talloires 19 E3
Tallow 8 B4
Talluskylä 71 E4
Talmont 17 D2
Tal'noje 81 E1
Talsi 78 C2
Talvik 67 D1
Tamames 27 D2
Tamar 6 B4
Támara 25 E3
Tamarite de Litera 29 D2
Tamási 80 B2
Tambre, R 24 A2
Tâmega, R 24 A4
Tamélos, Akr 60 B4
Tamiš 51 F1
Tammela 73 D3
Tammisaari 73 D4
Tamnava 52 C1
Tampere 73 D3
Tamsweg 41 D4
Tamworth 7 D2
Tana 67 E1
Tana *R* 67 E1
Tanafjorden 67 E1
Tanágra 59 E2
Tanagro 47 D2
Tanamea, Pso di 43 E2
Tanaro 23 E2
Tancarville, Pont de 13 E2
Tandådalen 75 D2
Tandragee 9 D2
Tandsbyn 69 E4
Tandsjöborg 75 E2
Tangerhütte 37 E3
Tangermünde 37 E3
Tanhua 67 F3
Taninges 19 E3
Tanlay 14 C4
Tann 38 C2
Tännäs 75 D1
Tanndalen 75 D1
Tannheim 40 A4
Tannila 71 D2
Tanumshede 74 C4
Taormina 49 D3
Tapa 78 C1
Tapia de Casariego 24 C1
Tar 43 F3
Tara 51 E3
Tara *R* 51 E4
Taracena 28 A3
Tara klisura 51 E4
Tarancón 28 A4
Taranto 47 E2
Taranto, G di 47 E2
Tarare 18 C3
Taraš 51 E1
Tarašča 81 E1
Tarascon (Ariège) 21 D4
Tarascon (Vaucluse) 22 B3
Taravo 23 E4
Tarayuela 28 C3
Tarazona 28 B2
Tarazona de la Mancha 32 B1
Tarbat Ness 3 D1
Tarbert (IRL) 8 B3
Tarbert (Strathclyde) 2 B4
Tarbert (Western Is) 2 B1
Tarbes 20 C4
Tarbet 2 C3
Tarcento 43 E3
Tarčin 51 D3
Tardets-Sorholus 20 B4
Tardienta 28 C2
Tärendo 70 C1
Tärendöälven 67 D4
Targon 20 C2
Târgovište 81 E3
Tarifa 31 D4
Tarm 76 B3
Tarmstedt 36 C2
Tarn 21 D3
Tarn (Dépt) 21 E3
Tärnaby 69 E2
Tarna, Pto de 25 D2
Tärnäsjön 69 E2
Tarn-et-Garonne 21 D3
Tarn, Gges du 21 F2
Tarnobrzeg 78 C4
Tarnos 20 B3
Tarnów 80 C1
Taro 23 F2
Tarouca 24 B4
Tarp 36 C1
Tarporley 6 C1
Tarquinia 44 B3
Tarragona 29 E3
Tarrasa 29 E2
Tàrrega 29 E2
Tarrekaise 69 F1
Tårs 76 C4
Tarsia 47 E3
Tartas 20 B3
Tartu 79 D1
Tarvasjoki 72 C4
Tarvisio 43 F2
Täsch 42 A3
Tåsinge 76 B3
Tåsjo 69 E3
Tåsjön 69 E3
Tassin 19 D3
Tåstrup 76 C3
Tata 80 B2
Tatabánya 80 B2
Tatarbunary 81 E2
Tatry 80 C1
Tau 74 A3
Tauber 38 C3
Tauberbischofsheim 38 C3
Taucha 37 E4
Tauerntal 43 E2
Tauerntunnel 43 E2
Taufers i. M. 42 C2
Taufkirchen 39 E4
Taulé 12 B3
Taunton 6 C3
Taunus 38 B2
Taunusstein 38 A2
Tauplitz 41 D3
Tauragė 78 C3
Taurianova 47 D4
Taurion 18 A3
Tauste 28 B2
Tauves 18 B4
Tavankut 51 E1
Tavannes 19 F2
Tavarnelle Val di Pesa 44 B2
Tavastila 73 E3
Tavaux 19 D2
Taverna 47 E3
Tavernelle 44 C3
Tavernes 22 C3
Tavignano 23 D3
Tavira 30 B3
Tavistock 6 B4
Tavolara, I 46 B2
Tavropós 58 C1
Tavropoú, Teh L 58 C1
Taw 6 B3
Taxenbach 40 C4
Taxiárhis 55 F3
Tay 3 D3
Tayinloan 2 B4
Tay, L 2 C3
Taynuilt 2 B3
Tayport 3 D3
Tayside 3 D3
Tazones 25 D1
Tczew 78 B3
Teano 46 B1
Teba 31 E3
Tebay 5 D3
Tech 29 F1
Techendorf 41 D4
Tecklenburg 36 B4
Tecuci 81 E2
Tees 5 E3
Teesside 5 E3
Teféli 64 C4
Tegéa 59 D4
Tegel 37 F3
Tegelen 11 E3
Tegernsee 40 B3
Teggiano 47 D2
Teguise 30 B4
Teide 30 A4
Teide *Mt* 30 A4
Teide, Pque Nac del 30 A4
Teignmouth 6 B4
Teijo 72 C4
Teil, le 22 B2
Teilleul, le 13 D3
Teisendorf 40 C3
Teisko 73 D3
Teixeiro 24 B1
Teixoso 26 C3
Tejeda, Sa de 31 E3
Tejo, R 26 A4
Tekeriš 51 E2
Tekija 53 E1
Tekirdağ 81 E4
Telč 41 E1
Telde 30 B4
Telemark 74 B3
Télendos, N 65 D1
Teleno 24 C2
Telese 46 C1
Telford 6 C2
Telfs 40 B4
Telgte 36 B4
Tellingstedt 36 C1
Telšiai 78 C2
Telti 46 B2
Teltow 37 F3
Témbi 55 E4
Tembleque 27 F4
Temerin 51 E1
Temmes 71 D3
Tempelhof 37 F3
Tempio Pausania 46 B2
Templemore 8 C3
Templin 37 F2
Temse 34 B3
Temska 53 E2
Tenala 73 D4
Ténaro, Akr 62 C4
Tenbury Wells 6 C2
Tenby 6 B3
Tence 22 A2
Tende 23 D2
Tende, Col de 23 D2
Tende, Colle di 23 D2
Tendilla 28 A3
Tenerife 30 A4
Tenhola 73 D4
Tenja 51 D1
Tennes 66 C2
Tenniöjoki 67 F3
Teno 67 E2
Tensta 75 F3
Tenterden 7 E3
Tentudia 30 C2
Teolo 43 D4
Teovo 53 E4
Tepelenë 54 A3
Teplá 39 E2
Teplice 39 F1
Tepsa 67 E3
Teramo 45 D3
Ter Apel 11 F2
Tera, R 24 C3
Terebovl'a 81 D1
Terena 30 C1
Terespol 78 C4
Terezino Polje 50 C1
Terges, Rib de 30 B2
Tergnier 14 B2
Terjärv 70 C3
Terlizzi 47 D1
Termas de Monfortinho 26 C3
Terme Luigiane 47 D3
Termini Imerese 48 C3
Terminillo 44 C3
Terminillo, Mte 44 C3
Termoli 45 E3
Terneuzen 11 D3
Terni 44 C3
Ternitz 41 F3
Ternopol' 81 D1
Térovo 54 C4
Térpilos 55 E2
Terpní 55 F2
Terpsithéa 58 C2
Ter, R 29 F2
Terracina 46 B1
Terra de Basto 24 B4
Terradets, Emb dels 29 D1
Terråk 69 D2
Terralba 46 A4
Terranova di Pollino 47 D2
Terranuova Bracciolini 44 B2
Terras de Bouro 24 A3
Terrassa 29 E2
Terrasson-la-Villedieu 21 D1
Terrenoire 18 C4
Terriente 28 B3
Terschelling 11 E1
Teruel 28 C3
Tervakoski 73 D3
Tervo 71 E4
Tervola 71 D1
Tervuren 34 B3
Terzaga 28 B3
Tešanj 51 D2
Teslić 51 D2
Tessin 37 E1
Tessy 13 D3
Teste, la 20 B2
Tetbury 6 C3
Teterev 79 E4
Teterow 37 E2
Tetica 32 A3
Tetijev 81 E1
Tetovo 53 D4
Tetrákomo 54 C4
Tettnang 42 B1
Teuchern 39 D1
Teufen 42 B2
Teulada 46 A4
Teupitz 37 F4
Teuva 72 C2
Tevere 44 C3
Teviot 5 D2
Tewkesbury 6 C2
Texel 11 D1
Thabor, Mt 19 E4
Thale 37 D4
Thalfang 35 D4
Thalgau 40 C3
Thalheim 39 E1
Thalmässing 39 D3
Thalwil 42 B2
Thame 7 D3
Thames, R 7 E3
Thanes, K e 54 A1
Thann 15 E4
Thannhausen 40 A3
Thaon 15 E4
Tharandt 39 E1
Tharsis 30 C2
Thássos 56 B2
Thássos, N 56 B2
Thatë, Mal i 54 C2
Thau, Bessin de 21 F3
Thaya 41 F2
Thégonnec 12 B3
Theil, le 13 E4
Themar 38 C2
Thenon 21 D1
Theológos (Stereá Eláda) 59 E2
Theológos (Thássos) 56 B2
Théoule 23 D3
Thérain 14 A2
Thérma (Ikaría) 61 D4
Thermá (Makedonía) 55 F2
Thérma (Samothráki) 56 C3
Thermaïkós Kólpos 55 E3
Thérma Lefkádas 61 D4
Thérmi 55 E2
Thermí 61 E1
Thermissía 59 E4
Thérmo 58 C2
Thermopíles 59 D2
Thérouanne 14 A1
Thespiés 59 E2
Thesprotía 54 B4
Thesprotikó 58 B1
Thessalía 55 D4
Thessaloníki 55 E2
Thessaloníki (Nomos) 55 F2
Thetford 7 F2
Theux 34 C3
Thèze 20 C3
Thézenay 17 E2
Thíamis 54 B4
Thiaucourt 15 D3
Thiberville 13 E3
Thiéblemont-Farémont 14 C3
Thiendorf 37 F4
Thiene 43 D3
Thiers 18 C3
Thiesi 46 A3
Thiessow 37 F1
Thillot, le 15 E4
Thimariá 57 D2
Thímena 61 E4
Thímena, N 61 E4
Thiní, Akr 59 E4
Thionville 15 D2
Thíra 64 C2
Thíra, N 64 C2
Thirassía, N 64 B2
Thirsk 5 E3
Thisted 76 B2
Thíva 59 E2
Thiviers 17 F4
Thizy 18 C3
Thoissey 19 D3
Tholen 11 D3
Tholey 38 A3
Thollon 19 E3
Tholó 58 C4
Tholopotámi 61 D2
Tholós 56 A2
Thomastown 8 C3
Thônes 19 E3
Thonon 19 E3
Thorens-Glières 19 E3
Thorikó 60 A3
Thorne 5 E4
Thornhill 5 D2
Thouarcé 17 E2
Thouars 17 E2
Thouet 17 E2
Thouría 62 C3
Thoúrio 57 D1
Thráki 56 C1
Thrakikó Pélagos 56 C2
Thrapston 7 E2
Threshfield 5 E3
Thueyts 22 A2
Thuile, la 19 E3
Thuin 34 B3
Thuir 21 E4
Thum 39 E1
Thun 19 F2
Thur 42 B1
Thüringen 40 A4
Thüringer Wald 38 C1
Thurles 8 C3
Thurn, Paß 40 C4
Thursby 5 D2
Thurso 3 D1
Thury-Harcourt 13 E3
Thusis 42 B2
Thy 76 B2
Thyborøn 76 B2
Tibro 77 D1
Tichvin 79 E1
Ticino 42 B4
Ticino *R* 42 B3
Tidaholm 77 D1
Tidö 75 E4
Tiefenbronn 38 B4
Tiefencastel 42 B2
Tiefensee 37 F3
Tiel 11 E3
Tielt 34 A3
Tienen 34 B3
Tiengen 42 A1
Tierbmesvarri 67 D2
Tiercé 17 E1
Tierga 28 B2
Tierp 75 F3
Tiétar, R 27 D3
Tigharry 2 A2
Tighnabruaich 2 B4
Tignes 19 E4
Tignes, Bge de 19 E4
Tiheró 57 D2
Tihío 54 C2
Tihuța 81 D2
Tiilikkajärvi 71 E3
Tiistenjoki 70 C4
Tijesno 50 B4
Tíjola 32 A3
Tikkakoski 73 D2
Tikkala 71 F4
Tikveš, Ez 53 E4
Tilburg 11 E3
Tilbury 7 E3
Tílissos 64 C4
Tillberga 75 E3
Tillières 13 F3
Tilly-sur-Seulles 13 E3
Tílos, N 65 E2
Timanfaya, Pque Nac de 30 B4
Timbáki 64 B4
Tímbano 56 B2
Tímfi, Óros 54 B3
Timfristós 58 C1
Timfristós *Mt* 58 C1
Timiș 80 C3
Timișoara 80 C3
Timmelsjoch 40 B4
Timmendorfer Strand 37 D1
Timok 53 E1
Timoleague 8 B4
Timrå 75 F1
Tímv. Peristéria 58 C4
Tinahely 9 D3
Tinchebray 13 D3
Tindari 49 D3
Tinée 23 D2
Tineo 24 C1
Tingáki 65 E1
Tinglev 76 B3
Tingsryd 77 E2
Tingvoll 68 B4
Tingvollfjorden 68 B4
Tinja 51 D2
Tinn 74 B3
Tinnsjø 74 B3
Tínos 60 C4
Tiñosillos 27 E2
Tínos, N 60 C3
Tiñoso, C 32 B3
Tintagel 6 A4
Tinténiac 12 C4
Tinto, R 30 C3
Tiobraid Árann 8 B3
Tione di Trento 42 C3
Tipasoja 71 E3
Tipperary 8 B3
Tipperary (Co) 8 B3
Tiranë 54 A1
Tirano 42 C3
Tiraspol' 81 E2
Tire 61 F3
Tiree 2 A3
Tirgo-Neamt 81 D2
Tirgoviște 81 D3
Tîrgu Frumos 81 E2
Tîrgu Jiu 81 D3
Tîrgu Mureș 81 D2
Tîrgu Secuiesc 81 D2
Tirig 29 D3
Tírintha 59 D4
Tiriolo 47 E3
Tírnavos 55 D4
Tirol 40 B4
Tirós 63 D3
Tirrenia 44 A2
Tirreno, Mare 48 C2
Tirschenreuth 39 E2
Tirso 46 B3
Tirstrup 76 C3
Tirteafuera, R 31 E1
Tisa 51 E1
Tiscar, Pto de 32 A2
Tisnaren 75 E4
Tišnov 41 F1
Tisvildeleje 76 C3
Tisza 80 C2
Tiszafüred 80 C2
Tiszavasvári 80 C2
Titaguas 28 C4
Titaríssios 55 D4
Titel 51 F1
Titisee 42 A1
Titlis 42 A2
Tito 47 D2
Titograd 52 C4
Titova Korenica 50 B3
Titova Mitrovica 53 D3
Titov Drvar 50 C3
Titovo Užce 51 F3
Titov Veles 53 E4
Titov vrh 53 D4
Titran 68 C3
Tittmoning 40 C3
Tiumpan Head 2 B1
Tivat 52 B4
Tiveden 75 E4
Tivenys 29 D3
Tiverton 6 B4
Tivissa 29 D3
Tivoli 44 C4
Tjaktjajaure 69 F1
Tjällmo 75 E4
Tjeggelvas 69 F1
Tjeldøya 66 B3
Tjeldstø 74 A2
Tjentište 51 E4
Tjøme 74 C4
Tjong 69 E1
Tjørnuvík 68 A3
Tjøtta 69 D2
Tkon 50 B4
Tobarra 32 B2
Tobercurry 8 B2
Tobermore 9 D1
Tobermory 2 B3
Toberonochy 2 B3
Toblach 43 E2
Toce 42 A3
Tocha 26 A3
Tocina 31 D2
Todi 44 C3
Todmorden 5 E4
Todorići 50 C3
Todtmoos 42 A1
Todtnau 42 A1
Toe Head (GB) 2 A1
Toe Head (IRL) 8 B4
Töfsingdalen 75 D1
Toft 3 F1
Tofte 74 C3
Toftir 68 A3
Tcftlund 76 B3
Tohmajärvi 71 F4
Toholampi 71 D3
Toijala 73 D3
Toivakka 73 D2
Toivala 71 E4
Tojšici 51 E2
Tok 39 F2
Tokaj 80 C2
Tolbuhin 81 E3
Toledo 27 F4
Toledo, Mtes de 27 E4
Tolentino 45 D2
Tolfa 44 C4
Tolga 74 C1
Tollarp 77 D3
Tollense 37 E1
Tølløse 76 C3
Tolmezzo 43 E2
Tolmin 43 F3
Toló 59 D4
Tolosa (E) 20 A4
Tolosa (P) 26 B4
Tolox 31 E4
Tolva 71 E1
Tolve 47 D1
Tomar 26 B3
Tomaševac 51 F1
Tomaševo 52 C3
Tomašica 50 C2
Tomaszów Lubelski 78 C4
Tomaszów Mazowiecki 78 C4
Tombebœuf 21 D2
Tomelilla 77 D3
Tomelloso 32 A1
Tomiño 24 A3
Tomintoul 3 D2
Tomma 69 D1
Tømmervøg 68 B4
Tomra 68 B4
Tomtabacken 77 D2
Tona 29 F2
Tonale, Pso del 42 C3
Tonara 46 B3
Tonbridge 7 E3
Tondela 26 B2
Tønder 76 B3
Tongeren 34 C3
Tongue 2 C1
Tonnay-Boutonne 17 D3
Tonnay-Charente 17 D3
Tonneins 20 C2
Tonnerre 14 C4
Tönning 36 B1
Tønsberg 74 D3
Tonstad 74 A4
Töpen 39 D2
Topeno 73 D3
Topla 50 A1
Toplica 53 E2
Topli Do 53 E2
Toplița 81 D2
Toploú 65 D4
Topola 53 D1
Topolčani 54 C1
Topol'čany 80 B2
Topólia 64 A3
Topolovnik 53 D1
Topusko 50 B2
Torà de Riubregòs 29 E2
Torano Castello 47 D3
Torbay 6 B4
Torbole 43 D3
Torcello 43 E3
Torchiarolo 47 F1
Tordera 29 F2
Tordesillas 25 D3
Tordesilos 28 B3
Tore 2 C2
Töre 70 C2
Töreboda 75 D4
Torella d. Sannio 45 E4

Torino

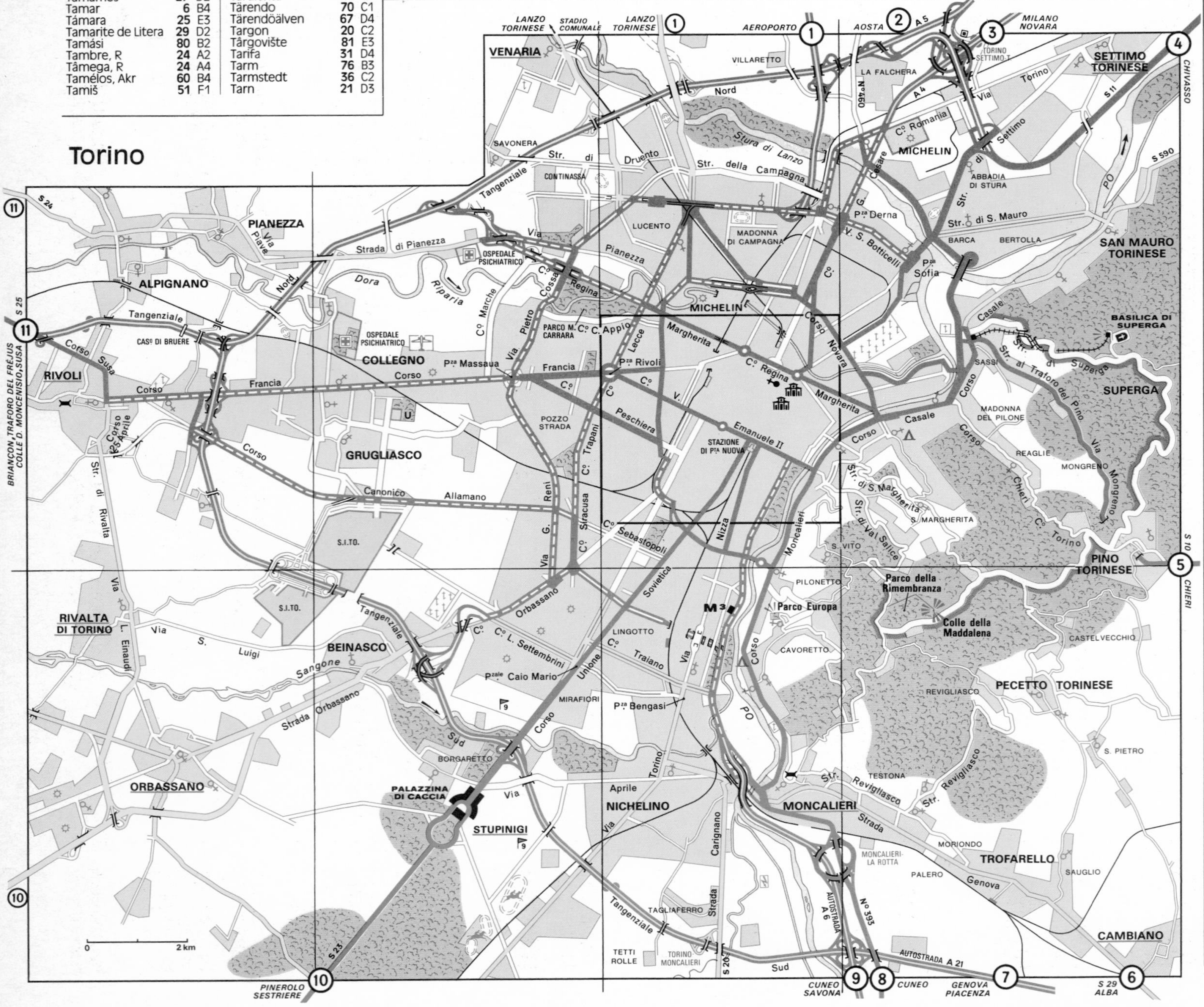

LANZO TORINESE
STADIO COMUNALE
AEROPORTO
AOSTA
MILANO NOVARA
CHIVASSO
VENARIA
SETTIMO TORINESE
VILLARETTO
LA FALCHERA
MICHELIN
PIANEZZA
ALPIGNANO
COLLEGNO
RIVOLI
GRUGLIASCO
SAN MAURO TORINESE
SUPERGA
BASILICA DI SUPERGA
PINO TORINESE
CHIERI
RIVALTA DI TORINO
BEINASCO
ORBASSANO
NICHELINO
MONCALIERI
PECETTO TORINESE
TROFARELLO
CAMBIANO
STUPINIGI
PALAZZINA DI CACCIA
Parco della Rimembranza
Colle della Maddalena
Parco Europa
PINEROLO SESTRIERE
CUNEO SAVONA
CUNEO
GENOVA PIACENZA
ALBA
AUTOSTRADA A 21
BRIANCON, TRAFORO DEL FREJUS COLLE D. MONCENISIO, SUSA
0
2 km

Toreno 24 C2
Torgau 37 F4
Torgelow 37 F2
Torhout 34 A3
Torigni 31 D3
Torija 28 A3
Torino 23 D1
Torio, R 25 D2
Torla 28 C1
Törmänen 67 E2
Törmänmäki 71 E2
Tormes, R 27 D2
Tornos 28 C1
Tornavacas 27 D3
Tornavacas, Pto de 27 D3
Torneälven 67 D3
Torneträsk 66 C3
Tornik 51 E3
Tornio 71 D2
Tornionjoki 70 C1
Tornjoš 51 E1
Toro 25 D3
Törökszentmiklós 80 C2
Toro, Monte 33 F1
Toróni 56 A3
Toropec 79 E2
Torpo 74 B2
Torpoint 6 B4
Torpshammar 75 E1
Torquay 6 B4
Torquemada 25 E3
Torralba de Calatrava 31 F1
Torrão 30 B1
Torre 26 B3
Torre Annunziata 46 C2
Torre Baja 28 B4
Torre Beretti 23 E1
Torreblanca 29 D4
Torrecaballeros 27 F2
Torrecampo 31 E2
Torre Canne 47 E1
Torrecilla 31 D4
Torrecilla en Cameros 28 A1
Torrecillas de la Tiesa 27 D4
Torre de Abraham, Emb de 27 E4
Torre de D. Chama 24 B3
Torre de Embesora 28 C4
Torre de Juan Abad 32 A2
Torre del Aguila, Emb de 31 D3
Torre de la Higuera 30 C3
Torre del Bierzo 24 C2
Torre del Campo 31 F2
Torre del Greco 46 C2
Torre del Mar 31 E4
Torredembarra 29 E3
Torre de Moncorvo 24 B4
Torre de Passeri 45 D3
Torre d. Impiso 48 B3
Torredonjimeno 31 F2
Torre Faro 49 D3
Torre Grande 46 A3
Torregrossa 29 D2
Torreira 26 B3
Torrejoncillo 26 C3
Torrejoncillo del Rey 28 A4
Torrejón de Ardoz 27 F3
Torrejón de la Calzada 27 F3
Torrejón el Rubio 27 D3
Torrejón-Tajo, Emb de 27 D3
Torre la Carcel 28 B3
Torrelaguna 27 F2
Torrelapaja 28 B2
Torrelavega 25 E1
Torrellano 33 C2
Torrelobatón 25 D3
Torrelodones 27 F3
Torremaggiore 45 F4
Torremegía 30 C1
Torre Mileto 45 F3
Torre Miró, Pto de 29 D3
Torremocha 27 D4
Torremolinos 31 E4
Torrent 32 C1
Torrente de Cinca 29 D2
Torrenueva 31 F1
Torre Orsaia 46 C4
Torre-Pacheco 32 C3
Torre Pellice 23 D2
Torreperogil 32 A2
Torres del Río 20 A4
Torres Novas 26 A4
Torres Vedras 26 A4
Torrevieja 32 C2
Torrico de San Pedro 26 C4
Torri del Benaco 42 C3
Torridon 2 B2
Torridon, L 2 B2
Torriglia 23 E2
Torrijas 28 C4
Torrijo 28 B2
Torrijos 27 E3
Tørring 76 B3
Torrita di Siena 44 B2
Torroella de Montgrí 29 F2
Torröjen 69 D3
Torrox 31 E4
Torsås 77 E3
Torsby 75 D3
Torshälla 75 E4
Tórshavn 68 A3
Torsken 66 B2
Torsminde 76 A2
Tórtoles de Esgueva 25 E3
Tortoli 46 B3
Tortona 23 E1
Tortorici 49 D3
Tortosa 29 D3
Tortosa, C de 29 D3
Tortosendo 26 B3
Toruń 78 B4
Torup 77 D2
Tørvikbygd 74 A3
Tory I 4 A1
Toržok 79 F1
Toscana 44 B2
Toscolano Maderno 42 C3
Tosenfjorden 69 D2
Toses, Collada de 29 E1
Tossa 29 F2
Tostedt 36 C2
Totak 74 B3
Totana 32 B3
Tôtes 13 F2
Totes Gebirge 41 D3
Tøtlandsvik 74 A3
Totnes 6 B4
Toucy 14 B4
Toul 15 D3
Toulon (Saône-et-Loire) 18 C2
Toulon (Var) 22 C4
Toulouse 21 D3
Toumbitsi 58 C3
Touques 13 E3
Touquet-Paris-Plage, le 14 A1
Tourcoing 14 B1
Tour-d'Auvergne, la 18 B4
Tour-du-Pin, la 19 D3
Tour-Fondue, la 22 C4
Touriñan, C 24 A1
Tourlida 58 C2
Tourmalet, Col du 20 C4
Tournai 34 A3
Tournan 14 B3
Tournay 20 C4
Tournoël 18 B3
Tournon-d'Agenais 21 D2
Tournon-St-Martin 17 F2
Tournon-sur-Rhône 22 B2
Tournus 19 D2
Tourouvre 13 E3
Tours 17 E1
Toury 14 A4
Toussuire, la 19 E4
Toutes Aures, Col de 22 C3
Touvet, le 19 E4
Toužim 39 E1
Tovariševo 51 E1
Tovarnik 51 E2
Tovdal selva 74 B4
Tovel, L di 43 D3
Tøvik 68 B4
Towcester 7 D2
Toysä 70 C4
Trabanca 24 C4
Trabancos, R 27 E2
Trabazos 24 C3
Traben-Trarbach 38 A3
Trabla 48 C3
Trabotivište 53 E4
Tracino 48 A4
Traenfjorden 69 D1
Trafalgar, C de 30 C4
Trafaria 26 A4
Trafoi 42 C2
Tragacete 28 B3
Trahiá 59 E4
Trahili 60 A2
Trahílos, Akr (Dodekánissa) 65 E2
Trahílos, Akr (Stereá Eláda) 59 D3
Trahílos, Akr (Stereá Eláda) 59 D2
Traiguera 29 D3
Traisen 41 E3
Traisen R 41 E3
Traiskirchen 41 F2
Traismauer 41 E2
Trajanova Tabla 53 E1
Trakai 78 C3
Trakošćan 50 B1
Tralee 8 A4
Tralee B 8 A3
Trá Lí 8 A4
Tramagal 26 B4
Tramariglio 46 A3
Tramatza 46 A3
Tramonti di Sopra 43 E2
Tramore 8 C4
Tranås 77 D1
Tranche, la 17 D3
Tranco, Emb del 32 A2
Trancoso 26 C2
Trandrandsfjällen 75 D2
Tranebjerg 76 C3
Tranemo 77 D2
Tranent 3 D4
Trani 47 D1
Tranòvalto 55 D3
Tranøy 66 B2
Tranquera, Emb de la 28 B2
Transilvania 81 D2
Transtrand 75 D2
Trápani 48 B3
Trápeza 59 D3
Trappstadt 39 D2
Trasacco 45 D4
Trasimeno, L 44 C2
Trás os Montes 24 B3
Trassem 15 E2
Trasvase Tajo Segura, Canal de 32 B1
Traun 41 D2
Traun R 41 D3
Traunkirchen 41 D3
Traunreut 41 D3
Traunsee 40 C3
Traunstein 40 C3
Travemünde 37 D1
Travnik 51 D3
Trayas, le 23 D3
Trbovlje 50 A1
Trbuk 51 D2
Trbušani 51 F3
Trdinov Vrh 50 A2
Trebbia 42 C4
Trebbin 37 F3
Trebević nac park 51 D3
Třebíč 41 E1
Trebinje 52 B3
Trebisacce 47 E2
Trebišnjica 52 B3
Trebišov 80 C2
Trebnje 50 A1
Třeboň 41 D2
Tréboul 12 A4
Trebsen 37 F4
Trebujena 30 C3
Trecastagni 49 D3
Trecate 42 B4
Tre Croci, Pso 43 D2
Tredegar 6 C3
Tredozio 44 B1
Treene 36 C1
Treffort 19 D3
Treffurt 38 C1
Trefynwy 6 C3
Tregaron 6 B2
Trégastel 12 B3
Tregnago 43 D3
Tregony 6 A4
Tréguier 12 B3
Trehörningsjö 69 F3
Treia (D) 36 C1
Treia (I) 45 D2
Treignac 18 A4
Trelleborg (S) 77 D3
Trelleborg (SF) 76 C3
Trélon 14 C2
Tremblade, la 17 D3
Tremestieri 49 D3
Tremezzo 42 B3
Tremiti, I 45 F3
Tremp 29 D1
Trenčín 80 B2
Trendelburg 36 C4
Trentino-Alto Adige 42 C3
Trento 43 D3
Trent, R 7 D1
Trepča (Crna Gora) 51 F4
Trepča (Kosovo) 53 D3
Tréport, le 14 A2
Trepuzzi 47 F1
Tresco 6 A4
Trescore Balneario 42 C3
Tresenda 42 C3
Tresfjord 68 B4
Tresjuncos 28 A4
Treska 53 E4
Treskavica 51 D4
Tres Mares, Pico de 25 E2
Trešnjevica 53 D2
Trešnjevik 52 C3
Trespaderne 25 F2
Třešť 41 E1
Trets 22 C3
Tretten 74 C2
Treuchtlingen 39 D4
Treuen 39 E2
Treuenbrietzen 37 F3
Treungen 74 B4
Trevélez 31 F3
Trèves 21 F3
Trevi 44 C3
Trévières 13 D2
Treviglio 42 C4
Trevignano Romano 44 C4
Treviño 20 A4
Treviso 43 E3
Trévoux 19 D3
Trezzo sull' Adda 42 B4
Trgovište 53 E3
Trhové Sviny 41 D2
Triánda 65 F2
Tría Nissiá 65 D2
Triaucourt 15 D3
Tribanj Kruščica 50 B3
Triberg 42 A1
Tribsees 37 E1
Tricarico 47 D1
Tricase 47 F2
Tricesimo 43 E3
Trichiana 43 E3
Trie 20 C3
Trieben 41 D3
Trier 35 D4
Trieste 43 F3
Trieste, G di 43 F3
Trifels 38 A3
Trifili 57 D2
Triglav 43 F2
Trigóna 54 C4
Trigueros 30 C3
Trihonída, L 58 C2
Trijueque 28 A3
Trikala (Makedonía) 55 E2
Trikala (Nomos) 54 C4
Trikala (Pelopónissos) 59 D3
Trikala (Thessalía) 55 D4
Trikeri 59 E1
Trilj 50 C4
Trillevallen 69 D4
Trillo 28 A3
Trilofo 59 D1
Trim 9 D2
Trimouille, la 17 F3
Trindade 24 B3
Třinec 80 B1
Tring 7 D3
Tringia 54 C4
Trinità d'Agultu e V. 46 A2
Trinitapoli 45 F4
Trinité, la 16 C1
Trinité-Porhoët, la 12 C4
Trino 23 E1
Triora 23 D3
Tripi 62 C3
Tripiti 56 A3
Tripiti, Akr 56 B4
Tripoli 59 D4
Triponzo 44 C3
Tripótama 58 C3
Triptis 39 D1
Trisanna 40 A4
Trischen 36 B1
Trittau 37 D2
Trittenheim 35 D4
Trivento 64 B2
Trizina 59 E4
Trlica 51 E4
Trnava 80 B2
Trnova Poljana 50 C4
Trnovo (Bosna i Hercegovina) 51 D3
Trnovo (Slovenija) 43 F2
Troarn 13 E3
Trofa 24 A3
Trofaiach 41 E3
Trofors 69 D2
Trogir 50 C4
Troglav, V. 50 C3
Trohalos 55 D4
Troia 45 F4
Tróia, Pen de 30 A1
Troina 48 C3
Troisdorf 35 D3
Trois Epis, les 15 E4
Trois-Moutiers, les 17 E2
Trois-Ponts 34 C3
Trojan 81 D4
Trojane 50 A1
Trollhättan 76 C1
Trollheimen 68 C4
Troms 66 C2
Tromsdalen 66 C2
Tromsø 66 C2
Trondheim 68 C4
Trondheimsfjorden 68 C3
Trondsheimsleia 68 C3
Tronö 75 F2
Tronto 45 D3
Troo 17 F1
Troon 4 C1
Tropea 47 D4
Trópea 58 C3
Tropojë 53 D3
Trosa 75 F4
Trossachs, The 2 C3
Trostan 4 B2
Trostberg 40 C3
Trouville 13 E2
Trowbridge 6 C3
Troyes 14 C4
Trpanj 51 D4
Trpezi 51 F4
Trpinja 51 D1
Trsa 51 E4
Tršić 51 E2
Trstenik (Kosovo) 53 D3
Trstenik (Pelješac) 52 A3
Trstenik (Srbija) 53 D2
Trsteno 52 B3
Trubčevsk 79 F3
Trubia 25 D1
Trubia, R 25 D1
Trubjela 52 B3
Truchas 24 C3
Truchtersheim 15 E3
Trujillo 27 D4
Trun 13 E3
Truro 6 A4
Trutnov 80 A1
Truyère, Gorges de la 21 E2
Tryde 77 D3
Trysilelva 75 D2
Tržac 50 B2
Trzebież 37 F2
Tržič Golnik 43 F2
Tsamandás 54 B4
Tsambika 65 F2
Tsangaráda 55 E4
Tsangário 54 B4
Tsaritsani 55 D4
Tsarkassiános 58 B3
Tsotili 54 C3
Tsoukaládes 58 A2
Tuam 8 B2
Tua, R 24 B3
Tuath, L 2 B3
Tubilla del Agua 25 E2
Tübingen 38 B4
Tubre 42 C2
Tučepi 50 C4
Tuchan 21 E4
Tudela 28 B1
Tudela de Duero 25 E3
Tuerto, R 24 C2
Tuffé 13 E4
Tuheljske Toplice 50 B1
Tuhkakylä 71 E3
Tui 24 A3
Tuineje 30 B4
Tukums 78 C2
Tulach Mhór 8 C3
Tulare 53 E3
Tulcea 81 E3
Tul'čin 81 E1
Tulla 8 B3
Tullamore 8 C3
Tulle 18 A4
Tullgarn 75 F4
Tullins 19 D4
Tulln 41 F2
Tullow 8 C3
Tulppio 67 F3
Tulsk 8 C2
Tumba 75 F4
Tunbridge Wells, Royal 7 E3
Tundža 81 E4
Tunnhovdfjorden 74 B3
Tunnsjøen 69 D3
Tuohikotti 73 E3
Tuoro sul Trasimeno 44 C2
Tupalaki 67 E2
Turaliči 51 E3
Turballe, la 16 C1
Turbe 51 D3
Turbie, la 23 D3
Turckheim 15 E4
Turda 81 D2
Turégano 25 E4
Turenki 73 D3
Turgutlu 61 F2
Turi 47 E1
Türi 78 C1
Túria, R 28 C4
Turija (Bosna i Hercegovina) 51 D2
Turija (Srbija) 53 D1
Turija (Vojvodina) 51 E1
Turinge 75 F4
Turis 32 C1
Turjak 50 A1
Türkheim 40 A3
Turku 72 C4
Turmiel 28 B3
Turnberry 4 C2
Turnhout 34 B2
Türnitz 41 E3
Turnov 80 A1
Turnu Măgurele 81 D3
Turnu Roşu 81 D3
Turracherhöhe 41 D4
Turre 32 B3
Turriff 3 D2
Tursi 47 E2
Turtola 70 C1
Turun ja Porin Lääni 72 C3
Tuscania 44 B3
Tuse 76 C3
Tušilović 50 B2
Tustna 68 B4
Tutin 53 D3
Tutrakan 81 E3
Tuttlingen 42 B1
Tuturano 47 F1
Tutzing 40 B3
Tuulos 73 D3
Tuupovaara 71 F4
Tuusniemi 71 E4
Tuusula 73 D4
Tuxford 7 D1
Tuzi 52 C4
Tuzla 51 D2
Tvedestrand 74 B4
Tverrfjellet 74 B1
Tvøroyri 68 A3
Tweed, R 5 E1
Twelve Pins, The 8 A2
Twimberg 50 A1
Twist 11 F2
Twistringen 36 B3
Tydal 69 D4
Tyin 74 B2
Tyin L 74 B2
Týn 41 D1
Tyndrum 2 C3
Tynemouth 5 E2
Tynkä 71 D3
Tynset 74 C1
Tyräjärvi 71 E2
Tyresö 75 F4
Tyrifjorden 74 C3
Tyringe 77 D3
Tyristrand 74 C3
Tyrnävä 71 D2
Tyrone 8 C1
Tysfjorden 66 B3
Tysnesøy 74 A2
Tysse 74 A2
Tyssebotn 74 A2
Tyssedal 74 A3
Tysvær 74 A3
Tywi 6 B2
Tywyn 6 B2

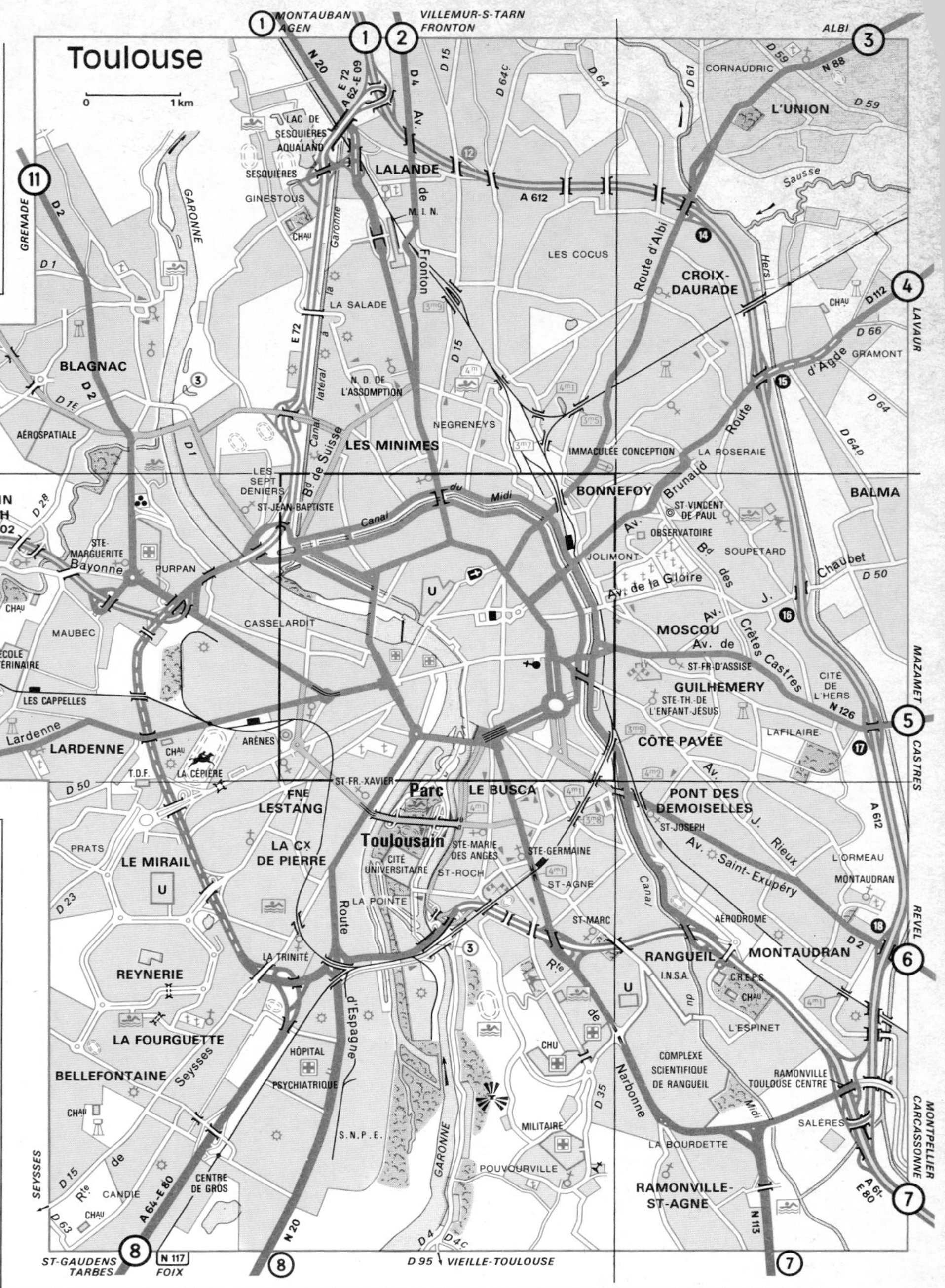

Toulouse
0
1 km
MONTAUBAN AGEN
VILLEMUR-S-TARN FRONTON
ALBI
CORNEBARIEU
BLAGNAC
TOULOUSE BLAGNAC
AÉROSPATIALE
LES MINIMES
LALANDE
CROIX-DAURADE
L'UNION
BONNEFOY
BALMA
ST-MARTIN DU TOUCH
MOSCOU
GUILHEMERY
CÔTE PAVÉE
LARDENNE
LESTANG
LA CX DE PIERRE
LE MIRAIL
Toulousain
Parc
LE BUSCA
PONT DES DEMOISELLES
RANGUEIL
MONTAUDRAN
REYNERIE
LA FOURGUETTE
BELLEFONTAINE
RAMONVILLE-ST-AGNE
ST-GAUDENS TARBES
FOIX
VIEILLE-TOULOUSE
GARONNE

U

Ub 52 C1
Ubaye 22 C2
Úbeda 31 F2
Überlingen 42 B1
Ubl'a 80 C1
Ubli (Crna Gora) 52 C3
Ubli (Lastovo) 52 A4
Ubrique 31 D4
Uchte 36 C3
Učka 50 A2
Uckange 15 D2
Uckfield 7 E4
Uclés 28 A4
Udbina 50 B3
Udbyhøj 76 B2
Uddevalla 76 C1
Uddheden 75 D3
Uddjaure 69 F2
Uden 11 E3
Udine 43 E3
Udovo 53 F4
Udvar 51 D1
Uebigau 37 F4
Uecker 37 F2
Ueckermünde 37 F1
Uelzen 37 D3
Uetersen 36 C2
Uetze 37 D3
Uffenheim 38 C3
Ugao 51 F4
Ugento 47 F2
Ugijar 32 A3
Ugine 19 E3
Uglič 79 F1
Ugljan 50 B3
Ugljan I 50 B3
Ugljane 50 C4
Ugljevik 51 E2
Ugra 79 F2
Ugrinovci 52 C1
Uherské Hradiště 80 B2
Uhingen 38 C4
Úhlava 39 E3
Uhrsleben 37 D3
Uig 2 B2
Uimaharju 71 F3
Uithoorn 11 D2
Uithuizen 11 F1
Ukkola 71 F4
Ukmergė 78 C3
Ukonselkä 67 E2
Ukraina 81 E1
Ukrina 51 D2
Ulcinj 52 C4
Uleåborg 71 D2
Ulefoss 74 B3
Uleila del Campo 32 B3
Ülëzë 53 D4
Ulfborg 76 B2
Uljanik 50 C1
Uljanovka 81 E1
Uljma 51 F1
Ullånger 69 F4
Ullapool 2 C1
Ulla, R 24 B2
Ullared 76 C2
Ullava 71 D3
Ulldecona 29 D3
Ullsfjorden 66 C2
Ullswater 5 D3
Ulm 38 C4
Ulmen 38 A2
Ulog 51 D4
Ulricehamn 77 D1
Ulrichsberg 41 D2
Ulsberg 68 C4
Ulsta 3 F1
Ulsteinvik 68 B4
Uludağ 81 F4
Ul'ugai'sa 67 E1
Ulva 2 B3
Ulverston 5 D3
Ulvik 74 B2
Ulvila 72 C3
Ulvsjö 75 E2
Ulzës, Liq i 53 D4
Umag 43 F3
Uman' 81 E1
Umbertide 44 C2
Umbrail, Pass 42 C2
Umbria 44 C3
Umbukta 69 E2
Umčari 53 D1
Umeå 70 B3
Umeälven 69 F3
Umhausen 40 B4
Umin Dol 53 E4
Umka 52 C1
Umljanović 50 C4
Una 50 C3
Unac 50 B3
Unari 67 E4
Unari L 67 E4
Uncastillo 28 C1
Unden 75 E4
Undersåker 69 D4
Undredal 74 B2
Uneča 79 E3
Unešić 50 C4
Unešov 39 E2
Ungeny 81 E2
Ungilde 24 C3
Unhais da Serra 26 B3
Unhošt 39 F2
Unije 50 A3
Universales, Mtes 28 B3
Unna 36 B4
Unnaryd 77 D2
Unnukka 71 E4
Unquera 25 E1
Unst 3 F1
Unstrut 37 E4
Unterach 41 D3
Unterhaching 40 B3
Unter-Schleissheim 40 B3
Unterwalden 42 B2
Unterwasser 42 B2
Unterweißenbach 41 D2
Upavon 7 D3
Upinniemi 73 D4
Upper L Erne 8 C2
Uppingham 7 D2
Upplands-Väsby 75 F4
Uppsala 75 F3
Uppsala Län 75 F3
Upton 6 C2
Uras 46 A4
Urbania 44 C2
Urbasa, Pto de 20 A4
Urbasa, Sa de 20 A4
Urbe 23 E2
Urbino 44 C2
Urbión, Sa de 28 A1
Urda 27 F4
Urdos 20 C4
Ure 5 E3
Uredakke 69 E3
Urepel 20 B4
Urfahr 41 E2
Urfeld 40 B3
Urho Kekkonens kansallispuisto 67 F3
Uri (CH) 42 B2
Uri (I) 46 A3
Uriage 19 E4
Urjala 73 D3
Urk 11 E2
Urla 61 E2
Urlingford 8 C3
Urnäsch 42 B2
Urnes 74 B2
Uroševac 53 D3
Urovica 53 E1
Urquiola, Pto 20 A4
Urshult 77 D2
Ursprungpaß 40 B3
Urtivaara 67 D3
Ururi 45 E4
Ury 14 B4
Urziceni 81 E3
Usagre 31 D2
Ušće 53 D2
Usedom 37 F1
Usedom I 49 E1
Useras 28 C4
Usingen 38 B2
Usk 6 C3
Usk R 6 C2
Uskoplje 52 B3
Üsküdar 81 F4
Uslar 36 C4
Ussat-les-Bains 21 D4
Ussé 17 E2
Usseglio 23 D1
Ussel 18 B4
Usseln 38 B1
Ustaoset 74 B2
Ustaritz 20 B3
Uster 42 B2
Ustevatn 74 B3
Ustibar 51 E3
Ustica, I di 48 B2
Ustikolina 51 E3
Ústí nad Labem 39 F1
Ustipača 51 E3
Ustka 78 B3
Ust'Užna 79 F1
Utajärvi 71 D2
Utåker 74 A3
Utbjoa 74 A3
Utebo 28 C2
Utelle 23 D3
Utena 79 D3
Utiel 28 B4
Utne 74 A3
Utrecht 11 E3
Utrecht (Prov) 11 D2
Utrera 31 D3
Utrillas 28 C3
Utsjoki 67 E1
Utsjoki R 67 E2
Uttendorf (Oberösterreich) 40 C3
Uttendorf (Salzburg) 40 C4
Utting 40 B3
Uttoxeter 7 D1
Uudenmaan Lääni 73 D4
Uukuniemi 73 F2
Uurainen 71 D4
Uusikaarlepyy 70 C3
Uusikaupunki 72 C3
Uvac 51 E3
Uvac R 51 F3
Uvdal 74 B3
Uzdin 51 F1
Uzel 12 C4
Uzerche 17 F4
Uzès 22 A3
Užgorod 80 C2
Uzin 79 E4
Uzunköprü 81 E4

V

Vä 77 D3
Vaajakoski 73 D2
Vääkiö 71 E2
Vaala 71 E3
Vaalajärvi 67 E3
Vaalimaa 73 E3
Vaals 34 C3
Vaarasiahti 71 E3
Vaasa 70 C4
Vaasan Lääni 70 C4
Vaassen 11 E2
Vabre 21 E3
Vác 80 B2
Vaccarès, Etang de 22 B3
Vacha 38 C1
Väddö 75 F3
Vadehavet 76 B3
Vadheim 74 A2
Vado Ligure 23 E2
Vadsø 67 F1
Vadstena 77 D1
Vaduz 40 A4
Vadvetjåkka 66 C3
Væggerløse 76 C4
Vaféika 56 B2
Vafiohóri 55 E2
Vågaholmen 69 D1
Vågåmo 74 C1
Vågan 66 B4
Vaganj 50 C4
Vaganski vrh 50 B3
Vágar 68 A3
Våge 74 A3
Vaggeryd 77 D2
Vágia 59 E2
Vagioniá 64 C4
Vagnhärad 75 F4
Vagos 26 A2
Vågsfjorden 66 B2
Vågsøy 74 A1
Vágur 68 A3
Váh 80 B2
Vähäkyrö 70 C4
Vahto 72 C4
Váï 65 D4
Vaiano 44 B2
Vaiges 13 E4
Vaihingen 38 B4
Vailly (Aisne) 14 B2
Vailly (Cher) 18 B1
Vainikkala 73 E3
Vaisaluokta 66 B3
Vaison-la-Romaine 22 B2
Vaksdal 74 A2
Vålådalen 69 D4
Valadares 24 A4
Valais 19 F3
Valalta 43 F4
Valamen 71 F4
Valandovo 53 F4
Val-André, le 12 C3
Valareña 28 B1
Valašské Meziříčí 80 B1
Valax 73 E4
Valberg 23 D2
Vålberg 75 D4
Valbiska 50 A2
Valbo 75 F3
Valbondione 42 C3
Valbonë 51 F4
Valbonnais 19 E4
Val Camonica 42 C3
Valcarlos 20 B4
Valdagno 43 D3
Valdahon 19 E2
Valdaj 79 E1
Val-d'Ajol, le 15 E4

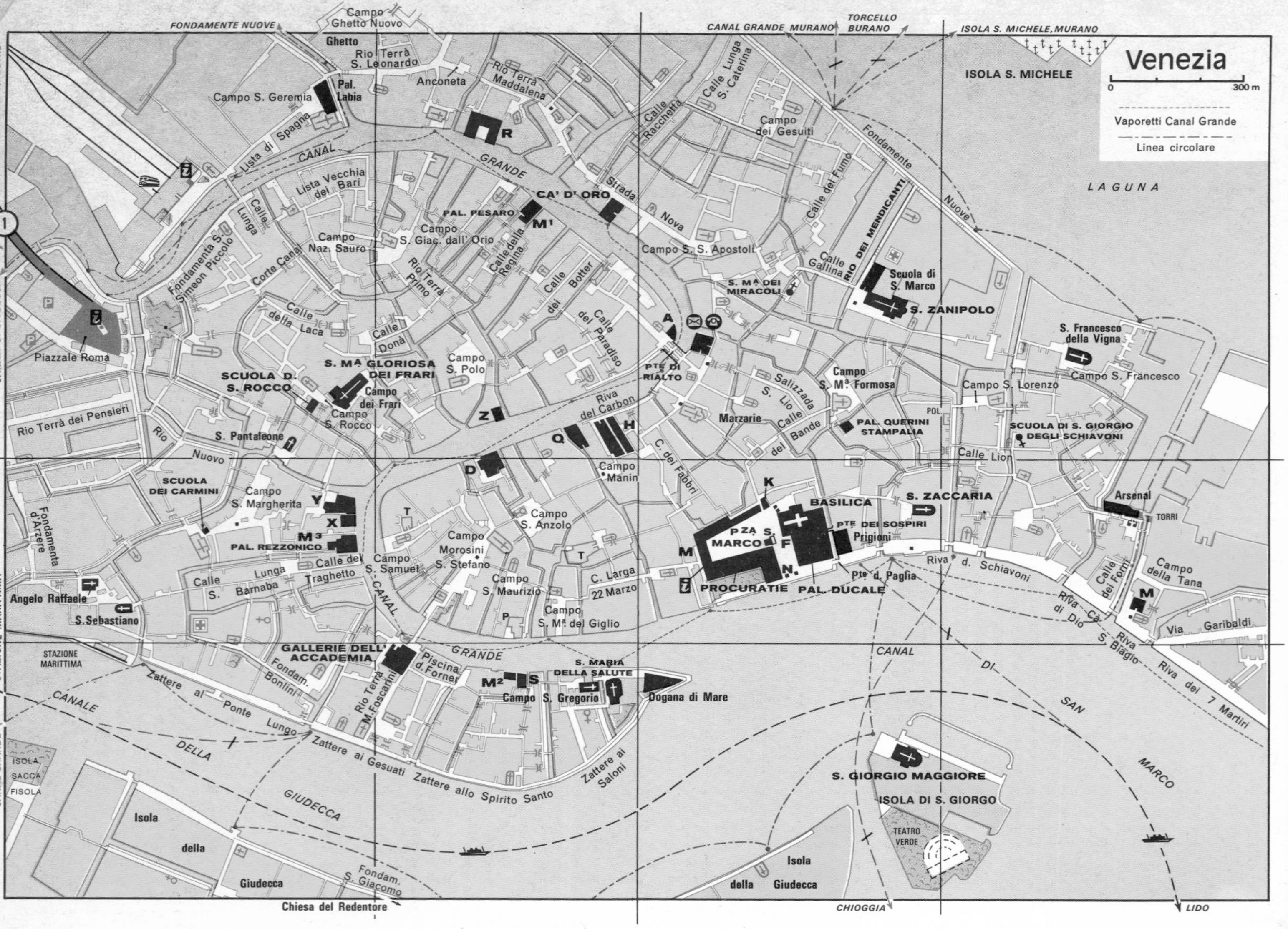
Venezia
0
300 m
Vaporetti Canal Grande
Linea circolare
FONDAMENTE NUOVE
Campo Ghetto Nuovo
Ghetto
Rio Terrà S. Leonardo
CANAL GRANDE MURANO
TORCELLO BURANO
ISOLA S. MICHELE, MURANO
ISOLA S. MICHELE
LAGUNA
ISOLA DI TRONCHETTO, MESTRE
CANALE D. GIUDECCA
Campo S. Geremia
Pal. Labia
Anconeta
Rio Terrà Maddalena
Calle Lunga S. Caterina
Campo dei Gesuiti
Fondamente Nuove
CA' D' ORO
PAL. PESARO
Campo S. Giac. dall' Orio
Campo SS. Apostoli
Piazzale Roma
SCUOLA D. S. ROCCO
S. MA GLORIOSA DEI FRARI
Campo dei Frari
Campo S. Rocco
Campo S. Polo
PTE DI RIALTO
S. MA DEI MIRACOLI
Scuola di S. Marco
S. ZANIPOLO
S. Francesco della Vigna
Campo S. Francesco
Campo S. Ma Formosa
Campo S. Lorenzo
PAL. QUERINI STAMPALIA
SCUOLA DI S. GIORGIO DEGLI SCHIAVONI
S. Pantaleone
SCUOLA DEI CARMINI
Campo S. Margherita
PAL. REZZONICO
Campo S. Anzolo
Campo Morosini S. Stefano
Campo S. Maurizio
Campo S. Ma del Giglio
BASILICA
S. ZACCARIA
PZA S. MARCO
PTE DEI SOSPIRI
Prigioni
Pte d. Paglia
PROCURATIE
PAL. DUCALE
Riva d. Schiavoni
Arsenal
TORRI
Campo della Tana
Via Garibaldi
Riva S. Biagio
Riva dei 7 Martiri
Angelo Raffaele
S. Sebastiano
STAZIONE MARITTIMA
FUSINA STAZIONE MARITTIMA
GALLERIE DELL' ACCADEMIA
S. MARIA DELLA SALUTE
Campo S. Gregorio
Dogana di Mare
CANAL GRANDE
CANALE DELLA GIUDECCA
Zattere al Ponte Lungo
Zattere ai Gesuati
Zattere allo Spirito Santo
Zattere ai Saloni
CANAL DI SAN MARCO
S. GIORGIO MAGGIORE
ISOLA DI S. GIORGIO
TEATRO VERDE
Isola della Giudecca
Fondam. S. Giacomo
Chiesa del Redentore
CHIOGGIA
LIDO

Villanueva de la Concepción 31 E3
Villanueva de la Fuente 32 A1
Villanueva de la Jara 32 B1
Villanueva de la Reina 31 F2
Villanueva de la Serena 31 D1
Villanueva de la Sierra 27 D3
Villanueva de las Torres 32 A3
Villanueva de la Vera 27 D3
Villanueva del Campo 25 D3
Villanueva del Duque 31 E2
Villanueva del Fresno 30 C1
Villanueva del Huerva 28 C2
Villanueva de los Castillejos 30 B2
Villanueva de los Infantes 32 A1
Villanueva del Rey 31 D2
Villanueva del Río y Minas 31 D2
Villanueva del Trabuco 31 E3
Villanueva de San Carlos 31 F1
Villa Opicina 43 F3
Villa Potenza 45 D2
Villaquejida 25 D3
Villaquilambre 25 D2
Villarcayo 25 F2
Villard-de-Lans 22 B2
Villar de Cañas 28 A4
Villardeciervos 24 C3
Villar de Domingo García 28 A4
Villardefrades 25 D3
Villar del Arzobispo 28 C4
Villar del Rey 26 C4
Villar de Peralonso 27 D2
Villarejo de Fuentes 28 A4
Villarejo de Orbigo 25 D2
Villarejo de Salvanés 27 F3
Villarente 25 D2
Villares de la Reina 27 D2
Villares del Saz 28 A4
Villargordo de Cabriel 32 B1
Villaricos 32 B3
Villarín de Campos 25 D3
Villarino 24 C4
Villarquemado 28 B3
Villarramiel 25 D3
Villarrobledo 32 A1
Villarroya 28 B1
Villarroya de la Sierra 28 B2
Villarroya de los Pinares 28 C3
Villarroya, Pto de 28 C3
Villarrubia de Santiago 27 F3
Villars 19 F3
Villars-les-Dombes 19 D3
Villarta de San Juan 27 F4
Villarubia de los Ojos 27 F4
Villasalto 46 B4
Villasana de Mena 25 F2
Villasandino 25 E3
Villa San Giovanni 47 D4
Villa Santa Maria 45 E4
Villasante 25 F2
Villa Santina 43 E2
Villasarracino 25 E2
Villasayas, Pto de 28 A2
Villaseco de los Reyes 27 D2
Villasequilla de Yepes 27 F4
Villasimius 46 B4
Villasor 46 A4
Villatobas 27 F4
Villatoro, Pto de 27 E3
Villatoya 32 B1
Villava 20 B4
Villavaara 67 F2
Villaverde del Río 31 D2
Villaviciosa 25 D1
Villaviciosa de Córdoba 31 E2
Villaviciosa de Odón 27 F3
Villavieja de Yeltes 26 C2
Villa Vomano 45 D3
Villé 15 E4
Villebois-Lavalette 17 E4
Villedieu, la 17 E3
Villedieu-les-Poêles 13 D3
Ville-en-Tardenois 14 C3
Villefagnan 17 E3
Villefort 22 A2
Villefranche-d'Albigeois 21 E3
Villefranche-de-Lauragais 21 E3
Villefranche-de-Lonchat 20 C2
Villefranche-de-Rouergue 21 E2
Villefranche-du-Périgord 21 D2
Villefranche-sur-Cher 18 A2
Villefranche-sur-Mer 23 D3
Villefranche-sur-Saône 19 D3
Villel 28 B4
Villemur 21 D3
Villena 32 C2
Villenauxe-la-Grande 14 B3
Villeneuve 22 B3
Villeneuve-de-Berg 22 A2
Villeneuve-de-Marsan 20 C3
Villeneuve-l'Archevêque 14 B4
Villeneuve-sur-Lot 21 D2
Villeneuve-sur-Yonne 14 B4
Villeréal 21 D2
Villers 13 E2
Villers-Bocage (Calvados) 13 D3
Villers-Bocage (Somme) 14 A2
Villers-Bretonneux 14 B2
Villers-Cotterêts 14 B3
Villers-devant-Orval 15 D2
Villersexel 19 E1
Villers-Farlay 19 D2
Villers la Ville 34 B3
Villers-le-Lac 19 E2
Villerupt 15 D2
Villerville 13 E2
Ville-sur-Tourbe 14 C3
Villeta Barrea 45 D4
Villiers-St-Georges 14 B3
Villingen-Schwenningen 42 A1
Villoldo 25 E3
Villoria 27 D2
Villotta 43 E3
Villuercas 27 D4
Vilnius 79 D3
Vilppula 73 D2
Vils (Bayern) 39 D3
Vils (Bayern) 39 E4
Vilsbiburg 39 E4
Vilseck 39 D3
Vilshofen 40 C2
Vilusi 52 B3
Vilvoorde 34 B3
Vimercate 42 B4
Vimianzo 24 A1
Vimieiro 30 B1
Vimioso 24 C3
Vimmerby 77 E2
Vimoutiers 13 E3
Vimpeli 71 D4
Vimperk 39 F3
Vinac 50 C3
Vinadio 23 D2
Vinaixa 29 D2
Vinalapó, R 32 C2
Vinaròs 29 D3
Vinay 19 D4
Vinça 21 E4
Vinča 52 C1
Vinchiaturo 45 E4
Vinci 44 A2
Vindafjorden 74 A3
Vindelälven 69 E2
Vindelfjällens N.R. 69 E2
Vindeln 70 B3
Vinderup 76 B2
Vindsvik 74 A3
Vingåker 75 E4
Vingelen 74 C1
Vinhais 24 C3
Vinica (Makedonija) 53 F4
Vinica (Slovenija) 50 A2
Viničani 53 E4
Vinje 74 B3
Vinkovci 51 D2
Vinnica 81 E1
Vinsternes 68 C4
Vinstra 74 C2
Vinstri 74 C2
Vintilänkaira 67 F3
Viñuelas 27 F3
Vinuesa 28 A2
Viotía 59 D2
Vipava 43 F3
Vipava *R* 43 F3
Vipiteno 43 D2
Vir (Bosna i Hercegovina) 50 C4
Vir (Hrvatska) 50 A3
Vir *I* 50 A3
Vira 50 C4
Vire 13 D3
Virgen 43 E2
Virgen de la Cabeza 31 E2
Virginia 8 C2
Virieu 19 D4
Virieu-le-Grand 19 D3
Virihaure 66 B4
Virkby 73 D4
Virkkala 73 D4
Virkkula 71 E1
Virksund 76 B2
Virmasvesi 71 E4
Virmutjoki 73 F3
Virolahti 73 E3
Virónia 55 F1
Virovitica 50 C1
Virpazar 52 C4
Virrat 73 D2
Virsbo 75 E3
Virserum 77 E2
Virsko more 50 A3
Virtasalmi 73 E2
Virton 15 D2
Virtsu 78 C1
Vis 50 C4
Vis *I* 50 C4
Visaurin 20 B4
Visby 77 F2
Visé 34 C3
Višegrad 51 E3
Višegradska Banja 51 E3
Viserba 44 C1
Viseu 26 B2
Viševica 50 A2
Viskan 76 C2
Viški kan 50 C4
Višnja Gora 50 A1
Višnjica 52 C1
Visočica 51 D4
Visočica *R* 53 F2
Viso del Marqués 31 F2
Visoki Dečani 53 D3
Visoko 51 D3
Visovac 50 B4
Visp 42 A3
Víssani 54 B3
Visselhövede 36 C3
Vissenbjerg 76 B3
Vissiniá 54 C2
Visso 45 D3
Vistabella del Maestrazgo 28 C3
Vistasväggi 66 C3
Vistheden 70 B2
Vistonída, L 56 C2
Visuvesi 73 D2
Vitaby 77 D3
Vítala 60 A2
Vitanovac 53 D2
Vitebsk 79 E2
Viterbo 44 C3
Vitez 51 D3
Vitigudino 27 D2
Vitína 58 C4
Vitina (Bosna i Hercegovina) 51 D4
Vitina (Kosovo) 53 E3
Vitlycke 74 C4
Vito d'Asio 43 E3
Vítoli 58 C1
Vitolište 55 D1
Vitomirica 53 D3
Vitoria-Gasteiz 20 A4
Vitorog 50 C3
Vitoša 81 D4
Vitovlje 50 C3
Vitré 13 D4
Vitrey 15 D4
Vitry-en-Artois 14 B1
Vitry-le-François 14 C3
Vítsa 54 B3
Vitsand 75 D3
Vittangi 67 D3
Vittangiälven 67 D3
Vitteaux 18 C1
Vittel 15 D4
Vittoria 49 D4
Vittoriosa 49 F4
Vittorio Veneto 43 E3
Vittsjö 77 D3
Vitznau 42 A2
Viù 23 D1
Vivaro 43 E3
Vivel del R Martín 28 C3
Viver 28 C4
Viverio 24 B1
Viverols 18 C4
Viveros 32 A1
Vivier, le 13 D3
Viviers 22 B2
Vivonne 17 E3
Vizcaya, G de 20 A3
Vizille 22 C2
Vižinada 43 F3
Vizítsa 59 E1
Vižnica 81 D2
Vizzavona 23 E4
Vizzavona, Col de 23 E4
Vizzini 49 D4
Vjosë 54 A2
Vlaardingen 11 D3
Vladičin Han 53 E3
Vladievci 53 F4
Vladimirci 51 E2
Vladimirovac 51 F1
Vladimirovo 53 F4
Vladimir-Volynskij 79 D4
Vlagtwedde 11 F1
Vlaháva 55 D4
Vlahérna (Ípiros) 58 B1
Vlahérna (Pelopónissos) 59 D3
Vlahiótis 63 D3
Vlahokerassiá 59 D4
Vlahomándra 58 C2
Vlahópoulo 62 B3
Vlanen 11 E3
Vlasenica 51 E3
Vlašić (Bosna i Hercegovina) 51 D3
Vlašić (Srbija) 51 E2
Vlasina Okruglica 53 E3
Vlasinsko jez 53 E3
Vlasotince 53 E2
Vlássio 58 C1
Vlásti 54 C3
Vlieland 11 D1
Vlihó 58 B2
Vlissingen 10 C3
Vlorë 54 A2
Vlotho 36 C4
Vltava 39 F2
Vobbia 23 E2
Voćin 50 C1
Vöcklabruck 41 D3
Vodice (Rijeka) 43 F3
Vodice (Šibenik) 50 B4
Vodna 53 D1
Vodňany 39 F3
Vodnjan 43 F4
Voe 3 F1
Vogatsikó 54 C3
Vogel 43 F2
Vogelsberg 38 B2
Vogelsdorf 37 F3
Voghera 23 E1
Vogošća 51 D3
Vohenstrauß 39 E3
Vöhringen 40 A3
Void 15 D3
Voikoski 73 E3
Vóïo, Óros 54 C3
Voiron 19 D4
Voiteur 19 D2
Voitsberg 41 E4
Vojakkala 70 C2
Vojens 76 B3
Vojka 52 C1
Vojmsjön 69 E2
Vojnić 50 B2
Vojnik 50 A1
Vojska 53 D1
Vojtanov 39 E2
Vojvodina 51 E1
Vólakas 56 A1
Volary 41 D2
Volchov 79 E1
Volchov *R* 79 E1
Volda 74 B1
Voldafjorden 68 B4
Volders 43 D2
Volendam 11 E2
Volga 79 F1
Volímes 58 A3
Volissós 61 D2
Volkach 38 C3
Völkermarkt 50 A1
Völklingen 15 E2
Volkmarsen 38 B1
Volkovija 53 D4
Volkovysk 78 C3
Volmunster 15 E3
Voločisk 81 D1
Volokolamsk 79 F2
Volonne 22 C3
Vólos 55 E4
Vožin 79 D3
Volpiano 23 D1
Volta 42 C4
Volterra 44 B2
Voltri 23 E2
Volturara Appula 45 E4
Volturino, Mte 47 D2
Volturno 46 B1
Volvic 18 B3
Vólvi, L 55 F2
Volyn' 79 D4
Volyně 39 F3
Vónitsa 58 B1
Vonnas 19 D3
Voors 11 E2
Voorschoten 11 D3
Voorthuizen 11 E2
Vopnafjórður 68 C1
Vörå 70 C4
Vorarlberg 40 A4
Vóras, Óros 55 D2
Vorau 41 F2
Vorchdorf 41 D3
Vordernberg 41 E3
Vorderrhein 42 B2
Vorderriß 40 B3
Vordingborg 76 C4
Vorë 54 A1
Voreppe 19 D4
Vorey 18 C4
Vóri 64 B4
Vória Píndos 54 C3
Vóries Sporádes 60 B1
Vøringfossen 74 B3
Vórios Evoïkós Kólpos 59 E2
Vório Stenó Kerkíras 54 A4
Vorma 74 C3
Vormsi 78 C1
Vorna 71 D3
Voroneț 81 D2
Vorsfelde 37 D3
Vorskla 79 F4
Võrtsjärv 78 C1
Võru 79 D2
Vosges (Dépt) 15 D4
Voss 74 A2
Votice 41 D1
Votonóssi 54 C4
Voúdia 63 F3
Vouga, R 26 B2
Vouglans, Lac de 19 D2
Vouhorína 54 C3
Vouillé 17 E2
Voukoliés 64 A3
Voúla 59 F3
Voulgára 58 C1
Vouliagméni 59 F3
Voulkariá, L 58 B2
Voúlpi 58 C1
Voulte, la 22 B2
Vouná Goúras 59 D1
Vouraïkós 58 C3
Voúrinos, Óros 55 D3
Vourkári 60 B3
Vourliótes 61 E3
Voúrvoura 59 D4
Vourvouroú 56 A3
Voutás 59 E2
Vouvant 17 D2
Vouvray 17 F1
Voúxa, Akr 64 A3
Vouzela 26 B2
Vouziers 14 C2
Voves 14 A4
Vovoússa 54 C3
Voxnan 75 E2
Vöyri 70 C4
Voz 50 A2
Vozarci 53 E4
Voznesensk 81 F2
Vrå 76 B2
Vraca 81 D4
Vraca pl 53 D4
Vračev Gaj 53 D1
Vračevšnica 53 D2
Vrådal 74 B3
Vraháti 59 D3
Vrahiónas, Óros 58 B3
Vrahnéika 58 C3
Vrams-Gunnarstorp 77 D3
Vrana 50 A3
Vrancei, M 81 E2
Vranduk 51 D3
Vranica 51 D3
Vranja 43 F3
Vranjak 52 B3
Vranje 53 E3
Vranjska Banja 53 E3
Vranovská přehr nádrž 41 E2
Vran pl 51 D4
Vransko 50 A1
Vransko jezero 50 B4
Vrástama 55 F3
Vratarnica 53 E2
Vratnica 53 E4
Vratnik 50 A2
Vratno 50 B1
Vravróna 60 A3
Vražogrnac 53 E1
Vrbanja 51 E2
Vrbanja *R* 50 C2
Vrbas 51 E1
Vrbas *R* 50 C2
Vrbaška 50 C2
Vrbas klisura 50 C3
Vrbljani 50 C3
Vrbnica 53 D4
Vrbnik 50 A2
Vrboska 50 C4
Vrbovec 50 B1
Vrbovsko 50 A2
Vrčin 52 C1
Vrdnik 51 E2
Vreden 11 F3
Vrela 53 D3
Vrelo (Hrvatska) 50 B3
Vrelo (Srbija) 53 E2
Vreoci 52 C1
Vresse 14 C2
Vrésthena 59 D4
Vreta Kloster 75 E4
Vrginmost 50 B2
Vrgorac 51 D4
Vrh Kapele 50 A2
Vrhnika 43 F3
Vrhpolje 50 C3
Vría 55 D3
Vrínena 59 D1
Vríssa 61 D1
Vrísses 64 B4
Vrissiá 59 D1
Vrissoúla 58 B1
Vrlika 50 C3
Vrnjačka Banja 53 D2
Vrnograč 50 B2
Vrondádos 61 D2
Vrondamás 63 D3
Vronderó 54 C2
Vrondissí 64 C4
Vrondoú 55 E3
Vrondoús, Óri 55 F1
Vrossína 54 B4
Vrouhás 64 D4
Vrpolje (Osijek) 51 D2
Vrpolje (Šibenik) 50 B4
Vršac 51 F1
Vršani 51 E2
Vrsar 43 F4
Vrsi 50 B3
Vrška Čuka 53 E1
Vrtac 52 C3
Vrtoče 50 B3
Vrutok 53 D4
Vučitrh 53 D3
Vučjak 53 F4
Vučje 53 E3
Vučkovica 53 D2
Vue des Alpes 19 E2
Vuka 51 D1
Vukovar 51 E1
Vulcano, I 49 D2
Vulture, Mte 47 D1
Vuohijärvi 73 E3
Vuohijärvi *L* 73 E3
Vuokatti 71 E3
Vuokkijärvi 71 E2
Vuokojaure 66 C3
Vuoksenniska 73 F3
Vuolijoki 71 E3
Vuollerim 70 B1
Vuolvojaure 69 F1
Vuonislahti 71 F3
Vuorji 67 D2
Vuosjärvi 71 D4
Vuoskuvarri 67 D2
Vuostimo 67 F4
Vuotso 67 E3
Vyškov 41 F1
Vyšnij Voločok 79 E1

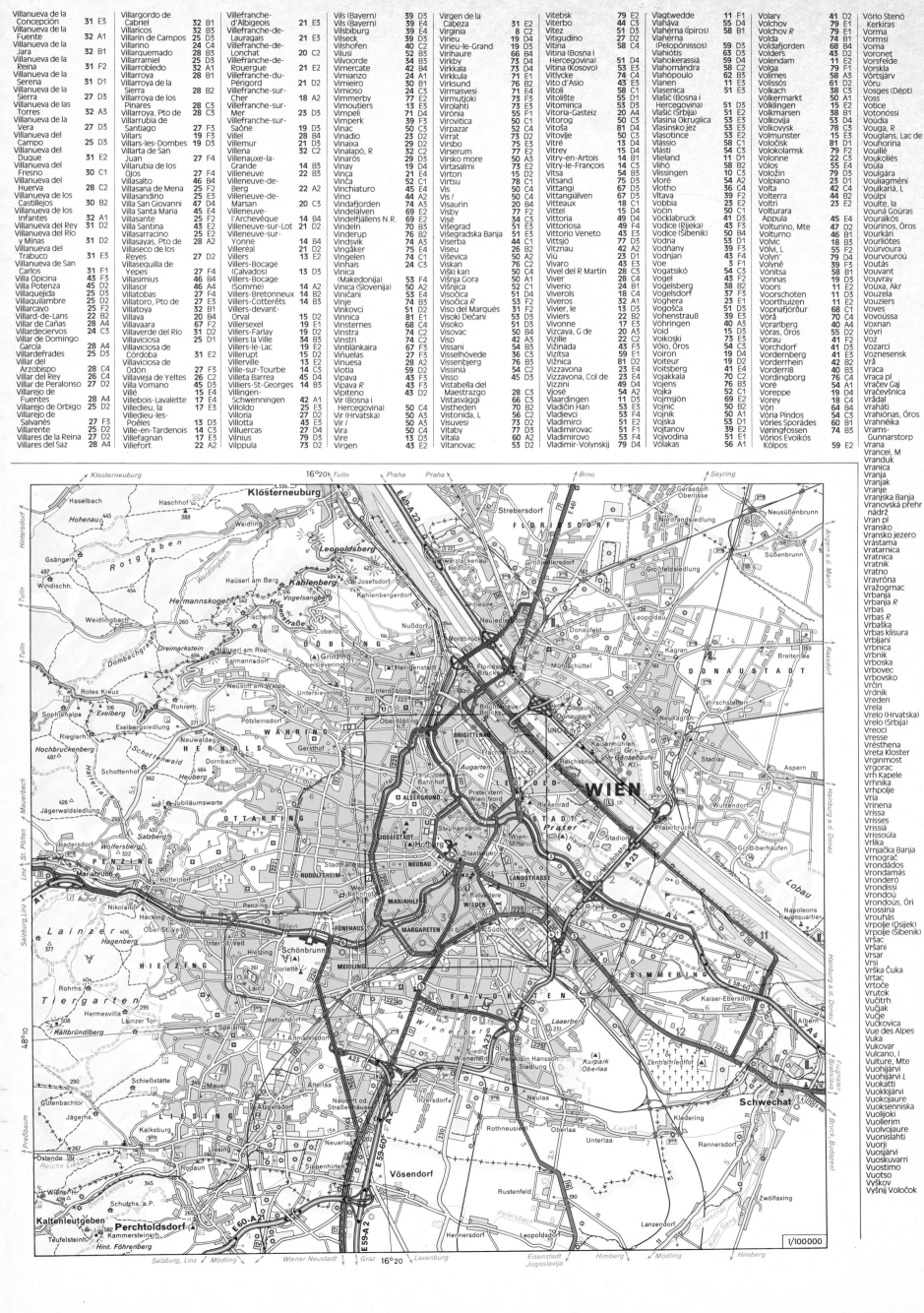

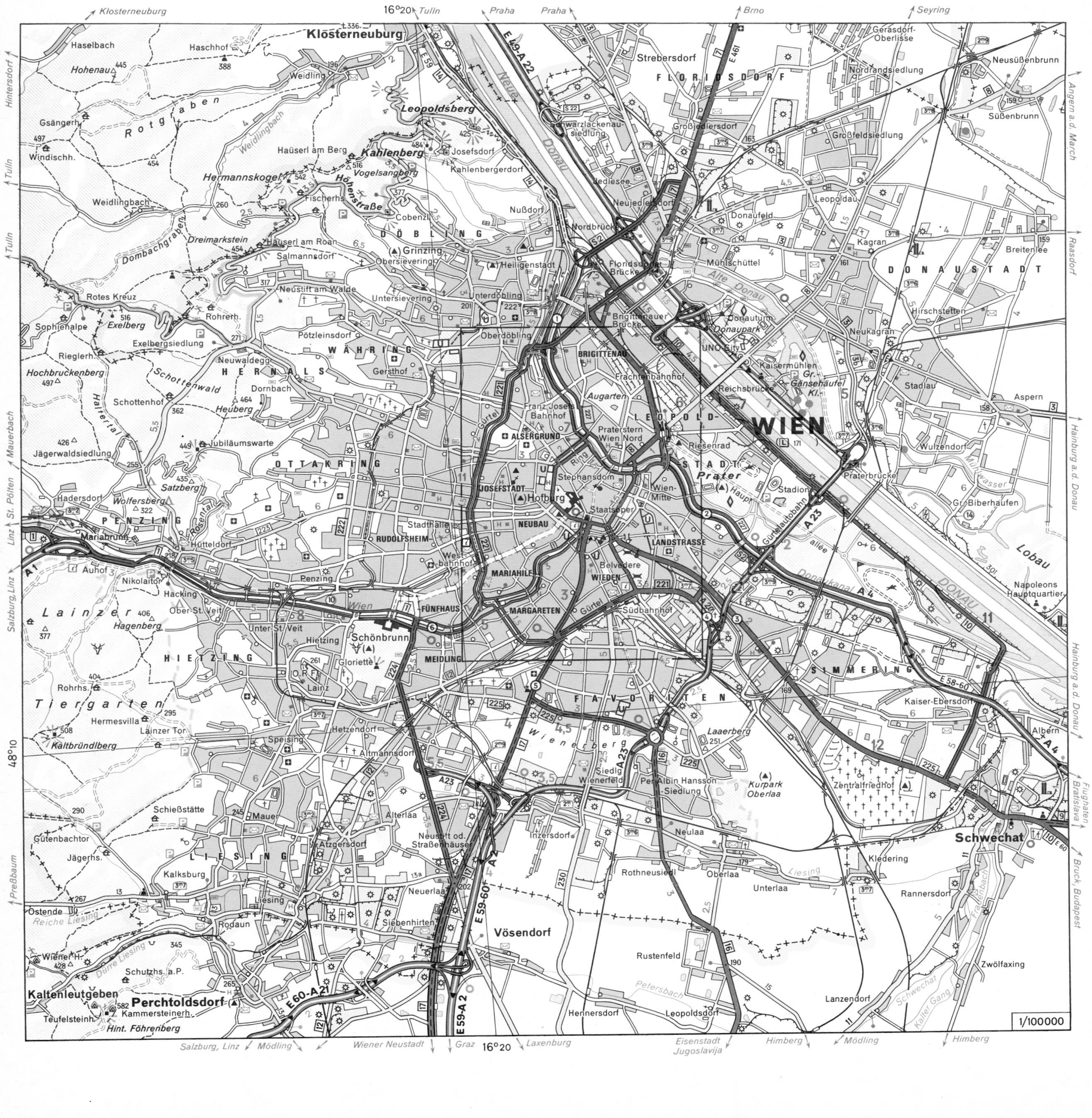

Klosterneuburg
Tulln
Praha
Brno
Seyring
Klosterneuburg
Leopoldsberg
Kahlenberg
Hermannskogel
FLORIDSDORF
DÖBLING
Grinzing
Heiligenstadt
WÄHRING
HERNALS
OTTAKRING
PENZING
HIETZING
Schönbrunn
MEIDLING
FAVORITEN
SIMMERING
DONAUSTADT
LEOPOLDSTADT
BRIGITTENAU
ALSERGRUND
JOSEFSTADT
NEUBAU
RUDOLFSHEIM
MARIAHILF
FÜNFHAUS
MARGARETEN
WIEDEN
LANDSTRASSE
LIESING
WIEN
Prater
Lainzer Tiergarten
Schwechat
Vösendorf
Perchtoldsdorf
Kaltenleutgeben
Lobau
Donau
1/100000
Salzburg, Linz
Mödling
Wiener Neustadt
Graz
Laxenburg
Eisenstadt Jugoslavija
Himberg
Bruck, Budapest
Flughafen Bratislava
Hainburg a.d. Donau
Raasdorf
Angern a.d. March
16°20
48°10

W

Waal 11 E3
Waalwijk 11 E3
Waasmunster 34 B3
Wabern 38 B1
Wachau 41 E2
Wachow 37 E3
Wächtersbach 38 B2
Waddeneilanden 11 D1
Wadebridge 6 A4
Wädenswil 42 B2
Wagenfeld 36 B3
Wageningen 11 E3
Waging 40 C3
Wagrain 41 D4
Wągrowiec 78 B4
Wahlstedt 36 C2
Waiblingen 38 B4
Waidhaus 39 E3
Waidhofen (Thaya) 41 E2
Waidhofen (Ybbs) 41 E3
Waidring 40 C3
Waischenfeld 39 D2
Waizenkirchen 41 D2
Wakefield 5 E4
Wałbrzych 80 B1
Walchensee 40 B3
Walcheren 10 C3
Walchsee 40 C3
Wałcz 78 B4
Wald 42 B2
Waldbröl 38 A2
Waldeck 38 B1
Waldenbuch 38 C4
Waldenburg 39 E1
Waldfischbach-Burgalben 38 A3
Waldheim 39 E1
Waldkappel 38 C1
Waldkirch 42 A1
Waldkirchen 41 D2
Waldkraiburg 40 C3
Wald-Michelbach 38 B3
Waldmünchen 39 E3
Waldsassen 39 E2
Waldshut 42 A1
Walensee 42 B2
Walenstadt 42 B2
Wales 6 B2
Wallasey 5 D4
Walldorf 38 B3
Walldürn 38 B3
Wallenfels 39 D2
Wallersdorf 39 E4
Wallerstein 38 C4
Wallingford 7 D3
Walls 3 F2
Walsall 7 D2
Walsrode 36 C3
Walsum 11 F3
Waltershausen 38 C1
Walton-on-the-Naze 7 F3
Waltrop 36 B4
Wanderup 36 C1
Wandlitz 37 F3
Wanfried 38 C1
Wangen 40 A3
Wangenbourg 15 E3
Wangerland-Hooksiel 36 B2
Wangerooge 36 B2
Wängi 42 B1
Wanna 36 B2
Wanne-Eickel 11 F3
Wantage 7 D3
Wantzenau, la 15 F3
Wanzleben 37 D4
Warburg 36 C4
Wardenburg 36 B3
Ware 7 E3
Waregem 34 A3
Wareham 6 C3
Waremme 34 C3
Waren 37 E2
Warendorf 36 B4
Warin 37 D2
Warkworth 5 E2
Warmensteinach 39 D2
Warminster 6 C3
Warnemunde 37 E1
Warnow 37 E2
Warrenpoint 9 D2
Warrington 5 D4
Warstein 38 B1
Warszawa 78 C4
Warszów 37 F1
Warth 40 A4
Wartha 38 C1
Warwick 7 D2
Warwickshire 7 D2
Wash, The 7 E1
Washington 5 E2
Wasselonne 15 E3
Wassen 42 B2
Wassenaar 11 D3
Wassenberg 11 E4
Wasseralfingen 38 C4
Wasserbillig 15 E2
Wasserburg 40 C3
Wasser-Kuppe 38 C2
Wassertrüdingen 38 C3
Wassigny 14 B2
Wassy 14 C3
Wasungen 38 C2
Watchet 6 B3
Waterfoot 4 B2
Waterford 8 C4
Waterford (Co) 8 C4
Waterford Harbour 8 C4
Waterloo 34 B3
Waternish Pt 2 B2
Waterville 8 A4
Watford 7 E3
Wattens 43 D2
Watton 7 F2
Wattwil 42 B2
Watzmann 60 C3
Waulsort 34 B4
Waveney 7 F2
Wavre 34 B3
Waxweiler 35 D4
Wear 5 E2
Wechsel 41 F2
Wedel 36 C2
Wedemark-Mellendorf 36 C3
Weener 36 A2
Weert 11 E3
Weferlingen 37 D3
Wegberg 11 E4
Wegeleben 37 D4
Weggis 42 A2
Węgorzewo 78 C3
Wegscheid 41 D2
Wehr 42 A1
Weibersbrunn 38 B2
Weichshofen 39 E4
Weida 39 D1
Weiden 39 D3
Weikersheim 38 C3
Weilburg 38 B2
Weil der Stadt 38 B4
Weilheim (Baden-Württemberg) 38 C4
Weilheim (Bayern) 40 B3
Weimar 39 D1
Weinfelden 42 B1
Weingarten 42 B1
Weinheim 38 B3
Weinsberg 38 B3
Weismain 39 D2
Weißbriach 41 D4
Weiße Elster 39 D1
Weißenbach 40 A4
Weißenberg 39 F1
Weißenburg 39 D3
Weißenfels 37 E4
Weißenhorn 40 A3
Weißenkirchen 41 E2
Weißensee 39 D1
Weißensee *L* 41 D4
Weissenstadt 39 D2
Weissenstein 19 F1
Weissfluhgipfel 42 C2
Weißkirchen 41 E4
Weißkugel 40 B4
Weitra 41 E2
Weiz 41 E3
Wejherowo 78 B3
Weldon 7 E2
Welgetschlag 41 D2
Welland 7 E2
Wellin 14 C2
Wellingborough 7 D2
Wellington 6 C3
Wellington Bridge 8 C4
Wells 6 C3
Wells-next-the-Sea 7 E1
Wels 41 D3
Welsberg 43 D2
Welschnofen 43 D2
Welshpool 6 C2
Weltenburg 39 D4
Welwyn Garden City 7 E3
Welzheim 38 C4
Wem 6 C1
Wemding 39 D4
Wemyss Bay 2 C4
Wendelstein 40 B3
Wenden 37 D3
Wengen 42 A3
Wenns 40 B4
Werbellinsee 37 F2
Werben 37 E3
Werdau 39 E1
Werder 37 F3
Werdohl 38 A1
Werfen 40 C3
Werl 36 B4
Werlte 36 B3
Wermelskirchen 35 D3
Wermsdorf 37 F4
Wernberg 39 E3
Werne 36 B4
Werneck 38 C2
Werneuchen 37 F3
Wernigerode 37 D4
Werra 38 C2
Wertach 40 A4
Wertach *R* 40 A3
Wertheim 38 C3
Werther 36 B4
Wertingen 39 D4
Wervik 34 A3
Wesel 11 F3
Wesenbeerg 37 E2
Wesendorf 37 D3
Weser 36 B2
Weser-Elbe-Kanal 37 D3
Wesselburen 36 B1
Wessobrunn 40 B3
West Auckland 5 E3
West Bridgford 7 D1
Westbury 6 C3
Westendorf 40 C4
Westenholz 36 C3
Westerburg 38 A2
Westerholt 36 A2
Westerland 36 B1
Westerlo 34 B3
Westernbödefeld 38 B1
Western Isles 2 B1
Wester Ross 2 C2
Westerstede 36 B2
Westerwald 38 A2
Westhofen 38 B3
West Kilbride 4 C1
West Linton 5 D1
West Loch Tarbert 2 B1
Westmeath 8 C2
West Mersea 7 F3
Weston-Super-Mare 6 C3
Westport 8 B2
Westray 3 E1
Westray Firth 3 E1
West Sussex 7 D4
West-Terschelling 11 E1
West-Vlaanderen 34 A3
Wetherby 5 E3
Wetter 38 A1
Wetteren 34 B3
Wettin 37 E4
Wettringen 11 F2
Wetwang 5 F3
Wetzikon 42 B2
Wetzlar 38 B2
Wexford 9 D4
Wexford (Co) 8 C4
Weyer-Markt 41 E3
Weyhausen 37 D3
Weyhill 7 D3
Weymouth 6 C4
Weyregg 41 D3
Whaley Bridge 5 E4
Whalsay 3 F1
Wharfe 5 E3
Whernside 5 D3
Whitburn 2 C4
Whitby 5 F3
Whitchurch 6 C1
White Bridge 2 C2
Whitehaven 5 D3
Whitehead 9 D1
Whiteness 3 F2
Whiten Head 2 C1
Whithorn 4 C2
Whitland 6 B2
Whitley Bay 5 E2
Whitstable 7 F3
Whittlesey 7 E2
Wick 3 D1
Wickford 7 E3
Wicklow 9 D3
Wicklow (Co) 9 D3
Wicklow Head 9 D3
Wicklow Mts 9 D3
Widnes 5 D4
Wiehe 39 D1
Wiek 37 E1
Wieliczka 80 C1
Wieluń 78 B4
Wien 41 F2
Wiener-Neudorf 41 F2
Wiener Neustadt 41 F3
Wienerwald 41 F2
Wies 50 A1
Wiesau 39 E2
Wiesbaden 38 B2
Wieselburg 41 E2
Wiesenburg 37 E3
Wiesensteig 38 C4
Wiesentheid 38 C3
Wiesenttal 39 D2
Wiesing 40 B4
Wiesloch 38 B3
Wiesmath 41 F3
Wiesmoor 36 B2
Wigan 5 D4
Wight, I of 7 D4
Wigton 5 D2
Wigtown 4 C2
Wigtown B 4 C2
Wijhe 11 E2
Wil 42 B2
Wildalpen 41 E3
Wildbad 38 B4
Wildeck 38 C1
Wildeshausen 36 B3
Wildon 41 E4
Wildspitze 40 B4
Wildstrubel 19 F2
Wilfersdorf 41 F2
Wilhelmina kan 11 E3
Wilhelmsburg (A) 41 E2
Wilhelmsburg (D) 36 C2
Wilhelmshaven 36 B2
Wilhering 41 D2
Wilkau-Haßlau 39 E1
Willebroek 34 B3
Willemstad 11 D3
Willingen 38 B1
Williton 6 B3
Wilmslow 6 C1
Wilnsdorf 38 A2
Wilsdruff 39 E1
Wilseder Berg 36 C2
Wilster 36 C2
Wilton 7 D3
Wiltshire 6 C3
Wiltz 15 D2
Wimborne Minster 6 C4
Wimereux 14 A1
Wincanton 6 C3
Winchcombe 7 D2
Winchelsea 7 E4
Winchester 7 D3
Windeck 35 D3
Windermere 5 D3
Windischeschenbach 39 E2
Windischgarsten 41 D3
Windsbach 39 D3
Windsor 7 D3
Winkleigh 6 B4
Winklern 43 E2
Winnenden 38 C4
Winnigstedt 37 D4
Winnweiler 38 A3
Winschoten 11 F1
Winsen (Celle) 36 C3
Winsen (Lüneburg) 36 C2
Winsford 6 C1
Winsum 11 E1
Winterberg 38 B1
Winterswijk 11 F3
Winterthur 42 B2
Wintzenheim 15 E4
Wipper 38 C1
Wipperfürth 35 D3
Wisbech 7 E2
Wischhafen 36 C2
Wishaw 5 D1
Wisła 78 B3
Wismar 37 D1
Wissant 14 A1
Wissembourg 15 F3
Wissen 38 A2
Witham 7 E1
Witham 7 E3
Withernsea 5 F4
Witney 7 D3
Wittdün 36 B1
Witte 37 E1
Witten 38 A1
Wittenberg 37 E4
Wittenberge 37 E3
Wittenburg 37 D2
Wittingen 37 D3
Wittlich 35 D4
Wittmund 36 B2
Wittstock 37 E2
Witzenhausen 36 C4
Władysławowo 78 B3
Włocławek 78 B4
Włodawa 78 C4
Wöbbelin 37 D2
Woburn 7 D2
Woburn Abbey 7 D2
Woensdrecht 11 D3
Woerden 11 D3
Wœrth 15 F3
Wohlen 42 A2
Woippy 15 D3
Woking 7 D3
Wokingham 7 D3
Woldegk 37 F2
Wolfach 38 B4
Wolfegg 40 A3
Wolfen 37 E4
Wolfenbüttel 37 D4
Wolfhagen 38 B1
Wolfratshausen 40 B3
Wolfsberg 50 A1
Wolfsburg 37 D3
Wolgast 37 F1
Wolin 37 F1
Wolin (Reg) 37 F1
Wolkenstein 43 D2
Wolkersdorf 41 F2
Wöllersdorf 41 F3
Wollersheim 35 D3
Wollin 37 E3
Wolmirstedt 37 E3
Wolsingham 5 E2
Wolsztyn 78 B4
Wolvega 11 E2
Wolverhampton 6 C2
Wolverton 7 D2
Wolznach 39 D4
Woodbridge 7 F2
Woodhall Spa 7 E1
Woodstock 7 D3
Wooler 5 E1
Worb 19 F2
Worbis 37 D4
Worcester 6 C2
Wörgl 40 C4
Workington 5 D2
Worksop 7 D1
Workum 11 E2
Wörlitz 37 E4
Wormerveer 11 D2
Wormhout 14 A1
Worms 38 B3
Worms Head 6 B3
Wörnitz 38 C3
Wörrstadt 38 A3
Wörth (Donau) 39 E3
Wörth (Main) 38 B3
Wörth (Rheinland-Pfalz) 38 B4
Worther See 43 F2
Worthing 7 E4
Wragby 7 E1
Wrath, Cape 2 C1
Wrecsam 6 C1
Wrexham 6 C1
Wriezen 37 F3
Wrocław 80 B1
Wroughton 7 D3
Września 78 B4
Wulfen 11 F3
Wullowitz 41 D2
Wümme 36 C3
Wümme *R* 36 C3
Wünnenberg 38 B1
Wünsdorf 37 F3
Wunsiedel 39 D2
Wunstorf 36 C3
Wuppertal 35 D2
Würzburg 38 C3
Wurzen 37 F4
Wurzen-Paß 41 D4
Wusterhausen 37 E3
Wustrow (Wismar) 37 D1
Wustrow (Rostock) 37 E1
Wuustwezel 34 B2
Wye, R 6 C3
Wyk 36 B1
Wymondham 7 F2

X

Xallas, R 24 A1
Xanten 11 F3
Xánthi 56 B2
Xánthi (Nomos) 56 B1
Xarrama, R 30 B1
Xàtiva 32 C1
Xeresa 32 C1
Xerovoúni 54 C4
Xerta 29 D3
Xertigny 15 E4
Xesta, Pto de la 24 B1
Xifianí 55 D2
Xilaganí 56 C2
Xilikí 59 D2
Xilís, Akr 63 D4
Xilókastro 59 D3
Xilopáriko 54 C4
Xilópoli 55 F2
Xilóskalo 64 A4
Xiniáda 59 D1
Xinó Neró 55 D2
Xinzo de Limia 24 B3
Xiró 59 E2
Xirokámbi 62 C3
Xirókambos 61 E4
Xirolímni 55 D3
Xistral 24 B1
Xódoto, Akr 64 C1
Xubia 24 B1
Xunqueira de Ambía 24 B2

Y

Yaiza 30 B4
Yalova 81 F4
Yanguas 28 B1
Yare 7 F2
Yarmouth 7 D4
Yarmouth, Great 7 F2
Ybbs 41 E2
Ybbs *R* 41 E3
Yebra 28 A3
Yecla 32 C2
Yeguas, Emb de 31 E2
Yeguas, R de las 31 E2
Yell 3 F1
Yell Sd 3 F1
Yelmo 32 A2
Yeltes, R 27 D2
Yenne 19 D3
Yeovil 6 C4
Yepes 27 F4
Yerville 13 F2
Yesa 20 B4
Yesa, Emb de 28 C1
Yeste 32 A2
Yeu, I d' 16 C2
Yèvre 18 B2
Y-Fenni 6 C2
Yildiz Dağlari 81 E4
Ylämaa 73 E3
Ylämylly 71 F4
Yläne 72 C3
Ylihärmä 70 C4
Yli-Kärppä 71 D2
Ylikiiminki 71 D2
Yli-Kitka 71 E1
Yli-li 71 D2
Yli-Muonio 67 D3
Yli-Nampa 71 D1
Yli-Olhava 71 D2
Ylistaro 70 C4
Ylitornio 70 C1
Ylivieska 71 D3
Ylläs 67 D3
Ylläsjärvi 67 E3
Ylöjärvi 73 D3
Yngaren 75 E4
Yonne 14 B4
Yonne (Dépt) 14 B4
York 5 E3
Yorkshire Dales Nat Pk 5 E3
Youghal 8 C4
Youghal B 8 C4
Yoxford 7 F2
Ypäjä 72 C3
Yport 13 E2
Yppäri 71 D3
Ypres 34 A3
Yr Wyddgrug 6 C1
Yser 14 B1
Yssingeaux 18 C4
Ystad 77 D3
Y Trallwng 6 C2
Ytterhogdal 75 E1
Yttermalung 75 D3
Yuncos 27 F3
Yunquera 31 E4
Yunquera de Henares 28 A3
Yuste 27 D3
Yverdon 19 E2
Yvetot 13 F2
Yvoir 34 B4
Yvoire 19 E3

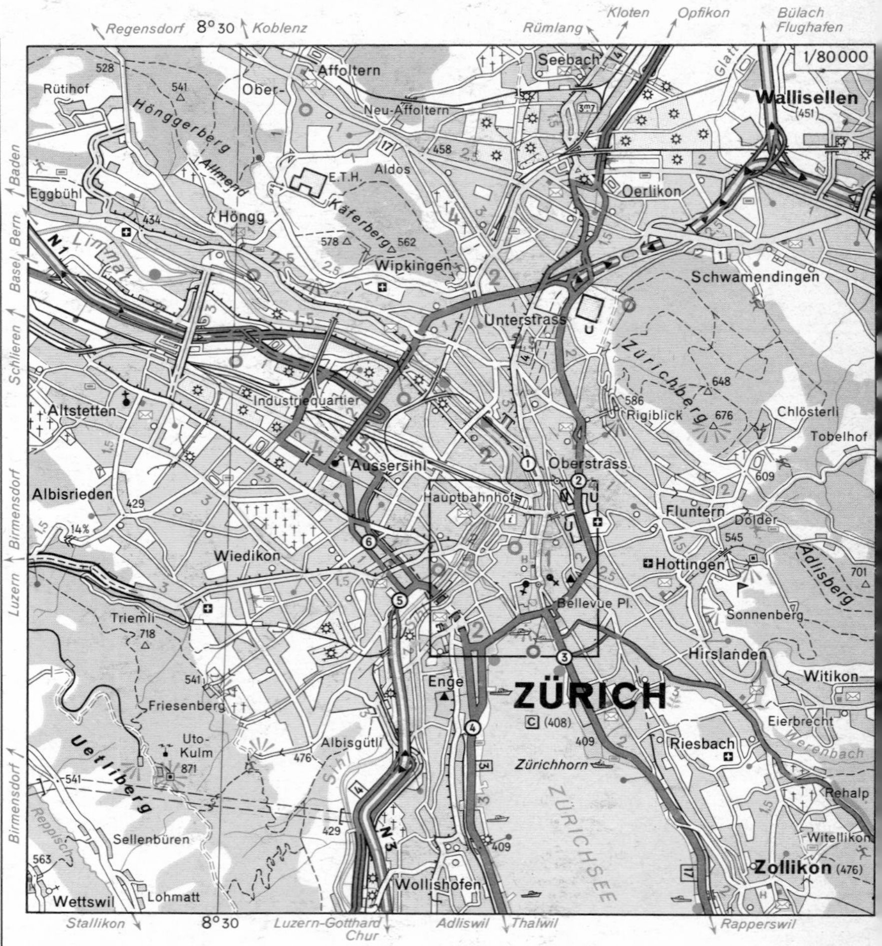

Regensdorf
8°30
Koblenz
Rümlang
Kloten
Opfikon
Bülach Flughafen
1/80 000
Wallisellen
Affoltern
Seebach
Rütihof
Neu-Affoltern
Hönggerberg
E.T.H.
Oerlikon
Eggbühl
Höngg
Käferberg
Wipkingen
Schwamendingen
Unterstrass
Altstetten
Industriequartier
Zürichberg
Rigiblick
Chlösterli
Tobelhof
Albisrieden
Aussersihl
Oberstrass
Hauptbahnhof
Fluntern
Dolder
Wiedikon
Hottingen
Adlisberg
Triemli
Bellevue Pl.
Sonnenberg
Hirslanden
Witikon
Friesenberg
Enge
ZÜRICH
Uto-Kulm
Albisgütli
Riesbach
Zürichhorn
Eierbrecht
Uetliberg
Rehalp
Sellenbüren
Wollishofen
ZÜRICHSEE
Witellikon
Zollikon
Wettswil
Lohmatt
Stallikon
Luzern-Gotthard Chur
Adliswil
Thalwil
Rapperswil
Baden
Basel
Bern
Schlieren
Birmensdorf
Luzern

Z

Zaandam 11 D2
Zabali 51 E1
Žabari 53 D1
Zablaće 50 B4
Žabljak (Durmitor) 51 E4
Žabljak (Titograd) 52 C4
Žabno 50 B1
Zabok 50 B1
Zabrdđe 51 E2
Zadar 50 B3
Zadarski kanal 50 A3
Zadvarje 50 C4
Zafarraya 31 E3
Zafóra, Ni 65 D2
Zafra 30 C1
Zaga 43 F2
Żagań 78 A4
Zaglavak 51 E3
Zagorá 55 E4
Zagória 54 C4
Zagorje 50 A1
Zagreb 50 B1
Žagubica 53 E1
Zagvozd 50 C4
Zahara de los Atunes 31 D4
Zahara, Emb de 31 D3
Zaháro 58 C4
Zahinos 30 C2
Zahna 37 E4
Záhony 80 C2
Zaidín 29 D2
Zajas 53 E4
Zaječar 53 E1
Zákinthos 58 B3
Zákinthos, N 58 A3
Zakopane 80 C1
Zákros 65 D4
Zala 80 B2
Zalaegerszeg 80 B2
Zalamea de la Serena 31 D1
Zalamea la Real 30 C2
Zalău 80 C2
Žalec 50 A1
Zaleščiki 81 D1
Zalew Wiślany 78 B3
Zalla 25 F2
Zálongo 58 B1
Zaltbommel 11 E3
Zalužnica 50 B3
Zambrana 20 A4
Zamora 25 D3
Zamość 78 C4
Záncara, R 32 A1
Zandvoort 11 D2
Zángano, Pto del 26 C4
Zanglivéri 55 F2
Zannone, I 46 A2
Zaorejas 28 B3
Zaostrog 51 D4
Zaovine Vežanja 51 E3
Zapadnaja Dvina 79 E2
Zapadnaja Dvina *R* 79 E2
Zapardiel, R 27 E2
Zapatón, R 26 C4
Zápio 55 E4
Zapponeta 45 F4
Zaprešić 50 B1
Zaragoza 28 C2
Zárakes 60 B2
Zaratán 25 D3
Zarautz 20 A3
Zarcilla de Ramos 32 B2
Zárkos 55 D4
Zarós 64 C4
Zaroúhla 59 D3
Zarrentin 37 D2
Žary 78 A4
Zarza la Mayor 26 C3
Zaškov 81 E1
Žatec 39 E2
Zatoka Gdańska 78 B3
Zaton 52 B4
Zavala 52 B3
Zavattarello 23 E1
Zavidovići 51 D3
Zavlaka 51 E2
Zavratnica 50 A3
Zawiercie 80 B1
Žažina 50 B2
Zbaraž 81 D1
Zbraslav 39 F2
Žďár nad Sázavou 80 B1
Zdenac 50 B2
Zdice 39 F2
Ždrelac 50 B3
Ždrelo 53 D1
Zdunje 53 E4
Zduńska Wola 78 B4
Zebë, Maj'e 53 D4
Zebreira 26 C3
Žednik 51 E1
Zeebrugge 10 C3
Zeeland 11 D3
Zefiría 64 A1
Zegovac 53 E3
Zegra 53 E3
Žegulja 52 B3
Zehdenick 37 F2
Zeist 11 E3
Zeitz 39 D1
Zejtun 49 F4
Žekovec 50 A1
Zele 34 B3
Zelengora 51 E4
Zelengora (Reg) 51 E4
Zelenika 52 B4
Zelenogorsk 79 D1
Železná Ruda 39 F3
Železnik 52 C1
Železniki 43 F2
Železnogorsk 79 F3
Želin 43 F3
Zelina 50 B1
Zélio 59 D2
Željezno Polje 51 D3
Željin 53 D2
Zell (D) 38 A3
Zell (Oberösterreich) 41 D2
Zell (Tirol) 43 D2
Zella-Mehlis 38 C2
Zell am See 40 C4
Zellerrain 41 E3
Zeltweg 41 E4
Zelzate 34 B3
Zemun 52 C1
Zenica 51 D3
Zen'kov 79 F4
Žep 51 E3
Žepče 51 D3
Zerbst 37 E4
Zeri 23 F2
Zermatt 42 A3
Zernez 42 C2
Zerqan 53 D4
Zestoa 20 A3
Zeta 52 C4
Zetel 36 B2
Zeulenroda 39 D2
Zeven 36 C2
Zevenaar 11 E3
Zevgaráki 58 C2
Zevgolatío 58 C4
Zevio 43 D4
Zêzere, R 26 B3
Žiča 53 D2
Zicavo 23 D4
Židlochovice 41 F1
Ziefsdorf 41 E2
Ziegenrück 39 D2
Zielona Góra 78 A4
Zierikzee 11 D3
Zierzow 37 E2
Ziesar 37 E3
Zi, Guri i 54 B2
Zijemlje 51 D4
Žilina 80 B1
Žilindar 51 F4
Ziller 43 D2
Zillertal 40 B4
Zimnicea 81 D3
Zinal 42 A3
Zingst 37 E1
Zinnowitz 37 F1
Zinnwald 39 F1
Zirbitzkogel 41 E4
Zirchow 37 F1
Žiri 43 F3
Žirje 50 B4
Zirl 40 B4
Zirndorf 39 D3
Zirndorf 42 B1
Zíros 65 D4
Zistersdorf 41 F2
Žitište 51 F1
Žitkovac 53 E2
Žitkoviči 79 D4
Žitomir 79 E4
Žitomislići 52 B3
Žitoradđa 53 E2
Zittau 39 F1
Živinice 51 D2
Živogošće 51 D4
Žizdra 79 F3
Zjum 53 D4
Zlarin 50 B4
Zlarin / 50 B4
Zlata 53 E2
Zlatar 51 F3
Zlatar Bistrica 50 B1
Zlatarevo 53 F4
Zlatari 53 D2
Zlatarsko jez 51 F3
Zlatibor 51 E3
Zlatica 51 E1
Zlatni Pjasăci 81 E3
Zlatokop 53 E3
Zletovo 53 F4
Zljebovi 51 E3
Žlobin 79 E3
Zlot 53 E1
Žlutice 39 E2
Zmajevo 51 E1
Žman 50 B4
Žmerinka 81 E1
Žminj 43 F4
Znamenka 81 F1
Znojmo 41 E2
Zöblitz 39 E1
Zoetermeer 11 D3
Zogaj 53 D4
Zollikofen 19 F2
Zoločev 81 D1
Zolotonoša 79 F4
Žoltyje Vody 81 F1
Zonári, Akr 65 F2
Zóni 57 D1
Zonianá 64 B4
Zonza 23 D4
Zoodóhos Pigí (Makedonía) 55 D3
Zoodóhos Pigí (Pelopónissos) 59 E4
Zörbig 37 E4
Zorita 27 D4
Zossen 37 F3
Zoúrvas, Akr 59 E4
Zoutkamp 11 E1
Zoutleeuw 34 B3
Zoúzouli 54 C3
Zrenjanin 51 F1
Zrin 50 B2
Zrinska gora 50 B2
Zrmanja 50 B3
Zrmanja *R* 50 B3
Žrnovnica 50 C4
Zrze 53 D3
Zschopau 39 E1
Zschopau *R* 39 E1
Zubcov 79 F2
Zubin Potoku 53 D3
Žuč 53 D2
Zucaina 28 C4
Zuckerhütl 40 B4
Zudar 37 F1
Zuera 28 C2
Zufre 30 C2
Zufre, Emb de 31 D2
Zug 42 A2
Zugspitze 40 B4
Zuid Beveland 11 D3
Zuidelijk-Flevoland 11 E2
Zuid Holland 11 D3
Zuidlaren 11 F1
Zújar 32 A3
Zújar, Emb del 31 D1
Zújar, R 31 D1
Žukovka 79 F3
Zuljana 52 A3
Zülpich 35 D3
Zumaia 20 A3
Zumárraga 20 A4
Zundert 11 D3
Zuoz 42 C2
Županja 51 D2
Žur 53 D4
Zürich 42 B2
Zurrieq 49 F4
Zürs 40 A4
Zurzach 42 A1
Zusmarshausen 40 A3
Žut 50 B4
Zuta Lokva 50 A2
Zutphen 11 E2
Žužemberk 50 A1
Zvečan 53 D3
Zvenigorodka 81 E1
Zvijezda nac park 51 E3
Zvikovec 39 F2
Zvolen 80 B2
Zvonce 53 F2
Zvorničko jez 51 E3
Zvornik 51 E3
Zweibrücken 15 E2
Zweisimmen 19 F2
Zwenkau 37 E4
Zwettl (Niederösterreich) 41 E2
Zwettl (Oberösterreich) 41 D2
Zwickau 39 E1
Zwickauer Mulde 39 E2
Zwiefalten 38 C4
Zwiesel 40 C2
Zwijndrecht 11 D3
Zwolle 11 E2
Żyrardów 78 C4
Żywiec 80 B1

Þ

Þingeyri 68 A1
Þingvallavatn 68 A2
Þingvellir 68 A2
Þistilfjörður 68 B1
Þjórsá 68 B2
Þórlákshöfn 68 A2
Þórshöfn 68 C1
Þórsmörk 68 B2